Yelena Dembo & Richard Palliser

the
Scotch game

EVERYMAN CHESS

Gloucester Publishers plc   www.everymanchess.com

First published in 2011 by Gloucester Publishers plc (formerly Everyman Publishers plc), Northburgh House, 10 Northburgh Street, London EC1V 0AT

British Library Cataloguing-in-Publication Data
A catalogue record for this book is available from the British Library.

ISBN: 978 1 85744 632 6

Distributed in North America by The Globe Pequot Press, P.O Box 480, 246 Goose Lane, Guilford, CT 06437-0480.

All other sales enquiries should be directed to Everyman Chess, Northburgh House, 10 Northburgh Street, London EC1V 0AT
tel: 020 7253 7887 fax: 020 7490 3708
email: info@everymanchess.com; website: www.everymanchess.com

Everyman Chess Series
Chief advisor: Byron Jacobs
Commissioning editor: John Emms
Assistant editor: Richard Palliser

Typeset and edited by First Rank Publishing, Brighton.
Cover design by Horatio Monteverde.
Printed and bound in the US by Versa Press.

Contents

Bibliography

Books

Beating the Open Games, Mihail Marin (Quality Chess 2008)

Dangerous Weapons: 1 e4 e5, John Emms, Glenn Flear and Andrew Greet (Everyman Chess 2008)

Garry Kasparov on Modern Chess, Part 4: Kasparov vs Karpov 1988-2009, Garry Kasparov (Everyman Chess 2010)

Play the Open Games as Black, John Emms (Gambit 2000)

Starting Out: The Scotch Game, John Emms (Everyman Chess 2005)

The Scotch Game, Peter Wells (Batsford 1998)

The Scotch Game for White, Vladimir Barsky (Chess Stars 2009)

Electronic

ChessBase Magazine, Mega Database 2010 (ChessBase), *New in Chess Yearbook* & TWIC

Introduction

The Scotch Game has been one of my favourite openings as White ever since I took it up a decade ago. It's far sounder than the majority of gambit lines available to White after 1 e4 e5, but like them leads to unbalanced positions in which the defender is likely to feel much less at home than in the generally more rational lines of the Ruy Lopez. In short, the Scotch leads to a complex, exciting early middlegame in which White can most certainly aspire to the advantage.

Throughout the 1990s Garry Kasparov was the main torch-bearer for the Scotch and under his patronage a large number of Grandmasters adopted the opening, no doubt attracted by the extremely original positions which arise after 4...♘f6 5 ♘xc6 bxc6 6 e5 ♕e7 7 ♕e2 ♘d5 8 c4 and then 8...♗a6 or 8...♘b6. In the first few years of the new millennium Black's other main defence, 4...♗c5, caused a number of players, including Kasparov, to lose some of their faith in the Scotch, not least because new defences were worked out after 5 ♘xc6 ♕f6 6 ♕d2. However, the wheel didn't take long to turn full circle, thanks to new discoveries being found for White after 5 ♗e3 and especially 5 ♘xc6 ♕f6 6 ♕f3!?. Indeed, nowadays the Scotch occupies a prominent part in the repertoire of Kasparov's sometime protégé, Magnus Carlsen, and is regularly employed as well by the likes of Alexander Morozevich, Teimour Radjabov and especially Sergei Rublevsky, not forgetting too the talented, young grandmasters Emanuel Berg, Gawain Jones and Ian Nepomniachtchi.

Having spent many months studying recent grandmaster games in and existing theory on the Scotch, it quickly became clear that this project was going to be far bigger than I ever could have envisaged. As such I was very pleased when Richard Palliser agreed to come onboard. Richard not only added to the number of new ideas I'd found, but also updated much of the existing work, while helping to present the theory and key motifs of each variation as clearly as possible.

Both your authors have to admit to a certain bias for White's cause in the Scotch, but this is very much a complete work and those who defend 1 e4 e5 should also find much of interest, as well as plenty of new ideas within. Now I just hope that you will enjoy your adventures with or against the Scotch as much as I've always done!

Yelena Dembo,
Athens,
December 2010

Chapter One
The Main Line: 8...♝a6 without 9 b3

1 e4 e5 2 ♘f3 ♘c6 3 d4 exd4 4 ♘xd4 ♘f6 5 ♘xc6 bxc6 6 e5 ♕e7 7 ♕e2 ♘d5 8 c4 ♝a6

Black refuses to retreat his knight, preferring to pin the pawn. This is a very aggressive approach and the resulting positions are some of the sharpest and most theoretical in the whole Scotch. That's no surprise, though, because if Black doesn't continue actively and aggressively, White will break the pin, thereby forcing the

knight to retreat to b6 after all when the bishop may well find itself misplaced on a6, biting against granite on c4.

The main line and White's most popular choice nowadays is 9 b3, shoring up the defence of c4 while preparing to develop the dark-squared bishop to b2 or even a3. That will be the subject of our next chapter, but here we will focus our attention on:

> **A: 9 ♘d2**
> **B: 9 g3**

Both approaches have their logic, as we will see; something which cannot be said of the other generally dubious ideas White has been known to try:

a) 9 ♕e4?! would not normally deserve attention, as it is totally pointless, since Black can repeat the position if he likes, inviting a draw by repetition. However, the issue is whether Black can do any better than that, and it seems that he can:

a1) 9...♘f6 10 ♕e2 is the repetition and, arguably, the best White can hope for!

a2) The main move has been 9...♘b6 and after 10 ♘d2 (safer is 10 ♘c3, transposing to a position we'll consider in note 'c' at the start of Chapter Five) 10...0-0-0! Black gained the advantage in two old Timman-Karpov games, but it seems that there is an even more promising continuation...

a3) 9...♘b4! is a simple, straightforward and strong response.

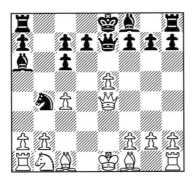

Following 10 ♘c3 (10 a3? runs into 10...d5! 11 cxd5 cxd5 12 ♕f3 ♘c2+ 13 ♔d1 ♘d4! with a large advantage for Black and 10 ♘a3 f6 is also unsatisfactory for White) 10...♖d8! Black threatens 11...d5 and White lacks a good response:

a31) 11 a3? is again ineffective: 11...d5 12 cxd5 (or 12 ♕b1 ♕xe5+ 13 ♗e2 d4 14 axb4 dxc3 15 ♖xa6 ♗xb4 16

♔f1 – 16 0-0 ♕xe2 17 bxc3 ♖d1 also loses – 16...♖d1+ 17 ♗xd1 c2 and Black wins, as analysed by Baklan and Kucyn) 12...cxd5 13 ♕f4 ♘c2+ sees Black win material.

a32) 11 ♖b1 d5 12 exd6 ♖xd6 13 ♕xe7+ ♗xe7 was also very difficult for White in T.Burg-M.Ragger, Groningen 2006.

a33) 11 c5 ♗xf1 12 ♔xf1 ♕xc5 13 ♗e3 ♕a5 just leaves Black a pawn ahead.

a34) 11 ♗e3 d5 12 cxd5 ♗xf1 13 d6 cxd6 14 ♕xb4 ♗xg2 15 ♖g1 ♗h3! 16 0-0-0 dxe5 17 ♖xd8+ ♕xd8 was good too for Black in K.Kristensen-E.Lund, Ballerup 2009.

a35) 11 ♗f4 d5 12 cxd5 (or 12 exd6 ♘c2+ 13 ♔d2 ♕xe4 14 ♘xe4 ♘xa1 with a large plus for Black in M.Kislov-R.Stern, Swidnica 2000) 12...cxd5 13 ♘xd5 ♘xd5 14 ♕a4+ (White was lost after 14 ♗xa6 ♕b4+ 15 ♕xb4 ♗xb4+ 16 ♗d2 ♗xd2+ 17 ♔xd2 ♘b4+ in E.Andreev-V.Baklan, Alushta 1997) 14...♕d7 15 ♕xd7+ (or 15 ♕xa6 ♗b4+ 16 ♔e2 ♕g4+ and Black wins) 15...♔xd7 16 ♗xa6 ♘xf4 17 0-0-0+ ♔e7 18 ♖xd8 ♔xd8 19 ♖d1+ ♔e7 20 g3 ♘e6 and White has nowhere near enough for his piece.

b) Another very strange-looking move is 9 h4?! In a position where White has no development, he chooses to play with a flank pawn, threatening... nothing!

Admittedly there are some ideas behind 9 h4, especially transferring the king's rook to the centre or queenside via the h3-square and preventing ...g5, but there are surely more pressing matters for White to attend to:

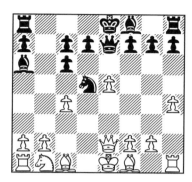

b1) The most direct response is 9...f6, after which 10 ♖h3 (consistent; White gains nothing from either 10 f4 ♕b4+ 11 ♔d1 ♗e7 or 10 exf6 ♘xf6 11 ♘c3 ♕xe2+ 12 ♗xe2 ♗c5, while outright bad is 10 e6? dxe6 11 g3 ♖d8) 10...fxe5 11 ♗g5 (11 ♖a3? is well met by 11...♘b4! 12 ♗g5 ♕e6 13 ♖c3 – 13 ♖e3? ♗c5! is decisive in view of 14 ♖xe5 ♘d3+ – 13...h6 14 ♗e3 c5 when Black is much better) 11...♘f6 12 ♖e3 (Black has the initiative too after 12 ♘d2 d5) 12...0-0-0 13 ♘d2 ♕f7 14 ♖xe5 ♗b4 15 0-0-0 was seen in D.Scerbin-P.Petran, Budapest 2000.

White's king's rook has certainly got into the game, but Black could have obtained good play with 15...♖he8 16 ♗xf6 gxf6 17 ♖xe8 ♖xe8.

b2) Also worthy of attention is 9...g6!? and after 10 a3 (threatening 11 ♗g5; otherwise, 10 ♖h3?! ♗g7 11 ♖a3 ♘b4 12 ♖a5 d5! 13 exd6 cxd6 14

♕xe7+ ♔xe7 is better for Black, as is 10 ♗g5?! ♕b4+ 11 ♘d2 ♕xb2 12 ♖b1 ♕xa2 13 e6 ♗g7 14 ♕f3 0-0! 15 cxd5 fxe6) 10...♘b6 11 ♗g5 ♕e6 Black already has some initiative.

c) 9 ♗d2?! prevents a check on b4, but the bishop is not well placed on d2: 9...♘b6 (9...0-0-0 10 ♘c3 ♖e8 11 f4 f6 is also quite good for Black) 10 b3 g6 11 ♗c3 ♗g7 12 g3 0-0 13 ♗g2 ♖fe8 14 0-0 ♗xe5 and Black was slightly for choice in J.Cabrera-H.Rego, Cuba 1999.

d) 9 f4?! is a logical move, fortifying the e5-pawn. However, it doesn't help White's development and the weakness of the pawn on f4 means that after 9...♕b4+ White must play 10 ♔d1 when Black is better after 10...♗c5 11 ♕e4 0-0 12 b3 (12 g4 ♖fe8 threatens 13...♘f6) 12...♕b6! 13 cxd5 ♗xf1 14 ♖xf1 ♗d4 15 ♗e3 ♗xe3.

A) 9 ♘d2!?

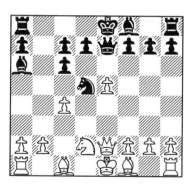

This hitherto slightly neglected move is an interesting alternative to the main line, 9 b3. White speeds up his queenside development and will only later play g3 and ♗g2. By starting with 9 ♘d2 instead of 9 b3 he also restricts Black's options. Most importantly, the move ...♛b4 no longer comes with check and if the e5-pawn falls, Black will not win it with tempo against the rook on a1. Finally, as the c4-pawn is now better protected, White begins to threaten ♛e4. That's the good news; the bad is that Black has a couple of quite reasonable responses, so 9 ♘d2 is unlikely to ever become more than an interesting sideline and a reasonable surprise weapon.

At this point we must chiefly examine:

A1: 9...♘b4
A2: 9...0-0-0
A3: 9...g6

Of these Line A1 seems to be too ambitious a try, but both A2 and A3 should grant Black decent-enough counterplay. First, though, we should examine the less-impressive alternatives:

a) 9...♘b6 is usually a concession in the 8...♗a6 variation: 10 b3 0-0-0 (10...d5 11 exd6 cxd6 12 ♗b2 f6 13 0-0-0 is a standard plus for White and 10...g6 11 ♗b2 ♗g7 12 0-0-0 also looks pleasant for him) 11 ♗b2 leaves Black's minor pieces in some danger of becoming marginalized on the queenside.

Indeed, all of 11...g6 12 0-0-0 ♗g7 13 f4 d5 14 ♛e3! dxc4 15 ♗xc4 ♗xc4 16 ♘xc4 ♘xc4 17 bxc4, 11...♖e8 12 ♛e3 f6 13 f4 g5 14 fxg5 fxe5 15 ♘e4 and 11...f6 12 exf6 ♛f7 13 0-0-0 gxf6 14 ♛f3 ♗g7 15 ♘e4 are very good for White, while after 11...d6 the simplest is 12 0-0-0 dxe5 13 ♛xe5 ♛xe5 14 ♗xe5 with a clear edge.

b) Another point of White's move order is to discourage 9...g5?!. That is a dynamic and important response to 9 b3, but here White can play 10 ♛e4!.

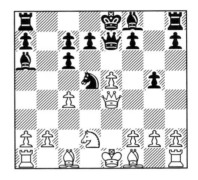

Suddenly Black faces problems as he must move his knight: 10...♘f4 (10...♘b6 11 b3 is good for White, who will quickly attack the protruding pawn on g5, and plain bad is 10...♘b4?! 11 a3 d5 12 ♛b1! when White wins a piece for little compensation) 11 h4! ♘g6 12 hxg5 ♛xg5 13 ♘f3 ♛e7 14 ♗d2 and White is much better.

c) 9...♘f4 is best met by 10 ♛e3! ♘g6 (10...♘e6 is possible, but more passive) 11 f4 and White can claim some advantage: for example, 11...f6 (alternatively, 11...d6 12 g3 ♛e6 13 ♗g2 ♘e7 14 0-0 was much better for White in L.Vajda-H.Holzmann, Balatonbereny 1996, as is 11...♕c5 12 ♘b3 ♕xe3+ 13 ♝xe3) 12 g3 ♕c5 13 ♕xc5 ♝xc5 14 exf6 gxf6 15 ♘b3 ♝b4+ 16 ♝d2 (16 ♔f2 ♝e7 17 ♝e3 is also good) 16...♖b8 17 0-0-0 and White had a clear plus in F.Gobet-P.Cladouras, Kecskemet 1987.

d) 9...♕b4?! is totally pointless: 10 a3 ♕b6 (or 10...♕a5 11 ♕e4 ♘b6 12 ♖b1) 11 ♕e4 ♘e7 12 b4 with a huge advantage for White.

e) And no better is the 9...♕h4?! 10 g3 ♕d4 11 a3 ♘b6 12 ♖b1 0-0-0 13 b4 ♕c3 of M.Langer-A.Shaffer, Dallas 2000, when simply 14 ♝b2 ♕c2 15 ♕e3 gives White a big advantage.

f) Finally, 9...f6!? is met by 10 ♕e4 ♘b6 11 exf6, but this may not be so bad for Black.

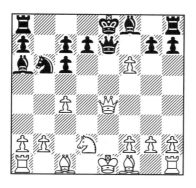

After 11...♕xe4+ 12 ♘xe4 ♝xc4! 13 ♝xc4 ♘xc4 14 0-0 ♔f7 White can hope to exploit his superior structure by playing b3 and fxg7, but Black seems to have enough counterplay in any case.

A1) 9...♘b4

An ambitious try, but there is no need to move the knight from d5 just yet.

10 ♘f3

With this simple response, White shows that he is more than capable of covering the c2-square.

10...c5

Securing the knight a retreat. Black might like to go 10...d5?!, but this is well met by 11 a3! ♝xc4 12 ♕d1 ♝xf1 13 ♔xf1 ♘a6 and now 14 ♕a4 (or 14 ♝e3!? ♕d7 15 e6 fxe6 16 ♘e5 with good compensation, as in N.Yaremko-M.Kravtsiv, Lvov 2006) 14...♘b8 15 ♝g5 has been shown by Ma.Tseitlin-A.Mikhalevski, Beersheba 1997, and subsequent games to give White promising compensation.

11 a3 ♘c6 12 ♝d2

White holds a slight edge, as Black has essentially renounced the ability to break with ...d5.

For example:

a) 12...f6 13 exf6 gxf6 14 ♝c3 is better for White.

b) So too was 12...d6 13 exd6 ♕xe2+ 14 ♝xe2 ♝xd6 15 ♝c3 0-0 16 0-0 ♖fe8

17 ♖fe1 in P.Koc-P.H.Nielsen, Pardubice 1995.

c) 12...♛e6 13 ♗c3 ♗e7 14 0-0-0 0-0 (or 14...f6 15 exf6 ♛xe2 16 f7+! ♚xf7 17 ♗xe2 with a slight edge in P.Svidler-V.Yemelin, St Petersburg 1995) 15 h4 ♖ae8 16 ♛e4 f6 17 ♗d3 and White had the upper hand in R.Har Zvi-Z.Almasi, Altensteig 1994.

d) Thus Black should probably try 12...0-0-0!?, especially as the natural 13 ♗c3?! runs into 13...d5! 14 exd6 ♖xd6! 15 ♛xe7 ♗xe7 when it was Black who had the edge in L.Oll-O.Kalinin, USSR 1986. Thus here White should either explore 13 0-0-0!? or settle for simplification with 13 ♗g5 f6 14 exf6 gxf6 15 ♛xe7 ♗xe7 16 ♗e3, retaining his structural advantage in both cases.

A2) 9...0-0-0

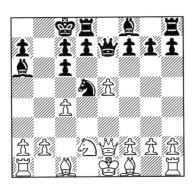

Just like it is after 9 b3 (Line B of our next chapter), this is a very obvious and natural try for Black.

10 b3

The alternatives are weaker: 10 ♛e4 ♘b6 transposes to note 'a2' to White's

9th move at the start of the chapter, while after 10 g3 ♖e8 11 f4 f6 12 ♛e4 ♘b6 Black is better.

10...g5

Another very thematic move. Black wants to bring his dark-squared bishop to g7, but advances the g-pawn two squares rather than one to both dissuade any notion of f4 and so that ♘f3 can be met by ...g4. This makes a lot of sense, but the text is by no means Black's only approach:

a) 10...♖e8?! doesn't achieve anything after 11 ♗b2 g6 (11...d6?? drops a piece to 12 ♛g4+ ♚b7 13 cxd5 and 11...♘f4 12 ♛e3 ♘g6 13 0-0-0 c5 14 f4 ♗b7 15 ♘f3 is also very good for White) 12 g3 ♗g7 13 0-0-0 ♘b6 14 f4 when White has a steady edge.

b) However, Black can play the very interesting 10...f6!, immediately challenging the central bridgehead.

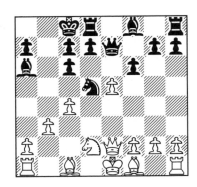

Now 11 ♛e4 ♘b4 gives Black the initiative, so White likely does best to play 11 ♗b2, but even then it seems that Black can pose some problems: 11...fxe5 12 0-0-0 (12 ♛xe5 ♛xe5+ 13

♗xe5 ♖e8 is plain bad for White) 12...♖e8! 13 g3 (alternatively, 13 ♘f3? e4 was much better for Black in J.Fernandez-S.Estremera Panos, Lleida 1991, as was 13 ♖e1?! ♘f6 14 g3 e4 in R.Heimrath-H.Grabher, Liechtenstein 1994) 13...♘f6 14 ♗h3 (14 ♘e4 ♔b8 15 ♗g2 ♕f7 16 ♕d2 ♘xe4 17 ♗xe4 ♗c8 saw Black slowly unravel in U.Voigt-D.Lobzhanidze, Wiesbaden 1996, with the advantage) 14...♔b8 15 ♖he1 (15 ♘f3 d6 is also good for Black) 15...d6 16 ♗g2 (or 16 ♘e4 ♗b7 17 ♗g2 h5 with an edge for Black in F.Peredy-L.Kovacs, Hungarian League 1996) 16...♗b7 17 ♕d3 ♕f7 and White had little compensation for her pawn in V.Savchenko-M.Fakhretdinova, Dagomys 2004.

c) Recently Black introduced the other immediate challenge to the e5-point, namely 10...d6!? in D.Howell-P.Svidler, Amsterdam 2010. Following the rather ambitious 11 ♕g4!? ♔b8 12 cxd5! ♕xe5+ 13 ♕e4 ♕xa1 14 ♕b4+ ♗b5 15 ♗xb5 ♕xc1+ 16 ♔e2 White had enough for the exchange, with the game concluding 16...♕c5 17 ♕xc5 dxc5 18 ♗xc6 ♗d6 ½-½. Thus White may do better with the more straightforward 11 ♗b2 and after 11...♘b4 (continuing actively; moreover, 12 exd6 was by now a serious threat with 12...♕f6 no longer possible in response) 12 ♕e4! (and not 12 ♘f3? here on account of just 12...dxe5, threatening to check on d3) White is perhaps a little better in a complicated and unexplored position: for example, 12...d5!? 13 cxd5

♗xf1 14 ♔xf1 cxd5 (or 14...♖xd5 15 ♘f3) 15 ♕e2 and White's king should prove the safer.

11 ♗b2 ♗g7 12 0-0-0!

There is no point in 12 ♕e4 ♘f4 13 0-0-0 ♗b7 14 ♕f5, as in J.Geller-A.Yakimenko, Krasnodar 2001, because after 14...♘g6 15 ♘f3 h6 Black is fine. Meanwhile 12 g3 leads to an important transposition, namely to Line C422 of our next chapter. However, with the text White manages to avoid the complications of that line, while keeping all his options open. This likely suffices for an edge, which is all the more reason why Black should not hope for a transposition after 10...g5, but should prefer 10...f6.

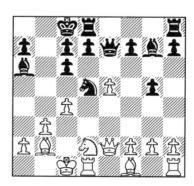

Black must now make a decision and it turns out that none of his options are especially good.

12...♘b6

The knight was not attacked, but Black wants to push either the d- or the f-pawn, after which an exchange of queens would unpin the pawn on c4.

Alternatively, Black could consider

putting more pressure on the e5-pawn, but after 12...♖de8 13 ♔b1 (also possible is 13 g3 followed by ♗g2) 13...♘f4 14 ♕e3 White would have the advantage.

Even worse, though, would be 12...♖he8?! in view of 13 h4! gxh4 14 ♕g4 with a big advantage in E.Najer-S.Sulskis, Pardubice 2004; the attack on the pawn on g5 is one of White's main ideas in this variation.

13 h4!

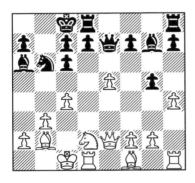

White is the first to strike a blow against the opponent's position and thus seizes the initiative.

13...g4

13...h6 14 ♕e3 would only make things worse for Black.

14 f4

White plays for maximum gain. 14 ♕xg4 ♗xe5 would be easier for Black, although White should still have something thanks to his better structure.

14...gxf3 15 ♘xf3 c5

Black gives up on the idea of ...d5 for a while and tries to activate his light-squared bishop.

16 ♕e1!

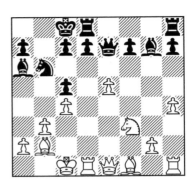

This frees the bishop on f1 while keeping an eye on e5, as well as creating possibilities for the queen on both flanks (with ♕a5 or ♕g3). No lesser game than T.Radjabov-V.Topalov, Nanjing 2009, continued 16...♗b7 17 ♗d3 h6 (another option was 17...♖de8, threatening to win the pawn; White would reply 18 ♖f1! ♖hg8 19 g4, retaining the advantage) 18 ♕g3 ♖dg8 19 ♖he1, leaving White ideally centralized and in full control of the position.

A3) 9...g6!?

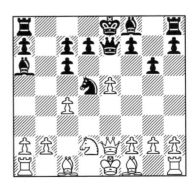

Line A2 can probably be considered

the main line after 9 ♘d2, but this is another logical approach from Black, taking immediate aim at e5.

10 b3

White decides to counter with a queenside fianchetto after all, which makes sense, especially when one considers most of the alternatives:

a) 10 ♘e4 runs into 10...♕b4+! 11 ♘d2 (and not 11 ♗d2?? ♕xb2 or 11 ♕d2? ♗xc4) 11...♗g7.

b) 10 a3?! prevents the check, but is slow and after 10...♗g7 11 ♘f3 ♘b6 12 b3 d6 13 ♗b2 ♘d7 White loses the e5-pawn.

c) 10 ♕e4 (forcing the knight to move) 10...f5! 11 exf6 (11 ♕d4?! ♘b4 12 ♕c3 c5 13 ♘f3 ♗g7 14 ♗g5 ♕e6 15 a3 ♘c6 16 0-0-0 0-0 left White too exposed in T.Micanek-P.Jerabek, Brno 1999) 11...♘xf6 12 ♕xe7+ ♗xe7 gives Black a lead in development and pressure down the f-file. The game T.Shadrina-R.Pokorna, Szeged 2006, continued 13 ♗e2 0-0 14 0-0 ♖ae8 15 ♗f3 ♗b4 16 b3 d5 17 ♖d1 g5 and Black was better.

d) 10 g3 ♗g7 11 ♕e4 (all of 11 ♘f3 0-0 12 ♗g5 f6 13 exf6 ♕b4+, 11 ♗g2 0-0 12 0-0 ♘b6 13 f4 f6 and 11 f4 0-0 12 ♕f2 ♘b4 are very good for Black) 11...♘b6 12 f4 0-0 13 b3 (as played in V.Diogo-D.Fernando, Almada 2008; otherwise, neither 13 ♗e2 f6 14 exf6 ♕xf6 nor 13 c5 ♗xf1 14 cxb6 ♗h3! 15 bxc7 d5 16 ♕e2 f6 is any improvement) 13...f6 14 ♗b2 fxe5 15 fxe5 d5 and Black is clearly on top.

e) Indeed, the only alternative worthy of further exploration is the recently topical 10 ♘f3!? ♕b4+! (10...♗g7 11 ♗g5! gives White an easy edge) 11 ♔d1!, giving up castling rights in a bid to leave Black's pieces poorly coordinated.

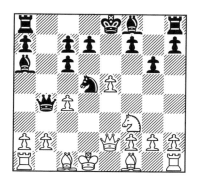

Now:

e1) After 11...♘b6 12 b3 ♗g7 13 ♕d2 ♕e7 (naturally White would be very happy to see an exchange of queens, leaving Black suffering from his offside minor pieces on the queenside and inferior structure) 14 ♕a5?! ♗b7 Black was better in V.Baklan-Z.Gyimesi, Austrian League 2005, but the somewhat more sensible 14 ♔c2 ♗b7 15 ♗b2 0-0 16 h4! improved and left White beginning to press in *Rybka-Pandix*, Leiden 2010. Very similar was the later 14 ♗b2 0-0 15 ♔c2 c5 16 h4! of I.Nepomniachtchi-P.Svidler, Moscow 2010, where the attempt to break out with 16...d5 only led to an unpleasant endgame for Black after 17 exd6 ♕xd6 18 ♗xg7 ♕xd2+ 19 ♘xd2 ♔xg7 20 ♘e4.

e2) Thus Black preferred to keep his knight in the centre while ruling out 12 ♕d2 with 11...♖b8!? in R.Ponomariov-P.Leko, Dortmund 2010. White eventually triumphed, but it's by no means clear that the endgame which arose after 12 ♕c2 ♘e7 13 b3 ♗g7 14 ♗d2 (maybe now is the time for 14 ♕d2!?, meeting 14...♕b6 with 15 ♗b2 and then a quick h4 à la *Rybka*) 14...♕b6 15 c5!? ♕b7 16 ♗xa6 ♕xa6 17 ♕c4 ♕xc4 18 bxc4 was better for him, with 18...f6!? a logical alternative to Leko's 18...h6.

Returning to 10 b3:

10...♗g7

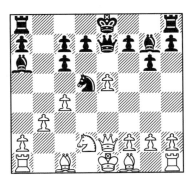

11 ♘f3

Another prudent decision, avoiding 11 ♗b2?! which is strongly met by 11...♘b4! 12 ♘f3 c5!, planning to attack the e5-pawn with ...♘c6. Indeed, after 13 g3 0-0 14 ♗g2 d5 15 0-0 (15 a3 ♘c6 16 0-0 ♖ab8 was also not what the doctor ordered for White in D.Petrosian-N.Grandelius, Sarajevo 2010) 15...♖ad8 16 ♖fd1 ♖fe8 Black was better in P.Svidler-M.Adams, Tilburg 1997.

11...0-0 12 ♗g5! f6 13 exf6 ♕xe2+ 14 ♗xe2 ♘xf6 15 0-0-0 d5

White has wisely elected to force simplification, but unsurprisingly Black has no problems whatsoever here and is fully equal.

B) 9 g3

White prepares to untangle his kingside pieces with a fianchetto, while supporting a possible f4-advance. This approach was fairly topical in the mid-late nineties, but methods have become established which promise Black sufficient counterplay.

B1: 9...g5
B2: 9...f6
B3: 9...0-0-0
B4: 9...♘b6
B5: 9...g6

Black's lesser options rather fail to convince:

a) 9...♕b4+ 10 ♘d2 ♘b6 (otherwise, 10...♗e7? 11 a3 ♕a5 was preferred in

J.Ocariz Gallego-R.Alonso Caamano, Mondariz 2004, but 12 ♕e4 would have driven back Black's knight with some advantage; perhaps, though, Black should settle for the 10...♖b8!? 11 ♕e4 ♘b6 12 ♗e2 g6 of O.Korneev-J.Gomez Esteban, Elgoibar 1998, although with 13 0-0!? ♗g7 14 ♖e1 0-0 15 c5! ♕xe4 16 ♘xe4 ♗xe2 17 cxb6 ♗g4 18 bxa7 ♖a8 19 ♗h6! White retains a clear pull) 11 ♕e4 (11 b3!? ♕c3 12 ♖b1 ♖b8 13 ♗b2 ♕c2 14 ♕d3 was also a little better for White in V.Rogovski-R.Gevorkyan, Kharkov 2003, but 11 a3 ♕a5 12 ♕e4?! doesn't achieve much here and after 12...0-0-0 Black had the initiative in B.Laubsch-D.Krajina, German League 2008) 11...0-0-0 (the solid 11...♗e7 12 ♗d3 would restrict White to just an edge) 12 ♗e2 ♗b7 13 0-0 ♕e7 14 a4! saw White beginning a strong attack in M.Rodriguez Garcia-F.Pascua Vilches, Palencia 1999.

b) The strange manoeuvre 9...♕c5 10 a3 ♕d4 consumes a fair amount of time and after the 11 ♘d2 ♘b6 12 ♖b1! of C.Severri Arrese-J.Ridameya Tatche, Barbera del Valles 2006, the queen will soon have to retreat, leaving White better.

c) 9...d6?! 10 ♗g2! (Krasenkow points out that Black is okay after 10 exd6 cxd6 11 ♕xe7+ ♘xe7) 10...dxe5 11 0-0 e4 (trying to return the pawn; 11...0-0-0 12 b3 would give White promising compensation and Black has to avoid 11...g6? because of Krasenkow's 12 ♕c2! ♘b4 13 ♕a4 0-0-0 14 a3)

sees Black waste no time opening up the centre.

Indeed, following the exchanges with 12 ♗xe4 f5 13 ♗f3 ♕xe2 14 ♗xe2 ♘b4 Black should be able to generate enough counterplay. However, White doesn't have to hurry to regain the pawn and 12 ♕c2! is strong: 12...♘b4 (the best of the bunch; both 12...♘b6 13 ♗xe4 0-0-0 14 b3 and 12...♘f6 13 ♘d2 0-0-0 14 ♘xe4 leave White somewhat better) 13 ♕a4 ♗b7 (13...♗xc4?! 14 a3 sees White picking up two pieces for the rook, with some advantage) 14 ♘c3 left White's queen very actively placed, which gave him promising compensation in the game S.Rublevsky-A.Aleksandrov, Polanica Zdroj 1997.

B1) 9...g5?!

This might be the choice of a player who has only really studied the 9 b3 g5 variation, but again this bold advance fails to convince when White hasn't potentially weakened himself on the long dark-square diagonal.

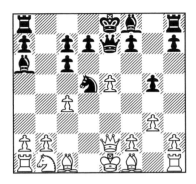

10 h4!?

White wastes no time pinpointing the downside to Black's ambitious advance.

Instead 10 b3 would give Black his desired transposition to Line C4 of our next chapter, but 10 ♗g2 ♗g7 11 0-0 isn't such a bad alternative for White. Now:

a) 11...♘b6 12 b3 0-0-0 (Black must avoid 12...♕xe5?? 13 ♕xe5+ ♗xe5 14 ♖e1, as pointed out by Tsesarsky and 12...♗xe5? 13 ♖e1 f6 14 ♗a3 ♕e6 15 ♕h5+ isn't too much better a pawn grab) 13 ♖e1 ♖de8 (White obtained a dangerous attack for the pawn after 13...♖he8 14 ♗b2 f6 15 a4! fxe5 16 ♘c3 ♔b8 17 a5 in F.Manca-M.Perez Candelario, Kusadasi 2006, with his knight en route to the juicy c5-square after ♘e4 and ♗a3) 14 ♗b2 sees White covering e5, while Black's minor pieces loiter a little forlornly on the queenside.

Moreover, Black's attempt to develop some counterplay on the kingside with 14...h5 (14...♕c5 15 ♘d2! ♗xe5? 16 ♗xe5 f6 rather backfired af-

ter 17 ♘e4! ♕xe5 18 ♕d2 in M.Narciso Dublan-J.Cubas, Linares 1996, and here 15...h5 isn't much of an improvement after 16 ♘e4 ♕e7 17 a4!; instead Black might challenge in the centre, but after 14...f6 again 15 a4!? fxe5 16 ♘c3 looks like excellent value for a pawn)

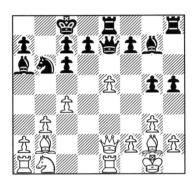

15 a4 (15 ♘d2!? with the idea of 15...h4 16 ♕g4 is also promising) 15...h4 in D.Pavlogianni-H.Markantonaki, Kallithea 2003, wouldn't have been overly convincing had White now counterattacked himself with 16 ♕e3 ♔b8 17 a5 ♘c8 18 ♘d2.

b) 11...0-0-0 12 ♖e1! (good prophylaxis; White can now move the queen away, whereas the immediate 12 ♕g4?! allows Black counterplay with 12...h5!) 12...♖de8 (unsurprisingly 12...♘b6 13 b3 d6 14 ♗b2 is somewhat in White's favour too) 13 ♕c2! ♕c5 was seen in E.Mukhametov-V.Likov, Omsk 1996, and now 14 ♘d2 followed by ♕a4 would have seen White retain the upper hand.

c) Perhaps, not withstanding the gash in his kingside structure, Black might consider 11...0-0!?, but after 12 ♖e1 ♖ae8 13 ♕h5! ♗xc4 14 ♗xg5 White secures the initiative in any case.

We now return to 10 h4:

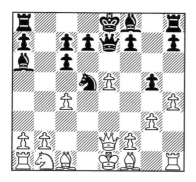

10...♗g7

Logically countering against e5.

Instead 10...gxh4 11 ♖xh4 ♘b6 (or 11...0-0-0 12 ♕e4 ♕b4+ 13 ♘d2 ♘b6 14 c5! ♕xe4+ 15 ♘xe4 ♗xf1 16 cxb6 with some advantage in V.Rogovski-P.Tishin, Alushta 2001) 12 ♘d2 0-0-0 13 b3 ♗g7 14 ♗b2 ♖de8 15 ♖e4! saw White making excellent use of his early rook deployment to keep Black's counterplay under control in V.Vehi Bach-A.Medina Garcia, Catalonian League 1999.

White must also be at least a bit better after 10...g4 11 ♗g2 ♗g7 12 0-0, having sealed the kingside, while he can meet 10...♘b6 11 ♘d2 ♗g7 with 12 hxg5 ♕xe5 13 ♕xe5+ ♗xe5 14 a4!, thereby securing some advantage.

11 hxg5

The correct capture, as 11 ♗xg5? runs into the powerful rejoinder 11...♗xc4! 12 ♗xe7 (the rook on a1 will fall after 12 ♕xc4? ♕xe5+) 12...♗xe2 13

♗xe2 ♘xe7 when it's Black who's better.

11...♗xe5 12 f4!

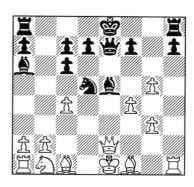

White preferred 12 ♖h4?! 0-0-0 13 ♖e4 ♖he8 14 f4 in A.Lastin-K.Andreev, St Petersburg 1997, but 14...♗d4 15 ♖xe7 ♖xe7 16 ♕xe7 ♘xe7 would have favoured Black thanks to his large lead in development. Neither is 12 ♘d2 0-0-0 13 ♔d1 ♖de8 14 ♘f3 ♗g7 too amazing for White, but after the text and 12...♗g7 13 ♕xe7+ ♘xe7 14 ♘d2 his structural plusses should continue to count for at least a little something.

B2) 9...f6

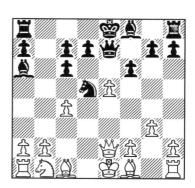

Black settles on a less-radical pawn push than 9...g5 in his bid to generate immediate counterplay.

10 e6!?

White sacrifices a pawn to keep the e-file closed and slow down Black's development. Such an approach is certainly tempting and becomes even more so when one examines the alternatives:

a) 10 exf6 ♘xf6 (10...♕xe2+ 11 ♗xe2 ♘xf6 12 ♗f4 0-0-0 13 0-0 d5 14 b3 ♗d6 15 ♗xd6 cxd6 is also fine for Black, A.Agayeva-K.Nadig, Oropesa del Mar 2000) 11 ♘c3 ♕xe2+ 12 ♗xe2 ♗c5 13 0-0 0-0 14 ♗f4 ♖ae8! gave Black sufficient activity to maintain the balance in M.Heika-T.Lochte, Freising 2001, since 15 ♗xc7 would have been met by 15...♘d5 16 cxd5 ♗xe2 17 ♘xe2 ♖xe2 18 dxc6 dxc6.

b) 10 b3 is another way of sacrificing the pawn, but with 10...fxe5 11 ♗g2 ♘f6 12 0-0 (White might prefer to regain the pawn with 12 ♗b2 ♕e6 13 ♕xe5, but 13...♗b4+ 14 ♘d2 ♕xe5+ 15 ♗xe5 0-0 clearly left Black without any problems in A.Rizouk-D.Leygue, St Affrique 2001) 12...♕e6 13 ♗b2 ♗d6 (safer than 13...♗c5 when 14 ♘c3!? 0-0 15 ♘a4 ♗b6? 16 ♘xb6 axb6 17 ♕xe5 ♕xe5 18 ♗xe5 regained the pawn with some advantage in R.Ponomariov-Z.Gyimesi, Pula 2000, and even 15...♗d6 16 ♕d2 would have given White decent compensation) 14 ♘d2 0-0 15 ♖ae1 ♖ae8 16 ♗c3 ♕e7 17 ♘f3 e4! 18 ♘d2 Black returned the pawn to

force exchanges, thereby maintaining the balance in I.Nataf-H.Rolletschek, Austrian League 2000.

c) 10 ♗g2? ♘b6! costs White a pawn for very little, as Black is able to meet 11 b3 with 11...♕xe5 12 ♕xe5+ fxe5.

Returning to the critical 10 e6:

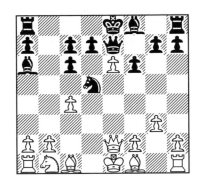

10...dxe6

Black accepts the offer, but quite possibly he should prefer to decline:

a) 10...♘b6 11 exd7+ (11 b3? ♕xe6 12 ♕xe6+ dxe6 13 ♗h3 was not the best of gambits in M.Narciso Dublan-M.Zivanic, Budapest 2001, because 13...♗c5 14 ♘c3 ♔f7 would have left White with clearly insufficient compensation) 11...♔f7 (otherwise, 11...♔xd7 12 ♗h3+ ♔e8 13 ♕xe7+ ♗xe7 14 b3 ♔f7 15 0-0 ♖ad8 16 ♗e3 gave White the initiative in G.Massenzano-N.Diaz Hollemaert, Buenos Aires 1993, and here 12 b3!? is also quite tempting, while after 11...♘xd7?! 12 b3 ♘e5 13 ♗e3 White enjoys a pleasant structural advantage) 12 ♕xe7+ ♗xe7 13 b3!? (Black was fine after the simplification with 13 c5 ♗xf1 14 cxb6 ♗h3 15 bxc7 ♗xd7 in

S.Rublevsky-Z.Almasi, Niksic 1997) 13...♘xd7 (it's not clear that the pawn has to be regained without delay and Black may do better with 13...♗c5!?) 14 ♗g2 (clearly the right square for the bishop, whereas 14 ♗e3?! ♘e5! 15 ♗e2 h5 16 h3 ♖ad8 misplaced it and gave Black the initiative in O.Maiorov-V.Tseshkovsky, Krasnodar 1997) 14...♗c5 sees Black developing a tempo and hoping to trouble White down the a1-h8 diagonal.

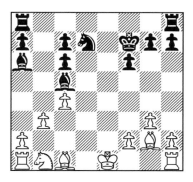

However, with the bold 15 0-0! (15 ♗e3 ♗xe3 16 fxe3 ♘e5 had earlier left Black pretty comfortably placed in V.Baklan-Z.Gyimesi, Vrnjacka Banja 1998) 15...♗d4 16 ♖d1 ♗xa1 17 ♖xd7+ ♔g6 18 ♖xc7 White picked up two pawns and thus full compensation for the exchange in A.Areshchenko-M.Zivanic, Balatonlelle 2001.

b) 10...0-0-0!? sees Black continuing aggressively and now White must decide what to do with his light-squared bishop:

b1) 11 ♗g2 ♘b6 (only now does the knight retreat; instead 11...♖e8 12 0-0

dxe6 13 ♖e1 ♔b8 14 ♕c2 gave White good play for the pawn thanks to Black's vulnerable queenside in O.Saez Gabikagogeaskoa-J.Diez, Islantilla 2007) 12 b3 ♕xe6! (simple and strong; 12...♖e8 was preferred in V.Novy-R.Wiesinger, Plzen 2004, but with 13 ♗h3!? dxe6 14 ♗g2 ♗b7 15 0-0 followed by a4 White would again have enjoyed good play for his pawn) 13 ♕xe6 dxe6 14 ♗xc6 ♗c5 leaves Black with a useful lead in development and thus the initiative.

b2) 11 ♗h3 ♔b8 (now after 11...♘b6 White can regain the pawn with an edge after 12 b3 dxe6 13 ♗a3 ♕e8 14 ♕xe6+ ♕xe6+ 15 ♗xe6+ ♔b8 16 0-0) 12 b3 (naturally White must avoid 12 exd7? ♕xe2+ 13 ♔xe2 ♗xc4+ 14 ♔f3 ♘b6 15 ♔g2 ♘xd7 16 ♖d1 ♗d5+ when Black is much better and he also does well to sidestep 12 0-0?! h5!) continues to offer the e6-pawn, but will White obtain enough for it?

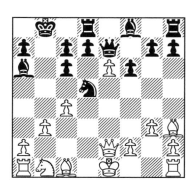

Indeed, following 12...dxe6 (12...f5!? is quite a tempting option too, intending 13 exd7 ♕xd7 14 0-0 g6 with easy and swift development) 13 a3 h5! White may not have had quite enough compensation in Ruan Lufei-Wang Yu, Shenzhan 2010, but in any case should now have preferred 14 &b2 to 14 0-0 h4.

11 &g2!

White correctly prioritizes kingside development, although of the alternatives variation 'c' is also tempting:

a) 11 ♕e4? f5 12 ♕c2 ♘b6 just leaves White with clearly insufficient compensation.

b) 11 b3?! ♕f7 12 &h3 &b4+ 13 &d2 e5 14 &xb4 ♘xb4 15 0-0 0-0 also favoured Black in I.Efimov-Y.Yakovich, Gausdal 1991.

c) 11 &h3!? f5 (White enjoys full compensation too after both 11...e5 12 0-0 ♖d8 13 b3 ♘b6 14 ♘c3 and 11...♔f7 12 0-0 g6 13 ♖e1 e5 14 ♘d2) 12 0-0 g6 13 ♖e1 ♔f7 14 ♘d2 &g7 15 &g2 ♖he8 16 ♘f3 left White well coordinated and with plenty of play for the pawn in M.Manakova-M.Savic, Zlatibor 2007.

11...♔f7

Black's king won't be entirely happy here, but neither are the alternatives a panacea for him:

a) 11...♖d8 12 0-0 (A.Bezemer-T.Ellenbroek, Purmerend 1993) 12...g6 13 ♖e1 ♔f7 14 b3 ♘b4 15 &e4 leaves Black's knight in potential danger and White with good compensation.

b) After 11...♕d7 12 0-0 ♘b6 13 b3 &d6 (or 13...0-0-0 14 ♘c3 &c5 15 ♖d1 &d4 16 &e3 e5 17 a4 and White enjoyed good attacking prospects in B.Lalic-F.Izeta Txabarri, Ubeda 1998) 14 ♖d1 0-0 15 ♕c2! Black faces certain difficulties on the c-file.

c) 11...0-0-0 12 0-0 (M.Heika-H.Appel, German League 2001) 12...h5!? 13 ♖e1 ♔b8 14 b3 isn't entirely clear, but again White must have at least enough for the pawn.

12 0-0 ♖d8

Black can also develop his kingside pieces with 12...♕c5 13 b3 &d6, but after 14 &b2 ♘e7 15 ♘d2 White enjoys good central and light-square control.

13 b3 c5

Black is determined to maintain his extra pawn! The text is not forced, but after both 13...g6 14 &a3! ♕d7 15 ♕e1 &xa3 16 ♘xa3 ♘e7 17 ♕a5 and 13...♘b4 14 ♘c3 f5 15 &e3 White has at least enough compensation.

14 ♖d1

White prepares to contest the d-file, but one can also make a good case for Chytilek's 14 ♘d2 followed by 15 ♘e4 and for the similar 14 &b2 g6 15 ♘d2 &g7 16 ♘e4 of M.Lantini-A.Tosoni, Italy 1998.

14...♘b6 15 ♘d2

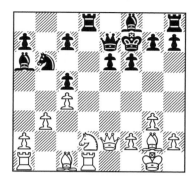

White keeps the rooks on, rather than help Black to untangle his kingside, and will follow up with 16 ♗b2 (or even 16 ♗a3, targeting c5) and 17 ♘e4 when his forces present a model of harmony. The same cannot be said of Black's and it's hard not to conclude that White likely enjoys more than enough play for the pawn.

B3) 9...0-0-0

Black keeps his central and kingside options open for a move, while hoping that White will transpose to Line B2 of our next chapter with 10 b3.

10 ♗g2!?

This requires White to be happy to sacrifice a pawn, but looks like the best way to avoid the aforementioned transposition. Others:

a) 10 ♗h3 ♖e8 11 0-0 ♘b6 12 ♘d2 ♕xe5 was seen in E.Grigorieva-M.Aseeva, St Petersburg 2001, when even 13 ♕xe5 ♖xe5 14 ♘f3 ♖e8 wouldn't have given White enough for her pawn.

b) 10 ♕e4 ♘b6 (or 10...♘f6 11 ♕e2 ♖e8 12 f4, as in S.Reppen-Wang Yu, Gibraltar 2008, when 12...♕b4+ 13 ♘d2 ♗c5 would have favoured Black) 11 b3 (11 c5?! ♗xf1 12 cxb6 ♗a6 13 bxa7 actually sees White temporarily win a pawn, but after 13...♔b7 14 ♗e3 d5 Black develops a strong initiative) 11...♖e8 12 f4 g5! began to undermine White's pawn-chain in T.Mihalincic-I.Bozanic, Zagreb 2009, and after 13 c5 ♗xf1 14 cxb6 ♗a6 15 bxa7 ♔b7 Black would have been slightly for choice.

10...♖e8!

Forcing White to sacrifice the pawn. Instead 10...♗xc4? 11 ♕xc4 ♕xe5+ 12 ♕e2 ♗b4+ 13 ♘d2 ♗xd2+ 14 ♗xd2 ♕xb2 15 0-0 was a badly unconvincing piece sacrifice in P.Scarella-G.Cuttica, Buenos Aires 1993, while White has good compensation after both 10...♘b6 11 b3 f6 12 ♗b2 (P.Janotta-J.Garodel, Toulon 2001) 12...fxe5 13 0-0 d5 14 ♕xe5 ♕xe5 15 ♗xe5 dxc4 16 ♖c1 and 10...f6 11 0-0 fxe5 12 ♕c2 ♘f6 (F.Peralta-C.Vittorino, Internet blitz 2004) 13 ♘d2 h5 14 ♕a4.

11 0-0

Fairly essential. White actually preferred 11 f4? in F.Amonatov-N.Purgin, Vladimir 2002, but with 11...f6 Black wins the pawn after all while also causing some discomfort to White's king.

11...♘b6

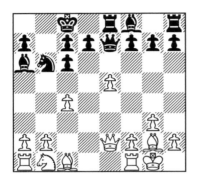

As we will see in Line D2 of our next chapter, Black can sometimes give up two pieces for a rook and two pawns in such a position, but here White hasn't spent a tempo on b3 and 11...♕xe5? 12 ♕xe5 ♖xe5 13 cxd5 ♗xf1 14 ♔xf1 ♖xe5 15 ♗e3 gives him excellent play against Black's vulnerable queenside.

12 b3

This looks a better try than the 12 ♖e1 f6 (12...♗xc4 13 ♕c2 f6 transposes) 13 ♕c2 of E.Shakenov-A.Achang, St Petersburg 2004, when 13...♗xc4 14 b3 ♗f7! 15 ♗b2 ♕c5 doesn't give White enough for the pawn.

12...♕xe5 13 ♕xe5 ♖xe5

Thus Black has snaffled a pawn, but at the risk that his queenside pieces will remain sidelined. Indeed, Black's attempts to activate them and White's

to prevent that happening will dominate play over the next few moves.

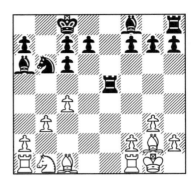

14 ♗f4!?

This looks like the best try. Instead 14 ♗b2 ♖e2 15 ♗d4 ♖e8 16 a4 c5 17 ♗e3 d6 18 ♘h3+ ♘d7 saw Black beginning to untangle when White didn't have quite enough in O.Saez Gabikagogeaskoa-V.Miguel Lago, Linares 1998, and after 14 ♖d1 f6 15 ♘c3 ♗b4 16 ♗b2 ♖he8 Black was also slightly for choice in S.Kowalczyk-H.Beekhuis, Hengelo 1998.

14...♖e8

We've followed the game M.Heika-H.Hepting, Fuerth 1999, and now 15 a4!?, threatening to entomb Black's knight in the corner, deserves close attention and should supply enough compensation.

B4) 9...♘b6

It may seem strange to retreat the knight voluntarily, but Black reasons that he is doing so with tempo and will be able to activate his queenside pieces with a quick ...d5.

10 b3

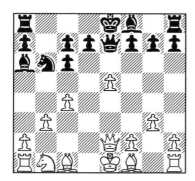

10 ♘d2 has long been considered less promising, but actually after 10...♛e6 11 b3 play has transposed to variation 'b' to White's 11th move, below, which he may well not object to. Thus Black might do better with 10...g6!? with a likely transposition into variation 'd' to White's 10th move in Line A3.

10...♛e6

Black prepares to develop his bishop along the a3-f8 diagonal, but practice has also seen:

a) 10...0-0-0!? is best met by 11 ♗b2, transposing to note 'b' at the beginning of Line B1 in our next chapter. Somewhat more aggressive was 11 a4? in L.Badjarani-Z.Abi Ayad, Iran 1993, but this would have backfired had Black found 11...♛b4+ 12 ♘d2 ♖e8.

b) 10...g6 11 ♗g2 ♗g7 12 0-0 0-0 13 f4!? (continuing to prioritize kingside development, but 13 ♗b2 should also lead to an edge for White: he meets 13...f6 with 14 ♗a3 and 13...d5 14 ♘d2 f6 15 e6! ♖fe8 16 ♖fe1 gave White the

initiative in B.Yildiz-N.Ozenmis, Kocaeli 2008) 13...♛e6 was seen in E.Relange-M.Waters, Buenos Aires 1992, and now 14 ♘c3 must promise White a pull.

c) 10...d5 may appear quite consistent, but actually after 11 ♗g2! (11 exd6 cxd6 12 ♗b2 ♛xe2+ 13 ♗xe2 0-0-0 14 ♘c3 was a little better for White too in L.Totsky-A.Syrchikov, Perm 1997) White's pressure down the long diagonal counts for more than Black's against c4.

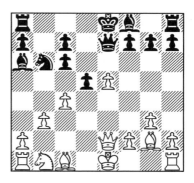

Indeed, after 11...♛d7 (11...♘xc4? 12 bxc4 ♗xc4 13 ♛e3 ♛b4+ 14 ♗d2 wasn't too convincing in M.Jenicek-L.Kozlovsky, Czech League 2006) 12 0-0 ♗e7 White had a couple of decent options in A.Mazara-F.Alvarez, Santo Domingo 2001: 13 ♘c3 and 13 a4!?.

d) 10...d6 11 ♗g2 ♗b7 12 ♗b2 dxe5 13 0-0!? should by now be quite a familiar concept and after 13...♘d7 14 ♖e1 White enjoyed promising play for the pawn in I.Salgado Lopez-P.Darini, Chalkidiki 2003.

11 ♗g2

Consistent with White's choice of

9th move, but by no means his only option:

a) 11 ♘c3?! ♗b4! 12 ♗d2 (O.Kauppila-D.Lardot, Helsinki 1998) 12...0-0 allows Black to become too active.

b) 11 ♗b2 ♗e7 (White was a little better after 11...d5 12 exd6 cxd6 13 ♘d2 in E.Malakhevich-A.Fatkulin, Kazan 2003) 12 ♗g2 0-0 saw Black wisely connect her rooks before advancing the d-pawn, thereby retaining approximate equality in M.Knotkova-J.Brudnova, Chrudim 1993.

c) 11 ♘d2!? ♗b4! (again the most active development; 11...♗c5 12 ♗b2 0-0 13 0-0-0 ♕e7 14 ♕e4 gave White a pull in J.Zawadzka-M.Palao, Turin 2006) 12 ♗b2 0-0 (12...0-0-0 13 0-0-0 ♖he8 14 a3 enables White to maintain control) 13 0-0-0! reaches a position in need of further tests.

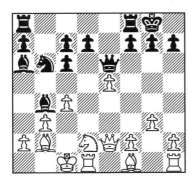

With Black's a-pawn currently impeded, White's king should be safe enough on the queenside and 13...♖fe8 (Black probably does better with the 13...♕e7 of H.Ingolfsdottir-J.Mohammed, Bled 2002, when he can meet 14

♘e4 with 14...♗a3, which should supply enough counterplay) 14 ♕h5! ♕e7 15 f4 slightly favoured White who had begun to attack on the kingside in M.Prizant-G.O'Toole, British League 2005.

11...♗c5!

Unlike in our last note, this is now the correct development for the bishop! That's because 11...♗b4+ no longer pins a knight and after 12 ♗d2 ♗xd2+ 13 ♘xd2 0-0 14 0-0 White had developed with tempo and secured an edge in E.Remete-J.Zalan, Hungarian League 2001.

12 ♗b2

Shoring up the defence of e5. Again White might like to exchange the dark-squared bishops, but now after 12 ♗e3 ♗xe3 13 ♕xe3 0-0 14 0-0 ♖ae8 Black was in time to develop decent counterplay in T.Gruskovnjak-M.Crepan, Bled 2000.

12...0-0 13 ♘d2 ♖ae8 14 0-0 d5

Only now does Black advance his d-pawn and after 15 ♖ac1 ♘d7 he had just enough counter-pressure to maintain the balance in V.Maksimenko-I.Kulish, St Petersburg 1993.

B5) 9...g6

A fairly popular response, after which play has often transposed to Line D2 of our next chapter following 10 b3 ♗g7 11 ♗b2. However, it seems that Black may have a simpler response to 10 b3, as we'll see shortly.

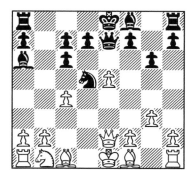

10 b3

Approved by theory, White pursues the transposition. Moreover, the alternatives aren't impressive:

a) 10 ♘d2 takes play back into note 'd' to White's 10th move in Line A3.

b) 10 ♗g2? could be considered consistent, but badly underestimates the pressure against e5: 10...♗g7! 11 0-0 (or 11 f4 f6! 12 b3 fxe5 13 ♗b2, as in M.Ragger-A.Kosten, Austrian League 2006, and now the simple 13...0-0 leaves Black somewhat for choice) 11...0-0 (but not 11...♗xe5?? 12 ♖e1 when White wins a piece) 12 ♖e1 ♖fe8! leaves White unable to defend his vulnerable pawns on e5 and c4:

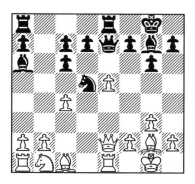

b1) 13 ♘a3 ♕c5?! (13...♘b6 looks like a better move order, transposing after 14 ♕c2 ♕c5) 14 ♕c2?! (returning the favour; he had to take his chance with 14 ♕d2!?, which wouldn't have been so clear) 14...♘b6 and Black found himself a clear pawn to the good after both 15 ♗f4 ♗xe5 in A.Danin-V.Feoktistov, Voronezh 2000, and 15 ♗e3 ♕xe5 in P.Petitcunot-H.Daurelle, French League 2003.

b2) The 13 ♗d2 of F.Mandon-A.Ladisic, Le Touquet 2009, should naturally be met by 13...♕c5.

b3) 13 ♘d2 ♕c5 14 ♕g4 (P.Rewitz-E.Sobjerg, Aarhus 1995) 14...♘b6 again sees Black picking up a pawn for almost no compensation.

10...f6!?

There are over 300 games with this position on ChessBase's *Mega Database* and in these Black has almost always opted for 10...♗g7, leading to the aforementioned transposition after 11 ♗b2, with the text having only occurred twice! No wonder that theory has rather neglected the move.

11 ♗b2

Retaining the tension must be correct. Indeed, after 11 exf6 ♕xe2+ 12 ♗xe2 ♘xf6 13 ♗b2 ♔f7 Black enjoyed easy development and equality in P.Bobras-J.Bernasek, Ceska Trebova 2007.

11...♗g7

This position has also arisen a few times from the move order 9 b3 g6 10 ♗b2 ♗g7 11 ♗b2 f6 (11...0-0 and 11...0-0-0 are much more common, as we'll see in Line D2 of Chapter Two; incidentally, after the former 12 ♗g2 f6 takes play into note 'a1' to White's 12th move, below). Now White must decide what to do about the pressure on e5.

12 exf6

This seems better-timed than the move before and now White can hope to exploit his superior structure in a queenless middlegame, but there are alternatives and critical ones at that:

a) 12 ♗g2 with a further divide:

a1) 12...0-0!? 13 e6?! (tempting, but too ambitious; instead the prudent 13 0-0 leaves Black with nothing better

than 13...fxe5, taking play into variation 'a2') 13...dxe6! (better than 13...♖fe8 14 0-0 dxe6 15 ♕d2 when White had good positional compensation in A.Motylev-P.Sinkevich, St Petersburg 1997) 14 ♕d2 f5! 15 cxd5 exd5+ gave Black two pawns, much the safer king and dangerous play for the piece in V.Parfenov-J.Grachev, St Petersburg 2002.

a2) 12...fxe5 13 0-0 0-0 14 ♕d2! (breaking the pin is a better try than 14 ♖e1, after which 14...♖ae8 15 ♕d2 ♘b6 16 ♗a3 c5 17 ♘c3 d6 didn't give White quite enough for the pawn in D.Carraro-D.Campagnoni, Argentina 2007, and neither here did 16 ♕a5 ♕f7 in L.Oms Fuentes-M.Panchanathan, Montcada i Reixac 2009) 14...e4! (14...♘b6?! 15 ♗a3 d6 16 ♗xc6 saw White regaining his pawn with some advantage after 16...♖ab8 17 ♘c3 ♔h8 18 ♖ae1 ♗b7 19 ♗xb7 ♖xb7 20 ♘e4 in D.Markin-C.Lissang, Pardubice 2009) 15 ♗xg7 ♕xg7 16 ♗xe4! regained the pawn and remained quite unclear in F.Tairi-S.Lejlic, Vaxjo 1998.

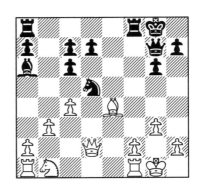

Now 16...♕xa1 17 ♗xd5+ cxd5 18 ♘c3 ♕xf1+ 19 ♔xf1 likely slightly favours White, as indicated by Tairi, but Black might consider 16...♖f7!?. Instead Tairi-Lejlic continued 16...♘e3 17 ♖e1 ♘g4 18 f3 ♘f6 19 ♘c3!? (19 ♘d3 ♘d5! is quite an annoying resource, as noted by Tairi in *Informant 71*) 19...♘xe4 20 ♘xe4 when it looked like White was beginning to get on top, but it seems that the calm 20...♖xf3! 21 ♘c5 ♗c8 should be okay for Black.

b) If White is determined to sacrifice the e-pawn for some play then 12 ♕d2!? also deserves attention. Certainly 12...♘b6 13 ♗g2 fxe5 14 0-0 ♗b7 15 a4 (15 ♕a5!?) 15...a5 16 ♘c3 0-0 17 ♗a3 d6 18 c5! saw White obtaining decent compensation in L.Vajda-E.Forgo, Zalakaros 1997.

12...♕xe2+ 13 ♗xe2 ♘xf6

Black keeps the bishops on and this seems more precise than 13...♗xf6 14 ♗xf6 ♘xf6 15 ♘d2 0-0-0 16 0-0-0 c5 17 ♗f3 ♖hf8 18 ♖he1 when the simplification had left White with a small but clear endgame pull in E.Handoko-I.Seitaj, Moscow Olympiad 1994.

14 ♘d2 0-0

This is quite a critical position for the assessment of 10...f6. Black still has his queenside weaknesses and his light-squared bishop is yet to rejoin the fray, but he will obtain counterplay down the e- and f-files, as well as with a timely ...♘e4 or ...♘d5. However, that activity may well not be enough for equality:

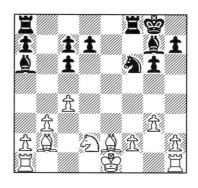

a) 15 0-0 ♖fe8 16 ♖fe1 c5?! 17 ♗f3 saw White taking control in N.Vyskocil-M.Rychtecky, Brno 2006, but Black would have been okay after 15...♖ae8 with the idea of 16 ♖ae1 ♘d5!.

b) 15 0-0-0 ♖ae8 16 ♖de1 (16 ♗f3!?) 16...♘e4 17 ♗xg7 ♔xg7 18 ♘xe4 ♖xe4 19 f3 ♖e7 20 ♗d1 ♖fe8 21 ♖xe7+ ♖xe7 22 ♔d2 gave White an edge thanks to his better structure, but Black was able to hold the endgame in B.Shovunov-I.Seitaj, Elista Olympiad 1998.

Conclusion

Only 9 ♘d2 and 9 g3 really deserve attention as alternatives to 9 b3. The former somewhat reduces Black's options, but unfortunately for White he has some problems to solve after 9...0-0-0 10 b3 f6! (but not 10...g5 11 ♗b2 ♗g7 in view of Radjabov's 12 0-0-0!), while 9...g6 forces him to be quite precise to avoid stumbling into an inferior position.

After 9 g3 Black should not lash out with 9...g5, but both 9...f6 and 9...0-0-0 are playable for him, not withstanding the decent positional compensation White obtains by giving up his e-pawn. Moreover, 9...♘b6 has more bite than one would expect and unsurprisingly 9...g6 is also in decent health for Black. Then 10 b3 usually leads after 10...♗g7 11 ♗b2 to the fairly critical Line D2 of our next chapter. Instead 10...f6!? deserves further attention, although on the current evidence it seems that White should be able to emerge with a pull.

Chapter Two
The Main Line:
8...♗a6 9 b3

1 e4 e5 2 ♘f3 ♘c6 3 d4 exd4 4 ♘xd4 ♘f6 5 ♘xc6 bxc6 6 e5 ♕e7 7 ♕e2 ♘d5 8 c4 ♗a6 9 b3

This is White's main move. He may well still fianchetto on the kingside and/or develop his knight to d2, but first shores up the c4-pawn and gives himself the useful option of supporting e5 with ♗b2. We will come across plenty of critical positions in this chapter, especially after all of the following options:

A: 9...♕h4
B: 9...0-0-0
C: 9...g5
D: 9...g6

The remaining alternatives are somewhat less challenging and give White good prospects of emerging with an edge:

a) 9...♕b4+ does not trouble White at all now that c4 is protected: 10 ♕d2 (this promises a long-term edge in a quiet position, but also possible is the more ambitious 10 ♗d2!? ♕b6 11 ♕e4 ♘b4 12 ♗e3 ♕a5 13 ♘d2, with the advantage) 10...♕xd2+ 11 ♔xd2! (a slightly unnatural recapture, but best as White prevents 11...♘b4) 11...♘f4 12 g3 ♘e6 13 ♗g2 g6 14 ♗b2 ♗g7 15 ♔c2 0-0-0 16 ♘d2 with a slight plus for White in J.Hector-T.Ernst, Swedish Team Championship 1999.

b) The rather inconsistent 9...♘b6 looks like a concession and here, unlike after 9 g3, it most certainly is!

White maintains some advantage with 10 ♗b2 d5 (otherwise, 10...♕e6 11 ♘d2 favours White also, as we'll see in the notes to Black's 10th move in Line A2 of our next chapter, and so too does the transposition 10...0-0-0 11 ♘d2, reaching a position which we considered at the start of Line A in our previous chapter) 11 exd6 ♕xe2+ 12 ♗xe2 cxd6 and now the most precise is 13 ♗f3! ♔d7 (or 13...♗b7 14 ♘c3 ♗e7 15 0-0-0 0-0-0 16 ♘e2 followed by ♘d4-f5 with some advantage) 14 0-0 ♖b8 15 ♗c3 f6 16 ♖e1 and White was much better in J.Santos-C.Boino, Lisbon 1999.

c) Of the immediate central challenges, 9...d6? is a blunder in view of 10 ♕e4 ♘b6 (even worse is 10...♘b4? 11 a3 d5 12 ♕e2) 11 ♕xc6+.

d) However, 9...f6 is in a sense quite a critical move, clearing a retreat square on f6 for the knight.

White must respond actively and precisely, but with 10 ♗b2 (10 exf6 ♘xf6 11 ♗b2 ♕xe2+ 12 ♗xe2 ♗c5 13 0-0 0-0 14 ♘d2 d5 15 ♗f3 ♖ae8 was a good indication of Black's aims in B.Thipsay-S.Iuldachev, Sangli 2000) 10...♘f4!? (alternatively, 10...0-0-0 transposes to Line B12, while 10...fxe5 11 ♕h5+ g6 12 ♕xe5 ♘f6 13 ♕xe7+! – note that 13 c5? fails to 13...♗xf1 14 ♔xf1 ♕xe5! 15 ♗xe5 ♗xc5! 16 ♗xf6 0-0 with advantage to Black, as pointed out by Mikhalevski – 13...♗xe7 14 ♘c3 ♗g7 15 0-0-0 gave White a stable edge in A.Motylev-S.Ovsejevitsch, Calcutta 2002) 11 ♕e3 (certainly not 11 exf6? ♘d3+ 12 ♔d2 ♕xe2+ 13 ♗xe2 ♘xb2 when Black was much better in L.Ljubojevic-B.Ivkov, Bugojno 1978) 11...fxe5 12 ♗xe5 ♘g6 13 ♗xc7! (13 ♗d4 ♕xe3+ 14 ♗xe3 0-0-0 15 ♘d2 ♖e8 16 0-0-0 c5 is nothing special) 13...♕xe3+ 14 fxe3 ♗c5 he does so, although here Black has some compensation for the pawn.

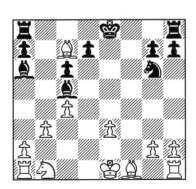

However, White should be better after 15 ♘c3! 0-0 (15...♗xe3 16 ♔e2 ♗b6 17 ♗d6 is unpleasant for the second player) 16 0-0-0 ♗xe3+ 17 ♔b1, which saw him returning the pawn to retain a structural advantage and slightly the more active pieces in E.Sveshnikov-J.Boudre, Val Maubuee 1990.

A) 9...♕h4

This bold approach has been surprisingly popular. Black frees his dark-squared bishop while bringing his queen to an aggressive square.

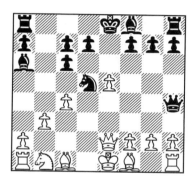

10 a3!

It may seem surprising that White plays this move, but not only is it very effective, it is also the only good move! Black has created some unexpected tactical difficulties for White's development and 10 a3 is the only way to alleviate them, as we can see from:

a) 10 ♗b2? ♗b4+! 11 ♔d1 (basically the only move; the problem being that 11 ♘d2?! ♘c3! is rather awkward for White: 12 ♕d3? ♘e4 13 g3 ♕h6! and 12 ♕f3? ♘e4 13 ♗c1 ♗c3! 14 g3 ♕e7 15 ♖b1 ♕xe5 are great for Black, so White really has to go 12 ♕e3! when after 12...♘e4 13 g3 ♕g4 14 f3 ♗xd2+ 15 ♕xd2 ♕xf3 16 ♕g2 he has some

compensation, but probably not enough) leaves White's king misplaced and Black able to save all his potentially-vulnerable minor pieces.

With 11...♘f4! (11...0-0?! 12 g3 intending ♕c2 helps White to sort things out) 12 ♕e4 (alternatively, 12 ♕f3 ♘e6 13 g3 ♕d8 14 a3 ♗e7 15 ♘d2 0-0 16 ♗d3 was seen in A.Hoffman-P.Leko, Buenos Aires 1994, and now 16...f6! would have retained some advantage, as pointed out by Leko, and 12 ♕e3 ♘e6! 13 g3 ♕d8 14 ♗g2 ♗c5 15 ♕d2 ♖b8 also seems promising for Black) 12...0-0! (instead 12...♕xf2 13 ♗d4 ♕h4 14 c5! ♕h5+ 15 g4! ♕xg4+ 16 ♔c2 ♗e2 17 ♗xe2 ♕xe2+ 18 ♕xe2 ♘xe2 leads to complications which are promising for Black, but the text is simpler) 13 g3 (Black wins after 13 ♗c3? ♗xc3 14 ♘xc3 ♕xf2) 13...♕h5+ 14 ♔c2 ♘h3 15 ♗d4, as in J.Kozamernik-J.Borisek, Bled 1999, and then Greenfeld's 15...c5 Black obtains a clear advantage.

b) Even worse is 10 g3?? which is a blunder in view of 10...♕d4 (or 10...♗b4+ 11 ♘d2 ♕d4 12 ♖b1 ♘c3) 11

♕c2 ♝b4+ 12 ♘d2 ♝xd2+ 13 ♕xd2
♕e4+ 14 ♕e2 ♕xh1 and Black wins.

c) Likewise, 10 ♘d2? ♕d4 11 ♖b1
♘c3 pretty much loses on the spot.

Returning to 10 a3:

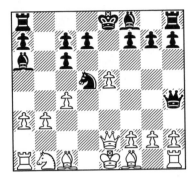

10...♘f4

Surprisingly Black has been unable
to find a way to exploit White's lack of
development and his pieces will soon
be pushed back after the text, but the
alternatives are no better:

a) 10...♝e7?? is a blunder. Then 11
g3 ♕d4 12 ♝b2 ♕c5 13 ♕d2 leaves
Black totally lost.

b) Not much better is 10...♝c5? 11
g3! ♝xf2+ (11...♕e7 12 ♝b2 ♘b6 13
♘d2 ♖b8 14 ♘e4 0-0 would also have
been very bad for Black in J.Palkovi-
I.Borocz, Hungarian League 2005, had
White found 15 ♕c2 threatening 16 b4,
and here 13...♕e6 14 ♘e4 ♝e7 15 h4!
was no improvement in V.Tseshkovsky-
N.Khoroshev, Tashkent 2010) 12 ♕xf2
♕e4+ 13 ♔d1! ♕xh1 14 ♘d2! when
Black might have netted the exchange,
but his queen and knight are both in
some trouble.

Black's best try is 14...0-0! (otherwise,
practice has shown that 14...♘c3+? 15
♔c2 ♘e4 16 ♘xe4 ♕xe4+ 17 ♝d3 gives
White fantastic compensation: for example, 17...♕g4 18 ♝f5 ♕h5 19 h4! f6
20 exf6! when Black's exposed king and
useless pieces leave him on the verge of
defeat; 14...f5? is met by 15 ♔c2! f4 16
gxf4 ♘xf4 and now Greenfeld's spectacular 17 e6!! ♘xe6 18 ♝b2 c5 19 ♝g2
♕xh2 20 ♖h1 when White wins; and,
finally, 14...f6 15 e6! dxe6 16 ♔c2 e5 17
♝b2 left Black in some trouble in
G.Jones-E.Lund, Klaksvik 2010) 15 ♔c2!
f6 (15...f5 16 ♝b2 f4 17 cxd5 was also
great for White in M.Calzetta-J.Krivec,
Leon 2001) 16 e6 dxe6, but now in
I.Nataf-D.McMahon, Mondariz 2000,
White should have played 17 ♝b2 ♘e3+
18 ♕xe3 ♕xh2 19 ♝d3! with a large advantage as his pieces are so powerfully
placed.

c) 10...0-0-0 11 g3 ♕e7 12 ♝g2 sees
White proceeding with his development, after which 12...f6 13 0-0! fxe5
14 ♝b2 followed by ♖e1 enables him to
regain the pawn with a clear edge.

d) Finally, 10...♖b8 also fails to trouble White: 11 g3 ♕d4 (11...♕e7 12 ♘d2 g6 13 f4 and ♘e4 is great too for White) 12 ♗b2 ♕b6 13 b4 ♘e7 14 ♗h3 c5 15 0-0 and White was much better in T.Nedev-J.Ridameya, Barbera 2000.

11 ♕e4

Pinning the knight is the most forcing continuation; other moves allow the knight to retreat to the more relevant e6-square.

11...♘g6

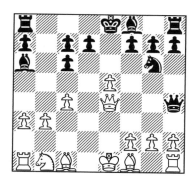

Now White must decide whether or not to exchange the queens.

12 ♕xh4

This leaves White with a slight but stable edge.

12 ♕e3 is a more ambitious alternative, with which White keeps the queens on and hopes to gain further time against Black's:

a) 12...♗e7 13 g3 ♕g4 (or 13...♕h5, as in S.Haslinger-E.Rapoport, Witley 1998, when 14 f4 f6 15 exf6 gxf6 16 ♗e2 ♕h3 17 ♗b2 0-0 18 ♘c3 gives White a clear edge) 14 h4! (14 ♗g2 0-0 15 0-0 f6 would allow some counter-

play) 14...♗b7 (14...♗c5? fails to 15 ♕xc5 ♕e4+ 16 ♗e3 ♕xh1 17 ♘d2, while 14...♕f5 is met by 15 f4! ♗c5 16 ♕xc5! ♕e4+ 17 ♔f2 ♕xh1 18 ♘c3 with the advantage) 15 f4 c5 16 ♗e2 ♕f5 17 ♖f1 and with 18 ♘c3 next up White is better.

b) 12...c5 13 ♗b2 ♗b7 (or 13...0-0-0?! 14 g3 ♕e7 15 ♗g2! ♘xe5 16 0-0 which gave White excellent compensation in G.Livshits-A.Mikhalevski, Tel Aviv 2002) 14 ♘c3 and White has an edge in view of the continuation 14...♕d4 15 ♕xd4 cxd4 16 ♘d5 ♗xd5 17 cxd5.

12...♘xh4 13 ♘d2

Similar is 13 ♗b2 ♗e7 (or 13...0-0-0 14 ♘d2 c5 15 g3 ♘f5 16 ♗g2 with the initiative, as given by Greenfeld) 14 g3 ♘f3+ 15 ♔e2 ♘g5 16 f4 ♘e6 17 ♘d2, with a steady plus, as is 13 ♘c3!? ♗c5 14 ♗b2 ♖b8 15 b4.

13...c5

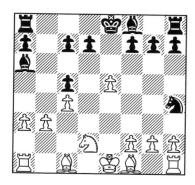

Black's other options are no better: 13...♗e7 14 g3 ♘f5 15 ♗b2 c5 16 ♗g2 ♖b8 17 0-0-0 gives White an edge, as did 13...d6 14 exd6 (or 14 g3!? ♘f5 15 ♗b2)

14...♗xd6 15 ♗b2 0-0 16 0-0-0 ♖ad8 17 g3 ♘g6 18 ♗g2 c5 19 ♖he1 in S.Lalic-N.Garcia Vicente, Debrecen 1992.

14 g3!

Even stronger than the natural 14 ♗b2 when after 14...♗b7 15 f3 (perhaps White should have tried 15 ♖g1!? ♗e7 16 f4 ♘f5 17 ♗d3 ♘d4, as he did in R.Reinaldo Castineira-M.Granados Gomez, Spanish Team Championship 2004, and now 18 ♗xd4 cxd4 19 ♗e4 retains an edge) 15...0-0-0 16 ♔f2 d6! Black was able to equalize in M.Muzychuk-A.Greenfeld, Neustadt 2009, with 17 exd6 ♗xd6 18 ♗xg7 ♖he8 19 ♖e1! ♖xe1 20 ♔xe1 ♖g8 21 ♗c3 ♘xg2+.

14...♘f5

After 14...♗b7 15 gxh4 ♗xh1 16 f3 White has a serious advantage, as the bishop is trapped on h1.

15 ♗g2

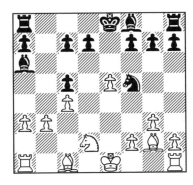

White has more than caught up in the development stakes and after 15...♖b8 16 ♗b2 ♗b7 17 ♗xb7 ♖xb7 18 0-0-0 ♘d4 19 ♗xd4! cxd4 20 ♔c2 c5 21 ♘e4 he was much better in E.Sevillano-M.Khachiyan, Stillwater 2007.

B) 9...0-0-0

A more sensible approach than 9...♕h4. Black brings his queen's rook into play, enabling him to pressure the e5-pawn with ...♖e8, while keeping all his pawn breaks open. He also hopes that his king will be safe enough on the queenside, but as we'll see, it's by no means unknown for White to launch an attack there.

At this juncture White must decide whether to complete his queenside fianchetto or to begin a second one:

B1: 10 ♗b2
B2: 10 g3

The remaining alternatives are somewhat less impressive:

a) 10 f4? g5! (the most incisive, although Black also obtains the initiative with 10...♖e8 11 ♕f2 ♕c5) 11 fxg5 (even worse is the 11 g3? gxf4 12 gxf4 of S.Huguet Mainar-P.Oatlhotse, Calvia Olympiad 2004, when the straightforward 12...♕h4+ 13 ♕f2 ♕xf2+ 14 ♔xf2

♗c5+ leaves White in some trouble) 11...♗g7 12 ♗b2 was seen in J.Holvason-F.Poetz, Fermo 2009, and now the simplest method of completing the undermining was 12...♘f4 13 ♕e3 ♕xg5, with some advantage for Black.

b) 10 ♗a3? only drives Black's queen to an active square: 10...♕g5 11 g3 ♗xa3 12 ♘xa3 ♖he8 left White under heavy central pressure in G.Souleidis-C.Richter, Emsdetten 2002.

c) 10 ♕b2?! ♘b6 11 ♗e2 ♖e8 12 ♗f4 (12 c5? ♕xe5 fails to help White) 12...g5! sees Black getting in a powerful advance with tempo and illustrates why White usually places his bishop, not queen, on b2.

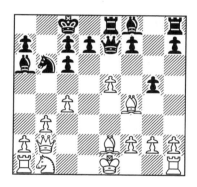

Indeed, after 13 ♗g3 ♗g7 14 ♘c3 (Black was somewhat better too after 14 ♘d2 f5 15 f4 gxf4 16 ♗xf4 d6 in V.Karasev-J.Emms, Leningrad 1990) 14...f5 White had to find 15 f4 just to stay in the game in L.Ljubojevic-Y.Seirawan, Wijk aan Zee 1986, and still remained somewhat worse after 15...gxf4 16 ♗xf4 ♗xe5.

d) Just like a move earlier, the un-

pinning 10 ♕e4 isn't especially impressive either and can quickly lead to complications. Now Black must decide which way to move the knight:

d1) 10...♘f6 11 ♕e2 (the queen has to go back, as 11 ♕f5? ♘g4 12 ♗b2 ♘xe5 costs White a pawn) 11...♖e8?! (refusing to repeat with 11...♘d5, which invites 12 ♕e4, but that is likely Black's best) 12 ♗b2 (after 12 exf6? Black wins the exchange with the neat manoeuvre 12...♕d8 13 ♗e3 ♕xf6, while 12 f4?! would have been too ambitious in J.Blackburne-J.Zukertort, London 1881, had Black seized the initiative with Marin's 12...d6 13 ♗b2 ♘d7) 12...♘d5 (White has too much for the queen after 12...d6 13 exf6! ♕d7 14 fxg7 ♗xg7 15 ♗xg7 ♖hg8 16 ♗d4 ♖xe2+ 17 ♗xe2, as pointed out by Marin, but perhaps Black might consider 12...d5!?) 13 ♕d2! ♘b6 (13...♘f6 14 ♗e2 ♘e4 would have left Black in trouble too in A.Fernandes-P.Dias, Lisbon 2003, after just 15 ♕d4) 14 ♗e2 sees White having gained from all the toing and froing by the queen and knight.

Black's pressure down the e-file isn't too scary here and after 14...f6 (otherwise, 14...g5 15 e6 ♖g8 16 exd7+ ♘xd7 17 ♘c3 maintained control and some advantage in B.Kovacevic-G.Benidze, Herceg Novi 2006, while the 14...g6 of A.Morozevich-A.Karpov, Russian Team Championship 2008, might have been met by 15 a4!?, threatening to entomb Black's knight on a8) 15 exf6 (a tempting alternative is 15 0-0!? fxe5 16 a4 ♔b8 17 a5 with promising compensation in J.Dworakowska-Shen Yang, Ningbo 2009) 15...gxf6 16 ♘c3 d5 (rather desperate, but White retains control and the upper hand after both 16...♖g8 17 g3 and 16...c5 17 0-0 ♗b7 18 ♖fe1) 17 0-0! dxc4 18 ♖fe1 White enjoyed a strong initiative for the pawn in J.Tenyi-L.Kovacs, Hungarian League 1993.

d2) Thus if Black doesn't want to repeat, he should move his knight to the queenside without delay. Moreover, 10...♘b6! 11 ♗e2 (11 ♗b2 ♗b7 12 ♕e3 was preferred in J.Geller-G.Kiselev, Saratov 1999, when 12...c5! followed by 13...d5 gives Black the initiative) 11...d5!? (11...♖e8 12 ♗b2 f6 would have been less impressive in J.Malec-A.Minczyk, Kolobrzeg 2003, had White come up with the standard sacrifice 13 0-0! fxe5 14 a4) 12 ♕f5+ ♕e6 13 ♕f4?! ♔b8 14 0-0 f6 saw White regretting his decision to retain the queens as Black seized the initiative in F.Zabala-R.Renteria, Barranquilla 1995.

B1) 10 ♗b2

Consistent and now Black must decide how he intends to develop counterplay. His main choices being:

> **B11: 10...♕g5**
> **B12: 10...f6**

However, practice has seen almost every legal idea being tried, including:

a) 10...♖e8 may appear consistent after Black's last, but 11 ♕d2! favours White as we saw with a repetition thrown in, above, in note 'd1' at the start of Line B.

b) 10...♘b6 11 g3 ♖e8 12 ♗h3!? (the more restrained 12 ♘d2 h5 13 ♗g2 h4 14 0-0-0 ♕e6 15 ♘e4 gave White a pleasant edge in M.Paragua-O.Annageldyev, Alushta 2004) 12...f6 13 0-0! fxe5 14 a4 was the course of the old game J.Mieses-R.Teichmann, Hastings 1895 *(see following diagram)*.

Once again we can see that the sacrifice of the central bridgehead has given White excellent compensation:

he enjoys two raking bishops, the knight is en route to e4 or a4, his king is much the safer and there is the threat to move the queen followed by 16 a5.

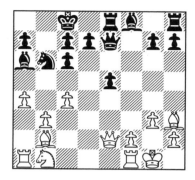

c) 10...♕b4+?! 11 ♘d2 ♘f4 (11...♝c5? would have cost Black material in B.Schippan-S.Zrinscak, Dortmund 2000, after 12 ♕f3!, unpinning and also threatening 13 a3) 12 ♕e3 ♘e6 13 ♕xa7 saw White net an important pawn in M.Rodriguez Boado-J.Bello Filgueira, Mondariz 2000.

d) 10...c5?! just encourages White to bring his bishop to a great diagonal and 11 g3 ♘b4 12 ♝g2 d5 13 0-0 dxc4 14 bxc4 gave him some advantage in H.Nakamura-J.Cabrejos Tovar, La Paz 2002.

e) After 10...♘f4?! 11 ♕e3 Black is able to preserve material equality, but not to equalize.

Following 11...♘g6 (White has a simple edge after 11...♕g5 12 g3 ♘e6 13 ♕xg5 ♘xg5 14 ♝g2, while the 11...g5?! 12 ♘d2 ♝g7 of M.Abdulyazanov-A.Belousov, Uljanovsk 2008,

should have been met by just 13 g3 followed by 14 ♕xa7) 12 ♕xa7 (Totsky's 12 ♝e2!? ♔b8 13 ♘d2 also suffices for a pull) 12...♝b7 13 ♝e2 ♘xe5 14 0-0 the exchange of pawns was slightly in White's favour, largely thanks to his safer king position in V.Tuzil-J.Juptner, Klatovy 1996.

f) Just like in Line B1 of the previous chapter, 10...g5 is quite well met by 11 h4! and after 11...♝g7 12 ♘d2 (12 hxg5!?) 12...♘b4 13 0-0-0 ♘xa2+ 14 ♔b1 ♘b4 15 ♕e3 White was slightly for choice in A.Stiri-M.Turov, Rethymnon 2009.

g) 10...g6 11 ♕d2 (11 ♕e4?! is well met by 11...f5!, but White should consider 11 ♘d2!? when 11...♝g7 12 0-0-0 ♜he8 13 g3 gives him an edge) 11...♘b6 12 ♝e2 ♝g7 13 ♕a5 ♝b7 likely gave Black just enough counterplay down the e-file and potentially against g2 to maintain a rough balance in M.Sulashvili-T.Sanikidze, Tbilisi 2000.

h) 10...♔b8 takes time to secure the a7-point against any ♕d2-a5 raid.

However, whether this is worth a

tempo isn't so clear and after 11 g3! (this appears the most promising; Black is better after 11 ♕f3?! ♘b4 12 ♕c3 c5, as pointed out by Van der Weide, and after the fairly popular 11 ♘d2 he can equalize with the thus-far neglected 11...♘b4!? 12 ♘e4 c5) 11...f6 12 ♕d2! (anyhow!) 12...♘b6 13 ♗g2 fxe5 14 0-0 d5 15 ♖e1 e4 16 ♘c3 gave White decent play for his pawn, thanks to his dark-square control and undermining prospects in J.Tisdall-R.Elseth, Oslo 1991.

B11) 10...♕g5

Black frees his bishop and hopes to generate pressure on the dark squares.

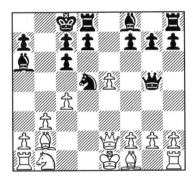

11 g3

Natural and best. Alternatively:

a) 11 a3? ♘f4 12 ♕f3 (or 12 ♕e4 d5) 12...♗b7 gave Black a strong, early initiative on the light squares in G.Szabo-M.Beinoras, Plovdiv 2008.

b) 11 ♕f3?! ♗b4+ 12 ♔d1 ♘f4! (ambitious but effective play from Black) 13 h4 ♕h6 14 g3 (14 ♗c1?! would have been well met by 14...d6 15 e6 ♕f6, ex-ploiting White's lack of development to pick up the loose rook on a1) 14...♘e6 15 ♗c1 (White didn't have to undevelop his only developed minor piece, but Adams was ready to meet 15 a3 with 15...♗e7 16 ♗c1 g5 17 hxg5 ♕g7, again with some initiative for Black) 15...♕g6 left Black much the better developed and for choice in J.Smeets-M.Adams, London 2008.

c) 11 ♘d2 ♗b4! (the only consistent approach; indeed, White was clearly better after 11...f6 12 h4 ♕h6 13 0-0-0 ♗c5 14 ♕f3 in V.Hort-W.Unzicker, German League 1984, and 11...♘f4 12 ♕e3! ♘xg2+ 13 ♗xg2 ♕xg2 14 0-0-0 c5 15 ♘e4 gives him a strong initiative for the pawn) 12 h4 (there's no time to cover the c3-square with 12 ♖c1?! in view of 12...d6, and Black also has the initiative after the 12 a3 ♘f4 13 ♕e3 ♗xd2+ 14 ♔xd2 of A.Peters-A.Scetinin, Mlada Boleslav 1992, and then 14...d5) 12...♕f5 gives Black easy counterplay with his pieces set to land on c2 and c3.

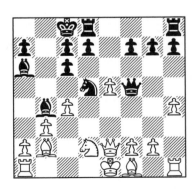

White really has to parry with 13 ♕d3, but after 13...♕xd3 14 ♗xd3 ♘f4

15 ♗f1 d5 16 0-0-0 dxc4 Black was fine in J.Tomczak-S.Sulskis, Warsaw 2007.

11...♗b4+

The alternative is 11...♖e8 when White must avoid 12 f4 ♕g6! 13 ♘d2 ♘b4, which gives Black the initiative, and especially 12 a3? ♗d6! (M.Mueller-K.Allen, Port Erin 2007). However, 12 ♘d2! ♕g6 13 ♗g2 ♕c2 14 ♘e4 forced the queens off and gave him the upper hand in B.Vuckovic-V.Tseshkovsky, Zlatibor 2006.

12 ♘d2

Slightly surprisingly 12 ♔d1 was preferred in Zhao Nan-K.Nuri, Acri 2006, when 12...♕f5!? followed by ...d6 would have given Black enough counterplay.

12...♘c3

Black's main try, continuing to harry.

Otherwise, 12...♗c3? would have been awkward for him in F.Samaritani-D.Pedersen, Aarhus 1992, had White found 13 h4!, since 13...♕h6 14 ♗xc3 ♘xc3 15 ♕f3 traps the errant knight.

A better alternative is 12...♖he8, but

13 f4 ♕g6 14 0-0-0 gave White an edge in A.Nechitailo-V.Moliboga, Kiev 2002.

13 f4!

Move order is important here. After the text, 13...♕e7? 14 ♕e3 costs Black a piece, but if White starts with 13 ♗xc3?! ♗xc3 14 f4 then Black can and should retreat to e7.

13...♕g6 14 ♗xc3

Necessary, as 14 ♕d3? ♘e4 costs White the exchange, while 14 ♕e3? ran into the cute 14...♘b1! in R.Freuler-J.Rindlisbacher, Thun 2008.

14...♗xc3 15 0-0-0!

The safest place for the king and, besides, 15 ♖c1?! is fairly well met by 15...♗xd2+!? 16 ♕xd2 ♕e4+ 17 ♔f2 ♕xh1 18 ♗g2 ♕xh2 19 ♖h1 and White's queen was in no way superior to Black's rooks in D.Mieles Palau-W.Palencia, Quito 2003.

15...d5

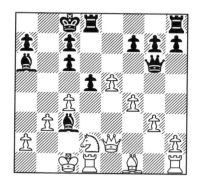

Black strikes back in the centre and hopes to show that even on the queen-side White's king isn't entirely safe, but now in J.Tomczak-M.Ragger, Gaziantep 2008, the simple 16 ♕d3 would have left White with a slight advantage.

B12) 10...f6

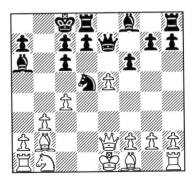

Black wastes no time opening the centre.

11 ♕e4!

This appears best, although of the alternatives 'd' may also be promising:

a) 11 g3 is playable but not overly promising, as we'll see by transposition in note 'a' to White's 11th move in Line B22.

b) 11 exf6 ♘xf6 (Black may do even better with 11...♕f7!?; certainly after 12 ♕f3 ♗b4+ 13 ♔d1 ♘xf6 14 a3 ♗c5 he had the initiative in A.Savickas-S.Sulskis, Kaunas 2008) 12 ♘c3 (neither does 12 ♕xe7 ♗xe7 13 ♘c3 particularly impress for White: 13...♗c5 14 ♗e2 ♖he8 15 0-0 d5 gave Black good, active counterplay in M.Zuriel-R.Pokorna, Turin Olympiad 2006) 12...d5! 13 0-0-0 ♕xe2 14 ♗xe2 ♗c5 15 f3 (a world-class player preferred 15 cxd5?! ♗xe2 16 ♘xe2 in V.Hort-F.Trois, Sarajevo 1980, but here 16...♘g4 would have been a little awkward for him) 15...♖he8 saw

Black equalize in V.Dragiev-V.Georgiev, Plovdiv 2003.

c) 11 ♘d2 fxe5 (likely even stronger than 11...♖e8, after which 12 ♕e4 ♘b6 13 f4 fxe5 14 fxe5 g6 15 0-0-0 ♗g7 was fine for Black in J.Zhang-B.Kovanova, Novokuznetsk 2008, and here practice has shown that 13...♗b7 14 0-0-0 fxe5 15 fxe5 g6 is also about equal) 12 0-0-0 (12 ♕xe5? ♕xe5+ 13 ♗xe5 ♖e8 leaves White in a bit of trouble down the e-file) 12...♖e8! (Black has also been known to return the pawn, but 12...♘f6 13 ♕xe5 ♕xe5 14 ♗xe5 ♘g4 15 ♗g3 ♗a3+ 16 ♔c2 ♖hf8 17 ♘f3 ♗c5 gave him no more than equality in S.Novikov-M.Turov, Sochi 2006) 13 g3 (naturally White must avoid 13 ♘f3? e4 and 13 ♖e1?! ♘f6 14 g3 e4 was hardly ideal either for him in R.Heimrath-H.Grabher, Liechtenstein 1994) 13...♘f6 gives White decent activity and some play for the pawn, but with his own king on the same side as Black's, it may well not be quite enough.

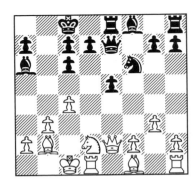

The game V.Savchenko-M.Fakhretdinova, Dagomys 2004, continued 14

♗h3 (14 ♘e4!? might be a better try, but 14...♔b8 15 ♗g2 ♕f7 16 ♕d2 ♘xe4 17 ♗xe4 ♗c8 still left Black likely slightly for choice in U.Voigt-D.Lobzhanidze, Wiesbaden 1996) 14...♔b8 15 ♖he1 d6 (or 15...♕f7!? 16 ♕f3 ♗b7 17 ♗xe5 ♗a3+ 18 ♔c2 c5 which returned the pawn to seize the initiative in T.Nedev-F.Elsness, Khanty-Mansiysk Olympiad 2010) 16 ♗g2 ♗b7 17 ♕d3 ♕f7 and Black was able to gradually untangle before putting her extra pawn to good use.

d) 11 ♕d2!? ♘b6 12 ♗e2 (the hasty 12 ♕a5?! runs into 12...♖b4+) 12...fxe5 (after 12...♔b8 13 0-0 fxe5 14 ♖e1 d6 15 c5! ♗xe2 16 cxb6 White had good attacking chances in A.Ciganikova-M.Beil, Prague 1995, and here Tseshkovsky's 14 a4!? is also quite tempting)

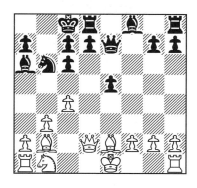

13 0-0 (the immediate 13 a4!? is possible too; after 13...♔b8 14 a5 ♘c8 15 ♘c3 ♕d6 16 ♗d3 White had decent compensation in R.Reinaldo Castineira-O.Korneev, Madrid 2000, and here Postny's 15...d5 16 cxd5 ♗b7 might be met by 17 a6! ♗a8 18 0-0 cxd5 19 ♖fc1,

ploughing straight ahead on the queenside) gives White typical compensation for the pawn and here, unlike in variation 'c', his king is on the opposite side to Black's, allowing him to attack!

B.Predojevic-I.Sokolov, Sarajevo 2005, continued 13...d5 (13...♔b8 14 ♖e1 maintains decent compensation, while after 13...♗b7 14 a4! White had begun to attack in S.Ptacnik-L.Burdik, Tatranske Zruby 2007, with the idea of 14...d5 15 a5) 14 cxd5 ♗xe2 15 ♕xe2 cxd5 and now 16 a4? saw White overestimate his queenside chances and allow Black good counterplay with 16...d4!, but the simple 16 ♗xe5 would have retained some advantage after 16...♘d7 17 ♕a6+ ♔b8 18 ♕b5+ ♘b6 19 ♖e1 ♕b4 20 ♘c3 (Postny).

Returning to 11 ♕e4:

11...♘b6

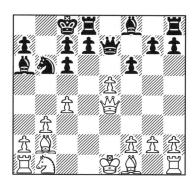

The knight has to retreat and 11...f5? 12 ♕xf5 g6 13 ♕e4 just cost Black a pawn for pretty much nothing in L.Van der Vegt-J.Van Ruitenburg, Leiden 2000.

12 ♘d2

There are alternatives:

a) 12 f4 ♗b7 (the 12...♖e8 13 ♗d3 fxe5 14 fxe5 of V.Gorkavij-A.Karabakhtsian, Krasnodar 2003, is also quite reasonable for Black after 14...♕c5) 13 ♘d2 fxe5 14 fxe5 c5 was about equal in D.Doncevic-J.De la Villa Garcia, San Fernando 1991.

b) 12 c5?! is a standard strike, but one which must always be well timed. Here's it's premature and 12...♗xf1 13 cxb6 ♗a6 14 bxa7 ♔b7 15 f4 (15 ♘d2 fxe5 16 0-0-0 d5 slightly favoured Black too in S.Beukema-P.Geuss, Maastricht 2008) 15...fxe5 16 fxe5 (G.Jacoby-J.Atri Sangari, Pinneberg 2006) 16...d5 leaves Black slightly for choice.

c) 12 ♗e2!? fxe5 13 0-0 ♕g5 (White has enough compensation too after 13...♖e8 14 ♘c3 followed by a4) 14 a4 was a humanlike and quite reasonable version of the standard sacrifice in *Shredder-ChessTiger*, Leiden 2003.

12...fxe5 13 0-0-0

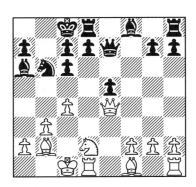

Giving up on any notion of a queenside attack, but White has the simple plan of regaining his pawn in the centre after which his structural advantage should count for something.

13...♖e8

Fighting to keep the queens on. Instead both 13...♗b7 14 ♕xe5 ♕xe5 15 ♗xe5 ♗a3+ 16 ♔c2 ♖hf8 17 f3 (C.Monsieux-N.Banerjee, Rheims 2004) and 13...c5 14 ♕xe5 ♕xe5 15 ♗xe5 (A.Matthaei-A.Hoffmann, Datteln 2002) give White a small but pleasant edge.

14 ♘f3 d6 15 c5!

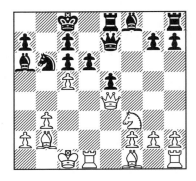

This key undermining thrust prevents Black from holding on to the pawn and after 15...♗xf1 16 ♖hxf1 d5 17 ♕f5+ White had regained it while retaining slightly the better prospects in S.Vajda-F.Amos, Eger 1995.

B2) 10 g3

It may seem slightly illogical not to complete the queenside fianchetto, but White reasons that there is no hurry to do so, preferring first to take control of the oft-important f4-square. Moreover, his dark-squared bishop might yet make a timely appearance on the a3-square, aiming to buy the white knight a fantastic home on c5.

At this stage Black's two main independent bids for counterplay are:

B21: 10...♖e8
B22: 10...f6

Instead 10...g5 transposes to the notes to Black's 10th move in Line C4 and 10...g6 11 ♗b2 to Line D2, while 10...♘b6 11 ♗b2 was seen to favour White in note 'b' to Black's 10th move at the start of Line B1. That just leaves:

a) 10...h5 11 ♗g2 h4 12 0-0 hxg3 13 hxg3 f6 14 ♖e1 fxe5 was rather ambitious from Black in B.Vuckovic-S.Brenjo, Vrsac 2007, and with the thematic 15 ♕d2! White could have counterattacked and enjoyed good compensation.

b) 10...♕b4+!? 11 ♗d2 ♕b6 12 ♘c3 ♘xc3 13 ♗xc3 ♗b4 14 ♕d2 c5 seemed okay for Black in A.Muzychuk-S.Sulskis, Gibraltar 2008. Thus White should try 12 ♕e4!? and soon after this chapter was written it occurred in no less a game than M.Carlsen-S.Sulskis, Khanty-

Mansiysk Olympiad 2010: 12...f5 (12...♘b4 13 ♘c3 ♗b7 14 ♗g2 should slightly favour White, even if Black takes the queens off with 14...♕d4!?) 13 ♕xf5! ♕d4 14 cxd5 ♗xf1 15 ♗c3! and White was slightly for choice in the complications, but with Mikhalevski's suggestion of 15...♗h3!? 16 ♗xd4 ♗xf5 17 dxc6 dxc6 Black would have developed counterplay on the light squares.

B21) 10...♖e8 11 ♗b2

The correct way to cover the e5-pawn. White's last did facilitate 11 f4?!, but 11...f6 12 ♕f2 ♕c5 would remind him that any advance of the f-pawn also has its drawbacks.

11...f6

Consistent. Black must increase the pressure down the f-file. Otherwise:

a) 11...♕b4?! 12 ♘d2! (but not 12 ♕d2 when 12...♘f6 13 ♗g2 ♘g4 gave Black enough counterplay in D.Musanti-J.Rosito, Villa Martelli 2002) 12...♕a5 was seen in V.Gashimov-S.Sulskis, Bydgoszcz 1999, and now 13 a3! would have been even stronger than the game's 13 f4 f6 14 ♕f3.

b) The simplest reply to 11...g5 is 12 ♕d2 (now this is correct as the knight can't retreat to f6 in response, whereas 12 ♘d2 ♘b4 transposes to note 'd' to Black's 12th move in Line C422, below) 12...♘b6 13 ♗d3 with a pull.

c) 11...h5 12 ♘d2 (12 ♕d2 ♘f6 13 ♗g2 ♘g4 14 f4 ♕b4?! 15 ♘c3 saw White doing well in F.De Araujo Lima-G.Batista, Brasilia 1998, but here 14...f6!? would have been a tougher nut to crack) 12...h4 13 ♗h3! (13 ♗g2 may also suffice for an edge, but it makes good sense to neutralize Black's play down the h-file) 13...f6 (or 13...♕g5?!, as in T.Luukkonen-S.Brenjo, Novi Sad 2009, and now 14 f4 would have left White somewhat better) 14 ♕e4 ♘b6 15 0-0-0 left White with harmonious development and an edge in B.Vuckovic-S.Brenjo, Belgrade 2007.

d) 11...g6 12 ♘d2 ♗g7 13 0-0-0 ♘b6 14 f4 f6 15 ♘f3 gave White an edge in A.Suarez Real-A.Naranjo Moreno, Burguillos 2008.

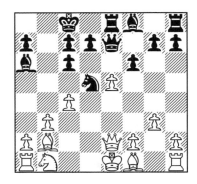

12 ♗g2!

Again we see White happy to give up the pawn on e5 for good development, pressure and potential attacking chances on the queenside. Moreover, here it's by far his best option:

a) 12 exf6?? ♕b4+ forces White to resign.

b) 12 f4?! fxe5 13 fxe5 ♕g5 14 ♘d2 ♗b4 left Black calling all the shots in D.Boskovic-M.Zivanic, Subotica 2000.

c) Even 12 ♕d2 ♘b6 isn't entirely ideal for White, logical though the queen move might appear. Now:

c1) 13 ♗g2 ♗xc4! 14 bxc4 ♘xc4 reveals the main problem.

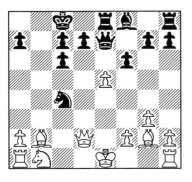

For the piece Black obtains a strong attack, forcing White to tread carefully. Following 15 ♕c2 (and not 15 ♕d4 ♘xb2 16 0-0?? ♕b4, as in J.Zezulkin-R.Stern, German League 2000) 15...♘xb2 16 ♕xb2 ♕xe5+ 17 ♕xe5 ♖xe5+ 18 ♔d2 (White must avoid 18 ♔f1? ♗b4, but might be able to get away with 18 ♔d1 because after Mikhalevski's 18...♗c5 19 f4 ♖e3 20 ♘d2 ♖he8 there is 21 ♗f1) 18...♗b4+ Black was well developed and had three pawns for the piece in R.Hasangatin-Z.Zyla, Koszalin 1998. This position isn't especially clear, but it does seem that an assessment of roughly level should be about right.

c2) 13 a4!? ♕b4! (Black must avoid 13...♗b8?! 14 a5 ♘c8 15 ♗h3!, which left her somewhat worse in A.Morozevich-Xie Jun, Pamplona 1998, as does 13...d6 14 ♗g2) 14 a5 (Xie Jun gained revenge in O.De la Riva Aguado-Xie Jun, Pamplona 1999, where 14 ♕xb4 ♗xb4+ 15 ♘d2 fxe5 didn't give White quite enough for the pawn) 14...♘d5 (Black might also consider the extremely unclear complications arising from 14...♕xb3!? 15 axb6 ♗b4) 15 ♗e2 ♕xd2+ (Black doesn't seem to have quite enough for the piece after 15...♕xb3?! 16 cxd5 ♗xe2 17 ♕xe2 ♗b4+ 18 ♔f1 ♕xd5 19 ♔g1!) 16 ♔xd2 ♗b4+ was again roughly balanced in M.Ragger-P.Ponkratov, Budva 2003.

c3) 13 ♗h3!? has received Kasparov's backing in his recent *Kasparov vs Karpov 1988-2009* and deserves further tests. Again Black might be tempted to sacrifice, but after the 13...♗xc4?! 14 bxc4 ♘xc4 15 ♕d4 ♘xb2 16 0-0! ♕xe5 of S.Krawczyk-M.Cajbel, Krynica 2003, White could have obtained a strong attack with 17 ♕xa7!.

12...fxe5

Black is right to grab the pawn, especially as 12...♕b4+ 13 ♕d2 ♘b6 (even worse is 13...♕xd2+?! 14 ♔xd2 ♗b4+, as in A.Szieberth-B.Lengyel, Budapest 1994, and now 15 ♔c1 gives White

some advantage) 14 0-0 fxe5 15 ♖e1 saw White regaining it with the upper hand in S.Abello-O.Adda, French League 2004.

13 ♘d2!?

Keeping the white king's options open. Practice has also seen much discussion of the alternatives:

a) 13 ♕d2?! ♘f6 14 ♗a3 ♕e6 saw White coming up short in A.Gomez Anadon-J.Fluvia Poyatos, Oropesa del Mar 2001.

b) After 13 0-0 we have a further divide, depending on how bold Black is feeling:

b1) 13...g6 14 ♕d2 ♘f6 15 ♖e1 gave White at least enough compensation in A.Hnydiuk-M.Kostyra, Police 2007.

b2) 13...♘b6 14 ♖e1 (14 a4!? ♘d5 15 ♘c3 ♘f6 16 ♗a3 is also tempting, as in D.Gormally-O.Niklasch, Tastrup 1997) 14...d5 saw Black trying to mobilize his central pawns in K.Wight-E.Wenaas, Toronto 2000, but now White has a pleasant choice between 15 ♕xe5 and the more ambitious 15 a4!?.

b3) 13...♘f6 14 ♘d2 (in line with our

last variation, White might consider too the 14 ♖e1 e4 15 ♕d2 of D.Genocchio-S.Navarro, Cortina d'Ampezzo 2003) 14...♗b7 15 ♖fe1 ♕f7 16 a3! (Van der Weide points out that 16 ♖ad1?! ♗c5 is a little annoying, but 16 ♕e3 ♔b8 17 ♖ad1 gave him enough for the pawn in K.Van der Weide-R.Wiesinger, Seefeld 2005) 16...e4 17 b4 saw White turning his superior development into a queenside attack in M.Mueller-H.Wegner, German League 1992.

b4) 13...♕f7 14 ♕d2 ♘b6 15 ♕a5 also saw White pressing on the queenside in H.Knoll-H.Baumgartner, Ansfelden 2003.

b5) 13...h5!? 14 ♕d2 ♘f6 is Black's most respectable option, striking back on the kingside.

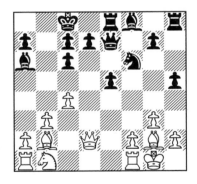

Now:

b51) 15 ♕a5 ♗b7 (15...♔b7? 16 ♗a3 gives White a strong initiative, such as after 16...♕f7 17 ♗xf8 ♖hxf8 18 ♘c3 e4 19 ♖ae1 h4 20 ♘xe4) 16 ♗a3! (16 ♕xa7?! ♕c5 would force the queens off and solve Black's problems) 16...♕e6 17 ♗xf8 (after 17 ♕xa7 h4 18 ♗xf8 Black's

kingside play gave him the initiative following 18...hxg3!? 19 fxg3! ♖exf8 in L.Oll-G.Giorgadze, Pula 1997) 17...♖hxf8! (the correct recapture, because 17...♖exf8 18 ♕xa7 h4 19 ♘c3 ♘g4 – 19...♖h6? 20 a4 hxg3 21 a5! was even worse for Black in Y.Hernandez Estevez-I.Herrera, Cuba 1993 – 20 h3 ♕h6 21 ♘e4 kept Black at bay on the kingside and gave White the initiative in Y.Dembo-S.Husari, Budapest 2001) 18 ♕xa7 ♕g4! 19 ♘a3 (more recently 19 ♘c3 ♕d4 20 ♕a5 h4 21 ♖ad1 ♕b6 was about equal in R.Khusnutdinov-M.Ragger, Moscow 2010) 19...h4 (and not 19...♕d4? 20 c5, which left White in charge in J.Rosito-G.Garcia, Buenos Aires 2003) 20 ♘c2 h3 gave Black sufficient counterplay in no lesser game than the highly-exciting G.Kasparov-A.Karpov, World Championship (Game 14), Lyons 1990, Kasparov's debut with the Scotch.

b52) 15 ♖e1! ♕c5 (White is also slightly better after 15...h4 16 ♖xe5 ♕f7 17 ♕a5, just as he was too following 15...♕b4 16 ♖xe5 ♖xe5 17 ♗xe5 in G.Jones-M.Hebden, British League 2007) 16 ♘c3 h4 (16...♕d4!? might be more critical, but White certainly has plenty of positional compensation after 17 ♕xd4 exd4 18 ♖xe8+ ♘xe8 19 ♘e4) 17 ♘a4 sees White settling for an edge, rather than engage in an attacking race as we saw in variation 'b51'.

Following 17...♕b4 18 ♕xb4 (18 ♗c3!? ♕d6 19 ♕e3 is also promising, T.Burg-P.Salnikov, Salekhard 2007)

18...♗xb4 19 ♖xe5 one of your authors enjoyed a pleasant advantage and went on to win in Y.Dembo-S.Husari, Budapest 2003.

We now return to White's attempt to avoid such a theoretical discussion with 13 ♘d2:

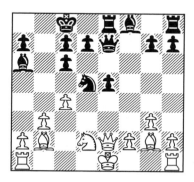

13...h5

Black strikes out on the kingside after all, but with White yet to commit his king there he might prefer one of:

a) 13...g6 14 0-0-0 ♗g7 15 ♘e4 saw White's much more active pieces fully compensate for the pawn in M.Maric-G.Markovic, Cetinje 1991, with ♕d2-a5 one plan, trying to bring the knight to c5 another.

b) 13...♘f6!? 14 0-0-0?! ♕c5 (14...g6? 15 ♖he1 saw White regain the pawn with some advantage in K.Toma-A.Chmielinska, Poraj 2003) 15 ♘e4 ♘xe4 16 ♕xe4 d5! left Black mobilizing his centre with a small plus in F.De Gleria-A.Kalka, German League 2001. Thus here White should prefer 14 0-0!, transposing to note 'b3' to his 13th move, above, while demonstrating that

his last merely kept his options open and didn't commit him to going for long castling.

14 0-0-0 ♕b4

After 14...h4 15 ♗e4! White clearly has plenty of compensation, with 16 ♗g6 then one idea.

15 ♘e4 ♕a5 16 ♔b1

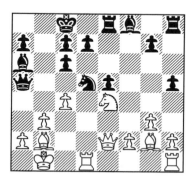

We've followed the game S.Rublevsky-V.Mikhalevski, Vilnius 1995, in which White had more than enough for the pawn, with Black vulnerable on all of e5, g5, h5 and d7.

B22) 10...f6

Black sees no need preface this with ...♖e8 and so attacks the central bastion without delay.

11 ♗g2

Prioritizing kingside development while again showing a willingness to sacrifice the e-pawn looks like White's best approach.

Alternatively:

a) 11 ♗b2 fxe5 sees Black declining a transposition back to Line B21 with 11...♖e8.

Now White again does best to turn to the kingside with 12 ♗g2 (otherwise, 12 ♕d2 ♘f6 13 ♗h3, as in E.Chorvatova-M.Savic, Balatonlelle 2001, enables Black to seize the initiative with 13...h5, while 12 ♘d2 ♘b4! 13 0-0-0 ♘xa2+ 14 ♔b1 ♘b4 failed to give White quite enough compensation in M.Killar-T.Kotrba, Czech League 2001) 12...e4!? (holding on to the pawn for the time being; instead 12...h5 13 0-0 h4 14 ♕xe5 ♕xe5 15 ♗xe5 enabled White to regain it with equality in H.Stefansson-J.Timman, Oviedo 1993) 13 0-0 (unfortunately for White, 13 ♕xe4 ♕b4+! 14 ♘d2 ♗c5 gives Black the initiative) 13...♘f6! (13...e3 is tempting, but turns out to be premature: 14 ♘c3! exf2+ 15 ♕xf2 ♘e3 16 ♖ae1 left White calling the shots in R.Ponomariov-F.Jenni, Lausanne 2000) when the issue is whether he can obtain enough compensation.

It's not so easy for White to do so, but 14 ♘d2! (Black was slightly for choice after 14 ♕e3 ♔b8 15 ♗d4 c5 16 ♗b2 d5 in E.Andreev-V.Tseshkovsky,

Krasnodar 2003, and also would have been in I.Vulicevic-D.Blagojevic, Vrnjacka Banja 1999, had he met 14 ♖d1 with 14...d5) 14...d5 15 b4!? may just do the trick and after 15...♕xb4? 16 ♗xf6 gxf6 17 ♖ab1 White had obtained a decisive attack in H.Van der Poel-L.Mostertman, Dieren 2004.

b) 11 e6 echoes White's play in Line B2 of the previous chapter. It's certainly quite thematic, but may come up a little short against accurate defence:

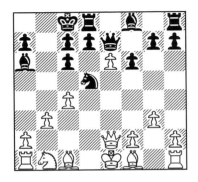

b1) 11...dxe6 12 ♗g2 (or 12 ♗h3?! f5 13 ♗b2 ♘b4 14 0-0, as in D.Markosian-V.Rakovich, Tula 2001, and now 14...h5 would have seen Black beginning his own attack) 12...♘b4 13 0-0 ♗b7 14 ♘c3 c5 15 ♗xb7+ ♔xb7 16 ♗e3 gave White more than enough for the pawn thanks to Black's weakened queenside in D.Marciano-G.Moncamp, Cannes 2000.

b2) 11...f5! 12 ♗g2 (12 ♗h3 was preferred in N.McDonald-M.Hebden, Southend 2007, and now Black should transpose into variation 'b1' with 12...dxe6) 12...♕f6 13 ♗b2 ♗b4+ 14

♔f1 was seen in A.Goloshchapov-A.Safin, Sangli 2000, and now the simple 14...♕xe6 would have left Black slightly for choice.

11...fxe5

Here 11...♘b4? rather leaps into nowhere and after 12 ♗b2 fxe5 13 0-0 e4 14 ♗xe4 White was doing pretty well in H.Strehlow-H.Jakoby, Gladenbach 1999.

12 0-0

Logical and it's hard to see why White would want to help Black untangle his kingside while crucially activating his queen with 12 ♗a3?! ♕g5! 13 0-0 ♘f6 14 ♗xf8 ♖hxf8. Unsurprisingly this left Black slightly for choice in J.Smeets-F.Jenni, Lippstadt 2003.

12...♘f6

Black prepares to advance his e-pawn and can now safely meet 13 ♗a3 with 13...♕e6. He has also been known to try:

a) Rather ambitious is 12...e4?!, trying to return to seize the initiative:

a1) 13 ♕xe4?! ♕f6! 14 cxd5 ♗xf1 15 ♗xf1 is the critical continuation.

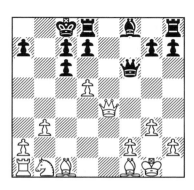

It may look like White will obtain a very dangerous attack for his material, but after 15...♗c5! (a key intermezzo; 15...♕xa1? 16 dxc6 dxc6 17 ♗a6+ ♔d7 18 ♗e2! would, indeed, give White strong attacking chances, as pointed out by Mikhalevski) 16 ♕c2 ♗d4! (16...♕xa1? fails to 17 ♗a6+ ♔b8 18 ♕xc5 ♔a8 19 ♗e3! ♕xb1+ 20 ♔g2 ♕e4+ 21 f3) 17 ♘c3 ♗xc3 18 ♗g5 ♕xg5 19 ♕xc3 it doesn't seem that he has more than sufficient play for the exchange.

a2) 13 ♕d2! ♘f6 (otherwise, 13...e3? misses White's key idea and after 14 ♕a5 Black lost material in A.Motylev-F.Naes, Ubeda 2000; Motylev has also analysed 13...♕b4!? 14 cxd5 ♗xf1 15 ♗xf1 ♕xd2 16 ♗xd2 cxd5 17 ♗a6+ ♔b8 18 ♘c3 c6, but after 19 b4! White should be slightly for choice) 14 ♕a5 ♔b7 (14...♗b7?! 15 ♗f4 only makes matters worse for Black) 15 ♗a3! (after 15 ♗f4 d5 16 ♘c3 ♖d7?! 17 ♗h3 Black lost the exchange for insufficient compensation in D.Pavasovic-F.Jenni, Leipzig 2002, but he improved with 16...♘h5! 17 cxd5 cxd5 18 ♘xd5 ♕c5 19 ♕xc5 ♗xc5 20 ♖fc1 ♗d4! and held his own in the complications in S.Collins-F.Jenni, Plovdiv 2003) 15...♕e6 16 ♗xf8 ♖hxf8 17 ♘c3 ♖de8 18 ♖ae1! leaves Black without a good move. White meets 18...♕e5 with 19 ♕b4+ ♔a8 20 ♘xe4 ♘xe4 21 ♖xe4 with some advantage, as b2 is defended, and the 18...d5 of J.Fidalgo Fernandez-A.Llorente Zaro, Mondariz 2004, should be met by 19

⊆d1 with very strong pressure.

b) 12...g6 is also well met by 13 ♕d2, after which 13...♞b6 14 ♕a5 ♚b7 15 ♗a3 ♕e6 leaves Black under some pressure.

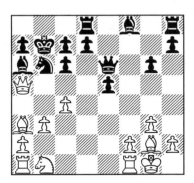

The game M.Lyell-P.Griffiths, British League 1997, continued 16 ⊆e1 (16 ♗xf8 ⊆hxf8 17 ♞c3 d5 18 ⊆ab1! also turned out rather well for White in J.Dovzik-F.Vrana, Slovakian League 2006) 16...♗g7 17 ♞c3 and, with ideas of ♞a4-c5 as well as of c5, White was doing pretty well.

c) 12...⊆e8 13 ♕d2 ♞f6 14 ♕a5 ♗b7 (14...♚b7?! 15 ♗a3 ♕f7 16 ♗xf8 ⊆hxf8 17 ♞c3 was even worse for Black with White's knight en route to c5 in P.Bobras-W.Janocha, Poraj 2003) 15 ♗a3 ♕e6 16 ♕xa7 saw White regain his pawn with an ongoing pull in G.Hernandez-G.Garcia, Guarapuava 1991.

13 ♗a3!

With Black's queen restricted to the centre and so away from the white king, White is again happy to exchange the bishops and here 13 ⊆e1 d5! 14

♗a3 ♕d7 didn't seem quite so effective for him in I.Ponter-P.Hutchings, Exeter 2006.

13...♕e6 14 ♕d2 e4

Instead both 14...♗b7 15 ⊆e1 and 14...♚b8 15 ♕a5 ♗b7 (V.Afromeev-Z.Igriashvili, Tula 2001) 16 ♗b2 leave White with good compensation, albeit possibly not more than that.

Black has also tried to decoy White's knight away from c5 with 14...♗xa3 15 ♞xa3 c5, as he did in V.Afromeev-E.Sosulin, Donskoj 2002 (note that here 15...d5? would have failed to 16 ♕a5 ♚b7 17 b4), but after 16 b4! the knight finds itself well placed to support the attack.

15 ♕a5 c5

Returning the pawn in a bid to slow down White's initiative. Instead after 15...♚b7 16 ♗xf8 ⊆hxf8 17 ♞c3 followed by ♞a4 White would enjoy his usual, fairly effective compensation.

16 ♗xc5 ♗xc5 17 ♕xc5

This position was reached in A.Morozevich-A.Huzman, Amsterdam 1995, where in view of the weakness of

Black's queenside and potentially slightly vulnerable e4-pawn, White enjoyed an ongoing pull.

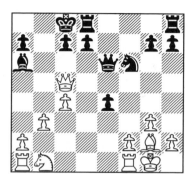

C) 9...g5!?

Black's most ambitious approach and a move which still seems slightly shocking some fifteen years after Anand introduced in his 1995 World Championship match with Kasparov. Black reasons that he can get away with weakening his kingside with White's bishop seemingly bound for b2 and so takes control of the important f4-square, while preparing to increase the pressure against e5 with ...♗g7.

At this juncture White must decide whether to proceed with natural development or to try and refute Black's ambitious advance:

> **C1: 10 ♗a3**
> **C2: 10 ♕e4**
> **C3: 10 h4**
> **C4: 10 g3**

Instead 10 e6? rather failed to convince after 10...♗g7 in D.Roberts-B.Addison, Swansea 2006, but it's surprising that 10 ♗b2 hasn't received more attention, especially when one considers that the bishop usually goes to b2 after all in the main line (C4). Indeed, following 10...♗g7 (10...♘f4 11 ♕e3 ♗g7 12 ♘d2 d6 was preferred in R.Hendriks-J.Berkvens, Dieren 1998, and now 13 h4 would have begun to undermine Black's position with some effect) 11 ♘d2!? (White holds back on developing his kingside; instead 11 ♕e4, 11 h4 and 11 g3 would transpose to Lines C2, C3 and C4 respectively) 11...0-0 (otherwise, 11...♘f4 12 ♕e3 takes play back into the note to Black's 10th, above, 11...♘b4 12 ♘e4 0-0-0 13 ♘g3 left White clearly better and even more than that after 13...♕e6?? 14 a3 in W.Tan-K.Nuri, Vung Tau 2008, and the 11...d6 of X.Sole Fabregat-J.Garriga Sole, Spain 1996, should have been met by 12 ♕e4, again with some advantage) 12 ♕e4 ♘f4 sees Black determined to keep his knight active, rather than retreat it to b6, but even this doesn't appear to suffice for equality.

His problem is that White can strike with 13 h4!? (13 0-0-0 was also a little better for White in A.Dunn-B.Addison, Cleveland 2003, as he will meet 13...d5 with 14 exd6), after which 13...d5 14 ♕f5 ♗xe5 15 ♕xe5 ♕xe5+ 16 ♗xe5 ♖ae8 17 0-0-0 ♖xe5 18 ♘f3 saw White regaining her pawn with an edge in M.Aseeva-G.Mukhin, St Petersburg 2007.

C1) 10 ♗a3

Kasparov's choice when surprised by 9...g5 in the stem game, but the resulting exchange sacrifice fails to bring White any advantage. Indeed, if anything he has to play quite accurately after it to maintain a rough balance.

10...d6!

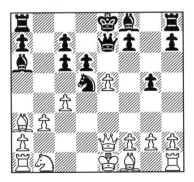

Black wastes no time opening up the centre as he aims to exploit the absence of White's bishop from the long dark-square diagonal.

11 exd6!

There's nothing better than this bold exchange sacrifice, especially as 11 ♕e4?! ♗g7 (11...f5 12 ♕xf5 ♗g7 13 ♗b2 would also have given Black the initiative in J.Van der Veen-M.Weeks, Hoogeveen 2006, had he found 13...♘b4!) 12 ♗b2 sees White losing time and after 12...♘b4! 13 a3 f5 (C.Sandor-E.Frosch, Balatonbereny 1996) 14 ♕e2 ♘d5 Black has the initiative.

11...♕xe2+ 12 ♗xe2 ♗g7!

The point of Black's play.

13 cxd5 ♗xe2

The correct way to pick up the exchange. Instead 13...♗b7?? would be a major error because Black will be overwhelmed by the white pawns after 14 dxc7! ♗xa1 (even worse is 14...cxd5? 15 ♗b5+, forcing mate) 15 d6 (Anand).

14 ♔xe2 ♗xa1

15 dxc6!

White relies on obtaining a passed c-pawn. Instead 15 ♖c1 0-0-0! left Black with the initiative and White struggling to prove quite enough compensation in G.Kasparov-V.Anand, World Championship (Game 8), New York

1995, while 15 ♘d2 ♗e5 16 dxc6 cxd6 transposes to our main line.

15...cxd6 16 ♘d2

The d-pawn is taboo: 16 ♗xd6? 0-0-0 saw Black's rooks taking powerful aim at the exposed white king in A.Billing-L.Balkan, Willingen 2006.

16...♗e5

We've followed the game P.Charbonneau-M.Khassanov, Montreal 2000, in which White's c-pawn and fairly well coordinated forces, not to mention the possible plan of ♘c4-e3-d5, gave him enough for the exchange.

C2) 10 ♕e4

This works well with 9 ♘d2 played instead of 9 b3, but here Black can again make good use of White's vulnerability down the long diagonal.

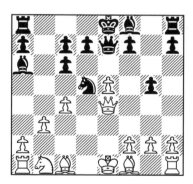

10...♗g7

Thematic, but this may not be Black's only promising approach:

a) 10...♘f6? 11 ♕f5 refuses to let the knight settle and is rather awkward for Black.

b) 10...♘b6 11 ♗a3 (or 11 ♘d2 ♗g7

12 ♗b2 d5! 13 cxd5 cxd5 14 ♕e3 ♗xf1 15 ♔xf1 0-0 and Black had the initiative in P.Kariz-S.Truta, Kranj 1999) 11...♕e6 12 ♗xf8 was seen in A.Haimi-S.Vuori, Helsinki 1997, and now 12...♔xf8 13 ♘d2 ♖e8 would have picked up the e-pawn for insufficient compensation.

c) The 10...♘f4!? of I.Corbacho Charneco-I.Cabezas Ayala, Almendralejo 2003, also deserves further attention. The critical line looks to be 11 ♗a3 ♕e6 12 ♗xf8 ♔xf8 13 ♘c3 ♘g6 with an unclear tussle ahead.

11 ♗b2 ♘f4! 12 ♘d2

White hasn't always developed thus, but after the more ambitious 12 h4 Black can achieve decent counterplay and rough equality with 12...0-0-0 (12...d5!?) 13 hxg5 (13 g3?! ♘g6 14 f4?! gxf4 15 gxf4 was far too ambitious in K.Van der Weide-R.Akhayan, Belgian League 2004, with 15...♗b7 but one route to a clear advantage for Black) 13...♕xg5 14 ♘d2 d5, as he did in B.Savchenko-A.Khruschiov, Moscow 2005.

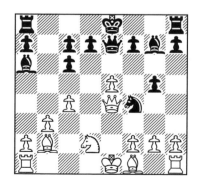

12...♘g6

This is why the knight went to f4: Black wants to win the e-pawn. He has also reacted in the centre, but after 12...d5 13 cxd5 ♗xf1 14 ♔xf1 cxd5 15 ♕a4+ ♕d7 16 ♕xd7+ ♔xd7 17 ♖d1! White was slightly for choice in K.Looijmans-U.Keil, Berlin 2004.

13 0-0-0!

White is right to sacrifice the e-pawn to seize the initiative. Instead after 13 ♘f3?! 0-0 (13...♕b4+ 14 ♔d1 would also have given Black the initiative in L.Demeestere-L.Delorme, La Fere 2008, had he gone 14...0-0 followed by ...d5) 14 0-0-0 f5! Black has the initiative and will shortly pick off the e-pawn after all.

13...♗xe5 14 ♗xe5 ♕xe5

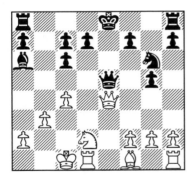

15 h4!

Breaking up Black's kingside structure looks like the best plan, especially as 15 ♕xe5+ ♘xe5 16 ♖e1 wouldn't have given White quite enough for the pawn in D.Vives Rodriguez-S.Bermudez Vives, Cenfotec 2003, after the simple 16...d6.

15...♕xe4 16 ♘xe4 gxh4 17 ♘f6+ ♔e7

This occurred in T.Thorhallsson-P.Landgren, Bergen 2001, where White was able to regain the first of his pawns on d7, leaving the position about even.

C3) 10 h4!?

This worked well in Line B1 of our last chapter (with 9 g3 played instead of 9 b3), but even with the advance not supported it's quite a critical test and tempting option.

10...♗g7

Invariably played. Instead 10...gxh4 11 ♗b2 (W.Orton-A.Khruschiov, Internet blitz 2005) 11...♘f4 12 ♕e4 ♘g6 13 ♘d2 does leave Black a pawn up, but with his structure a wreck on both flanks White must have at the very least good compensation.

11 ♗b2 0-0-0

Alternatively:

a) 11...♘f4?! has been fairly popular, but after 12 ♕e3 h6 (12...♘g6 13 hxg5 ♘xe5 14 ♘c3 ♘g6 15 ♕xe7+ ♘xe7 16 0-0-0 left White somewhat for choice thanks to his pressure down the d- and h-files in O.Pritchard-B.Kay, Queenstown 2009) 13 ♘d2 (13 g3 ♘g6 14 f4 gxf4 15 gxf4 is less effective in view of 15...h5! 16 ♗d3 ♗h6 which was okay for Black in J.Van der Wiel-M.Erwich, Amsterdam 2002) 13...♘g6 White has quite a pleasant choice:

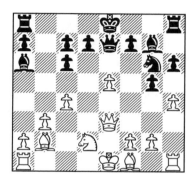

a1) 14 hxg5 hxg5 15 ♖xh8+ ♗xh8 16 0-0-0 ♗xe5 17 ♗xe5 ♕xe5 was seen in S.Haslinger-L.Cako, Hoogeveen 2008, and now 18 ♖e1 would have given White enough for his pawn.

a2) 14 0-0-0!? ♘xh4?! 15 g3 ♘g6 16 f4 gave White excellent play in P.Wells-S.Mannion, Halifax (rapid) 2005.

a3) It's not clear why, though, Wells refrained from his earlier suggestion of 14 ♘f3! g4 (Black tried 14...gxh4 15 0-0-0 0-0 in J.Smeets-J.Timman, Amsterdam 2002, but now 16 ♗d3 would have left White clearly better) 15 h5 gxf3 16 hxg6 fxg6 17 gxf3 g5 (White was somewhat for choice too after 17...♗b7 18 ♗d3 in H.Ten Hertog-S.Mannion, Cappelle la Grande 2006) 18 ♗d3 'which favours White', as he noted in his classic work.

b) 11...h6 12 ♘d2 (stronger than 12 ♕e4 when 12...♘f4 13 ♘d2 ♘g6 14 ♘f3 ♗b7 15 0-0-0 0-0-0 gave Black enough counterplay in Lim Chuing Hoong-Anasrullah, Kuala Lumpur 2005) 12...0-0-0 13 0-0-0 ♖de8 14 g3 ♘b6 15 f4 ♗b7 (15...♔b8 covered a7 in C.Munoz-G.Melendez, San Salvador 2008, but now 16 ♕f2 with the threat of 17 c5 leaves White much better) 16 hxg5 hxg5 17 ♖xh8 ♗xh8 was seen in J.Dworakowska-S.Vijayalakshmi, Moscow 2001, and now 18 ♘e4! retains an edge, as 18...gxf4 19 gxf4 f6? fails to 20 ♘xf6 ♗xf6 21 exf6 ♕xe2 22 ♗xe2 ♖xe2? 23 f7.

c) 11...g4 12 ♘d2 (P.Homatidis-A.Dounis, Panellhnia 2005) 12...f5 13 exf6 is also a small but pleasant advantage for White.

Returning to 11...0-0-0:

12 ♘d2

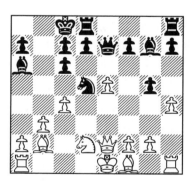

This looks like the most challenging approach. Instead 12 hxg5 ♖de8! (as played in G.Livshits-T.Nabaty, Israeli League 2008, but Black should avoid the 12...♘f4?! 13 ♕e3 ♘g6 of

R.Griffiths-G.Vereb, Budapest 2008, because 14 ♘d2 leaves White somewhat in front) 13 ♘d2 ♘f4 appears to give Black enough counterplay down the e-file and the long diagonal.

12...♘b4

As Black just appears to be worse after this, he should give serious attention to 12...♘f4!? which has been quite rare. White responded with 13 ♕e3 in M.Haast-B.Bok, Geldrop 2007, but after 13...♖de8 Black seems to have enough counterplay to maintain the balance.

Instead the immediate 12...♖de8 runs into 13 hxg5 ♘f4 (13...♗xe5?! 14 ♗xe5 ♕xe5 15 ♕xe5 ♖xe5+ 16 ♔d1 leaves White clearly better thanks to the strong, cramping pawn on g5) 14 ♕g4 ♗xe5 15 0-0-0 f6 (Black also failed to equalize with both 15...♗xb2+ 16 ♔xb2 ♕e5+ 17 ♔b1 in A.Van Beek-I.Khmelniker, Plovdiv 2008, and 15...h5 16 ♕f5 c5 17 ♘f3 in J.Van der Wiel-M.Okkes, Dutch League 1995) 16 ♘f3 when White retained the initiative and a pull in I.Kurnosov-S.Azarov, Bucharest 2008.

13 0-0-0!

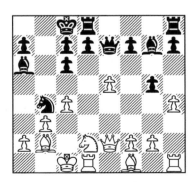

Boldly sacrificing the a-pawn. The materialistic 13 ♔d1?! c5 14 hxg5 was preferred in S.Haslinger-O.De Abreu, Benidorm 2009, but after 14...d6 Black would have enjoyed good compensation.

13...♘xa2+

Black has also been known to decline the challenge, but 13...c5 14 a3 ♘c6 15 hxg5 ♕xg5 (15...♘d4!? improved in T.Burg-R.Van Kampen, Dutch League 2010, but with 16 ♕e3 ♕xe5 17 ♕xe5 ♗xe5 18 b4! White could have maintained a pull) 16 ♖h5 left Black's kingside weak and White with some advantage in E.Wiersma-M.Weeks, Hoogeveen 2005.

14 ♔b1 ♘b4

This critical position was reached in M.White-M.Yeo, Liverpool 2008, and now Palac's 15 ♕e3 retains a clear edge, with Black's kingside weaknesses more important than the slight damage to the white king's pawn shield. Moreover, White may do even better with 15 hxg5!? since 15...♕xg5 16 ♘e4 ♕g6 17 ♖h4! gives him a powerful initiative.

C4) 10 g3

Finally we come to White's main move, preparing a second fianchetto while keeping Black's knight out of f4.

10...♗g7

If Black wants to go long he might begin with 10...0-0-0 when both 11 ♗b2 ♗g7 12 ♗g2 and 11 ♗g2 ♗g7 12 ♗b2 transpose to Line C42, below. Instead 11 ♗a3?! (11 h4!? is likely a better independent try and after 11...gxh4 12 ♖xh4 ♗g7 13 ♗b2 ♖de8 14 ♖h5! f6 15 ♕d2 ♘b6 the position wasn't clear in C.Vitoux-A.Kosten, Pau 2008) 11...♘b4! 12 ♗b2 ♗g7 13 ♗h3 (13 ♗g2 ♘d3+! 14 ♕xd3 ♗xe5 15 ♗xe5 ♕xe5+ 16 ♕e3 ♕xa1 failed to give White anywhere near enough for the exchange in B.Macieja-A.Karpov, Warsaw 2003) 13...♖he8 14 0-0 (I.Doukhine-D.Frolov, Samara 2003) 14...♗xe5 favours Black according to Kosten. It may, although White does have some compensation after 15 ♘c3.

11 ♗b2

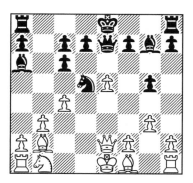

We've reached an important position in which Black must decide which side to house his king:

C41: 11...0-0
C42: 11...0-0-0

Of these the former is more consistent with 9...g5 and likely the better option, but both appear superior to the

rare 11...d6 12 ♕e4 ♘b6 of T.Tatarko-R.Cizmar, Slovakian League 2000, when White could have seized the initiative with 13 h4!?.

C41) 11...0-0?!

This doesn't seem especially harmonious in conjunction with 9...g5 and, indeed, White can obtain the upper hand by avoiding the endgame which Black is hoping for.

12 ♘d2!

Best. White prepares to go long, but he can also deploy his light-squared bishop:

a) After 12 ♗g2 Black should go for the aforementioned endgame with 12...♖ae8 (otherwise, 12...d6?! 13 0-0 ♗xe5 14 ♗xe5 dxe5 15 ♕d2 ♘b6 16 ♗xc6 sees White regaining his pawn with some advantage, just as 12...f6 13 ♕d2! ♘b6 14 0-0 fxe5 15 ♗a3 d6 16 ♗xc6 did in M.Makropoulou-B.Trabert, Pula 1997) 12...♖ae8 13 0-0 ♗xe5 (13...♘b6 14 ♖e1 f6 was preferred in G.Livshits-J.Jirka, Olomouc 2001, but now 15 ♕e3 with the idea of 16 ♗a3 would have given White a plus) 14 ♕xe5 ♕xe5 15 ♗xe5 ♖xe5 16 cxd5 ♗xf1 17 ♔xf1 cxd5.

We will see plenty more of this famous Scotch endgame in both Line C421 and Line D2, below. Black has two pawns and the open e-file for his rooks, but White too is not without his chances. He will aim to restrain Black's rooks as well as his central pawns, hoping to gradually pick them and/or the slightly loose a-pawn off. In general with the pawn on g5 (in Line D2 it will be back on g6 which does make a difference), it seems that Black does best to have his king on the queenside (Line C421), where it supports his potentially vulnerable a7-, c7- and d7-pawns.

Here White should continue 18 ♘d2! (beginning to exploit the hole on c5 while leaving the c-file clear for the rook; instead 18 ♘c3?! c6 19 ♘a4 saw the knight heading for c5, but Black was better after 19...♖fe8 in P.Phoobalan-B.Adhiban, Chennai 2004, with ...f5 and ...♔g7-f6 one way to proceed, making good use of the space

obtained by having the pawn on g5, not g6) 18...g4! (best, as 18...f6 19 ♘f3 ♖e7 20 h4 g4 21 ♘h2 sees White picking up a pawn with a plus and 18...c6 19 ♘f3 also left him a little better in A.Murariu-Z.Zhao, Oropesa del Mar 1998; the pawn does control some useful squares on g5, but Black must remain alert to the fact that it can become a target) 19 f3, opening the kingside and thereby securing enough counterplay to maintain a rough balance.

b) 12 ♗h3!? has been quite rare, but gives White useful pressure against d7 and after 12...♖fe8 13 0-0 d6 14 ♕d2 he had the initiative in V.Diepeveen-M.Erwich, Belgian League 2008.

12...♘b4!

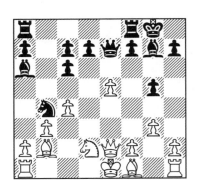

The knight moves before it is pushed, since White must now attend to the defence of c2, and this is Black's best method of obtaining some counterplay. Alternatively:

a) 12...f6?! was powerfully rebuffed in the classic Scotch encounter, G.Kasparov-P.Nikolic, Linares 1997, where 13 ♕h5! ♘b4 14 h4! g4?! (otherwise, 14...♘c2+? 15 ♔d1 ♘xa1 16 hxg5 leaves White with a very strong, likely decisive attack, while Kasparov points out that 14...♕e8 15 ♕xe8 ♖axe8 16 0-0-0 is also in White's favour) 15 ♔d1! left White on top, with Black's knight in trouble on b4 and his kingside rather loose.

b) 12...♖fe8?! 13 0-0-0 ♘b6 (or 13...d6?, as in R.Sanchez-E.Kloster, Merida 1997, when the direct 14 ♕h5 would have been pretty strong) 14 f4 gxf4? (14...d5 improves, but still leaves White somewhat for choice after 15 h4) 15 gxf4 f6 saw everything going wrong for Black in I.Nataf-Y.Pelletier, Bermuda 1999, and now 16 ♖g1 would have led to an extremely strong attack.

c) 12...d6, as in D.Dzhakaev-A.Tsamriuk, Krasnodar 2003, is also rather inadvisable, again because of 13 h4.

13 0-0-0!

Just as in Line C3, White must be prepared to give up the a-pawn to mobilize all his forces. Instead 13 h4? turned out to be rather too speculative after 13...♘c2+ 14 ♔d1 ♘xa1 15 hxg5 ♕xg5 in M.Calzetta Ruiz-J.Jirka, Olomouc 2001.

13...♘xa2+ 14 ♔b1 ♘b4 15 h4

Undoubtedly White enjoyed good attacking chances and compensation here in V.Kotrotsos-K.Kokolias, Athens 2004, although further tests are required before we can definitely conclude that White is better.

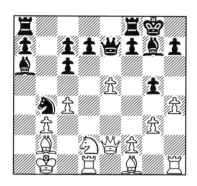

C42) 11...0-0-0!

Black removes his king from a potential attack on the kingside and will now use it to defend his potentially vulnerable queenside pawns should White go in for the two pieces against rook and two pawns endgame.

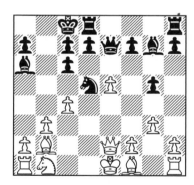

At this stage, with apologies to the reader, we come to a further divide:

C421: 12 ♗g2
C422: 12 ♘d2

The former leads to the aforementioned endgame, but White should probably avoid this particular version with Black's king on c8 and his pawn on g5. As well as with Line C422, White can avoid such a fate with 12 ♕e4?!, but this just makes matters worse and leaves Black with a number of dangerous responses:

a) One continuation he must avoid, however, is the 12...♕b4+? 13 ♘d2 ♘b6 of S.Jacob-K.Heffter, Schoeneck 1996, because 14 c5! ♕xe4+ 15 ♘xe4 leaves White clearly for choice.

b) 12...♘b4 13 a3 was seen in R.Koltsov-A.Novitsky, Peterhof 2007, and now 13...♗b7! would have given Black a dangerous initiative.

c) 12...f5 13 ♕xf5 ♖hf8 14 ♕e4 ♘f6! (14...♘b4!?) 15 ♕e2 ♘g4! 16 ♕xg4 ♗xe5 was quite dangerous in P.Charbonneau-M.Khassanov, Montreal 2000.

d) 12...♘f6 13 ♕c2 ♘g4 14 ♗g2 was also pretty tempting for Black in *Shredder-Rebel*, Maastricht 2001, when the machine should have begun to attack 14...h5!.

C421) 12 ♗g2

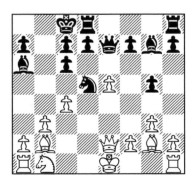

Presumably being a fan of meeting 9...g6 with 10 g3 (Line D2) followed by going in for the endgame, White adopts an identical policy here.

12...♖de8

Black's main choice, but of the alternatives unsurprisingly the closely-related 'd' is also pretty critical:

a) 12...♕b4+? 13 ♘d2!? (the simpler 13 ♕d2 is also rather effective) 13...♖de8 14 a3 ♕a5 15 0-0 ♘c3 16 ♕e3 turned out rather well for White in G.Hernandez-R.Henao, Guarapuava 1992.

b) 12...h5?! 13 ♘d2 g4 14 ♕e4 ♘b6 would have failed to trouble White in K.Sorri-M.Mujunen, Heinola 1997, and actually just left him much better had he gone 15 0-0-0.

c) 12...♘b6 13 0-0 f6 (Black may do better with the 13...d5 14 ♘d2 h5 of Z.Revesz-J.Lamdan, Parsippany 2008, when 15 ♖fe1 is only slightly better for White) 14 ♕d2 ♗b7 15 a4! sounded a powerful charge in D.Gonzalez Gandara-G.Jimenez Martin, Azkotia 1991.

d) 12...♖he8 13 0-0 ♗xe5 14 ♕xe5 ♕xe5 15 ♗xe5 ♖xe5 16 cxd5 (White is unable to trap the black knight after 16 ♘d2? ♘c3) 16...♗xf1 17 ♔xf1 cxd5 reaches the same position as our main line, but with Black's king's rook on e5, not his queen's.

Unsurprisingly play can easily transpose and here we will mainly focus on lines where Black doesn't play or delays ...♖de8 for some time:

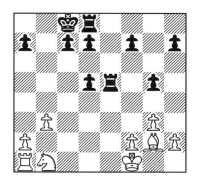

d1) 18 ♘d2 g4! (18...f6 19 ♘f3 ♖ee8 wasn't so clear in G.Berg-E.Sung, Parsippany 2006) 19 f4 ♖h5! 20 ♔f2 c6 slightly favoured Black in J.Zorko-D.De Val, Nova Gorica 2004.

d2) 18 ♗f3 f5 19 h3 holds Black up on the kingside, but after 19...c6 20 ♘d2 ♔c7 White was devoid of a good plan and Black slightly for choice in W.Wilke-H.Knoll, Vienna 2006.

d3) 18 ♘c3 c6 19 ♖c1 demonstrates one of White's main plans: he would like to control Black's pawns with ♘a4-c5 and b4, after which ♖c3-a3/b3 may cause problems:

d31) 19...♔b8?! enables White to proceed with his plan and after 20 ♘a4 ♔c7 21 ♘c5 ♖de8 (N.Fercec-N.Nikcevic, Cannes 1996) 22 ♘d3 ♖e2 chances look about equal.

d32) The alert 19...♔b7! enables Black to meet 20 ♘a4 (otherwise, 20 ♗f3 f5 21 h3 ♖g8 saw Black mobilizing his kingside pawns in M.Jakivchik-M.Guda, Ternopil 2003, and 20 ♘e2 ♖de8 21 ♗f3 ♔b6 left him slightly for choice in C.Nowicki-C.Petri, Ruhrgebiet 1997) with 20...d6.

Then 21 ♘b2 ♖de8 reaches a position we'll see in the notes to Black's 19th move in our main line, below, but here Black could also consider the seemingly-retrograde 21...♖ee8!?, with the idea of 22 ♘d3 ♔b6 23 ♘b4 ♖c8 followed by ...a5 and only then some form of action on the kingside.

Returning to 12...♖de8:

13 0-0

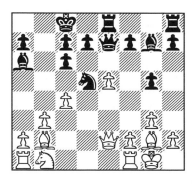

13...♗xe5!

Here too Black is advised to go in for the endgame. Otherwise, 13...f5 14 ♖e1 ♘b6, as in A.Mack-G.Rees, British League 2008, leaves White much better after 15 a4, as did 13...h5 14 ♖e1 h4 15 ♕d2 ♘b6 16 ♕a5 in P.Kuehn-F.Winiwarter, Naumburg 2002.

14 ♕xe5

White can also add one to the move order with 14 ♕d2!? ♗xb2 15 ♕xb2 ♕e5 (best, since 15...♘f6 16 ♘c3 ♗b7 17 b4 gave White good compensation in W.Tjipueja-P.Green, Calvia 2004, and 15...♕f6 16 ♕a3 ♘b4 17 ♘d2 favoured him if anyone in J.Pinkava-A.Potapov, Pardubice 2008) 16 ♕xe5 ♖xe5.

14...♕xe5 15 ♗xe5 ♖xe5 16 cxd5 ♗xf1 17 ♔xf1 cxd5

It is firmly our belief that this represents Black's most promising version of the endgame. Admittedly he must be careful that his king doesn't become a target, but it is well placed to support his otherwise slightly fragile queenside pawns. Moreover, it's a definite boon having the pawn on g5 not g6, since a timely ...g4 may cramp White and in any case one of Black's main plans is to open lines for his rooks with a kingside pawn advance, aiming to stretch White's defences.

18 ♘c3

White sends the knight towards the c5-square. This is his best plan with the pawn back on g6 and likely here too. Alternatively:

a) 18 ♗f3 c6 19 ♘c3 ♔c7 20 ♖c1 (the most active square for the rook; 20 ♖d1 has also been tried, but after 20...f5 21 ♗e2 ♖f8 Black had achieved an ideal kingside mobilization and was better in A.Bitalzadeh-M.Ragger, Groningen 2006) 20...♔d6 21 ♘a4 h5 22

♘b2 h4 saw Black pressing on the king-side with a definite plus in D.Pavasovic-I.Bozanic, Bled 1996, although both here and in Bitalzadeh-Ragger White managed to hold.

b) 18 ♘d2?! g4! prevents White from stopping ...♖e2 with ♗f3. Now a rook exchange would clearly be in Black's favour, but in any case he has scored well from here, such as after 19 b4 (or 19 f3 h5 20 ♔f2 ♖he8, which prepared to invade on e2 or e3 in M.Velcheva-I.Turova, Plovdiv 2008) 19...♖he8 20 ♘b3 c6 21 ♘d4 ♔c7 22 ♖c1 ♔b6! 23 f3 h5 24 ♔f2 ♖e3 and Black's rooks were invading in G.Hakimifard-S.Tajik, Tehran 2008.

c) 18 ♘a3 c6 19 ♘c2 makes some sense, but is a slightly defensive ma-noeuvre and Black was likely for choice after 19...h5 20 ♖d1 h4 in A.Aresh-chenko-M.Hebden, Gibraltar 2008.

18...c6

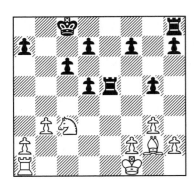

Wisely keeping White's bishop blunted. Instead 18...d4 19 ♘e2 c5 20 ♘c1 d6 21 ♘d3 doesn't necessarily favour White, but there's no need to give both his minor pieces good roles.

19 ♖c1

There has certainly been a fair amount of practical experience with this version of the endgame, also here including:

a) 19 ♗f3 transposes to note 'a' to White's last move.

b) 19 ♖d1?! h5! 20 h3 h4 21 ♘e2 (as played in V.Vehi Bach-F.Jenni, Neuchatel 1998; otherwise, 21 g4 ♖he8 just left Black dominating in M.Prizant-F.Stephenson, Dovedale 2008) 21...hxg3 22 fxg3 ♖h6! leaves White tied down and Black threatening to invade down the f-file.

c) 19 ♖e1?! ♖he8 20 ♖xe5 ♖xe5 21 ♘e2 ♔c7 was not what the doctor ordered for White in L.Winter-D.Lobzhanidze, Griesheim 1999. Without the rooks on, Black finds it easy to activate his king and will gradually advance his central pawns, with White unable to do little more than look on.

19...♔d8!?

Black decides that his king belongs on e7. This has been quite popular, but a natural alternative is to advance it with 19...♔b7 and after 20 ♘a4 ♖e7! (20...d6 may be an imprecision because of 21 ♘b2! ♖he8 22 ♗f3 a5 23 ♘d3 when the b4-break gave White the initiative in A.Suarez Real-L.Venner, French League 2006) 21 ♘c5+ ♔b6 22 ♗f3 d6 23 ♘d3 a5! Black had the initiative in B.Kreiman-G.Giorgadze, Ubeda 1999, with 24 b4 now met by 24...♖a7.

20 ♗f3

White activates his bishop, but this may not be best, as we can see from a perusal of the alternatives:

a) 20 ♘a4?! h5 21 ♘c5 may seem very thematic, but after 21...♖he8 22 a4 a5! followed by ...g4 Black was somewhat for preference in M.Van Wissen-L.Van Beek, Hengelo 2002.

b) 20 h3!? ♖he8 (perhaps Black should prefer 20...h5!? followed by ...g4) 21 ♗f3 ♔e7 22 ♘a4 ♔d6 23 ♘b2 (23 ♘c5 f5 24 ♘d3 followed by b4 also gave White good counterplay in E.Vovsha-L.Kaufman, Parsippany 2005) 23...♖5e7 24 ♘d3 a5 was unclear and likely about level in B.Macieja-A.Delchev, Budapest 2000.

c) 20 ♘e2!? g4 keeps White's bishop out of play and prepares an advance of the h-pawn.

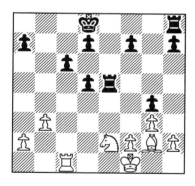

However, after 21 b4 (21 f3 h5 22 ♔f2 ♖he8 23 ♖c2 was preferred in no lesser game than A.Morozevich-V.Mikhalevski, Zurich 2009, and now Mikhalevski has indicated that 23...a5 was best) 21...♖he8 22 ♘d4 a6 23 a4 ♔e7 24 b5 White was able to simplify the position with equality in J.Broekmeulen-T.Gharamian, Bethune 2003.

20...h5 21 ♗e2 ♔e7

Black can also consider both 21...h4!? and the 21...f5 22 ♖d1 g4 23 ♖d4 h4 24 ♔g2 of T.Thorhallsson-G.Giorgadze, Elista Olympiad 1998, when 24...♔e7 would have given him an edge, as indicated by Mikhalevski.

22 ♗d3

We've followed the game L.Ruan-N.Kosintseva, Nizhnij Novgorod 2007, in which Black had improved her king and kingside pawns, while keeping her rooks on good squares. At this point 22...f5?! 23 ♘e2! h4 24 ♖c5 gave White good counterplay, but with the simple 22...h4! 23 ♘e2 hxg3 24 hxg3 ♔d6 Black would have remained slightly for choice.

C422) 12 ♘d2!

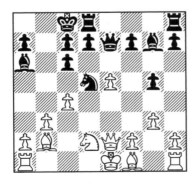

White avoids the endgame while preparing to go long.

12...♖he8

Logically increasing the pressure against e5, but of the alternatives 'd' has been quite popular of late and may even be Black's best option:

a) 12...♖de8 13 0-0-0 ♘b6 (likely the best of the bunch; instead 13...h5?! 14 ♔b1 sees White improving his position with some advantage, 13...f6? runs into the unpinning 14 ♕f3 and 13...c5 14 ♗g2 ♘b4 15 f4! left White doing very well in O.Kanmazalp-T.Demirel, Antalya 2008) 14 f4 (White plays as per our main line, but with Black's rooks on e8 and h8, not d8 and e8, the case for 14 ♖e1!? becomes even more convincing) 14...gxf4 (Black must challenge without delay: 14...♔b8? 15 ♔b1 just left White much better in I.Nataf-J.Netzer, French League 2004, because it's now too late for 15...gxf4 16 gxf4 f6? as 17 exf6 ♗xf6 18 ♕xe7 wins material with Black no longer able to exchange bishops with check) 15 gxf4 f6! 16 exf6 ♗xf6 17 ♕xe7 ♗xb2+ 18 ♔xb2 ♖xe7 is very likely to transpose to our main line, such as after 19 ♗d3 ♖f8. That is okay for Black, but perhaps here White can go 19 a4!?, since Black's rooks aren't quite so well placed after 19...d5!? 20 a5 ♘d7.

b) 12...f5 is a little too simplistic because White's structural advantage must count for something after 13 exf6 ♕xe2+ 14 ♗xe2 ♘xf6 15 0-0-0, as indeed it did in A.Maksimenko-F.Jenni, German League 2006.

c) 12...♔b8?! 13 ♗g2 ♖he8 (E.Salihbegovic-P.Den Boer, Groningen 2007) 14 0-0-0 gives White a pleasant edge with Black about to be left with two rather misplaced minor pieces on the queenside.

d) 12...♘b4!? recently received the backing of Karjakin and is quite critical.

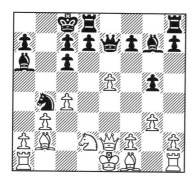

Now:

d1) 13 ♔d1?! is well met by 13...c5! 14 ♗g2 ♗b7 15 ♗xb7+ ♔xb7 when White comes under central pressure: for example, 16 ♕e4+ ♘c6 or 16 f4 d6! 17 ♕e4+ (S.Gaston-L.Verat, Paris 2001) 17...♘c6.

d2) 13 ♕e4?! is also best avoided, because of 13...♖he8! 14 f4 gxf4 15 gxf4 (P.Simacek-F.Jenni, Brno 2006) 15...♕h4+ 16 ♔d1 d6! when the centre opens with some advantage to Black.

d3) 13 ♘f3 and then:

d31) 13...g4? 14 ♘h4 ♕g5 (14...♗xe5? 15 ♕xe5 ♕xe5+ 16 ♗xe5 ♖he8 is too clever because 17 ♔d2 ♖xe5 18 a3 traps and wins the knight on b4, as pointed out by Postny) 15 a3 ♗xe5 (15...♘d5 would be safer, but White is somewhat for choice after 16 ♕d2) 16 f4! saw White win material in Wang Hao-F.Jenni, Calvia Olympiad 2004.

d32) The more prudent 13...c5 buys the black knight a retreat square.

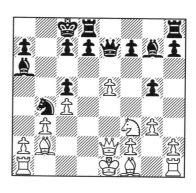

Moreover, Black hopes to place e5 under some pressure, but White is able to complete his development with 14 ♗g2 ♗b7 (alternatively, after the 14...♖he8 15 0-0 ♗b7 16 ♖fe1 h6 of M.Mueller-K.Volke, German League 2004, White should start an attack with 17 a3 ♘c6 18 b4!?, while 14...g4 15 ♘h4 ♗xe5? 16 0-0 was a misguided pawn grab in K.Van der Weide-C.Richter, Dutch League 2005, in view of the tactics down the e-file and the weakness of g4) 15 0-0 (there's no need to drive the knight back just yet, although 15 a3 ♘c6 16 0-0 may also suffice for an edge: 16...h5?! 17 ♖fe1 h4 18 b4! hxg3 19 hxg3 clearly favoured White in G.Jones-A.Vuilleumier, Dresden 2007, and even the superior 16...d6! 17 ♖fe1 ♖he8 18 ♕c2 dxe5 19 ♕f5+ ♔b8 20 ♘xg5 f6 21 ♘f3 gives White a pull, having blunted the bishop on g7) 15...f5 (perhaps not best, but White will meet 15...h5 with 16 ♖fe1 and 15...♘c6 16 ♖fe1 h5 17 a3 favours him too, as we saw, above, via 15 a3) 16 a3 ♞c6 17 b4, which gave him slightly the better attacking chances in R.Khusnutdinov-S.Azarov, Moscow 2010.

d33) 13...♖he8!? delays worrying about the knight's perilous situation for a while longer and after 14 a3 (it's not clear that there's anything better; 14 ♗h3?! has also received some testing, but after 14...h5! 15 a3 ♞d5! 16 ♕d2 g4 Black was slightly ahead in G.Jones-G.Gajewski, Heraklion 2007, with one key idea being 17 ♕a5 ♚b7 18 cxd5 ♕f6! when it seems to be White's king which is the weaker of the two) 14...g4! reaches quite a sharp and critical position.

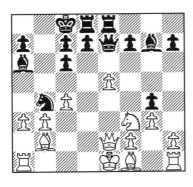

Following 15 ♞h4 (15 axb4!? gxf3 16 ♕e3 ♕xb4+! 17 ♗c3 ♖xe5! favoured Black in S.Rublevsky-A.Onischuk, Foros 2007, but here 17 ♚d1! ♗b7 18 ♚c2 c5 19 ♗d3 d6 isn't at all clear, as pointed out by Kosten; Black has a number of weak pawns and this position could really do with a test or two) 15...♗xe5 16 0-0-0 ♞a2+ 17 ♚c2 ♕f6 18 ♗xe5 ♖xe5 19 ♕d2 ♖de8! (but not the

19...♖e6 of B.Reefat-S.Ganguly, Kelamabakkam 2000, because of Kosten's 20 ♕d4!) 20 ♗d3 (20 ♚b1 ♖e2! gave Black enough counterplay too in B.Macieja-H.Kallio, Stockholm 1999; indeed, it's White who must be careful here with 21 ♕xd7+ ♚b7 22 ♗xe2 ♖xe2 23 ♕d4! the prudent defence, after which 23...♞c3+ 24 ♚c1 ♞a2+ is a perpetual) 20...d5 21 ♖he1 d4 22 ♖xe5 ♖xe5 23 f3 ♞c3 24 ♖f1 ♕d6 the position remained pretty complex but was about even in S.Rublevsky-S.Karjakin, Poikovsky 2010.

d4) White has also tested the bold 13 0-0-0!?, leading to another divide:

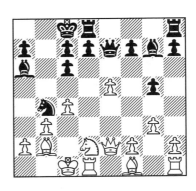

d41) 13...♞xa2+ 14 ♚b1 ♞b4 15 f4 (supporting e5, but 15 ♕e3!? c5 16 ♞e4 ♗b7 17 ♗h3 deserves attention too, after which 17...f5 18 ♗xf5 ♖hf8 19 g4 ♗xe5 20 ♖he1 ♗xh2 21 f3 gave White good play for the two pawns in 'Frigderi'-'Flying Saucers', Internet freestyle 2006, and 17...h5!? 18 f4 also looks like enough compensation) 15...♖he8 (invariably played, but Black might test L'Ami's assertion that after 15...gxf4 16 gxf4 ♗b7 17 ♘e4 c5 'White has decent compensation, but not more than that') 16 ♘e4 (16 ♕e4!? is another idea, but after the 16...f6 of Y.Dembo-Z.Borosova, Beijing 2008, I (YD) should have played 17 exf6 ♗xf6 18 ♕xe7 ♗xe7 19 fxg5 ♗xg5 20 ♘f3 with enough compensation, in view of Black's currently inactive pieces on the queenside) 16...gxf4 17 gxf4 c5 18 ♗g2 ♗b7 19 ♖he1 ♗h8 (19...♔b8 20 ♕f2 ♕f8?! 21 ♘xc5 ♗xg2 22 ♗a3! a5 23 ♘a6+ saw White regaining his pawn with ongoing attacking chances in T.Nedev-E.L'Ami, Plovdiv 2008, and here even 20...♕e6 21 ♕xc5 looks to favour White) 20 ♕f2 ♔b8 saw Black clinging on to his extra pawn in J.Zezulkin-M.Walach, Chotowa 2007.

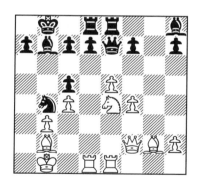

However, with 21 ♗h1!? White would have left c5 en prise and retained pretty decent compensation.

d42) Black has also declined the pawn with 13...c5, but neither is this a complete panacea for him: 14 f4 (or 14 ♗g2 when 14...d5?! 15 a3 ♘c6 16 f4 left White much better in E.Berg-A.Vuilleumier, Sarajevo 2010, and after the pref-

erable 14...♗b7 15 ♗xb7+ ♔xb7 of J.Zezulkin-T.Thannheiser, German League 2007, White can retain a pull with 16 ♔b1) 14...♗b7 15 ♗g2 ♘d3+!? 16 ♕xd3 ♗xg2 17 ♖he1 (17 ♖hg1!? ♗c6 18 ♘e4 also deserves attention) 17...gxf4 18 gxf4 ♗h6 (or 18...♗c6 19 ♕h3 h5 20 ♔b1 ♗h6 21 f5 and White was advancing with an ongoing pull in G.Jones-R.Williamson, Liverpool 2008) 19 ♖e2 ♗c6 20 ♖f1 (improving over 20 f5?! whereupon 20...♕h4! 21 ♔b1 d5 gave Black decent counterplay in T.Abergel-S.Maze, Pau 2008) 20...♕h4 was seen in A.Kolev-E.Postny, Kallithea 2009, and now with 21 ♖ef2 White could have maintained a small edge.

After that important digression, we return to Black's straightforward attempt to include his king's rook in the game with 12...♖he8:

13 0-0-0!

Indirectly defending the pawn because capturing it would cost Black his knight, whereas 13 ♘f3? does just drop the pawn to 13...g4.

13...♘b6

Thus Black's knight has been forced offside and that may well cost him once the centre opens up.

14 f4

White's invariable choice, but one can also make a good case for the 14 ♖e1!? ♔b8 15 h4 of D.Yashnev-N.Pokazanjev, Rybinsk 2000, and 14 h4!? g4 15 f4 gxf3 16 ♘xf3, with an edge in both cases. Indeed, considering White's difficulties in proving an advantage from the tabiya after move 18, below, it wouldn't be surprising if both these options become a lot better explored in the future.

14...gxf4 15 gxf4 f6!

Black might prefer not to challenge and risk his queenside pieces being left out of play, but he must before White consolidates his advantage and begins to increase the pressure, such as with 16 ♕f2 and 17 ♘e4.

Instead 15...♕h4 16 ♖g1 ♗h8 (Z.Plecsko-M.Walzl, Zalakaros 2000) 17 ♕g4 forces the queens off with some advantage and Black would also have been in trouble after 15...♕f8 16 ♖g1 f6 in A.Murariu-A.Toth, Sozina 2004, had White gone 17 ♕f2.

16 exf6

Black should have enough counterplay after 16 ♗h3?! fxe5 17 ♖he1 ♔b8! followed by ...d5, as pointed out by Van der Weide, but Postny's 16 ♖e1!? looks like the last try to maintain a little something after 16...fxe5 17 fxe5 d5 18 ♕e3 dxc4 19 ♘xc4 ♘xc4 20 bxc4.

16...♗xf6 17 ♕xe7 ♗xb2+ 18 ♔xb2

♖xe7

Thus White has managed to get the queens off, but cannot afford to dally with Black set to gang up on his f-pawn, as well as hoping to break with ...d5.

19 ♗h3

White counters Black's ideas (the d-pawn is now pinned and f5 will save the f-pawn from attack), but he can also consider:

a) 19 ♖g1 ♖f8 20 c5 ♗xf1 21 cxb6 was analysed by Van der Weide and now 21...♗h3! keeps matters rather unclear.

b) 19 a4 d5! (but not the slow 19...♔b8?! 20 a5 ♘c8 of J.Hector-J.Timman, Malmo 2001, when 21 ♘f3 favours White) 20 a5 ♘d7 21 ♗h3 ♖e2 gave Black decent counterplay in M.Mueller-F.Jenni, Zurich 2006.

c) 19 ♗d3 looks quite tempting, trying to tie Black to h7, but 19...♖f8 20 ♖hf1 ♘d5! brings the knight back into the game with some effect. Here White might go 20 ♖de1!?, but the tricky tactical line 20...♖xe1 21 ♖xe1 ♖xf4 22

♖e8+ ♔b7 23 ♘e4 d6 24 ♖e7 ♘d5! 25 ♖xh7 ♔b6 is hardly at all clear.

19...♖f8 20 ♖he1

Perhaps 20 f5!? is White's final try to obtain a little something.

20...♖xe1 21 ♖xe1

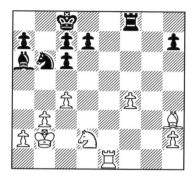

This position was reached in S.Rublevsky-R.Ponomariov, Foros 2006, where 21...♔d8?! 22 f5 ♗c8 23 ♘f3 favoured White, but it didn't take Black long to improve and equalize with the fearless 21...♖xf4! 22 ♖e8+ ♔b7 23 ♘e4 d6 in O.De la Riva Aguado-M.Perez Candelario, Ayamonte 2006.

D) 9...g6

Finally we come to Black's main choice and a very sensible one at that. He plans to increase the pressure against e5 and without weakening his kingside anywhere near as much as 9...g5 does.

At this juncture White has two main options:

> **D1: 10 f4**
> **D2: 10 ♗b2**

Alternatively:

a) 10 g3 ♗g7 11 ♗b2 is another common route into Line D2, although here Black can also consider 10...f6!?, as we saw in Line B5 of the previous chapter. Moreover, if he is happy to debate the endgame with his king on the queenside then 10...0-0-0 is an option, after which 11 ♗b2 (11 ♗a3?! is well met by 11...♘b4!, after which 12 f4 g5!? 13 ♗b2 gxf4 14 a3 ♘d5 left Black with the initiative in J.De la Villa Garcia-M.Illescas Cordoba, Pamplona 1998) 11...♗g7 takes play into Line D21.

b) Similarly misguided was 10 ♕e4? f5! 11 ♕d4 ♘b4 in C.Belger-G.Voelsgen, Willingen 2006.

c) 10 ♘d2 fails to really trouble Black, as we saw in Line A3 of Chapter One.

d) 10 ♗a3 echoes White's play in Line C1, but grants Black a number of decent options:

d1) 10...♕g5 11 g3 (or 11 ♗xf8 ♖xf8 12 ♘d2 0-0-0 13 ♘f3, as in K.Albert-

L.Nagy, Hungarian League 2002, and now 13...♕f5 is about equal) 11...♘c3 12 ♘xc3 ♗xa3 13 ♘e4 ♕e7 14 ♘f6+ ♔f8 15 ♗g2 ♗b4+ 16 ♔f1 ♖d8 was okay for Black in G.Kasparov-V.Ivanchuk, Amsterdam 1994.

d2) 10...♕h4!? brings the queen to her most aggressive square and is undoubtedly an improvement on Line A for Black.

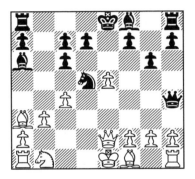

Following 11 ♗b2 (and not 11 ♗xf8? because of 11...♕d4!, picking up the exchange) 11...♗b4+ 12 ♘d2 (as played in H.Krieger-M.Daub, German League 2004; otherwise, 12 ♔d1?! ♘f4 13 ♕e4 would have given Black, not White, the initiative in A.Szieberth-J.Estrada Nieto, Hungarian League 1997, had he gone in for 13...0-0 14 ♗c1 g5!) 12...♘c3 Black clearly has no problems.

d3) However, 10...♕xa3?! 11 ♘xa3 ♗b4+ 12 ♕d2 ♗xd2+ 13 ♔xd2 is a little too simplistic, and here 13...♘f4 (or 13...♘b4 14 g3 0-0-0 15 ♗h3 ♔b8 16 ♘c2 with an edge for White in V.Kupreichik-E.Kolesnik, Minsk 2004)

14 g3 ♘e6 15 ♗g2 was a little better for White in A.Cvicela-M.Sycova, Prievidza 1998.

d4) 10...♘b4!? 11 ♗b2 (11 g3? ♘c2+! 12 ♕xc2 ♕xe5+ 13 ♕e2 ♗g7 14 ♘c3 ♕xe2+ 15 ♔xe2 ♗xc3 cost White a pawn in A.Abdollah Zadeh-N.Grandelius, Lund 2010) 11...♗g7 is quite a crafty idea. After 12 a3 (White can also consider 12 f4!? 0-0, as in M.Heidrich-O.Zhuravleva, Pardubice 2009, when matters aren't too clear after 13 a3 ♘d5 14 ♕d2) 12...♘d5 13 g3 (13 ♘d2 c5 14 0-0-0 0-0 15 g3 ♖ab8 gave Black enough counterplay in M.Muzychuk-M.Savic, Subotica 2008) 13...0-0 14 ♗g2 ♖ae8 we have a position from Line D222 but with White having the extra move a3, which may leave his queenside a little unstable in the endgame after 15 0-0 ♗xe5 16 ♗xe5 ♕xe5 17 ♕xe5 ♖xe5 18 cxd5 ♗xf1 19 ♔xf1 cxd5.

d5) 10...d6 was how Black responded in Line C1 and here too it's hardly a bad option. Following the necessary exchange sacrifice 11 exd6! ♕xe2+ 12 ♗xe2 ♗g7 13 cxd5 ♗xe2 14 ♔xe2 ♗xa1 White can try to exploit the difference in the placement of Black's g-pawn with 15 ♖c1! 0-0-0 16 f4, but whether this suffices for an advantage isn't at all easy to say.

D1) 10 f4

White shores up the defence of e5 and now the battle will revolve around whether Black can remove that central bastion and, if so, at what price. At this point he usually opts for one of:

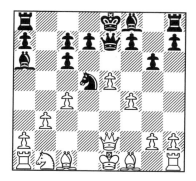

D11: 10...♗g7
D12: 10...f6
D13: 10...♕b4+

On occasion practice has also seen:

a) 10...♗h6?!, as in K.Krasko-J.Prizant, Tula 2004, should just be met by 11 ♕f2 followed by ♗a3 with an edge.

b) 10...g5!? is a somewhat more pointed and radical idea, moving the g-pawn a second time. Following 11 fxg5 (Black also has decent counterplay after 11 f5 0-0-0 12 ♗b2, as in E.Berg-A.Smith, Gothenburg 2010, and then 12...♕c5, while he should meet the 11 ♗a3?! of A.Motylev-V.Ivanchuk, Moscow (blitz) 2002, with Kasparov's suggestion of 11...♘b4! 12 f5 d5) 11...♗g7 12 ♗b2 0-0 (12...♕xg5!? 13 ♘d2 0-0-0, as pointed out by Kasparov, is another option in this fascinating and neglected sideline) 13 ♕e4 ♕xg5 14 cxd5 wouldn't have been at all clear in

D.Pavasovic-I.Balinov, Pula 2003, had Black gone in for 14...♖fe8! 15 ♘d2 ♗xf1 16 ♖xf1 ♗xe5.

c) 10...d6!? wastes no time getting in a central challenge, but has been surprisingly rare here, despite some attention from the strong German Grandmaster and respected theoretician, Jan Gustafsson. Here 11 ♗b2 (11 ♕f2?! was certainly no improvement and actually left Black slightly for choice following 11...♘f6 12 ♗a3 ♕e6 13 ♗e2 dxe5 14 fxe5 ♗xa3 15 ♘xa3 ♘d7 in M.Müller-J.Gustafsson, German League 2009) 11...♗g7 was seen in N.Ronchetti-J.Gustafsson, Reggio Emilia 2008, whereupon 12 ♕f2 ♘b6 is unclear and in need of testing.

d) Another rather neglected approach has been 10...0-0-0 and after 11 ♕f2 ♕c5 (but not 11...♘b6? 12 c5) 12 ♕d2 ♘xf4! (Black must sacrifice, as 12...♘e7? 13 ♗a3 ♕b6 14 ♘c3 d6 15 ♘a4 just leaves White somewhat for choice) 13 ♕xf4 ♗g7 14 ♗b2 ♖he8 15 ♘d2 Black has interesting play for the piece.

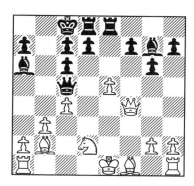

Now 15...♗xe5! (this seems stronger than throwing more wood on the fire with 15...♖xe5+!? 16 ♗xe5 ♗xe5 17 b4 ♕e7, not that this was exactly clear in S.Rublevsky-G.Todorovic, Novi Sad 2000) 16 ♗xe5 ♖xe5+ 17 ♔d1 ♖f5 18 ♕g3 d5 gave Black roughly enough for his piece and remained pretty unclear in Y.Dembo-G.Todorovic, Budapest 2001.

D11) 10...♗g7?!

This may appear a very logical follow-up to 9...g6 and has been pretty popular, but just appears a little misguided in view of White's strong response.

11 ♕f2!

White wastes no time unpinning, thereby forcing Black to decide what to do with his knight. Otherwise:

a) Not for the first time 11 ♕e4? runs into 11...f5! when Black is slightly for choice after 12 ♕f3 ♘b4.

b) 11 ♕f3? ♘b4 12 ♕c3 would have been even worse for White in R.Borondo Garcia-A.Gimenez Carretero,

Seville 2001, had Black gone 12...f6 13 ♗b2 fxe5 14 fxe5 d6.

c) 11 g3?! f6! 12 ♗a3 (A.Gotsi-I.Koniou, Greece 1995) 12...♘b4 is also pretty good for Black.

d) 11 ♗a3? ♘xf4! 12 ♗xe7 ♘xe2 13 ♗f6 ♗xf6 14 exf6 ♘f4 cost White a pawn in A.Gara-D.Papagorasz, Paks 1996.

Thus it can be seen that not only is 11 ♕f2 strong, it is also rather essential!

11...♘b6

Now Black's minor pieces may well, of course, find themselves a little out of play on the queenside, but neither are the alternatives a panacea for him:

a) 11...♘f6 and then:

a1) White should avoid 12 ♗d3? ♘g4! 13 ♕e2 ♘xe5! which cost him material in A.Turzo-D.Jakovenko, Budapest 1995.

a2) 12 ♗a3 ♘g4 (or 12...♕e6 13 ♗e2 ♘e4 14 ♕f3 with an edge for White in B.Trabert-E.Stavropoulou, Athens 2003) 13 ♕e2 (13 ♗xe7? ♘xf2 14 ♔xf2 ♗xe7 favours Black, who will activate his unopposed bishop with ...f6) 13...♕e6 14 ♘d2 d6 (14...f5?! enabled White to take control with 15 h3 ♘h6 16 ♘f3 in A.Delchev-A.Sidorenko, Bled 2002) 15 h3 ♘h6 16 0-0-0 0-0-0 17 ♘e4 dxe5 (Black later tried in 17...♕f5 in A.Shabalov-J.Granda Zuniga, Buenos Aires 2005, and here Postny's 18 g3!? dxe5 19 ♖xd8+ ♖xd8 20 ♗b2 definitely deserves attention) 18 ♘c5 saw White's knight land on its favourite square and gave him good compensation for the pawn in A.Pulido-D.Otero, Cuba 2000.

a3) 12 ♗e2! is simple and strong, continuing to harry the knight:

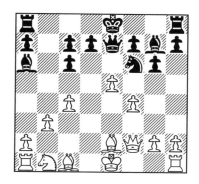

a31) 12...♘e4 13 ♕e3 ♘d6! (a better try than 13...f5?! when 14 ♗a3 d6 15 ♘d2 g5? failed to 16 exd6! in A.Goloshchapov-A.Moiseenko, Ordzhonikidze 2000; here 15...♘xd2 improves, but isn't enough for equality after 16 ♕xd2, whereas the earlier deviation 14...♕e6?! 15 ♘d2 ♘xd2 16 ♕xd2 0-0-0 17 ♕a5 ♗b7 18 c5 left White clearly better in C.Stanetzek-A.Zude, Bad Wiessee 2001) 14 0-0 (improving over 14 ♕f3 ♘f5 which seemed okay for Black in O.Kulicov-S.Okrugin, Tula 2002) 14...♘f5 15 ♕f2 leaves White slightly better.

a32) 12...0-0 13 ♗a3! d6 14 ♘c3 is also a little better for White.

a33) 12...d6?! refuses to move the knight, but after 13 ♗f3 (13 ♗a3 ♕e6!? doesn't seem so clear, but White might consider 13 0-0!? dxe5 14 ♗a3 ♕e6 15 ♘c3 which gave him promising compensation in H.Lodes-A.Zude, Bad Wi-

essee 2006) 13...0-0 14 0-0 ♗b7 15 ♗a3! (even stronger than 15 ♗b2 ♘d7 16 exd6 cxd6 17 ♗xg7 ♔xg7 18 ♘c3 with an edge in J.Van der Wiel-A.Beliavsky, Groningen 1994) 15...♘d7 (G.Halvax-J.Kociscak, Herceg Novi 2008) 16 ♘c3 White is somewhat for choice, with 17 ♖ad1 set to increase the pressure against d6.

b) 11...♘b4!? 12 a3! (taking up the challenge; instead 12 ♗b2 ♗b7 13 a3 ♘a6 doesn't seem too bad for Black) 12...♗xe5! 13 fxe5 ♕xe5+ is Black's most uncompromising defence, but the complications appear to favour White.

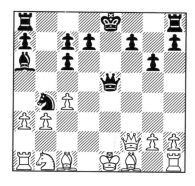

The critical line runs 14 ♔d1 (White can also consider Mikhalevski's simpler idea of 14 ♕e2!? ♘c2+ 15 ♔f2 ♕xe2+ 16 ♗xe2 ♘xa1 17 ♗b2 0-0 18 ♗xa1 when the bishop-pair should give him the upper hand) 14...♕xa1 15 axb4! ♕xb1 16 ♕e3+ ♔d8 17 ♕c3 ♖e8 18 ♗d3 ♕a2 19 ♗b2 ♗xc4 (essential, since 19...c5? 20 ♔c2 cost Black her queen and the game in N.Zdebskaja-E.Matseyko, Kharkov 2005) 20 bxc4 when Black can save his queen, but White is for choice with his powerful bishops.

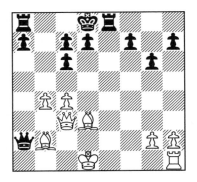

J.Lautier-A.Mikhalevski, Paris 2000, continued 20...c5! (20...♖b8 21 ♔d2 ♕a4 22 b5 also favoured White in J.Smeets-E.Garcia, Chalkidiki 2003) 21 ♔d2 ♕a6 22 bxc5, reducing Black's extra pawns by one while retaining a pull, but White may do even better with 21 b5!? ♕a4+ 22 ♔c1, after which his king is certainly somewhat the safer.

We now return to 11...♘b6:

12 ♗a3

Once again White causes problems down the a3-f8 diagonal, but of the alternatives 'a' is also a promising possibility:

a) 12 c5!? ♗xf1 13 cxb6 ♗a6 14 ♗a3 d6 (or 14...♕d8 15 bxc7 ♕xc7 16 ♗d6 ♕a5+ 17 ♕d2 ♕xd2+, as in V.Tseshkovsky-P.Harikrishna, Hastings 2002/3, and now Postny's 18 ♔xd2! f6 19 ♘c3 leaves White much better) 15 bxc7 is a very logical way of undermining Black on the dark squares.

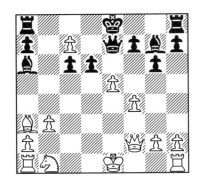

The second player must respond with 15...c5, but after 16 ♘c3 ♕xc7 17 0-0-0 ♕a5 18 ♗b2! dxe5 19 ♘d5 White remained slightly for choice in V.Tseshkovsky-V.Arbakov, Krasnodar 2002.

b) 12 ♗e2 should be met by 12...d6!, after which 13 ♗a3 ♕e6 doesn't seem clear, but White should prefer that to 13 0-0 dxe5 which didn't give him quite enough play in H.Van der Poel-A.Bouwmeester, Dutch League 2000.

c) 12 ♗b2? 0-0 13 ♘d2 f6 saw e5 falling with some advantage for Black in L.Snyder-M.Aigner, San Francisco 2002.

12...d6

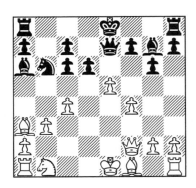

A better try than 12...♕e6?! when 13 c5! was strong in D.Dochev-N.Mina, Agios Kirykos 2004, because 13...♗xe5 14 fxe5 ♕xe5+ 15 ♔d1 ♕xa1 16 ♔c1 ♘c4 (White has a winning attack down the long diagonal after 16...♘d5? 17 ♗xa6 0-0 18 ♗b2) 17 bxc4 would have left both members of Black's royal family in some danger.

13 ♘c3

The c5 break is an important idea, but not here: 13 c5? ♗xe5! 14 fxe5 ♕xe5+ 15 ♔d2 ♕xa1 favoured Black in S.Ganguly-N.Babu, Mumbai 2003.

13...0-0

White is now able to meet 13...f6 with 14 c5, but the attempt to prevent such ideas with 13...c5 simply left Black much worse after 14 ♗e2 ♗b7 15 0-0 0-0 16 ♖ad1 f6 17 exd6 cxd6 18 ♘b5 in G.Jones-T.Nixon, Scarborough 2004.

14 ♗e2!

White too decides that his king is best housed on the kingside. He preferred 14 0-0-0 in H.Kummerow-M.Herrmann, Dresden 2007, but here 14...c5 shouldn't be too bad for Black.

14...c5 15 0-0

This looks like a fairly pleasant edge for White. He retains his structural plusses and Black is still some way from being able to resolve the central tension.

D12) 10...f6

Black undermines without delay, having realized that he is now better able to meet 11 ♗a3 than he is after 10...♗g7.

11 exf6

Giving up the bridgehead, but White hopes for a pull in a queenless middlegame. Alternatively:

a) 11 ♕d2?! ♘b6 12 ♗a3 (misguided here, but even worse is 12 ♗b2?! fxe5 13 c5 ♗xf1 14 cxb6 ♗a6, which left Black doing very well in V.Kraft-M.Kreuzer, German League 2001) 12...c5 13 ♗e2 fxe5 failed to give White enough compensation in T.Hacquebord-E.Oosterom, Utrecht 2009.

b) 11 ♕e4 ♘b6 12 ♗b2 (safer is 12 ♘d2 fxe5 13 ♕xe5 when 13...♗g7 14

♕xe7+ ♔xe7 15 ♗a3+ gave White a pull in J.Van der Wiel-E.Oosterom, Leiden 2008, but Black improved with 13...♕xe5+ 14 fxe5 ♗g7 to equalize in V.Belov-M.Ragger, Budva 2009) 12...♗g7 13 ♘d2 fxe5 14 fxe5 was tried by one of your authors in Y.Dembo-M.Savic, Herceg Novi 2001, but 14...0-0 would have given Black the initiative, thanks to the pressure against e5 and his safer king.

c) 11 ♗a3 echoes White's play in Line D11 and was once played by Kasparov:

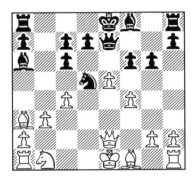

c1) 11...♕f7?! is the safe-looking response, but following the sharp line 12 ♕d2! (12 exf6+? ♔d8 only caused White problems down the e-file in D.Derakhshani-U.Ashwini, Vung Tau 2008) 12...♘b6 13 c5! ♗xf1 14 cxb6 ♗a6? (after 14...axb6? the powerful intermezzo 15 e6!! gave White some advantage in G.Kasparov-A.Karpov, Tilburg 1991, but 14...♗xa3 15 b7! ♖b8 16 ♘xa3 restricted him to an edge in R.Barten-A.Skulteti, correspondence 1995) 15 bxc7 fxe5 (Black's bold idea)

16 ♕a5 ♕xf4! 17 ♕xa6 ♕h4+ 18 ♔d1! (White rejects the draw and is prepared to return the extra material and more to seize a strong initiative) 18...♕d4+ 19 ♔c2 ♕e4+ 20 ♕d3 ♕xg2+ 21 ♘d2 ♗xa3 Black emerges from the complications in some trouble after 22 ♖hf1! with the large threat of 23 ♕a6, after which White won without too much trouble in H.Repp-V.Tammemagi, correspondence 1992.

c2) 11...♘b4! 12 ♗b2 ♗h6! (Wells points out that both 12...c5?! 13 ♘c3 fxe5 14 a3! and 12...fxe5 13 a3 ♘d5 14 ♕xe5 ♘f6 15 ♗e2 ♗g7 16 ♘d2 are promising for White) 13 a3! (the knight must be kicked; 13 ♕f2?! threatened to trap it in J.Van der Wiel-N.Pedersen, Dutch League 2005, but after 13...♗b7 14 a3 ♘a6 Black enjoyed promising activity) 13...♘d5 sees both sides losing time and entails an exchange sacrifice by Black.

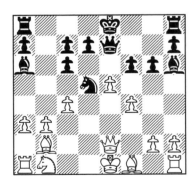

White accepted the offer with 14 exf6 ♕xe2+ 15 ♗xe2 ♘xf4 16 f7+ ♔xf7 17 ♗xh8 ♖xh8 in E.Sutovsky-P.H.Nielsen, Reykjavik 2004, but Black enjoyed full compensation thanks to his very active pieces. Thus White should probably prefer 14 g3!?, although after 14...0-0 (but not 14...fxe5?! 15 ♕xe5 ♘f6 16 ♕xe7+ ♔xe7 17 ♘d2 with advantage to White) 15 ♕e4 ♘b6 Black still had enough counterplay in D.Rombaldoni-N.Grandelius, Reykjavik 2009.

11...♘xf6

Black has no desire to simplify, but it may be the case that he does better with 11...♕xe2+!? 12 ♗xe2 ♗b4+ 13 ♗d2 (perhaps White should prefer 13 ♔d1!?, since 13...♘xf6 14 ♗d2! ♗xd2 15 ♘xd2 c5 16 ♗f3 gave him a pull in N.Olenin-V.Genba, Dagomys 2009, but not here 14 ♗e3, as 14...0-0 15 a3 ♗d6! gave Black the initiative in Ni Hua-E.Vladimirov, Tripoli (rapid) 2004) 13...♗xd2+ 14 ♘xd2 when he is able to keep his knight active.

Following 14...♘xf4 15 ♖f1!? (15 g3 ♘xe2 16 ♔xe2 0-0 was fine for Black in Ni Hua-E.Vladimirov, Tripoli 2004) 15...♘xg2+ (15...♘xe2!? 16 ♔xe2 ♔f7 17 ♔d3 ♖ae8 is a simpler alternative,

as played by a certain leading Scotch exponent in T.Radjabov-G.Kasparov, Linares 2004) 16 ♔f2 ♘f4 White is able to maintain his passer on f6, but that has come at the cost of a pawn and this position was hardly at all clear in S.Rublevsky-V.Tseshkovsky, Krasnoyarsk 2003.

12 ♗b2 0-0-0

Unsurprisingly the less ambitious 12...♗g7 13 ♘d2 ♕xe2+ 14 ♗xe2 gave White a small but clear edge in I.Nataf-H.Daurelle, French League 2003.

13 ♘d2!

Black can keep the queens on after this, but 13 ♕xe7?! ♗xe7 14 ♘c3 ♖he8 would give him the initiative thanks to his active, centralized rooks.

13...♕f7

Black would like to break with 13...d5?!, but practice has shown 14 0-0-0 d4 to give White a few routes to the advantage. Of these 15 ♖e1! is likely the simplest and after 15...♕xe2 16 ♗xe2 c5 (Wells has suggested 16...♗d6, but after 17 c5! White has some advantage, while both 16...♗b4

17 ♗f3 and 16...♗h6 17 g3 gave him an edge in D.Bucher-F.Sanchez Aller, Aviles 2000, and A.Beliavsky-Z.Almasi, Niksic 1997, respectively) 17 ♗f3 White is slightly for choice with Black's central pawns well blockaded.

14 0-0-0 ♗g7

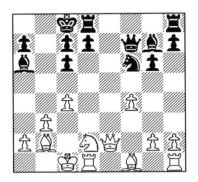

We've followed the game O.Sepp-S.Zjukin, Tallinn 2006, in which Black still hoped to obtain counterplay down the central files, but here 15 ♕f2!? ♔b8 16 ♗e2 ♖he8 17 ♖he1 is one way for White to maintain control and the upper hand.

D13) 10...♕b4+

Black exploits the fact that 11 ♕d2? drops a pawn to 11...♘xf4 to transfer his queen to the g1-a7 diagonal, while disrupting White's development.

11 ♗d2 ♕b6

The point of Black's play, whereas 11...♘xf4?? would now be far too clever and cost him a piece after 12 ♕e4.

12 ♕f3

White breaks the pin and prepares to develop his kingside, but there are important alternatives:

a) 12 ♕e4 f5! (the standard response to the queen's arrival on e4; otherwise, 12...♘b4? 13 ♘c3 ♗b7 14 a3! f5 15 ♕b1 ♘a6 16 b4 left White clearly better in D.Pavasovic-B.Rogulj, Dresden 1998, and so does 12...♘e7? 13 ♘c3 ♗g7 14 ♘a4, as pointed out by Mikhalevski) 13 ♕f3 is another way of bringing the queen to a good square on f3.

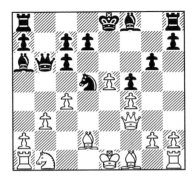

Here White may find it harder to advance on the kingside, but at the same time Black has been deprived of the ...f6 break. Play remains similar to our main line, though, and may continue 13...♘b4 (or 13...♕d4 14 ♘c3 ♘xc3 15 ♗xc3!? ♗b4 16 ♖c1 with an edge for White in B.Macieja-G.Vescovi, Bermuda 2003) 14 ♔d1! ♗b7 15 ♘c3 c5! (Black failed to equalize after 15...0-0-0 16 a3 ♘a6 17 b4 in J.Fluvia Poyatos-M.Panchanathan, Montcada i Reixac 2009) 16 ♘d5 ♗g7 (White is a little better after 16...♘xd5 17 cxd5, but Black can consider 16...♕c6 17 ♗xb4 cxb4 which wasn't too clear in F.De la Paz Perdomo-D.Otero, Havana

2001) 17 ♔c1 (17 ♗xb4?! cxb4 18 ♔c2 ♗xd5 19 cxd5 d6 favoured Black thanks to his unopposed dark-squared bishop in I.Nataf-E.Bacrot, Cannes 2002) 17...♕c6 18 ♗xb4 cxb4 and in this unbalanced position Black had enough counterplay in D.Eschbach-B.Marzolf, German League 2002.

b) 12 ♘c3 ♗b4 (more challenging than 12...♘xc3?! 13 ♗xc3 ♗b4 14 ♗xb4 ♕xb4+ 15 ♕d2 ♕xd2+ 16 ♔xd2 which gave White a small but clear edge in G.Jones-M.Panchanathan, Parramatta 2010) 13 ♕d3! (better than 13 ♕f3 ♘xc3 14 ♗xc3 when Black can consider 14...♕a5!?, as well as 14...♗b7 15 0-0-0 c5 which was fine for him in B.Gelfand-A.Karpov, Linares 1992) 13...♗xc3 (likely not best; indeed, Black should look into 13...♘xc3!? 14 ♗xc3, as in J.Hector-T.Ernst, Lidkoeping 1999, and then 14...0-0 which looks like a better try for equality, as does 13...0-0 14 0-0-0 ♘xc3 15 ♗xc3 d5 of G.Jones-R.Nielsen, Klaksvik 2010) 14 ♗xc3 has received some attention from theoreticians and looks like a decent sacrifice of the f-pawn.

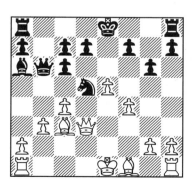

The game Z.Vuckovic-D.Blagojevic, Yugoslavia 1993, continued 14...♘xf4 (otherwise, 14...♘xc3 15 ♕xc3 gave White a pull in J.Hector-H.Olsen, Gentofte 1999, and 14...♕e3+?! 15 ♕xe3 ♘xe3 16 ♔f2 ♘xf1 allows him even more than that after Vuckovic's 17 e6!) 15 ♕d2 ♘e6 and now 16 h4!? would have been a decent alternative to the game's 16 0-0-0 0-0-0 17 ♗a5!.

12...♕d4

Black moves his queen again, but once more it's not so clear that he should be so keen to simplify. Thus 12...♘b4!? looks like a better try and after 13 ♔d1 ♗b7 14 ♘c3 c5! (important prophylaxis; instead 14...0-0-0 15 a3 ♘a6 16 b4 caused some problems for Black's huddle of pieces on the queenside in D.Petrosian-M.Asbahi, Teheran 2005) 15 ♕e3 (15 ♘d5?! was shown to be too ambitious after 15...♗g7 16 ♗xb4 cxb4 17 ♔c2 ♗xd5 18 cxd5 0-0, which left Black's king the safer in R.Fontaine-D.Marciano, French League 2002) 15...♕e6 16 ♘b5 ♘a6! (the correct way to cover d7; otherwise, 16...0-0-0?! 17 ♘xa7+ ♔b8 doesn't give Black enough compensation after Postny's 18 a3 and 16...♔d8?! 17 ♗e2 gave White the initiative in T.Nedev-Z.Gyimesi, Plovdiv 2003) 17 ♔c2 ♗g7 18 ♖e1 0-0 Fontaine's decision to switch sides had given him enough counterplay in J.Lautier-R.Fontaine, Aix les Bains 2003.

13 ♘c3 ♘xc3 14 ♕xc3

Just as with his pawn on f5 (note 'a' to White's 12th move, above), it's hard to believe that White isn't a little better on account of his superior structure, although some stubborn defenders have been happy to take the black side.

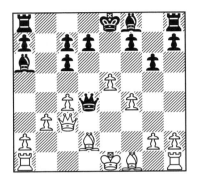

14...♗c5

Black can activate the other bishop with 14...c5, but after 15 ♗d3! ♗b7 (or 15...♗g7 16 ♕xd4 cxd4 17 0-0 with an edge in J.Lautier-E.Bacrot, Cannes 2002) 16 ♕xd4 cxd4 17 0-0 ♗g7 (17...d6 18 ♖ae1 gave White the initiative down the central files in S.Rublevsky-G.Vescovi, Poikovsky 2003) 18 ♗b4 White stays slightly in front.

15 0-0-0 ♕xc3+ 16 ♗xc3 ♖f8 17 g3 0-0-0 18 ♗h3

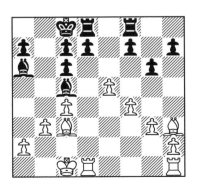

By this point in O.De la Riva Aguado-S.Crouan, Montpellier 2000, there could be no doubting that White enjoyed a very pleasant advantage, being all set to increase the pressure against the target on d7.

D2) 10 ♗b2 ♗g7

Invariably played and after 10...♘f4?! 11 ♕d2 ♘e6 12 g3 h5 13 ♗g2 ♗h6 14 f4 White was clearly for choice in S.Macak-V.Musil, Tatranske Zruby 2000.

11 g3

White begins a second fianchetto. Instead 11 ♕e4? is ineffective because of 11...f5!, making the most out of the pin down the e-file. Note too that here 11 ♘d2 is much less effective than with Black's pawn on g5 and after 11...♘b4 Black has good counterplay, as we saw in the note to White's 11th move in Line A3 of the previous chapter.

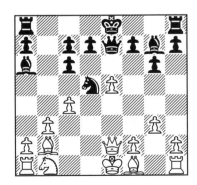

After 11 g3, just as in Line C4, Black must decide which side to send his king:

With his pawn on g5 Black is advised not to go short, but with the pawn safely back on g6 it is a much safer option and his more-common choice. We should also mention:

a) 11...♘b6 12 ♗g2 0-0 13 0-0 transposes to Line D221 after 13...♖fe8 or to Line D222 if Black prefers the move 13...♖ae8

b) 11...d6 transposes after 12 ♗g2 0-0 to note 'b' to Black's 12th move at the start of Line D22.

c) 11...f6!? has been underestimated by theory, as we saw in Line B5 of Chapter One.

d) 11...♕b4+ 12 ♕d2 ♕xd2+ 13 ♔xd2 ♘b6 14 ♔c2 0-0 15 ♘d2 gave White a standard edge in the game M.Makropoulou-E.Stavropoulou, Kallithea 2003.

D21) 11...0-0-0

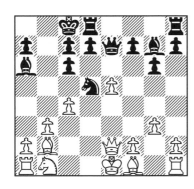

Again we see Black deciding to use

his king to support his potentially vulnerable pawns should the rook and two pawns against two pieces endgame arise. Such a decision remains viable, but isn't quite as effective as with the pawn on g5 because Black will be slower to mobilize his kingside pawns and White may be able to make good use of the f3-square; a square which with the pawn on g5 Black frequently takes control of with a quick ...g4. Moreover, here White may find it possible to disrupt Black's rooks and gradual build-up with a timely f4.

12 ♗g2

White agrees to the endgame. This isn't essential, but the alternatives aren't overly promising:

a) 12 ♘d2 ♘b4 (more active than 12...♖de8 when 13 0-0-0 ♘b6 14 f4 was a little better for White in J.Magem Badals-C.Montolio Benedicto, Linares 2002) 13 ♘f3 c5 14 ♗g2 ♗b7 was about equal in J.Bejtovic-A.Smith, Valby 2008.

b) 12 f4 f6! 13 exf6 (White does well to refrain from breaking with 13 ♕f2 ♘b6! 14 c5 because of 14...♗xf1 15 cxb6 fxe5!! which gave Black a strong attack for the piece in V.Baklan-V.Mikhalevski, Vlissingen 1999) 13...♕xe2+ 14 ♗xe2 ♗xf6 15 ♗xf6 ♘xf6 is equal according to Mikhalevski.

12...♖he8

Not for the first nor the last time we see the issue of: which rook? Black can also keep a rook on h8 and it's not clear that 12...♖de8 13 0-0 ♗xe5 14 ♕xe5

♕xe5 15 ♗xe5 ♖xe5 16 cxd5 ♗xf1 17 ♔xf1 cxd5 18 ♘c3 (perhaps by analogy with the note to White's 18th move in our main line, 18 f4!? should be considered here) 18...c6 19 ♖c1 gives him a worse version of the endgame:

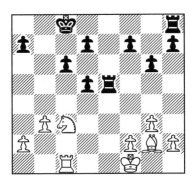

a) Indeed, after 19...♔b8!? 20 ♘e2 (only now that the knight is further from c5) 20...♔b7 21 ♘d4 a5 Black was set to mobilize his rooks and kingside pawns, with rough equality in B.Vuckovic-G.Todorovic, Vrnjacka Banja 2005.

b) Fleeing the c-file with 19...♔d8 has also been tried and after 20 ♘a4 h5 (White had good play on the queenside after 20...g5 21 ♘c5 g4 22 ♘d3 ♖e7 23 b4! in R.Zelcic-R.Rasmussen, Elista Olympiad 1998) 21 ♘c5 h4 22 ♘d3 ♖ee8 23 ♖c5 White had enough counterplay to maintain a rough balance in M.Ashley-A.Mikhalevski, Budapest 1997.

13 0-0 ♗xe5 14 ♕xe5 ♕xe5 15 ♗xe5 ♖xe5 16 cxd5 ♗xf1 17 ♔xf1 cxd5 18 ♘c3

Invariably played here. Instead 18

♘d2 lacks purpose when there's no pawn on g5 to attack with ♘f3, but White might consider 18 f4!? ♖h5 (B.Maiorov-A.Lukjanenko, Voronezh 2003) 19 ♘c3 c6 20 h4, which definitely keeps Black at bay on the kingside for the time being.

18...c6

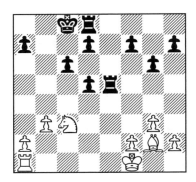

19 ♖c1!

Definitely the right square for the rook. Indeed, it achieves little after 19 ♖d1?! ♔c7 20 ♗f3 f5, which left Black beginning to take control in I.Papadopoulos-M.Ragger, Aghia Pelagia 2004.

White has also manoeuvred his knight to d3, but 19 ♘e2 ♔c7 20 ♘f4 ♔d6 21 ♘d3 ♖ee8 didn't overly trouble Black in R.Mamedov-M.Ragger, Heraklion 2004.

19...♔b8

The right square in turn for the black king. Instead 19...♔b7?! is well met by the vigorous 20 b4! and after 20...a5 21 b5 White most certainly had the initiative in A.Hnydiuk-P.Stempin, Polish Team Championship 1997.

Meanwhile it's a little too early to push the d-pawn: 19...d4 20 ♘e2 d3 21 ♘f4 saw the errant pawn fall in D.Khamrakulov-B.Amin, Heraklion 2004.

20 ♘a4

White wastes no time improving his knight and rook, but he can also consider 20 ♗f3 ♖de8 21 h4 h6 22 ♘a4, which was unclear and likely about equal in E.Relange-V.Mikhalevski, Budapest 1996.

20...♖e7 21 ♗f3 ♖de8

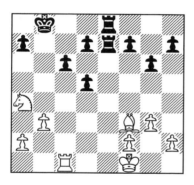

Black is yet to open lines for his rooks, but neither is White doing too much and the endgame was roughly level in B.Macieja-M.Grabarczyk, Plock 2000.

D22) 11...0-0

A more popular choice than going long, not only because the king will be quite safe on the kingside, but also because Black doesn't have to go in for the endgame.

12 ♗g2

Fairly essential. Otherwise 12 ♘d2?

worked well in Line C41, but here Black's king is much safer and 12...d6! 13 0-0-0 (White tried 13 ♕e4 in G.Jones-J.Smeets, London 2009, but the temporary queen sacrifice 13...♗xe5! 14 cxd5 cxd5 15 ♕e3 ♗xb2! 16 ♕xe7 ♖fe8 leaves Black doing pretty well) 13...♗xe5 14 ♘f3 ♗xb2+ 15 ♕xb2 ♘f6 16 ♗d3 c5 17 ♖he1 (Kosten) shouldn't give White anywhere enough for the pawn after 17...♕d8 18 ♘g5 ♗b7.

After 12 ♗g2 Black must decide which rook to bring to e8 and we have a further but final divide:

> **D221: 12...♖fe8**
> **D222: 12...♖ae8**

However, Black doesn't have to move either rook and on occasion has preferred one of the following:

a) Yet again 12...f6!? has been surprisingly rare, but should give Black enough counterplay, as we saw in note 'a' to White's 12th move in Line B5 of Chapter One.

b) 12...d6 13 0-0 ♗xe5 (White is for

choice too after 13...dxe5 14 ♕d2 ♖fd8 15 ♕a5) 14 ♗xe5 dxe5 15 ♖e1 sees Black picking up the e5-pawn and without running into anything nasty on the a3-f8 diagonal.

However, after 15...♖ad8 (S.Granara Barreto-E.Cervetto, Villa Martelli 2008) 16 ♕xe5 White regains his pawn with an ongoing pull, but Black should prefer that to 15...♖fe8? 16 ♕d2 which cost him material in E.Epstein-C.Airapetian, Seattle 2000.

c) 12...♕b4+ 13 ♕d2 ♕xd2+ 14 ♔xd2 ♘e7 15 ♖e1 gave White a clear edge in L.Milov-T.Ahlich, Nuernberg 2007.

D221) 12...♖fe8

By no means a bad deployment, but not the best move order if Black wants to debate the endgame.

13 0-0

13...♘b6

Avoiding the endgame, but Black can also consider:

a) 13...♖ab8 14 ♖e1 (White may do even better with the 14 f4!? ♘b6 15 ♕f2

♗b7 16 ♘c3 of M.Lammers-W.Schmidt, Munich 2008) 14...♘b6 15 ♕c2 favours White, since he was able to meet 15...f6 with 16 e6! in S.Stoljarov-M.Ginzburg, Rimavska Sobota 1996.

b) 13...f6 14 ♕d2 ♘b6 15 exf6 ♗xf6 16 ♘c3 was likewise quite pleasant for White in D.Khalifeh-E.Al Rufei, Istanbul 2000.

c) After 13...♗xe5 14 ♕xe5 ♕xe5 15 ♗xe5 ♖xe5 16 cxd5 ♗xf1 17 ♔xf1 cxd5 some quite strong players have gone 18 ♘c3 when 18...c6 19 ♖c1 ♖ae8 will be seen by transposition in note 'c1' to Black's 13th move in Line D222. However, White can do better here with 18 f4!.

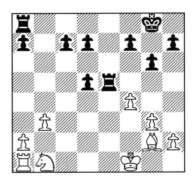

This either drives Black's rook offside or forces him into a pawn sacrifice, although even here Black may be able to maintain a rough balance: 18...♖e3 (invariably played, but perhaps Black can consider too 18...♖h5!? 19 h4 ♖e8 20 ♗f3 ♖f5, which saw the machine garner some counterplay in *Shredder-GANDALF X*, Paderborn 2002) 19 ♗xd5 ♖ae8 (19...c6 20 ♗g2 ♖d3 21 ♘a3 ♖e8 22 ♖e1 is a little better for White, as noted by Wells) 20 ♘d2! ♖e2 (Kasparov claimed a clear advantage after 20...♖d3 21 ♘e4 ♔g7 22 ♗c4, but 22...♖d4! didn't seem so bad for Black in P.Simacek-V.Talla, Ostrava 2005; indeed, after 23 ♘c3 ♖d2 24 ♖d1 ♖xd1+ 25 ♘xd1 c6 the resulting endgame isn't too clear at all) 21 ♖d1 ♖xh2 22 ♗g2! (preventing Black doubling on the seventh) 22...♖e7! (otherwise, 22...d6 23 ♔f2 was a little better for White in J.Zezulkin-R.Biolek, Czech League 2002, and Black must avoid 22...♖h5? 23 ♘e4) 23 a4 (beginning to advance the queenside pawns, but White may do better with 23 ♔f2!? or 23 ♘c4!?) 23...♖h5 was about equal and soon agreed drawn in A.Motylev-A.Moiseenko, Moscow 1999.

14 ♖e1 f6

Black decides to exploit his pressure down the d-file, but he has also tested:

a) After 14...d5 15 ♕c2! (15 ♕d2 is also promising, at least so long as White meets 15...♗xc4 with 16 ♕c2!) White unpins with some advantage, since Black can't capture on c4.

In G.Kasparov-I.Sokolov, Yerevan Olympiad 1996, the World's leading Scotch authority proceeded to obtain a clear advantage after 15...♖ad8 (Kasparov points out that White is also much better after both 15...♘d7 16 cxd5 cxd5 17 ♘d2! ♗b7 18 ♕xc7 ♘xe5 19 ♖ac1 and 15...♕c5 16 ♘d2 ♘d7 17 ♘f3 dxc4 18 ♗d4! ♕a5 19 ♗c3 ♕c5 20 b4 ♕b6 21 e6) 16 ♘d2 ♕c5 17 ♖ac1 d4? 18 ♘f3. Black can improve with 17...dxc4, but after 18 bxc4 White is better, as 18...♗xe5?! 19 ♘b3 ♕xc4 20 ♗xe5 ♖xe5 21 ♖xe5 ♕xc2 22 ♖xc2 ♖d1+ 23 ♗f1 ♖xf1+ 24 ♔g2 (Marin) costs Black material and here Kasparov's energetic 18 ♘e4!? ♕b4 19 ♗c3 ♕b5 20 ♘f6+ ♗xf6 21 exf6 is also promising.

b) 14...♕c5 15 ♘d2 d5 16 ♖ac1 kept c4 covered and so retained an edge in I.Hakki-W.Sarwat, Cairo 1997.

c) However, Black might consider the 14...♗b7!? of P.Masic-N.Puric, Bijeljina 2001, when Masic observes that 15 ♘d2 d6 isn't too clear.

15 e6

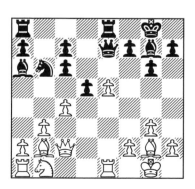

White only wants to open lines on his terms. Sometimes, as we've seen, he can sacrifice the e-pawn, but here 15 ♕d2?! fxe5 16 ♗a3 ♕f7 failed to supply quite enough compensation in E.Tomilova-I.Derbentseva, St Petersburg 2005.

15...♗b7!?

Calmly covering c6. Black should avoid the 15...d5? of V.Marques-M.De Souza, Sao Paulo 1999, on account of 16 ♕c2, but can equalize with the straightforward 15...♕xe6 16 ♕xe6+ ♖xe6 17 ♖xe6 dxe6 18 ♗xc6 ♖d8, as he did in D.Marciano-E.Bacrot, Meribel 1998.

16 a4

White tries to destabilize Black's forces on the queenside, but with 16...♕b4 Black was able to maintain the balance in I.Papadopoulos-N.Krutika, Denizli 2003.

D222) 12...♖ae8 13 0-0

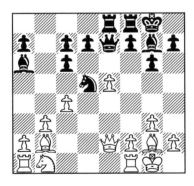

13...♘b6

Black should avoid 13...f6?! 14 ♕d2 fxe5 15 cxd5 ♗xf1 16 ♗xf1, which left White doing pretty well in A.Averjanov-A.Solomaha, Alushta 2002, but with his

queen's rook on e8 he might well prefer to go in for the endgame with 13...♗xe5 14 ♕xe5 ♕xe5 15 ♗xe5 ♖xe5 16 cxd5 ♗xf1 17 ♔xf1 cxd5 and now:

a) 18 f4 ♖e3! 19 ♗xd5 gives White definite chances of obtaining the upper hand when it comes with tempo against a rook on a8, but here it doesn't and 19...♖d3 leaves Black quite actively placed.

White really must cover his back rank with 20 ♗f3, but even after 20...♖e8 21 ♔f2 c6 (H.Klek-I.Balog, Szeged 2008) 22 ♗e2! ♖de3 23 ♗d1 ♖e1 Black retains a small initiative.

b) 18 ♘d2 c6 19 b4 ♖fe8 20 ♗f3 ♔f8 21 ♘b3 ♔e7! clamped down on the c5-square, but Black was at least okay with his king bound for d6 in A.Ahmad-P.Mahesh Chandran, Tehran 2001.

c) Thus White usually goes in for 18 ♘c3 c6 and then one of:

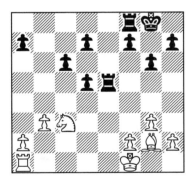

c1) 19 ♖c1 ♖fe8 (this position frequently arises too from a 12...♖fe8 move order) 20 ♗f3 ♔f8 (thematic, but Black can consider too 20...♔g7!? followed by ...h5) 21 ♘a4 ♔e7 22 ♘c5 ♔d6 23 ♘d3

(Black was also okay after 23 b4 ♖b8 24 ♘d3 ♖ee8 in V.Baklan-M.Erwich, Hoogeveen 2004) 23...♖5e7 24 b4 ♖a8! 25 a4 a5 26 b5 was about even when P.Leko-Z.Almasi, Ubeda 1997, came to a slightly premature halt.

c2) 19 ♘a4 wastes no time heading for c5, but after 19...♖a8 (Black goes back to support his a-pawn and prepares to meet b4 with ...a5; of the many alternatives 19...g5!? 20 ♘c5 ♖e7 deserves particular attention and gave Black enough counterplay in R.Ponomariov-J.Plaskett, Hastings 1998/99) 20 ♘c5 ♖e7 21 ♖d1 ♔f8 Black brought his king back to the centre and was okay in S.Sulskis-S.Zjukin, Tallin 2006.

c3) The rare 19 h4!? is a decent try to halt Black up on the kingside and after 19...h5 20 ♖c1 f5 21 ♘e2! ♔f7 22 ♖c5 White had the initiative in S.Macak-S.Hubschmid, Winterthur 2007, but here too Black may do better to whisk his king straight back to the centre.

c4) 19 ♖d1!? introduces the idea of ♖d4-a4, tying Black down to his vulnerable a-pawn.

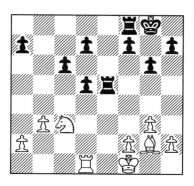

Now:

c41) 19...♖fe8 20 ♗f3 ♔f8 (centralizing the king; instead 20...f5 21 ♘e2! ♔g7 22 ♖d4 gave White the initiative in B.Socko-K.Jakubowski, Polish Team Championship Krynica 1997) 21 ♘e2 ♔e7 22 ♖d4 ♖b8 (Black later improved with 22...♔d6! 23 ♖a4 ♖a8 and after 24 ♖a5 ♔c7 25 b4 a6 26 ♘c1 ♔b6 27 ♘b3 the position was unclear but about equal in S.Rublevsky-V.Tseshkovsky, Sochi 2005, and here Black was also okay after 24 h4 ♖ee8 25 ♖a5 ♖eb8 26 ♘f4 ♖b6 in R.Zelcic-Z.Plenkovic, Omis 2004) 23 ♖a4 ♖b7 24 b4 ♔d6 25 a3 saw White prioritize the activation of his rook and after the thematic continuation 25...♖e8 26 ♘d4! h5?! (rather pointless here; instead Black should have taken steps against White's plan with the prophylactic 26...♔e5!? 27 ♘b3 ♖c7!, which would likely still have been okay for him) 27 ♘b3 ♖e7 28 ♘c5 ♖c7 29 h4 he had taken control and went on to win by arranging to break through with b5 in S.Rublevsky-J.Geller, Dagomys 2004.

c42) Black may do better with 19...♖b8!?, preventing b4 and preparing to activate the rook via b4: 20 ♗f3 (or 20 ♘a4 ♖e7 21 ♘c5 ♖b4! and Black had good counterplay in J.Bejtovic-E.Lund, Copenhagen 2009) 20...a5!? (Jakovenko's idea; instead 20...♔f8 21 ♖d4 ♔e7 22 ♖a4 ♖b7, as in R.Mamedov-B.Amin, Heraklion 2002, enables White to activate his king and begin his own play after 23 ♘e2!? ♔d6

24 ♔e1) 21 ♘a4 (the 21 ♖d4 of J.Geller-
D.Jakovenko, Sochi 2005, is most simply
met by the immediate and consistent
21...♖b4) 21...d6 (21...♔g7!? followed by
pushing the kingside pawns could well
be a better plan and may even leave
Black slightly for choice) 22 ♖c1 c5 23
♘c3?! (23 ♖d1! d4 24 ♘b2 was the correct way to blockade) 23...d4 24 ♘d5?!
♔g7 25 ♖c4 g5! 26 g4 f5! saw Black
opening lines for his rooks with some
advantage in J.Nelson-T.Bae, Donostia
2010.

After that discussion of a popular
version of the endgame, we return to
Black's main alternative to it, 13...♘b6:

14 ♖e1

Shoring up e5. With both king's
rooks on the f-file White has also tried
14 f4!? and after 14...f6 15 ♘d2 fxe5 16
fxe5 ♗xe5 (Black may do better with
16...d5 17 ♖xf8+ ♖xf8 18 ♕e3 dxc4,
which was fairly unclear in R.Nolte-
K.Sundararajan, Olongapo City 2010)
17 ♖xf8+ ♕xf8 18 ♘e4 he had typical
compensation for the pawn, in view of
Black's currently inactive queenside
minor pieces, in M.Ragger-A.Kosten,
Austrian League 2006.

14...f6

Just as in Line D221, 14...d5 offers
White a couple of routes to the advantage, of which 15 ♕d2! (heading towards a5 now that the rook has vacated a8, although 15 ♕c2 ♕b4 16 ♗c3
♕c5 17 ♘d2 also sufficed for a pull in
J.Mellado Trivino-D.Fernando, Loures
1997) 15...♕d7, as in R.Abdel Aziem-

W.Sarwat, Cairo 1999, and now 16 ♘a3
would have seen White taking control
of the position.

Here Black should also avoid
14...♕e6?! 15 ♘d2, which left him low
on effective counterplay in L.Kritz-
H.Jonkman, Dieren 2002, but he might
consider 14...c5!?, which saw him beginning counterplay after 15 ♕c2 f6 in
N.Halyavskiy-D.Goltsov, Serpukhov
2004.

15 ♕e3!

The most testing continuation.
White must, of course, avoid 15 f4?
fxe5 16 fxe5 ♕c5+ and 15 e6, as we saw
him employing with the other rook on
e8, allows Black to equalize with the
simple 15...♕xe6 (but not 15...c5? 16
♘c3 ♕xe6 17 ♕xe6+ ♖xe6, as in
M.Devereaux-M.Hebden, British League
2007, when 18 ♘d5 would leave White
doing pretty well) 16 ♕xe6+ ♖xe6 17
♖xe6 dxe6, as he did in S.Gashimov-
Y.Yudkovsky, Tallinn 1997.

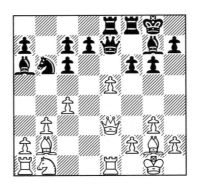

After 15 ♕e3 practice has seen:

a) 15...fxe5 16 ♗a3 is White's point
and an idea which would clearly be less

effective without a rook on f8, which is why White doesn't try it in Line D221. However, after 16...c5 (but not 16...d6? 17 ♗xc6 when the c5 breakthrough will give White some advantage) 17 ♗xc5 d6 Black was okay in P.Simacek-F.El Taher, Olomouc 2005.

b) 15...♕f7 16 ♘d2 fxe5 17 ♗a3 d5!? (17...d6? 18 ♗xc6 would again be just what White is hoping for) 18 ♗xf8 ♖xf8 19 ♖ad1 didn't give Black quite enough for the exchange in J.Tomczak-B.Amin, Gaziantep 2008.

c) 15...c5 was quite an ambitious idea in B.Gonzalez-B.Amin, Dresden Olympiad 2008, and after 16 a4! fxe5 17 a5 ♘c8 18 ♘c3 White should have promising compensation.

d) 15...♕e6!? 16 ♗a3! (better than 16 ♘d2 fxe5 17 ♘e4 ♕f5 when Black had good counterplay in A.Areshchenko-M.Erwich, Oropesa del Mar 2001) 16...♖f7 17 ♘c3 fxe5 18 ♖ad1 gave White typical and sufficient play in R.Ponomariov-E.Bacrot, Lausanne 1999.

Conclusion

This has been a long and important chapter, but also one which contains a number of exciting positions. The tricky try 9...♕h4 shouldn't work so long as White remembers 10 a3! and the idea of meeting 10...♗c5 with 11 g3!. Instead after 9...0-0-0 Black can pretty much win the e5-pawn by force, but White obtains good compensation

thanks to his freer development and queenside prospects. It's tempting to keep the dark-squared bishop flexible with 10 g3, but then Black has the option of 10...g5 and so 10 ♗b2 may be a simpler route to a likely plus for White.

The bold 9...g5 remains just as topical in late 2010 as when Anand introduced it in 1995. However, White should not fear it. Indeed, all of 10 g3 ♗g7 11 ♗b2 0-0-0 12 ♘d2, 10 h4!? and the strangely neglected 10 ♗b2 ♗g7 11 ♘d2 give him good chances of emerging with the advantage. Thus 9...g6 should still be considered the main line when Black seems to be able to gain enough counterplay after 10 f4 with both 10...f6 and 10...♕b4+, as well as the underrated 10...g5!? and 10...d6. Likewise after 10 ♗b2 ♗g7 11 g3 0-0 12 ♗g2 Black can duck the endgame and obtain sufficient counterplay with either rook to e8 followed by 13 0-0 ♘b6.

Finally, we cannot finish without a word on the endgame. Black's best version appears to be that with his king on the queenside and g-pawn well placed on g5, after which the onus may even be on White to demonstrate that he can maintain a rough balance. Instead with the pawn on g6 Black has usually gone short, reaching a typically unbalanced situation in which the better prepared player, in terms of knowing variations *and* understanding the key motifs, is likely to triumph.

Chapter Three
The Main Line: 8...♞b6 without 9 ♞c3

1 e4 e5 2 ♞f3 ♞c6 3 d4 exd4 4 ♞xd4 ♞f6 5 ♞xc6 bxc6 6 e5 ♛e7 7 ♛e2 ♞d5 8 c4 ♞b6

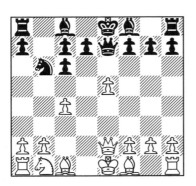

Black retreats his knight without delay. This might appear less challenging than 8...♝a6, but White can still find his queenside coming early pressure, especially the c4-pawn. At this stage play traditionally continued 9 ♞d2, but in recent years the more ambitious 9 ♞c3!? has come to the fore. We'll consider that topical approach in our next

chapter, focussing here on development by White which keeps c4 well protected.

A: 9 ♞d2
B: 9 b3

The former used to be considered the main line after 8...♞b6; the latter is a closely-related approach, shoring up c4 and preparing to cover the e5-pawn with ♝b2, after which play can easily transpose to 9 ♞d2 lines.

White has also tried a couple of other moves here:

a) 9 f4?! is rather premature, as it doesn't contribute to White's development. Black effectively counters with the immediate 9...♛e6 10 ♞d2 d5 and now 11 exd6 ♝xd6! (quick development is especially important here, as White has severely weakened his position with f4) 12 ♞e4 0-0!, which sees Black ignoring the threat of 13 c5 because the white king is too exposed in the centre.

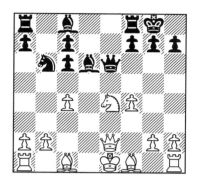

Indeed, White is advised to take refuge in the prudent 13 ♘xd6 (after 13 c5 ♗a6! 14 ♕f3 ♗xf1 15 ♔xf1 ♖fe8 16 cxd6 cxd6 Black will soon win the piece back with some advantage, while 13 b3? ♗e7 is practically winning for Black in view of the imminent ...♖e8) 13...♕xd6 14 ♗e3 ♗a6 15 ♕c2 (15 c5? ♕e7 16 ♕f3 ♘d5 17 ♔f2 ♗xf1 18 ♖hxf1 ♕f6 is again very good for Black), although even here after 15...♕e6 16 ♔f2 ♖fe8 17 ♖e1 ♘xc4 Black is better.

b) On the other hand, 9 g3 is a serious move and gives Black a choice:

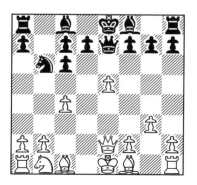

b1) The standard move, 9...♕e6, is Black's usual choice when 10 ♘d2 a5 transposes to Line A12, below. Instead 10 ♘c3?! is well met by 10...♗b4 11 ♗d2 0-0 12 ♕e4 d6, and after 10 b3 Marin likes 10...♗b4+!? (10...a5 is another option and will probably transpose elsewhere in this chapter) 11 ♗d2 a5 12 ♗g2 0-0 13 0-0 and now 13...f6 (13...♖e8 14 f4 f6 is also good) 14 ♘c3 fxe5 15 f4 d5 with advantage for Black.

b2) 9...g6!? is the other logical option: 10 b3 (after 10 ♗g2 ♗g7 11 0-0 0-0 12 ♖e1 ♖e8 13 ♗f4 ♗a6 14 ♘d2 g5 15 ♗e3 ♕xe5 16 ♕g4 h6 White did not have much for her pawn in T.Kosintseva-M.Sebag, Istanbul 2003; this reminds us why an early b3 is often seen, shoring up c4 and enabling White to protect e5 with ♗b2) 10...♗g7 11 f4 (alternatively, 11 ♗b2 0-0 12 ♗g2 ♖e8 13 0-0 ♗xe5 14 ♗xe5 ♕xe5 15 ♕xe5 ♖xe5 and Black had the advantage in E.Kuzevanova-E.Golcman, Pardubice 2009; neither is 12 f4 an improvement here in view of 12...d6 or just 12...f6 13 exf6 ♗xf6 14 ♕xe7 ♗xe7 15 ♗g2 d5) 11...f6! (the standard reaction to f4) 12 ♗a3 d6 13 ♗g2 fxe5 14 ♘c3 exf4 15 ♗xc6+ ♗d7 16 ♗xd7+ ♔xd7 and Black was much better in V.Baklan-J.De Jong, Ghent 2007.

A) 9 ♘d2

The traditional move, as played by Kasparov in the first significant 8...♘b6 game of the modern era, Game 16 of the 1990 World Championship match.

However, this approach has lost much of its popularity in the last few years, partly because of the rise in popularity of 9 ♘c3 and because of Black's good results and sound theoretical standing after 9...a5.

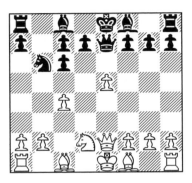

The purpose of putting the knight on d2 is clear: the c4-pawn, often the main target of Black's counterplay, is now better protected. However, on d2 the knight hinders the development of the dark-squared bishop, which usually has to enter the game via b2. It is this issue that Black's 9...a5 response aims to exploit. Unlike after 9 ♘c3, the plan of ...♗a6 and ...d5 is much less effective here, but Black's other ideas gain in strength because of the more passive development scheme White employs. Indeed, at this point the second player can choose between:

A1: 9...a5
A2: 9...♕e6!?
A3: 9...♗b7

Line A1 can very much be considered the main line, but Lines A2 and A3 very much have the right to exist to. Creative and experimental minds may also wish to consider both:

a) 9...g6!? is another logical way to play and deserves to be explored further. After 10 b3 (alternatively, 10 ♘f3?! ♕b4+ is very annoying and 10 ♘e4!? transposes to 9 ♘c3 g6 10 ♘e4, although Black is okay here, as we'll see in Line B of the next chapter) 10...♗g7 11 ♗b2 (9 b3 g6 10 ♗b2 ♗g7 11 ♘d2 is another route to this position) 11...d6! Black seems to be okay, as shown by the possible continuation 12 f4 0-0 13 g3 (13 ♘f3 is, as ever, annoyingly met by 13...♗g4) 13...dxe5 14 ♗xe5 ♗xe5 15 ♕xe5 ♕xe5+ 16 fxe5 ♖e8 17 ♗g2 ♖xe5+ 18 ♔f2 ♗g4 19 ♖he1 ♖ae8 20 ♖xe5 ♖xe5 21 ♖e1, as given by Wells. Here Black's extra pawn does not mean much and will probably soon be lost, but, of course, the opening has been a success for him.

b) 9...d6 (or 9...d5) is insufficient for equality after 9 ♘c3, but here the knight isn't so well placed for the resulting structure and thus Black's chances are comparatively better: 10 exd6 (10 c5 is simply met by 10...♘d5, while both 10 ♘f3?! ♗g4! and 10 f4 dxe5 11 ♕xe5 ♕xe5+ 12 fxe5 ♗e6 are uncomfortable for White) 10...cxd6 (but not the compliant 10...♕xe2+?! 11 ♗xe2 cxd6 12 ♗f3 ♗b7 13 0-0 0-0-0 14 a4, which was great for White in L.Vajda-A.Bezgodov, Budapest 1996)

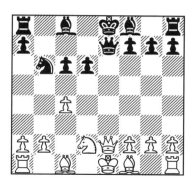

11 b3 ♗g4 and now we have the following:

b1) 12 ♕xe7+ ♗xe7 13 ♗b2 0-0 14 ♗d3 (14 ♗e2 ♖fe8! 15 ♗xg4 ♗f6+ 16 ♔d1 ♗xb2 17 ♖b1 ♗d4 was fine for Black in D.Pavlovic-D.Blagojevic, Herceg Novi 2008) 14...d5! 15 h3 (Black is fine after both 15 0-0 ♗b4! and 15 cxd5 ♗b4! 16 f3 ♖ad8 17 fxg4 ♖fe8+ 18 ♔d1 ♘xd5 19 a3 ♗xd2 20 ♔xd2 ♘f4, as pointed out by Wells) 15...♗h5 16 cxd5 (16 g4 ♗g6 17 ♗xg6 fxg6 18 cxd5 ♗b4 is another line stemming from the indefatigable Wells, with advantage to Black) 16...♗b4 and Black had the initiative in R.Shankar-M.Sorokin, Calcutta 1999.

b2) 12 f3 ♗e6 13 ♗b2 (13 ♗a3?! is well met by 13...♕f6 14 ♖c1 d5 15 ♗xf8 ♔xf8 intending ...♖e8) 13...d5 14 cxd5 ♘xd5 eyes the e3-square and has given Black good counterplay in several games that have reached this position, amongst them an important clash between two opposing experts, S.Rublevsky-A.Beliavsky, Yugoslav Team Championship 2000.

A1) 9...a5

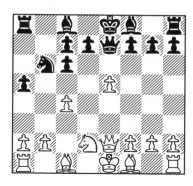

As just mentioned this thrust is very logical and undoubtedly a critical test of White's set-up. The first player can now be bold and fianchetto regardless, or try to do without an early b3:

A11: 10 b3
A12: 10 g3

That second option isn't the only way of holding back on b3, but the alternatives aren't especially challenging:

a) 10 h4?! is well met by 10...a4! 11 g3 (or 11 ♖h3?! d5!, as given by Emms) 11...♖a5! 12 f4 ♗a6 and Black had the upper hand in A.Shirov-S.Agdestein, Oslo 1992. Note that after 9...a5 Black is not just waiting for White to play b3 before pushing ...a4; he often goes ahead with ...a4 in any case, preventing b3 altogether.

b) 10 ♕e3 and other such moves are best met by the simple 10...g6. Black develops, applies pressure to the e5-

pawn and waits to see how White is going to resolve the issue of his dark-squared bishop.

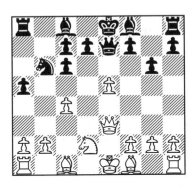

After 11 f4 ♗g7 12 ♘f3 ♗a6 Black was most certainly fine in J.Breukelman-J.Op den Kelder, Hengelo 2003.

c) 10 ♕e4 can again be met by 10...g6, although this is one instance when 10...d5!? is actually possible, since it attacks the queen and thus White cannot ignore it: 11 exd6 (11 cxd5 cxd5 12 ♗b5+ ♗d7 13 ♗xd7+ ♕xd7 was equal in J.Hector-T.Wedberg, Orebro 2000) 11...cxd6 12 ♗e2 ♕xe4 13 ♘xe4 ♗e6 14 c5 (14 b3 d5 15 cxd5 ♗xd5 gives Black the initiative according to Marin) 14...dxc5 15 ♗e3 ♘d5 and thanks to his active pieces, Black was fine in T.Radjabov-V.Topalov, Bilbao 2008.

Returning to 10...g6, play may continue 11 ♗d3 (11 b3 ♗g7 12 ♗b2 0-0 13 ♗e2 ♖e8 14 f4 d5 15 ♕f3 f6 saw some simple and purposeful play by Black give him an edge in A.Drei-I.Efimov, Reggio Emilia 2000) 11...♗g7

12 0-0 0-0 (but not 12...♗xe5?! 13 ♖e1 ♗f6 14 ♘f3 with advantage for White)

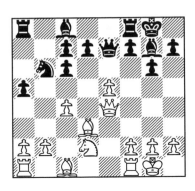

13 ♘f3 (13 f4? is clearly mistaken in view of 13...d5 14 ♕e2 f6! 15 exf6 ♕xe2 16 ♗xe2 ♗xf6 when Black was much better in T.Fogarasi-M.Hebden, Cappelle la Grande 1993), and now the most logical continuation is 13...♗a6 (13...♘a4!? 14 ♗g5 ♕b4, as proposed by Emms, and Wedberg's 13...f5!? are other intriguing possibilities), whereupon after 14 ♗g5 f6!? (Emms' 14...♕e6 is also playable) 15 ♗h4 (worse is 15 exf6?! ♕xe4 16 ♗xe4 ♗xf6 17 ♗xf6 ♖xf6 18 b3 d5 with tremendous pressure) 15...♖fe8 Black has the upper hand.

d) Finally, Black has nothing to worry about after either 10 f4 ♗a6 or 10 ♘f3 ♗a6 11 b3 a4.

A11) 10 b3 a4 11 ♗b2

As we'll see in Line B1, below, this position can also arise from the move order 9 b3 a5 10 ♗b2 a4 11 ♘d2. With the bishop on c1, White might try to keep the rooks on, but such a policy is ill-advised: 11 ♖b1?! axb3 12 axb3 ♕e6 13 ♕e4 ♗b4 14 ♗d3 ♖a2 and Black had the initiative in M.Ahn-R.Swinkels, Eupen 2006.

11...axb3 12 axb3

Not, of course, 12 ♘xb3? as Black then replies with 12...♕b4+ 13 ♕d2 ♘xc4.

12...♖xa1+ 13 ♗xa1 ♕a3

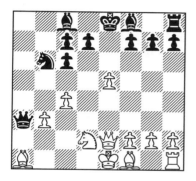

Black keeps creating threats, so as not to allow White to develop. With ...♗b4 and quick castling coming White's position looks desperate, but the truth is somewhat different. In fact Black has no efficient way to open up the position and White is able, with care, to parry all the immediate threats. Indeed, if anything the onus is on Black to continue actively and create counterplay before White consolidates, as otherwise his structural defects and the passivity of his queenside minor pieces will become a serious problem.

An interesting alternative to the standard 13...♕a3 was seen in S.Zhigalko-A.Aleksandrov, Rethymnon 2003: 13...♗b7!? 14 ♗b2 ♕g5 15 g3 (15 h4 ♕g6 is no problem for Black) 15...♗b4 16 ♗g2 0-0 and Black's position seems pretty much okay, since the queen is quite influential on the kingside. The black minor pieces stuck on the queenside may be a source of worry for the future, but White in turn must make some concessions in order to castle, so most likely the mutual exchange of inconveniences leads to approximate equality. In any case, the text move is more ambitious, continuing to pester White.

14 ♕d1

Absolutely forced, as 14 ♗c3?? ♕c1+ 15 ♕d1 ♕xc3 loses on the spot, while 14 ♗d4? c5 15 ♗e3 ♕a1+ dropped the e5-pawn in M.Danielsen-G.Tallaksen, Bergen 2005.

14...♗b4 15 ♗d3

And here 15 ♕b1?? ♕a5 16 ♕b2 ♗xd2+ forced White to resign in Z.Fayvinov-L.Kaufman, Washington 2002.

15...♕a5

Preventing castling and keeping an eye on e5. Instead 15...♗xd2+?! 16 ♔xd2 0-0 17 ♕c2 h6 18 ♗b2 ♕e7 19 f4 (Emms) is a good example of White obtaining a solid plus after weak play by Black.

The main alternative is 15...♕a2, which also prevents castling and threatens to win the b3-pawn. However, it turns out that things are not so simple after 16 ♗d4! and now we have the following:

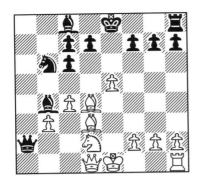

a) The critical but overly risky approach is 16...♗xd2+ 17 ♕xd2 ♕xb3 and now White should play 18 e6!, opening lines against the black king. Indeed, White obtains very promising play after 18...dxe6 (Black also has problems after both 18...fxe6 19 0-0 ♕a3 20 ♗xg7 ♖g8 21 ♖a1 ♕e7 22 ♗c3 with a powerful initiative for White, and 18...f6 19 exd7+ ♗xd7 20 0-0 0-0 21 ♕e3!, threatening ♖b1 and ♗c5) 19 0-0 f6 (19...♘xc4 20 ♗xc4 ♕xc4 21 ♗xg7 ♖g8 22 ♖d1 ♕h4 23 ♗e5 sees White attacking on the weakened dark squares with some effect) 20 ♖b1 ♕a3 21 ♕e3 ♕e7 22 ♗c5 ♕d8 23 ♖d1 when his initiative persists and it is not at all easy for Black to untangle.

b) 16...0-0!? 17 ♗e3 ♕a5 (worse is 17...♖e8 18 0-0! ♖xe5 19 ♗f4 ♖e8 20 ♖e1 and Black has problems, as most of his pieces are out of play) 18 0-0 ♕xe5 was played in K.Van der Weide-R.Ris, Haarlem 2007. Here White has some compensation for the pawn, but it may not be enough and so this may well be Black's best option at this stage.

c) 16...c5 is Marin's preference, deflecting the bishop from the queenside. After 17 ♗e3 ♕b2 18 f4 d5 19 exd6 cxd6 20 0-0 f5 21 ♖f2 ♕c3 Black has counterplay.

Returning to 15...♕a5:

16 ♔e2!

White radically solves the problem of the pinned knight. His next move will be ♕c2, preventing an exchange of bishops on c3, and then ♘f3, securing the e5-pawn. Should this happen, Black will be left without any real play and his position will become critical. He must under no circumstances allow White a free hand here.

Otherwise, White achieves nothing with 16 ♗d4 in view of 16...♗c3! (16...♗b7 17 ♗b2 d6 may also be acceptable) 17 ♗xc3 ♕xc3 18 ♕e2 0-0 (already Black can force a repetition with 18...♕c1+ 19 ♕d1 ♕c3) 19 0-0 ♖e8 20 ♘f3 (or 20 f4 d5 21 ♖f2 g6 with equality) 20...g6 when Black is certainly not worse.

A misguided move order is 16 ♗b2 d6 (I also like the more forcing 16...d5!?

17 ♕c2 dxc4 18 bxc4 and now 18...♕a4 with constant threats) 17 ♕c2 dxe5 18 ♔e2 and now the simplest is 18...♕c5 with an edge for Black.

16...d6!

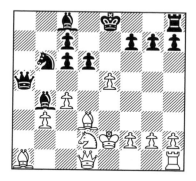

Black must not delay and should immediately strike at White's centre. Quite obviously e5 is much more sensitive than c4 and so it becomes the target of Black's activity.

Instead 16...♗c3 may appear logical, but after 17 ♗xc3 ♕xc3 18 ♕a1 White retains the upper hand. We can also appreciate two further points behind 16 ♔e2 after:

a) 16...0-0?! is too slow: 17 ♕c2 ♖e8 (hardly any good are both 17...d5? 18 ♗d4! and 17...♗xd2 18 ♕xd2 ♕c5 19 ♖e1) 18 ♘f3 and White has secured his steady edge.

b) 16...d5?! hits at the wrong spot, so White can play 17 ♕c2 ♗xd2! (Black gets rid of a potentially useless bishop; note that White was also threatening 18 ♗d4, causing some discomfort to the black queen) 18 ♕xd2 ♕xd2+ 19 ♔xd2 dxc4 20 bxc4 ♗e6 21 ♖c1 when

he retains a slight but permanent edge, thanks to his better pawn structure and bishop-pair.

17 f4!?

White ambitiously bolsters e5, counting on his space advantage.

17 exd6? is a serious mistake in view of 17...0-0! 18 d7 (18 dxc7 ♖e8+ 19 ♘e4 f5! also wins for Black) 18...♗xd7 19 ♘f3 ♖e8+ 20 ♔f1 ♗g4 and there is no acceptable defence to 21...♖e1+, as pointed out by Emms.

White's safest option is 17 ♘f3, which should be met by 17...♗g4 18 ♕c2 (18 exd6? is still wrong due to 18...0-0! and 18 h3 ♗xf3+ 19 ♔xf3 dxe5 was fine for Black in B.Vuckovic-I.Ivanisevic, Zlatibor 2007) 18...dxe5 (17 ♕c2 dxe5 18 ♘f3 ♗g4 is another way of reaching this position).

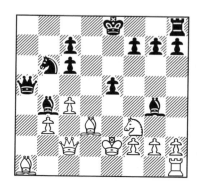

Here 19 h3! (19 ♗xh7? fails to 19...♖xh7! 20 ♕xh7 ♕a2+ 21 ♔e3 ♕xb3+ 22 ♔e2 ♗xf3+ 23 gxf3 ♕xc4+ 24 ♕d3 ♕a2+ and Black wins, while 19 ♗e4 is best met by 19...0-0! 20 h3! ♗xf3+ 21 ♗xf3 f5 when Black is better) 19...♗xf3+ 20 gxf3 gave White compensation in E.Sharapov-A.Nechaev, Simferopol 2003, although it is difficult to say whether it suffices for more than equality.

17...dxe5

At this point I would give serious consideration to 17...♘d7!? 18 ♘f3 dxe5 19 fxe5 ♘c5, as played in E.Sharapov-I.Nester, Lubawka 2008, and which feels promising for Black.

18 fxe5 ♗g4+!

An important move. Black tried the weaker 18...♗c3?! 19 ♗xc3 ♕xc3 20 ♘f3 in H.Nakamura-S.Ernst, Bermuda 2002, and was worse.

19 ♘f3 ♘d7!

Black has managed to secure enough counterplay to prevent White from establishing a steady edge. From here the game B.Macieja-A.Kosten, Izmir 2004, continued 20 ♔f2 (20 h3?! ♗xf3+ 21 ♔xf3 ♗c3 would drop the e5-pawn) 20...♘c5?! (Black enjoys a good position, but this is misguided; after 20...0-0! 21 ♕c2 g6 White has problems to solve with both his airy king and the weak e5-pawn) 21 ♗c2 ♘e6 22 h3 (per-

(perhaps 22 ♕e2!? would have been preferable) 22...♗xf3?! (why exchange the bishop?) 23 ♕xf3 and even here 23...0-0 24 ♖d1 ♕a2 25 ♕e2 would have been okay for Black.

A12) 10 g3

The most serious alternative to 10 b3.

10...♕e6

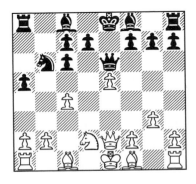

We've made this our main move because the pressure on c4 causes the most discomfort to White, although it is not the only good option for Black:

a) 10...a4?! has, apart from the obvious idea of preventing b3, the less obvious intention of attacking the e5-pawn with ...♖a5. Still, here I would advise Black not to spend time moving his a-pawn again. After the further 11 ♗g2 ♖a5 12 0-0! ♗a6 13 ♖b1! (preparing b4) 13...♖xe5 (after 13...♕xe5 14 ♕d1! ♕f5 15 ♖e1+ ♗e7 16 b4 White has fantastic compensation for the pawn) 14 ♕d3 (here 14 ♕d1?! ♘xc4 15 ♘f3 ♖d5 16 ♕xa4 ♖a5 is only unclear) 14...♖e1 (an unusual move so early in the opening, but practically forced here; instead 14...♕d6?! 15 ♕c3 ♗e7 16 ♘e4 was very good for White in S.Rublevsky-P.Svidler, Frankfurt (rapid) 2000) 15 b3, in view of Black's retarded development White had very good compensation in M.Goodger-A.Richardson, British League 2004.

b) 10...♗a6 is a logical and good move: 11 b3 (alternatively, 11 ♕e4 ♕e6 12 a3 a4 13 h4!? d5 14 exd6 cxd6 was equal in E.Berg-S.Brynell, Stockholm 2007, while White cannot proceed with 11 ♗g2? in view of 11...♘xc4! 12 ♘xc4 ♕b4+) 11...♕e6 12 ♗g2 ♗b4 13 ♗b2 0-0 14 0-0 d5 and Black was fine in S.Shankland-R.Laxman, Philadelphia 2008.

c) Neither is there anything wrong with 10...g6!?. After 11 ♗g2 (11 ♘e4 ♗g7 12 f4 0-0 already gives Black the initiative) 11...♗g7 12 0-0 0-0 13 ♖e1 ♖e8 14 ♘f3 (White was worse after 14 f4 a4 15 ♖b1 d5 in G.Arzumanian-V.Varavin, Alushta 2001) 14...♗a6 15 b3 d5 Black was again fine in V.Gashimov-T.Meszaros, Litohoro 1999.

11 b3

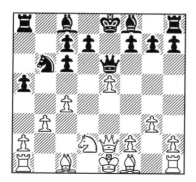

White plays this while he can, hoping to secure both c4 and e5. In comparison to Line A11, here Black's queen cannot come to attack the queenside, but on the other hand his dark-squared bishop is free to come to b4, pinning the knight and creating different sorts of problems. In any case, though, the alternatives appear weaker from White's perspective:

a) 11 ♗g2?! ♗b4 12 0-0 0-0! (12...♗xd2?! 13 ♕xd2 ♕xc4 14 b3 ♕b4 15 ♕xb4 axb4 16 ♗d2 gave White an edge in J.Lautier-J.Emms, Harplinge 1998, and here Emms notes that 13...♘xc4!? 14 ♕d4! 0-0 15 f4 ♘b6 16 f5 ♕c4 17 ♕f2 gives White dangerous attacking prospects)

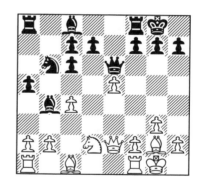

13 f4!? f6 (actually the greedy 13...♗xd2!? 14 ♕xd2 ♕xc4 15 b3 ♕c5+ may also be good for Black) 14 ♗e4 (Black keeps his nose in front too after 14 b3 fxe5 15 fxe5 ♖xf1+ 16 ♘xf1 ♗c5+) 14...fxe5 15 ♘f3 ♕xc4 left Black dominating in F.Erwich-J.Smeets, Hengelo 2002.

b) 11 h4 d5!? (11...♗a6 12 b3 ♗b4

13 ♗h3 ♕e7 was about equal in S.Silivanov-A.Mukhaev, Moscow 2000) 12 ♗h3 ♕e7 13 ♗xc8 ♖xc8 14 h5 h6 15 cxd5 cxd5 16 ♕b5+ ♕d7 17 ♕xa5 ♗e7 (Marin) gives Black decent play for the pawn.

c) 11 f4!? ♗b4 12 a3 ♗xd2+ 13 ♗xd2 ♗a6 again left c4 already pretty vulnerable in J.Timman-L.Johannessen, Malmo 2002, and sadly it seems that this approach is likely too ambitious from White.

d) Finally, please note that we saw the position after 11 a3 a4 12 ♕e4 ♗a6 in note 'b' to Black's 10th move, above, and there too the second player enjoys easy counterplay.

11...♗b4

The arguably less-incisive 11...a4 also makes sense and after 12 ♗b2 axb3 (12...♗b4 would keep play in our main line) 13 axb3 ♖xa1+ 14 ♗xa1 ♗b4 15 ♗g2 0-0 Black is fine.

12 ♗b2 a4

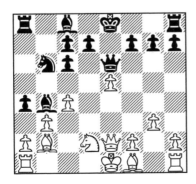

Black consistently tries to create problems for White, thereby remaining true to his opening strategy. This isn't the only approach, though, and after 12...0-0 13 ♗g2 d5 14 0-0 he doesn't even have to transpose with 14...a4. Black preferred a light-square approach with 14...♕g6!? in F.Corrales Jimenez-V.Bhat, Badalona 2010, which continued 15 a3!? (15 ♖fc1 would have been a safer approach) 15...♗xd2 16 ♕xd2 dxc4 17 ♖ac1 and now Black should have taken his chances in the critical line 17...cxb3! 18 ♗xc6 (or 18 ♖xc6 ♗e6 19 ♖xc7 ♖ac8 and again Black's queenside duo of knight and pawn on b3 forces White to be careful) 18...♗a6 19 ♗xa8 ♗xf1 20 ♔xf1 ♖xa8 21 ♖xc7 ♕e6 when White certainly isn't better, but may be able to hold the balance despite Black's strong presence on the light squares.

13 ♗g2

White achieved nothing after 13 f4 0-0 14 ♗g2 f6 15 0-0 axb3 16 axb3 ♖xa1 17 ♗xa1 fxe5 18 fxe5 ♖xf1+ 19 ♗xf1 d5 in F.Guilleux-C.Lecuyer, French League 2006.

13...0-0

Black castles and will play ...d5 next move. In general it is hard to approve of the move 13...a3?! here or later, as it unnecessarily releases the queenside tension. At certain specific moments the move might cause White some inconvenience, but unfortunately that is not the case here: 14 ♗d4 c5 (or 14...♖a5 15 0-0 c5 16 ♗e3 with an edge in T.Nedev-J.Tisdall, Panormo 2001, as 16...♕xe5?! 17 ♕d3 is very risky with ♖fe1 coming) 15 ♗xa8 ♘xa8 16 ♗e3 and Black didn't have adequate compensation for the exchange in I.Mastoras-J.Barkhagen, Gausdal 1992, despite his superiority on the light squares.

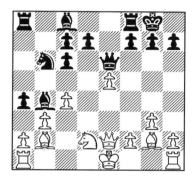

14 0-0 d5

Again Black does not benefit from inserting 14...a3 15 ♗d4 and now 15...d5 16 f4 (or 16 cxd5 cxd5 17 ♖fc1 with an edge) 16...♕g6 17 ♕f2! ♗xd2 18 ♕xd2 dxc4 19 ♗c5 ♖e8 20 bxc4 ♞xc4 21 ♕c3 ♗a6 22 f5 ♕h6 23 e6 (Postny) results in a big advantage for White. Again we can see how resolving the queenside tension only frees White's hand.

15 f4

Another logical move is 15 ♞f3!?, intending to free White's kingside majority with the help of ♞d4 and then f4. In this particular position Black actually does best to finally play 15...a3! (alternatives such as 15...♗a6 16 ♞d4 ♕g6 17 ♖ac1 c5 18 ♞c2 and 15...♕g6 16 ♞h4 ♕g4 17 ♗f3, A.Areshchenko-K.Georgiev, Gibraltar 2005, give White the advantage), after which 16 ♗d4 (16

♗c1?! ♗c3 is bad for White) 16...c5!? (16...♗a6 17 ♗xb6 cxb6 is also fine for Black) 17 cxd5 (17 ♗e3 ♗a6 pressured c4 and was good for Black in P.H.Nielsen-R.Dautov, Bad Lauterberg 1991) 17...♕xd5 (but not 17...♞xd5? 18 ♞g5) 18 ♕e3 (alternatively, Wells analyses 18 ♗e3 ♗a6 19 ♕c2 ♗xf1 20 ♖xf1 ♖ad8! 21 ♞g5 ♕d3 22 ♕xd3 ♖xd3 as good for Black) 18...♗a6! reaches an unclear position, but one where White is the one who has to be careful, as Black's pieces are very active.

15...♗c5+

Black should avoid a mechanical blockade with 15...f5?! in view of 16 ♞f3 dxc4 17 ♞d4 with good compensation for White. It seems viable, though, for him to increase his control over the light squares through 15...♕g6!? 16 ♞f3 ♗g4 with a good game, but, still, the text is more forceful.

16 ♔h1

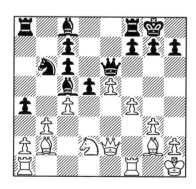

16...a3?!

Now this move is once again mistaken. Timing really can be everything in chess! Here Black can obtain a promising position with 16...♕g6! 17 ♘f3 (so far M.Velcheva-E.Djingarova, Sofia 2004) 17...dxc4 18 bxc4 ♗g4, with appreciable pressure on White's position, especially the c4-pawn.

17 ♗c3 f5?!

Black is following the wrong plan and soon ends up worse.

18 ♖ac1 ♗a6 19 ♘f3 ♖fd8 20 ♘g5 ♕e7 21 e6!

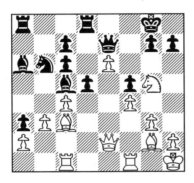

Now White's advantage acquires distinct proportions, and he eventually triumphed after many adventures in G.Buchicchio-A.Gupta, Kochin 2004.

A2) 9...♕e6!?

This is Black's main move against 9 ♘c3. Here it is less popular, but by no means bad. Indeed, why shouldn't Black play just like in our next chapter? There is less pressure on c4, but at the same time also on d5. Moreover, results have been generally encouraging, so this must count as a very sound alternative for the second player.

10 b3

This is White's main option, focus-

sing on quickly castling long. Black can react in several ways; the most critical is, as always, 10...a5. Otherwise, White has:

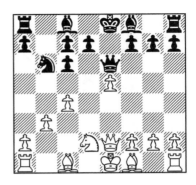

a) 10 ♕e4 sees White follow the same course as he does after 9 ♘c3 ♕e6. The reader is advised to study Line C of our next chapter for a better understanding of the situation, but with the knight passively placed on d2, White has no hope of an advantage: 10...g6 (Black plays just like he does against 9 ♘c3 and there is nothing wrong with this approach; 10...d5 11 exd6 cxd6 should equalize too and 10...♗a6 has also produced good results: for example, 11 ♗e2 ♗b4 12 b3 ♗c3 13 ♖b1 ♕xe5 14 0-0 ♕xe4 15 ♘xe4 ♗b4 followed by ...0-0 was better for Black in J.Timman-M.Adams, Sarajevo 1999) 11 ♗d3 ♗g7 12 f4 0-0 13 0-0 d5 14 ♕e2 f6 and Black was fine in S.Sanchez Castillo-S.Vajda, Bled 2002.

b) 10 g3 ♗b4! (likely even better than 10...a5 which takes play back into Line A12) 11 a3 ♗xd2+ 12 ♗xd2 0-0!? (12...a5 13 ♕e4 ♗a6 14 c5 ♗xf1 15

♔xf1 f5 also makes good sense and was promising for Black in S.Collas-A.Rizouk, Malaga 2002) 13 0-0-0 (13 c5? is a blunder in view of 13...♘a4 14 ♗g2 ♘xc5) 13...a5 sees Black enjoying a good position.

10...a5!

Thematic and promising. Instead 10...♗e7 is a passive move, not suited to this line. White can obtain an advantage with 11 ♗b2 0-0 12 g3! (12 0-0-0 d5 is okay for Black and after 13 exd6 cxd6 14 ♕f3 d5 15 ♗d3 ♕h6! he even had some initiative in V.Ivanchuk-Z.Almasi, Monte Carlo (rapid) 2001) 12...d5 13 exd6 cxd6 14 ♕xe6 ♗xe6 15 ♗g2

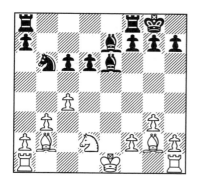

15...d5 16 cxd5 cxd5 (perhaps Black does better to recapture with a piece) 17 0-0 ♖fc8 18 ♘f3, as he did in L.Oll-G.Garcia, New York 1997.

Likewise, 10...♗a6 is usually out of place when White has fortified c4 so well. After, for example, 11 ♗b2 ♗b4 (or 11...0-0-0 12 0-0-0 ♗e7 13 ♕e3 followed by ♗d3 and White is obviously better; please also note the threat of

13...f6? 14 c5) 12 0-0-0 0-0 13 ♕h5 ♕e7 14 ♔b1 ♗a3 15 ♗a1 White had a stable edge in K.Neumeier-K.Nickl, Oberpullendorf 2002.

However, 10...♗b4 is a decent alternative. After 11 ♗b2 0-0 12 0-0-0! d5 (12...♕e7!? is another idea, intending to exchange the dark-squared bishops; White found nothing better than 13 ♔b1 ♗a3 14 ♗c3 ♗b4 and an early repetition in S.Rublevsky-A.Beliavsky, Yugoslav Team Championship 1999, as both 14 ♗a1?! d5 and, a move earlier, 13 ♘e4 ♖e8 are problematic) 13 exd6 ♕xd6 14 ♕e3 ♗a3 15 ♗d3 ♗g4 16 f3 ♖ae8 17 ♘e4 ♗xb2+ 18 ♔xb2 ♕e5+ 19 ♔c2 f5 Black has good counterplay, as indicated by Piket.

11 ♕e3

11 ♗b2 is energetically met by 11...a4! (11...♗b4 12 a3! gave White the advantage in no less a game than G.Kasparov-A.Karpov, World Championship (Game 16), Lyons 1990)

12 ♕e3 ♗b4! (worse is 12...axb3?! 13 axb3 ♖xa1+ 14 ♗xa1 ♗b4 15 ♗d3 d6 16 0-0 with an edge for White,

P.Svidler-I.Sokolov, Groningen 1995) 13 ♗d3 d6! and now the best White can do is 14 0-0-0! (White suffers after both 14 exd6 ♕xe3+ 15 fxe3 cxd6 16 ♗xg7 ♖g8 17 ♗d4 c5 18 ♗f6 axb3 19 axb3 ♖xa1+ 20 ♗xa1 ♖xg2 and 14 0-0?! a3 15 ♗c1 ♕xe5) 14...axb3 15 axb3 d5, but even here Black has the better chances, as he also does after 15...0-0 16 ♕e4 ♕h6 17 ♕xc6 ♖a6.

11...♗b4

11...a4 is another good option, transposing after 12 ♗b2 to the previous note.

12 a3 ♗xd2+ 13 ♗xd2

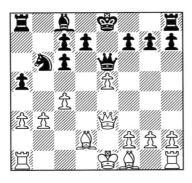

We've followed the game T.Thorhallsson-R.Hardarson, Gardabaer 1991, and now after the simple 13...a4 Black is better. Thus the ball is currently very much in White's court after 9...♕e6!?, especially if 10 b3 only plays into Black's hands. Expect further developments here over the coming months!

A3) 9...♗b7

People rarely play the Scotch like this nowadays, generally preferring more active options. Here Black puts the bishop on a potentially good diagonal, but at the same time shouts his intention of playing the positionally sub-optimal ...c5 to open it up. Moreover, this set-up does nothing to solve the problem of the stranded knight on b6 or to fight against White's bridgehead on e5, although on the other hand, quick development cannot be too bad.

10 b3

The most logical way to play. 10 h4?! is usually a waste of time so early in the game, even more so when Black is developing fast, and after 10...0-0-0 11 b3 d6 12 f4 (12 exd6? ♕f6! was very good for Black in R.Ramesh-M.Kazhgaleyev, Yerevan Olympiad 1996) 12...dxe5 13 fxe5 ♕e6 (Wells) Black is better.

Likewise, 10 f4 c5 11 ♘f3 0-0-0 12 a4 d6 13 a5 ♘d7 14 ♖a3 g6 gave Black good play in J.Hector-J.Barkhagen, Linkoping 2001. Indeed, one can't help but feel that White should not neglect his development for so long.

10...a5

Now that White has offered a target for this advance, Black obliges. Practice has also seen 10...0-0-0 11 ♗b2 and now:

a) 11...d5 12 0-0-0 ♕e6 13 ♕e3 ♗b4 14 cxd5 cxd5 15 ♘f3 was better for White in T.Shaked-I.Morovic Fernandez, Groningen 1997.

b) 11...♕e6 12 0-0-0 ♗e7 13 f4 ♖he8 was N.Padevsky-R.Kholmov, Dresden 1956, and again White would have been better had he now played 14 ♕f2 followed by 15 ♗d3.

c) The simplest way to meet 11...d6 is 12 0-0-0 dxe5 13 ♕xe5 ♕xe5 14 ♗xe5 with a permanent plus, as in E.Najer-S.Sulskis, Ohrid 2001.

d) Note too that this is not a good moment for 11...g5 (or 11...g6), in view of 12 e6 ♖g8 13 exd7+ ♘xd7 14 ♕xe7 ♗xe7 15 ♗d3 with a slight advantage.

e) Thus the critical approach is 11...c5, continuing the old standard plan. Black opens up the bishop, controls the d4-square, and prepares to later put pressure on the e5-pawn by means of ...g6, ...♗g7 and ...d6 or ...f6. He hopes that he can thus force White to exchange on d6 or f6, after which his active pieces will compensate for the resulting small structural defects.

White will also castle long and then try to support his centre; the ensuing positions can sometimes become similar to those seen in the 8...♗a6 lines: 12 0-0-0! d6 (the over-optimistic 12...♕g5?! resulted after 13 h4 ♕g6 14 ♖h3 ♗xg2 15 ♗xg2 ♕xg2 16 ♖g3 in Black's complete disorganization in I.Gaponenko-M.Lomineishvili, Rimavska Sobota 1992) 13 exd6 (White is also better after both Fogarasi's 13 f4 and 13 ♘f3 d5 14 cxd5 ♘xd5, as in H.Stefansson-J.Emms, Gausdal 1992, and then 15 ♕d2) 13...♕xd6 (or 13...cxd6 14 ♕g4+ ♕e6 15 ♗e2 with an edge), and now White has the strong idea 14 h4!, preparing to activate the king's rook.

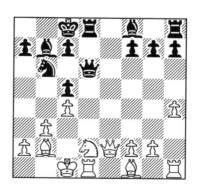

Following 14...h5 15 ♖h3 ♕h6 16 ♖e3 ♗d6 17 g3 White had a big advantage in S.Smagin-J.Emms, Copenhagen 1992.

While the old-fashioned 10...0-0-0 might not cut the mustard, 10...g6!? is quite logical and appears to give Black a decent-enough set-up. After the mutually consistent 11 ♗b2 (11 a4!? should always be met by 11...a5, although it is not clear here who benefits from the advance of both a-pawns) 11...♗g7 12 0-0-0 0-0-0 13 f4 c5 (13...d6 14 ♘f3 dxe5 15 ♘xe5 c5 was seen in M.Pribyl-S.Apel, Policka 1993, and is also reasonable; Black often accepts this structure, compensating for it with piece pressure in the centre) 14 ♘f3 (White should fortify e5; after 14 ♘e4 d6 15 ♕g4+ ♔b8 Black had pressure in V.Ivanchuk-M.Adams, Frankfurt (rapid) 2000 14...♖he8 (or the immediate 14...d6 15 exd6 ♕xe2 16 ♗xe2 ♗xb2+ 17 ♔xb2 ♖he8! with complex play in S.Rublevsky-P.Svidler, Tomsk 2001; it is important to include ...♖he8 before White has vacated f3 for his bishop) 15 g3 f6 16 ♗g2 and now in S.Rublevsky-M.Adams, Frankfurt (rapid) 2000, Black should have played 16...d6 with balanced chances.

Returning to 10...a5:

11 ♕e3

White shows his intention to develop his light-squared bishop quickly, most likely to d3. The alternative is to proceed with the natural plan of 11 ♗b2, but here Black can throw a spanner in the works with 11...a4!:

a) 12 g3? axb3 13 axb3 ♖xa1+ 14 ♗xa1 ♕a3 15 ♕d1 ♗b4 16 ♗g2 ♕a2! is rather annoying for White.

b) Even after 12 f4 axb3 13 axb3 ♖xa1+ 14 ♗xa1 ♕a3 15 ♕d1! (worse is 15 ♗d4?! ♗b4 16 ♔f2 c5 17 ♗e3 0-0 and Black is somewhat for choice) 15...♗b4 Black had the upper hand in D.Dochev-M.Kazhgaleyev, Pardubice 1996. Just as in variation 'a' play resembles the 9 b3 a5 variation, but in a favourable version for Black.

c) Perhaps White does best not to flinch and play 12 0-0-0!? ♕e6 13 ♕e4 axb3 14 axb3 ♗b4 which looks equal.

In view of such lines, White has also held up ...a4 with 11 a4, but this compromises his queenside structure and after 11...♕e6 (11...d6 12 exd6 cxd6 13 ♗b2 was preferred in the old game

E.Sveshnikov-A.Adorjan, Budapest 1967, and now 13...f6 14 0-0-0 ♕xe2 15 ♗xe2 d5 is about equal; had the pawn been back on a2 we would be able to speak of a slight edge for White, but here Black has b4 for his pieces and the b3-pawn may prove weak) 12 ♗b2 ♗b4 13 0-0-0 0-0! Black seems okay, which may not be the case after the more usual 13...0-0-0 14 ♘f3 ♕h6+ 15 ♔b1 when Black's only idea is 15...d6, but then 16 exd6 cxd6 17 ♕c2 should be better for White.

These lines may help to explain why no less a player than Radjabov recently preferred 11 ♕e3:

11...a4

Black is consistent, although the presence of the queen on e3 also enables him to consider the ...a4-a3 idea: 11...♕e6!? and now if 12 ♗b2 ♗b4 13 ♗d3 a4 14 0-0 a3 Black has the initiative, as after 15 ♗d4? c5! 16 ♗xc5 ♗xd2 17 ♕xd2 ♕c6 he wins a piece.

12 ♖b1

12 ♗b2 axb3 13 axb3 ♖xa1+ 14 ♗xa1 ♕a3 should by now be a familiar scenario and again White has difficul-

ties containing Black's initiative after 15 ♗c3 (15 ♕c3 ♗b4 is even worse) 15...♗c5 16 ♕d3 (16 ♗b2? ♕xb2 17 ♕xc5 ♔d8 and ...♖e8 is unpleasant for White) 16...♕c1+ 17 ♔e2 ♗a6, which certainly gave Black the upper hand in D.Brumen-U.Krstic, Zagreb 1997.

12...axb3

It may not be that important, but it is likely more accurate to play 12...c5 first, intending to transpose with 13 ♗b2 axb3 14 axb3, as pointed out by Mikhalevski.

13 axb3

An unusual recapture is 13 ♖xb3!?, but it makes sense here as two black minor pieces are situated on the b-file. Now Black does best to reject the a2-pawn with 13...c5, because after 13...♖xa2?! 14 ♘e4 ♕xe5 White has 15 ♘c5! ♕xe3+ 16 ♖xe3+ ♔d8 17 ♘xb7+ ♔c8 18 c5 ♔xb7 19 cxb6 cxb6 20 ♖f3 f6 21 ♗d3 with some advantage (Mikhalevski).

13...c5! 14 ♗b2 ♖a2!?

Black persists with his annoyance tactics, aiming to sacrifice the exchange on b2 and win the e5-pawn, although 14...g6 is perfectly viable and likely fine for him.

15 ♗d3!?

And White seems to value the e5-pawn more than the others, resorting to radical measures. The saner 15 ♘e4 would be met by 15...♖xb2 16 ♖xb2 ♕xe5 with unclear play; Black's hold on the dark squares is important here.

15...♗xg2 16 ♖g1 ♗c6 17 ♘e4!

Suddenly the position appears very threatening for Black: he has no kingside development and all White's pieces are very active. However, after 17...♗xe4 18 ♕xe4 (18 ♗xe4!? ♕e6 19 f4 g6 would have been similarly unclear and perhaps a better choice) 18...♕e6 (to stop the projected e6 sacrifice before playing ...g6; after the immediate 18...g6 19 e6 ♖g8 20 exd7+ ♘xd7 21 ♔f1 ♗g7 22 ♗xg7 ♕xe4 23 ♗xe4 ♖xg7 Black can defend, but this was not easy to decide on in a rapid game) 19 ♖g3 g6 20 f4 ♗e7 Black had everything in order in T.Radjabov-V.Ivanchuk, Cap d'Agde (rapid) 2009.

Indeed, despite his passive-looking position, there does not seem to be any real danger. White's only positive idea is to push f5, but this was quickly nipped in the bud by 21 ♔f1 ♖f8 22 ♕f3 f5!.

B) 9 b3

This crafty move order was a little neglected in some older works on the Scotch. With it White may hope to engineer a favourable transposition to certain 9 ♘d2 lines, while reducing Black's options. However, 9...a5 remains an eminently sensible response and, again, Black has some decent, creative alternatives.

> **B1: 9...a5**
> **B2: 9...♕e6**

There's also:

a) Just like after 9 ♘d2, there's no obvious reason why 9...g6!? hasn't been more popular.

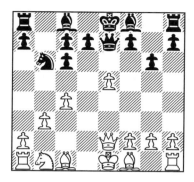

Indeed, as we saw near the start of Line A, 10 ♗b2 ♗g7 11 ♘d2 d6! gives Black good counterplay. Perhaps that explains why White has tried 10 f4 (after 10 ♗a3?! d6, 11 exd6?? ♕xe2+ 12 ♗xe2 ♗g7 is something to watch out for, but here even 11 f4 ♕e6! 12 g3 dxe5 13 ♗xf8 ♔xf8 favours Black), although following 10...♗g7 11 ♗b2 (11 ♗a3 comes at a moment when ...♕e6 is not good, but after the logical 11...c5 12 ♘c3 ♗b7 13 0-0-0 0-0 14 ♕f2 d6 Black had an excellent position in A.Mikhalchishin-V.Zheliandinov, Lviv 1998) 11...0-0 12 ♘d2 d6! (this is the standard way to counter White's central preponderance in this line) 13 0-0-0 dxe5 14 fxe5 a5 15 ♕e3 ♖e8 16 ♖e1 a4 Black was better in A.Pridorozhni-E.Najer, Moscow 2004.

b) However 9...d6 and 9...d5 are not very good here, as White retains the option of bringing out his knight to c3: 10 exd6 cxd6 11 ♘c3 should also give White a slight plus.

c) 9...♕h4!? is a little-played but interesting idea.

The point is that 10 ♗b2 (10 ♕e3 ♗b4+ 11 ♗d2 a5 12 ♗d3 0-0 13 0-0 f6 was okay for Black in B.Bayer-O.Lehner, Austrian League 2008) 10...♗b4+ 11 ♘d2 0-0 12 a3 ♗xd2+ 13 ♕xd2 d6 even gives Black the initiative. Definite food for thought!

d) Finally, even 9...♗b7 demonstrates that White has scarcely cut down Black's options, as after 10 ♗b2 0-0-0 11 ♘d2 play reaches Line A3.

B1) 9...a5

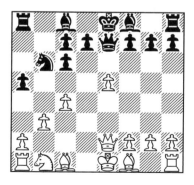

The most popular and most consistent reaction to 9 b3. In his bid to avoid a transposition to Line A11, White has tried a number of ideas here, but it may well be that he has nothing better than to accept the transposition, as we will see.

10 ♗b2

White has tried other moves here, but it seems that only with the text can he really hope for any advantage.

a) 10 ♘d2 can be met by 10...a4, likely reaching Line A11 after 11 ♗b2, or by 10...♕e6 taking play into Line A2.

b) 10 ♘c3?! transposes to note 'b' to White's 10th move in Line B of our next chapter.

c) 10 ♗a3?! is well met by the vigorous 10...d6!, enabling Black to maintain the right to castle kingside.

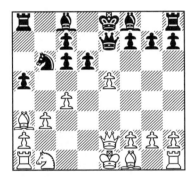

At this point 11 f4 (otherwise, 11 exd6 cxd6 12 ♘d2 ♗g4 is, of course, fine for Black, while the positional pawn sacrifice 11 c5?! dxc5 12 ♘d2 a4 13 ♕e4 ♕e6 does not provide White with adequate compensation) 11...♕e6 (11...a4 12 ♕e4 g5!? also appears promising) 12 ♘d2 (Marin analyses 12 ♕e4?! dxe5, with the idea of 13 ♗xf8 ♖xf8 14 fxe5 f5!, as good for Black) 12...a4 13

♗b2 (White must refrain from 13 ♘e4? axb3 14 ♘g5 ♕g4!, and both 13 b4?! dxe5 14 ♕xe5 ♕xe5+ 15 fxe5 ♗e6 and 13 exd6?! axb3! 14 d7+ ♔xd7 15 ♗xf8 b2 give Black a great position too) 13...d5! (a promising idea stemming from Marin, whose analysis we will now follow; Black wants to play ...♗b4, castle and then break with ...f6) 14 ♕e3 ♗b4 15 ♗c3 ♗xc3 16 ♕xc3 f6 17 ♗d3 fxe5 18 0-0 (again White must avoid 18 fxe5?! 0-0 as his king becomes too exposed) 18...axb3 19 axb3 ♖xa1 20 ♕xa1 sees some accurate defence from White enable him to claim equality after 20...0-0 21 ♕xe5 (or 21 fxe5 ♖xf1+ 22 ♗xf1 ♕h6 with good counterplay for Black) 21...♕xe5 22 fxe5 ♖xf1+ 23 ♔xf1 ♗e6.

d) 10 a4?! hopes to quash Black's counterplay by blunting his knight and light-squared bishop, but is too ambitious. The b4-square has been badly weakened and if Black manages to get his pawn to d5, the resulting pressure on c4 and the weakness of White's queenside will tell.

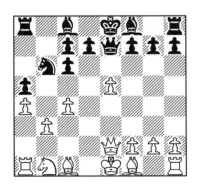

Thus the correct path for the second player is 10...♕e6 (an interesting attempt to complicate is 10...♕b4+ 11 ♘d2 ♕c3 12 ♖b1 ♗b4 which forces White to tread carefully; still, after the correct 13 ♕e4 c5 14 ♗d3 ♗b7 15 ♕e2, as in A.Grosar-T.Matkovic, Makarska 1994, and then 15...0-0 the position is only unclear) 11 g3 (11 ♗a3?! ♗xa3 12 ♘xa3 0-0 13 f4 d5 14 exd6?! ♕xd6 was a total disaster for White in H.Lopez Aguilar-A.Zarate, Mexico 2001, and 11 ♗b2 ♗b4+ 12 ♘d2 0-0 13 0-0-0 ♕h6! was also very good for Black in R.Hendriks-G.Garcia, Hoogeveen 1998) 11...♗c5 12 ♗g2 0-0 13 ♗b2, which occurred in E.Sutovsky-M.Adams, Reykjavik 2003, and now after the logical 13...d5! it is clear that Black has the upper hand.

e) 10 g3 a4 11 ♗a3 (11 ♗b2?! isn't ideal either, as we'll see in the note 'a' to White's 11th in our main line, below) 11...♕e6 is again pretty comfortable for Black.

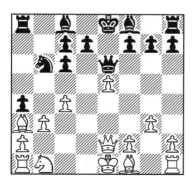

Indeed, White must once again be careful, as shown by the line 12 b4?

♗b7 13 f3 ♗e7 14 ♘d2 0-0 which creates a vivid image of White's great lag in development. Thus 12 ♗g2! is correct, although even here after 12...♗xa3! (Black should not be tempted by 12...axb3 13 axb3 ♗b4+?! 14 ♗xb4 ♖xa1 15 0-0 with very good compensation for White) 13 ♘xa3 axb3 14 axb3 0-0 (Marin gives 14...♕e7 15 ♘c2 ♖xa1+ 16 ♘xa1 0-0 17 0-0 f6 as equal, which seems correct) 15 0-0 f6 Black had a slight initiative in J.Sole Bove-X.Duran Albareda, Spain 1997.

Returning to 10 ♗b2:

10...a4

Black is again consistent and now White must make an important decision.

11 ♘d2

It seems that this natural and sensible move is best, accepting transposition to Line A11. Indeed, the alternatives are rather unimpressive and may well just leave White worse:

a) 11 g3?! runs into 11...axb3 12 axb3 ♕b4+ 13 ♘d2 ♖xa1+ 14 ♗xa1 ♕a5! (intending 15...♗b4; in the resulting play White's g3-move turns out to be a waste of precious time) 15 ♗b2 (15 ♕d1 ♗b4 16 ♗b2 d5! 17 exd6 0-0 is excellent for Black) 15...♗b4 16 ♗g2 (Black is better after both 16 ♕d3 0-0 and 16 ♔d1 0-0 17 ♘e4 d5, the latter occurring in W.Chikhaoui-M.Marin, Turin Olympiad 2006, but perhaps with 16 ♕e3!? 0-0 17 ♗g2 White might be able to maintain the balance) 16...♕a2 17 ♗c1 ♕xb3 and Black has won a pawn, for which White has negligible compensation.

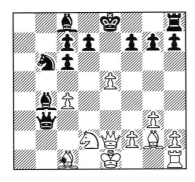

After 18 0-0 (18 c5 is answered by 18...♕c4) 18...♗xd2 19 ♗xd2 ♕xc4 20 ♕h5 Marin considers that White has compensation thanks to his bishop-pair, but after 20...0-0 21 ♖c1 ♕d3 the bishops remain rather passive and therefore it seems that Black is just better.

b) 11 f4?! suffers from the same problem as 11 g3, namely 11...axb3 12 axb3 ♕b4+ 13 ♘d2 ♖xa1+ 14 ♗xa1 ♕a5! and again White is under pressure: 15 ♗d4 ♗b4 16 g3 c5 17 ♗e3 and now the accurate 17...♕a2! 18 ♔f2 ♗b7

19 ♖g1 0-0 leaves Black much better.

c) 11 ♕e3?! prepares to bring the bishop out to d3, but Black has a strong counter in 11...axb3! 12 axb3 ♖xa1 (also good was 12...♕b4+ 13 ♕c3 ♖xa1 14 ♗xa1 ♘a4 15 ♕xb4 ♗xb4+ 16 ♔d1 ♘c5 with a big plus in M.Stefanova-S.Vajda, Predeal 2007) 13 ♗xa1 ♕b4+ 14 ♘d2 ♕a3 when he most certainly has the initiative, thanks to his active queen and White being a long way from castling.

d) Similarly 11 ♕f3?! should be met by 11...axb3! 12 axb3 ♖xa1 13 ♗xa1 ♕b4+ 14 ♘d2 ♕a3.

e) 11 ♕c2 is perhaps a more serious option, although of course such a move, with almost all the other pieces at home, can hardly be called critical. White keeps the queen closer to the attacked queenside, but the further waste of time allows Black to seize the initiative with 11...♕g5! 12 g3 ♗b4+ 13 ♘d2 0-0 14 f4 axb3 (perhaps even better is the active 14...♕e7!? 15 ♗g2 ♕c5, preventing White from castling) 15 axb3 ♖xa1+ 16 ♗xa1 and now in T.Kosintseva-S.Guliev, Moscow 2004, 16...♕e7! 17 ♗d3 ♕c5 18 ♗xh7+ ♔h8 19 ♗d3 d5 would have given Black a powerful initiative.

B2) 9...♕e6

This makes less sense than after 9 ♘d2 and 9 ♘c3, although it transpires that pressuring c4 is not Black's only idea behind the queen move; he also prepares to play ...♗b4 and ...d5.

10 ♗b2

White is correct to keep play in independent waters. Instead 10 ♘d2 would take play into Line A2, which wasn't especially promising for the first player and neither are the alternatives at this juncture:

a) 10 a3 prevents ...♗b4 but loses further time. Moreover, it weakens the b3-c4 pawn chain, so the obvious reaction is 10...a5 (10...g6 11 ♗b2 ♗g7 12 ♘d2 0-0 13 f4 d6 14 ♘f3 ♗a6 is also perfectly fine, as in R.Voigt-M.Mueller, Altenkirchen 1999) 11 ♘d2 g6 12 ♗b2 ♗g7 13 f4 0-0 when Black is ahead in development and ready to break in the centre.

b) 10 ♗d2 is again met by 10...a5 11 ♗c3 a4 12 ♕b2 d5 13 ♘d2 ♕g6 with an edge, as in J.Oresky-J.Krejci, Ceska Trebova 2008.

c) 10 ♕e3 g6 11 ♗b2 ♗g7 12 ♗d3 d6 13 f4 dxe5 14 0-0 ♘d7 15 f5 ♕d6 was complicated but not worse for Black in M.Amrutha-G.Hakimifard, Tehran 2007.

10...a5

As usual, this move is Black's main idea against set-ups with b3. However, he should give close consideration to 10...♗b4+! since 11 ♘d2 transposes to a position considered in the notes to Black's 10th move in Line A2, where he was able to obtain decent-enough counterplay.

11 ♕c2!

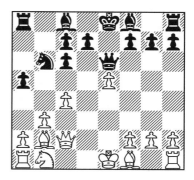

An unusual move, but with a certain point behind it. Instead of moving the queen to e3 or e4 in preparation for ♗d3, White wants to bring out the light-squared bishop with a gain of tempo on h7. There is the added advantage that the queen is less exposed on c2, but also the drawback that the e5-pawn becomes even weaker now.

Instead 11 ♘d2 would hardly be an ideal transposition (see the notes to White's 11th move in Line A2), while 11 f4?! ♗b4+ 12 ♘d2 0-0 13 ♕e3 d5 is good for Black.

11...♗b4+

Yet another plus of putting the queen on c2 is that 11...d5?! is unattractive, in view of the potential hanging pawn on c7. Indeed, 12 cxd5 ♘xd5 13 ♗c4 gives White a definite plus.

12 ♘d2 a4 13 ♗d3 ♕h6!

A good move, keeping White tied to his knight and forcing him to abandon the a-file. The alternatives show that Black cannot afford to play in too routine a fashion: for example, after 13...axb3?! 14 axb3 ♖xa1+ 15 ♗xa1 d6 16 0-0 dxe5 17 ♘f3 (Postny suggests 17 f4, but it does not seem to have the desired effect after 17...exf4 18 ♗xg7 ♕e3+) 17...f6 18 ♗xh7 f5 19 ♗xe5 ♖xh7 20 ♗xc7 ♘a8 21 ♘g5 White has the advantage, and neither is 13...a3?! any good after 14 ♗c3 ♗xc3 15 ♕xc3 d6 16 0-0 dxe5 17 ♖ae1 with a large advantage for White in M.Zumsande-H.Zieher, Hamburg 2005.

14 ♖d1 axb3 15 axb3 ♖a2

Black is trying hard, but White now gets to castle when he has a slight but clear edge.

16 0-0 0-0

16...♗a3 is well met by 17 ♗xa3!? (Postny's 17 ♖b1 0-0 18 ♕c3 ♗xb2 19 ♖xb2 ♖xb2 20 ♕xb2 also suffices for an edge) 17...♖xc2 18 ♗xc2 and in view of Black's passive pieces, White has a serious advantage.

17 ♕b1 ♖a5 18 ♘f3

White has consolidated and his position is definitely superior. Now in F.Vallejo Pons-P.Leko, Linares 2004, Black decided to lash out with 18...d5, but with 19 exd6! cxd6 20 ♘d4 White's better-placed pieces could have secured him an edge.

Conclusion

9 ♘d2 has declined in practice for good reason. Apart from 9...a5, which is quite sufficient, Black has several other decent lines. This stems from the passive placement of the knight on d2, which allows Black greater freedom in the centre and clogs up White's already slow development. 9...♕e6 in particular poses White some problems.

Unfortunately for fans of a set-up with the queen's bishop fianchettoed, the interesting move order with 9 b3 is not a panacea either. After 9...a5 White has tried a number of ways to avoid a transposition to the line 9 ♘d2 a5 10 b3 a4 11 ♗b2, but without much success. Black also has some decent independent paths to explore against 9 b3, but he should be aware that this is one position where 9...♕e6 may be best avoided. Vallejo's idea of 11 ♕c2 is certainly a serious threat to the continuation 10 ♗b2 a5.

Chapter Four
The Main Line:
8...♘b6 9 ♘c3

1 e4 e5 2 ♘f3 ♘c6 3 d4 exd4 4 ♘xd4
♘f6 5 ♘xc6 bxc6 6 e5 ♕e7 7 ♕e2 ♘d5
8 c4 ♘b6 9 ♘c3

A: 9...a5
B: 9...g6!?
C: 9...♕e6

The modern approach. Rather than spend time shoring up c4 and e5 with an early b3, White develops his knight to its most aggressive square and refuses to block the dark-squared bishop.

We now consider three options for Black: the typical queenside advance 9...a5, fianchettoing with 9...g6, and pressuring the c4-pawn with 9...♕e6.

Line C can undoubtedly be considered Black's main continuation, but Lines A and B may well have been unfairly neglected, as we will see. However, Black should restrict any creative urges to those lines; his lesser alternatives are generally unimpressive here:

a) Black should certainly avoid immediately fighting back in the centre: 9...d5?! (or 9...d6?!) 10 exd6 cxd6 (10...♕xe2+ 11 ♗xe2 cxd6 12 ♗f3 ♗b7 13 b3 0-0-0 14 0-0 also gives White a pleasant plus), since White can build on his better structure and development by means of 11 ♗g5 f6 (or 11...♕xe2+ 12 ♗xe2 ♗e6 13 ♗f3 ♖c8 14 b3 h6 15 ♗e3 with the standard structural edge) 12 ♗f4 ♗e6 (P.Vas-

117

A.Ebenfelt, Vadso 2008), and now strong is 13 c5! dxc5 14 0-0-0 with appreciable pressure.

b) 9...♕b4?! 10 a3 ♕b3 was a creative effort to trouble the c4-pawn in K.Van der Weide-T.Michalczak, Senden 2004, but after the accurate sequence 11 ♘e4! ♗a6 12 ♘d2 ♕c2 13 ♕d3 ♕xd3 14 ♗xd3 d5 15 exd6 ♗xd6 (or 15...cxd6 16 0-0) 16 0-0 0-0-0 17 b3 White avoids all the pitfalls and emerges with a definite advantage.

c) 9...♗a6 may seem a little illogical at this point, but is not so bad. Here White should avoid 10 b3?!, which allows Black to seize the initiative with 10...0-0-0 11 ♗b2 ♖e8!), but he does better with 10 ♕e4.

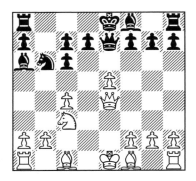

Then 10...♕e6 takes play into Line C1, below, but Black might consider too 10...f6!?, since after 11 exf6 (perhaps White must look into the more ambitious 11 c5!?) 11...gxf6 12 ♕xe7+ ♗xe7 13 b3 0-0-0 he had enough counterplay to maintain a rough balance in D.Sadvakasov-A.Ivanov, Los Angeles 2000.

d) Finally, the old plan of quickly castling queenside after 9...♗b7 is rather passive. This is best highlighted by the accurate 10 ♗d2! and then:

d1) White is somewhat better after 10...♕e6 11 f4 c5 (or 11...a5 12 ♕e4 g6 13 ♗d3 ♗g7 14 0-0 0-0 15 ♕e2, R.Zelcic-D.Rogic, Zadar 2005) 12 ♘b5 ♕c6 13 ♖g1 a6 14 ♘c3 0-0-0, as in D.Pavasovic-D.Rogic, Zadar 2005, and then 15 g3 ♕e6 16 0-0-0.

d2) 10...g6 11 ♘e4 ♗g7 12 ♘f6+ ♗xf6 13 exf6 ♕xe2+ 14 ♗xe2 is also rather pleasant for the first player.

d3) Similar is 10...d5 11 exd6 ♕xe2+ 12 ♗xe2 cxd6 13 0-0-0.

d4) 10...0-0-0 11 0-0-0 ♖e8 (no improvement is 11...g6 12 h4 h6 13 f4, J.De la Villa-O.Korneev, Mondariz 2000, nor Sepp's 11...f6, which should be met by 12 exf6! ♕xf6 13 h4) 12 f4 f6 13 exf6 (so far A.Motylev-Zhang Zhong, Linares 2001) 13...♕f7 14 ♕f2! (better than 14 fxg7 ♗xg7 15 ♕d3 c5 with compensation) 14...gxf6 15 c5 with an edge.

A) 9...a5

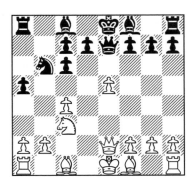

With this move Black tries to create counterplay on the queenside, by getting ready to meet b3 with ...a4. Indeed, he clearly hopes to provoke b3 by applying quick pressure to the c4-pawn.

10 ♕e4

This is the obvious way for White to develop: he opens up a path for the light-squared bishop to come to d3, eyeing Black's king should it go short, and retains central control. At the same time, by removing the queen from the a6-f1 diagonal, White discourages Black's possible central breaks and increases the protection of c4. It seems that all this should make ...a5 look out of place, but in fact Black is able to drum up counterplay without delay, exploiting the negative aspects of White's whole development scheme, namely a slight loss of time, the potential exposure of the queen on e4 and the relative lack of protection for the c4-pawn.

White might wish to look to the alternatives, but they are generally pretty unimpressive:

a) 10 a3?! ♝a6 11 ♕e4 ♕e6 12 b3 a4! is, as usual, problematic for White.

b) This is not the right moment for 10 b3?! in view of 10...a4 11 ♖b1 (even worse is 11 ♝b2? ♕b4! 12 ♕c2 axb3 13 axb3 ♖xa1+ 14 ♝xa1 ♕a5 and e5 dropped off in A.Murariu-L.Vajda, Bucharest 2002; note that here 12 a3 isn't a panacea either, since after 12...♕xb3! 13 ♖b1 ♝a6 14 ♕e4 ♝xc4 15 ♝a1 ♝d5 16 ♖xb3 ♝xe4 17 ♖xb6 cxb6 18 ♞xe4

♝xa3 Black wins) 11...axb3 12 axb3 ♕e6 13 ♕e4 ♝b4 14 ♝d2 d5 15 exd6 cxd6 16 ♝d3, as occurred in S.Crouan-A.Kosten, Sautron 2005.

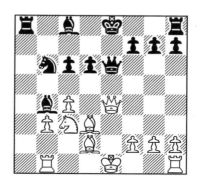

The problem is that Black breaks with 16...d5! 17 cxd5 cxd5 18 ♕xe6+ fxe6 19 ♔e2 d4 20 ♞e4 ♝xd2 21 ♔xd2 and after 21...♖a2+! 22 ♝c2 d3 23 ♔xd3 0-0 enjoys highly promising compensation.

c) 10 f4 runs into 10...♝a6! 11 b3 a4 12 ♕c2 (12 ♝b2? ♕b4 13 ♕c2 ♝c5 was bad for White in R.Swinkels-J.Van den Bersselaar, Maastricht 2007; after 14 ♝d3 h6 the white king, stuck in the centre, will be a constant cause for concern) 12...d5 13 ♝e3 dxc4 14 ♕e4 ♝b7 15 bxc4 ♕a3 and Black had a strong initiative in D.Smerdon-G.Lane, Canberra 2009.

d) 10 g3? a4 11 ♝g2 is also unfortunate in view of 11...♝a6 12 b3 ♕b4 13 ♕b2 ♖b8 with a clear plus for Black.

e) The most popular alternative has been 10 ♝d2, but even this leads to difficulties for White unless he is careful after 10...♝a6! and then:

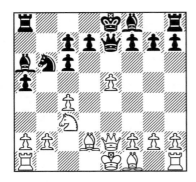

e1) 11 b3 a4 12 ♕e3! (precise; otherwise, 12 f4?! ♕a3! 13 ♗c1 ♕b4 14 ♕c2 ♕a5 15 ♖b1 axb3 16 axb3 ♗b4 17 ♗d2 d5 gave Black the initiative in S.Ganguly-P.Thipsay, Mumbai 2003, and after 12 ♕e4 g6 13 ♗d3 ♗g7 14 f4 0-0 15 0-0 d6 Black also has the upper hand) 12...g6! (Black is not afraid of ghosts) 13 ♘e4 ♗g7 14 ♘f6+ ♗xf6 15 exf6 ♕xe3+ 16 ♗xe3 0-0 17 0-0-0 d5 18 ♗xb6 cxb6 19 cxd5 ♗xf1 20 ♖hxf1 cxd5 with an equal position in E.Sutovsky-I.Ivanisevic, Subotica 2008.

e2) 11 ♕e4?! g6 (Black simply develops) 12 ♗d3 (Black is better after any of 12 ♖c1?! ♗g7 13 c5 ♗xf1! 14 ♗a6 15 bxc7 ♗xe5 16 ♔d1 f5! 17 ♕e3 f4 18 ♕e4 0-0, 12 f4 ♗g7 13 0-0-0 0-0 and 12 0-0-0 ♕e6) 12...♗g7 and now White has often played the mistaken 13 0-0? (however, 13 f4 0-0 14 b3 f6, as in R.Swinkels-I.Khmelniker, Vlissingen 2006, and then 15 f5 fxe5 16 fxg6 d5 is good for Black; so too is the 13 0-0-0?! 0-0 14 f4 of K.Toma-J.Zawadzka, Chotowa 2007, in view of 14...a4! followed by ...♕e6 hitting c4) 13...0-0 14 ♖ae1

♖fe8 15 ♕g4 intending ♘e4.

Unfortunately for the first player, Black can meet this with 15...d5! (15...h5 is also interesting) 16 b3 (16 exd6? ♕xd6 gives Black great play along the open files) 16...dxc4 17 ♗xc4 (17 bxc4 ♖ad8! 18 ♗g5 ♕d7! is very good for Black according to Delchev) 17...♘xc4 18 bxc4 h5! 19 ♕e4 ♕c5 and in M.Parligras-A.Delchev, Nova Gorica 2004, Black was much better.

We now return to White's main move, 10 ♕e4:

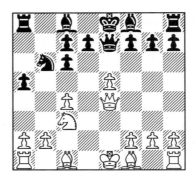

10...g6!

Definitely best. Black should try to attack e5 as quickly as possible before White manages to develop his pieces and coordinate them. The alternatives allow White to do just that and emerge with an edge:

a) 10...a4? 11 ♗e2 ♖a5 12 f4 ♗a6 13 ♗d2 ♕e6 14 ♘b5! was quite bad for Black in R.Mamedov-L.Gogochuri, Baku 2001.

b) 10...♗b7? 11 ♗e3 g6 12 0-0-0 ♗g7 13 f4 0-0 14 h4 ♖fe8 15 h5 d5 16 ♕c2 also gave White a big plus in

S.Karjakin-V.Varavin, Alushta 2001.

c) Even the more reasonable 10...♕e6 proves one move too slow after 11 ♗d3 g6 (and not 11...a4? 12 0-0 ♖a5 13 ♗f4 or the 11...d5? 12 exd6 cxd6 13 ♗e3 ♕xe4 14 ♗xe4 of G.Pinter-T.Meszaros, Paks 1998, with a clear plus for White in both cases; Black also found himself in trouble after 11...♗b4 12 ♗d2 ♗a6 13 b3 d5 14 exd6 cxd6 15 a3! ♗xc3 16 ♗xc3 in M.Dzhumaev-R.Jumabayev, Voronezh 2010) 12 0-0 ♗g7 13 f4 0-0 (G.Antal-L.Amoros Aguilar, Barcelona 2003) 14 c5 ♘d5 15 ♗d2 when White has a steady edge.

d) However, Black can start with 10...♗a6 when 11 ♗d3 (11 ♗e2 ♕e6 12 b3 ♗b4 13 ♗d2 0-0 14 0-0 f5 appears fine for Black) 11...g6 12 0-0 ♗g7 is very likely to transpose below, such as after 13 ♗f4 0-0, to note 'a' to White's 13th move.

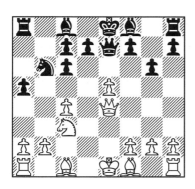

11 ♗d3

Again the most natural move. White can also try to shore up his defences on the dark squares before Black breaks with ...f6 or ...d6:

a) 11 ♗e3 ♗g7 12 f4 ♕b4 (Black can consider too 12...0-0, as he obtains good compensation after 13 c5 ♘d5 14 ♘xd5 cxd5 15 ♕xd5 ♖b8 16 0-0-0 d6!, T.Sauerwald-J.Dahm, Bergneustadt 1999) 13 0-0-0 was seen in K.Singer-S.Zawadzki, Wisla 2000, but after 13...♖b8 14 ♖d2 0-0 Black has good play; a combination of ...♘a4, ...d6 and ...f5/...f6 will lead to a strong attack.

b) No better seems 11 f4 ♗g7 12 ♗e2 (12 ♗d2?! 0-0 13 0-0-0 d5 14 cxd5 cxd5 15 ♘xd5 ♘xd5 16 ♕xd5 ♗e6 17 ♕c6 ♗xa2 was good for Black in B.Socko-S.Guliev, Kusadasi 2006, while 12 ♗d3 transposes to the notes to White's 12th in our main line, below) 12...0-0 13 0-0 ♗a6 14 ♗e3 (14 b3?! f6 was already better for Black in S.Kabir-L.Johannessen, Dhaka 2002), and now 14...f5! gave Black the advantage in N.Rutter-M.Hebden, Nuneaton 1999, as c4 was hard to defend.

11...♗g7 12 0-0

Alternatively, 12 f4 0-0 is similar to our last note and Black obtained good play after 13 ♗e3 ♕b4 14 0-0-0 ♖b8 15 ♖d2 ♘a4 in D.Lintchevski-S.Zhigalko, Kirishi 2005, while 12 ♗f4 is likely to transpose to the notes to White's 13th move, below.

12...0-0

White's main problem in this position is the defence of the e5-pawn, which is the target of Black's central breaks. Compared to similar positions after 9...♕e6 10 ♕e4 g6 (Line C3), it is not at all clear that Black's queen is worse placed on e7. From there it has access to the dark squares, while the addition of ...a5 makes ...♗a6 ideas all the more potent.

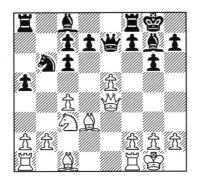

13 ♖e1

After 13 ♗f4?! White faces difficulties with the defence of e5:

a) 13...♗a6 14 ♖ac1 (14 ♖ae1? ♕b4 dropped a pawn in R.Edouard-J.Lopez Martinez, Salou 2006, while the 14 b3 of D.Pavasovic-S.Ernst, Wijk aan Zee 2004, should be met by 14...♖ae8! threatening ...f6) 14...♖fe8 15 ♖fe1 ♕b4 16 b3 (16 a3 ♕xb2 is, of course, bad for White), and now comes the strong break 16...d5! 17 ♕f3 ♘d7 (or Smeets' 17...a4) 18 ♕g3 ♘c5 when Black was better in A.Muzychuk-J.Zawadzka, St Petersburg 2009.

b) Probably even more accurate is 13...♖e8!, which led to a similar situation after 14 ♖ae1 ♗a6 in S.Ganguly-R.Shetty, Calcutta 2001. Black intends ...♕b4, putting both e5 and c4 in danger, and despite his seemingly harmonious development, White finds it tricky to defend his pawns.

Once again 13 f4?! may seem logical, but it is not good, partly because the position of Black's queen gives him the option of a timely check on c5. Moreover, after 13...♗a6! it is hard to find a good move for White.

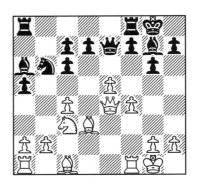

The main difficulty is that 14 b3? (14 ♗d2? runs into 14...♘xc4! 15 ♗xc4 ♕c5+, but can one really call either 14 ♔h1 ♖ae8 intending ...f6 or 14 ♖f2 f6! an ideal solution for White?) 14...d5! 15 ♕f3 (hardly any better is 15 ♕e2 dxc4 16 bxc4, as in M.Zumsande-L.Trent, Internet blitz 2004, and now 16...f6, opening up the long diagonal, but White cannot play 15 cxd5? because of 15...♕c5+ 16 ♗e3 ♕xc3) 15...f6 (or simply 15...dxc4 16 bxc4 ♘xc4) 16 exf6 (16 e6 f5 drops the e6-pawn) 16...♗xf6 17 ♗b2 dxc4 supplied a large advantage for Black in W.Murawski-I.Nester, Gdansk 2007.

13...♗a6 14 b3

Even for grandmasters this variation has proved tough. Indeed, White blundered a pawn with 14 ♗f4? ♕b4 in R.Zelcic-A.Delchev, Dresden 2003.

14...♖ae8 15 ♗f4

Again 15 f4?! f6 leaves White in trouble.

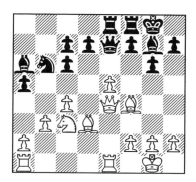

So far White has done his best to keep control over the position, but here Black could still obtain the better chances with 15...♕b4! 16 ♖ac1 d5 17 ♕f3 ♘d7, increasing the pressure on White's position. Instead 15...f6 was seen in S.Macak-A.Ashton, British League 2005, whereupon White blundered a pawn with 16 c5? (he should have played 16 ♖ac1! and answered 16...fxe5 with 17 ♗e3, intending c5 with decent positional compensation) 16...♗xd3 17 ♕xd3 ♕xc5, and after 18 e6 the precise 18...♖xe6! would have left White struggling.

B) 9...g6!?

This is a normal developing move, similar to 9...♕e6 10 ♕e4 g6 (Line C3). It appears to promise Black a good game and it's hard to explain its lack of popularity.

10 ♘e4

The critical move, threatening ♗g5

and hoping to exploit the weakening of the f6-square. Other tries allow Black to complete kingside development and obtain active play:

a) 10 f4 ♗g7 11 ♗e3 (neither do the alternatives promise anything good for White: 11 ♗d2 ♗a6 12 ♕e4 0-0, 11 g3 0-0 12 a4 d5, and 11 ♘e4 0-0 12 ♗e3 d6 13 c5 dxe5! 14 cxb6 axb6, M.Yeo-J.Henshaw, London 1978, are all promising for Black) 11...♗a6 12 b3 0-0 13 ♕d2 f6 and Black was better in L.Duarte-L.Rodi, San Luis 2007.

b) 10 ♕e4 ♗g7 11 f4 0-0 12 ♗d3 is simply met by 12...♗a6! 13 0-0 (or 13 ♗e3 f5 14 exf6 ♕xf6) 13...♗xc4 14 ♗xc4 ♕c5+ 15 ♗e3 ♕xc4, but here 12 ♗e3 (F.Saez-J.Boudre, St Affrique 2002) 12...d6 is also better for Black.

c) 10 b3 ♗g7 11 ♗b2 0-0 12 0-0-0 ♗xe5 was again bad for White in M.Tan-R.Pruijssers, Groningen 2005.

10...♕e6!

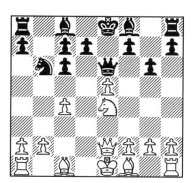

Correct; Black allows the threatened check and it turns out that White's position is rather loose. Moreover, he must avoid 10...♗g7? 11 ♗g5 (11 ♘f6+ is also good) 11...♕b4+ (but not 11...♕xe5?? 12 ♗f6!, while 11...♕e6 12 ♘f6+ ♔f8 13 0-0-0 ♗a6 14 b3 also leads to a unfortunate position for Black) 12 ♕d2! ♕xd2+ 13 ♔xd2 and Black's position is unpleasant, since 13...♗xe5 is met by 14 ♘f6+ ♗xf6 (14...♔f8? 15 ♗h6+ ♔e7 16 ♗g7! ♖d8 17 ♖e1 ♔d6 18 ♘e4+ is winning for White) 15 ♖e1+ ♔f8 16 ♗xf6 ♖g8 and in V.Baklan-D.Blagojevic, Budva 2002, amongst others, 17 ♖e7 would have led to a clear plus for White.

11 ♗d2

Other options:

a) 11 ♘f6+ ♔d8 does not cause Black as much discomfort as one might assume: 12 ♗d2 (or 12 ♗g5 h6 13 ♗d2 ♗e7 which is similar) 12...♗e7 13 0-0-0 ♗a6 14 b3 (14 ♕f3 ♗xc4 was better for Black in F.De Gleria-M.Feygin, Essen 2002) 14...♗xf6 15 exf6 ♕xf6 and it's not just that White has lost a pawn, but that a queen exchange on b1 is hard to avoid.

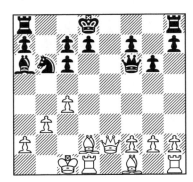

That said, White retains considerable positional compensation, in view of the misplaced black minor pieces,

his domination on the dark squares and Black's lack of coordination, but no quick threats can be generated and so his compensation likely only suffices for equality.

b) 11 ♗g5 ♗b4+ 12 ♔d1 ♗e7 13 ♗xe7 ♕xe7 14 ♕e3, as in O.Maiorov-V.Malaniuk, Krasnodar 1999, doesn't give White anything after 14...0-0.

c) 11 c5?! ♘d5 12 f4 a5 threatens ...♗a6 and is good for Black.

11...♗g7 12 ♘f6+

Black's counterplay comes quickly after 12 f4 0-0 13 0-0-0 (again 13 c5 ♘d5 14 0-0-0 a5 prepares ...♗a6 with the upper hand) 13...d6 14 exd6 (V.Gurevich-J.Fleck, German League 2000) 14...cxd6 15 ♗b4 ♖e8! which leaves White under pressure.

12...♗xf6 13 exf6 0-0 14 0-0-0 d6

No good is 14...♗a6?! 15 ♕f3! ♗xc4 16 ♕f4 ♔h8 17 ♖e1, as in J.Zezulkin-M.Grabarczyk, Krakow 1999, but Black can consider the positional exchange sacrifice 14...♕xf6!? 15 ♗h6 ♗a6 16 ♗xf8 ♖xf8.

15 ♗c3 ♘a4

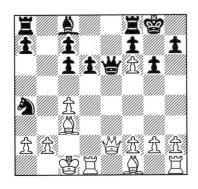

At this point the game I.Khamrakulov-J.Iruzubieta, Lisbon 2001, was agreed drawn, but surely Black already has the initiative and so might have continued?

C) 9...♕e6

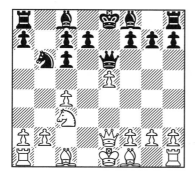

The main line. Black opens up a path for his dark-squared bishop, usually to come out to b4, and at the same time prepares to free his position with ...♗a6 and ...d5, after which the pressure on c4 will force White to exchange on d5 (or d6). These are noble aims, but one might also say that Black is playing a little strangely. It is not exactly clear how well the queen is placed on e6 (we saw earlier how it can become useful on c5 or b4 at some point), while White can even consider sacrificing the c4-pawn, provided Black has to eventually capture with a pawn there, in order to retain his space advantage in the centre.

10 ♕e4

This is White's most popular move. He follows suit and allows the light-squared bishop to be developed ac-

tively, removes the queen from the dangerous f1-a6 diagonal and keeps an eye on the c6-pawn, discouraging ...d6.

Practice has also seen:

a) The most sensible alternative to 10 ♕e4 is 10 ♗d2, defending against ...♗b4 in advance and preparing long castling. However, Black can now prevent this altogether when it turns out that White's chosen plan is not optimal: 10...♗a6! 11 b3 ♗a3 (11...♗c5 has also been played by some strong players, but it doesn't make so much sense; the main line is 12 ♕e4 – 12 f4!? has been condemned by Van der Wiel on the basis of 12...0-0-0 13 ♘e4 ♗d4 14 0-0-0 f6 15 exf6 ♖he8, but White seems to be better after 16 ♖e1 gxf6 17 ♕h5 – 12...0-0-0! 13 ♗d3 ♖de8 14 f4 f6 15 a4 and now best is 15...fxe5! 16 a5 exf4 17 0-0-0! with an unclear position, although Black's duo of problematically-placed minor pieces on the queenside does not inspire much confidence).

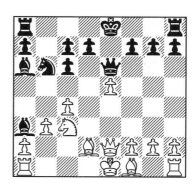

With two simple moves Black has prevented castling and obtained a lead in development. Suddenly White's lack of piece coordination begins to show, with Black ready for ...d5. Indeed, after 12 ♕e4 0-0! (another adequate move is 12...♕g6 and then 13 ♕f3 ♕e6 14 ♕e4 sees White unable to avoid repetition, as after 14 ♕g3 0-0 15 ♗d3 f6 Black has the initiative; meanwhile Mikhalevski has suggested 12...0-0-0!?, with the idea of 13 c5 ♗xf1 14 cxb6 d5 15 bxa7 ♔b7 16 ♕d4 c5 when Black is much better) 13 f4 ♖ae8 14 ♗d3 f5 Black has the upper hand.

b) 10 f4 is logical and often employed later on, but here it is premature in view of 10...♗b4 11 ♗d2 a5 (11...d6 12 a3 ♗xc3 13 ♗xc3 0-0 14 0-0-0 ♕g6 15 ♕e3 ♘a4 also gave Black good play in A.Strikovic-E.Van den Doel, Bajada de la Virgen 2005) 12 ♕e4 d5 13 cxd5 cxd5 14 ♕f3 0-0 with an excellent game for Black.

c) 10 b3 does not make much sense in this move order. After all, why commit the knight to c3 (where it is hanging) so early? Black can respond in many ways, the most obvious being 10...a5 (10...♗b4 is the other good option, and after 11 ♗d2 0-0 12 f4 d6! or 11 ♗b2 0-0 12 a3 ♗c5 13 g3 ♗d4 14 f4 d6 Black has the advantage) and then:

c1) 11 ♕e4 a4 12 ♖b1 axb3 13 axb3 transposes to note 'b' to White's 10th in Line A, which was fine for Black.

c2) 11 ♕e3 ♗b4 (also good is Marin's 11...a4 12 c5 ♘d5 13 ♘xd5 ♕xd5 14 b4 ♗a6) 12 ♗d2 (or 12 a3 ♗xc3+ 13 ♕xc3 a4 threatening ...♗a6) 12...a4 13 ♖c1 axb3 14 axb3 0-0 15 ♗d3

(A.Motylev-M.Sosnicki, Polanica Zdroj 1999), and now 15...d6! gives Black the initiative.

c3) 11 a4?! allows the strong 11...♗b4! 12 ♗b2 0-0 13 0-0-0 f5 14 h4 ♖b8 with an edge for Black.

c4) 11 g3 a4 12 ♖b1 axb3 13 axb3 ♗b4 14 ♗d2 0-0 15 ♗g2 ♖e8 was good for Black in the family clash R.Kaufman-L.Kaufman, Fredericksburg 2001.

c5) 11 ♗b2 a4! 12 ♕e3 ♗b4 13 0-0-0 (13 a3? is bad in view of 13...♗xc3+ 14 ♕xc3 axb3, as is 13 ♖d1?! axb3 14 axb3 f6) 13...♕e7 14 ♔b1 axb3 15 axb3 ♗a3 16 ♗a1 is unclear but harder for White to handle.

Returning to 10 ♕e4:

Now Black usually chooses between 10...♗b4 and 10...g6, but he can also force the pace by attacking c4. Thus we must consider:

C1: 10...♗a6
C2: 10...♗b4
C3: 10...g6

Other options are:

a) 10...a5?! takes play back into note 'c' to Black's 10th move in Line A.

b) 10...♗b7 is passive and does not mix well with Black's plans. Indeed, White is assured of an edge here: for example, 11 ♗d3 (another good option is 11 f4 g6 12 a4 a5 13 ♗d3 0-0-0 14 0-0 ♗c5+ 15 ♔h1 with a plus in V.Tseshkovsky-I.Kovalenko, Sochi 2008) 11...♗b4 (alternatively, 11...0-0-0 12 0-0 ♖e8 13 ♖e1 g6 14 a4 a5, as in T.Gruskovnjak-F.Rodman, Bled 2000, and now White is better after 15 ♗f4, or 11...d6 12 exd6 cxd6 13 0-0 ♕xe4 14 ♘xe4 h6 15 ♗f4 with a clear advantage for White in Yu Ting-Li Ruofan, HeiBei 2001) 12 ♗d2 0-0-0 13 0-0-0

13...♗xc3 14 ♗xc3 ♘a4 15 ♗a5, as in A.Lastin-A.Zakharov, Nizhny Novgorod 1999, and White has a steady edge.

c) 10...♗e7 also fails to inspire: 11 ♗d3 f6 (11...d5 12 exd6 cxd6 didn't solve Black's problems after 13 0-0 ♗d7 14 ♗f4 f5 15 ♕d4 in E.Goossens-F.Schwicker, French League 2008) 12

exf6 ♕xe4+ 13 ♘xe4 gxf6 14 ♗f4 ♗a6 15 ♘d2 with an edge for White in E.Cosma-J.Ambats, Buenos Aires 1992.

d) The direct 10...d5 11 exd6 cxd6 was popular for a while after its adoption by Ivan Sokolov, but is ultimately insufficient for equality.

White's best is 12 ♗d3! (after the alternatives Black manages to level the chances: 12 ♗f4 d5! 13 cxd5 ♘xd5 14 ♕xe6+ ♗xe6 15 ♘xd5 ♗xd5 and the strong bishop on d5 secured equality for Black in T.Oral-I.Sokolov, Selfoss 2002, while 12 ♗e3 ♕xe4 13 ♘xe4 ♗f5 14 ♘c3 ♗e7 15 ♗e2 0-0 was equal in S.Rublevsky-J.Lautier, Kallithea 2002) 12...f5 (likewise, 12...♕xe4+ 13 ♗xe4 ♗d7 14 b3 0-0-0 15 0-0 gave White a slight edge in S.Rublevsky-A.Kunte, Bled Olympiad 2002, as did 12...♗a6 13 ♗e3 ♕xe4 14 ♗xe4 ♖c8 15 c5! in A.Hnydiuk-K.Pinkas, Polanica Zdroj 2004) 13 ♕xe6+ ♗xe6 14 b3 d5 15 cxd5 ♗b4 16 ♗d2 ♘xd5 17 ♘xd5 ♗xd2+ 18 ♔xd2 ♗xd5 19 ♖ae1+ and White had a slight but permanent advantage in M.Parligras-L.Rama, Istanbul 2002.

C1) 10...♗a6

Black develops with tempo, but White is able to keep a grip on the central situation.

11 b3

White sensibly protects c4, restricting the enemy minor pieces, whereas 11 f4 d5! is fine for Black, since 12 cxd5 cxd5 13 ♘xd5 ♘xd5 14 ♕a4+ c6 15 ♗xa6 ♗b4+ gave him excellent compensation in J.Sequera-V.Sanchez, Cali 2007.

Instead 11 c5 starts some tactics, but Black had good play after 11...♗xf1 12 cxb6 (not, of course, 12 ♖xf1? ♗xc5) 12...f5 (12...♗c4 13 bxc7 ♗b4 also provided compensation in S.Keskinen-N.Sammalvuo, Lahti 1999) 13 ♕e3 ♗xg2 14 ♖g1 ♗d5 15 b7 ♖d8 16 ♕xa7 ♕xe5+ in E.Sveshnikov-L.Gostisa, Celje 2003.

11...0-0-0

The logical continuation of Black's play. Instead 11...♗b7?! 12 ♗d3 0-0-0 13 0-0 f6 14 exf6 ♕xf6 15 ♗b2 was very good for White in M.Parligras-I.Sofronie, Curtea de Arges 2002, but 11...♗b4

is a very important option, taking play into Line C2 after 12 ♗d2.

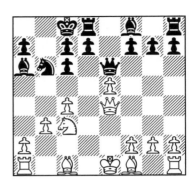

12 ♗b2!

The best square for the bishop, adding to the protection of e5. Having gone 9 ♘c3 White might not want to develop his bishop to b2, but the alternatives are unconvincing:

a) 12 ♗e2?! attempts to close the e-file, but runs into 12...f5, as played in F.Manca-J.Timman, Saint Vincent 2000, and after the further 13 ♕d4 c5 14 ♕e3 ♖e8 15 f4 g5 Black has an obvious initiative.

b) 12 c5?! fails to 12...♗xf1 13 cxb6 d5!, as in J.Smeets-E.Van den Doel, Leeuwarden 2005.

c) Hardly any better is 12 f4 f6 13 c5?! (13 ♗d2 fxe5 is also good for Black) 13...♗xf1 14 cxb6 ♗a6 15 bxa7 ♔b7 with excellent compensation for Black in P.Kotsur-D.Pavasovic, Dubai 2001.

d) Finally, 12 ♗d2 ♖e8 13 c5 ♗xf1 14 cxb6 ♗a6 15 bxa7 ♔b7 was similarly promising for Black in S.Shankland-A.Onischuk, Saint Louis 2009.

12...♗b7

The immediate 12...♖e8 is no improvement after 13 f4! (White should refrain from 13 c5 ♗xf1 14 cxb6 d5 15 bxa7 ♔b7, which favoured Black if anyone in B.Macieja-D.Sermek, Vidmar Memorial 2001, and neither was White's surprising decision to repeat this in S.Rublevsky-I.Sokolov, Poikovsky 2010, exactly a roaring success) 13...f6 (or 13...♗c5 14 0-0-0 f6 15 ♕f3) 14 0-0-0 (the recent development 14 a4!? ♔b8 15 a5 ♘c8 16 0-0-0! also deserves serious consideration; after 16...fxe5 17 ♕xe5 White had an edge in R.Robson-A.Onischuk, Lubbock 2010, and should have met 17...♕f7 18 ♕d4 ♗b4?! with the vigorous 19 c5! ♗xc3 20 ♗xc3 ♗xf1 21 ♖hxf1 ♕xb3 22 ♖f2 ♔a8 23 ♖b2 ♕a3 24 ♕c4, thereby maintaining a strong initiative) 14...fxe5 15 c5! (now the time is right for this blow) 15...♗xf1 16 cxb6 ♗a6 17 bxa7 and White had the initiative in D.Pavasovic-D.Rogic, Bizovac 2005. This c5 breakthrough is a typical idea in this line and may prove effective, but White must time it correctly.

Instead the unchallenging 12...♗c5 13 ♗d3 f6 14 exf6 ♕xf6 15 0-0 saw White enjoy a pleasant edge in D.Brandenburg-J.Smeets, Hilversum 2008.

13 0-0-0

White has brought his king to safety and the e5-pawn is secure, whereas Black has not managed to develop any counterplay. White certainly enjoys a plus in this position (and similar ones), and the following play shows why Black usually opts for more dynamic approach early in the opening.

13...♖e8

White is better too after all of 13...c5 14 ♘d5 f5 15 ♕d3, 13...♗b4 14 ♗d3 and, as in A.Motylev-I.Sofronie, Eforie Nord 2000, 13...d5 14 exd6 cxd6 15 ♗e2.

14 f4 d5

And here 14...g6 15 ♗d3 ♗h6 was played in J.Willemze-V.Mikhalevski, Vlissingen 2000, when White could have played 16 c5 with the advantage.

15 cxd5 cxd5 16 ♕c2

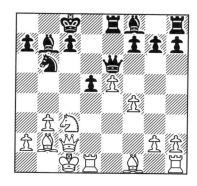

With his centre secure, White has clearly stabilized his advantage.

16...♔b8

Black cannot play 16...♕h6 17 g3 ♖xe5? 18 ♘b5 ♖e7 19 ♗e5 as his king ends up under a strong attack.

17 ♔b1

Another way to play is 17 ♗d3!? d4 18 ♘e4 ♘d5 19 ♘c5 with the upper hand, but not 17 ♘b5?! c5 18 f5 ♕h6+ 19 ♔b1 d4 when Black threatens ...♘d5-e3/b4 and has the initiative.

17...g6 18 a4

A standard way of discomforting the knight on b6, although White also retains the advantage with either 18 ♗e2 c5 19 ♗f3, G.Kasparov-M.Adams, Internet 2000, and the more dynamic 18 ♘b5!? c5 (18...c6 19 ♘d4 ♕c8 20 ♕d2! c5 21 ♖c1 is also very good for White) 19 f5 gxf5 20 ♘d6 ♗xd6 21 exd6 ♕xd6 22 ♗xh8 ♖xh8 23 ♕xf5 and White is on top, as analysed by Kosten.

18...c5?

This impulsive move allows White to increase his advantage. Black had to control the b5-square with 18...a6!?, although after 19 ♗e2 ♗b4 20 ♖hf1 White is still better.

19 ♗b5!

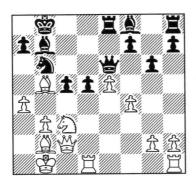

Now Black is in big trouble and was practically forced to give up the exchange in J.Timman-I.Sofronie, Budva 2009.

C2) 10...♗b4

For a long time this direct move, pinning the knight, preparing castling and intending ...d5, was Black's main choice. However, after a couple of wins by Kasparov and, finally, the win by Radjabov we will now follow, black players began to abandon this sub-variation and switch to the more flexible 10...g6 (Line C3).

11 ♗d2 ♗a6!

Black must play for ...d5, otherwise his opening play makes little sense, as becomes clear after an examination of the alternatives:

a) 11...♗xc3 12 ♗xc3 d5 13 cxd5 (a simple but strong approach) 13...cxd5 14 ♕b4 ♖b8 was seen in A.Kurilin-M.Leonov, Donskoj 2007, and now 15 ♕c5 gives White an edge. Here Black preferred 14...♘d7 in D.Sadvakasov-R.Ziatdinov, Philadelphia 2003, but without changing the assessment after 15 ♗b5 ♗a6 (or 15...c6 16 ♗a4) 16 ♗a4 0-0-0 17 0-0-0.

b) 11...0-0 12 ♗d3 gains an important tempo for White. After 12...g6 (the forcing 12...f5 13 exf6 ♕xe4+ 14 ♘xe4 ♗xd2+ 15 ♔xd2 d5 16 cxd5 cxd5 17 ♘c5 ♖xf6 18 f3 resulted in an unpleasant position for Black in N.Bojkovic-B.Hund, Batumi 1999) 13 0-0 ♗a6 14 b3 White was slightly better in S.Brunello-P.Pace, Porto San Giorgio 2004, although 14...f6 would have kept his advantage within manageable bounds.

c) 11...♗b7 12 f4 ♗xc3 13 ♗xc3 f5 14 ♕d4 is also pleasant for White.

d) Finally, do note that Black cannot play the immediate 11...d5?! because of 12 cxd5 ♘xd5 13 ♗d3 when White is much better.

12 b3

White should refrain from the erroneous 12 c5?! ♘c4 13 ♗xc4 ♗xc4 14 f4 ♗xc3 15 ♗xc3 ♗xa2 when Emms considers Black to be slightly better and I fully agree.

12...♗xc3

Black proceeds with his main plan. Instead 12...0-0 13 ♗d3 g6 14 0-0 f6 is very slightly better for White, as we saw above, while Black got himself into lots of trouble after 12...0-0-0? 13 c5! ♗xf1 14 cxb6 ♗xc3 (14...♗xg2 15 bxa7 ♔b7 16 ♕xb4+ wins for White) 15 ♗xc3 in A.Seyb-B.Ter Akopyan, Oberhaching 2006.

13 ♗xc3 d5

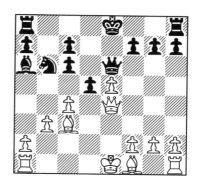

14 ♕h4

White puts his queen on the most active square, at the same time staying in touch with c4, and refrains from the exchange on d5 for as long as possible, so as not to free up Black's pieces. Moreover, the resulting pin of the c4-pawn after Black captures there will keep Black's minor pieces tied up, as he cannot allow White to recapture on c4 without punishment.

14 ♕f3 dxc4 15 ♗e2 has similar intentions, but the queen is less well placed on f3 and after 15...0-0 16 0-0 ♖fe8 17 ♖fe1 ♖ad8 18 ♖ac1 (or the similar 18 ♗f1 c5 19 ♖ad1 h6 of R.Ponomariov-B.Spassky, Cannes 1998) 18...c5 19 ♗f1 ♘d5 the position was unclear in L.Ljubojevic-B.Spassky, Montreal 1979.

Meanwhile the reason for refraining from the exchange on d5 becomes obvious after 14 cxd5 cxd5 when Black obtains good play: for example, 15 ♕b4 (or 15 ♕d4 ♗xf1 16 ♖xf1 ♖c8 17 b4 ♘a4, which was fine for Black in N.Nestorovic-A.Toth, Zlatibor 2007)

15...♗xf1 16 ♖xf1 (16 ♔xf1 ♘d7 gives Black good counterplay, such as after 17 ♗d4 a5 18 ♕b7 0-0 19 ♕xc7 ♕f5) 16...♘d7! 17 0-0-0 c5 18 ♕b7 ♘b6 and Black was better in M.Castiglione-D.Schwarz, Topilcianky 1997. Thus a premature exchange on d5 only serves to increase the mobility of Black's c- and d-pawns, and here White isn't yet ready to apply pressure to them.

14...dxc4

A critical position.

15 ♖c1!?

When played by Radjabov this was a novelty and it became the straw that broke the camel's back for Black. He already had problems to solve after the main move, 15 ♗e2, and 15 ♖c1 set new ones, which proved too much.

Instead 15 0-0-0?! is ill-advised; since White plans to exploit his structural advantage, it makes no sense to place the king on the queenside. After 15...0-0 16 g3 ♘d5 17 ♗xc4 ♗xc4 18 ♕xc4 a5 Black was for preference in M.Aigner-J.Becerra Rivero, Las Vegas 2007.

Many games have been played, though, with the simple and logical move 15 ♗e2, with which White prepares to castle and set his kingside majority in motion, while it is not clear what Black can do:

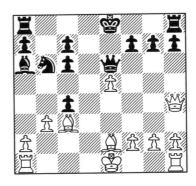

a) 15...0-0 was tried by some players hoping to avoid the fate of Kasparov's opponents after 15...♘d5, below, but it fails to equalize: 16 0-0 ♘d5 (several games have shown that none of 16...f5 17 ♖ac1, 16...c5 17 ♖fe1 nor 16...♖fe8 17 ♖ac1 are any better) 17 ♗xc4 (a safe move and the best; Kasparov once recommended 17 ♗d4, but after 17...♖fe8 18 ♖fe1 ♘b4 Black had counterplay in J.Zezulkin-D.Sebastian, German League 2003) 17...♗xc4 18 ♕xc4 sees White having obtained a stable advantage.

The only real question is whether Black can relieve himself of his weaknesses. To this end he usually opts for 18...a5 (18...♘xc3 19 ♕xc3 ♖ad8 20 ♖ac1 was difficult for Black in K.Kulaots-O.Sepp, Puhajarve 2001) 19 ♖ac1 ♖fb8, as in the stem game, A.Mikhalchishin-A.Onischuk, Batumi

1999, but now White should play 20 f4! ♕h6 (no better is 20...♘e3 21 ♕xe6 fxe6 22 ♖fe1! ♘d5 23 ♗e4 and Black will soon start to lose some of his weak pawns) 21 ♗d2 with a serious plus.

b) 15...♘d5 16 ♗xc4 (again this simple move is best; in his first attempt Kasparov chose 16 ♗d4?! and after 16...c5?! 17 ♗xc5 ♘c3 18 ♗xc4 ♕xe5+ 19 ♗e3 ♘e4 20 0-0 ♗xc4 21 bxc4 he had an edge in G.Kasparov-M.Adams, Sarajevo 1999, but 16...♘e7! secures Black counterplay and after 17 0-0 ♘f5 18 ♕f4 ♘xd4 19 ♕xd4 0-0 Kasparov feels that Black has good prospects) and now:

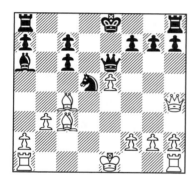

b1) Karjakin's 16...g5?! is well met by 17 ♗xd5! cxd5 (or 17...♕xd5 18 ♕d4! – 18 ♕xg5 may also be promising, although with 18...♖d8 19 ♕g4 h5 20 ♕f3 ♕xf3 21 gxf3 ♖g8 Black was able to find enough counterplay in E.Sutovsky-S.Karjakin, Pamplona 2004 – 18...♕xd4 19 ♗xd4 0-0-0 20 0-0-0 and White had a stable edge in M.Godena-E.Dervishi, Bratto 2004; note that here 18...♕xg2? 19 0-0-0 is probably win-

ning for White, who has a very powerful attack) 18 ♕xg5 c5 19 0-0-0 d4 (19...♗b7?! 20 f4 was very good for White in E.Sutovsky-H.Stefansson, Reykjavik 2004) 20 ♗a5!? (Sutovsky's suggestion) 20...♖c8 21 ♖he1 when White has the better chances.

b2) 16...♗b5 17 0-0 g5 18 ♕d4 was also better for White in B.Macieja-J.Timman, Willemstad 2001.

b3) 16...♗xc4 17 ♕xc4 0-0 (Black does not manage to equalize with 17...g5 18 0-0 ♘f4 19 ♕xe6+ ♘xe6 20 ♖fd1 ♔e7 21 f3, or here 19...fxe6 20 ♗d2! ♘e2+ 21 ♔h1 h6 22 ♗e3 with a clear plus for White) 18 0-0 ♖fe8 19 ♗b2 and again White had a useful structural edge in P.Marusenko-A.Law, British League 2000.

We now return to Radjabov's 15 ♖c1:

15...0-0

There is nothing better: 15...♘d5 16 ♗xc4 ♗b5 17 0-0 0-0 18 ♖fd1 is much better for White, while 15...♕g6 (Wang Hao-S.Karjakin, Al Ain 2008) 16 g3! 0-0 17 ♗e2 also fails to convince for the second player. However, as this book was going to press, Karjakin actually repeated 15...♕g6. It was only in a blitz game, albeit against Carlsen and after 16 ♗b4 f6! 17 ♕h3, 17...♕e4!? would have been a worthy alternative to the game's 17...♗c8, with a decent position for Black in both cases. One has to wonder, though, just what the talented young Russian has found against 16 g3...

16 ♗e2

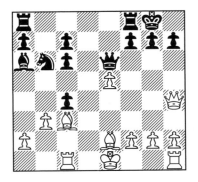

16...♘d5

No better is 16...♘d7 17 f4 (but not 17 0-0?! ♘xe5 which equalized in B.Macieja-V.Korchnoi, Mallorca Olympiad 2004) 17...♘c5 (or 17...f6 18 0-0 fxe5 19 ♗g4 ♕e8 20 ♕h3! ♖d8 21 ♗e6+ ♔h8 22 ♖fd1 with a clear plus for White) 18 0-0 cxb3 19 f5 ♕h6 (19...♕d5 20 ♗xa6 ♘xa6 21 ♖fd1 is no improvement) 20 ♕xh6 gxh6 21 ♗xa6 ♘xa6 22 axb3 and White is much better in this simplified position.

White has the initiative too after 16...f6 17 0-0 fxe5 18 ♖fe1.

17 ♗a1?!

This move allows Black to complicate things. White can guarantee himself a safe plus with the simple 17 ♗xc4! ♗xc4 18 ♕xc4 f6 (18...♖fe8?! 19 ♗a1 f6 20 0-0 fxe5 21 ♕xc6 was even worse for Black in A.Naumann-J.Gustafsson, Internet blitz 2006) 19 ♗a1 thanks to his better structure and minor piece.

17...♘b4

Perhaps 17...♕f5!? 18 0-0 ♘f4 would

have been a better practical choice, as this way Black creates some counter-threats.

18 bxc4 ♖ad8

Going for the pawn with 18...♘xa2 leads to serious problems: 19 ♖d1 c5 (19...♘b4 20 0-0 c5 21 f4 transposes, while 19...f5 20 0-0 ♘b4 21 ♖d2 will be followed by ♖fd1 when White's pressure is strong) 20 0-0 ♘b4 21 f4 ♕f5 (Black collapsed after 21...f5? 22 exf6! ♕xe2 23 ♖d7 in A.Kolev-Van der Veen, Hoogeveen 2005) 22 ♕g3 and White is much better.

19 0-0 ♘d3 20 ♖c3 ♘xe5 21 ♖e3 ♘g6

21...f6 22 f4 ♘g6 23 ♕xh7+ ♔xh7 24 ♖xe6 would be a favourable simplification for White.

22 ♕g5!

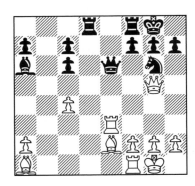

Black has been forced on to the defensive and White now concluded matters with a string of powerful moves in T.Radjabov-S.Karjakin, Dos Hermanas 2005: 22...♕d7 23 h4! f6 24 ♕a5 ♕c8?! 25 ♖g3 ♕e6 (25...♖f7 26 h5 ♘f4 27 ♗g4 f5 28 ♗f3 also sees White apply unbearable pressure on the black king) 26

♖e3 ♕c8 27 ♖e1 ♘xh4? (this loses by force, but Black's position was highly unpleasant in any case) 28 ♖h3! ♘g6 (Postny points out the line 28...♘f5 29 ♗g4 g6 30 ♗xf5 gxf5 31 ♖g3+ ♔h8 32 ♕e5!, spectacularly forcing mate) 29 ♕h5 ♕e6 30 ♕xh7+ ♔f7 31 ♖g3 1-0.

C3) 10...g6

Marin's preference in *Beating the Open Games* (much of the following analysis is based on Marin's detailed study of this variation), and Black's best option after 10 ♕e4. Black opts for piece pressure against e5, hoping to increase the effect of a later central break. Undoubtedly this solid and sound continuation is better than the once common 10...♗b4. Do note, though, that Black has not completely abandoned the idea of playing ...♗b4 and may choose to do so when the position requires it.

11 f4

The most obvious move, strengthening the e5-pawn that is the bridgehead of White's set-up. Practically every other reasonable move

every other reasonable move has been tried, though:

a) 11 ♗f4?! has the defect of physically preventing f4, which has consequences for the e5-pawn in the future. Moreover, this is one of those instances when Black does best to switch plans and opt for 11...♗b4!, intending quick pressure against c4 and ...d5.

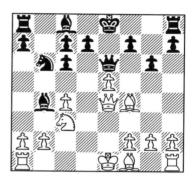

Note that the weakness of the f6-square does not really matter, as the white knight is pinned and the e4-square occupied. Moreover, Black already threatens 12 ...♘a4, solving the problem of the stray knight once and for all. Following 12 ♗d2 (12 ♖c1 ♘a4 13 ♗d2 ♘xc3 14 ♗xc3 ♗xc3+ 15 ♖xc3 0-0 was equal in J.Tomczak-I.Chirila, Szeged 2008, as was 12 ♗d3 ♘a4 13 0-0 ♗xc3 14 bxc3 ♘c5 in T.Nabaty-Y.Yemelin, Neustadt an der Weinstrasse 2009) 12...0-0 13 0-0-0! (and not 13 ♗d3? ♗a6 14 b3 ♖ae8 intending ...d5 or ...d6, or 13 a3? ♗xc3! 14 ♗xc3 ♘a4, hitting the bishop and eyeing the b3-square) 13...♖b8! (protecting the bishop in preparation for ...d5) 14 h4

(14 a3?! is again met by 14...♗xc3 15
♗xc3 ♘a4, while 14 ♗d3 ♖e8 15 f4
♗a6 16 b3 d5 is Black's idea and gives
him the upper hand) 14...♗a6 15 b3
(White cannot afford 15 c5?! ♗xc3
when Postny points out that 16 ♗xa6?
fails to 16...♗xb2+! 17 ♔xb2 ♘a4+ 18
♔a3 ♘xc5 19 ♕c4 ♖b6! 20 ♕xc5 ♖xa6+
21 ♗a5 ♖b8 22 ♖b1 ♖bb6! and Black
wins in view of the dual threats of ...d6
and ...♕e7, but even after 16 ♗xc3 ♘d5
Black was better in J.Lautier-P.Leko, Cap
d'Agde 2003) 15...d5 Black has good
play.

b) 11 ♗d3 is a logical move and now
11...♗g7 leads to a further divide:

b1) 12 ♗f4?! is again inadvisable in
view of 12...♗a6 13 0-0-0 (13 b3 d5! 14
cxd5 cxd5 is better for Black, as the
typical tactic 15 ♘xd5? ♕xd5! 16 ♕xd5
♘xd5 does not work as the bishop is
hanging on f4, as pointed out by
Marin) 13...♗xc4 14 ♗xc4 ♕xc4 (or
14...♘xc4) 15 ♕xc4 ♘xc4 and Black was
better in M.Turov-M.Grabarczyk, Cappelle la Grande 1998.

b2) 12 0-0 is most simply met by

12...0-0! (accepting the pawn with
12...♗xe5 allows White compensation
after 13 ♖e1 ♗xc3 14 bxc3, but
12...♗a6 13 c5 ♗xd3 14 ♕xd3 ♘d5
should be fine for Black) 13 c5 (or 13
♖e1 ♗a6 14 b3 f6 with equality in
F.Amonatov-V.Varavin, Vladimir 2002)
13...♘d5 14 f4 d6 with equality.

b3) 12 f4 0-0 13 0-0 (White is not yet
ready for 13 c5 ♘d5: for example, 14
0-0 d6! sees Black hit back in the centre
and equalize after 15 exd6 cxd6 16
♘xd5 cxd5 17 ♕xe6 fxe6 18 cxd6 ♖d8,
as in K.Van der Weide-J.De Jong, Hilversum 2006; here the dynamic 13...d5!? is
also worthy of serious consideration)
13...♗a6 (intending 14...d5, but the
immediate 13...d5 is playable, as 14
cxd5 cxd5 15 ♕f3 f6 16 exf6 ♕xf6 17
♘xd5 ♘xd5 18 ♕xd5+ ♗e6 supplies
compensation, while it's also hard to
find anything wrong with the 13...f5!?
14 exf6 ♕xf6 of V.Schneider-
A.Fejzullahu, Marianske Lazne 2008) 14
b3 d5!

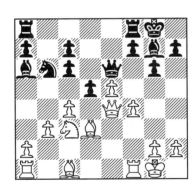

15 cxd5 (or 15 ♕f3 dxc4 16 ♗e4
cxb3 17 ♖f2 bxa2 18 ♖fxa2 ♗c4 with

an edge for Black) 15...cxd5 16 ♕e2 ♗xd3 17 ♕xd3 and now Black must strike with 17...f6 (17...c5 is also reasonable, but one might be slightly concerned by 18 ♗a3 ♖ac8 19 ♘b5 f6 20 ♘xa7 ♖a8 21 ♗xc5! ♖xa7 22 ♗xf8 ♗xf8 23 exf6 ♗a3, as given by Marin, and then 24 f5! looks dangerous) 18 ♘b5 fxe5 19 ♘xc7 ♕d6 20 ♘xa8 e4 with at least equality for Black in R.Griffiths-P.Sowray, Coulsdon 2008.

c) With the humble 11 ♗d2 White forestalls ...♗b4 and wishes to play a quick c5 in the case of ...♗g7, so I think that the most accurate reaction is 11...♗a6!

12 c5 (alternatively, 12 b3 ♗g7 13 f4 0-0 14 c5 ♗xf1 15 ♖xf1, as in O.Chebotarev-M.Marin, Moscow 2005, and now after 15...d5 16 ♕e3 ♘d7 17 ♘e2 Marin considers White to better, but Black seems more than okay after the logical 17...f6; in fact, one might even say that White is in some trouble here) and now:

c1) The complicated 12...♗xf1 13 cxb6 f5 14 ♕e3! ♗xg2 15 ♖g1 f4 16 b7

♖d8 17 ♕xf4 ♗d5 18 ♕e3 has been heavily analysed by Marin, but seems somewhat favourable for White.

c2) Thus Black should play 12...♘c4! with excellent counterplay and the initiative.

d) 11 ♗e3?! does not contribute to either the defence of e5 or the c3-knight, and so Black can play 11...♗b4 12 ♖c1 (12 ♗d2 would take play back into variation 'a') 12...f5 13 ♕d4 (hardly any better is 13 ♕f4 d6! 14 ♕h4 dxe5 15 ♗h6, as in B.Macieja-M.Marin, Spain 2006, and now 15...♘a4 with an obvious plus for Black) 13...c5 14 ♕f4 0-0 15 ♗e2 (15 a3 ♗xc3+ 16 ♖xc3 ♖e8 also fails to convince for White in view of 17 ♗xc5? ♕xe5+!, as pointed out by Marin) 15...♖e8 and Black has the upper hand.

e) White also cannot possibly expect much from the meek 11 ♗e2 ♗g7 12 f4 0-0 13 0-0 f6.

f) And 11 ♗g5 should simply be met by 11...♗g7 12 f4 h6 13 ♗h4 d5, again with good play for Black.

Finally, we return to 11 f4:

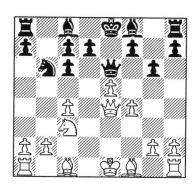

11...d5

This move, forcing the clarification of the central tension, has become Black's main choice here and leads to approximate equality. Moreover, the alternatives fail to convince:

a) 11...♗g7?! is perhaps the most logical move, but with e5 securely defended, White can afford to press forward with 12 c5! (12 ♗d2 d5 13 cxd5 cxd5 14 ♕b4 c6 15 0-0-0 ♕e7 16 ♕xe7+ ♔xe7 17 ♘e2 f6 18 ♘d4 ♔f7 fails to trouble Black, as Marin points out) 12...♘d5 (12...d5?! is just mistaken here in view of 13 cxd6 cxd6 14 ♕xc6+ ♗d7 15 ♕xd6 ♕xd6 16 exd6, with a clear edge for White in D.Sadvakasov-Peng Xiaomin, Las Vegas 1999) 13 ♗c4 ♗b7 (13...♘xc3 14 bxc3 is also slightly better for White) 14 0-0 0-0 (or 14...♕e7 15 ♕d4! ♘xc3 16 bxc3 with the usual edge) 15 ♖d1 ♕e7 16 ♘xd5 cxd5 17 ♗xd5 ♕xc5+ 18 ♗e3 ♗xd5 19 ♖xd5 and White had a safe edge in D.Brandenburg-C.Richter, Haarlem 2007.

b) 11...♗a6 12 b3 ♗g7 13 ♗b2 0-0 14 0-0-0 was also slightly better for White in J.Dworakowska-A.Greenfeld, Coventry 2005.

c) So too would have been 11...♗b4 12 ♗d2! (wisely breaking the pin; 12 ♗e3?! f5 13 ♕d3 ♗a6 14 b3 d5 gave Black good counterplay in T.Nabaty-V.Golod, Haifa 2010) 12...0-0 13 ♗d3 ♗a6 14 b3 d5 15 cxd5 cxd5 in T.Nedev-B.Avrukh, Kallithea 2008, had White now chosen 16 ♕xb4 ♗xd3 17 ♗e3.

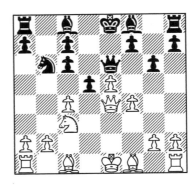

12 ♕c2!?

A tricky move, after which Black must play accurately to equalize. As we will see, White forces Black to recapture on d5 with a piece, so as not to allow ♘b5, awkwardly hitting c7. Again White also has several other options:

a) 12 cxd5 seems rather simplistic, but it is not clear that Black solves all of his problems after 12...cxd5

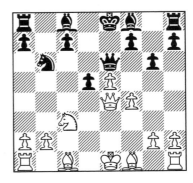

13 ♕e3!? (13 ♕c2 is also possible, intending ♘b5, but Black seems to have no problems after 13...c6 14 ♗d3 and now the precise 14...♗c5 15 ♗d2 0-0 prevented White's plan of 0-0 and f5, and equalized in S.Haslinger-S.Collins,

Hastings 2007/08) 13...c6 14 ♗d3 f6. Marin feels that Black has counterplay here, but after the logical 15 0-0 ♗e7 16 ♘e2 White may well retain a slight edge, although of course there is still a lot to play for. Black should prevent ♘d4 with 16...c5, after which White can simply continue developing or opt for the dynamic 17 exf6 ♕xf6 18 ♗b5+ ♔f7 19 f5!? gxf5 20 ♘g3 ♖f8 21 ♗d3 with a dangerous initiative.

b) However, 12 ♕d4 is well met by Marin's 12...c5! 13 ♕f2 d4 14 ♘e4 f5.

c) 12 exd6 cxd6 is too tame, as Black's spatial issues are resolved: for example, 13 ♗e3 (13 ♗d2 f5 14 ♕xe6+ ♗xe6 15 b3 ♗g7 is also fine for Black) 13...♗g7 14 0-0-0 (after 14 ♕xc6+ ♗d7 15 ♕f3 0-0 White's lack of development is a serious cause for concern) 14...d5 (with 14...♗xc3 15 ♕xe6+ ♗xe6 16 bxc3 0-0-0 Black also equalized in S.Movsesian-Z.Almasi, German League 2002, while 14...0-0!? 15 ♕xe6 ♗xe6 should be okay too) 15 cxd5 ♘xd5 16 ♕xe6+ ♗xe6 17 ♘xd5 ♗xd5 18 ♗c5 0-0-0 with equality in Li Chao-D.Vocaturo, Wijk aan Zee 2010.

d) Finally, White tried 12 ♕f3 ♗e7 13 ♗e3 0-0 14 ♗xb6 axb6 15 cxd5 cxd5 16 ♕xd5 c6 in D.Pavasovic-H.Stevic, Sibenik 2008, but it seems to me that Black has good compensation and White should tread carefully here.

12...♗b4!

Once again Black does best to play this move, increasing the pressure and, significantly, pinning the knight.

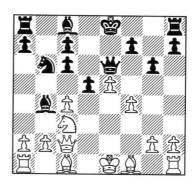

Alternatively, he can capture the offered pawn, but then White obtains good compensation after either 12...dxc4 13 ♘e4 ♗e7 (even worse was 13...f5?! 14 exf6 ♗b4+ 15 ♔f2 in J.Dworakowska-Li Ruofan, Moscow 2004) 14 ♗e2 0-0 15 0-0, or 12...♘xc4 13 ♗xc4 dxc4 14 ♘e4 ♗e7 15 ♗e3. In both cases Black's weak pawns may later fall and it isn't clear how he is going to drum up counterplay.

Incidentally, the point of White's last move is revealed after 12...♗g7?! 13 cxd5 ♘xd5 (13...cxd5? 14 ♘b5 wins the house) 14 ♗c4 with a pleasant advantage. Finally, 12...a6 was recently introduced in T.Nabaty-V.Mikhalevski, Haifa 2010. It enables Black to meet 13 cxd5 with 13...cxd5, but after 13 ♗e3 ♗e7 14 c5 (14 0-0-0!? may be promising too) 14...♘c4 15 ♗xc4 dxc4 16 0-0 White had a small but clear edge.

13 cxd5

White can also consider sacrificing the pawn, but 13 a3 ♗xc3+ 14 ♕xc3 dxc4 should give Black enough counterplay thanks to his use of the d5-square.

Indeed, the precise 15 ♗e2 0-0 16 0-0 f6 17 ♗e3 ♘d5! returned the pawn to force exchanges and an early draw in I.Nataf-D.Harika, Reykjavik 2010.

13...♘xd5

13...♕xd5 14 ♗d2 should be slightly better for White, whereas after 14 ♗d3 ♗xc3+ 15 bxc3 ♕c5! things are not so clear (Atalik).

14 ♗d2 ♘xc3?!

As White can improve after this, it is hard to recommend it. Instead Black should probably follow Atalik's plan of 14...0-0 15 ♗e2 (or 15 ♗c4!? ♗xc3 16 bxc3 ♕e7 with complex play, but White could certainly look into this position in his quest for an advantage) 15...♕e7 16 ♘xd5 cxd5 17 ♖c1 ♗f5 18 ♗d3 ♗xd2+ 19 ♕xd2 ♗xd3 20 ♕xd3 ♕b4+ 21 ♕d2 ♕b6 which seems fine for him.

15 ♗xc3?!

White has at his disposal here the strong intermediate move 15 a3! ♗c5 and now after the correct recapture 16 ♕xc3 (but not 16 ♗xc3 0-0 17 ♖d1 ♕a2!? with a certain degree of annoyance) 16...♕d5 17 ♗e3 ♗b6 18 ♗xb6 (and not 18 ♔f2 ♕e4!) 18...axb6 19 ♗e2 he enjoys a slight plus thanks to his superior pawn structure.

15...♕f5 16 ♕xf5 ♗xc3+ 17 bxc3 ♗xf5

We've followed D.Pavasovic-S.Atalik, Valjevo 2007, which had resulted in a simplified ending, where White's better structure is compensated by Black's control of the open b-file and his more active rooks. White does not really have grounds for pressing for the win, and Black may even get chances himself if White is not careful.

Conclusion

White must meet 9...♕e6 with 10 ♕e4, as other moves appear weak. Then there is a good reason why 10...♗b4 has disappeared from practice and 10...g6 has emerged as Black's main choice. By not immediately committing his bishop to b4, Black retains more options and can react to White's attempts accordingly. That said, with 11 f4 White can still aspire to an advantage and after 11...d5, as well as 12 ♕c2, 12 cxd5 deserves attention.

Black has two interesting alternatives to his main move, 9...♕e6. For some reason, neither 9...a5 nor 9...g6 has even been popular, but it is certainly hard to pinpoint specific instances where White can cause any problems. Indeed, one really has to conclude that the ball is in his court here and it wouldn't be a surprise if these lines were to enjoy an upsurge in popularity over the next year.

Chapter Five
The Main Line: Early Deviations

1 e4 e5 2 ♘f3 ♘c6 3 d4 exd4 4 ♘xd4 ♘f6 5 ♘xc6

White insists on the Scotch Game and this critical approach is the only one we will be covering. Instead 5 ♘c3 takes play into the so-called Scotch Four Knights, which can easily lead to quite a positional, manoeuvring struggle and on which the interesting reader will coverage in, for example, John Emms' *Starting Out* work.

5...bxc6

Invariably played. Moreover, it's clearly inaccurate to recapture the other way: 5...dxc6?! 6 ♕xd8+ ♔xd8 7 f3 ♗e6 (or 7...♗c5 8 ♗c4 ♔e7 9 ♗f4 ♗b6 10 g4 ♗e6 11 ♘d2 and White was slightly better in T.Kos-M.Crepan, Ljubljana 1997, while here 8...♗e6 9 ♗xe6 fxe6 10 ♘d2 also gives White an edge) 8 ♗e3 ♘d7 9 ♘d2 ♗c5 10 ♔f2 ♔e7 (10...f5 is simply met by 11 ♗d3) 11 ♗c4 ♖ad8 12 ♖ad1 ♗b6 13 ♗xe6 ♔xe6 14 ♘b3 and White had a comfortable edge in R.Zelcic-Tu Hoang Thai, Elista Olympiad 1998. To put it very simply, after 5...dxc6 White has all the advantages of an Exchange Ruy Lopez with none of the disadvantages!

After the correct recapture on c6, White must do something about the e4-pawn and the most logical approach is to push it forward, kicking the knight on f6, as we have seen. Perhaps intimidated by the amount of theory involved in these lines, as well as by the unique 'strangeness' of the resulting play, white players have sometimes sought to play more simply with 6 ♗d3. This approach is certainly valid, but it fails to pose Black any problems.

A: 6 ♗d3

B: 6 e5

Of the alternatives to 6 e5, only 6 ♗d3 has any merit and has been occasionally tried by strong players. Otherwise:

a) 6 ♘d2 is passive and after 6...d5 7 exd5 cxd5 8 ♗b5+ ♗d7 9 ♗xd7+ ♕xd7 10 0-0 ♗e7 Black cannot possibly have any problems, being ahead in development and enjoying the better control of the centre. We will soon see this scenario reoccurring in other lines as well.

After 11 c4 (11 ♘f3 0-0 12 ♗g5 h6 13 ♗h4 ♖fe8 14 ♖e1 ♕b5 15 b3 was fine for Black and agreed drawn in S.Tiviakov-L.Fressinet, Pamplona 2005) 11...0-0 12 cxd5 ♘xd5 13 ♘e4 ♖ad8 14 ♕f3 ♖fe8 Black was actively placed, which compensated for his slight structural weaknesses in E.Sveshnikov-A.Morozevich, St Petersburg 1993.

b) 6 ♘c3 can be met by 6...d5!? (6...♗b4 transposes to the Scotch Four Knights), and now:

b1) 7 exd5 cxd5 8 ♗b5+ ♗d7 9 0-0 ♗e7 10 ♗xd7+ (10 ♗g5 c6 11 ♗d3 0-0

gives Black good play – Emms) 10...♕xd7 11 ♗g5 c6 12 ♗xf6 ♗xf6 13 ♖e1+ ♗e7 14 ♕e2 ♖c8 is no problem for Black, who will follow up with ...♖c7 and ...0-0.

b2) 7 ♗d3 ♗e7 8 0-0 0-0 9 e5?! (9 ♗f4 ♖b8 10 ♖b1 ♗e6 looks saner, but is still fine for Black) 9...♘g4 10 ♗f4 f6! 11 exf6 (Wang Yue-G.Kaidanov, Beer Sheva 2005) 11...♗d6! 12 ♕d2 ♕xf6 gives Black the initiative.

c) Finally, the odd 6 ♕d4 is well met by 6...♗d6!, intending ...♕e7, ...♗e5 and ...d5 – a typical idea. After 7 ♗d3 ♕e7 8 0-0 0-0 Black has excellent prospects and many possibilities, such as ...♗b7 and ...c5.

A) 6 ♗d3

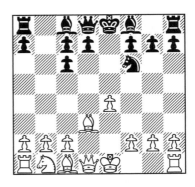

6...d5!

It is our firm conviction that this obvious move is the best counter to 6 ♗d3. As we will see, it promises Black a very good game and at least equality. However, several black players often prefer to meet this system (and 6 ♘c3/d2 as well) with a slower approach, especially when playing weaker opponents, in order to avoid mass simplification (such as after exd5 and ♗b5+). Their usual choice is 6...d6 and then ...g6, leading to a complex game. This approach, while not entirely optimal, has certain merit; compared to the 4...g6/d6 systems of our final chapter, here White has committed his light-squared bishop to d3, which is by no means its ideal square. Despite that White should be able to achieve a slight edge thanks to his structural advantage, but this set-up is a perfectly acceptable way of meeting these rare lines when easy equality will not do for Black.

Some sample lines after 6...d6: 7 0-0 (7 ♘c3 g6 8 ♕e2 ♗g7 9 e5 is direct but doesn't bring any benefits after 9...dxe5 10 ♕xe5+ ♗e6 11 0-0 0-0 12 ♗g5 ♖b8 by when Black even had some initiative in S.Karjakin-S.Djuric, Panormo 2002) 7...g6 and now:

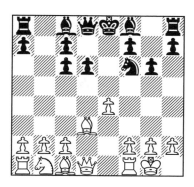

a) 8 ♕e1 ♗g7 9 e5 dxe5 10 ♕xe5+ ♗e6 11 ♗g5 (R.Zelcic-D.Rogic, Pula 1996) 11...0-0 is again fine for Black.

b) So is the similar 8 ♖e1 ♗g7 9 e5 dxe5 10 ♖xe5+ ♗e6 11 ♖e1 0-0 when White has the better structure, but Black was very active after 12 ♘d2 ♖b8 13 ♘b3 ♕d6 14 h3 ♘d5 15 ♗e4 ♖fe8 in O.Maiorov-M.Kazhgaleyev, Yalta 1995.

c) 8 b3! reaches the best set-up for White. After 8...♗g7 9 ♗b2 0-0 10 ♘d2 White slowly focuses all his pieces on the e5-square, planning to eventually make a break there under favourable circumstances: for example, 10...♖e8 11 ♖e1 (also interesting is the direct 11 f4!?, after which 11...♘xe4 12 ♗xg7 ♘xd2 13 ♕xd2 ♔xg7 14 f5! ♖e5 15 f6+ ♔g8 16 ♕f4 gave White good compensation in D.Pavasovic-D.Mastrovasilis, Istanbul 2003) 11...d5 12 e5 ♘d7 13 f4 f6 14 exf6 ♗xf6 15 ♗xf6 ♘xf6 16 ♕f3 when Barsky claims a slight advantage for White and one has to agree. Black was not, of course, forced to push ...d5 here, but in any case only with this counter-fianchetto approach can White obtain something real against 6...d6.

We now return to the critical 6...d5:

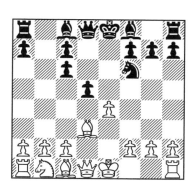

7 exd5

White opts for the safe approach, hoping to make the game quite dry. Alternatively:

a) 7 0-0 is a pointless pawn sacrifice. After 7...dxe4 8 ♕e1 (similarly, Black has the better chances after 8 ♕e2 ♕e7 9 ♗a6 ♗g4 10 ♕c4 ♕c5 11 ♕xc5 ♗xc5 12 ♗b7 ♖b8 13 ♗xc6+ ♗d7 thanks to his better development) 8...♕e7 9 ♕c3 White can hope to regain the pawn, but that's all and 9...♕c5 10 ♖e1 ♗e6 11 ♗xe4 ♘xe4 12 ♖xe4 0-0-0 was fine for Black in K.Chernyshov-N.Pedersen, Budapest 2006.

b) 7 e5!? is critical. Black must meet it aggressively and be well prepared, as there is a lot of danger hidden in this line. The correct reply is 7...♘g4! when White does best to sacrifice the pawn by playing 8 0-0 (instead 8 ♗f4? is powerfully met by 8...g5! 9 ♗g3 ♗g7 10 ♕e2 0-0 when the pawn will drop anyway; moreover, after the further 11 0-0 ♖e8 12 f4 gxf4 13 ♗xf4 ♘xe5 14 ♗xe5 ♖xe5 Black was a clear pawn up in S.Golac-M.Zerdo, Neum 2003) 8...♗c5 and:

b1) 9 ♗f4 is again well met by 9...g5! 10 ♗g3 (the 10 ♗d2 of I.Nataf-Z.Gyimesi, Paris 1995, is nothing after 10...0-0) 10...h5 (threatening to win the bishop) 11 ♗e2 (11 h3? h4 12 ♗h2 ♘xh2 13 ♔xh2 was played in the old game J.Meyer-M.Euwe, Amsterdam 1922, and after the logical 13...♕e7 Black would have been clearly better) 11...h4 12 ♗xg4 hxg3 13 hxg3 f5 14 ♗h5+ ♔f8 15 g4 ♕e7 and Black was much better in Pasternak-E.Lasker, Switzerland 1898, particularly in view of the bishop being locked out of play on h5.

b2) 9 h3 ♘xe5 10 ♖e1 ♕f6 11 ♕e2 0-0! is also very good for Black, since White cannot afford to go in for 12 ♕xe5? ♕xf2+ 13 ♔h1 ♗xh3! 14 gxh3 ♕f3+ 15 ♔h2 ♗d6 16 ♖e3 ♕xe3 17 ♗xe3 ♗xe5+ 18 ♔g2 ♗xb2, as pointed out by Emms.

b3) However, after 9 ♕e2 Black must tread carefully, as shown by Barsky's analysis. His best course of action is likely the dynamic 9...♕e7! 10 ♗f4 g5!.

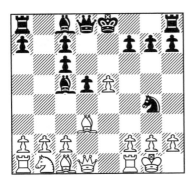

Now White does best to retreat with 11 ♗d2 (11 ♗g3?! again runs into 11...h5! and after the 12 ♗a6 ♗xa6 13 ♕xa6 ♕e6! 14 h3 h4! 15 ♗h2 ♘xh2 16 ♔xh2 of V.Tomescu-A.Musat, Bucharest 1993, 16...♕xe5+ would have left White with a horrible position), when Black should proceed bravely with 11...♘xe5 12 ♖e1 ♗d6! and after 13 ♕h5 (alternatively, 13 f4?! gxf4 14 ♗xf4 f6! 15 ♘d2 was played in M.Kaminski-E.Bacrot, Elista Olympiad 1998, but after 15...0-0 16 ♘f1 ♖b8! 17 ♖ab1 ♖b4 White has no compensation; Barsky also examines the possibility of 13 ♗c3 f6 14 ♘d2 0-0 15 ♘f1 when the simple 15...♗e6 prepares to unpin with ...♖ae8 and ...♕d7, and here too it is hard to see any compensation either) 13...h6 14 h3 Barsky feels that White has good compensation.

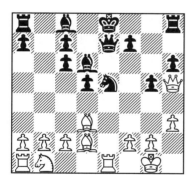

Black is, indeed, unable to castle and it is possible for White to open up some lines with f4, but with his queen-side pieces still sleeping, it is hard to believe that White is able to generate any meaningful threats. After a normal move such as 14...♔f8, intending ...♔g7 followed by bringing the other pieces into play, White is surely hard pressed to prove his compensation.

c) 7 ♕e2 defends the e-pawn, but allows Black to obtain the bishop pair: 7...dxe4 8 ♘c3 (worse is 8 ♗xe4?! ♘xe4 9 ♕xe4+ ♕e7 10 ♕xe7+ ♗xe7 when the two bishops will have their say) 8...♗b4 9 ♗xe4 (P.Ruiz-A.Pena, Cartagena de Indias 2007) 9...♘xe4 10 ♕xe4+ ♕e7 with simple equality.

d) Neither does 7 ♘d2 trouble Black in any way, so 7...♗d6 8 0-0 (8 exd5 ♕e7+ 9 ♕e2 ♕xe2+ 10 ♗xe2 cxd5 is fine too for Black) 8...0-0 9 ♖e1 (the ambitious 9 f4?! fails to 9...♗g4 10 ♕e1 ♘xe4 11 ♗xe4 dxe4 12 ♕xe4 ♕d7 with a clear plus as ...♖ae8 is coming) 9...♖e8 10 exd5 ♖xe1+ 11 ♕xe1 cxd5 by when Black was somewhat better in D.Collas-L.Verat, Cannes 1996.

e) Even less impressive is 7 ♗g5 ♗e7 8 e5 ♘g4 9 ♗f4 f6.

Finally, before we return to 7 exd5, do note that 7 ♘c3 would take play back into note 'b2' to White's 6th move, above.

7...cxd5

This position greatly resembles the Scotch Four Knights; the only difference is that the moves ♘c3 and ...♗b4 have not been played. Black has nothing to complain about here, as he is the only one with a central pawn, he has easy development and White's pieces are still at home. In fact, the first player is completely unable to do anything productive for a long time and is placing his hopes on the slight structural advantage he would enjoy in a simplified position.

Well, chess is not as simple as that; first there is a middlegame to be played, where Black's own positional plusses will come into effect and give him good play. It is for this reason that white players reaching this position usually try a strategy different to simply bringing their pieces out. They seek to take advantage of not having played ♘c3 by quickly undermining the black centre with c4. It is quite a different story for Black to have a single isolated pawn in the centre than a mobile pawn duo ready to advance.

8 ♗b5+

Before proceeding with the c4-plan, White exchanges yet another pair of minor pieces, further reducing Black's potential.

The other option is 8 0-0 ♗e7 9 c4 (alternatively: 9 ♘c3 0-0 is very similar to the Scotch Four Knights, but the bishop is already back to e7, which may

mean a gain of tempo for Black; after 9 b3 0-0 10 ♗b2 the disruptive 10...♗g4!? is attractive; and Black was at least equal after 9 ♗g5 0-0 10 ♘d2 ♗g4 11 ♕c1 ♘h5 12 ♗xe7 ♕xe7 13 ♖e1 ♕g5 14 g3 ♖ae8 in N.Fercec-A.Fejzullahu, Feugen 2006)

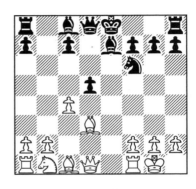

9...0-0 (as we will see in the main line too, Black always prefers to exchange the pawns and open lines for his pieces, rather than support d5 with ...c6) 10 cxd5 (there is no point in delaying this exchange: for example, 10 ♗g5 ♖b8 11 ♕c2 dxc4 12 ♗xc4 ♕d6 threatens ...♘g4 and puts White on the defensive) 10...♘xd5 11 ♗e4 (Black is fine too after 11 ♕f3 ♗e6 12 ♖e1 ♗d6) 11...♗e6 12 ♘c3 ♘xc3 13 bxc3 ♕xd1 14 ♖xd1 ♖ad8, but this is absolutely fine for Black: for example, 15 ♗f4! (15 ♗e3 c5 16 ♗f3?! ♖xd1+ 17 ♖xd1 ♖b8 18 h3 ♖b2 already saw White on the back foot in A.Nimzowitsch-S.Tarrasch, San Sebastian 1911; indeed, White must be accurate here) 15...♗f6 16 ♗xc7 ♖c8 17 ♗a5 ♗xc3 18 ♗xc3 ♖xc3 19 ♗d5 and White managed to achieve his hard-fought half-point in H.Stevic-A.Beliav-sky, Bled Olympiad 2002.

We should also note that 8 ♕e2+ puts the queen on an open file, which is rarely ideal in such positions: 8...♗e7 9 0-0 0-0 10 ♗f4 (or 10 ♗g5 h6 11 ♗h4 ♖e8) 10...♖b8 11 b3 ♖e8 and White is on the defensive once again.

8...♗d7 9 ♗xd7+ ♕xd7 10 0-0 ♗e7

It is mainly this position that black players are keen to avoid when they prefer 6...d6. White has managed to exchange two sets of minor pieces and will play c4 next, negating Black's central space advantage. Black does not, of course, face any problems, but admittedly it can be difficult to play for a win from here. He must rely almost entirely on active piece play, hoping to provoke weaknesses.

11 c4

By refraining from this move, White runs the risk of ending up worse: for example, 11 ♘d2 0-0 12 b3 (or 12 ♘f3 ♖fe8 13 ♗e3 ♗d6) 12...a5! (latching on to the hook on b3; instead 12...♘g4 only led to exchanges and an early

draw after 13 ♗b2 ♗f6 14 ♗xf6 ♘xf6 in H.Stevic-R.Ponomariov, Khanty-Mansiysk Olympiad 2010) 13 a4 ♗b4 (hitting the dark squares) 14 ♗b2 ♖a6 (centralizing the rook) 15 ♘f3 ♖e8 16 ♕d3 ♖d6 and in just a few moves Black had obtained an excellent position in J.Mellado Trivino-M.Adams, French League 2001.

11...dxc4!

It is not a good idea to play 11...c6 12 cxd5 cxd5, as then the black pawn may become weak on d5. White has a minute advantage here.

12 ♕c2

White must try to regain the pawn. Instead 12 ♕xd7+ ♘xd7 13 ♖e1 ♖d8 14 ♗d2 ♘c5 is already better for Black.

12...0-0 13 ♕xc4

If 13 ♘d2 then 13...c3 14 ♕xc3 ♘d5 15 ♕c2, as in M.Godena-J.Parker, Mondariz 2000, and now 15...♘b4 16 ♕c4 ♖fd8 with the initiative for Black.

13...♖ab8

13...♗d6 14 ♘c3 ♖ab8 is similar.

14 ♘c3 ♖b4

Black activates his pieces with gain

of time and if anyone must be careful here it's White. Indeed, with 15 ♕e2 ♗c5 16 h3 ♕f5 17 a3 ♖bb8 18 ♗e3 ♖fe8 19 ♖ad1 ♗xe3 20 fxe3 ♕e5 Black had forced a weakness on e3 and went on to grind out the full point in the all-grandmaster clash R.Zelcic-A.Graf, Turin Olympiad 2006.

B) 6 e5

So White puts the question to the black knight. At this stage 6...♕e7 is, of course, very much the main line, but we should also examine the three possible knight moves, two of which are not entirely unknown at club level.

> **B1: 6...♘e4**
> **B2: 6...♕e7**

If Black is to move the knight, then the former is his best try, as can be seen from examining both:

a) 6...♘g8? is obviously a bad move. White is much better after anything reasonable: for example, Barsky gives 7 ♗d3 ♗c5 (or 7...g6 8 0-0 ♗g7 9 ♘c3 d6 10 ♕f3 d5 11 ♖e1 with a clear plus in A.Lopez Andujar Ocana-I.Khamrakulov, Madrid 2001) 8 0-0 ♘e7 9 ♘c3 d5 10 exd6 ♗xd6 (also bad is 10...cxd6 11 ♘e4 ♗b6 12 ♕h5) 11 ♕h5 h6 12 ♘e4 with a clear advantage.

b) 6...♘d5?! seems similar to 6...♕e7 7 ♕e2 ♘d5, but the following analysis shows exactly why 6...♕e7 is indispensable. The main line is not a matter of who benefits most from the queen moves; Black must go down that path in any case. Here 7 c4! is strong, immediately kicking the knight from the centre.

Already one significant difference with the main line is revealed – Black cannot pin the c4-pawn and retain the knight in the centre with ...♗a6. Thus he has tried:

b1) 7...♘b6 is just quite passive and White obtains an advantage by simple means: 8 ♗d3 d6 (alternatively: 8...♗e7 9 0-0 0-0 10 ♕c2 h6 11 ♘c3 d6 12 ♗f4 ♗e6 13 ♖ad1 saw some good and purposeful play from White in J.Petro-

Z.Szilagyi, Miskolc 1994, but he should have answered 13...♘xc4 with 14 ♘e2! ♘b6 15 ♘d4, thereby securing a clear advantage; 8...♗c5 also enables White to develop with straightforward play through 9 0-0 0-0 10 ♘d2 ♕e7 11 ♘f3 h6 and now one good move is 12 ♗c2! planning ♕d3; and, finally, 8...d5 9 cxd5 cxd5 10 0-0 ♗c5, as in A.Rudolf-K.Martin, British League 2005, followed by 11 ♕c2 ♕e7 12 ♗f4 supplies a clear plus) 9 exd6 cxd6 (or 9...♗xd6 10 0-0 0-0 11 ♘c3 ♗e6 12 b3 ♕f6, as in Y.Dembo-Chen Peng An, Beijing (blitz) 2008, and then 13 ♕c2 with a standard edge)

10 0-0 ♗e7 11 ♕c2 h6 12 ♘c3 0-0 13 ♗f4 d5 (13...♗e6 14 b3 is slightly better for White as well) 14 cxd5 ♘xd5 was seen in N.Kurenkov-B.Savchenko, St Petersburg 2005, and now the simplest was 15 ♘xd5 cxd5 16 ♗c7! ♕d7 17 ♖ac1 with an edge.

b2) 7...♘e7 also fails to inspire: 8 ♗d3 ♘g6 (otherwise, 8...g6 9 0-0 ♗g7 10 ♖e1 0-0 11 ♘c3 d6 12 ♗f4 ♖e8 13 exd6 cxd6 14 ♘e4 is very good for White, as is 8...d6 9 exd6 cxd6 10 0-0 d5 11 ♕e2) 9 0-0 d6 (9...♗e7 10 ♕h5! d6 11 exd6 cxd6 12 ♗xg6 fxg6 13 ♕f3 also looks pretty bad for Black) 10 exd6 ♗xd6 (10...cxd6 11 ♗e4 is even worse) 11 ♖e1+ ♗e6 and in the game S.Dujkovic-N.Chadaev, Herceg Novi 2006, White could have played 12 ♕c2 0-0 13 c5 (Barsky) with an edge.

b3) With 7...♗b4+ Black tries to exchange a pair of pieces, in order to ease his cramp, but after 8 ♗d2 ♗xd2+ 9 ♕xd2

9...♘e7 (9...♘b6 10 ♗d3 0-0 11 0-0 d5 12 exd6 cxd6 13 ♘c3 is typically good for White) 10 ♘c3 0-0 (White is much better too after 10...d5 11 exd6 ♕xd6 12 ♕xd6 cxd6 13 0-0-0 ♔d7 14 ♘e4) 11 0-0-0 Black is very passive, his pieces are stuck on the back ranks and ...d6 is impossible arrange. Thus White is much better and could seriously consider a kingside attack with h4 and g4.

B1) 6...♘e4

This move has been tried by some strong players on occasion. Black simply plans to support the knight in the centre with ...d5 and play along similar lines to the Open Variation of the Ruy Lopez. Indeed, if necessary, the knight can retreat to e6 via c5. While 6...♘e4 is playable, White is able to obtain an advantage against it. One important point is that an exchange on e4 will not result in Black attacking a knight on f3 when White would have to lose time.

7 ♘d2!

With most other moves well met by 7...d5, White forces Black to decide what to do with his knight.

7...♘c5

Keeping the game fairly complex. Instead 7...♘xd2 8 ♗xd2 is a little too simplistic and passive for Black, who will find it hard to create counterplay:

a) 8...♗c5 9 ♕g4! g6 10 ♕g3 (10 ♗h6 also makes good sense) 10...h6 11 ♗d3 ♕e7 12 0-0 a5 and in M.Kuijf-J.Bollen, Ellmedingen 1978, White could have secured a big plus with 13 ♖ad1 followed by ♗c3 and ♖fe1.

b) 8...g6 9 ♗c4 ♗g7 10 0-0 0-0 11 ♗b4 is unpleasant for Black.

c) 8...d6 9 ♗c3! ♕g5 (or 9...♗e6 10 exd6 cxd6 11 ♕d2 with a clear plus) 10 h4! ♕g6 11 ♕d4 is also nice for White.

d) 8...♕h4 prevents ♕g4 ideas, but after 9 ♗d3 ♗c5 10 0-0 0-0 11 ♕f3 ♖b8 (P.Adamek-P.Zvara, Ceske Budejovice 1997), and then 12 b4! ♖xb4 (worse is 12...♗xb4 13 g3 ♕e7 14 ♖ab1) 13 ♗xb4 ♕xb4 14 c3 White is on top.

e) 8...d5 has been Black's most-popular choice, but after 9 ♗d3 White's bishops are well co-ordinated and he enjoys a structural advantage.

Now 9...♕h4 (otherwise, White is typically better after 9...♗e7 10 ♕h5, while 9...♗e6 10 0-0 ♕d7 11 f4 ♗c5+ 12 ♔h1 ♗f5 was the course of R.Zelcic-S.Baumegger, Portoroz 1998, when White should have played 13 ♕f3! 0-0 14 ♗xf5 ♕xf5 15 ♕c3 with a clear advantage) 10 0-0 ♗c5 11 c4! (the typical plan of pressurizing Black's doubled pawns on the c-file) 11...0-0 (11...dxc4? 12 ♕a4 is plain bad) 12 ♖c1 ♗d4 (no better are 12...♖d8 13 cxd5 ♖xd5 14 ♗c4! ♖xe5 15 ♕f3 and 12...♗g4 13 ♕a4 ♗d4 14 ♗c3 ♗xc3 15 ♖xc3 d4 16 ♖b3!,

with pressure on Black's queenside) 13 ♗c3! (after the exchange of bishops Black has no counterplay and will be permanently worse) 13...♗xc3 (if 13...♗b6 then 14 ♗b4) 14 ♖xc3 ♗e6 (14...d4 15 ♖a3 also doesn't help) 15 f4 and White had a steady structural advantage in P.Vallejo Pons-V.Korchnoi, Vera 2004.

Before returning to 7...♘c5, we should note that naturally 7...d5? is bad: 8 ♘xe4 dxe4 9 ♕xd8+ ♔xd8 10 ♗e3 ♗e6 11 0-0-0+ ♔e8 12 ♖d4 with a clear advantage for White.

8 ♘f3

8...♗e7

Black completes his development before undertaking anything in the centre. Alternatively:

a) 8...d5 9 exd6 cxd6 (or 9...♗xd6 10 ♗c4) 10 ♗e2 ♗e7 11 0-0 0-0 is better for White, provided he doesn't waste time and hits Black's weak spots by following the course of B.Yildiz-R.Pokorna, Dresden 2007: 12 ♘d4! ♗d7 13 ♗f3 d5 (or 13...♕b6 14 ♗e3) 14 c4! ♘e4 15 cxd5 cxd5 16 ♗e3.

b) 8...♘e6 tries to forestall ♘d4 by White, but after the plausible 9 ♗d3 ♗e7 10 0-0 0-0 11 c3 White is set to play the knight move anyway and stands slightly better.

9 ♘d4!

An important move, planning to invade the f5-square.

9...0-0 10 ♗e2 ♖e8

Black might break out, but after 10...f6 11 exf6 ♗xf6 12 0-0 again White has an edge.

11 0-0 ♗f8 12 f4 d6 13 ♗f3!

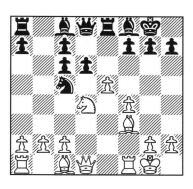

White clearly has appreciable pressure, having responded vigorously to the pressure on e5. The game E.Schmittdiel-L.Gostisa, Buekfuerdo 1995, continued 13...♗b7 (13...dxe5 14 fxe5 was perhaps better, albeit still good for White) 14 b4 dxe5 15 fxe5 and Black's queenside weaknesses had become clearly visible to the naked eye.

B2) 6...♕e7

Time and practice have proven this to be best. Black voluntarily inconveniences his dark-squared bishop, but forces White to reply in kind. Now some very complicated and unusual play commences, as we have already seen. Indeed, in Chapters 1-4 we examined the important variations 7 ♕e2 ♘d5 8 c4 ♗a6 and 8...♘b6. Thus here we'll examine both sides' alternatives in that critical sequence.

7 ♕e2

Essential because White cannot play 7 f4? d6 when he simply loses the e5-pawn.

7...♘d5

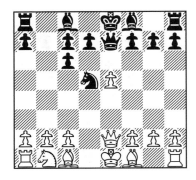

We are approaching the key tabiya of the 4...♘f6 variation. Of course, Black must avoid 7...♕b4+?? 8 c3 and 7...♘g8 is as bad as it was one move earlier. The presence of the queen on e2 somewhat complicates White's development, but not much after 8 g3! and then:

a) 8...d5 was seen in A.Areshchenko-G.Kuzmin, Sudak 2002, and should be met by 9 c4! ♕b4+ 10 ♘d2 ♗c5 11 ♗g2 ♘e7 12 0-0 0-0 13 ♘b3 dxc4 14 ♗d2 when Black loses c4, after which c6 and c7 may follow.

b) 8...♕e6 9 ♘d2 ♗c5 10 ♘f3 ♘h6 11 ♗g2 ♘g4 12 0-0 d5 13 c4 ♗a6 was a commendable effort to play actively in V.Ortiz Fernandez-A.Acebal Muniz, Oviedo 2003, but comes unstuck after the simple 14 b3.

c) 8...f6 9 f4 fxe5 10 fxe5 ♕e6 weakened White's kingside in L.Vajda-B.Itkis, Bucharest 1998, but White could opt for long castling after 11 ♘c3 ♘h6 12 ♗f4 with the advantage.

d) Another disruptive attempt with 8...a5 9 ♘c3 ♗a6 10 ♕e4 ♗xf1 11 ♔xf1 d5 falls short after 12 exd6 ♕xe4 13 d7+ ♔xd7 14 ♘xe4 with a clear advantage.

e) 8...g6 9 ♗g2 ♗g7 10 0-0! and, as 10...♘f6? 11 ♘c3 only makes matters worse for Black, the second player faces serious difficulties untangling his kingside:

e1) The 10...♖b8 11 ♖e1 ♘h6 12 ♘d2 0-0 13 ♘f3 f6 of J.Mieses-E.Lasker, Hastings 1895, could have been strongly met by 14 e6! ♘f5 (or 14...dxe6 15 ♘d4) 15 exd7 ♕xe2 16 ♖xe2 ♗xd7 17 b3 with an obvious plus.

e2) Unfortunately, 10...♗xe5? is met by 11 ♖e1 f6 12 c3 threatening 13 f4.

e3) After 10...♘h6 11 b3 ♕e6 12 ♗a3 f6 (12...♗xe5 is still bad: 13 c3) 13 ♘d2 ♔f7 14 ♘f3 ♘f5 15 ♖ae1 White was pretty much winning in I.Gonzalez-A.Acebal Muniz, Oviedo 2000.

8 c4

Just as after 6...♘d5?!, attacking the knight immediately causes the most discomfort. White has tried some other moves here, mostly aiming to play c4 later and in this way trick the opponent into an inferior sub-variation, mainly because Black cannot yet play ...♗a6. However, Black has at least one good response against each of these ideas:

a) 8 g3 is the most popular alternative and works well against 8...♗a6 players; if they want to try and transpose to their main system, they have to abandon ideas with a quick ...0-0-0 and play something like 8...g6 here, but then White delays c4 further. However, Black can take up the opportunity to invite a favourable transposition with 8...♕e6!, leading to:

a1) 9 c4 ♘b6 transposes to 8 c4 ♘b6 9 g3 ♕e6, which may seem like a moral victory for White but in fact this is not such a good line for him, as we noted at the beginning of Chapter Three.

a2) 9 h4?! is too ambitious and runs into 9...♘b4! 10 c4 (10 a3? is a serious mistake in view of 10...♗a6! 11 c4 ♗xc4 12 ♕xc4 ♕xc4 13 ♗xc4 ♘c2+ 14 ♔e2 ♘xa1 15 b4 a5 with a clear advantage for Black) 10...♕f5!, as given by Emms, After the further 11 ♘a3 ♗c5 12 ♗f4 0-0 Black is much better.

a3) Thus the main independent move is 9 ♗g2, after which 9...f6 (Black rushes to eliminate the e5-pawn, so that his knight can retreat to f6 if hit by c4) 10 0-0 fxe5 11 ♖e1 ♗d6! (even stronger than the 11...♗c5 of B.Gonzalez-E.Dervishi, Turin Olympiad 2006)

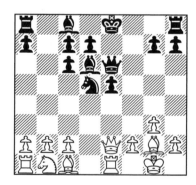

12 ♘d2 0-0 13 ♘e4 ♗e7 14 ♘g5 ♗xg5 15 ♗xg5 ♕f5 gives White has no compensation for the pawn.

b) 8 h4 intends a quick ♖h3 to activate the rook and was once a favourite with John van der Wiel, but appears too speculative. Since the move is largely irrelevant in the fight for the centre, Black can afford to play 8...a5.

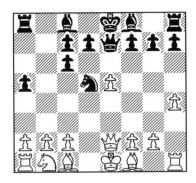

This keeps all Black's options open and after 9 c4 (9 ♗g5? ♛e6 10 c4 ♘b6 11 ♘d2 was preferred in R.Sebe Vodislav-I.Danilov, Bucharest 2000, and now 11...♗b4 12 a3 ♗xd2+ 13 ♗xd2 ♗a6 is very good for Black) 9...♗a6 10 b3 (10 ♖h3?! ♘b6 11 b3 ♛e6 followed by ...♗b4 and ...0-0 also seems promising) 10...f6 11 ♗b2 fxe5 12 ♛h5+ g6 13 ♛xe5 ♘f6 14 h5 ♛xe5+ 15 ♗xe5 ♗b4+ Black certainly has the upper hand.

c) 8 ♘d2 is strongly met by 8...g6! when Black puts the e5-pawn under immediate pressure:

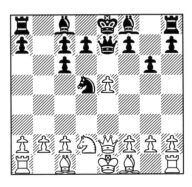

c1) 9 b3? loses material after 9...♛c5 10 ♛e4 ♛c3.

c2) 9 ♘e4 ♗g7 10 c4 ♗a6 (or 10...f5!? 11 ♘g5 ♗a6) 11 ♗g5 (no better is 11 f4 0-0 12 ♛f2 ♛b4+ 13 ♘d2 ♘b6) 11...♛xe5 12 ♘c5 ♛xe2+ 13 ♗xe2 and now Black is better after 13...♘b4! (but not 13...♗xb2? 14 ♖b1 ♗c3+ 15 ♗d2 when two black pieces are hanging).

c3) 9 ♘f3 should be countered by the forcing 9...♛b4+! 10 ♛d2 (10 c3? runs into 10...♘xc3!) 10...♖b8! 11 c4 (Black also has the upper hand after 11 c3 ♛e4+ 12 ♛e2 ♛xe2+ 13 ♗xe2 ♗g7 14 0-0 0-0 and 11 ♗d3 ♘f4! gives him the initiative) ♛xd2+ 12 ♗xd2 ♘b4 13 ♔d1 c5! 14 ♗c3 ♗g7 when White again finds himself on the defensive.

c4) Thus White probably has to go in for 9 c4, but this is fairly well met by 9...♗a6!.

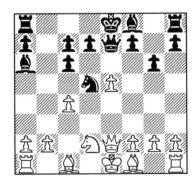

Indeed, as we saw in Line A3 of Chapter One, via the move order 8 c4 ♗a6 9 ♘d2 g6, White has certain problems to solve here.

d) Note too that the other transpositional idea 8 b3?! is met by 8...♕b4+! 9 ♗d2 ♕b6 with the initiative. Here White certainly cannot afford to become embroiled in the line 10 ♘c3?! ♕d4 11 ♕e4 ♗c5 12 ♕xd4 ♗xd4 13 ♘xd5 cxd5 14 0-0-0 ♗xf2.

e) Finally, there is no point in 8 ♕e4 g6 9 ♗c4 (otherwise, 9 ♗d3 ♗g7 10 f4 0-0 11 0-0 d6 is better for Black, but White has missed his chance for 9 c4 in view of 9...f5! 10 ♕d4 ♘b4) 9...♗g7 10 0-0 0-0 11 ♖e1 d6 12 ♗xd5 cxd5 13 ♕xd5 ♖b8 when White is undeveloped and just worse.

We now return to the main line and 8 c4:

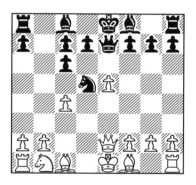

Here Black has two real options, 8...♘b6 and the more complicated 8...♗a6, but some mention must be made of the weaker alternatives:

8...♕b4+

The idea of this check is to gain the f4-square for the knight.

Instead 8...♘b4?! allows White to expand with 9 a3 ♘a6 10 b4! g6 11 f4 ♗b7 12 ♗b2 ♗g7 and now after simply 13 g3 0-0 14 ♗g2 it is obvious that

Black's position is bad.

Likewise, 8...♕c5?! does not contribute to Black's cause after the simple 9 a3. As soon as the c1-bishop is protected, White will start gaining time on both the black knight and queen.

9 ♘d2 ♘f4

9...♗a6 seems annoying, but after simply 10 ♕e4 ♘b6 11 ♗e2 g6 12 f4 White is clearly better.

10 ♕e4

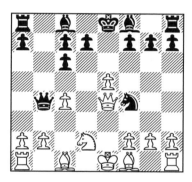

10...♘e6

The alternatives are even worse: 10...♘g6 11 ♗d3 ♗e7 12 0-0 0-0 13 ♘f3 f5 14 ♕e2 d5 15 ♕c2 is much better for White, and so is 10...g5 11 a3 ♕b6 12 ♘f3 ♗c5 13 ♕c2.

11 g3!

An important move. With the knight blockading on e6, Black's only logical plan from a positional viewpoint is to play ...c5 and put his light-squared bishop on b7. By first occupying the long diagonal himself, White prevents this plan and leaves Black in a very passive and fairly senseless position.

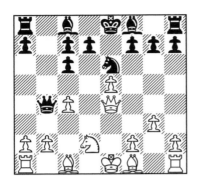

11...♗b7

Black insists on his plan, but he will have to lose further time. Other tries:

a) 11...♗c5 12 ♗g2 a5 13 0-0 a4 14 ♖b1 ♘d4 15 ♕d3 0-0 16 ♘e4 was much better for White in S.Videki-M.Nemeth, Balatonlelle 2003.

b) So was 11...g6 12 a3 ♕c5 13 b4 ♕d4 14 ♖b1 ♗b7 15 ♗g2 ♗g7 16 ♗b2 ♕xe4+ 17 ♘xe4 in W.Tan-C.Aplin, Da Nang 2008.

12 ♗g2 0-0-0

Or 12...♖b8 13 0-0 c5 14 ♕d3 ♗xg2 15 ♔xg2 with a steady edge in R.Shankar-D.Sharma, Muzaffapur 1998.

13 a3 ♕b6 14 0-0

By now in M.Pasman-E.Shvidler, Beer Sheba 1984, White's advantage was obvious: he controls much more space, his position has a lot of potential

and Black is very passive.

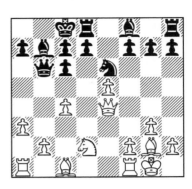

Conclusion

Although 4...♗c5 has been pretty popular in recent years, 4...♘f6 remains the main line of the Scotch. After 5 ♘xc6 bxc6 White gains nothing by avoiding the critical 6 e5. Admittedly some have played for a draw with 6 ♗d3, but the issue is really whether White will make one in the face of powerful and determined play from Black.

In turn Black should not deviate after 6 e5 from the main line sequence 6...♕e7 7 ♕e2 ♘d5 and he should prepare one of the two main defences to 8 c4. That 8th-move isn't forced, but the alternatives, while tricky for an inexperienced player to face, don't bring White much joy against a precise reaction.

Chapter Six

The 4...♗c5 Variation: 5 ♘xc6 ♛f6 6 ♛d2

1 e4 e5 2 ♘f3 ♘c6 3 d4 exd4 4 ♘xd4 ♗c5 5 ♘xc6

White deals with the pressure against d4 by responding just as he does after 4...♘f6. This approach was a cornerstone of Kasparov's Scotch repertoire and a variation in which unsurprisingly he introduced a number of important ideas.

5...♛f6!

A useful intermezzo which forces White to move his queen earlier than he'd like to, but at lower levels Black frequently recaptures the knight without delay:

a) 5...dxc6?! 6 ♛xd8+ ♚xd8 gives Black very little in return for the loss of castling rights and the damage to his structure. Following 7 ♘c3 ♗e6 8 ♘a4!? ♗b4+ 9 c3 ♗d6 10 ♗e3 White enjoyed a pretty pleasant edge in S.Pavlovic-I.Milosavljevic, Dimitrovgrad 2003.

b) Wells noted back in 1998 that 5...bxc6 'is virtually unknown at the highest level', a state of play which has remained true until this day.

If Black wants to go in for this structure he usually flicks in 4...♗b4+ 5 c3 ♗c5 when after 6 ♘xc6 bxc6 (Line A1 of Chapter Eleven) White's knight can't use the c3-square. Here it can, but in any case Black's position isn't too bad, at least so long as he continues actively with a rapid ...♛h4:

a) 6 ♗c4 ♕h4! 7 ♕e2 (wisely avoid-ing 7 0-0?! when even 7...♘f6 8 g3 ♕h3 9 ♕f3 0-0 10 ♘c3, as in E.Petrushko-A.Petrushin, Ilichevsk 2007, and then 10...d6 leaves Black with the initiative) 7...♘f6 8 e5 ♘d5 (or 8...♘g4!? 9 g3 ♗xf2+ 10 ♕xf2 ♘xf2 11 gxh4 ♘xh1 12 ♘c3 with something of a mess in S.Bromberger-G.Giorgadze, Sants 2006) 9 ♘d2 0-0 10 ♘e4 ♗e7 11 g3 ♕h3 12 ♗g5 ♖e8 was okay for Black in M.Zum-sande-M.Solleveld, Haarlem 2009.

b) White likely does better with the more restrained 6 ♗d3 and then:

b1) 6...♘f6?! 7 e5! ♕e7 (7...♘d5 8 ♕g4 takes aim at g7) 8 0-0 ♘d5 9 a3 a5 10 c4 ♘b6 11 ♘d2 d5?! 12 exd6 cxd6 13 ♖e1 ♗e6 14 ♕h5 left Black under heavy pressure in J.Jens-G.Crippa, Arco 2000.

b2) After 6...♘e7 White has often gone in for 7 0-0 0-0 8 ♘c3 ♘g6 9 ♘a4, but this doesn't seem too bad for Black after the solid 9...♗b6. Instead 7 ♘d2!? deserves attention and after 7...♘g6 8 ♘b3 ♗e7 9 0-0 0-0 10 f4 d6 11 ♕h5 White had obtained a decent attacking set-up and the initiative in M.Hennigan-N.Davies, Wrexham 1994.

b3) 6...♕f6 7 0-0 ♘e7 8 ♘c3 ♘g6 (Black must avoid both 8...d6? 9 e5! and 8...0-0?? 9 ♕h5) 9 e5 ♕e7 10 ♘e4 gives White the initiative and after 10...0-0?! 11 ♕h5 ♗d4 12 ♘g5 h6 13 ♘f3 he was somewhat for choice in O.Biti-J.Jambresic, Sibenik 2005.

b4) Thus 6...♕h4! is again the best approach when White must be careful not to castle into a sudden attack.

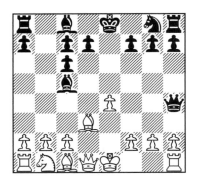

After 7 ♕e2 (instead 7 ♕f3 leaves the queen a little exposed and Black can meet 7...♘f6 8 ♗f4 with 8...d5!? or just 8...d6 when 9 e5 ♘d5 10 ♗g3 ♕b4+ 11 ♘d2 0-0 gave him the initia-tive in M.White-S.Haslinger, Hastings 2008/09) 7...♘f6 8 h3! (taking control of the g4-square; 8 ♗e3 ♗xe3 9 ♕xe3 0-0 10 ♘d2 ♖e8 11 0-0 d6 12 ♖ae1 was preferred in no less a game than M.Carlsen-G.Kamsky, Khanty-Mansiysk 2007, but with 12...♘d5 13 ♕g3 ♕xg3 14 hxg3 ♘b4 Black could have main-tained a rough balance) 8...0-0 (8...d5!? also deserves attention, with the idea of 9 exd5+ ♔f8 10 0-0 ♗xh3!; then White has nothing better than 11 ♗e3 ♗d6 12 gxh3 ♕xh3 13 f4 ♕g3+ with a draw, but even after 9 g3 ♕h5 10 ♕xh5 ♘xh5 Black should have sufficient counterchances) 9 g3 ♕h5 10 g4!? (a more ambitious try than 10 ♕xh5 ♘xh5 11 ♘c3 when 11...d5! 12 ♗d2 ♖e8 13 ♔f1 ♘f6 14 ♖e1 ♗d4 was okay for Black in V.Malisauskas-M.Godena, Novi Sad 2009, and here 12 exd5 cxd5 13 ♘xd5 ♗b7 would have given him good compensation) 10...♕e5! (keeping the queen in play; instead 10...♕h4?! 11 ♘d2 ♘e8 12 ♘b3 sees White taking control and he was somewhat for choice after 12...♗e7? 13 ♘d4! ♗c5 14 ♘f5 in A.Motylev-Liang Chong, Moscow 2001) 11 g5 (unfortunately for White, 11 f4 ♕e7 12 g5? fails to 12...♘xe4! 13 ♗xe4 ♖e8, as pointed out by Marin) 11...♘e8 12 f4 ♕e7 13 ♘d2 d5 14 ♘b3 ♗b6 15 a4 a5 the position was unclear but about equal in I.Nataf-P.Charbonneau, Montreal 2008.

Returning to the main move, 5...♕f6.

6 ♕d2

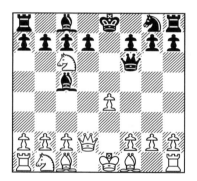

Kasparov's invariable choice when he reached this position, but of late 6 ♕f3!? has become topical, as we'll see in our next chapter. Now Black usually recaptures with his d-pawn, but he isn't forced to:

A: 6...dxc6
B: 6...bxc6
C: 6...♕xc6

A) 6...dxc6

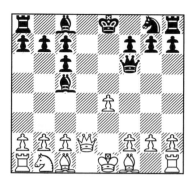

White must now decide how to continue his development:

A1: 7 ♗d3
A2: 7 ♘c3

On occasion he has also tested two other ideas we'll see plenty more of in this chapter, but played immediately both seem a little premature:

a) 7 ♕f4?! hopes for an immediate clarification of the position, but Black doesn't have to oblige. Instead with 7...♕e7! he utilizes the delay in White's development to create threats and grab the initiative: 8 ♗d3 (Black also had the initiative after 8 ♘c3 ♘f6 9 ♗e3 ♗b4 10 ♗d3 ♘g4 11 ♗d2 ♗c5 12 f3 ♘f2 13 ♖f1 ♗d6 in A.Razmyslov-A.Rizouk, Seville 2003) 8...♘f6 9 ♗e3 ♗xe3 10 ♕xe3 ♕b4+ 11 ♘d2 ♕xb2 12 0-0 ♘g4 13 ♕g3 ♕e5 and White had inadequate compensation for the pawn in L.Kritz-A.Leniart, Warsaw 2005.

b) 7 ♗c4 is best met by the direct 7...♗e6. It is true that exchanges generally favour White in this structure, but here Black gains time to develop and is the first to create threats, particularly against the pawn on e4 after 8 ♗xe6 ♕xe6 9 ♘c3 ♘f6 10 0-0 0-0.

Now White must make room for his bishop, but after 11 ♕f4 (no better are 11 ♕e2 ♖fe8 12 ♗f4 ♗d4 or 11 ♕g5 ♗d4 12 ♕f4 ♗e5) 11...♖fe8 12 ♕xc7 ♘xe4 13 ♘xe4 ♕xe4 14 ♕xb7 ♖ab8 15 ♕c7 ♕xc2 Black had won the opening battle in V.Vavpetic-Z.Zvan, Kranj 1999.

A1) 7 ♗d3

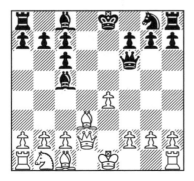

White hurries to complete the development of his kingside, but this approach doesn't put Black under any immediate pressure.

7...♗e6

The most logical move, especially since with the d-file blocked Black can castle long, but he can also prefer to focus on kingside development:

a) 7...♘e7 and then:

a1) 8 ♕f4 ♘g6 9 ♕xf6 gxf6 reaches quite a typical position for the ...♘e7 approach, which we'll see much more of in Line A24, below. Here Black stands well after 10 ♘c3 ♘h4 11 ♔f1 ♖g8 or 10 ♘d2 ♘e5 and 10 ♗e2 ♘h4 11 0-0 ♖g8 12 g3 f5 is also quite nice for the second player.

a2) 8 ♘c3 ♘g6 9 0-0 0-0 10 ♕g5 (hardly any good is 10 ♘a4 ♗d6 11 ♕g5 ♕xg5 12 ♗xg5 ♘f4 13 ♖fe1 ♘xd3 14 cxd3, A.Sabahi-C.Sengul, Antalya 2008, and then 14...♖e8; or the 10 ♔h1 ♘e5 11 f4 ♘xd3 12 ♕xd3 b5 13 ♕f3 b4 14 e5 ♕g6 of M.Lazic-M.Godena, Turin 2002, with an edge for Black in both cases) 10...♕xg5 11 ♗xg5 h6 12 ♗d2 ♖d8 13 ♘a4 ♗d4 14 ♗c3 ♘f4 gave Black the initiative in P.Llaneza Vega-M.Vilar Lopez, La Roda 2000.

a3) 8 0-0 ♘g6 9 ♕g5 (White hurries to get the queens off, partly because the alternative plan, 9 ♔h1 ♘e5 10 ♗e2, can simply be met by 10...♘g4) 9...♕xg5 (Black also equalizes after both 9...♗d4 10 ♘c3 ♕xg5 11 ♗xg5 f6 12 ♗c1 ♘e5 13 ♗e2 ♗e6, as he did in J.Smeets-E.L'Ami, Groningen 2003, and with the 9...♘e5 10 ♕xf6 gxf6 11 ♗e2 ♖g8 12 ♗f4 ♗g4 13 ♗xg4 ♖xg4 14 ♗xe5 fxe5 of J.Broekmeulen-R.Janssen, Dutch League 2007) 10 ♗xg5 f6 11 ♗d2 ♘e5 12 ♗e2 ♗e6 13 ♘c3 0-0-0 14 ♖e1 ♖he8 was equal in J.Broekmeulen-N.Pedersen, Hertogenbosch 2003.

Here Black's active and better-developed forces offset his structural problems.

b) 7...♕e7 prepares ...♘f6 followed by kingside castling and is also a reasonable way to play: for example, 8 0-0 ♘f6 9 ♘c3 0-0 10 ♕g5 h6 11 ♕g3 (better is 11 ♕h4!? when 11...♘g4 12 ♕xe7 ♗xe7 13 ♗f4 gave White an edge in V.Baklan-V.Malaniuk, Donetsk 1998) 11...♘h5 12 ♕f3 ♕h4 13 ♗e2 ♘f6 was seen in S.Rublevsky-A.Morozevich, Maikop 1998, and now Black is fine after the logical 14 ♕f4 ♕xf4 15 ♗xf4 ♖e8.

8 0-0

Continuing his plan, but again there are alternatives:

a) 8 ♘c3 0-0-0 once more sees Black developing smoothly and he even has chances to grab the initiative here.

Indeed, after 9 ♘a4 (we'll see plenty more of this disruptive idea in Line A2) 9...♗d4 10 0-0 ♘h6 11 c3 (or 11 ♕g5 ♘g4 12 ♕xf6 gxf6 13 ♗e2 b5 14 ♘c3 ♘e5 with equality in M.Ragger-G.Gajewski, Aviles 2003) 11...♗e5 12 f4 in A.Strikovic-D.Campora, Seville 2001, Black might have made a temporary piece sacrifice with 12...♘g4! 13 fxe5 ♕xe5 14 g3 b5 and thereby obtained strong counterplay. Thus here White might prefer 9 ♕f4, but practice has shown that Black is fully equal after 9...♕xf4 10 ♗xf4 ♘e7: for example, 11 ♗g3 h5! (a standard reaction to the retreat of the bishop to g3) 12 f4 f5 13 ♗f2 was seen in M.Dluzniewski-D.Sadzikowski, Polanica Zdroj 2008, when 13...♗xf2+ 14 ♔xf2 fxe4 15 ♘xe4 ♘d5 would have left White on the defensive.

b) 8 ♕f4 is again a little too simplistic: 8...0-0-0 (8...♗b4+ !? is a tempting alternative and after 9 c3 0-0-0 10 ♕g3 ♗d6 11 f4 ♗xf4 12 ♗xf4 ♖xd3 13 ♕xd3 ♕xf4 14 ♘d2 ♘f6 Black had the upper hand in B.Savchenko-B.Grachev, Cheboksary 2006) 9 ♕xf6 ♘xf6 10 h3 (Black is on top after all of 10 f3 ♘d7, 10 ♘c3 ♘g4 11 0-0 ♘e5 and 10 ♗g5 ♗d4 11 ♘c3 h6 intending ...♘g4-e5) 10...♖he8 and Black is fine, especially since the natural 11 ♘c3? fails to 11...♘xe4!.

8...0-0-0

Taking stock we can see that Black has castled and will develop his king-side next. He already exerts some pressure down the d-file and White's position is not a model of development and coordination. Indeed, it's hard to believe that such a position can be promising for White and practice has rather borne this out.

9 ♕g5

Forcing the queens off is again quite logical, but White has also tried:

a) 9 ♘c3 ♗c4 (9...♘h6!? is also pretty reasonable and after 10 ♕f4 ♘g4 11 h3 ♘e5 12 ♕xf6 gxf6 Black was able to attack on the kingside in Z.Varga-V.Tkachiev, Rabac 2004) 10 ♕e2 (10 ♘a4 doesn't really achieve anything after just 10...♗xd3 11 cxd3 ♗d4) 10...♗xd3 11 cxd3 ♔b8 12 ♗e3

♗d4 13 ♖ac1 ♘e7 14 ♕d2 ♕e6 was fine for Black in G.Kacheishvili-P.Lukacs, Debrecen 1992.

b) 9 ♕e2 ♘h6 (this might be prefaced by 9...h5!? and after 10 e5?! ♕e7 11 ♘d2 ♘h6 12 ♔h1 ♘g4 13 ♘f3 ♗d5 Black was better in J.Ehlvest-J.Fernandez Garcia, Pamplona 1991, while 10 ♔h1 ♘h6 11 ♘d2 ♘g4 12 ♘f3 ♖de8 13 c3 ♕d8 14 ♗c2 f6 15 b4 ♗d6 gave him the initiative in B.Erdos-E.Remete, Mako 2009) 10 h3 ♖he8 (perhaps White should have played it safe with 10 ♘d2, since here 10...g5!? 11 ♕h5 ♖hg8 12 ♘c3 ♕g7 13 ♗d2 f6 saw Black menacing aggressive intent in D.Sebastian-T.Straeter, German League 2005) 11 ♘d2 ♗b8 12 ♘f3 ♕e7 13 ♗e3 f6 was about equal in the gane F.Sebe Vodislav-S.Kapnisis, Oropesa del Mar 1999.

c) 9 ♕f4 ♕xf4 (also nothing wrong with 9...♗d4) 10 ♗xf4 ♘e7 11 ♘d2 ♘g6 12 ♗g3 ♗d4! 13 ♖fb1 h5! highlights the problems White can face finding a role for his dark-squared bishop.

On the kingside the bishop becomes

a target and here 14 h3 h4 15 ♗h2 would have left Black ahead in the attacking stakes in R.Lau-R.Sherbakov, European Cup 1992, after 15...♘e5.

9...♗d4

Naturally there's nothing wrong either with 9...♕xg5 10 ♗xg5 f6 11 ♗d2 (a little passive, but safer than 11 ♗f4, after which the 11...g5!? 12 ♗g3 of J.Lachowicz-E.Hofer, Mureck 2007, should have been followed up with the consistent 12...h5! 13 h4 ♗d4) 11...♘e7 when Black has good play on the dark squares and down the d-file, with his knight set to come to either e5 or f4.

White can try to prevent this outcome with 12 ♔h1, but after 12...g5!? (12...♗d4 is also pretty logical) 13 f4 gxf4 14 ♗c3 ♖hf8 15 ♖xf4 in R.Servat-L.Bronstein, Buenos Aires 1991, 15...♘g6 would have revealed that he had failed in his aims. Instead 12 ♘c3 gets on with development, but after 12...♘g6 13 ♘a4 ♗d4 14 ♗c3 ♘e5 15 ♗e2 ♗c4 Black had at the least no problems in J.Bejtovic-B.Thorfinnsson, Valby 2008.

10 ♘c3

There's no need for White to fear an exchange on c3, but 10 ♕xf6 ♘xf6 11 ♘d2 has also been seen when 11...c5! 12 h3 ♖he8 leaves Black well centralized.

Again we see White is yet to complete his development and with 13 ♖e1 (13 ♘f3? cost White a pawn after 13...c4 14 ♘xd4 ♖xd4 15 ♗e3 ♖dd8 in K.Eisenbeiser-C.Martin Luis, Budapest 2003) 13...c4 14 ♗xc4 ♗xc4 15 ♘xc4 ♖xe4 Black guaranteed himself full equality at least in F.Sebe Vodislav-A.Bochkarev, Bucharest 2001.

10...♕xg5 11 ♗xg5 f6 12 ♗c1 ♘e7 13 ♘e2 ♗b6 14 ♔h1 c5!

After a logical sequence, we again see Black making good use of his c-pawn to pose problems. The game R.Lagerman-T.L.Petrosian, Kemer 2007, continued 15 b3 ♞c6 16 ♞f4 ♝f7 17 ♞d5!?, but now 17...♝xd5 18 exd5 ♖xd5 wouldn't have given White quite enough for his pawn.

A2) 7 ♞c3

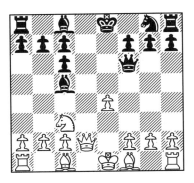

As there is hardly a better square for the knight, it is no surprise that White usually develops it without delay to c3. Black must now decide whether to continue his own development or to try to disrupt White's:

A21: 7...♕e7
A22: 7...♝b4
A23: 7...♝e6
A24: 7...♞e7
A25: 7...♝d4

White has the idea of 8 ♞a4, but it's not entirely clear that it counts as a concrete threat, so unsurprisingly prac-

tice has also seen some lesser options:

a) 7...♞h6?! is hardly effective, as is shown by 8 ♕f4 ♕e7 (White is better too after both 8...♞g4 9 f3 ♞e5 10 ♝e3 ♕xf4 11 ♝xf4 and 8...♕g6 9 ♕e5+ ♝e7 10 f3) 9 ♝e3 ♝d6 10 ♕g5 f6 11 ♕h5+ ♞f7 12 f4! ♝b4 13 ♝d3 ♝xc3+ 14 bxc3 ♝e6 15 0-0 b6 16 a4 with a clear edge for White in S.Tiviakov-Z.Gyimesi, Groningen 1999.

b) 7...a6 has the obvious idea of safeguarding the bishop from the threat of ♞a4, but there are more constructive ways of doing so, as we will see. White can obtain an edge in more than one way against this slow move, the most consistent being 8 ♕f4 ♝e6 9 ♕g3 0-0-0 10 ♝e3 ♝xe3 11 ♕xe3 ♕d4 (Black tried 11...♕h6? in B.Macieja-V.Ivanchuk, Moscow 2001, but it completely failed against White's reaction of 12 f4 ♞f6 13 ♝d3 ♖he8 14 0-0! ♕xh2+ 15 ♔xh2 ♞g4+ 16 ♔g3 ♞xe3 17 ♖f3 ♞c4 18 f5 when Ivanchuk was in some trouble) 12 ♕xd4 ♖xd4 13 ♝d3 with the usual safe edge.

c) 7...♝d7 has been tried fairly often, but it compares unfavourably to the more common 7...♝e6 as the bishop is less active on d7. White should respond in a similar manner to how he plays in Line A23, namely with 8 ♝d3 0-0-0 (Black is under pressure after both 8...♞e7 9 0-0 0-0-0 10 ♞a4 ♝d6 11 ♕a5 ♕e5 12 ♕xe5 ♝xe5, as in N.Guliev-Z.Mamedjarova, Baku 2001, and then 13 ♞c5, and the 8...♝d4 9 0-0 0-0-0 10 ♞e2 ♝c5 11 ♖b1! ♞h6 12 b4 ♝e7 13

♗b2 of Y.Berthelot-M.Mesli, French League 2002) 9 ♘a4!.

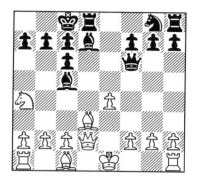

With Black's light-squared bishop on e6 he can obtain sufficient counterplay with 9...♗d4, as we saw in note 'a' to White's 8th move in Line A1. Here, however, the pseudo-active 9...♗d4?! gave White some advantage after 10 0-0 c5 11 ♕a5 ♕c6 12 ♗f4! c4 13 ♗e2 ♔b8 14 ♖ad1 in D.Pavasovic-Wong Meng Kong, Istanbul Olympiad 2000. Neither, though, is the meek 9...♗b6?! at all ideal for Black: 10 ♘xb6+ cxb6 11 a4! ♘e7 12 0-0 h6 13 ♕e3 ♔b8 14 ♕g3+ ♔a8 15 a5 already left him close to being lost in O.Chebotarev-A.Kuznetsov, St.Petersburg 1998, without White really having had to do anything special. Thus Black should retreat with 9...♗d6, but after 10 ♕a5 ♕d4 (10...♔b8 11 ♗g5 ♗b4+ 12 ♕xb4 ♕xg5 13 ♘c5 is also good for White) 11 0-0 c5 12 ♘c3 ♔b8 13 ♘b5 ♗xb5 14 ♕xb5, which Pavasovic has twice been fortunate enough to reach as White, the bishop-pair promises the first player a long-lasting plus.

d) The same ♘a4 and ♕a5 method applies after 7...♗g4 too: 8 ♗d3 0-0-0 9 0-0 ♘e7 10 ♘a4! ♗d6 (10...♗b6? 11 ♘xb6+ cxb6 12 a4 is clearly bad for Black) 11 ♕a5 ♕e5 12 ♕xe5 ♗xe5 13 ♗e3 and had a plus in T.Abergel-G.Michalet, Issy les Moulineaux 2002.

e) Against 7...♕g6 White should undertake some action with 8 f4!? (here the standard 8 ♕g5 fails to bring any dividends, in view of 8...♗d4 9 ♕xg6 hxg6 10 ♗f4 ♘f6 11 ♗d3 ♘g4 12 0-0 ♗e5 13 ♗xe5 ♘xe5 followed by ...g5, which was fine for Black in S.Bohnenblust-C.Boschetti, Swiss League 1996) 8...♗d7 9 ♗d3 a6, but must then find a way to untangle his pieces and house his king.

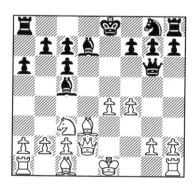

Here in L.Mkrtchian-M.Shukurova, Bled Olympiad 2002, the correct solution was 10 f5! ♕g4 11 g3 followed by ♕f4 with the advantage.

A21) 7...♕e7

Black partially subtracts his fifth move, but wants to classically develop his knight to f6.

8 ♕g5!

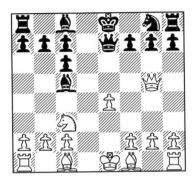

Naturally White is happy to offer the exchange of queens, especially with Black having already moved his queen twice.

Instead 8 ♗d3 ♘f6 9 h3 (it's too late for 9 ♕g5?!, because after 9...h6 10 ♕xg7? ♗xf2+! 11 ♔xf2 ♖g8 the queen is trapped, as noted by Mikhalevski) 9...♗e6 10 0-0 0-0-0 11 ♕e2 ♘d7 12 ♘a4 ♗d6 13 f4 f6 14 ♗e3 g5 gave Black the initiative and was a good demonstration of his aims in M.Paragua-M.Godena, Milan 2001.

8...f6

Kicking the queen away, but now the knight won't be able to come to f6 after all. Thus Black might prefer one of:

a) 8...♘f6?! is best met by 9 ♗e3! intending 0-0-0 and then:

a1) 9...♗b4? fails to 10 e5! ♘g4 (or 10...♘e4?! 11 ♕xg7! ♖f8 12 a3!, as in I.Nataf-A.Kharitonov, Koszalin 1999, and now Mikhalevski gives the nice variation 12...♗a5 13 ♗d3! ♘xc3 14 ♗d2 ♕c5? 15 b4 ♗xb4 16 axb4 ♕xb4

17 e6! f6 18 0-0! with a winning position) 11 ♕xg7! ♖f8 12 ♕g5 ♗xc3+ 13 bxc3 ♕a3 14 ♗d2 with a clear plus in M.Paragua-D.Isonzo, Milan 2001.

a2) 9...♗xe3?! 10 ♕xe3 0-0 11 ♗d3 ♖e8 12 0-0 ♕b4 13 ♕c1 ♗e6 14 a3 was also better for White in L.Cernousek-M.Kislov, Trinec 2003;

a3) 9...♗d6 improves, but can be answered by the simple 10 ♗e2! h6 11 ♕h4 0-0 12 ♗d4 ♖e8 (A.Motylev-V.Ivanchuk, Moscow (rapid) 2002) 13 f3 with a steady edge, rather than the 10 ♗d4 0-0 11 0-0-0 h6 12 ♕h4 b5 13 ♗d3 ♘d7 14 ♕xe7 ♗xe7 15 f4 ♘c5 of S.Tiviakov-E.Van den Doel, Leeuwarden 2002, which was less clear and probably fine for Black.

b) 8...♗d4 9 ♕xe7+ ♘xe7 10 ♗f4 f5 sees Black allow the queens to come off, but does look quite active for him.

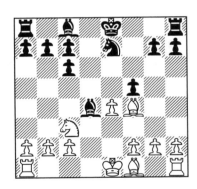

However, White can defuse any activity with the vigorous 11 0-0-0! ♗xf2 (or 11...♗xc3 12 ♗xc7! ♗d7 13 bxc3 fxe4 14 ♖e1 with some advantage in this open position in J.Van der Wiel-O.Korneev, Elgoibar 1998) 12 ♗c4!?

(Mikhalevski), with the safer king, an attack on c7 and thus a powerful initiative.

c) 8...♛xg5 9 ♝xg5 should give White a small but steady edge, such as after 9...f6 10 ♝f4 ♝d6 11 ♝e3.

9 ♛g3

The best square, eyeing c7 as well as g7.

9...♝e6

White also obtained the initiative after 9...♝d6 10 f4! ♞h6 11 ♝e2 ♝d7 12 ♝e3 b6 13 0-0 0-0-0 14 a4 in M.Paragua-P.Kotsur, Doha 2003.

10 ♝e3

Forcing Black to make a decision over his bishop, whereas nothing was promised by 10 ♝d3 0-0-0 11 ♝e3 ♞h6 12 ♝xc5 ♛xc5 13 h3 g5! 14 0-0-0 ♞f7 in V.Kotrotsos-A.Mastrovasilis, Ermioni 2005.

10...♝d6

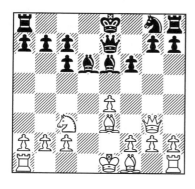

White has more than caught up in the development stakes and now has two routes to a pleasant advantage:

a) 11 f4 ♞h6 12 ♝e2 0-0-0 13 0-0 ♝c5 14 ♞a4 ♝xe3+ 15 ♛xe3 saw White

secure an edge in B.Macieja-A.Mastrovasilis, Antalya 2004.

b) 11 ♝f4 ♝xf4 12 ♛xf4 0-0-0 13 ♝d3 ♞h6 14 0-0-0 ♛c5 15 h3 ♞f7 16 ♖he1 supplied a steady plus in B.Vuckovic-A.Shchekachev, Paris 2004.

A22) 7...♝b4

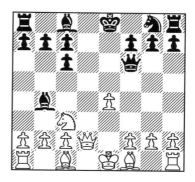

Black decides to ruin White's structure with an exchange on c3, but this is not such a good idea: the pawn ending after the exchange of all the pieces remains, generally-speaking, winning for White and he is not really bothered by the resulting structural defect in the middlegame either. On the contrary, his bishop-pair becomes quite strong, especially in conjunction with the obvious plan of castling short followed by pushing the e- and f-pawns.

8 ♝d3

White opts for the simplest approach, but there is a promising alternative: 8 ♛e3!? ♛e7 9 ♝d2 ♞f6, as in A.Mikhalchishin-V.Zheliandinov, Ptuj 2000, and then 10 0-0-0!? with an edge, since 10...♞g4?! doesn't work out well after 11 ♕g3 ♗c5 12 ♗e1 when the knight will be kicked back.

8...♗e6

White's simple plan comes into operation after both 8...♘e7 9 0-0 0-0 10 a3 ♗d6 11 f4 and 8...♗xc3 9 bxc3 ♘e7 10 0-0 0-0 11 ♖b1. In neither case does Black have an easy way to oppose this plan.

9 0-0 0-0-0 10 ♕e3!

Now that Black has castled long, White switches his attention to the queenside.

10...♔b8

Black's position is already quite grim and the alternatives are hardly inspiring:

a) 10...♗xc3 11 bxc3 ♔b8 was seen in S.Voitsekhovsky-N.Purgin, St.Petersburg 2000, and now 12 ♖b1 gives White the useful ideas of e5, c4 and ♗b2, with a powerful initiative.

b) 10...♕d4 11 ♘e2 ♕xe3 12 ♗xe3 a6 13 ♘d4 saw Black eliminate the main danger in S.Docx-W.Bor, Belgian League 2003, but his structural defect remained, as did White's unquestion-

able edge.

11 ♕g3 ♕g6 12 ♘e2 ♘e7

Again the exchange of queens by means of 12...♕xg3 13 ♘xg3 ♘f6 14 ♗g5 would leave White on top. Thus the text was preferred in B.Vuckovic-B.Ferrandi, Calvi 2007, where 13 ♗e3 h5?! (a misguided advance, thanks to which Black loses the option of ...hxg6 in the event of an exchange of queens) 14 a3 ♗d6 15 ♕xg6 ♘xg6 16 f4 saw White's pawns beginning to roll with some intent.

A23) 7...♗e6

With this move Black puts his bishop on a more active square than d7, but White is ready with a powerful rejoinder.

8 ♘a4!

The star move. Rather than try to catch up in development, White places his knight on the rim just to attack Black's bishop. This may seem totally amateurish and against all the standard principles of opening play, but it works! By losing his dark-squared bishop from the g1-a7 diagonal Black will find that he has fewer tactical opportunities later on and, moreover, there isn't an ideal retreat square. Thus it seems that White obtains just enough time to develop, restore some harmony in his position and obtain certain chances to secure a permanent edge.

On the other hand, the alternatives have not fared too well. We examined the natural 8 ♝d3 by transposition in note 'a' to White's 8th move in Line A1, while Black obtains easy and good counterplay after 8 ♛f4 0-0-0! 9 ♛xf6 ♘xf6.

After 8 ♘a4 Black must decide what to do with his bishop, with his two most important choices being:

A231: 8...♜d8
A232: 8...♝d6

That leaves:

a) 8...♝d4 9 c3 ♝b6 allows White a simple edge after 10 ♝d3 ♘e7 11 ♘xb6 axb6 12 0-0 0-0 13 ♛f4.

b) 8...♝b6 9 ♘xb6 axb6 10 a3 ♘e7 11 ♝d3 0-0 12 ♛f4 ♛xf4 13 ♝xf4 ♜ac8 was seen in S.Rudolf-H.Wall, Willingen 2004, and now after 14 0-0-0 White is simply better.

c) 8...♝e7 is rather passive, but at least it keeps the bishop out of harm's way. In addition, this retreat takes the sting out of ♛a5, because it will no long carry the threat of ♝g5. In fact it is

by no means so simple for White to prove an advantage here, but with 9 ♝d3 he has good prospects of emerging with one:

c1) 9...♛d4 10 ♘c3 ♘f6 11 ♛e3! (it seems that only this accurate move promises White anything; Black was certainly fine after 11 ♘e2 ♛c5 12 0-0 0-0-0 13 ♛e1 ♘g4 14 ♘f4 ♝d6 15 h3 h5! 16 ♘xe6 fxe6 in N.Gavrilakis-A.M.Botsari, Athens 1996) 11...♛b6 (after 11...♛xe3+ 12 ♝xe3 ♘g4 13 ♝f4 the knight does not manage to come to e5 in time to disturb White) 12 0-0 0-0-0 13 h3 and White, having prevented the annoying manoeuvre ...♘g4-e5, maintains his modest plus.

c2) 9...b5 allows the bishop to return to c5, at the cost of weakening the queenside, and after 10 ♘c3 ♝c5 11 f4 ♜d8 12 ♛e2 ♛e7 13 ♝e3 ♘f6 14 h3 ♝xe3 15 ♛xe3 White was better in D.Makalov-A.Smirnov, Dagomys 2004.

c3) 9...0-0-0 10 ♛e3 (it is important to deny Black the option of ...♛d4 and nothing comes from 10 ♛a5 ♚b8 11 ♝e3 b6) 10...b6 11 0-0 was seen in

A.Felsberger-A.Sorin, Moscow Olympiad 1994. Now with 11...♕h4 12 ♘c3 ♘f6 Black could have obtained fairly decent play, but his structural defects should still enable White to claim a tiny plus.

A231) 8...♖d8

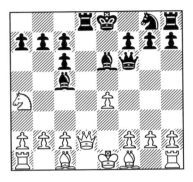

The most popular continuation, trying to retain the bishop on the active g1-a7 diagonal.

9 ♗d3

White has no choice, as 9 ♕f4? is a blunder in view of 9...♗xf2+! 10 ♔xf2 (10 ♕xf2? ♖d1+ 11 ♔e2 ♗g4+ 12 ♔e3 ♕d4+ loses immediately) 10...♕d4+.

9...♗d4

This is the idea behind 8...♖d8. Even here the modest retreats of the bishop remain acceptable, although Black has, of course, lost the option of queenside castling, which allows White good chances for an edge:

a) 9...♗e7 10 0-0 ♘h6 (White is better too after 10...♕d4 11 ♘c3 ♘f6 12 ♘e2 ♕c5 13 ♘f4) 11 h3 0-0 12 ♕e3 b6 13 f4 ♕d4 14 ♕xd4 ♖xd4 15 ♘c3 and White enjoyed an advantage in

D.Kamphausen-O.Gutt, Bergisch Gladbach 2006, having been just in time to prevent the activation of Black's pieces.

b) 9...♗d6 10 ♕a5! highlights the difference with 8...♗d6 (Line A232). White can now afford this annoying move and after 10...b6 11 ♕c3 ♕xc3+ 12 ♘xc3 ♘e7 13 f4 f6 14 ♗d2 he enjoyed a steady edge in R.Hendriks-A.Meijere, Dieren 1997. Here he also enjoys an edge after the ambitious 10 f4!? ♕h4+ (otherwise, 10...♘h6 is met by 11 ♕c3 ♕xc3+ 12 ♘xc3 f6 13 h3, while 10...♕d4 11 ♘c3 ♗b4 12 a3 ♗a5 13 b4 ♗b6 14 ♗b2 is good too for White) 11 ♕f2 ♗b4+ 12 ♘c3 ♕xf2+ 13 ♔xf2 ♗c5+ 14 ♗e3 ♗xe3+ 15 ♔xe3, as in E.Grzybowski-S.Kurpiewski, Augustow 1997.

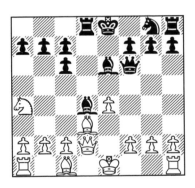

10 0-0!

One point behind Black's play is that the seemingly natural 10 c3?! runs into the powerful blow 10...♗xf2+! and after the forcing sequence 11 ♕xf2 ♖xd3! (but not the inaccurate 11...♕xf2+? 12 ♔xf2 ♖xd3 because of Yusupov's 13 ♘c5 ♖d8 14 ♘xb7 ♖b8 15 ♘c5 ♘e7 16 b3 intending ♗a3 and ♘xe6, with a big plus for White) 12 ♕xf6 ♘xf6 13 ♘c5 ♖d8 14 ♘xb7 ♖b8 15 ♘c5 ♖b5! 16 b4 ♘xe4! 17 a4 (17 ♘xe4? ♖e5 is clearly bad for White, who is losing his extra piece) 17...♖xc5! 18 bxc5 ♗c4 Black's prospects are no worse, despite the exchange minus; his pieces are very active and the white king exposed. Black's compensation is enduring and very dangerous, as was shown by 19 ♗e3 0-0 20 ♗d4 ♖b8 21 0-0-0 ♗e2, with a strong initiative in M.Hennigan-J.Parker, British League 2006.

Neither does 10 ♕f4 work: 10...b5! 11 ♕xf6 ♘xf6 12 ♘c3 ♘g4 13 ♘d1 0-0 and White was worse in M.Aseeva-S.Bezgodova, St.Petersburg 2000.

10...b5!?

White was by now threatening 11 c3, so Black decides to meet it head-on. The alternatives have not fared so well: a) 10...♘e7?! 11 c3 ♘g6 (with 11...a6 Black tried to be smart in A.Vouldis-U.Garbisu, Rotterdam 1998, but after the simple 12 ♕e2 ♗a7 13 ♗e3 ♗xe3 14 ♕xe3 b6 15 f4 White obviously has the upper hand, while 11...b5 12 cxd4 ♕xd4 is bad because of 13 ♕a5! ♕xd3 14 ♘c5 with a serious plus) 12 ♕e2 ♗e5 13 f4 and Black's pieces are being pushed back.

b) 10...♘h6 is simply met by 11 h3 0-0 (or 11...a6 12 ♕f4 ♕xf4 13 ♗xf4 with an edge) 12 c3 b5 13 cxd4 ♕xd4 14 ♕c2 and White is better, J.Dukhin-B.Kovanova, Serpukhov 2002.

c) The sensible 10...a6 was chosen in some top-level games, including the one where Kasparov introduced his then new concept of 8 ♘a4. Black safeguards his bishop, but this gives White just enough time to untangle:

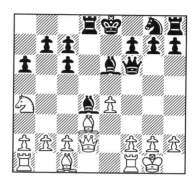

c1) Kasparov settled for the simple and likely best 11 ♘c3, and after 11...♘e7 (or 11...c5 12 ♘d5! ♗xd5 13 exd5 ♘e7, as in M.Golubev-A.Onischuk, Alushta 1994, when 14 c3 ♗e5 15 ♕e2 0-0 16 ♖e1 would have left White better) 12 ♘e2 ♗b6 (White regains his pawn with some advantage after 12...♗xb2?! 13 ♗xb2 ♕xb2 14 ♖ab1) 13 ♕f4 ♘g6?! (relatively better, but similarly favourable for White is 13...♕xf4 14 ♘xf4) 14 ♕xf6 gxf6 15 ♘g3 h5 16 ♗e2 he was comfortably better in G.Kasparov-N.Short, World Championship (Game 17), London 1993.

c2) White has also tried 11 ♕a5, attacking the weak spot on c7, but then 11...b6! (11...b5?! 12 ♘c3 ♗b6 13 ♕xa6 does not provide Black with enough compensation, and no improvement are any of 11...♕e7?! 12 ♗f4!, 11...♗e5 12 f4 or 11...♕e5?! 12 ♕xe5 ♗xe5 13

♘c5 ♗c8 14 a4 ♘e7 15 ♔h1 0-0 16 f4, the last occurring in V.Tseshkovsky-A.Stambulian, Krasnodar 2001) 12 ♕xa6 ♗c8 13 ♕a7 b5 14 ♘c5 ♕e5 15 ♗e3 ♗xe3 16 fxe3 ♘f6 reaches a complicated position which has been debated in some games. It seems that White does not have any advantage here: for example, D.Pavasovic-D.Flores, Internet blitz 2000, saw 17 ♗e2! 0-0 18 ♘d3 ♕xe4 with approximate equality.

d) 10...♕h4 11 ♕g5! ♕xg5 12 ♗xg5 ♘e7 13 ♖fd1 gives White a small edge.

e) So too does 10...♕e7 11 c3 ♗f6 12 ♕e3.

11 ♘c3

The knight must return to c3, as here White cannot go in for the position after 11 c3?! bxa4 12 cxd4 ♕xd4 when Black has good play: 13 ♕g5 ♘e7 14 ♗c2 ♕c4 15 ♕xg7 ♖g8 16 ♕c3 ♕xc3 17 bxc3 ♗h3 18 g3 ♗xf1 19 ♔xf1 and here in B.Golubovic-H.Kummer, Oberwart 1999, White had compensation for the exchange, but it is not possible to speak of any advantage.

11...♘e7

Black cannot possibly count on equality after either 11...♗xc3 12 bxc3 ♗c4 13 a4 or the 11...♘h6 12 a4 a6 13 ♕f4 ♘g4 14 ♕xf6 gxf6 15 ♘e2 of T.Shaked-B.Spassky, Hoogeveen 1998.

12 a4!

This strong move clarifies White's advantage. Now Black's queenside is destabilized and further weakened.

12...a6

Alternatively, 12...b4 13 ♘e2 c5 14 ♘xd4 ♕xd4 (even worse is 14...♖xd4?! 15 ♕e3 0-0 16 ♕g3, which saw White beginning to really press on the dark squares in A.Hnydiuk-P.Liwak, Czestochowa 1998) 15 ♕f4 c4 16 ♗e2 has been shown to give White an advantage, including by, amongst others, the game J.Nunn-G.Flear, Isle of Man 1994.

13 axb5

Both the 13 ♔h1 0-0 14 f4 ♗xc3 15 bxc3 of N.Sedlak-D.Rybansky, Balatonlelle 2001, and 13 ♕f4 ♕xf4 14 ♗xf4, as tried in several games, promise White the upper hand too, but the text is the most consistent approach.

13...axb5

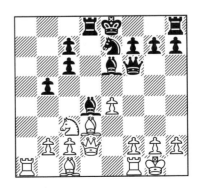

Now a simple solution is 14 ♛f4!? ♛xf4 15 ♝xf4 ♝b6 16 ♖fe1, with an obvious edge. In any case, though, White has the upper hand and slowly but surely increased his advantage with 14 ♔h1 0-0 15 f4 ♛h4 16 ♞e2 ♝b6 17 f5 ♝c4 18 b3 ♝xd3 19 cxd3 in V.Ivanchuk-F.Amonatov, Odessa (rapid) 2007.

A232) 8...♝d6!

It seems that this is Black's best option. Instead of renouncing the option of castling queenside, he simply retreats the bishop to the most natural square and will continue his development. Now White must either accept the fact that moving the knight to a4 was time-consuming or waste even more time trying to activate it via c5. It looks like Black is exposed to f4 followed by e5, but in fact he can easily meet this plan.

9 ♛e3

White frees his dark-squared bishop and introduces the ideas of a timely ♞c5 or ♛g3. With his light-squared

bishop still on f1 he must avoid 9 ♛a5? ♛d4, but has also tried:

a) 9 f4?! is aggressive but leaves White too exposed on the kingside. The simplest response is 9...♞h6! 10 h3 (10 e5? ♝xe5 11 fxe5 ♛h4+ 12 ♛f2 ♛xa4 is Black's idea) 10...0-0-0 11 ♛f2 ♖he8 and Black's initiative was growing in S.Kristjansson-S.Azarov, Oropesa del Mar 1998.

b) 9 ♝d3 aims to complete development, but things are again not so simple after the incisive 9...♞h6!? (9...0-0-0 is also possible) 10 h3 (or 10 ♛g5 ♛xg5 11 ♝xg5 ♞g4 12 h3 ♞e5 13 ♝e2 f6 14 ♝e3 ♞c4 with the initiative in N.Panagiotakos-F.Bellia, Rethymnon 2009) 10...0-0-0 11 ♛e3 ♔b8 (N.Udovnichenko-V.Kiriushin, Belorechensk 2007) 12 0-0 ♖hg8. Here Black prepares ...g5-g4, but it's not easy to see where White's play is.

9...♞h6

Again we see this development of the knight and now the threat of ...♞g4 forces White to expend another tempo. Moreover, once White has gone h3 he will lose the option of offering a queen exchange with ♕g3, which turns e5 into a decent post for the black queen.

10 h3 0-0

Simple and good, but an interesting alternative is 10...♕g6, provoking a weakness: 11 g4 0-0 12 ♗d2 ♖fe8 (earlier 12...b5 13 ♘c3 b4 was unclear in D.Pavasovic-O.Korneev, Nova Gorica 2002, and it is interesting that Pavasovic himself chose this line as Black in a later game) 13 0-0-0 b5 14 ♗d3 bxa4 15 e5 f5 and Black had good play in J.Kozamernik-D.Pavasovic, Rogla 2002.

11 ♗e2

Other moves do not fare any better:

a) 11 g4 ♕e5 (but not 11...♕h4 12 ♕g5! ♕xg5 13 ♗xg5 with an edge for White) 12 g5 (Black has the initiative after 12 ♗d2 ♗d5 13 ♗d3 ♖ae8 14 ♘c3 f5) 12...♕a5+ 13 ♗d2 (or 13 ♘c3 ♘f5! 14 exf5 ♗d5! with a big plus; this and other lines have been pointed out by Wells) 13...♕xa4 14 b3 (no better is 14 gxh6 ♕xc2) 14...♕a3 15 gxh6 g6 and White is definitely worse.

b) 11 ♗d3 is more sensible, although 11...♕e5 (or 11...♖fe8 12 0-0 ♕h4) 12 ♘c3 ♗c5 is fine for Black.

11...♖fe8 12 ♘c3 ♗e5

The correct piece here. Black might like to go 12...♕e5?!, but after 13 f4 ♕a5 14 ♗d2 White had an edge in Su.Polgar-Xie Jun, 7th matchgame, Jaen 1996.

13 0-0 ♖ad8 14 ♔h1 ♗c8

We've followed the game M.Narciso Dublan-J.Candela Perez, Zamora 1996,

where it was clear that it was Black who enjoyed a light initiative.

A24) 7...♘e7

When 7...♗e6 was looking under a cloud and before the advent of 7...♗d4, this move was Black's main choice. Black renounces ideas of castling long for a while, preferring to concentrate on fighting for the central dark squares by bringing his knight to g6.

8 ♕f4

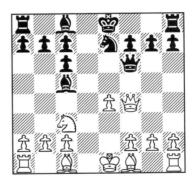

The main move. White hopes the fact that the c7-pawn is attacked means he will be able to exchange the queens, at the same time freeing his pieces for further development. As we will see, this is his only reasonable way to proceed and the method 7...♗d4 is designed to prevent. That said, it turns out that Black is not too perturbed by the queen exchange and can even try to avoid it by sacrificing the c-pawn.

Alternatively:

a) 8 ♗d3 takes play into a position we saw in note 'a1' to Black's 7th move in Line A1.

b) 8 ♘a4?! is hardly effective here: 8...♗d6 9 f4 (both 9 ♗d3 ♘g6 10 ♛g5 ♛d4 11 ♘c3 h6 12 ♛e3 ♛e5 13 ♗d2 ♘f4 14 ♛xf4 ♛xf4 15 ♗xf4 ♗xf4, as in L.Fantin-U.Krstic, Cannes 1997, and the 9 ♛g5 ♛e6 10 ♗d3 h6 11 ♛e3 ♘g6 of P.Pascal-J.Lamorelle, Cannes 2000, fail to achieve anything either) 9...♘g6 (9...0-0 is another good option: 10 ♛f2 ♘g6! 11 g3 – the ambitious 11 e5?! runs into 11...♘xe5 12 fxe5 ♛xe5+ 13 ♗e3 ♗g4 with fantastic compensation for Black in I.Balinov-*Deep Blue Junior*, Vienna 1997 – 11...♖e8 12 ♗d3 b5 13 ♘c3 b4 and Black had the upper hand in P.Boukal-Z.Straka, Czech League 2004) 10 g3 ♗g4! and now:

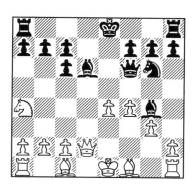

b1) 11 h3?? lost to 11...♗f3 12 ♗g2 ♗xf4! 13 gxf4 ♘h4 in B.Savchenko-E.Tomashevsky, Cheboksary 2006.

b2) Again 11 e5?! ♘xe5 12 fxe5 ♗xe5 13 ♗e2 ♗xe2 14 ♛xe2 0-0-0 seems very dangerous for White.

b3) 11 ♛f2 0-0-0 12 ♗d3 ♗b4+ 13 ♗d2 ♗xd2+ 14 ♔xd2 ♖d4 gave Black a serious initiative in M.Ragger-E.Romanov, Peniscola 2002.

b4) Maybe safest is 11 ♗e2 ♗xe2 12 ♛xe2, as in B.Macieja-M.Sarwinski, Grodzisk Mazowiecki 2007, but after the simple 12...0-0 Black is fine.

c) 8 f4 fights for the dark squares, but after 8...b5 9 ♗d3 0-0 10 ♛e2 ♛h4+ 11 g3 ♛h3 12 ♗e3 ♗g4 13 ♛f2 ♗xe3 14 ♛xe3 ♖fe8 Black had the upper hand in J.Dworakowska-I.Naumkin, San Marino 2006.

d) Finally, nothing came out of 8 ♗c4 0-0 9 0-0 ♗e6 10 ♛e2 ♘g6 11 ♗xe6 ♛xe6 12 ♗e3 ♗xe3 13 ♛xe3 ♘e5 in T.Oral-J.Kalivoda, Czech League 1993, where Black was fully equal.

Returning to 8 ♛f4 and now Black must decide what to do about the queens:

A241: 8...♗e6
A242: 8...♛e6

Of those the former is the most natural continuation, the latter a radical pawn sacrifice devised by Romanishin. Practice has also seen:

a) 8...♛d6?! is one way to avoid the

exchange taking place on f6, but the queen is not well placed on d6. White should retain a slight edge with 9 ♗e3 (Kasparov once tried 9 ♗e2, but it didn't work out too well after 9...♘g6 10 ♕g3 f5 11 f4 ♕d4! 12 ♗d3 ♗b4! 13 exf5? ♗xc3+ 14 bxc3 ♕xc3+ 15 ♔f2 0-0! by when Black had a strong initiative in G.Kasparov-V.Anand, Frankfurt (rapid) 1999) 9...♗b4 (otherwise, 9...0-0 10 ♕xd6 ♗xd6 11 f4 is a simple edge, as are both 9...♗xe3 10 ♕xe3 0-0 11 ♗c4! and the 9...♘g6 10 ♕xd6 ♗xd6 11 g3 0-0 12 f4 ♖e8 13 a3 ♘f8 14 ♔f2 of P.Kotsur-D.Kaiumov, Dubai 2000) 10 ♕xd6 cxd6 11 0-0-0, which undoubles Black's pawns, but leaves him a little weak on d6.

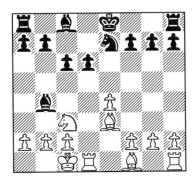

Following 11...♗xc3 (no better was 11...♗e6 12 ♘e2 d5 13 ♘f4 dxe4 14 ♖d4 ♗c5 15 ♘xe6 fxe6 16 ♖xe4 in D.Marciano-P.Van der Sterren, German League 1999, or 11...d5 12 ♗d4 0-0 13 a3 ♗xc3 14 ♗xc3 in T.Oral-A.Aleksandrov, Prague 2000) 12 bxc3 d5 13 ♗d4 (13 exd5 ♘xd5 14 ♗d4 0-0 15 c4 is also good) 13...f6 14 e5 ♔f7 15

exf6 gxf6 16 f3 White had a plus thanks to his pair of bishops in D.Pavasovic-A.Aleksandrov, Dubai 2001.

b) Exchanging with 8...♕xf4?! 9 ♗xf4 is even worse: 9...♗d6 (or 9...♗b6?! 10 ♘a4!, hunting down the bishop-pair) 10 ♗xd6 cxd6 11 0-0-0 ♔d7 12 ♗c4 f6 and now the most precise is 13 ♖d3 ♔c7 14 ♖g3 g6 15 h4 h5 16 ♘e2, which took aim at Black's weaknesses on e6 and g6 in J.Kozamernik-F.Sorcnik, Slovenian League 2002.

c) Although the knight may prove useful on e7 after an exchange on f6, supporting an ...f5 break, 8...♘g6!? is a logical move, which has even been tried at the highest levels with decent results: 9 ♕xf6 gxf6 10 ♗d2 (nothing is promised by either 10 ♘a4 ♗d6 11 ♗e3 f5 12 exf5 ♗xf5 13 0-0-0 0-0-0, as in E.Relange-A.Onischuk, Halle 1995, or 10 f4 h5 11 ♗d2 ♗d6 12 f5 ♘e5 13 ♗e2 b6 14 0-0-0 ♗b7) 10...♖g8 leaves Black's structure a wreck, but his pieces are very active and he has sufficient pressure against White's kingside.

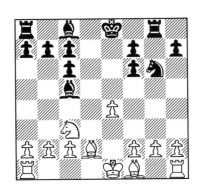

In no lesser game than G.Kasparov-V.Topalov, Las Palmas 1996, 11 ♘a4 (11 f4 is well met by Wells' suggestion of 11...♘h4 12 ♘a4 ♗e7 13 ♔f2 b5 14 g3 bxa4 15 gxh4 f5! with good counterplay) 11...♗d6 12 0-0-0 ♗e6 (attacking the a2-pawn) 13 ♘c3 0-0-0 (Black has a good game, as White will not find it easy to complete his development) 14 g3 ♗g4! (but not 14...f5? 15 ♗g5 ♖d7 16 ♗h3!? fxe4 17 ♗xe6 fxe6 18 ♘xe4 with a serious edge for White according to Kramnik) 15 ♗e2 ♘e5 was fine for Black.

d) Finally, if Black wants to keep the queens on then he should opt for Line A242 and not 8...♕g6? 9 ♕xc7 0-0 10 ♕g3 which failed to supply any real compensation in N.Burnoiu-E.Pessi, Bucharest 2003.

A241) 8...♗e6!

The most logical developing move, albeit one which allows a serious weakening of Black's pawn structure – or does it? In fact, the doubled f-pawns are not such a big deal. Black can easily force through a later ...f5 to open the centre and eliminate one of them, while practice has shown that his piece activity fully makes up for the structural deficiencies of his kingside.

9 ♕xf6

White really must follow up with this consistent exchange. Instead 9 ♗e3 ♕xf4 10 ♗xf4 0-0-0 11 ♘a4 ♗b4+ 12 c3 ♗d6 13 ♗xd6 cxd6 was fine for Black in S.Tatai-M.Godena, Bratto 2003,

as was 9 ♘a4 ♕xf4 10 ♗xf4 ♗d6 11 ♗xd6 cxd6 12 0-0-0 0-0-0 13 ♘c3 f5 in H.Kadhi-N.Short, Tripoli 2004.

9...gxf6

Already the position is quite critical. White lags in development and must be careful not to be destroyed by Black's initiative. Simple play will not do the job, rather White has to embark on some precise action to damage the coordination between Black's pieces.

10 ♘a4!

This motif should be pretty familiar by now! Moreover, here other moves are just too complacent, as shown by:

a) The 10 ♗d2 0-0-0 11 f3 ♗f2+ 12 ♔d1 of S.Jeric-O.Korneev, Nova Gorica 2004, gives Black the initiative after 12...♘g6.

b) 10 f4 should always be met by 10...f5 and here after 11 ♗d2 (11 ♘a4!? ♗b4+ 12 c3 ♗d6 13 e5 b5! has been condemned for White by Wells, but actually after 14 exd6 cxd6 15 ♗d2 bxa4 16 c4 things are not entirely clear) 11...0-0-0 12 0-0-0 ♖hg8 13 g3 h5! and Black's initiative is acquiring menacing proportions. One top-level game went 14 ♗h3! h4 15 ♘a4! ♗f2! 16 ♗b4 ♖xd1+! 17 ♖xd1 (17 ♔xd1?! hxg3 18 hxg3 ♔d8 is worse) 17...hxg3 18 hxg3 b5! 19 ♗xe7 bxa4 and thanks to White's careful defence, the position was pretty much equal in V.Anand-A.Shirov, Linares 1997.

c) 10 ♗d3 ♖g8 11 ♗f4 0-0-0 (11...♖xg2? 12 ♗g3 would trap the errant rook) 12 ♗g3 h5! 13 0-0-0 ♘g6 14 h4 ♘e5 15 ♗e2 ♘g4 16 ♖xd8+ ♔xd8 17 ♘d1 a5 gave Black decent counterplay right across the board in M.Krupa-D.Semcesen, Olomouc 2010.

10...♗b4+

Best, as Black forces some form of concession from White.

10...♗d6 11 ♗e3 f5 12 ♗d4 ♖g8 13 e5 was seen in D.Pavasovic-E.Romanov, Warsaw 2005, where after the logical 13...♗b4+ 14 c3 ♗a5 Black is likely okay, but the text move is much more interesting. On the contrary, 10...♗b6?! 11 ♗d2 ♖g8 12 f4 f5 13 e5 0-0-0 14 ♘xb6+ cxb6 15 0-0-0 was a comfortable edge for White in K.Arakhamia Grant-V.Smyslov, Roquebrune 1998, although Black's light-square blockade was not so easy to break.

11 c3

This leaves the knight out on the rim and weakens the d3-square, but it gains time. The alternative is 11 ♗d2 ♗xd2+ 12 ♔xd2 0-0-0+! 13 ♗d3 when White has much the better structure, but here too Black is just in time to obtain sufficient counterplay:

a) 13...b6 14 ♖ae1 c5 15 ♔c1 ♘c6 16 ♘c3 (or 16 a3 ♘d4 17 ♘c3 ♖hg8 18 g3 ♘b3+ with equality in S.Rublevsky-A.Aleksandrov, Poikovsky 2004) 16...♖hg8 17 g3 ♘b4 and Black had no problems in D.Pavasovic-Z.Hracek, Rabac 2004, with the ...f5 break back on the agenda.

b) 13...f5 14 ♖ae1 fxe4 15 ♖xe4 was preferred in N.Sedlak-M.Kozakov, Valjevo 2000, and after 15...♖hg8 Black should be fine.

11...♗d6 12 ♗e3!

White fights for the c5-square.

12...b6!

And naturally Black covers it. Worse was 12...f5?! 13 ♗d4! ♖g8 14 e5 b5 15 exd6 cxd6 16 ♘c5 dxc5 17 ♗xc5 with a serious positional advantage for White in A.Moroz-G.Timoshenko, Enakievo 1997.

13 f4!

White must play this move too, so as to be ready to answer ...f5 with e5. Otherwise, with an open centre, holes everywhere and no development, he will be exposed to all kind of attacks:

for example, 13 ♗a6?! ♖g8 14 g3 f5 15 exf5 ♘xf5 was good for Black in M.Mrva-Z.Hracek, Czech League 2005.

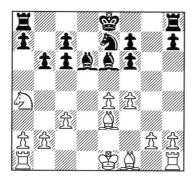

13...0-0-0

The obvious move, but there are alternatives:

a) 13...♗d7 intends 14...c5 but is rather tame and after 14 c4 ♗b4+ 15 ♗d2 ♗xd2+ 16 ♔xd2 0-0-0 17 ♘c3 ♘g6 18 g3 White was better in J.Lautier-A.Shirov, Monte Carlo (rapid) 1998.

b) 13...c5 at once is again met by 14 c4!. White concedes control of the d4-square, but the resulting stability is worth it. That said, Black is okay after 14...0-0-0 15 ♘c3 ♘c6 16 0-0-0 ♖he8, as in A.French-R.James, Swansea 2006. Here it will be difficult for White to make any real progress, although the position is not all that enticing for Black.

c) 13...♖g8!? is quite a smart move, preventing the development of White's other bishop. Following 14 g3 (White acquiesces to another slightly weakening, but it's hard to find anything better; 14 c4 f5 15 e5 ♗b4+ 16 ♔f2 0-0-0 was certainly okay for Black in J.Zorko-

S.Jeric, Ptuj 2005) 14...f5?! (this move is ill-timed here; a better option is 14...♗d7!?, intending to put the light-squared bishop on the recently-weakened long diagonal after ...c5) 15 e5 ♘d5 16 ♗f2 ♗e7 and now in J.Isaev-M.Godena, Dresden Olympiad 2008, White should have prepared c4 (17 c4?! ♘b4 gave Black has a dangerous initiative in the game) with 17 0-0-0, thereby maintaining a stable edge.

14 ♔f2

This is played to prevent ...f5.

Instead 14 ♗e2 is met by the standard ploy 14...f5 15 e5 ♘d5 16 ♗d2 ♗e7 with good play for Black in D.Rensch-V.Bhat, Berkeley 2008; Black's pieces have good outposts and a later ...f6 will dissolve the doubled pawns.

14...c5

So Black switches plans!

15 c4

Alternatively, 15 b3 ♗d7 16 g3 ♗c6 17 ♗g2 ♖he8 was comfortable for Black in A.Kovchan-M.Matlakov, Dagomys 2009.

15...♘c6 16 ♘c3 f5

We can see that Black enjoys a very pleasant position. In fact, it is White who must tread carefully to maintain equality with 17 e5 (17 exf5?! ♗xf5 18 ♖d1 ♖he8 19 ♘d5 ♘b4 was better for Black in J.Magem Badals-A.Kovalev, Batumi 1999, while 17 ♗d3? fails to 17...♗xf4) 17...♗f8! 18 ♗e2! (to the point; instead 18 b3?! ♘b4! saw Black develop a strong initiative in *Deep Fritz*-V.Kramnik, 3rd matchgame, Manama 2002, and not much better was 18 ♘d5!? ♘d4 19 ♖d1 c6 in D.Rensch-V.Bhat, Lubbock 2009) 18...♘d4. This is equal, although it is clear that Black is more equal than White, if you catch the drift!

A242) 8...♕e6!?

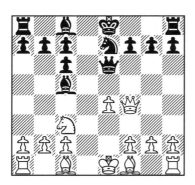

Romanishin's idea. Black willingly gives up the c7-pawn, but acquires a large lead in development should White accept the offer.

9 ♕xc7!

The first in a string of precise moves which seems to call Black's concept into question. However, after less critical moves Black has an easy game:

a) 9 ♗d3 0-0 10 0-0 ♘g6 11 ♕g5 and now Black has doing fine with Romanishin's 11...♕e5, but maybe even simpler is 11...♘e5 12 ♗f4 f6 13 ♕h5 ♗d7 14 ♖ad1 ♖ad8 with equal chances in O.Touzane-G.Flear, Montauban 2000.

b) 9 ♕g5 ♗d4 10 ♗d3 ♘g6 11 0-0 ♕e5 12 ♖b1 0-0 13 ♘e2 ♗b6 14 ♘g3 ♕xg5 15 ♗xg5 ♗e6 was again pretty much okay for Black in D.Pavasovic-O.Romanishin, Bled 1999.

c) 9 ♕g3 0-0 10 ♗d3 ♘g6 11 0-0 (otherwise, 11 ♗e3 ♗xe3 12 ♕xe3 f5 13 f3 f4 14 ♕f2 ♘e5 did not inspire in S.Martinovic-M.Godena, Lido Estensi 2000, but perhaps White can investigate the 11 f4!? f5 12 e5 ♕f7 13 a3 ♗e6 14 ♗e3 ♗e7 15 ♕f3 of M.Kobalia-E.Magerramov, Dubai 2002, since he may have a little something here) 11...♕e5 12 ♘e2 ♕xg3 13 ♘xg3 ♘e5 14 ♗e2 a5 15 a4 ♗e6 16 h3 f6 and Black was fine in A.Areshchenko-S.Fedorchuk, Kharkov 2001.

9...♗b4

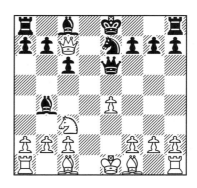

This move has proved to be the most effective:

a) 9...0-0 was Romanishin's initial idea, but it seems White can emerge with a plus: e.g. 10 ♕g3 f5 (10...♘g6? 11 f4 f5 12 e5 b5 13 ♗d3 ♗b7 14 ♗e3 was plain bad for Black in I.Nataf-S.Fedorchuk, Ohrid 2001) 11 e5 b5 (and no better was 11...f4? 12 ♗xf4 ♕f7 13 ♘e4 ♗d4 14 0-0-0 c5 15 ♗g5! in A.Motylev-A.Beliavsky, Novi Sad 2000) 12 f4 ♘d5 13 ♘xd5 ♕xd5 was seen in D.Pavasovic-O.Romanishin, Solin 2002, and now the simple 14 ♕b3 favours White.

b) 9...♗d6!? is another option, but White should retain a plus with 10 ♕a5 b5 11 ♗e3! (improving over 11 ♗d3 0-0 12 0-0 ♕e5 13 f4 ♕d4+ 14 ♔h1 ♗b4 15 ♕c7 ♗d6 with a repetition in H.Stevic-B.Lalic, Jahorina 2003) 11...b4 12 ♘a4 ♕xe4 13 0-0-0 ♘d5 14 ♘c5 ♕f5 15 ♗d3.

10 ♗e3!

Less good is 10 ♗d2 ♗xc3 11 ♗xc3 ♕xe4+ 12 ♔d2 (or 12 ♗e2 ♘d5 13 ♕e5+ ♕xe5 14 ♗xe5 0-0 15 c4 ♖e8 with decent counterplay down the e-file) 12...♘d5 13 ♕e5+ ♕xe5 14 ♗xe5, as in A.Strikovic-O.Romanishin, Calvia 2006, and now after 14...f6 15 ♗g3 ♗f5 Black should be fine.

10...♗xc3+ 11 bxc3 ♕xe4 12 ♗d3 ♕e6 13 0-0

White's structure has been damaged, but thanks to his active queen and bishop-pair he was slightly for choice in G.Sax-P.Skatchkov, Pardubice 1996.

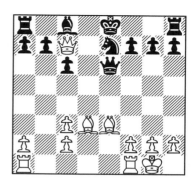

A25) 7...♗d4!

With Black having taken action against his plans of ♘a4 and ♕f4, White has rather struggled to trouble Black here. Usually he has now opted for one of:

A251: 8 ♗c4
A252: 8 ♗d3

There's also:

a) 8 ♘a4 may seem a little strange here, but it aims to discomfort the black bishop with the threat of 9 c3. Unsurprisingly, though, it has been shown to be rather ineffective: 8...a6! (but not 8...b5?! 9 c3! ♗xf2+ 10 ♕xf2 ♕xf2+ 11 ♔xf2 bxa4 12 ♗f4 ♖b8 13 ♖b1 ♗e6 14 c4 ♘f6 15 ♗d3 which gave White excellent compensation in M.Kosegi-D.Schwarz, Slovakian League 2006) 9 c3 (neither 9 f4 ♗a7 10 e5 ♕h4+ 11 g3 ♕e7 12 ♕c3, as in N.Kharmunova-S.Bezgodova, Serpukhov 2004, and then 12...♘f6, nor the 9 ♗d3 ♘e7 10 0-0 b5 11 ♘c3 ♗b7 12 a4

0-0 13 ♔h1 ♖ad8 14 f4 b4 of I.Nataf-L.Christiansen, Kapuskasing 2003, are effective; indeed, in both cases Black has the initiative) 9...♗a7 10 b4 ♗d7 (or 10...♗g4 11 f3 ♗e6 12 ♗b2 ♖d8 13 ♕c2 ♘e7 14 ♗d3 ♘g6 with advantage to Black in B.Mitrovic-J.Kocicsak, Sibenik 2007) 11 ♗d3 ♘e7 12 0-0 ♘g6 13 ♕g5 ♕xg5 14 ♗xg5 f6 15 ♗c1 0-0-0 and Black had the initiative in C.Theoharides-M.Lodhi, Calvia Olympiad 2004.

b) 8 f4?! is weakening, especially since e5 is not yet a threat. Black's strongest reply is 8...♘h6!, although practice has shown that 8...♗e6 9 e5 ♕h4+ is hardly a bad alternative. Following 9 e5 (9 ♘e2? is a blunder in view of 9...♗xb2 10 e5 ♗xc1 11 ♘xc1 ♕g6) 9...♕h4+ 10 g3 ♕d8 Black has made a number of moves with his queen which has returned to base, but just look at White's overextended and undeveloped position!

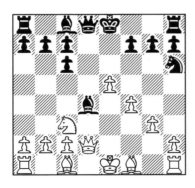

Indeed, White must avoid 11 ♘e2? because of 11...♕d5! 12 ♕xd4 ♕xh1, as in A.Danin-J.Geller, Vladimir 2002,

while 11 ♘e4?! ♗f5 12 ♗g2 ♘g4 13 ♕e2 ♕d7 14 ♗d2 0-0-0 left him under heavy pressure in I.Khamrakulov-S.Estremera Panos, Andorra 2001. Thus he likely does best with 11 ♗g2, but 11...0-0 12 ♘e4 f6 13 c3 ♗b6 14 ♕xd8 ♖xd8 still gave Black an edge in D.Batsanin-P.Smirnov, Togliatti 2003.

c) 8 ♘d1 aims to quickly dislodge the bishop from d4, but such a move can hardly be threatening. Indeed, Black has an easy game after 8...♗e6 (8...♗g4!? 9 f3 ♗e6 is similar and also playable is 8...♘e7 9 c3 ♗b6) 9 ♕g5 ♕g6!, fighting to only exchange the queens on his terms.

Following 10 f3 f6 11 ♕xg6+ hxg6 12 ♗e3 (12 c3 was no improvement in the later I.Nataf-J.Degraeve, Val d'Isere 2004, and after 12...♗c5 13 ♗e3 ♗d6 14 f4 g5 15 fxg5 ♖xh2 16 ♖xh2 ♗xh2 Black was better) 12...0-0-0 (Black can also consider 12...♗b6!? 13 ♗xb6 cxb6! 14 ♘e3 b5 15 c4 a6 with equality) 13 ♗xd4 ♖xd4 Black had at least equality in the game I.Nataf-J.Dorfman, Val d'Isere 2004.

A251) 8 ♗c4

White develops the bishop to its most active square, but Black won't mind exchanging it, since White is a long way from exploiting his superior structure.

8...♘h6

Black can also try the immediate 8...♗e6 9 ♗xe6 fxe6, bringing a pawn into the centre while preparing to increase the pressure against f2.

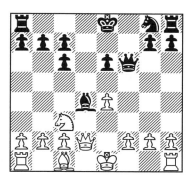

However, this may be less accurate due to 10 ♘d1! (White must seek to exchange queens; otherwise, he will face trouble down the open files, as he has after 10 0-0 0-0-0 and then, for example, 11 ♕e1 ♘h6! 12 ♗e3 ♘g4 13 ♗xd4 ♕f4! 14 g3 ♕h6 15 h4 ♖xd4 16 ♕e2 ♕g6 with a powerful initiative for Black on the kingside), after which 10...0-0-0 11 ♕g5 ♕f7 12 ♗e3 ♘f6 13 f3 h6 14 ♕a5 ♔b8 15 0-0 ♘h5 16 ♗xd4 ♖xd4 17 ♘e3 resulted in approximate equality in S.Tiviakov-S.Mamedyarov, San Sebastian 2006.

9 h3

White usually plays to restrict the black knight. Instead 9 0-0 ♘g4 10 ♕f4 ♕e7 (also fine is 10...0-0, as played by Tkachiev) 11 h3 ♘e5 12 ♗e2, as in T.Franke-T.Michalczak, Dortmund 2003, and then 12...♘g6 leads to equality and demonstrates an unusual route for the black knight to take to g6.

9...♗e6!

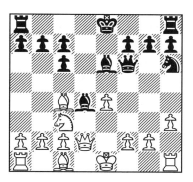

The most promising course, aiming to castle queenside and seize the initiative on the kingside.

10 ♗xe6

Instead 10 ♗b3 0-0-0 11 0-0 ♖he8 12 ♕g5 was agreed drawn here in J.Rosito-H.van Riemsdijk, Serra Negra 2002, but Black can, of course, take the pawn with 12...♗xc3 13 bxc3 ♕xc3 when it's not clear that White has quite sufficient compensation.

10...fxe6 11 ♘d1

After 11 0-0 countering in kind with 11...0-0 makes sense now that the f-file is open. Then 12 ♘d1 ♘f7 13 c3 ♗b6 14 ♕e2 was seen in A.Motylev-V.Tkachiev, 2000, when Black might have seized the initiative with 14...♕e5.

11...0-0-0 12 ♕e2

Black was better also after 12 ♕g5 ♕f8 13 c3 ♗b6 14 ♗e3 ♘f7 15 ♕h5 ♘d6 16 ♕e2 ♗xe3 17 ♕xe3 b6 in S.Tiviakov-O.Korneev, Khanty-Mansiysk 2005.

12...♘f7!

This multipurpose retreat appears to be even stronger than Aronian's aggressive 12...g5, after which he clearly had no problems following 13 c3 ♗b6 14 ♗e3 ♘f7 15 ♗xb6 axb6 16 ♘e3 h5 in I.Nataf-L.Aronian, Moscow 2003.

13 0-0

Worse is 13 c3 ♗b6 14 ♗e3 ♘e5 15 0-0 ♘d3 when Black has the advantage.

13...♖d7 14 c3 ♗b6 15 a4 a5 16 ♗e3 ♖hd8

By this point Black clearly had the upper hand in J.Van der Wiel-A.Stefanova, Wijk aan Zee 2004, and it seems that White needs to look to improve before 12...♘f7.

A252) 8 ♗d3

The most logical move, preparing to castle while not allowing ...♗e6 to come with tempo.

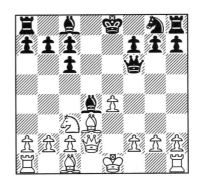

8...♘e7

The black knight sets off on the long journey to e5. Here 8...♘h6 is not as good as after 8 ♗c4, because there is no tempo gain when the knight comes to e5. Thus White can play 9 0-0 ♘g4 10 ♕f4 ♕e7 11 h3 ♘e5 12 ♗e3 ♘xd3 13 cxd3 with a slight edge.

9 0-0

Invariably played, but this isn't forced:

a) 9 ♘d1 is quite harmless: 9...♕g6 10 ♕g5 ♗e6 11 0-0 ♕xg5 12 ♗xg5 f6 13 ♗e3 0-0-0 14 ♗xd4 ♖xd4 gave Black easy equality in Z.Varga-L.Lenic, Sibenik 2007.

b) 9 f4!? is ambitious, but requires further attention. Black countered in kind with 9...h5!? in M.Parligras-M.Arnelind, Paleohora 2009, but after 10 ♘d1 ♗b6 11 ♘f2 h4 12 ♕e2 ♗a5+?! 13 ♔f1! h3 14 g4! ♗b6 15 ♖g1 ♗d7 16 ♖g3 he was beginning to regret such an approach.

9...♘g6!

Black should have no problems after the simple 9...0-0 10 ♕g5 ♕xg5 11

♗xg5 ♘g6 12 ♖ad1 (nothing is promised either by 12 ♘d1 ♘e5 13 ♗e2 ♗e6 or 12 ♗d2 ♘e5) 12...♗e6 13 a3 a5 14 ♗e2 ♗xc3 15 bxc3 f5, which was equal in D.Lintchevski-D.Howell, Budva 2003, but the text move is more promising.

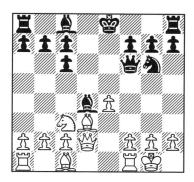

White is now faced with a dilemma over how to proceed. Should he seek the exchange of queens to free his queenside, or should he try to push f4 and discomfort the black pieces, not fearing ...♘e5-g4 in response?

10 ♔h1

White opts for the second plan and this is his most ambitious choice. However, it also allows Black to bring his knight to e5, which will give him good counterchances.

There are various alternatives here, which aren't so critical but are also less risky, including:

a) It turns out that nothing is offered by the standard 10 ♕g5, in view of 10...♕d6 (or even the simple 10...♕xg5 11 ♗xg5 f6 12 ♗c1 ♘e5 13 ♗e2 ♗e6 14 ♘d1 0-0-0 15 ♖e1 h5, which was fine for Black in J.Smeets-

E.L'Ami, Groningen 2003) 11 ♘e2 h6 12 ♕h5 ♗b6 (J.Broekmeulen-M.Kazhgaleyev, Zwolle 2004) 13 ♗d2 0-0 14 ♗c3 ♗e6 with approximate equality.

b) 10 ♘d1 prepares to defend against Black's aggressive ideas, but hardly disturbs the second player: 10...0-0 11 ♕g5 ♕d6 12 ♗e3 (A.Stambulian-V.Malaniuk, Krasnodar 2001) 12...♘e5 13 ♗e2 ♗e6 with equality.

c) 10 ♕e1 makes way for the dark-squared bishop to be developed, but Black has more than one way to meet it:

c1) 10...♘e5 11 ♗e2 (White must prevent the knight from coming to g4; if 11 ♗e3? then 11...♗h3! 12 ♘e2 – surprisingly 12 ♔h1?? ♗xg2+ 13 ♔xg2 ♕f3+ 14 ♔g1 ♕g4+ has been considered a draw by perpetual, but actually Black wins after 15 ♔h1 ♘f3 16 ♕e2 ♗e5 17 ♖g1 ♕h3 18 ♖g2 0-0-0 and ...♖d6-g6 – 12...♗xe3 13 fxe3 ♕g5 with an obvious advantage for Black) 11...g5! (11...h5!? has been tried too, intending to bring the knight to g4 after all, but it is risky; the text, securing a nice central post on e5 for the knight, is solid and sound) 12 ♔h1 ♗e6 13 ♘a4 0-0-0 14 c3 ♗b6 and Black is certainly not worse.

c2) 10...♗e5!? is Bacrot's idea, exploiting White's temporary lack of control over f4. Following 11 ♖b1 (both 11 ♗c4 0-0 12 ♗e3 ♘f4 and 11 ♘e2 ♗xb2 12 ♗xb2 ♕xb2 13 f4 ♕b6+ 14 ♔h1 ♕c5 are good for Black) 11...♘f4 12 ♗xf4 (worse is 12 ♘e2?! ♘xd3 13 cxd3 ♕d6, as in C.Bauer-E.Bacrot, Aix les Bains 2003, when after 14 d4 ♗xd4 15 ♘xd4 ♕xd4 16 ♗f4 0-0 17 ♗xc7 ♖e8 18 ♖d1 ♕xb2 Black is better) 12...♕xf4 13 g3 any queen retreat will leave Black satisfied with his position, the most promising probably being 13...♕h6.

d) 10 ♘e2!? is White's most forceful continuation and likely his best try for an advantage:

d1) Capturing the offered pawn has been tried in practice and shown to be risky: 10...♗xb2?! 11 ♗xb2 ♕xb2 12 ♖ab1 ♕f6 (12...♕xa2 13 ♖b3 prepares ♕c3 and spells trouble) 13 f4 0-0 was A.Bellaiche-M.Rebreyend, French League 2001, and now 14 ♕e3 intends e5, leaving Black under pressure and White with good compensation.

d2) Safer is 10...♗b6 and after 11 ♘f4 (otherwise, 11 ♘g3 h5!? does not allow White to complete his development in peace and after 12 ♗e2 ♗g4 13 ♕g5 ♕xg5 14 ♗xg5 f6 15 ♗d2 ♘e5 16 ♗xg4 hxg4 17 ♗c3 ♖d8 18 ♖ad1 ♔f7 Black was equal in T.Radjabov-G.Sargissian, Antalya 2004) 11...♘e5

(Black should, of course, avoid exchanges; Svidler recently tried 11...♕h4, but White would have had some initiative after 12 a4 a5 13 e5!) 12 ♗e2 0-0 13 ♕c3 (perhaps 13 ♘d3 ♘g6, as in E.Vorobiov-V.Tkachiev, Kazan 2005, and then Postny's suggestion 14 ♔h1!? ♖e8 15 f3 with the idea of ♕e1-g3 may offer White a little something) 13...♖e8 14 ♗e3 (14 ♔h1!? prepares f3 as an answer to ...♗g4 and may give White a slight edge after 14...♗d7 15 a4! a5 16 ♗e3) 14...♗g4 15 ♗xg4 ♗xe3! 16 ♘h5 (16 ♕xe3 ♘xg4 17 ♕g3 ♘e5 18 ♘h5 ♕h6 was also equal in A.Stiri-J.Houska, Athens 2005) 16...♕h6 17 ♗e2 ♗b6 the position was equal in B.Vuckovic-A.Karpatchev, Marseille 2004.

10...♘e5

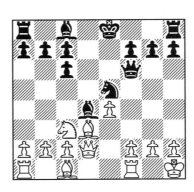

Now White again faces an important decision with Black being about to play ...♘g4, which will create immediate threats against the white king.

11 ♗e2

White opts for defensive measures and to retain his bishop for now, but he also has:

a) 11 ♕g5? is mistaken in view of 11...♕xg5 12 ♗xg5 f6 13 ♗d2 ♗e6 14 ♔g1 0-0-0 with a clear plus for Black,

b) 11 ♘e2 ♗b6 12 ♘f4 gave White the advantage after 12...♘xd3 13 ♕xd3 ♗d7 14 a4 0-0-0 15 a5 ♗c5 16 ♕e2 ♖he8 17 ♘d3 in V.Tseshkovsky-A.Aleksandrov, Vrnjacka Banja 2005, but Black should have preferred 12...0-0 with equal chances.

c) 11 f3 could be met by 11...♗e6!? followed by ...0-0-0.

d) Fairly critical is 11 f4, but it doesn't offer White anything after 11...♘g4!.

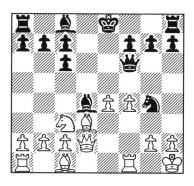

Then 12 ♕e1 (certainly not 12 ♘d1?? ♘xh2 and 12 e5?! is risky for White after the 12...♕h4 13 g3 ♕h5 of S.Voitsekhovsky-A.Gavrilov, Vladimir 2004) 12...♘xh2! (the knight sacrifice is forced, as after 12...0-0? 13 h3 or 12...♗d7 13 e5 the black pieces will be pushed back with gain of time) 13 ♔xh2 ♕h6+ 14 ♔g3 ♕g6+ results in a draw by perpetual check, as it did in Ni Hua-M.Krasenkow, Shanghai 2001.

11...♘g4 12 ♘d1

White does not have much choice here: 12 ♗f3? h5 is already very good for Black and the further 13 ♘d1? ♗e5 14 h3 ♘h2 forced White to resign in G.Livshits-V.Mikhalevski, Ramat Aviv 2004, while 12 ♗xg4 ♗xg4 13 f3 0-0-0! 14 ♕e2 (or 14 ♕f4 ♕xf4 15 ♗xf4 ♗e6!?) 14...♗e6 15 ♘d1 g5 16 ♗e3 (A.Bellaiche-K.Bordi, French League 2002) 16...♗e5 is pretty good for Black with 17...h5 next up.

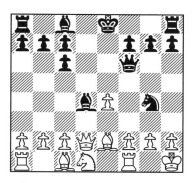

12...♕d6!

Black can also consider 12...♗e6!? intending to castle long. Play can continue 13 h3 (bad is 13 f3? ♘xh2! and not much better 13 c3?! ♗b6 14 h3 ♖d8 15 ♕f4 ♕xf4 16 ♗xf4 ♘f6 17 ♗f3 0-0 with the initiative for Black, as White's pieces are badly placed) 13...0-0-0! 14 ♗xg4! (White loses after 14 hxg4?? ♕h4+ 15 ♔g1 ♗e5 16 g3 ♗xg3 17 fxg3 ♕xg3+, while 14 ♕f4? ♗e5 15 ♕xf6 ♘xf6 16 ♗d3 ♘h5 was also bad for him in R.Asylguzhin-S.Kayumov, Dubai 2002) 14...♗xg4 15 hxg4 ♗xb2 16 ♕xd8+ (16 g5?! ♕g6 sees e4 drop) 16...♕xd8 (similar is 16...♖xd8 17 ♗xb2

♕h4+ 18 ♔g1 ♕xg4 19 e5 with a complex position) 17 ♗xb2 ♕h4+ 18 ♔g1 ♕xg4 by when the position was dynamically balanced in A.Danin-E.Ubiennykh, Serpukhov 2003.

Also possible is the calm 12...0-0, but after 13 h3 ♖d8 (A.Morozevich-V.Tkachiev, Cannes (rapid) 2001) 14 ♗xg4! ♗xg4 15 hxg4 ♗xb2 (or 15...♕h4+ 16 ♔g1 ♗xb2 17 ♘xb2 ♖xd2 18 ♗xd2 ♕xg4 19 f3 ♕h5 20 ♘d3 with an edge, as analysed by Postny) 16 ♕xd8+ ♖xd8 17 ♗xb2 ♕h4+ 18 ♔g1 ♕xg4 19 e5 White's extra pieces may prove more effective than Black's queen and pawns.

13 f4?!

This move allows another perpetual, but Black may and probably should try for more. However, it looks like White must improve his play earlier in the opening, since by now Black enjoys a very good game, as we can also see from:

a) 13 g3 h5 14 c3 ♗b6 15 ♕g5 ♕e5 16 f3 ♕xg5 17 ♗xg5 ♘e5 and Black had the initiative in D.Pavasovic-

N.Pedersen, Bled Olympiad 2002.

b) The best move for White may even be 13 ♗xg4, although Black is clearly fine after 13...♗xg4: for example, 14 ♕g5 (14 ♘e3 ♗e6 15 f4 f6 16 ♕e2 0-0-0 was good for Black in M.Paragua-G.Timoscenko, Bled Olympiad 2002) 14...♕g6 15 ♕f4 ♕h5 16 f3 ♗e6 17 ♕g3 0-0-0 and Black was more than comfortable in I.Nataf-A.Onischuk, Cap d'Agde (rapid) 2002.

13...h5!?

Black wishes to retain his knight on g4. There is an immediate draw available, though, with 13...♘xh2 14 ♔xh2 ♕h6+ 15 ♔g3 ♕g6+, as in S.Rublevsky-A.Onischuk, Poikovsky 2002 and G.Sax-V.Erdos, Croatian Team Championship 2010.

14 c3

14 e5 ♕d8 does not improve things and after the careless 15 ♗f3?? ♘xh2 White had to resign in J.Kozamernik-D.Pavasovic, Ljubljana 2004.

14...♗b6 15 ♕xd6 cxd6

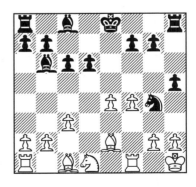

The outcome of the opening is that Black has an edge, due to White's uncoordinated and undeveloped pieces, and he went on to win in A.Danin-A.Lastin, Moscow 2007.

B) 6...bxc6

Just like the same recapture a move earlier, this approach has never really caught on at the top level, but is by no means uncommon at lower levels. Black finds himself less actively placed than in Line A, but his position remains fairly solid, playable and no more than a little worse.

7 ♘c3

White can and likely should prioritize kingside development with 7 ♗d3 ♘e7 (perhaps the rare and radical 7...♘h6!? is a better try; 8 0-0 0-0 9 ♘c3 d6 10 ♕g5 ♕xg5 11 ♗xg5 ♘g4 12 h3 ♘e5 13 ♗e2 f5 seemed fine for Black in D.Ionescu-S.Tikhomirov, Bucharest 1999, although White likely does better with 10 ♘a4!?) 8 0-0 when Black must decide whether to go for early counter-play or to solidly complete his development:

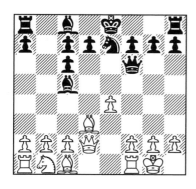

a) 8...♘g6 9 ♔h1 ♘e5 10 ♗e2 d6

(White was a little better too after 10...♕h4 11 f4 ♘g4 12 ♗xg4 ♕xg4 13 ♖f3 in A.Suarez Real-G.Flear, Barcelona 2006) 11 f4 ♘g4 12 ♗xg4 ♗xg4 13 f5! ♕d4 14 ♕e1 left Black's pieces a little offside and White with the initiative in P.Svidler-V.Yemelin, St Petersburg 1993.

b) 8...d5 9 ♘c3 (9 ♕f4 should also lead to an edge) 9...♗e6 (we'll see 9...0-0 in variation 'c2', below) 10 exd5 cxd5 11 ♕f4 ♕xf4 12 ♗xf4 ♔d7 13 ♖ad1 c6 14 ♘a4 gave White a small but clear edge in T.Shaked-V.Korchnoi, Cannes 1998.

c) 8...0-0 9 ♘c3 sees White first prepare to meet ...d5 before expanding with ♔h1 and f4. Now:

c1) 9...d6? isn't as solid as one might think on account of 10 e5! ♕h4 (Black loses a piece after 10...dxe5?? 11 ♘e4 and 10...♕xe5?? 11 ♖e1 ♕f6 12 ♘e4 ♕h4 13 g3 also wins material, as pointed out by Postny, while 10...♕e6 11 exd6 ♗xd6 12 ♖e1 ♕d7 13 ♘e4 ♘g6 14 ♘xd6 cxd6 15 b3 ♗b7 16 ♗b2 gave White a very pleasant advantage in M.Kobalija-M.Sorokin, Tomsk 2004) 11 ♘e4 ♗f5 12 ♘xc5 dxc5 13 ♗xf5 ♘xf5 14 ♕d3 ♕g4 15 h3 ♕g6 16 ♖d1, which left White with a certain structural advantage in R.Reinaldo Castineira-Z.Azmaiparashvili,Internet blitz 2003.

c2) After 9...d5 10 ♕f4 (10 ♕g5 is also possible and after 10...♕xg5 11 ♗xg5 f6 12 ♗f4 ♗b6 13 exd5 ♘xd5 14 ♘xd5 cxd5 15 ♖fe1 White again enjoyed an edge in P.Wells-I.Semenova,

Zalakaros 1998) 10...♕xf4 11 ♗xf4 ♗b6 (Black found himself badly low on counterplay after 11...dxe4? 12 ♘xe4 ♗b6 13 ♖fe1 ♘d5 14 ♗d2 in A.Motylev-I.Sokolov, Neum 2000) White has tried a number of ideas, with one simple and strong continuation 12 ♘a4!? dxe4 (White's superior minor piece gave him a plus too after 12...♗e6 13 ♘xb6 cxb6 14 a3 ♖ad8 15 exd5 ♘xd5 16 ♗g3 in S.Rublevsky-I.Sokolov, Neum 2000) 13 ♘xb6 cxb6 14 ♗xe4 ♗f5 15 ♗xf5 ♘xf5 16 c3, which supplied a small but clear edge in M.Spal-M.Jaros, Klatovy 2003.

c3) 9...♘g6 10 ♔h1! d6 (the immediate 10...♗b4 isn't too disruptive on account of 11 ♘d5! cxd5 12 ♕xb4 dxe4 13 ♗xe4 c6 14 ♗e3 with a pull for White in S.Zhigalko-Y.Glyzin, Minsk 2005) 11 f4 ♗b4 reaches quite an important position.

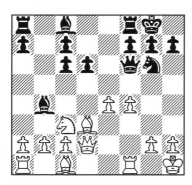

Having gone f4 White is no longer so keen to open the position with 12 ♘d5, but should prefer to sacrifice a pawn to dent Black's fairly solid set-up: 12 ♕e1 (the closely-related 12 ♕f2!? ♗xc3 13 bxc3 ♕xc3 14 ♖b1 ♕f6 15 ♗b2

of G.Lane-S.Azarov, Bled Olympiad 2002, might be even more precise) 12...♗xc3 13 bxc3 ♖e8 (Black came under strong pressure after 13...♗b7?! 14 ♖b1 ♖ab8 15 c4 c5 16 ♕a5 in M.Parligras-K.Markidis, Nicea 2003) 14 ♕g3! ♕xc3 15 ♖b1 f6 16 ♗b2 saw White's extra space and bishop-pair at least fully compensate for the pawn in E.Andreev-V.Belikov, Alushta 2001.

We now return to 7 ♘c3:

7...♘e7

Along with 7...d6 the most natural, but there are other alternatives:

a) 7...♘h6?! hopes to target f2, but is well met by 8 h3!.

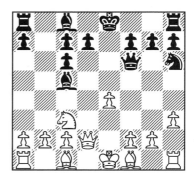

Indeed, after 8...0-0 9 ♗d3 d6 10 0-0 ♕g6 11 ♕g5 ♕xg5 (11...a5 12 ♘a4 ♗d4 13 c3 ♗a7 was preferred in I.Nataf-N.Short, New Delhi 2000, but here White can retain a plus with Postny's 14 ♖e1 ♗d7 15 b3) 12 ♗xg5 ♗e6 13 ♘a4 White begins to hunt down the bishop-pair with a small but clear edge.

b) 7...♕g6!? attempts to tie White down to g2 and after 8 ♕g5 d6 9 ♕xg6 hxg6 practice has shown Black's position to be very solid: for instance, 10 ♗d2 ♘f6 11 f3 ♘h5 12 ♘e2 was seen in F.Remiro Juste-D.Adla, Aragon 2005, whereupon 12...f5 would have equalized. Thus here White might prefer 8 f4!? and after 8...♘f6 (the classical counter 8...♘e7 9 ♗d3 d5! was a safer approach by Black in J.Smeets-I.Sokolov, Dutch League 2002, and here Postny considers 10 ♘a4 dxe4 11 ♘xc5 exd3 to be roughly balanced) 9 ♗d3 ♘g4 10 e5! ♕h6 11 ♕e2 ♘f2 12 ♘e4! ♘xh1 13 ♘xc5 ♕xh2 14 ♗e3 White had dangerous compensation for the exchange in A.Motylev-P.Acs, Dubai 2002.

c) 7...d6 8 ♗d3 ♘e7 9 0-0 transposes to variation 'c1' in the notes to White's 7th move, above, after 9...0-0?, but here Black can do better. One thematic approach is 9...♕h4!? 10 ♘a4 ♗b6 11 ♕g5 ♕xg5 12 ♗xg5 f6 13 ♗d2 ♔f7, which was about equal in D.Sadvakasov-G.Timoscenko, Istanbul Olympiad 2000, another 9...♘g6 10 ♔h1 ♗d4 11 f4 0-0, relying on Black's active pieces and pressure against c3 to keep White's expansion in check.

Here 12 ♘e2 ♗b6 13 f5 ♘e5 14 ♕e1 (U.Krstic-D.Gazarek, Pula 2001) 14...♖e8 15 ♕g3 h6 seems solid enough for Black, but a bold player might prefer 12 e5!? dxe5 (and not 12...♗xc3? 13 exf6 ♗xd2 14 fxg7 ♔xg7 15 ♗xd2, which left White with a clear plus in I.Vujacic-M.Cvorovic, Cetinje 2005) 13 ♘e4 ♕d8 14 f5 ♘f4 15 f6, which gave White enough kingside chances for his pawn in R.Mamedov-S.Skembris, Istanbul 2001.

8 ♘a4

Hunting down the bishop-pair is a very logical try. White must avoid 8 b3? ♗xf2+! which left him rather embarrassed in Z.Hracek-J.Smejkal, Czech League 1995, but again 8 ♗d3 is a decent option and after 8...0-0 9 0-0 play has transposed to note 'c' to White's 7th move, above.

8...♗b6

A critical alternative is the attempt to preserve the bishop with 8...♗d6!? 9 f4 ♘g6 10 g3 (but not 10 e5? ♗xe5 11 fxe5 ♕h4+, picking up the knight on a4) 10...0-0.

Now 11 e5? ♖e8 12 ♗e2 ♘xe5! 13 fxe5 ♕xe5 gives Black a powerful attack for the piece and 11 ♗g2?! ♗a6 12 ♕e3 ♖fe8 13 ♗d2 ♘e7 14 0-0-0 ♘d5 gave him the initiative in J.Ehlvest-P.Blatny, Stratton Mountain 2000. However, with the prudent 11 ♕e3! ♖e8 12 ♗d2 ♕e7 13 ♗g2 ♗b4 14 0-0-0 White retained an edge in V.Ivanchuk-N.Short, Dubai (rapid) 2002.

9 ♗d3 0-0 10 0-0 d5?!

As Black is about to lose the bishop-pair, he should probably not be in such a hurry to open things up. Instead after 10...♘g6 11 ♔h1 d6 12 f4 ♖e8 13 ♖b1 c5 14 b3 ♗b7 15 ♗b2 ♕h4 his position didn't seem too bad in M.Galyas-D.Howell, Budapest 2003.

Another solid option is 10...d6 and after 11 c3 (or 11 ♔h1 ♕h4! 12 b3 f5 13 exf5 ♗xf5 14 ♘xb6 axb6 and Black's kingside activity compensated for White's bishops in M.Paragua-N.Maiorov, Genoa 2004) 12 ♖e1 ♗h3 13 ♗f1 ♗e6 14 c4 c5 Black was okay in A.Morozevich-N.Short, Wijk aan Zee 2000.

11 ♕f4 ♕xf4

Black can keep the queens on, but he also failed to equalize with both 11...♕d4 12 ♘xb6 cxb6 13 ♕d6 in L.Nisipeanu-C.Caminade, Naujac 2000, and 11...♕e6 12 exd5 ♘xd5 13 ♕h4 in R.Kholmov-E.Kristiansen, Dresden 2002.

12 ♗xf4 ♘g6 13 ♘xb6 cxb6 14 ♗d6! ♖d8 15 ♗c7 ♖d7 16 ♗g3

With a simple but strong sequence White has netted the bishop-pair while

displacing Black's rook, and unsurprisingly practice has confirmed that he has a rather pleasant edge here.

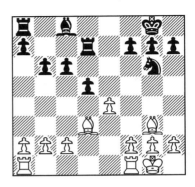

C) 6...♕xc6

Black decides to keep his structure intact. This is another option which is far from unknown at club level, but the queen doesn't achieve too much on c6 and, as in Line B, White has good chances of obtaining an advantage.

7 ♗d3

Holding back on the development of the queenside gives White some useful extra options, but it's also possible to begin with 7 ♘c3 and only then 8 ♗d3.

7...♘e7

Again the knight heads for g6, but Black might do better to exploit the now-vacant f6-square with 7...♘f6!? 8 0-0 0-0 (but not 8...d6? on account of the vigorous 9 b4!, after which 9...♗d4? 10 a4! a6 11 ♗b5! axb5 12 axb5 won material in A.Turzo-T.Gacso, Aggtelek 1995, and even the superior 9...♗b6 leaves Black in trouble after both 10 ♗b2 and 10 ♕g5) 9 ♘c3, reaching a position where both queens are a little misplaced.

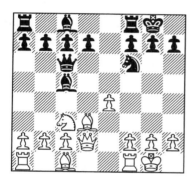

Naturally Black must avoid 9...d5? 10 ♘xd5 ♘xd5 11 exd5 ♕xd5?? 12 ♗xh7+, but as well as the solid 9...♖e8 he can consider 9...♗d4!?. White should take up the challenge with 10 ♕f4! when it would be a brave man who went in for 10...♗xc3 11 bxc3 ♕xc3 12 ♖b1, but 10...d6 11 ♘e2 (or 11 ♗d2 a6 when Black will develop in relative comfort with 12...♗e6) 11...♗e5 12 ♕h4 ♘d7! 13 c3 ♘c5 remained very solid for Black and about equal in J.Van der Wiel-J.Piket, Gouda 1997.

8 0-0 0-0 9 b4!?

This energetic advance is a key weapon in White's armoury in this line, but here he also has good chances of an edge after 9 ♘c3 d6 10 ♘d5!, as in J.Langreck-C.Boor, Mason 1998, since 10...♘xd5 11 exd5 ♕b6 12 c3 leaves White with the initiative and certain prospects on the kingside.

9...♗d4

Black hints at deploying his bishop on the kingside. The alternative is 9...♗b6, but after 10 ♗b2 both White's bishops rake the black kingside and 10...d6 11 ♘c3 ♕e8 12 ♖fe1 leaves him with a pretty pleasant advantage.

10 c3 ♗f6

And so the bishop goes to the kingside after all. With Black having induced c3, 10...♗b6 becomes a slightly better option than a move earlier, although 11 ♗b2 a5 12 b5! ♕g6 13 e5 ♕h5 14 c4 still gave White the initiative in M.Santo Roman-D.Anic, French League 2002.

11 ♕e2!

White improves his queen, while hoping that Black will either grab on c3 or cut off his queen from the defence of his kingside with 11...d6. This is a more precise move order than 11 b5 ♕b6 12 ♕e2 because here 12...♘g6 13 ♗e3 ♕a5 14 f4 d6 left White a little overextended and Black with enough counterplay in Y.Dembo-I.Mihalincic, Pula 2002.

11...♕e6

Keeping the queen in touch with the kingside. This isn't enough to equalize, but neither are the alternatives especially attractive:

a) 11...♗xc3? 12 b5 ♕f6 13 ♘xc3 ♕xc3 14 ♗b2 clearly gives White excellent attacking prospects with two raking bishops.

b) 11...d6 12 ♗b5!? ♕b6 13 ♗e3 c5 14 ♗d3 leaves White all set to advance with f4 and with the initiative.

c) 11...g6!? 12 ♗h6 ♖e8 13 ♕f3 gives White quite a dangerous attacking position, but perhaps Black should go in for this since 13...♔h8 14 ♘a3 a6 15 ♖ac1 d5! began counterplay and wasn't so clear in F.Galassi-M.Godena, Porto Mannu 2008.

12 f4 d6 13 ♕c2 ♘c6

Black tried to dissuade ideas of e5 with 13...♔h8 in A.Bellaiche-D.Anic, Val d'Isere 2002, but 14 ♘d2 a5 15 b5 kept White in front.

14 a3 a5 15 b5!?

Boldly advancing and not worrying about the tactical defence 15...♘d4!?, since then 16 ♕b2 ♕b3 17 e5! sees White retaining the initiative.

15...♘b8 16 ♗e3

White's extra space clearly gave him a pull here in A.Grischuk-A.Graf, Yerevan 2001, and it wasn't long before he broke through down the e- and f-files after 16...g6 17 ♘d2 ♘d7 18 ♖ae1 ♕e7 19 e5!.

Conclusion

Kasparov championed 5 ♘xc6 ♕f6 6 ♕d2 in the Nineties, but it's not clear that he would play it were he to venture a Scotch nowadays. Even after the oft-condemned 7...♗e6 Black seems to be okay, at least so long as he meets 8 ♘a4 with 8...♗d6, and 7...♘e7 8 ♕f4 ♗e6! definitely promises him plenty of counterplay to offset his structural deficiencies. However, the main reason for the decline of 5 ♘xc6 ♕f6 6 ♕d2 has been the emergence of 7...♗d4!, retaining the bishop on the key g1-a7 diagonal, which just seems to give Black easy equality. Indeed, it's little wonder that many Scotch aficionados have switched to those lines we will now consider in the next four chapters!

Chapter Seven

The 4...♗c5 Variation: 5 ♘xc6 ♕f6 6 ♕f3

1 e4 e5 2 ♘f3 ♘c6 3 d4 exd4 4 ♘xd4 ♗c5 5 ♘xc6 ♕f6 6 ♕f3!?

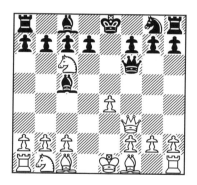

This somewhat shocking move, considered something of a harmless sideline until around about 2005, has now come firmly to the fore and is currently White's main try in the 5 ♘xc6 ♕f6 variation. The offer to exchange the queens is unexpected, in that White's main trump has always been considered his superior pawn structure and in one fell swoop he agrees to incur some

structural damage of his own. While the exchange on f3 does not entirely negate his endgame possibilities on the kingside, it does make it much more difficult to obtain a passed pawn there.

However, there are other factors in play as well the damage to White's pawns should Black exchange on f3. First, White solves the issue of f2 in a most convenient manner, avoiding messing up his development, as he does with 6 ♕d2. In addition to obtaining easy and rapid development, the queen exchange may well be to his advantage, as it usually is in similar lines. In fact White does not really intend to win in the endgame; rather his main plan is to play a complex middlegame where his superior central presence and development should count for something.

Before we examine 6 ♕f3 in some detail, it should be noted that both that and 6 ♕d2 are White's main tries for a reason, as we can see from a brief perusal of the alternatives:

a) 6 f4?! is too ambitious and turns Black's dark-squared bishop into something of a monster, which gives him, not White, an early initiative: 6...dxc6 7 ♕f3 (or 7 ♘c3 ♘h6 8 ♕f3 ♕h4+ when 9 ♕g3 ♕xg3+ 10 hxg3 ♘g4 is slightly in Black's favour, but White should prefer that to 9 g3?! ♗g4! 10 ♕g2 ♕h5 11 ♗e2 0-0-0 12 h3 ♗xe2 13 ♕xe2 ♕g6 14 g4 ♖he8 15 ♗d2 ♘f5, which left him in some trouble in L.Barczay-O.Romanishin, Dortmund 1982) 7...♕h4+ already sees Black forcing a concession.

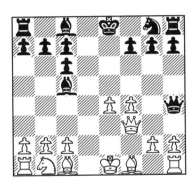

White's problem is that 8 g3? is again well met by 8...♗g4! when 9 ♕d2 0-0-0 would be rather good for Black, but even after the prudent 8 ♕g3 ♕xg3+ 9 hxg3 ♘f6 10 ♗d3 ♘g4 11 ♖f1 Black would have been for choice in K.Bjerring-W.Riedel, Munich 1993, had he settled for the simple 11...0-0.

b) 6 f3?! dxc6 7 ♘c3 ♗e6 8 ♗d2 (or 8 ♗d3 0-0-0 9 ♕e2 ♘e7 10 ♗e3 ♗b4 11 ♗d2 ♘g6 12 0-0 ♘f4 with some advan-

tage for Black in S.Hrisoglou-A.Leniart, Halkidiki 2005) 8...0-0-0 9 ♕e2 ♘e7 10 0-0-0 was seen in B.Gyorky-K.Horvath, Debrecen 2002, and now 10...♘g6 would have confirmed that the initiative belonged to Black.

c) 6 ♕e2 isn't so bad, but unlike after 6 ♕d2 White is not preparing to trade the queens with ♕f4 and, of course, ♕f3 would now cost him a tempo over the main lines of this chapter. Here Black should respond with 6...bxc6 7 ♘c3 (unfortunately for White 7 g3? runs into 7....♗a6! and the more creative 7 ♘d2 ♘e7 8 ♘b3 ♗b6 9 c4 d6 10 c5 dxc5 11 ♕f3 of V.Dragiev-M.Stoinev, Sofia 2004, would only have left White slightly worse had Black gone 11...♕e5) 7...♗d4, increasing the pressure down the long, dark-square diagonal.

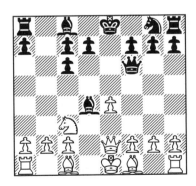

In V.Ivanchuk-D.Jakovenko, Moscow (blitz) 2009, White countered in 6 ♕d2-like fashion with 8 ♘a4 (the rather defensive 8 ♘d1 ♘e7 9 c3 ♗b6 10 ♕c2 ♘g6 11 ♗e2 had been seen in H.Murtez-Bj.Thorfinnsson, Saint Vincent 2005, when 11...0-0 12 0-0 ♖e8 leaves Black a little better) 8...♛e7 9 c3 ♝b6 10 g3 d6 (the alternative was 10...♘f6!? 11 e5 ♘d5 followed by ...f6, borrowing an idea from the 4...♘f6 variation) 11 ♝g2 ♝d7 12 0-0 ♘f6 13 e5!? when again play was not dissimilar to certain lines after 4...♘f6, and here Black returned the pawn to equalize with 13...dxe5 14 ♖e1 e4 15 ♝xe4 ♘xe4 16 ♛xe4 ♛xe4 17 ♖xe4+ ♝e6.

Returning to 6 ♛f3 when Black faces a major choice:

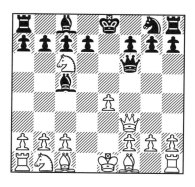

A: 6...♛xf3
B: 6...dxc6
C: 6...bxc6

It may seem surprising, but practice has shown that the immediate exchange on f3, which is how Black often responded when 6 ♛f3 first became topical, offers White simple, risk-free play with good chances of an advantage. Indeed, nowadays Black tends to refrain from exchanging on f3, prefer-

ring to retain the tension between the queens, as we'll see in Lines B and C. Those who adopt 6 ♛f3 should note too that 5...♛f6 wasn't forced and that Black's 5th-move alternatives were covered at the start of our last chapter.

Black's only other possibility is 6...♛xc6?! which retains the queens, but simply leads to a worse middlegame without much counterplay for him after 7 ♘c3.

At this juncture Black has tried to complete his development in a number of ways:

a) 7...b6 8 ♘d5 ♝b7? 9 ♝b5! won material in N.Ninov-M.Le Moal, Gap 2008.

b) 7...♝b4 8 ♝d2 ♘f6 (better than 8...♛f6?! 9 ♛g3 which saw White generating some strong threats in R.Arheit-S.Farias, Villa Ballester 2005) 9 0-0-0! (just to show that 6 ♛f3 isn't entirely a modern conception, 9 ♝d3 0-0 10 0-0 d6? 11 ♘d5! saw White exploiting the potential weakness of h7 to win a piece in R.Skuja-A.Ostrauskas, Minsk 1957; here Black does better with 10...♖fe8, not that it is enough to equalize after 11 ♖fe1 a6 12 ♕g3) 9...0-0 was seen in O.Koeller-I.Valencia, Giessen 1992, and now Barsky's 10 e5 leaves White very much calling the shots.

c) 7...♘f6 8 ♗d3 0-0 9 0-0 d6 saw Black developing quite classically in H.Kaiser-O.Kroener, Templin 2004, but with 10 ♘d5 White retains a pleasant pull.

d) 7...♘e7 has been Black's main choice, hoping that ideas of a timely ♘d5 and ♗g5 will be less effective than they are with the knight on f6.

However, in any case White's forces are better coordinated and he should emerge with a comfortable plus:

d1) 8 ♗d3 is the most straightforward approach, but after 8...0-0 9 0-0 ♘g6 (as played in J.Hernandez Velasco-C.Valverde Lujan, Valladolid 1993; otherwise, 9...d6 10 ♕g3 gives White a pull and the premature 9...f5?! 10 ♗g5 ♘g6 11 ♗b5 ♘e5 12 ♕g3 ♕e6 13 ♖ae1 d6 14 exf5 ♕xf5? 15 ♗e7! cost Black the exchange in G.Pitl-S.Torok, Budapest 2007) 10 ♘d5 ♕d6 White is restricted

to just a small pull with 11 ♗e3.

d2) 8 ♗b5 is based on a little tactic. Whether White should be so keen to drive the black queen to a potentially better square is not so clear, although after 8...♕e6 (Black was a little worse after 8...♕b6 9 ♗d3 0-0 10 0-0 ♗d4 11 ♘b5 ♗e5 12 ♗e3 in A.Wirig-S.Brunello, Steinbrunn 2005, but he might consider 8...♕g6!? 9 ♗f4 a6 10 ♗d3, as in R.Babayev-A.Golosnyak, Uelzen 2007, and then 10...d6 11 e5 ♕e6, which leaves him close to equality) 9 0-0 0-0 10 ♕d3 (keeping pieces on, since 10 ♘d5 ♗d6 11 ♗f4 didn't lead anywhere after 11...♗xf4 12 ♘xe7+ ♕xe7 13 ♕xf4 ♕b4 in P.Mittelberger-H.Eisterer, Hartberg 1992) 10...a6 11 ♗c4 ♕e5 12 ♗e3 b5 13 ♗b3 White has an edge, as pointed out by Barsky.

d3) The aggressive 8 ♗d2!? 0-0 9 0-0-0 of C.Ramirez-F.Escandon, Roque Saenz Pena 1997, deserves further attention, since White certainly has the initiative after, say, 9...d6 10 h4.

A) 6...♕xf3 7 gxf3

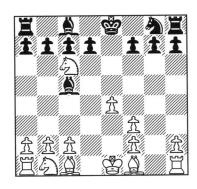

Thus both sides will emerge from the early exchanges with structural damage, but White can obtain a slight but durable edge whichever way Black recaptures:

A1: 7...dxc6
A2: 7...bxc6

A1) 7...dxc6

This is how Black usually recaptures in the 6 ♛d2 variation, but here the queens have gone and White still has some chances in a pure pawn endgame.

8 ♗e3!

The critical move, immediately challenging Black's bishop before the second player is able to enforce a blockade on the key central squares, f4 and e5. The alternatives give him time to do just that with ...♘e7-g6 and are unsurprisingly weaker:

a) 8 ♘d2 ♘e7 9 ♘b3 ♗d6 10 ♗d2 ♘g6 11 ♗c3 f6 12 h4 ♗e5 13 ♘d4 was seen in N.Zhukova-Shen Yang, Ekater-

inburg 2006, and after the blockading 13...♗d7 14 h5 ♘f4 it's hard to see any problems for Black.

b) 8 ♖g1 ♘e7 9 ♗e3 ♗xe3 10 fxe3 ♖g8 (10...0-0 11 ♗c4 b5 12 ♗d3 f5 13 ♘d2 fxe4 14 ♗xe4 ♗f5 was also okay for Black in M.Vujic-I.Solomunovic, Novi Sad 2008) 11 ♘c3 ♗d7 12 ♗c4 ♗e6 13 ♗xe6 fxe6 14 ♔e2 ♖d8 15 ♖ad1 ♔f7 saw Black equalize comfortably in T.Radjabov-V.Gashimov, Rimavska Sobota 1996. These future super-GMs were very young back then, but had perhaps already realized that one day 6 ♛f3 would become pretty topical!

c) 8 ♗f4 ♗d6 9 ♗e3 makes no sense after 9...♘e7 10 ♘d2 ♘g6 11 0-0-0, as in G.Lettieri-M.Olszewski, Belfort 2005, and now simply 11...♗e6 12 ♘c4 ♗f4 completes Black's ideal blockade.

d) Finally, with 8 ♗c4!? White can take play into Line B2, below.

Moving the bishop to e3 always poses a serious dilemma for Black in the 6 ♛f3 variation. Should he exchange on e3 or retreat the bishop? Both options represent some sort of concession: a retreat to d6 or e7 means abandoning a good diagonal, but an exchange on e3 helps strengthen White's central control and leaves him less susceptible to ideas of ...f5.

8...♗xe3

Here there does not seem to be a choice, as the alternatives are clearly weaker:

a) 8...♗d6?! 9 ♘d2 (White goes for the bishop pair, but 9 f4 also looks promising: for example, 9...♘h6 10 h3 f5 11 e5 ♗e7 is better for White according to Lukacs and Hazai, and also after 9...f5 10 e5 ♗b4+ 11 c3 ♗a5 12 ♘d2 White is somewhat better) 9...♗e6 (9...♘e7?! 10 f4 f6 11 ♘c4 is very good for White) 10 ♘c4 ♘e7 11 f4 f5 12 e5 and White has an obvious advantage.

b) 8...♗b6 stays on the g1-a7 diagonal, but 9 ♘c3 ♗e6 10 0-0-0 ♘e7 11 ♖g1 0-0 12 f4 was slightly better for White in S.Dujkovic-D.Lekic, Neum 2005.

c) 8...♗e7 9 ♘d2 ♘f6 10 0-0-0 0-0 11 ♘b3 was similarly pleasant for White in M.Godena-L.Yurtaev, Turin Olympiad 2006, thanks to his possibilities of kingside expansion.

9 fxe3

Now White's plan is generally to develop his knight to d2 and then to bring it to either b3 or c4.

9...♗e6

After this relatively popular choice White gains the option of exchanging the remaining bishops with ♗c4, but in any case Black is unable to equalize:

a) 9...♘f6 10 ♘d2 ♗e6 11 ♖g1 0-0 12 ♘b3 was slightly better for White in D.Andreikin-D.Howell, Yerevan 2006.

b) The active 9...f5 failed to equalize after 10 ♘c3 fxe4 (or 10...♘e7 11 ♖g1 g6 12 ♗d3, retaining a pull, as given by Barsky) 11 ♘xe4 ♗f5 12 ♗d3 ♘e7 13 0-0-0 0-0-0 14 ♖hg1 in Z.Corrales Jimenez-J.Perez Rodriguez, Holguin 2008.

c) 9...♘e7 10 ♘c3 ♗e6 11 ♖d1 0-0 12 ♔f2 ♖fd8 13 ♗e2 saw White preparing to advance with f4 and to make a favourable exchange of rooks in S.Novikov-P.Dvalishvili, Moscow 2010.

10 ♖g1!?

This move is likely the most irksome for Black, as he cannot yet meet it with castling. That said, 10 ♘d2 is also promising when one example saw 10...♘e7 11 ♗c4 ♗xc4 12 ♘xc4 ♖d8 13 ♔e2 c5 14 ♖hg1 g6 15 ♖ad1 with an edge for White in Zhang Penxiang-G.Vescovi, Taiyuan 2006.

10...g6 11 ♘d2

Now 11...0-0-0 12 ♘b3 ♘f6 13 ♘d4 gives White a clear edge. He can also

meet 11...♘f6 with 12 ♘b3 and the same plan, although 12 ♗c4 ♗e7 13 ♔e2 b6 14 ♗xe6 ♔xe6 15 f4 ♖ad8 16 e5 was no less effective a way of retaining the upper hand in I.Nataf-B.Lajthajm, Budva 2003, which White went on to win after making good use of the e4-square for his knight and by bringing his rook to d4.

A2) 7...bxc6

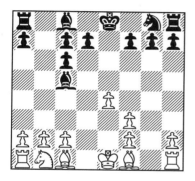

A more challenging approach than the recapture with the d-pawn and one which can lead to a more complicated fight for control of the centre.

8 ♗e3!

Again this move is the most incisive and after it White's further course of action will depend on how Black resolves the tension between the bishops. White has also delayed ♗e3 by a move or two, but the alternatives are generally less impressive:

a) 8 ♘c3 ♘e7 9 h4 reveals an important concept against Black's plan of ...♘g6: White will kick the knight without delay and so cause problems. Now:

a1) 9...h5 halts the white h-pawn, but after 10 ♗e3 (of course!) 10...♗xe3 11 fxe3 d6 12 0-0-0! (better than 12 ♗e2 ♘g6 13 f4 when Black was okay after 13...♗g4! 14 ♗xg4 hxg4 15 h5 ♘e7 in T.Radjabov-V.Akopian, Elista 2008) 12...♖h6 (or 12...♗e6 13 ♘e2 ♗c4 14 b3 ♗xe2 15 ♗xe2 with an edge, V.Tseshkovsky-D.Lekic, Herceg Novi 2005) 13 ♗e2 ♘g6 14 ♖dg1 ♖xg1+ 15 ♖xg1 g6 16 f4 White had a steady advantage in V.Tseshkovsky-V.Zvjaginsev, Vrnjacka Banja 2005.

a2) 9...♖b8!? is more annoying for White. Then 10 ♘a4 ♗d4 11 c3 ♗f6 12 ♘c5 was seen in V.Tseshkovsky-M.Klauser, Biel 2006, but after 12...h5 White's position isn't so ideal with Black able to meet ♘d3 with ...♗a6.

a3) Black was also fine after 9...0-0 10 ♘a4 ♗d4 11 c3 ♗f6 12 ♘c5 ♖b8 13 ♘d3 ♘g6 in V.Tseshkovsky-D.Rodin, Voronezh 2009, and so the conclusion must be that White should prevent the ...♗d4-f6 manoeuvre, when the bishop eyes White's h-pawn and joins in the fight for control of e5, by playing an early ♗e3.

b) 8 ♘d2 takes play into Line C2 and is not such a bad try for the advantage, as we'll see there.

c) 8 ♖g1 seeks to cause some discomfort, but in this particular case it doesn't work out too well: 8...♘e7! 9 ♗e3 (9 ♖xg7? loses the exchange to 9...♘g6 and after 10 ♗h6 ♗d4 11 ♘c3 d6 12 0-0-0 ♗xg7 13 ♗xg7 ♖g8 14 ♗f6 ♘e5 White hasn't enough compensation, as pointed out by Tyomkin) 9...♗xe3 10 fxe3 ♖b8 11 ♗c4 d5 saw Black commencing counterplay and equalizing in B.Laubsch-W.Bode, German League 2007.

d) 8 ♗c4!? is a more reasonable move, after which 8...♘e7 9 ♘c3 d6 10 ♖g1 ♗d4 11 ♗e3 ♗f6 12 0-0-0 ♗e6 13 ♗b3 0-0 was seen in S.Granara Barreto-J.Hase, Necochea 2007, and now the simple 14 f4 gives White a plus. Still, the main line is more forcing and causes Black more problems.

8...♗xe3

Unfortunately for Black, avoiding this exchange brings nothing but trouble:

a) 8...♗b6 runs into the powerful 9 c4!.

The threat to trap the bishop on the queenside forces 9...♗xe3 (otherwise: 9...♖b8? 10 c5! ♗a5+ 11 ♔d1 is a disaster and 11...♘f6 12 ♔c2 d6 13 cxd6 cxd6 14 ♗xa7 cost Black a clear pawn in A.Zontakh-V.Yemelin, St Petersburg 2006; 9...♘e7?! 10 c5 ♗a5+ 11 ♘d2 is also pretty good for White; and 9...d6

10 c5 ♗xc5 11 ♗xc5 dxc5 12 ♘c3 promises him a pleasant plus too) 10 fxe3 d6 (nothing is changed by 10...♘e7 11 ♘c3 d6 12 c5 ♗e6 13 0-0-0 ♖d8 14 ♖d4 0-0 15 ♖a4 when Black was under pressure in B.Savchenko-K.Georgiev, Moscow 2006, and here Renet points out that 13...0-0-0 14 ♖g1 g6 15 ♗a6+ ♔b8 16 ♖d4 dxc5 17 ♖dd1 f5 18 ♘a4 gives White a strong initiative) 11 ♖g1 g6 (11...♘e7 12 ♘c3 0-0 13 0-0-0 is more of the same) 12 ♘c3 ♘e7 (Black tried the active 12...f5 13 0-0-0 ♘f6 in E.Can-L.Lenic, Kemer 2007, but was worse after 14 ♗d3 fxe4 15 ♘xe4 0-0 16 ♘xf6+ ♖xf6 17 ♗e4) 13 0-0-0 ♗e6 14 f4 f5, as occurred in Ruan Lufei-T.Sachdev, Teheran 2007, and after the typical 15 c5 White is better.

b) Rather passive is 8...♗e7 9 c4 ♗f6 10 ♘c3 d6 11 c5! ♗e6 12 0-0-0 ♔e7 13 ♗a6 ♖b8 14 ♖d2 ♗e5 15 f4 ♗xc3 16 bxc3 by when White had achieved a sizeable plus in B.Savchenko-V.Orlov, St Petersburg 2005.

9 fxe3

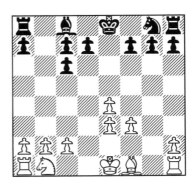

The outlines of the battle have been

drawn and they don't look too pleasant for Black, simple though the position might appear to be. White has a central preponderance, an open g-file and will eventually have the more active pieces. In addition, his central pawn trio can begin to advance. It looks like Black must strike against e4 with ...f5, but this fails to have the desired impact, as we shall see. Therefore the conclusion is that White has a steady edge.

9...♘e7

Alternatively:

a) Black can hardly achieve anything with 9...d5 10 ♘c3 ♘f6 11 exd5 cxd5 12 ♘b5 and in general an early ...d5 brings only trouble for the second player.

b) 9...d6 can be met by, amongst others, 10 ♖g1 ♘e7 11 c4 g6 12 ♘c3 ♗e6 13 f4 f6 14 0-0-0 0-0-0 15 c5 with an edge in N.Vyskocil-Z.Vojacek, Brno 2006.

c) 9...♖b8!? should always be considered, as it gives Black the option to activate his rook while forcing White to play a move he perhaps wouldn't like to:

c1) 10 ♗c4 ♘e7 (10...♖xb2 11 ♗b3 traps the rook) 11 ♘c3 (11 ♘d2 can be well met by 11...f5 12 e5 d5 with equal chances) 11...0-0 12 0-0-0 d6 13 f4 was seen in O.Kulicov-S.Kapnisis, Litohoro 2006, and now after 13...♗e6 Black is okay.

c2) The simpler 10 b3 is likely a better try: 10...♘f6 (another possibility is 10...♘e7 11 ♘c3 f5 12 e5 ♘g6 13 f4 d6 14 exd6 cxd6 15 ♖d1 when White re-

tains some edge, while 10...d6 should be met by the typical idea 11 ♖g1 ♘e7 12 ♖g5!? with the initiative) 11 ♖g1! (with the idea to bring the rook via g5 to a5, which is a logical way to take advantage of the move ...♖b8) 11...0-0 12 ♘c3 ♖e8 (12...d6 13 0-0-0 ♖e8 14 ♖d4 is also better for White) 13 ♖g5! d5 14 ♗d3 h6 15 ♖g2! dxe4 16 ♗xe4 and White had the advantage in G.Vescovi-G.Milos, Guarulhos 2006.

10 ♘c3

Straightforward and correct. Instead 10 c4 is no longer appropriate, as White will be a tempo down on the 8...♗b6 lines and this allows Black to equalize, as he did with 10...d6 11 ♘c3 0-0 12 f4 f5 13 ♗g2 fxe4 14 ♗xe4 ♗e6 15 b3 d5 in D.Smerdon-K.Georgiev, Gibraltar 2007.

10...d6

Having ruled out e5 in response, Black is now ready to break with ...f5 and this forces White to play with precision.

Unsurprisingly the immediate 10...f5 is well met by 11 e5! (worse is 11

♣d3 fxe4 12 ♞xe4 ♜b8 13 0-0-0 0-0
with equality) 11...d6 12 ♜g1 g6
(12...♞g6 13 exd6 cxd6 14 0-0-0 d5 15
♞e2 is also preferable for the first
player, but perhaps 12...0-0!? 13 exd6
cxd6 14 0-0-0 ♜f6 can be considered)
13 exd6 cxd6 14 0-0-0 ♗d7 15 h4 ♗c7
16 ♣c4 when White was better in
E.Najer-A.Naiditsch, Moscow 2007.

Instead Black played a very interesting idea in Y.Iwasaki-N.Pokazanjev,
Kemerovo 2007: 10...0-0!? 11 ♣c4 ♗h8
12 0-0-0 f5 13 e5 f4! 14 ♜he1 fxe3 15
♜xe3 ♞f5 and stood well. However,
White's play was hardly critical and he
should have started with 11 ♜g1 or 11
0-0-0, with the former transposing to
our main line after 11...d6.

11 ♜g1!

White's main move has actually
been 11 0-0-0, but here Black can try
11...f5 (otherwise, 11...0-0 should be met
by 12 ♜g1 and not the hasty 12 f4 f5,
which seems okay for Black, but note
can be made of the creative 11...g5!? 12
♜g1 h6 13 f4 ♞g6 14 e5 dxe5 15 ♣g2
♣d7 16 ♞e4 ♗e7, which turned out well
in J.Tomczak-M.Bartel, Warsaw 2009) 12
e5!? (daring, but 12 ♜d4 0-0 13 f4 fxe4
14 ♜xe4 ♞f5 15 ♣c4+ ♗h8 didn't give
White anything in S.Rublevsky-
P.Simacek, Ohrid 2009) 12...dxe5 13 ♣c4
♣d7 (or 13...♞g6 14 ♜hg1 ♗e7 15 h4
♗f6 16 h5, again with good compensa-
tion, as in A.Muzychuk-A.Stefanova,
Krasnoturinsk 2008) 14 ♜hg1 g6 15 e4
with good compensation in A.Kornev-
M.Kobalia, Moscow 2005, although one

can hardly tell if it is enough for the advantage. Indeed, overall the more forcing text move appears preferable.

11...0-0

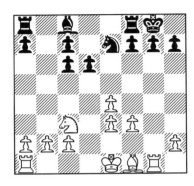

Natural, but in fact attention
should be paid to 11...g6!? now that the
dark-squared bishops have been exchanged. The downside is that it gives
White the option of pushing h4-h5
later and here White should probably
try 12 f4 f5 13 ♣d3 ♜b8 14 b3 ♣e6 15
♗d2, using the king to protect the central pawns and intending to take on f5
followed by pushing e4, which should
supply some edge.

12 f4!

White must be incisive and not allow Black to equalize with 12 0-0-0 f5.

12...f5

Very similar is 12...♜b8!? 13 b3 f5 14
♣c4+ ♗h8 15 e5! dxe5 16 0-0-0 ♞g6
and now White's best try is the sacrifi-
cial 17 ♜d3! (one might also look into
Lukacs and Hazai's suggestion of 17
♞e2!?) 17...♜a8 (alternatively, 17...exf4?
loses to 18 ♜xg6! hxg6 19 exf4; after
17...e4?! 18 ♜d2 White doubles rooks

on the d-file when he is much better; and, finally, 17...c5 18 ♖f1 ♗b7 19 ♘a4 ♗e4 20 ♖d2 gave White an edge in Ni Hua-I.Naumkin, Cappelle la Grande 2007) 18 ♘a4. Here Black can take up the challenge, but after 18...exf4 (18...e4?! 19 ♖d2 is again bad for Black) 19 ♖xg6! fxe3! 20 ♖xc6! (but not 20 ♖g1? f4 with a big plus for Black in Zhang Zhong-V.Akopian, Turin Olympiad 2006) 20...f4 21 ♘c3 ♗f5 22 ♖d4 f3 23 ♖f4 ♗g6 24 ♘d5 White manages to stop the pawns in time. It's still not trivial, but it seems that White is the one playing for the win here.

13 ♗c4+

Again the check is best, especially as 13 ♗d3 fxe4 14 ♘xe4 ♗f5 is just equal.

13...♔h8 14 e5!

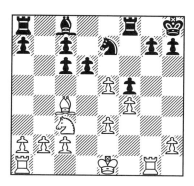

White pushes on with this interesting pawn sacrifice, which enables him to continue fighting for the upper hand.

14...dxe5 15 0-0-0

So what does White have for the pawn? His pieces are much the more active, he controls the d-file and can increase the pressure in various ways. Moreover, Black has problems coordinating and his pawns are weak, especially on the queenside. Overall, it seems that White's compensation is very promising and he doesn't even need to do anything concrete; simply slowly turning the screw should suffice.

15...exf4

This is an understandable decision, but the open files can only really benefit the white rooks. Still, Black faces a difficult choice:

a) 15...e4 allows White a simple advantage with either 16 ♘a4 ♘g8 17 ♘c5 ♘f6 18 h3 or 16 ♖d4 ♘g8 17 ♘a4 ♘f6 18 h3.

b) Again Black likely does best to retain the tension with 15...♘g6, although here too White seems to be on top after 16 ♖d3! (or even 16 ♘e2!? when 16...♘h4? 17 ♖g3 e4 18 ♘d4 was very bad for Black in A.Bitalzadeh-V.Rothuis, Dutch League 2007, but even 16...a5 17 a4 exf4 18 exf4 ♗a6 19 ♗xa6 ♖xa6 20 ♖d7 gives White an advantage in the endgame thanks to his active pieces, E.Najer-V.Akopian, Sochi 2007) 16...a5 (otherwise, 16...exf4? once more runs into 17 ♖xg6! fxe3 18 ♖xc6 f4 19 ♖xc7 when White's extra piece was somewhat more important than Black's passed pawns in J.Valmana Canto-P.Harikrishna, San Sebastian 2006, while after 16...e4 17 ♖d2 White is steadily on top) 17 ♘e2, as in S.Haslinger-R.Berzinsh, British League 2007. Here after 17...e4 18 ♖a3 White has a strong initiative and Black's extra pawn doesn't really matter at all.

16 exf4 ♖b8

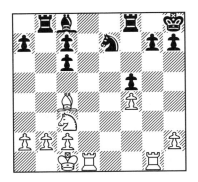

We've followed the game D.Howell-J.Werle, London 2009, where White improved his pieces with 17 ♖de1 ♘g8 18 ♘a4 ♗d7 19 ♘c5 ♖bd8 20 ♖g3. That sufficed for some advantage and Howell went on to win, but perhaps an even simpler way to secure a serious plus was 17 ♖g3!? ♘g8 (and again not 17...♘g6?? 18 ♖xg6! hxg6 19 ♖d3) 18 ♖e3 when the sorry state of the rook on b8 and the bishop on c8 is telling.

B) 6...dxc6

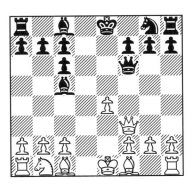

Black recaptures as he tends to after 6 ♕d2, preparing to bring his light-squared bishop to e6 and to generate play down the d-file after an early ...0-0-0 or ...♖d8. At this point a fair amount of practice has shown that White does best to develop one of his knight or light-squared bishop as actively as possible.

> **B1: 7 ♘c3**
> **B2: 7 ♗c4**

Before it became clear that those were the critical lines, there was also a fair amount of debate with the alternatives:

a) 7 ♕g3 is an important try after 6...bxc6 (Line C2), but here 7...♘e7 8 ♗d3 ♘g6 9 0-0 ♕e5 is fine for Black, as it was in E.Struth-H.Immer, German League 1995, when 10 ♘d2 ♕xg3 11 hxg3 ♗e6 would have been about equal.

b) 7 ♗e2 ♗e6 8 ♘c3 0-0-0 9 ♕xf6?! (a little premature; instead after 9 0-0 one route to equality is the simple 9...♕xf3 10 ♗xf3 ♘f6, but White must avoid 9 ♗d2? which blundered a key pawn to 9...♗xf2+! 10 ♔xf2 ♖xd2 in C.Stanetzek-D.Korth, German League 2007) 9...♘xf6 10 ♗g5 h6! left Black with the initiative and slightly for choice in N.Grunina-T.Sterliagova, Volgograd 1996.

c) 7 ♗d3 ♕xf3 (7...♗e6 8 0-0 ♕xf3 9 gxf3 0-0-0 10 ♘c3 ♘e7 was also fine for

Black in A.Latfullin-O.Sanzhina, Salek-hard 2006) 8 gxf3 ♝e6 9 ♝e3 was tried in P.Marxen-B.Lengyel, Budapest 2004, when 9...♝xe3 10 fxe3 0-0-0 followed by ...♞e7 would have been fine for the second player.

d) Neither should Black fear 7 ♛xf6 ♞xf6 8 f3 (after 8 ♝d3 Black has a fairly pleasant choice between 8...♝e6 9 0-0 0-0-0 and 8...0-0 9 0-0 ♜e8, likely followed by improving the knight via d7, with equality in either case) 8...♝e6 (invariably played, but again 8...0-0!? 9 ♞d2 ♜e8 is fine too and after 10 ♞b3 ♝b6 11 c4 in J.Dworakowska-V.Golubenko, Dresden 2007, Black might well have battled for the initiative with 11...♞d7), since his somewhat better development clearly offsets his structural problems.

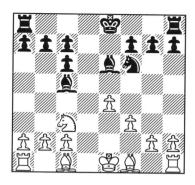

9...0-0-0 10 ♝d2 (alternatively, 10 ♝g5?! h6 11 ♝xf6 gxf6 12 ♝d3 was seen in T.Al Hassan-Z.Basil Ghazala, Dubai 2005, when 12...h5 would have left Black somewhat for choice, as pointed out by Renet, while 10 ♝d3 can be met by either 10...♜he8 11 ♝g5 h6 12 ♝h4 ♝d4, with easy play for Black, or by the 10...h6!? 11 ♚e2 g5 12 ♞a4 of S.Lalic-K.Bhatia, British League 2008, and then 12...♝e7, with rough equality) 10...♝f2+ 11 ♚e2 (White was a little worse too after 11 ♚d1 ♞d7 12 ♝d3 ♞e5 in P.Rewitz-N.Borge, Copenhagen 1995) 11...♝d4 12 ♝e3 c5 gave Black any advantage which was going in K.Chernyshov-Z.Gyimesi, Balatonbereny 1994.

d3) 9 ♝d3 ♞d7 10 f4?! f6 11 ♞d2 0-0-0 12 ♚e2 was pretty ambitious from White in K.Chernyshov-W.Spyra, Krynica 1995, and now the undermining 12...g5 would have given Black the upper hand.

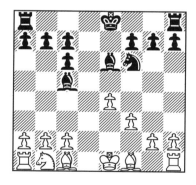

Now:

d1) 9 ♝g5?! h6! 10 ♝h4 0-0-0 11 ♞c3 g5 12 ♝g3 ♞h5 saw Black putting his superior development to good use in A.Berelovich-A.Naumann, Internet blitz 2005.

d2) 9 ♞c3 is also a little misguided:

d4) White's main continuation is 9 ♞d2 0-0-0 (Renet's idea of 9...a5!? 10 ♝c4 a4 11 ♝xe6 fxe6 12 ♚e2 b5, seizing a fair amount of space on the queenside, also deserves attention) 10 ♘b3, but this doesn't, of course, drive Black's bishop from the key g1-a7 diagonal:

d41) 10...♗xb3!? 11 axb3 ♖he8 12 ♗d2 (as tried in I.Nataf-C.Matamoros Franco, Evora 2006; otherwise, 12 ♗e2 ♖d7 13 c3 ♘d5! 14 b4 ♘e3 15 ♗xe3 ♗xe3 favours Black, as pointed out by Renet and 12 ♗d3 ♘d5 13 ♗d2 ♘b4 14 ♗xb4 ♗xb4+ was equal in M.White-J.Cox, Gausdal 2007) 12...♘d5 13 g3 ♘e3 14 ♗xe3 ♗xe3 15 ♔e2 ♗c5 16 ♗h3+ ♔b8 17 ♖hd1 ♖d6 (Renet) is fine for Black, with a draw looking quite likely.

d42) 10...♘b6 11 ♗d2 (Black equalized after 11 ♗e2 ♘d7 12 ♗f4 f5 13 exf5 ♗xf5 in L.Kritz-A.Naumann, Austrian League 2005) 11...♘d7! (Black frees his pawn, while the knight may reappear on any of c5, e5 or f6) 12 ♗c3 was seen in A.Naumann-J.Borisek, Szeged 2007, when the thematic 12...f5 was called for. Annotating for ChessPublishing.com, the indefatigable Re-

net supplies the lines 13 ♗xg7?! ♖he8 14 ♘d2 fxe4 15 ♘xe4 ♘c5 16 ♗e2 ♘xe4 17 fxe4 ♖g8 18 ♗f6 ♖df8 19 e5 ♖xg2, when Black regains his pawn with some advantage, and 13 exf5 ♗xf5 14 0-0-0 ♘f6 15 ♗c4 ♗e3+ 16 ♗d2 ♗xd2+ 17 ♖xd2 ♖xd2 18 ♘xd2 ♖e8, giving Black sufficient counterplay to maintain the balance.

e) 7 ♘d2 dissuades a queen exchange on f3, while again preparing to bring the knight to b3, but after 7...♗e6 (unsurprisingly 7...♕xf3 8 ♘xf3 ♘e7 9 ♗f4 ♗b6 10 ♗c4 ♘g6 11 ♗g3 sufficed for an edge in S.Shurygin-V.Malaniuk, Koszalin 2001) White faces a further choice:

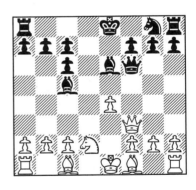

e1) 8 ♘b3 ♗b6 (White was a little better after 8...♗xb3 9 axb3 ♕xf3 10 gxf3 ♘e7 11 ♗e3 ♗xe3 12 fxe3 in A.Delorme-J.Boudre, St Affrique 2006, but Black might consider 8...♗d6!?; then White probably has nothing better than 9 ♕xf6 ♘xf6 10 f3 after all when 10...c5 11 ♗e3 b6 is pretty solid for Black, since 9 ♗e2?! ♕e5! 10 ♗d2 ♘f6 11 ♗c3 ♕xe4 12 ♕xe4 ♘xe4 13

♗xg7 ♖g8 14 ♗d4 0-0-0 left Black on top in G.Jones-S.Mamedyarov, Bastia (blitz) 2010) 9 ♕g3 (otherwise, 9 ♗d3 is well met by Sakelsek's 9...a5 when 10 0-0 a4 11 ♘d2 a3 gives Black the initiative, but probably White should try that or 9 ♗d2, not that Black then has any problems after 9...0-0-0, since the text is unimpressive) 9...0-0-0 (the immediate 9...♕g6 is also fine for Black and after 10 ♗d3 ♘f6 11 ♗f4 0-0-0 12 ♕xg6 hxg6 13 ♔e2 ♖h5! he was able to seize a small initiative on the kingside in S.Novikov-A.Feoktistov, Voronezh 2006) 10 ♗d3 ♕g6! 11 ♕xg6 (the misguided 11 ♗g5 ♘f6 12 f3? ♘h5 cost White material in G.Antal-V.Bhat, Lubbuck 2009) 11...hxg6 12 ♔e2 ♘f6 13 ♗e3 was seen in E.Andreev-V.Zhidkov, Nabereznye Chelny 2007, and now the simple 13...♗xe3 14 ♔xe3 ♘g4+ would have left Black slightly for choice.

e2) Thus White does better with 8 ♗d3, not that he has any advantage after 8...0-0-0 9 0-0 and then:

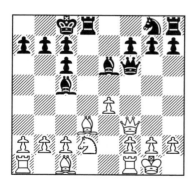

e21) 9...♘e7 10 ♕xf6 gxf6 11 ♘b3 ♗b6! (keeping control of d4) 12 ♗e3 ♖hg8 13 ♔h1 (the later 13 ♖fe1 ♘g6 14 ♗xb6 axb6 15 ♖e3 ♘f4 16 g3 c5 gave Black the initiative in T.Kos-Z.Zvan, Bled 2001, as does 13 ♗xb6 axb6 followed by ...c5) 13...♘g6 (but not 13...♗xe3? 14 fxe3 ♖g6 because of 15 ♘d4, as pointed out by Nunn) 14 ♗xb6 axb6 15 f4 ♘e7 was fine for Black in A.Huzman-J.Nunn, Wijk aan Zee 1993.

e22) Nunn later suggested 9...♗d4!? and after 10 ♕xf6 ♘xf6 11 ♘f3 ♗b6 Black was okay in M.Ragger-E.Romanov, Belfort 2005.

B1) 7 ♘c3

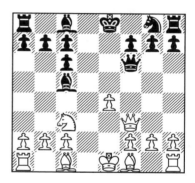

The knight may not seem so well placed here, but White facilitates the important concept of ♗e3 and may later follow up by regrouping the knight via e2.

7...♗e6

Black's main choice, but this may not best:

a) The misguided 7...♘e7?! of I.Bulmaga-A.Karlovich, Kharkov 2008, should be met by 8 ♕xf6 gxf6 9 ♗f4 with some advantage.

b) 7...♕xf3 8 gxf3 ♗e6 (after 8...♘e7
9 ♗e3! ♗xe3 10 fxe3 ♗e6 11 0-0-0 0-0
12 ♘e2 ♖ad8 13 ♘d4 ♗c8 14 ♗c4
White had regrouped his pieces to
emerge with an edge in A.Hnydiuk-
T.Warakomski, Karpacz 2008) 9 ♗f4
(otherwise, 9 a3 doesn't really trouble
Black after 9...0-0-0 10 ♗e3 ♗b6, but
White should look into both 9 ♗e3 and
9 ♘a4!?) 9...0-0-0 10 ♖g1 g6 11 ♗d3
♗d4! 12 ♗g3 ♘e7 was fine for Black in
D.Vinckier-C.Vinsard, La Fere 2006.

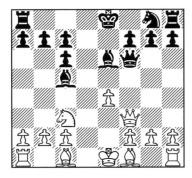

8 ♗e3!

Simple and effective, if not the only
route to the advantage:

a) However, 8 ♘a4?! does not work
out well here: 8...♗b4+ 9 c3 ♗d6 10
♗e3 (10 ♕xf6? ♘xf6 11 f3 would, of
course, fail to 11...b5) 10...♕e7 11 ♗d4
f6 12 b4 ♘h6 13 h3?! was the course of
D.Sadvakasov-S.Mamedyarov, Astana
2006, when Black could have seized the
initiative and some advantage with
13...0-0 14 ♘c5 a5.

b) 8 ♕g3 0-0-0 (White is a little better after 8...♘h6 9 ♗e2, but not 9 ♗g5?
♗xf2+, while the 8...♗d4!? 9 ♗f4 0-0-0

10 0-0-0 ♖d7 of D.Lintchevski-
N.Matinian, Rybinsk 2008, should be
met by 11 ♗d3!, intending 11...♗xc3 12
bxc3 with strong pressure against g7) 9
♗e3! is quite an ambitious try, but the
complications seem to favour White:

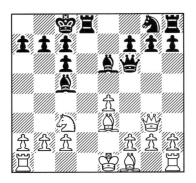

b1) 9...♗d6? 10 f4 ♗b4 is what Black
would like to play, but after 11 ♗xa7!
g5 (11...b6? fails to 12 ♗a6+ ♔d7 13
0-0-0+ ♔e8 14 f5, as analysed by Lukacs
and Hazai) 12 fxg5 ♕g7 13 ♗f2 h6 14
gxh6 ♕xh6 15 ♗d3 Black clearly didn't
have enough for his pawns in V.Belov-
D.Svetushkin, Rijeka 2010.

b2) 9...♗b4? 10 ♗g5 picks up the exchange.

b3) 9...♗d4 10 ♗xd4 ♖xd4 11 f4
♘e7 12 ♗d3 ♔b8 13 0-0 ♖hd8
(13...♖dd8? allowed White's pawns to
advance with some effect in A.Motylev-
E.Romanov, Krasnoyarsk 2007, where
14 f5! ♗c8 15 e5 ♕h6 16 ♖ae1 gave
White a strong initiative) 14 f5 ♗c8 15
♖ae1 sees White retaining a useful
pull.

b4) The simple 9...♗xe3 10 ♕xe3
♔b8 was tried in I.Kurnosov-E.Ubilava,

New Delhi 2008, and now 11 ♗d3 ♘e7 12 f4 ♖he8 13 0-0 would preserve an edge.

8...♗b4

Otherwise, 8...♛e7 9 ♗xc5 ♛xc5 10 0-0-0 ♘f6 11 h3 0-0 12 ♔b1 b5 13 ♗d3 ♘d7 14 ♛g3 ♘b6 15 f4 gave White an edge in B.Savchenko-S.Mamedyarov, Moscow (blitz) 2007, while 8...♗xe3 9 ♛xe3 ♛e7 10 0-0-0! ♘f6 11 f4 0-0 12 h3 b6 13 g4 saw him logically beginning to attack in A.Martorelli-R.Mandolini, Porto San Giorgio 2009.

9 ♛xf6!

White shouldn't fear an exchange on c3. He has also tested 9 ♗d2, but after 9...0-0-0 10 ♗d3 (or 10 ♛xf6 ♘xf6 11 f3 ♘d7 12 0-0-0 f5 13 a3 ♗d6 14 exf5 ♗xf5 15 ♗g5 ♖de8 and the 6...dxc6 specialist had enough counterplay to maintain a rough balance in G.Jones-S.Mamedyarov, Bastia (rapid) 2010) 10...♛e7 11 a3 ♗c5 12 ♗e3 ♘f6 13 h3 ♘d7 Black was fine in G.Gomez-J.Perez, Tunja 1991.

9...♘xf6 10 f3 ♖d8

As pointed out by Lukacs and Hazai, 10...0-0-0 11 a3 ♗xc3+ 12 bxc3 looks a little better for White, in view of his bishop-pair and more useful majority, and he might even consider an advance of the a-pawn.

11 a3!

Forcing the issue is a better try than 11 ♗e2 ♘d7 12 ♔f2 ♘b6! 13 g4 a5 14 a3 ♗xc3 15 bxc3 ♘a4, which saw Black seizing the initiative in D.Petrosian-T.L.Petrosian, Teheran 2005.

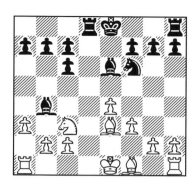

11...♗a5

Now if Black tries 11...♗xc3+ 12 bxc3 ♘d7 White can cause some disruption with 13 ♗f4 (Lukacs and Hazai).

12 ♔f2

This looks a little better for White who will follow up with 13 ♗e2 and then consider ideas involving kingside expansion, as well as of a timely ♘a4, hunting down the bishop-pair.

B2) 7 ♗c4

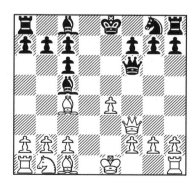

A reactive idea, preparing to meet ...♗e6 with a favourable trade of bishops.

7...♕xf3

Black frees his knight for duty without allowing his kingside structure to be shattered, but there are a number of alternatives and quite important ones at that:

a) 7...♞e7 8 ♕xf6 gxf6 9 ♗f4 ♗b6 (or 9...♗d6 when one good approach is 10 ♗e3 ♞g6 11 ♞d2 f5 12 g3 0-0 13 f4 ♗e6 and now in G.Szabo-O.Romanishin, Bucharest 2008, 14 ♗d3 would have left White doing pretty well) 10 ♞d2 (White was also a little better after 10 ♞c3 ♞g6 11 ♗g3 h5 12 h4 ♞e5 13 ♗e2 ♗e6 14 ♞a4 ♗a5+ 15 c3 in S.Rublevsky-A.Naiditsch, Poikovsky 2009, but here Black likely does better with 12...♗e6 and 13 ♗xe6 fxe6 14 0-0-0 ♖g8, which seemed okay for him in N.Vyskocil-T.Roussel Roozmon, Brno 2008) 10...♞g6 11 ♗g3 h5 is quite a radical approach from Black.

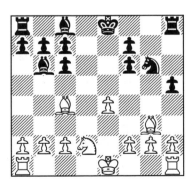

After 12 h3 ♗e6 13 ♗xe6 fxe6 14 ♞c4 0-0-0 15 ♔e2 ♖d4 he had sufficient counterplay to maintain the balance in T.Radjabov-E.Bacrot, Odessa (rapid) 2007, but White does better

with 12 h4. Then 12...♗e6 13 ♖d1! ♔e7 14 ♔e2 ♖ad8 15 ♗b3 f5 16 exf5 ♗xf5 17 ♖he1 retained an edge in Ni Hua-G.Sargissian, Turin Olympiad 2006, as did 12...♞e5 13 ♗b3 ♖g8 14 ♞c4 ♞xc4 15 ♗xc4 ♗e6 16 ♗e2 in I.Kurnosov-E.Romanov, Krasnoyarsk 2007.

b) 7...♗e6 is somewhat more obliging and after 8 ♕xf6 (White can also exchange immediately on e6: 8 ♗xe6 ♕xe6 9 ♗e3 ♗b4+ 10 ♞d2 0-0-0 11 c3 ♗d6 12 0-0 ♞f6 13 ♗g5 ♔b8 14 ♗xf6 gxf6 15 ♞b3 gave him a pull too in S.Sulskis-D.Svetushkin, Port Erin 2007; note here that 10...♗xd2+ 11 ♗xd2 ♞f6 12 0-0 ♞xe4? fails to 13 ♖fe1 f5 14 ♕e3 when White regains his pawn with some advantage) 8...♞xf6 9 ♗xe6 fxe6 10 f3 0-0 (or 10...e5 11 ♔e2 ♔f7 12 ♗e3 ♗xe3 13 ♔xe3 g5 14 ♞d2 with an endgame edge in P.Negi-K.Lahno, New Delhi (rapid) 2006) 11 ♞d2 ♞d7 (11...♞h5?! 12 ♞b3 ♗b6 would have allowed White some advantage in M.Dillmann-H.Tabatt, German League 2002, had he found the standard idea of 13 c4) 12 ♞c4 a5 13 a4 ♞b6 14 ♞e5 ♗d6 15 ♞d3 c5 16 ♗e3 White had a small but clear edge in Ni Hua-Yang Wen, Beijing 2008.

c) 7...♕g6 8 ♞d2 (more effective than 8 h3 ♞f6 9 ♗d3 ♞d7 10 ♗f4 when in S.Crouan-J.Le Roux, Nantes 2006, the thematic 10...♗d4 11 c3 ♞e5 would have been fine for Black) 8...♞f6 9 0-0 ♗g4 10 ♕c3! 0-0 11 e5 gave White the initiative in M.Glienke-L.Caglio, Palau 2009.

d) 7...♗d7 8 ♘c3 ♕xf3 9 gxf3 ♘e7 10 ♗e3 saw an early draw offer in G.Waldmann-K.Hofmair, Austrian League 2008, but White should really have continued, since he enjoys a standard pull with ♖g1 followed by f4 next up.

e) 7...♕e7!? 8 ♗e3 ♘f6 9 ♗xc5 ♕xc5 10 ♘d2 was tried in A.Danin-I.Lysyj, Moscow 2010, when 10...♗e6!? would have restricted White to a tiny pull, but he might also explore 8 0-0!? ♘f6 9 ♘c3 followed by ♗e3 or even ♗g5.

We now return to the queen exchange on f3:

8 gxf3

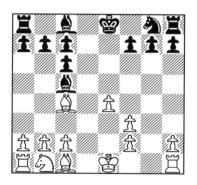

8...♘e7

The logical follow-up, but again there are alternatives:

a) 8...♗e6 9 ♗xe6 (this seems better than 9 ♘d2 ♘e7 10 ♗xe6 fxe6 11 ♘c4, since 11...0-0 12 ♔e2 b5 13 ♘e5 ♗d6 14 ♘d3 c5 15 ♗e3 c4 16 ♘c5 e5 turned out okay for Black in Z.Varga-J.Gustafsson, Budapest 2004) 9...fxe6 10 ♗e3 (Black should meet 10 h4 with 10...♘e7, rather than 10...♘f6?! 11 h5!

0-0 12 ♗e3 ♗d6 13 ♘d2 ♘d7 14 ♔e2, which gave White an edge in V.Zvjaginsev-I.Khairullin, Sochi 2007) 10...♗xe3 11 fxe3 leaves White with the better central control.

Indeed, he should emerge with a pull, since Black can't easily advance his e-pawn and after 11...♘f6 (or 11...♘h6 12 ♘d2 ♖f8 13 ♔e2 ♔e7 14 ♖hg1 and with f4 on the cards, White was better in D.Fingerov-K.Reshetkov, Odessa 2008) 12 ♘d2 0-0-0 13 ♘c4 ♖hf8 14 ♔e2 ♘d7 15 ♖hg1 White had a small but clear edge in P.Andrieux-X.Lebrun, French League 2003.

b) The 8...♗h3 of M.Sanchez-C.Risueno, Albacete 1994, should just be met by 9 ♖g1 g6 10 ♗f4, again with a pull.

c) 8...♔e7 9 ♗f4 ♗b6 10 a4 a5 11 ♘d2 ♗e6 12 ♗xe6 ♔xe6 13 ♘c4 ♘e7 14 ♖g1 led to a similar outcome in S.Jazbinsek-T.Kranjec, Celje 2006.

d) Perhaps Black might consider 8...♘f6!?, meeting 9 ♗f4 with 9...♗d6 and 9 ♖g1 with 9...g6 10 ♗g5 ♘d7 followed by ...f6 and ...♗d6.

9 ♗e3

A simple and logical approach. White has also tried 9 h4!?, but after 9...♘g6 (9...♗e6 10 ♗xe6 fxe6 11 ♗e3 ♗d6 12 ♘d2 0-0 13 h5 c5 14 ♔e2 ♘c6 15 c3 b6 16 ♖ag1 gave White an edge thanks to his kingside possibilities in I.Nataf-K.Sundararajan, Edmonton 2005) 10 h5 ♘e5 11 ♗e2 f5! 12 f4 ♘g4 13 ♗xg4 fxg4 the resulting unbalanced position was no more than approximately level in H.Stevic-K.Georgiev, Sibenik 2008.

9...♗xe3

This exchange isn't forced, but both 9...♗b6 10 ♖g1 ♘g6 11 ♘d2 ♗e6 12 f4 0-0 13 f5 ♗xe3 14 fxe3 ♗xc4 15 ♘xc4 in S.Granara Barreto-L.Perdomo, Argentina 2006, and the 9...♗d6 10 f4 ♗e6 11 ♘d2 of S.Haslinger-V.Georgiev, Hastings 2007/08, give White a pretty pleasant pull.

10 fxe3

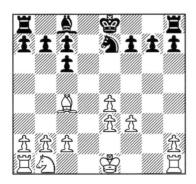

10...f5

This isn't enough to equalize, but is the best way of obtaining some counterplay. Instead 10...b5?! looks a little suspicious and after 11 ♗d3 ♗d7 12 a4 a6 13 ♘d2 ♘c8 14 ♘b3 White was somewhat better in G.Shankar-A.Melekhina, Chicago 2008.

11 ♘c3

White can also iron out his pawns with 11 exf5 ♘xf5 12 ♔f2 ♔e7 13 ♘c3 ♗e6 14 ♗xe6 ♔xe6 15 ♖ad1. This was enough for a small edge in O.Terletsky-E.Dedkov, Lvov 2005, but the text is likely more promising.

11...fxe4 12 ♘xe4 ♗f5

We've followed the game A.Delorme-G.Miralles, Cannes 2005, when it was time to probe and begin to increase White's small advantage with 13 ♘c5.

C) 6...bxc6

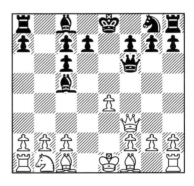

This has become established as Black's main choice at grandmaster level. His light-squared bishop may still emerge on the h3-c8 diagonal after ...d6, while early counterplay against b2 is often on the agenda with ...♖b8 and/or ...♗d4, as well as sometimes ...a5-a4.

At this point White's two main moves are:

C1: 7 ♕g3
C2: 7 ♘d2

We should also note:

a) 7 ♕xf6?! ♘xf6 gives Black easy play with the ...d5 break now on the agenda: 8 ♗d3 (or 8 f3 0-0 9 ♘c3 d5! 10 ♗d3 ♖e8 11 ♗f4 ♗f5 and already Black was slightly for choice in J.Rinas-A.Conde, Villa Ballester 2008) 8...0-0 (there's nothing wrong either with 8...d5 and if 9 ♘c3 then 9...0-0 10 0-0 ♖b8) 9 0-0 ♖e8 10 ♘c3 was the course of A.Neumann-S.Schmid, Giessen 1993, and here 10...♖b8 would have given Black the initiative.

b) 7 ♘c3 was an important line after the alternate recapture on the c6-square,

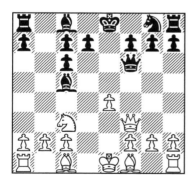

but here the idea of ♗e3 packs much less punch after 7...d6 (Black should avoid 7...♕xf3 8 gxf3 d6 when 9 ♗e3! ♗xe3 10 fxe3 ♘e7 11 ♖g1 g6 12

0-0-0 ♗e6 13 h4 gave White an edge in A.Muzychuk-L.Galojan, Rijeka 2010, but can consider both the 7...♖b8 8 ♕g3 of J.Van Egmond-D.Van der Meiden, Alkmaar 1985, and then 8...♗d4, as well as 7...♗d4!?, again preventing 8 ♗e3, and after 8 ♕g3 h5 9 h4 ♘e7 10 ♗g5 ♕e5 11 ♕xe5 ♗xe5 12 0-0-0 ♗xc3 13 bxc3 d6 Black was okay in E.Perelshteyn-J.Friedel, Tulsa 2008).

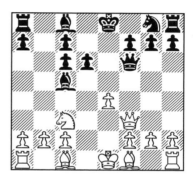

White's problem is that 8 ♗e3 (8 ♕g3 is the alternative, taking play into note 'b' to Black's 7th move in Line C1) 8...♗xe3 (8...♗b4!? is also possible) 9 ♕xe3 ♘e7 followed by ...0-0 gives Black pretty comfortable play with both ...♘g6, seizing control of some important dark squares, and ...♖b8 on their way. However, 8 ♗c4 a5! 9 ♗b3 ♕xf3 10 gxf3 ♘e7 11 ♖g1 ♗d4 failed to trouble Black in H.Yaramis-M.Geenen, Kemer 2007, and even after the more popular 8 ♗e2 ♕xf3 (Skembris' 8...♗d4!?, with the idea of 9 0-0 ♕xf3 10 ♗xf3 ♖b8, might be an even simpler solution for Black) 9 ♗xf3 ♘e7 10 0-0 0-0 11 ♖d1 it's hard to speak of any advantage for White, despite some high-level testing:

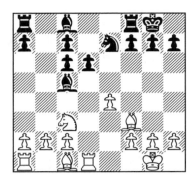

b1) 11...a5 12 ♘a4 ♗a7 13 c4 ♘g6 (Black might well have broken with 13...f5! when Barsky has suggested 14 c5!? fxe4 15 ♗xe4 ♗f5 16 ♗xf5 ♖xf5 17 ♖e1 ♘d5 18 ♗d2 dxc5 19 f3, but it doesn't seem that White has enough compensation here after 19...♘b4) 14 c5 dxc5?! (rather ugly; correct was 14...♘e5 15 ♗e2 ♗g4!, maintaining the balance) 15 ♗e3 c4 16 ♗xa7 ♖xa7 17 ♗e2 ♖b7 18 ♖ac1 gave White an edge in V.Ivanchuk-P.Leko, 2nd matchgame, Mukachevo (rapid) 2007.

b2) 11...f5! 12 exf5 ♗xf5 13 ♗g5 ♖ae8 was proposed in the first draft of this chapter, as an active way for Black to gain the initiative. It was then seen in H.Stevic-A.Shirov, Khanty-Mansiysk Olympiad 2010, where 14 ♖d2 d5 15 ♘a4 ♗d6 16 ♗e3 ♘g6 17 ♗h5 ♖e4! 18 ♗xg6 ♗xg6 gave Black a definite pull, although White managed to hold the resulting inferior endgame.

c) 7 ♗e2 ♕xf3 (Black must avoid 7...♕e6? on account of 8 ♕c3, but an-

gling for a transposition to variation 'b' with 7...d6 8 0-0 ♕xf3 9 ♗xf3 ♘e7 is a much better alternative; White avoided it with 10 ♖d1 in L.Shytaj-S.Brunello, Martina Franca 2008, but after 10...a5! 11 ♘c3 a4 Black had good counterplay) 8 ♗xf3 (invariably played, but even here attention should be given to 8 gxf3!? which left White slightly for choice after 8...♘e7 9 ♗e3 ♗xe3 10 fxe3 a5 11 ♘c3 ♗a6 12 ♖d1 in A.Danin-K.Rjabzev, St Petersburg 2009) leaves White with the better structure, but his bishop isn't especially well placed on f3.

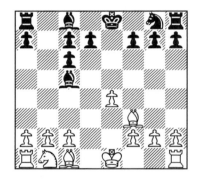

Indeed, after 8...♘e7 (8...♘f6!? is a decent alternative and after 9 ♘c3 0-0 10 0-0 ♖e8 11 ♗f4 ♗d4 12 ♗xc7 ♗xc3 13 bxc3 ♘xe4 Black had equalized in B.Borsos-V.Inkiov, Saint Affrique 2008) 9 0-0 (9 ♘c3 d6 would again take play into variation 'b') 9...0-0 10 ♘c3 ♘g6 (Barsky's 10...♗d4 11 ♘e2 ♗f6 12 c3 ♖b8 13 b3 d6 is a similar, sensible approach) 11 ♘a4 ♗e7 12 b3 ♗f6 13 ♖b1 d6 Black was fine in V.Yemelin-V.Tkachiev, Dagomys 2008.

C1) 7 ♕g3

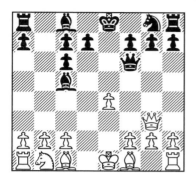

White keeps the queens on and has hopes of developing aggressively after ♘c3 with some combination of ♗e3, ♗g5 and f4. For a while this was even the main line of the 6 ♕f3 variation, but then Black found a way to exploit the queen's position on g3 to develop decent counterplay.

7...h5!?

Battling for the initiative, but even after a more classical approach White has struggled to demonstrate much:

a) 7...♘e7 8 ♗d3 ♘g6 9 0-0 d6 (here too 9...h5!? comes into consideration when Lukacs and Hazai have pointed out the line 10 ♕xc7 ♘e5 11 ♕a5 d6 12 ♘d2?! h4 13 h3 ♖h6! when Black will have a pretty strong attack after 14...♖g6; White avoided such greed in K.Chernyshov-A.Aleksandrov, Abu Dhabi 2005, with 10 ♘c3 d6 11 ♘a4 ♗d4 12 c3 h4 13 ♕g5, but here 13...♕xg5 14 ♗xg5 ♗e5 would have retained a rough balance, as pointed out by the aforementioned Hungarian analysts, and perhaps Black might also

consider 10...h4!?) 10 ♘d2 ♘e5 11 ♘c4 (Black need not fear the resulting exchange, but 11 ♗e2 0-0 also leads nowhere for White, with the f-pawn pinned and 12 ♔h1 met well enough by 12...♕g6) 11...♘xc4 12 ♗xc4 0-0 13 c3 ♗e6 14 ♗a6 ♗c8 15 ♗d3 a5 was fairly solid and okay for Black in A.Grosar-K.Opl, Austrian League 2001.

b) After 7...d6 8 ♘c3 Black has usually been keen to get the queens off after all, but quite possibly he shouldn't be in such a hurry:

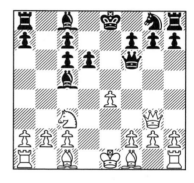

b1) 8...♕g6 9 ♗d2 (Black seems to be okay after 9 ♕xg6 hxg6 10 ♘a4 ♗d4 11 c3 ♗e5, while 9 ♗d3 can be met by either 9...a5!?, whereupon the early complications resolved themselves in rough equality after 10 e5 ♕xg3 11 hxg3 dxe5 12 ♖xh7 ♖xh7 13 ♗xh7 ♘f6 14 ♗d3 ♗e6 in V.Tseshkovsky-E.Tomashevsky, Kazan 2005, or by 9...♘f6 10 ♘a4 ♗d4 11 c3 ♗b6 12 f3 ♘d7 13 ♗f4 f6, which was very solid for Black in T.Radjabov-L.Aronian, Wijk aan Zee 2009) 9...♘f6 (after 9...♖b8 10 ♗d3 ♗d4 11 ♘e2!? ♗xb2 12 ♖b1 ♖b6 13 0-0

♕xg3 14 hxg3 ♘e7 15 ♗a5 White had decent enough play for his pawn at this stage in A.Morozevich-V.Laznicka, Khanty-Mansiysk 2009, but Black might also have considered 11...♗e5!? 12 ♕xg6 hxg6 13 f4 ♗f6) 10 f3 0-0 (10...♗e6 11 0-0-0 ♕xg3 12 hxg3 ♘d7 13 g4 ♘e5 14 g5 ♗b6 15 b3 saw White seizing some useful space and with it an edge in Li Chao-G.Sargissian, Khanty-Mansiysk 2009) 11 0-0-0 and now:

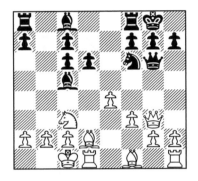

b11) White has the initiative after 11...♖b8 12 ♕xg6 hxg6 13 ♘a4! ♗f2 14 ♗a5 and is also likely for choice here with Mikhalevski's 12 ♘a4.

b12) 11...♘d7 12 ♕xg6 hxg6 13 h4! a5 14 h5 gxh5 15 ♖xh5 g6 16 ♖h2 gave White the initiative on the kingside this time in A.Morozevich-P.Leko, Moscow 2009.

b13) Perhaps Black does best with a suggestion of various commentators, namely the immediate 11...a5!? followed by ...♗a6.

b2) 8...♗d4!? is quite provocative, but after 9 ♘a4 (9 ♗c4 ♗e6 10 ♗b3 h5

was fine for Black in F.Bentivegna-S.Brunello, Bratto 2006, with the idea of 11 h4 ♘e7) 9...♕e7 10 ♕d3 White is losing time too and 10...♗b6 11 f3 f5!? 12 ♕c3 ♗d7 13 ♘xb6 axb6 14 ♗d3 fxe4 15 fxe4 ♘f6 gave Black enough counterplay against e4 to maintain the balance in Ni Hua-D.Jakovenko, Tai-yuan 2006.

b3) 8...♘e7 9 ♗c4 (Black develops counterplay after 9 ♗e3 with the logical 9...♗xe3 10 ♕xe3 0-0 11 ♗e2 ♖b8, while 9 f4 0-0 10 ♘a4 ♗b6 11 ♗d3 ♖e8 12 ♘xb6 axb6 13 0-0 ♗a6 left him very solidly placed in S.Barbeau-Bj.Thorfinns-son, Montreal 2009) 9...♖b8 10 0-0 ♘g6 11 ♗e3 ♗b6 12 ♘a4 0-0 13 ♘xb6 axb6 gave White the bishop-pair, but only a tiny plus at most in G.Jones-L.Sobolevsky, Dresden 2007.

Returning to the more ambitious 7...h5!?:

8 h4

White has also let the h-pawn advance, but after 8 ♘c3 h4 9 ♕f3 h3 10 ♘a4 ♗d6 he finds his kingside coming under early pressure.

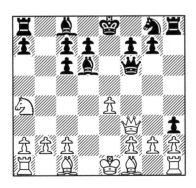

Now 11 ♗e3 ♖h4 (analysing for ChessPublishing.com, Peter Wells pointed out that 11...hxg2 12 ♗xg2 ♛xf3 13 ♗xf3 ♖xh2 14 ♖xh2 ♗xh2 would have been pretty risky for Black, with one dangerous counter being 15 0-0-0 d6 16 ♗g2 ♗d7 17 ♖h1 ♗e5 18 f4 ♗f6 19 e5! dxe5 20 ♘c5, but Black should consider 11...♗e5!? 12 0-0-0 d6 when he may be able to retain the initiative) 12 0-0-0 ♛xf3 13 gxf3 ♘e7 14 ♘c3 f6 15 ♖g1 g5 16 ♖g4! remained quite complex, but was about equal in T.Radjabov-E.Inarkiev, Baku 2008.

8...♘h6 9 f3 d5

Tempting, but Ftacnik points out that Black might delay this with 9...0-0!? 10 ♘c3 ♖e8 11 ♗e2 (11 ♗g5?! ♘f5 12 ♛f4 ♛e6 causes problems only for White) 11...d5, which he rightly feels is also enough for equality.

10 ♘c3

Naturally White should avoid greed. Both 10 ♛xc7? 0-0 and 10 exd5? 0-0 leave Black with a dangerous initiative thanks to his much safer king.

10...♗d4!

Grischuk's idea which was largely responsible for extinguishing interest in 7 ♛g3. Previously Black had preferred 10...♗b4 11 ♗d2 dxe4, but after 12 0-0-0! White has the initiative and 12...e3 13 ♗xe3 ♗xc3 14 bxc3! (the earlier 14 ♗g5 ♗xb2+ 15 ♔b1 ♗e6? 16 ♗xf6 ♗xf6 would have turned out rather well for White in S.Rublevsky-V.Tkachiev, Poikovsky 2007, had he found 17 ♛xc7 0-0 18 ♛xc6 ♖ab8+ 19

♔c1 ♖b2 20 ♗c4, but the correct way to sacrifice the queen was 15...♖b8! 16 ♗xf6 gxf6 17 c3! ♗f5+ 18 ♖d3 ♗a3+ 19 ♔c2 ♔f8! with ongoing complications and reasonable compensation) 14...♘f5 (14...0-0? 15 ♛g5 was something of a disaster for Grischuk in the earlier S.Rublevsky-A.Grischuk, 4th match-game, Elista 2007) 15 ♛xc7! (a fearless improvement over 15 ♛g5 ♘xe3 16 ♛xe3+ ♛e7 17 ♛xe7+ ♔xe7 which was only equal in Ni Hua-E.Najer, Ergun 2006) 15...♘xe3?! (Black should settle for 15...0-0 16 ♗d2 when White is slightly better, but everything remains to play for) 16 ♖d6 ♛e7 17 ♛xc6+ ♔f8 18 ♛xa8 ♛xd6 19 ♛xc8+ ♔e7 20 ♛b7+ ♔f6 21 ♗d3 sees White emerging from the complications with a clear advantage, as analysed by Marin.

11 ♗d2 ♖b8 12 0-0-0 ♗e5!

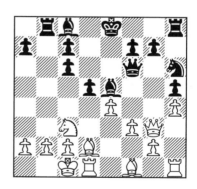

The attack on his queen, allied to the pressure down the long diagonal, is quite awkward for White.

13 f4!?

Rublevsky's second try, but this may be too ambitious. In S.Rublevsky-

A.Grischuk, 6th matchgame, Elista 2007, he had grabbed a pawn with 13 ♕g5 ♕d6 14 exd5, but after 14...0-0 15 ♗c4 (Kosten points out 15 dxc6?? loses material to 15...♕b4 16 b3 ♗xc3) 15...cxd5 16 ♗xd5 (Black enjoys a strong initiative after 16 ♗b3 c6! 17 ♕xh5 ♘f5 18 ♘e2 a5!) 16...♕xd5 17 ♘xd5 ♗xb2+ 18 ♔b1 ♗c3 Black was able to force a draw and he might even be able to do better than that with the tempting exchange sacrifice 16...♖xb2!? 17 ♔xb2 ♕xd5, as proposed by both Kosten and Marin.

13...♗d4 14 ♕d3 ♗g4

Black's bishops dominate their counterparts and White really has nothing better than to plunge into the complications.

15 e5 ♗xc3!

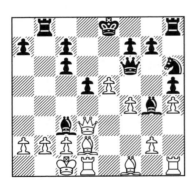

16 ♕xc3

After 16 exf6 ♗xb2+ 17 ♔b1 ♗xf6+ 18 ♔c1 ♗b2+ 19 ♔b1 Black might again force a draw, although it's also tempting to continue with 19...♗xd1!?.

16...♕e6 17 ♖e1 0-0 18 ♗e3 ♖fd8 19 ♕c5 a5!

Thanks to his light-square blockade

and queenside possibilities Black enjoyed promising counterplay in S.Rublevsky-A.Grischuk, 7th matchgame, Elista (rapid) 2007.

C2) 7 ♘d2

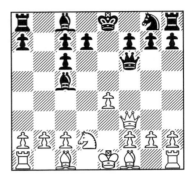

White accepts that ♗e3 is off the agenda for the time being, but hopes that he might yet get it in after first prodding Black's bishop while keeping it off the important a1-h8 diagonal with ♘b3. Moreover, he now has the option of recapturing on f3 with the knight and has chances to outplay his opponent in the resulting typically unbalanced and strategically complex middlegame.

7...♕xf3

Black's main choice, but this is far from forced. Indeed, of the many alternatives, he should pay particular attention to the solid 'a' and the enterprising 'b' and 'c':

a) After the solid 7...d6 White has tried three main systems:

a1) 8 ♗d3 ♕xf3 (otherwise, the bishop redeployment 8...♗d4?! no longer convinces, since after the 9 0-0 ♞e7 10 c3 ♝e5 11 ♛e2 ♞g6 of W.Van den Brande-H.Renette, Belgian League 2009, White could have removed the troublesome bishop with 12 ♞c4, thereby gaining some advantage, but Black might consider 8...a5, transposing into variation 'c2', below) 9 ♞xf3 (one might expect White to prefer 9 gxf3 ♞e7 10 ♞b3, but after 10...♝b6 11 a4 a5 12 ♝e3 f5 13 ♝xb6 cxb6 14 ♜g1 fxe4 15 fxe4 0-0 he didn't have any advantage to talk of in T.Radjabov-P.Eljanov, Kemer 2007) 9...♞e7 10 0-0 (after 10 ♝d2 ♝g4 11 h3 ♝xf3! 12 gxf3 f5 13 ♝g5 fxe4 14 fxe4 ♞g6 15 ♚e2 0-0 it was Black who enjoyed the initiative in B.Savchenko-V.Kramnik, Moscow (blitz) 2007) 10...0-0 11 c3 (Black was also okay after 11 ♜e1 ♞g6 12 ♝e3 ♝xe3 13 ♜xe3 ♜e8 14 ♜ae1 ♝g4 in D.Brandenburg-S.Ernst, Groningen 2007) 11...a5 12 ♞d4 ♝a6 13 ♝xa6 ♜xa6 14 ♜e1 ♜e8 gave White at most a small edge in M.Peschansky-V.Pechenov, Tula 2001.

a2) 8 ♞b3 ♝b6 forces Black to be a little careful with ♝d2-c3 on its way.

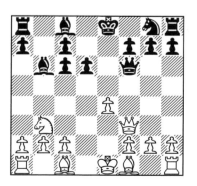

At this point 9 a4 a5 10 ♝d2 ♛xf3 11 gxf3 ♞e7 transposes to variation 'a' in the notes to White's 11th move in our main line, below. Moreover, White should likely slightly expose Black's a-pawn thus, since after 9 ♝d2 ♛xf3 (but not 9...♝e6?! 10 ♝c3 ♛h6? 11 ♝a6! when the threat of a4-a5 left Black in some trouble in I.Nataf-L.Fressinet, Besancon 2006, and here even after 10...♛xf3 11 gxf3 f6 12 ♜g1 White is slightly for choice) 10 gxf3 ♞e7 (the knight heads for g6; here 10...♞f6?! isn't a good alternative, in view of 11 ♜g1 0-0, as in D.Brandenburg-A.Van de Oudeweetering, Dutch League 2007, and then simply 12 ♝c3) 11 ♜g1 (Black was okay too after 11 ♝c3 0-0 12 ♜g1 ♞g6 13 ♞a5 ♝d7 14 ♞c4 f6 15 ♞xb6 axb6 in T.Abergel-L.Fressinet, Pau 2008, while he should meet Kurnosov's 11 c4!? with 11...♝e6, again maintaining a rough balance) 11...0-0 12 c4 ♝e6 13 ♝c3 ♞g6 14 h4?! f6 15 h5 ♞e5 it was Black, not White, who had seized the initiative in A.Lazar-D.Pavasovic, Bled 2008.

a3) 8 ♝e2 has been Radjabov's latest try, although after 8...♛xf3 9 gxf3 ♞e7 (the more ambitious 9...f5!? turned out okay after 10 ♞b3 ♝b6 11 a4 a5 12 ♜g1 g6 13 ♝e3 ♝xe3 14 fxe3 fxe4 15 fxe4 ♞h6 16 e5 ♞f7 17 exd6 cxd6 18 0-0-0 ♚e7 in D.Brandenburg-A.Naiditsch, German League 2010, but White might test 10 ♜g1 g6 11 e5!?, sacrificing a pawn to cause some problems on the long dark-square diagonal after 11...dxe5 12 ♘c4 ♗d6 13 ♗d2 ♗e6 14 f4) it's again not so easy to see any advantage for White:

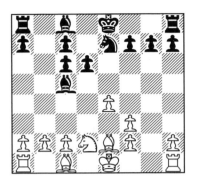

a31) 10 ♘b3 ♗b6 11 ♖g1! (again 11 ♗e3 fails to impress: 11...0-0 12 c4 ♗xe3 13 fxe3 f5 14 exf5 ♘xf5 gave Black easy counterplay in F.Munoz-O.Castro Rojas, Barranquilla 1972) 11...0-0 12 a4 a5 13 ♗e3 ♗xe3 14 fxe3 c5! (improving over 14...♗a6 15 ♗xa6 ♖xa6 16 ♘d4 when White's more active knight gave him a pull in T.Radjabov-D.Jakovenko, Nanjing 2009) 15 f4 ♗b7 16 e5 ♗d5 was okay for Black in Li Chao-G.Sargissian, Khanty-Mansiysk (blitz) 2009.

a32) 10 ♖g1!? g6 11 h4 f5 12 h5 (consistent, but perhaps White should look into 12 ♘b3!? ♗b6 13 a4 a5 14 ♗g5) 12...♗e6 13 ♘b3 ♗b6 14 ♗e3 ♗xe3 15 fxe3 fxe4 16 fxe4 gxh5 17 ♗xh5+ ♘g6 18 ♗xg6+ hxg6 19 ♖xg6 ♖h4! saw Black regaining his pawn and he soon drew in T.Radjabov-E.Inarkiev, Astrakhan 2010.

b) Keeping the queens on with 7...♕e7!? has been quite rare, but has received support from Ftacnik in his annotations for ChessBase. The critical line seems to run 8 ♗d3 ♘f6 9 0-0 0-0 10 ♘b3 ♗b6 11 c4! (more challenging than 11 a4 a5 12 ♗e3 d6 13 ♖fe1 ♖e8 14 h3 h6, which was pretty solid for Black in I.Nataf-V.Tkachiev, Aix-les-Bains 2007) 11...a5 (the pin gives White the initiative after 11...d6 12 ♗g5) 12 a4 d6 13 c5!.

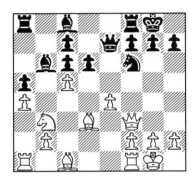

This was a highly thematic pawn sacrifice in Ni Hua-E.Inarkiev, Nizhnij Novgorod 2007, but with 13...dxc5 14 ♗g5 ♖d8! (Ftacnik) Black may be able to maintain a rough balance, such as after 15 ♖fd1 h6 16 ♗xf6 ♕xf6 17 ♕xf6 gxf6 18 ♗c4 ♗e6 19 ♖dc1 ♖ab8, shot though his structure is.

c) 7...a5!? strikes out on the queenside and dissuades ideas of ♘b3, unless White wants to follow up with a4, while preparing a timely exchange of light-squared bishops with ...♗a6. Now:

c1) 8 ♗c4 ♕xf3 9 ♘xf3 d6 10 ♗d2 ♘f6 11 ♗d3 ♘g4 12 0-0 f6 13 h3 ♘e5 was fine for Black in B.Savchenko-P.Leko, Moscow (blitz) 2007.

c2) 8 ♗d3 d6 9 0-0 (9 ♕g3 ♘e7 10 0-0 is a more ambitious approach, but after 10...h5! 11 ♘c4 h4 12 ♕f4 ♕xf4 13 ♗xf4 ♗e6 White failed to obtain any advantage in S.Rublevsky-S.Grigoriants, Moscow 2006) 9...♕xf3 10 ♘xf3 f6 11 c3 ♗a6 12 ♗xa6 ♖xa6 13 ♗d2 ♘e7 was very solid for Black who was able to keep his king in the centre in E.Moser-O.Korneev, Balaguer 2007.

c3) Perhaps White does best to take up the challenge with 8 ♘b3!?, which has only recently received some attention.

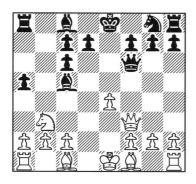

With 8...♗b6 9 a4 d6 10 ♗d2 ♕xf3 11 gxf3 ♘e7 play transposes to note 'a' to White's 11th move in our main line, below, which gives him chances for a plus, but Black should prefer that to 8...♗b4+?! 9 c3 a4 10 cxb4 ♕xf3 11 gxf3 axb3 12 a3 ♘f6 13 ♗c4 d5 14 ♗xb3, which left White fully in charge in S.Haslinger-J.Woolley, Halifax (rapid) 2010.

d) Black might like to break with 7...d5, but after 8 exd5 ♕xf3 (8...cxd5?! 9 ♗b5+ ♔f8 10 0-0 ♖b8 11 ♗e2 ♕xf3

12 ♗xf3 ♘f6 13 ♘b3 ♗d6 14 ♗e3 just gave White a pretty pleasant edge in J.Timman-V.Korchnoi, Wijk aan Zee 2008) 9 ♘xf3 cxd5 10 ♗b5+ ♗d7 11 ♗xd7+ ♔xd7 White must have a pull, as he maintained with 12 ♘e5+ ♔e6 13 ♘d3 ♗d6 14 ♘f4+ ♗xf4 15 ♗xf4 ♔f5 16 ♗e3 ♘f6 17 0-0-0 in I.Ibragimov-J.Friedel, San Diego 2006.

e) 7...♗d4 is a thematic-enough idea, but after the 8 c3 ♕xf3 9 gxf3 ♗f6 of B.Muhren-Shen Yang, Yerevan 2006, and then Barsky's 10 ♘c4 White has an edge.

f) White also emerges with a pleasant plus after 7...♖b8 8 ♘b3 ♗e7 (Z.Plenkovic-M.Zelic, Split 2008) 9 ♕g3 d6 10 ♗d3.

g) Finally, 7...♗b6 8 a4! disturbed Black's bishop without delay in L.Williams-J.Cobb, Cardiff 2008, and after 8...♕xf3 9 gxf3 ♘e7 10 a5 White has the initiative.

We now return to the exchange of queens on f3:

8 gxf3

White settles for the standard clump of pawns in the centre, while facilitating ideas of ♖g1 and still intending to unravel with ♘b3. He has also recaptured with the knight, but after 8 ♘xf3 ♘f6 (the right square for the knight here, as 8...♘e7 9 ♗d3 0-0 10 0-0 d5 11 ♗f4 ♗b6 12 ♖fe1 ♘g6 13 ♗g3 left White slightly for choice in A.Stamatovic-M.Boskovic, Belgrade 2008) 9 ♗d3 Black might just continue solidly with Kosten's 9...d6!? 10 0-0

②d7 11 ♗d2 a5, although in practice he has usually preferred the more active 9...d5.

Now:

a) 10 e5?! ②e4! (better than 10...②d7?! 11 0-0 0-0 12 ♖e1 ♖e8 13 ♗d2 ♗b6 14 ♗f1 ②c5 15 c4 ♗g4 16 ②d4 with a tiny edge for White, which soon grew after 16...②e4?! 17 ♗e3 ♗d7 18 ②b3 when Black was hampered by the doubled c-pawns in Ni Hua-J.Rowson, Liverpool 2007) 11 0-0 0-0 12 c3 ♖e8 13 ♗f4 ♗b6 14 ②d4 g5! enabled Black to equalize in S.Haslinger-A.David, Liverpool 2007.

b) 10 exd5 cxd5 11 0-0 0-0 still enables White to aspire to a little something and after 12 ♗f4! (driving Black's bishop back to b6, whereas 12 ♖e1 ♗b7 13 ♗e3 ♗d6 14 ♗d4 c5 15 ♗xf6 gxf6 16 c4 dxc4 17 ♗xc4 ♗xf3 18 gxf3 ♗e5 saw the presence of opposite-coloured bishops make a draw rather likely in V.Ivanchuk-P.Leko, 8th matchgame, Mukachevo (rapid) 2007) 12...♗b6 13 ♖fe1 ♗b7 14 a4 a5 15 ♗e3 he was slightly for choice in M.Godena-

B.Ivanovic, Heraklion 2007.

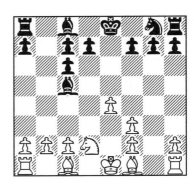

8...②e7

As so often the best square for the knight when White has the doubled f-pawns, enabling Black to get in a counterstrike with ...f5. Alternatively:

a) 8...②f6?! 9 ②b3 ♗e7 (otherwise, 9...♗b6 10 ♖g1 0-0 11 ♗h6 ②e8 12 a4 a5 13 ♗e3 gives White the initiative and after 9...♗d6 10 ♗e3 ②h5 11 0-0-0 ♗f4 12 ②d4 g6 13 ♗h3 ♖b8 14 ②e2 ♗xe3+ 15 fxe3 he was slightly for choice in T.Kos-B.Abramovic, Ptuj 2000) sees Black developing along quite traditional lines, but such an approach is a little too solid and slow here.

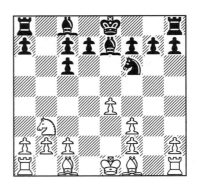

Indeed, after the 10 ♖g1 (White was also for choice following 10 ♗e3 d6 11 0-0-0 a5 12 a4 ♗e6 13 ♘d4 ♗d7 14 h4! 0-0 15 h5 in I.Ibragimov-M.Scekic, Ledyards 2006) 10...♖g8 of F.Schmenger-G.Schmidt, Binz 1995, White can obtain a pleasant advantage with 11 ♗e3 d6 12 0-0-0.

b) Once again Black might like to break with 8...d5, but neither is this a panacea for him:

b1) 9 ♘b3! ♗d6 (9...♗b6 10 a4 a5 11 ♖g1 g6 12 ♗d2 followed by directing the bishop to c3 is quite pleasant for White) 10 ♗e3 (better than 10 c4 when Black should counter with Lukacs and Hazai's idea of 10...a5!, after which 11 ♗e3 a4 12 ♘c5 ♘e7 13 ♗d4 f6 is unclear, as they point out, as is 11 ♖g1 dxe4 12 fxe4 g6; however, White might consider 10 ♗d2!? ♘e7 11 ♗c3, which left her a little better after 11...f6 12 0-0-0 ♔f7 13 h4 in K.Burdova-M.Korenova, Plzen 2000) 10...♘e7 (White should meet the 10...♘f6 of K.Chernyshov-B.Molnar, Szekszard 1994, with 11 ♗d4! followed by 12 ♖g1 or 12 e5) 11 0-0-0! f5 12 ♗d4 fxe4 13 fxe4 dxe4 was quite murky in S.Haslinger-P.Wells, Treforst 2008, but White would have remained slightly for choice after 14 ♗xg7.

b2) The seemingly more dynamic 9 ♖g1 allows Black to counter with 9...♘e7! (surprisingly Topalov once settled for the less combative 9...g6 and after 10 ♘b3 ♗d6 11 h4 dxe4 12 fxe4 ♘f6 13 f3 0-0 14 ♗e3 a5 15 0-0-0 White

was beginning to press in T.Radjabov-V.Topalov, Wijk aan Zee 2008) 10 ♘b3 (the rook is, of course, trapped after 10 ♖xg7?! ♘g6) 10...♗d6.

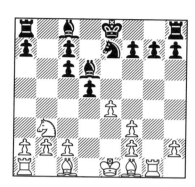

This seems fully acceptable for the second player, since after 11 ♖xg7!? (otherwise, 11 h4!? 0-0 12 ♗e3 a5 13 0-0-0 a4 14 ♘c5 has been proposed by Lukacs and Hazai, but Black should be okay after 14...♘g6; however, that is better for White than the 11 c4?! dxe4 12 fxe4 of G.Jones-T.Michalczak, Porto San Giorgio 2007, when the simple 12...♘g6 would have left Black with the initiative, as pointed out by Kosten) 11...♘g6 12 ♗h6 ♗xh2 13 0-0-0 ♗e5 (but not the 13...♗d6? of T.Radjabov-A.Motylev, Biel 2007, on account of 14 exd5 when the centre opens to Black's detriment) 14 exd5 cxd5 15 ♖xd5 ♗xg7 16 ♗xg7 ♖g8 17 ♗f6 ♘e7 gives White sufficient compensation for the exchange, but Kosten is surely right that he has no more than that.

c) 8...a5 is a little less impressive than it was a move before and after the 9 ♘b3 ♗b4+ (Black can again consider too 9...♗b6, but here White might just ignore the a-pawn with 10 ♗e3, rather than block with 10 a4 and so transpose to our main line after 10...♘e7) 10 c3 ♗e7 of V.Zorman-D.Gliksman, Slovenian League 1991, White could have retained the upper hand with 11 ♖g1 ♗f6 12 ♗g5.

d) 8...g6 9 ♘b3 ♗f8 10 ♗d2 ♗g7 11 0-0-0 ♖b8 12 ♗a5 began to probe, with an edge in E.Goossens-R.Michiels, Belgian League 2007.

e) 8...♗e7 9 ♘c4 (9 ♖g1 g6 10 ♘b3 ♗f6 11 c3 ♘e7 would also have been a little better for White in I.Nataf-L.Gofshtein, French League 2010, had he gone 12 ♗e3) 9...d6 (T.Kos-J.Fuksik, Sisak 2000) 10 ♖g1 g6 11 ♗e3 is again quite pleasant for White.

Returning to 8...♘e7:

9 ♘b3 ♗b6

The bishop doesn't have to retreat here, but after 9...♗d6 10 ♗e3 ♘g6 11 0-0-0 ♗e5 in K.Jongsma-R.Van Gompel, Haarlem 1995, White could have secured an edge by restricting Black's light-squared bishop with 12 ♘a5!.

10 a4!

An important and testing advance to flick in. White preferred the more routine 10 ♗e3 ♗xe3 11 fxe3 in B.Zachariassen-J.Ingvaldsen, Norwegian League 2002, but with 11...f5 12 e5 f4! Black could have seized the initiative.

A more common alternative has been 10 c4 c5! 11 ♗e3 (after 11 ♖g1 0-0 12 ♗d2 d6 13 h4 ♗d7 14 h5 the position was unclear, but a draw agreed in A.Khalifman-A.Pashikian, Moscow 2010, while here 13 ♗c3 f6 14 f4 ♗b7 seemed unbalanced and okay too for Black in D.Brandenburg-M.Vasilev, Wijk aan Zee 2007) 11...d6, leaving Black's bishop entombed, but with the ...f5 and ...a5 advances high on the agenda.

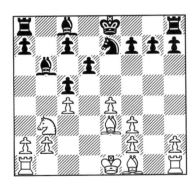

Following 12 0-0-0 (Black's aims were well illustrated by 12 f4 ♗b7 13 f3 f5 14 ♗d3 0-0 15 0-0 a5 16 a4 ♖ae8 when he was the one pressing despite the still-blunted bishop in R.Tischbierek-Z.Sturua, Berlin 1997) 12...a5 (only now, as 13 a4? ♗d7 would cost White a pawn) 13 ♖g1 a4 14 ♘d2 0-0

15 ♘b1 f5 Black was actively placed and with good counterplay in K.Chernyshov-D.Lybin, Frydek-Mistek 1997.

However, White might take play into our main line with 10 ♖g1 0-0 11 a4 a5. Black preferred 11...a6 here in F.Calandri-M.Sciortino, Porto San Giorgo 2003, but then 12 a5 ♗a7 13 ♗e3 would have clamped Black's queenside, with a pull.

10...a5

Best. Again 10...a6 is well met by 11 a5 ♗a7 12 ♗e3 ♗xe3 13 fxe3 with a grip.

11 ♖g1!?

Beginning to probe, but there are important alternatives:

a) 11 ♗d2 d6 reaches an important position, which can also come about from both a 7...d6 and a 7...a5 move order, as we have seen.

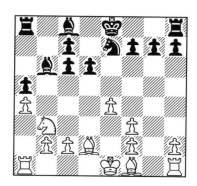

At this point White has often played as per the main line with 12 ♖g1 (12 ♗c3 is the other way of targeting g7, but after 12...0-0 13 ♖g1 f6 14 h4 Black would have been okay in I.Nataf-G.Sargissian, German League 2006, had

he activated his knight with 14...♘g6 15 h5 ♘f4; however, perhaps if White decides Black is going to castle short in any case, he might begin with 12 ♗e3!? and after 12...♗xe3 13 fxe3 0-0 14 0-0-0 g6 15 ♗c4 ♔g7 16 ♖d2 his position was slightly the easier to handle in G.Jones-A.Naiditsch, Warsaw (blitz) 2010, and this approach could do with further testing) 12...0-0 (Black does well not to commit his knight just yet; 12...♘g6 13 ♗e3 ♗xe3 14 fxe3 ♘e5 15 ♗e2 g6 16 f4 left White a little better in T.Radjabov-L.Aronian, Bilbao 2008) 13 ♗e3, reaching something of a topical tabiya:

a1) 13...♗a6 14 ♗xa6 ♖xa6 15 0-0-0 ♗xe3+ 16 fxe3 c5 17 e5! broke through to give White a pull in S.Rublevsky-E.Inarkiev, Dagomys 2010.

a2) 13...♗a7 14 0-0-0 f5 15 e5! dxe5 16 ♗c4+ ♔h8 17 ♗xa7 ♖xa7 18 ♘c5 was similar and this thematic pawn sacrifice gave White at least enough compensation in S.Rublevsky-A.Naiditsch, Halle 2010.

a3) Those two games both arose from a 7...d6 move order, but in S.Haslinger-M.Meyer, German League 2010, play had transposed via 7...a5 and even here 13...f5 14 e5!? (pretty ambitious and White may do better with 14 ♗xb6!? cxb6 15 0-0-0, especially as both 15...fxe4 16 ♖xd6 exf3 17 ♗c4+ ♔h8 18 ♖e1 and 15...d5 16 exd5 ♘xd5 17 ♗c4 give him the initiative) 14...dxe5 15 ♗c4+ ♘d5 16 0-0-0 ♗b7 17 h4 ♔h8 18 ♗c5 ♖f6 19 ♖g5 h6 20 ♖gg1 gave White enough for his pawn thanks to Black's queenside holes.

a4) Black's most logical try is 13...♗xe3 14 fxe3, leaving him a tempo ahead (...d6) of our main line, below.

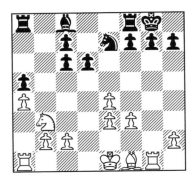

This is likely enough for him to claim equality, although after 14...c5 (14...f5!? 15 ♗c4+ ♔h8 16 e5 is quite a critical line and one which may well receive a test or two in 2011) 15 0-0-0 ♗b7 16 ♗b5 ♗c6 17 e5! ♖fd8 (in his second encounter with Rublevsky, at the 2010 Poikovsky tournament, Naiditsch tried to improve with the active 17...♗xb5 18 axb5 a4, but 19 ♘d2 d5 20 ♘b1! still left the leading Scotch exponent with a little something) 18 exd6 cxd6 19 ♗xc6 ♘xc6 20 ♘d2 Black's weaknesses down the d-file gave White a small but clear edge in no less a game than V.Anand-L.Aronian, Bilbao 2008.

b) Assuming the position has come about via a pure 7...♕xf3 8 gxf3 ♘e7 move order, White doesn't need to lose a tempo with his dark-squared bishop and 11 ♗e3 is quite a thematic choice:

b1) 11...♗xe3 12 fxe3 d6 13 0-0-0 (White should give close attention to

13 ♘d4!?, waiting for 13...0-0 before going 14 0-0-0 and after 14...f5 15 e5! dxe5 16 ♗c4+ ♔h8 17 ♘b3 f4 18 exf4 exf4 19 ♖he1 ♘f5 20 ♖e5 he was able to regain his pawn while maintaining the upper hand in G.Jones-N.Kabanov, Khanty-Mansiysk Olympiad 2010) 13...♗e6 14 ♘d4 ♗d7 15 ♖g1 g6! saw Black frustrating the white pieces by refusing to castle short in F.Vallejo Pons-V.Kramnik, Linares 2004, and after 16 ♖d2 c5 17 ♘b5 0-0-0 18 ♘c3 a draw was already agreed.

b2) Despite Kramnik's example, 11...0-0 12 0-0-0 ♗xe3+ 13 fxe3 d6 14 ♖g1 ♗e6 15 ♘d4 ♗d7 has also been seen in practice.

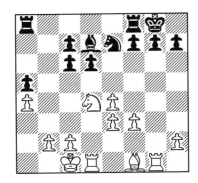

White has a small pull, but after 16 ♖g5 h6 17 ♖g3 ♔h7 18 ♗d3 g6 Black's defences remained tight in A.Filippov-V.Akopian, Khanty Mansiysk 2007, just as they did after the later 16 f4!? ♖ad8 17 ♖g5 (one might make a decent case too for the anti-...f5 measure 17 ♗d3!?) 17...c5 18 ♘b5 f6 19 ♖g1 ♗xb5 20 ♗xb5 f5 21 ♗c4+ ♔h8 of S.Haslinger-T.Nyback, German League 2010.

Returning to 11 ♖g1:

11...0-0 12 ♗e3 ♗xe3 13 fxe3 f5!?
Black lashes out in a bid for counter-play. He might prefer the more re-strained 13...d6 when 14 0-0-0 would take play into variation 'b2' in our last notes and here White can also consider the immediate 14 ♘d4.

The other central break is 13...d5?!, but this creates weaknesses and after 14 0-0-0 ♖e8 15 ♘c5 White enjoyed quite a pleasant edge in C.Ferreira Lopes-B.Oliveira Maroneze, Brazil 2003.

14 e5!
Here this pawn advance doesn't en-tail a pawn sacrifice, but is again strong and naturally White had no in-tention of opening the f-file for Black's forces.

14...f4

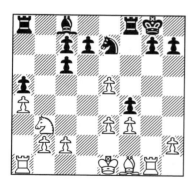

Black is determined to create some counterplay, but after 15 ♗c4+ (15 e4 ♘g6 16 ♗c4+ ♔h8 is another possible order of moves) 15...♔h8 16 e4 ♘g6 17

♖g5 there was no need for White to offer a draw in D.Brandenburg-T.Nyback, Jyvaskyla 2010. Presumably he was worried about the weakness of e5, but after 17...♖e8 18 e6! d6 19 ♖xa5 ♖xa5 20 ♘xa5 ♘e5 and then 21 ♗e2 ♗xe6 22 ♘b3 or even 21 ♔f2!? ♘xc4 22 ♘xc4 ♗xe6 23 ♘d2 White's outside passed a-pawn should most certainly count for something.

Conclusion

6 ♕f3 is hardly a new invention, but only over the last six years has it begun to be taken seriously and nowadays it is taken pretty seriously indeed! The immediate exchange of queens on f3 only plays into White's hands and nei-ther is 6...dxc6 likely enough for equal-ity after either 7 ♘c3 or 7 ♗c4, with the development of the dark-squared bishop to e3 an important weapon in White's armoury in all cases.

Black likely does best with 6...bxc6, fighting not to allow White a small but stable edge after an early ♗e3. More-over, 7 ♕g3 has rather fallen from grace due to the active riposte 7...h5!?, but with 7 ♘d2 White can still aspire to a pull. One suspects that 7...d6 and 7...a5 might turn out to be Black's best move orders, with the tabiya seen in note 'a' to White's 11th move in Line C2 likely to receive a fair bit more testing in 2011.

Chapter Eight

The 4...♗c5 Variation: 5 ♗e3 without 5...♛f6 6 c3 ♘ge7 7 ♗c4

1 e4 e5 2 ♘f3 ♘c6 3 d4 exd4 4 ♘xd4 ♗c5 5 ♗e3

A different approach from White! Rather than damage Black's structure, as we've seen him do in Chapters 1-7, White simply develops and now the threat of 6 ♘xc6 rather limits Black's options.

> **A: 5...♗b6**
> **B: 5...♗xd4**
> **C: 5...♛f6**

Line C is the critical response and there the main line runs 6 c3 ♘ge7 7 ♗c4, which we'll consider in our next chapter, but first we will come across the various ways both sides can deviate from that sequence.

This all just leaves:

a) The position after 5...♘xd4 6 ♗xd4 ♗xd4 7 ♛xd4 will be seen by

transposition in the notes to Black's 6th move in Line B.

b) 5...♛h4? rather asks for trouble after 6 ♘c3 with the threat of 7 ♘f5:

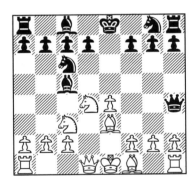

b1) 6...♘ge7? covers the f5-square, but after 7 ♘f3 ♛h5 8 g4! White nonetheless picked up the bishop in K.Krondraf-F.Frink, Znojmo 2003.

b2) 6...♗b4 7 ♗d3 d6 8 0-0 ♗xc3 9 bxc3 ♘f6 saw Black losing time with his bishop, having first misplaced his queen in P.Richmond-R.Long, Cardiff

1998; factors which White should have exploited with 10 f3 0-0 11 ♞b5.

b3) 6...♝xd4 7 ♝xd4 ♞xd4 8 ♛xd4 ♛f6 (8...♞f6? 9 g3 ♛h5 10 e5 ♛g4 11 ♛e3+ left Black in huge trouble in M.Zuriel-A.Miserendino, Olivos 2002, since moving the knight allows 12 ♞d5) 9 e5 ♛b6 10 ♛xb6 axb6 saw Black get the queens off in I.Elo-I.Karacsony, Pecs 1998, but after 11 ♝d3 White's superior development and the cramping e5-pawn would have given him a large advantage once again.

b4) 6...♝b6 7 ♞f5 ♛f6 sounded the retreat in P.Kuijpers-R.Loerke, Les Dicqs 2002, but with 8 ♞d5! ♛e5 (8...♛xb2 9 ♝xb6 cxb6 10 ♖b1! ♛e5 11 ♛d3 followed by f4 leaves Black in huge trouble) 9 ♝d3 White could have obtained a crushing initiative.

b5) 6...d6 7 ♞db5! ♝g4 8 ♛d2 is also clearly better for White, since there's no good way for Black to defend c7.

A) 5...♝b6 6 ♞f5!

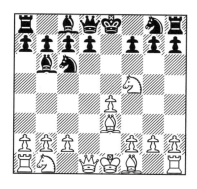

White wastes no time pinpointing

one downside to the early development of Black's bishop.

6...♝xe3

After this exchange followed by 8 ♞c3 White will obtain easy development and a firm grip on the d5- and f5-squares, thereby leaving Black with quite a passive position. This explains why Black should prefer 4...♝b4+ 5 c3 ♝c5 6 ♝e3 ♝b6 if he wants to play in this manner, which denies White's queen's knight the c3-square, as we'll see in Line A2 of Chapter 11. Here practice has also seen:

a) 6...g6 7 ♝xb6 axb6 (7...gxf5? is clearly misguided in view of 8 ♝d4 ♞f6 9 ♞c3) 8 ♞e3 d6 9 ♞c3 ♝e6 (preferable to the 9...♞ge7 10 h4! f5 11 h5 f4 12 ♞ed5 g5 of S.Tartakower-R.Spielmann, Vienna 1913, when 13 h6 would have left White clearly better) 10 ♝e2 ♞ge7 (Black preferred 10...♞h6 in K.Van der Weide-J.Freundorfer, Bad Wiessee 2006, but with 11 ♞ed5 White can retain an edge) 11 ♛d2 f5 12 exf5 ♞xf5 13 ♞xf5 ♝xf5 saw Black getting in his main pawn break in R.Zacarias-R.Kropff, Asuncion 2006, but after 14 0-0-0 followed by ♖he1 White retains the initiative.

b) 6...♛f6 isn't so bad either, although with 7 ♝xb6 axb6 8 ♞c3 ♞ge7 9 ♞e3 White retains a small but clear edge thanks to his grip on the d5-square.

c) 6...d5? 7 ♞xg7+! ♚f8 was an ambitious try in T.Gruskovnjak-M.Crepan, Bled 2000, and now 8 exd5 ♚xg7 9 dxc6 ♕xd1+ 10 ♔xd1 leaves Black with insufficient compensation.

d) Likewise 6...d6? 7 ♘xg7+ ♔f8 8 ♗xb6 axb6 9 ♘h5 ♕h4 10 ♘g3 left White a pawn to the good in J.Dworakowska-Z.Wiliczkiewicz, Zakopane 2000.

7 ♘xe3 ♘f6

Usually played. With 7...♘ge7 the knight does support ...f5, but after 8 ♘c3 0-0 9 ♕d2 d6, as in A.Kolev-A.Mastrovasilis, Chalkida 2009, and then 10 f4! followed by 0-0-0 any such break would clearly be pretty risky.

8 ♘c3 0-0

Closely-related play arises after 8...d6 9 ♕d2 0-0 (White has the initiative too after the 9...♗e6 10 0-0-0 a6 of M.Magnucka-E.Smolak, Krynica 2001, and then 11 f4 0-0 12 ♗e2 followed by g4) 10 0-0-0 ♖e8 11 f3 when 11...a6 12 g4 sounds the charge, as did 11...♗e6 12 g4 ♘d7 13 h4 ♘b6 14 f4 f6 15 g5 ♗f7 16 ♗e2 and by now White enjoyed some attack in H.Munoz Sotomayor-F.Yee, Valencia 2000.

9 ♕d2!

With Black low on counterplay, going long followed by pushing the king-side pawns is both tempting and strong.

9...♖e8 10 f3 d6 11 ♗e2!?

With 11 0-0-0 White would have taken play back into our last note, but perhaps surprisingly the text is at least as strong, supporting an advance of the f- and g-pawns, while there's no hurry for White to castle.

11...a6

Black relies on his b-pawn. The alternative is 11...♘e5 12 0-0-0 ♗d7, but after 13 ♖hg1!? (avoiding any counterplay with 13 g4 b5) 13...a6 14 g4 followed by g5 and f4 White has good attacking chances, but even worse for Black was 13...♗c6?! 14 ♘f5 a6 15 g4 ♔h8 (or 15...b5 16 g5 ♘fd7 17 f4) 16 g5, which saw him coming under serious pressure in S.Smagin-W.Unzicker, Dortmund 1992.

12 g4!

Undoubtedly the initiative belongs to White and he enjoys good prospects on the kingside, as we can see from both 12...b5 13 g5 ♘h5 14 ♘cd5!, threatening 15 f4, and 12...♖b8 13 g5 ♘d7 14 h4 ♘f8 15 0-0-0 followed by pushing the f- and h-pawns.

B) 5...♗xd4 6 ♗xd4 ♘f6

Black opts for quick development and pressure against d4. He can also hoover off another pair of pieces with 6...♘xd4?! 7 ♕xd4, but unsurprisingly White's space advantage gives him a pleasant pull here.

Following 7...♕f6 (7...♘f6? runs into 8 e5 and after 8...♘g8 9 ♘c3 ♘e7 10 0-0-0 0-0 11 ♗d3 d5 12 exd6 cxd6 13 ♖he1 ♘c6 14 ♕f4 White was somewhat for choice in T.Thorhallsson-B.Bjornsson, Reykjavik 1997) 8 e5 Black has tried a number of ideas, but only the continued attempt to get the queens off gives him a playable if worse position:

a) 8...♕e7?! 9 ♘c3 gives White a strong, early initiative and after 9...d6? 10 ♘d5 he was already winning material in R.Strohhaeker-J.Babutzka, Schoeneck 2005.

b) 8...♕g6?! 9 ♘c3! ♘e7 (9...♕xc2 10 ♘d5!, with some advantage, is White's idea) 10 ♗d3! ♕xg2 11 0-0-0 ♕g5+ 12 f4 ♕h6 left Black a pawn up in J.Kvisla-M.Jacobsen, Moss 2006, but his position would have been most unenviable had White gone 13 ♘b5.

c) 8...♕c6?! 9 ♘c3 ♘e7 (9...♕g6? 10 ♘d5 ♕xc2 11 ♗d3 ♕c6 12 ♗b5! ♕c2 13 ♗a4 cost Black heavy material in P.Svidler-N.Starke, Darmstadt (simul) 2000) 10 0-0-0 0-0 (White was threatening 11 e6) 11 ♗d3 d6 12 exd6 saw White winning a pawn in L.Perez Rodriguez-M.Vilar Lopez, Banyoles 2002.

d) 8...♕b6 9 ♕xb6 axb6 10 ♘c3 is Black's best, but only leads to a cramped, rather depressing position as we can see:

d1) 10...♖a5 makes good use of the semi-open file to prevent any notion of 11 ♘d5, but after 11 f4 f6 (11...♘e7 12 0-0-0 ♖c5 13 g3 0-0 14 ♗h3 ♖d8 15 ♖d2 d5 16 exd6 cxd6 17 ♖e1 left White doing pretty well too in B.Mela-F.Sones, Buenos Aires 2001) 12 b4 ♖a8 13 ♘d5 ♔d8 14 ♗c4 fxe5 15 fxe5 the knight had reached d5 after all and White was somewhat better in L.Spacek-K.Novacek, Most 1999.

d2) 10...♘e7?! 11 0-0-0 0-0 12 a3 ♘g6 13 ♘d5 ♘xe5 14 ♘xc7 ♖a5 15 ♗b5 left Black's position a complete wreck in L.Antol-F.Frink, Trencianske Teplice 2005.

d3) 10...f6 is Black's best try, although after 11 f4!? fxe5 12 fxe5 ♖a5 (12...♘e7 13 0-0-0 ♘c6 ♗c4 leaves White's nose clearly in front, with the idea of 14...♘xe5?! 15 ♖he1 d6 16 ♘b5) 13 ♘b5 ♔d8 14 b4! ♖a4 15 a3 ♘h6 16 ♗c4! ♘g4 17 ♗b3 ♖a8 18 e6 White enjoys a dangerous initiative. That said, with the 18...c6! (18...dxe6? 19 0-0-0+! ♔e7 20 ♖he1 c6 21 ♘d6 ♖xa3 22 ♘xc8+ ♖xc8 23 ♖xe6+ saw White regaining his pawn with some advantage in V.Babula-Z.Varga, Zemplinska Sirava 2004) 19 ♘d6 ♔c7 20 0-0-0 dxe6 of M.Krakops-V.Zhuravliov, Riga 1993, Black can restrict White to just an edge after 21 ♖he1!.

Returning to 6...♘f6:

7 ♘c3

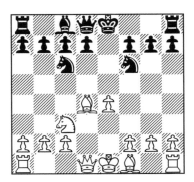

7...0-0

Black continues to refuse to develop White's queen to a powerful, central square, but he has also been known to try:

a) 7...d6 8 ♗e3 ♗e6 9 ♗e2 ♕d7 was the solid continuation of F.Hidalgo Santana-P.Heimbacher, Tenerife 2005, but after 10 ♕d2 White's bishops must give him a small but pleasant advantage.

b) 7...♕e7?! 8 ♗xf6! ♕xf6 9 ♘d5 ♕d8 (White is somewhat for choice after 9...♕xb2 10 ♘xc7+ ♔d8 11 ♘d5!, in view of his safer king) 10 f4 0-0 11 ♕d3 followed by 0-0-0 gives White control and the initiative.

c) 7...♘xd4?! 8 ♕xd4 reaches a position which can also come about from the Scotch Four Knights, i.e. 4...♘f6 5 ♘c3 ♗c5 6 ♗e3 ♘xd4 7 ♗xd4 ♗xd4 8 ♕xd4. Just as at move 6, Black shouldn't be keen to help White develop so smoothly and after 8...d6 9 0-0-0 0-0 10 e5! the first player has unsurprisingly scored pretty well in practice.

8 ♗e3 ♖e8

After 8...d6 White would revert back to the attacking mechanism we saw in Line A: 9 f3 ♗e6 10 ♕d2 followed by advancing the kingside pawns.

9 ♗c4! d6

White's last had left the e-pawn taboo: 9...♘xe4?! 10 ♘xe4 ♖xe4 fails to 11 ♗xf7+ ♔h8 12 0-0 with a very pleasant advantage for White thanks to his bishop-pair.

10 f3

White shores up e4 and may castle on either side. Meanwhile Black is a little low on counterplay and there can be little doubt that White enjoys an easy pull.

C) 5...♕f6

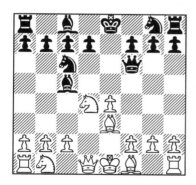

Black's main and most ambitious move. Rather than meekly retreat the bishop or exchange on d4, he prefers to continue his development and provoke complications. Indeed, while White usually defends his knight at this point, he also has a sharp alternative, taking immediate aim at c7.

C1: 6 ♘b5
C2: 6 c3

C1) 6 ♘b5!?

White wastes no time striking against Black's softest spot, c7. This is tempting, but does ask quite a lot of his own position.

6...♗xe3

Naturally Black should exchange and damage White's structure. Otherwise, 6...♗b4+? 7 c3 ♗a5 8 ♘d2 a6 9 ♘d4 ♘ge7 10 ♘c4 b5 11 ♘xc6 ♘xc6 12 ♘xa5 ♘xa5 13 a4 ♘c4 14 ♗d4 left White in complete control in N.Dobrev-A.Kulago, San Sebastian 2009, and even worse was 6...♗d6? 7 ♘1c3 a6 8 ♘d5 ♕d8 9 ♘xd6+ cxd6 10 ♗b6 when Black could have resigned in J.Chamorro Villoria-S.Pastrana Alvarez, Leon 2006.

7 fxe3

7...♕h4+

Black forces a further concession before retreating his queen to guard c7. This is both critical and best, as we can see by comparing:

a) 7...♕e5?! 8 ♘d2 ♔d8 (there's no time for 8...♘ce7? on account of 9 b4!, renewing the threat of ♘f3 and after 9...♔f8 10 ♗d3 c6 11 ♘f3 ♕b8 12 ♘bd4 d5 13 0-0 White was doing pretty well in J.Gonzalez-G.Aguado Rodriguez, Mosto-les 2008) 9 ♗d3 ♘f6 10 0-0 d6 11 ♘f3 (but not 11 ♘c4? ♕xb5 12 ♘xd6 ♕c5 13 ♘xf7+ ♔e7 14 ♘xh8 ♕xe3+ 15 ♔h1 ♗g4 when it was Black who was clearly better in M.Langer-J.Friedel, Las Vegas 2009) 11...♕e7 12 ♕e1 ♘g4 13 ♕g3 g6 14 ♘fd4 left White clearly for choice in O.Kulicov-A.Okara, Alushta 2005.

b) After 7...♔d8 8 ♘1c3 ♘ge7 un-surprisingly Black will face difficulties for some moves as he tries to coordi-nate his forces.

White should continue aggressively with 9 ♕d2 (best; 9 ♕f3?! d6 10 ♗e2 ♘e5 11 ♕xf6 gxf6 12 0-0 f5 13 ♘d5 c6 14 ♘xe7 ♔xe7 15 ♘c3 fxe4 16 ♘xe4 ♗e6 saw Black successfully untangling and equalizing in H.Remmler-O.Kor-neev, Böblingen 2003) 9...a6 10 ♘d4 d6 (or 10...♘e5 11 0-0-0 d6 12 ♗e2 ♗e6 13 h3 h5 14 ♘f3 ♔d7 15 ♖hf1, which re-

tained a pull in A.Areshchenko-E.Zude, Coventry 2005) 11 0-0-0 and after 11...♗d7 (11...b5?! 12 ♘d5 ♕e5 13 ♘xe7 ♘xe7 would have left Black's po-sition quite loose in M.Langer-K.Cao, Stillwater 2009, had White found 14 ♗d3 followed by ♘f3 and e5) 12 h3 b5 13 g4 ♕e5 14 ♘f3 ♕c5 15 ♘d5 White was slightly better in E.Valeanu-V.Tuchila, Bucharest 2008.

c) 7...♕d8 8 ♕g4! g6 (surprisingly 8...♘f6? has been tried and equally surprisingly White has often rejected the simple 9 ♘xc7+! ♔xc7 10 ♕xg7 when after both 10...♔e7 11 ♕xh8 ♕b6 12 ♘c3 ♕xe3+ 13 ♗e2 ♘b4 14 ♖f1 and 10...♖g8 11 ♕xf6 ♘b4 12 ♘c3! ♘xc2+ 13 ♔f2 ♘xa1 14 ♘d5 ♕d8 15 ♕d6 his advantage is already decisive; Black should also avoid 8...♔f8?!, which left White doing pretty well after 9 ♕g3 d6 10 ♘1c3 a6 11 ♘d4 ♘e5 12 0-0-0 ♘f6 13 ♗e2 g6 14 ♖hf1 in R.Sprangers-W.Roggeveen, Vlissingen 2006) 9 ♕f4 d6 10 ♗c4 sees White transferring the centre of operations from c7 to f7.

This is quite an effective plan, as

shown by 10...♞e5 (otherwise, 10...f5? 11 exf5 ♝xf5 12 e4 was just all over in R.Prasca-A.Hernandez, Paracotos 2005, while 10...♝e6? 11 ♝xe6 fxe6 12 0-0 ♞ge7 13 ♞1c3 ♞e5 would have left White doing very well in T.Burg-S.Lepot, La Fere 2005, had he gone 14 ♖ad1) 11 0-0 ♛d7 (essential; Black is crushed after 11...♛e7? 12 ♞1c3 c6 13 ♞xd6+! ♛xd6 14 ♝xf7+ ♚e7, as in R.Batkovic-B.Jevtic, Belgrade 1993, and then 15 ♖ad1 ♛f6 16 ♛g3, while 12...g5 is no help on account of the 13 ♛f2 c6 14 ♝xf7+! ♚d7 15 ♞d4 of R.Swinkels-D.De Vreugt, Hoogeveen 2004) 12 ♞d2 (12 ♞1a3!? is promising too and after 12...a6 13 ♞d4 ♛e7 14 ♞f3 ♞xc4 15 ♞xc4 ♝e6 16 e5 White most certainly had the initiative in R.Zelcic-G.Kuba, Pula 2003) 12...a6 13 ♞c3 c6 14 ♝b3 ♛e7 15 ♞c4 ♞xc4 16 ♝xc4 ♝e6 17 ♝xe6 ♛xe6 18 ♖ad1 0-0-0 19 ♛xf7 ♛xf7 20 ♖xf7 ♞h6 when Postny has suggested that Black is only slightly worse, but surely White must be clearly better after 21 ♖f4.

Returning to 7...♛h4+:

8 g3 ♛d8!

Now defence is the right plan. More active is 8...♛xe4, but following 9 ♞xc7+ ♚d8 (usually played, although after 9...♚f8!? 10 ♞xa8 ♛xh1 11 ♛d2 ♛e4 12 ♞c3 ♛e5 13 0-0-0 the position doesn't seem too clear; here White might prefer the 11 ♛d6+ ♞ge7 12 ♞d2 of A.Gad-D.Marholev, Amantea 2008, when 12...♛xh2 13 0-0-0 h5 14 ♝b5 gives him enduring and fairly promising compensation) 10 ♞xa8 ♛xh1 (otherwise, 10...d5?? 11 ♞c3 ♛xh1 12 ♞xd5 left Black without a move in H.Kummerow-F.Denig, Recklinghausen 2005, while 10...♞f6 11 ♛d6 ♛xh1 12 ♞d2 should favour White on account of his safer king: for example, 12...♛d5 13 ♛c7+ ♚e7 14 0-0-0 ♛xa2 15 ♞b3 ♛a4 was seen in M.Velcheva-I.Paulicka, Sunny Beach 2006, when 16 ♝g2 would have left White with the initiative, but that is preferable for Black to 14...♛e5?! 15 ♞c4 ♛xc7 16 ♞xc7 ♞d8 17 ♞d6, which saw him being squashed in L.Kritz-P.Hohler, Triesen 2005) 11 ♛d6 while both queens are actively placed, White's enjoys the more threatening position.

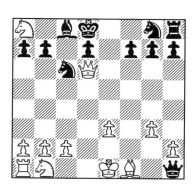

Here 11...♘ge7 (perhaps Black should investigate 11...♘f6!?) 12 ♘d2 keeps Black's queen out of f3 and after 12...♕xh2 (12...♕d5?? dropped a piece to 13 ♕c7+ ♔e8 14 ♕xc8+! ♘xc8 15 ♘c7+ in S.Shyam-S.Das, New Delhi 2007) 13 0-0-0 ♘f5 14 ♕f4 White enjoys the initiative and decent play for the pawn.

9 ♕g4

White must try to cause some problems with his queen. After 9 ♗c4?! ♘f6 10 0-0 0-0 followed by ...d6 and ...♘e5 Black clearly has a pleasant edge on account of his superior structure, while 9 ♘1c3 a6 10 ♘d4 ♘f6 11 ♕d2 was seen in E.Borulya-B.Latzke, German League 2006, and now just 11...0-0 12 ♗g2 ♖e8 13 0-0 d6 would have left Black slightly for choice.

9...g6

Natural and effective, although not everyone has been so convinced and practice has also seen:

a) 9...♔f8 avoids weakening the pawns, but it will then take Black even longer to coordinate his forces and after 10 ♕f4 d6 11 ♘1c3 ♘e5 (alternatively, 11...a6 12 ♘d4 ♘e5 13 0-0-0 ♘g6 14 ♕f2 ♕f6 15 ♕d2 ♘8e7 16 ♗c4 followed by ♖hf1 was excellent for White in L.Rojas-H.Lopez Silva, Santiago 2006, while 11...♘f6 12 0-0-0 ♕e7 13 h3 a6 14 ♘d4 ♗d7 15 g4 ♖e8 16 ♗g2 ♕e5 17 ♖hf1 left White slightly for choice in A.Kolev-E.Van den Doel, Bajada de la Virgen 2005, but Black might consider the 11...♘ge7!? 12 ♗c4 ♘e5 of

L.Bensdorp-A.Van Weersel, Leeuwarden 2005, when 13 ♗b3 h5 begins counterplay) 12 ♗e2 ♘f6 13 0-0-0 followed by 14 h3 White had a pull in K.Nuri-J.Krejci, Sibenik 2007.

b) 9...g5!? is a more radical approach and after 10 ♘1c3 (otherwise, 10 ♕h5 ♘e5 11 h4?! d6 12 ♗e2 a6 13 ♘d4 c5 14 ♘f5 ♗xf5 15 exf5 ♘f6! already left Black doing pretty well in M.Langer-A.Onischuk, Stillwater 2005, and here White should prefer 11 ♘d2 d6 12 h3 with approximate equality) 10...♘e5! (more precise than 10...d6 11 ♕e2 a6 12 ♘d4 ♘e5 when 13 ♕f2 ♗e6 14 ♗e2 ♕f6 15 ♘f5 invaded the hole on f5 with an edge in M.Langer-E.Santarius, Tulsa 2008) Black's knight finds an excellent outpost.

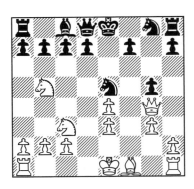

It looks like White should improve his pieces with 11 ♕e2 d6 12 h3 (12 ♗g2 c6 13 ♘d4 ♗g4 14 ♗f3 was preferred in I.Mutschnik-O.Romanishin, Nettetal 2004, and now 14...♘xf3+ 15 ♘xf3 ♕f6 16 ♖f1 0-0-0 17 0-0-0 would have been roughly level) 12...c6 13 ♘d4 ♘f6 14 0-0-0 ♕e7 15 ♕f2, angling to play down the f-file, but Black is well placed on the dark squares and after 15...♗e6 16 ♗e2 0-0-0 17 ♘f5 ♗xf5 18 exf5 ♘ed7 began to take over the initiative in P.Bontempi-O.Jovanic, Nova Gorica 2008. Thus 9...g5!? very much deserves further attention.

10 ♕f4 d6

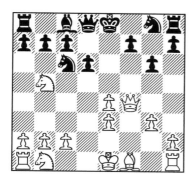

11 ♗c4?!

White plays as he does with his pawn back on g2 (note 'c' to Black's 7th move), but the weakening of his kingside will make an important difference. Indeed, White should likely prefer 11 ♘1c3! when 11...a6 (Black has to avoid 11...♘f6? 12 ♘xc7+ ♕xc7 13 ♕xf6, but after both 11...♘e5 12 0-0-0 a6 and 11...♗e6 12 0-0-0 a6 13 ♘d4 ♘e5 play is very likely to transpose below) 12 ♘d4 ♘e5 13 ♗e2 (perhaps 11...a6 is slightly imprecise, as here White should consider 13 0-0-0 ♗g4 14 ♖d2!?, whereupon 14...♕d7 15 h3 ♗e6 16 ♘f3 supplied a pull in E.Doluhanova-E.Levushkina, Kharkiv 2006) 13...♗e6 (or 13...♗h3 14 0-0-0 ♘f6, as in K.Stokke-K.Strand, Gjovik 2008, when

15 ♖hg1! would have given White the initiative) 14 0-0-0 ♘f6 15 ♖hf1 ♘fd7 16 ♘f5! (as played in R.Swinkels-E.L'Ami, Hoogeveen 2006; instead 16 g4 ♕e7 17 ♘d5 ♗xd5 18 exd5 h6 was very solid for Black and about equal in G.Jones-P.Sowray, Hereford 2006) 16...gxf5 17 exf5 ♗xa2 18 ♘xa2 leaves Black with a firm grip on e5, but White should be better in view of his mobile kingside majority.

11...♘e5 12 0-0 ♗h3!

This is why Black checked on h4. Otherwise, there was little point in the check, as we can see from 12...♕e7? 13 ♘1c3 g5 14 ♕f2 c6 15 ♗xf7+ ♔f8 16 ♗e6+ ♔g7 17 ♗xc8 ♖xc8 18 ♘d4 ♘h6 19 ♕e2, which left White clearly for choice in H.Rasch-E.Agdestein, Gibraltar 2007, and even the superior 12...♕d7 13 ♘1a3 a6 (Y.Abramova-S.Bezgodova, Voronezh 2009) 14 ♗e6! ♕e7 15 ♗xc8 ♖xc8 16 ♘c3 with a slight plus for White.

13 ♗xf7+

White grabs the pawn before Black can evacuate his king to safety. He might not want to, but after 13 ♘1c3 ♕d7 (and not 13...♗xf1?? 14 ♖xf1 ♕d7 on account of 15 ♗e6! ♕c6 16 ♘d4 when Black had to resign in M.Langer-A.Yermolinsky, Stillwater 2009) 14 ♗xf7+ ♘xf7 15 ♘d5 0-0-0 16 ♕xf7 ♗xf1 17 ♕xf1 c6 Black emerges with the upper hand in any case.

13...♔d7

White has netted a pawn, but his kingside is a wreck and the initiative has undoubtedly passed into Black's hands.

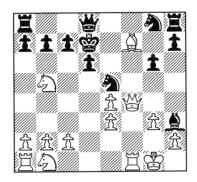

At this point White doesn't seem to have anything better than 14 ♘1c3 (saving the rook with 14 ♖d1? only makes matters worse after 14...♕e7) 14...g5 15 ♕f2, but after 15...♘h6 the exchange was lost for insufficient compensation in A.Gavrilova-B.Schink, Crete 2007.

C2) 6 c3

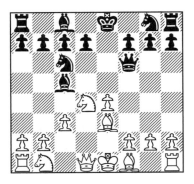

White shores up the defence of his knight and will emerge with an ideal two-abreast pawn centre should Black exchange on d4. At this point Black usually facilitates castling while sup-

porting a ...d5 counterstrike, but he also has a tricky queen move:

C21: 6...♕g6
C22: 6...♘ge7

The fairly uncommon alternatives are somewhat less challenging:

a) 6...d6 7 ♕d2 (but not 7 ♗c4?! because of 7...♕g6 8 0-0 ♘e5 and after 9 f3 ♘xc4 10 ♕a4+ c6 11 ♕xc4 ♗e6 12 ♕e2 ♘e7 13 ♘d2 0-0 14 ♘2b3 ♗b6 Black was fine in R.Staufcik-M.Butula, Czech League 1997) 7...♘ge7 (otherwise, 7...♘xd4 8 cxd4 ♗b6 9 ♘c3 gives White an easy edge and 7...♗d7 8 ♘a3! the initiative) 8 ♘b5 ♗xe3 9 ♕xe3 targeted c7 to give White a pleasant edge in R.Zelcic-N.Zinina, Cattolica 1993.

b) 6...a6 7 ♗e2 ♘ge7 8 0-0 0-0 9 f4 saw White expanding in V.Zotin-H.Burreh, Naumburg 2002, and after 9...d5 10 e5 he undoubtedly has an edge.

c) 6...b6 7 ♗e2 ♗b7 8 0-0 0-0-0 was quite an ambitious try in G.Koskoska-J.Charest, Istanbul 2000, but after 9 b4! ♗d6 10 f4 White would have been for choice.

d) 6...♘xd4?! 7 cxd4 ♗b6 8 ♘c3 c6 9 ♗c4 would be ideal for White and already leaves him clearly better.

e) 6...♗xd4?! 7 cxd4 ♘ge7 8 ♘c3 prevents ...d5 and after 8...♘g6 9 d5 White is again somewhat for choice.

f) 6...♗b6 7 ♘a3 ♘ge7 sees Black angling for ...d5, but 8 ♘c4 gives White an edge after 8...♗xd4 9 cxd4 d5 10 e5.

C21) 6...♛g6

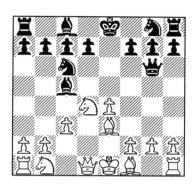

Black's most important alternative to 6...♘ge7. It looks tempting to pressure e4 and g2, but Black is moving the queen again and White can try to seize the initiative. Now we have:

> **C211: 7 ♘b5**
> **C212: 7 ♘d2**
> **C213: 7 ♛e2**
> **C214: 7 ♛f3**

Those have been White's most common approaches, but we should also note:

a) 7 ♘f5? ♗xe3 8 ♘xe3 ♛xe4 is a rather optimistic sacrifice. White hopes to gain time kicking the black queen back, but a key pawn has been lost and after 9 ♗d3 (or 9 ♘d2 ♛e7 10 ♛g4 g6 11 ♛g3 d6 12 ♗b5 ♘f6 13 0-0-0 0-0 when White didn't have enough compensation in A.Szieberth-P.Lukacs, Budapest 2000) 9...♛e5 10 0-0 ♘ge7 11 ♘a3 d5 12 ♖e1 ♗e6 Black was slightly for choice in O.De la Riva Aguado-J.Oms

Pallise, Seville 2004.

b) 7 ♘xc6?! ♗xe3 8 ♘d4 is another approach which can't exactly be described as critical or important. White should be able to regain the bishop, but after 8...♗h6 (Black can also repeat with 8...♗f4 9 ♛f3 ♗c1 10 ♛e2 ♗f4 or go 8...♗xd4 9 ♛xd4 ♘e7 10 ♘d2 0-0, as Romanishin earlier had) 9 ♘f5 ♘e7 10 ♘xh6 ♛xh6 one can't exactly talk of any advantage for him.

Indeed, after 11 ♗d3 ♘g6 12 0-0 0-0 13 ♖e1 ♘e5 14 ♘a3 d6 15 ♘c4 ♗g4 chances were balanced in A.Stiri-O.Romanishin, Athens 2007.

c) 7 f3.

This makes a fair amount of sense, shoring up e4 while enabling White to cover g2 with his queen.

Now:

c1) 7...♘f6?! was tried in L.Sanchez Silva-J.Baena Canada, Burguillos 2008, but after 8 ♘b5!? (the simpler 8 ♕d2 should suffice for an edge) 8...♗xe3 9 ♘xc7+ ♔d8 10 ♘xa8 White is likely doing pretty well, despite the cornered knight, thanks to his safer king and solid structure.

c2) 7...♘xd4 8 cxd4 ♗b6 9 ♕d2 ♘e7 10 ♘c3 0-0 11 ♗d3 d6 rather gave away the centre in J.Hartikainen-R.Nevanlinna, Finnish League 1997, where 12 ♘a4 would have given White a pleasant edge.

c3) 7...♘e5?! 8 ♘b5 ♗xe3 9 ♘xc7+ ♔d8 10 ♘xa8 b6 11 ♕a4 saves the knight with some advantage.

c4) 7...b6 dissuades a raid on c7, but after 8 ♘d2 ♗b7 9 ♘2b3 White has an edge.

c5) 7...♘ge7 has been Black's main move and after 8 ♕d2 (again 8 ♘b5!? very much comes into consideration, rare though it's been here; after 8...♗xe3 9 ♘xc7+ ♔d8 10 ♘xa8 b6 in D.Fiala-M.Jaros, Plzen 2000, White might have gone 11 ♘a3! ♗b7 12 ♘c4 ♗g5 13 ♘axb6 axb6 14 ♘d6, which would have left him with the initiative and surely for choice) 8...0-0 (otherwise, the gambit 8...d5 9 ♘b5 ♗xe3 10 ♕xe3 0-0 transposes to variation 'c52', below, but Black should consider 8...a6!? 9 ♘c2 ♗xe3 10 ♘xe3 0-0, since 11 c4 d6 12

♘c3 f5 left him actively placed and with decent counterplay in Z.Zhao-G.Lane, Melbourne 1999) White must be a little careful as he trails in terms of development:

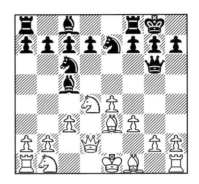

c51) 9 ♗c4 ♘xd4 10 cxd4 was seen in M.Rodriguez Garcia-J.Baena, Barcelona 2000, and now 10...d5! 11 exd5 ♗d6 would have given Black decent compensation, but he might do even better with 9...♘e5!? 10 ♗b3 b6, thereby seizing an early initiative.

c52) 9 ♘b5 is likely a more critical and better try. After 9...♗xe3 10 ♕xe3 d5 11 ♘xc7 ♖b8 Black's lead in development compensates for the pawn, although White might be slightly for choice after 12 ♘d2!? dxe4 13 ♘xe4 ♗f5 14 0-0-0!.

d) 7 ♗e2!? has been quite rare, but is quite a tempting gambit. Following 7...♕xg2 (White has the initiative after 7...♗xd4?! 8 cxd4!, while 7...♘xd4 8 cxd4 ♗b4+ 9 ♘c3 ♕xe4?! 10 0-0 ♗xc3 11 bxc3 d5?! 12 ♖e1 ♗e6 13 ♗g5 ♕g6 14 h4 left Black in huge trouble in C.Husson-A.Le Diouron, French League

2008; in the latter line, 9...♛xg2 is perhaps a better pawn to grab, although with 10 ♝f3 ♝xc3+ 11 bxc3 ♛g6 12 h4 White retains promising compensation) 8 ♝f3 ♛g6 9 ♘d2 it's now White who is much the better developed.

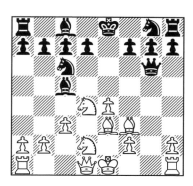

The game H.Welten-H.Jonkman, Vlissingen 2001, continued 9...♛f6 10 ♘c4 (10 ♛a4!? followed by going long was the alternative) 10...♘xd4 11 cxd4 ♝b4+ and now 12 ♚e2! would have left White well coordinated, with a strong centre and decent compensation.

C211) 7 ♘b5!?

The most critical and ambitious choice, wasting no time going after c7.

7...♝xe3 8 ♘xc7+

The consistent follow-up. With Black's queen on g6, not f6, White might also wonder about 8 fxe3?!, but after 8...♚d8 9 ♘d2 (9 ♛f3 is also insufficient: 9...♘f6 10 ♘d2 d6 11 h3 ♖e8 12 0-0-0 ♘xe4 13 ♘xe4 ♛xe4 14 ♛xf7 ♛xe3+ 15 ♖d2 ♛e1+ left Black doing pretty well in Y.Malinarski-H.Jonkman, Hoogeveen 2003) 9...♘f6! Black's queen

continues to exert awkward pressure and is definitely now quite well placed on g6.

Indeed, after 10 ♛a4? ♘g4 Black is clearly doing pretty well, just as he was with 10 ♝e2? ♛xg2 11 ♝f3 ♛g5 12 ♛e2 ♛h4+ in S.Lalic-P.Wells, Torquay 1998. Neither did 10 ♛b3 ♘g4 11 0-0-0? ♘f2 12 ♝e2 ♘xh1 13 ♖xh1 d6 exactly turn out well for White in K.Rathnakaran-P.Negi, Mangalore 2008, and quite possibly he has nothing better than 10 ♛c2, restricting Black to just an edge with 10...♘g4 11 ♘c4 a6.

8...♚d8 9 ♘xa8

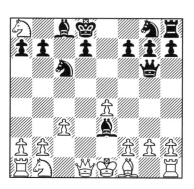

9...♗h6

Instead 9...♗c5 10 ♘d2 b6 11 b4 must leave White at least slightly for choice, but 9...♗f4 has been fairly common:

a) 10 f3? ♗xh2 11 ♕a4 ♗g3+ 12 ♔d1 would have favoured Black in N.Kharmunova-F.Steil Antoni, Kemer 2007, after just 12...b6 and ...♗b7.

b) 10 ♕c2!? b6 11 g3 improved in M.Ikonomopoulou-F.Steil Antoni, Kemer 2007, and following 11...♗b8 12 ♘a3 ♗b7 13 ♘xb6 axb6 14 0-0-0 White has the initiative.

c) 10 ♕f3 has been White's main move and then:

c1) The 10...♗c1?! of M.Ragger-J.Krivec, Maribor 2003, should be met by 11 ♘d2 ♗xb2 12 ♖b1 ♗a3 13 ♗b5 with some advantage.

c2) 10...♗e5 11 ♘d2 ♘f6, as in C.Allor-M.Kumar, Mallorca 2004, and then 12 ♗b5 also leaves White doing well.

c3) 10...♗b8 11 ♘d2 ♘f6 (otherwise, 11...♘e5 12 ♕g3 ♕f6 13 0-0-0 ♘e7 14 ♗e2 b6 15 ♖hf1 left White much better in M.Hoehn-R.Holzer, Bruchkoebel 2002, while 11...b6 12 ♕e3 reveals White's idea and after 12...f5 13 exf5 ♕xf5 14 ♗d3 ♕f4 15 ♕xf4 ♗xf4 16 ♘c4 ♗b7 17 ♘axb6 axb6 18 0-0 ♗c7 19 ♖fe1 ♘f6 20 a4 ♖e8 21 ♖xe8+ ♔xe8 22 b4 he retained a small but clear advantage despite the exchanges in S.Lakatos-C.Koch, correspondence 2001) 12 0-0-0 was P.Hromada-L.Ostrowski, Moravia 2003, where again

12...b6 13 ♕e3 gives White the initiative and likely the upper hand.

c4) 10...♗h6 11 ♗e2 (but not 11 ♕f5?! ♕xf5 12 exf5 b6 13 ♘a3 ♗b7 14 ♘xb6 axb6 15 ♘c4 ♔c7 when Black had the initiative in D.Campora-V.Tkachiev, Biel 1995) 11...♘f6 12 0-0! ♘xe4 13 ♗d3 gives White the initiative, with Black's king not entirely happy in the centre.

10 f3

Introduced in F.Lopez Fuentes-J.Avila Jimenez, Barcelona 2001, this simple move shores up e4. So too does 10 ♘d2 and after 10...b6 11 f3 ♗b7 12 ♘xb6 axb6 13 ♘c4 ♔c7 14 ♕b3 White has the initiative.

10...b6

Naturally Black plays to pick up the cornered knight.

11 ♘a3 ♗b7 12 ♘xb6 axb6 13 ♕b3

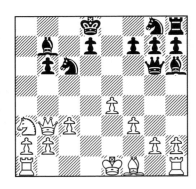

The position certainly isn't entirely clear, but White is likely for choice. By attacking b6 he will obtain the initiative and his king should feel safer on the f2-square than Black's does on d8 or c7.

C212) 7 ♘d2

White's most popular choice in practice, but that may say more about the surprise value of 6...♕g6 than any objective merits of White's simple defence.

7...♘f6

8 ♕f3

A whole host of alternatives have been tried, but pretty much all of them have failed to convince:

a) 8 f3?! is rather slow and after 8...d5! 9 ♘b5 (further defence won't do, as shown by 9 ♕e2 ♗xd4 10 ♗xd4?! ♘xd4 11 cxd4 dxe4 12 ♘xe4 0-0 13 ♘xf6+ ♕xf6 which already left Black much better in D.Van den Dikkenberg-E.Van der Beld, Dutch League 1996, or 9 ♕c2 ♗xd4! 10 cxd4 0-0 with the safer king and ongoing pressure against e4 for Black; instead the combative 9 ♗b5!? was tried in E.Berg-I.Morovic Fernandez, Saint Vincent 2000, but after 9...♕xg2 10 ♖g1 ♕xh2 11 ♖xg7 ♗d7 12 ♕b3 ♕h4+ the complications favoured Black) 9...♗xe3 10 ♘xc7+ ♔f8 11 ♘xa8 in A.Eliseev-H.Jonkman, Inter-

net (rapid) 2002, 11...dxe4! would have given Black a dangerous attack for the exchange.

b) 8 ♕c2?! is rather well met by 8...♘g4! and after 9 0-0-0 (again it's too early for 9 ♘b5 and 9...♗xe3 10 fxe3 ♔d8 11 ♘c4 ♕g5 is in Black's favour) 9...♘xe3 10 fxe3 0-0 11 ♘2f3 d6 12 ♘f5 in G.Marinelli-M.Scacco, Bratto 2004, the simple 12...♖e8! would have left Black on top.

c) 8 ♕e2 ♘g4! is again a slightly awkward raid for White to face and 9 ♘c2 ♘xe3 10 ♘xe3 ♘e7 11 ♘b3 ♗b6 12 ♘f5 ♕f6 13 ♘xe7 ♕xe7 14 g3 0-0 15 ♗g2 d6 left Black with the bishop-pair and slightly for choice in R.Roszkowski-A.Leniart, Grodzisk Mazowiecki 2007.

d) 8 ♘f5 ♗xe3 9 ♘xe3 0-0 (but not the greedy 9...♘xe4?! because 10 ♗d3! ♘xf2 11 ♗xg6 ♘xd1 12 ♗xf7+ ♔xf7 13 0-0+! ♔e7 14 ♖axd1 gives White a strong initiative for the pawn) 10 ♗d3 d5! 11 exd5 ♕xd3 12 dxc6 reaches quite an important position.

Will White emerge with the better pawns or can Black make him pay for his light-square weaknesses and un-castled king? Now 12...b6 13 ♕f3 ♗e6 14 c4 b5 15 0-0-0! ♕g6 16 h4 saw White seizing the initiative in J.Degraeve-N.Mitkov, Pula 1997, but with 12...♖e8! Black can set some problems, although 13 ♘b3 ♕b5 (13...♕a6!? is also possible) 14 a4!? (after 14 cxb7?! ♗xb7 Black will surely at least regain his pawn on g2) 14...♕xc6 15 0-0 b6 16 ♘d4 ♕e4 failed to bring him any advantage in view of White's well-placed knights in J.Hoogendoorn-A.Van de Oudeweetering, Leeuwarden 2001.

e) 8 f4 ♘xd4 (the right trade; instead 8...♗xd4 allows the intermezzo 9 f5!, but again Black might consider 8...♘g4!?, after which 9 ♗g1 ♘xd4 10 cxd4 ♗b4 11 ♗d3 0-0 should give him enough counterplay to maintain a rough balance) 9 cxd4 (now 9 f5?! runs into 9...♘xf5! 10 ♗xc5 ♘h6! 11 ♕f3 d6 12 ♗d4 ♘hg4 with an extra pawn for Black, as pointed out by Nataf) 9...♗b4 10 f5 ♕g4 11 ♕xg4 (after 11 e5 ♕e4! White should allow the repetition with 12 ♔e2 ♕g4+ 13 ♔e1 ♕f4, since 12 ♕f3 ♕xf3 13 gxf3 ♘d5 14 ♗f2 d6 can only favour Black if anyone) 11...♘xg4 12 ♗f4 d5 13 h3 (clearly preferable to 13 ♗d3?! dxe4 14 ♗xe4 ♘f6 15 0-0 ♘xe4 16 ♘xe4 ♗xf5 when Black was doing well in P.Wells-J.Hector, Oxford 1998) 13...♘f6 (and not 13...♘h6? 14 f6!) 14 e5 ♘e4 15 g4 g6 was unbalanced but about equal in E.Handoko-J.Ehlvest, Bali 1999.

f) 8 ♗e2 d5! (here it's risky to grab the pawn: 8...♕xg2 9 ♗f3 ♕g6 10 ♕e2! ♘e5 11 0-0-0 ♘xf3 12 ♘2xf3 gave White decent compensation in J.Fabian-S.Marek, Slovakian League 1999; but Black might consider 8...d6!?, with the idea of 9 0-0 ♗h3 10 ♗f3 ♘e5) 9 exd5 ♘xd5 10 ♗f3 ♘xe3 11 fxe3 ♘e5 12 0-0 0-0 13 ♗e4 ♕h6 favoured Black slightly with her bishops in E.Stavropoulou-M.Ikonomopoulou, Athens 2003.

Finally we return to White's most active defence of the e-pawn, 8 ♕f3:

8...♘g4!

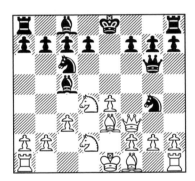

Again Black chases down the bishop-pair. Naturally he must avoid 8...0-0?? 9 ♘xc6 and 8...♗b6? 9 ♘b5 is also inadvisable, but 8...♘e5 is possible and after 9 ♕f5 (perhaps White should try 9 ♕g3!?) 9...d6 10 ♕xg6 hxg6 11 f3 0-0 12 0-0-0 ♖e8 13 ♘c2 ♗b6 14 ♘c4 ♗xe3+ 15 ♘2xe3 ♘c6 the position was about equal in J.Moawad-H.Jonkman, Cairo 2003.

9 ♘f5

White might also consider 9 ♘2b3, but after 9...♘xe3 10 ♕xe3 ♗b6 Black again enjoys a small initiative thanks to his bishops.

9...♞xe3 10 ♞xe3 0-0 11 ♞d5 ♞e5 12 ♛g3

We've followed the game B.Kharashkina-O.Stjazhkina, St Petersburg 2001, in which White no doubt hoped that the active knight on d5 would compensate for the loss of the bishop-pair, but Black can kick it away with 12...♛xg3 13 hxg3 c6 when he must be at least equal.

C213) 7 ♛e2

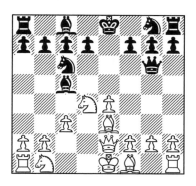

White makes use of the tactic 7...♛xe4? 8 ♞xc6 ♝xe3 9 ♞d4 to indirectly defend the e-pawn. At first the move looks quite attractive and it has received a fair bit of testing, but the drawback is, of course, that the light-squared bishop is blocked in; a factor which should enable Black to equalize.

7...♞xd4!

Correct. Black must counter the threat of 8 ♞b5 and 7...♝xd4?! 8 cxd4 ♞f6 (8...♛xe4? now fails to 9 ♞c3 ♛f5 10 d5 ♞ce7 11 d6! cxd6 12 ♞b5 with

some advantage for White) 9 f3 0-0 10 ♞c3 would only give White a strong centre and the bishop-pair to boot.

8 ♝xd4

White wants to develop his knight as actively as possible. The obvious choice is 8 cxd4 ♝b4+ (invariably played; 8...♝b6 9 ♞c3 ♞e7 10 d5 0-0 was preferred in D.Darcia-M.Aseeva, Melitopol 1992, but after 11 h4 h5 12 0-0-0 White has a dangerous-looking initiative with f3 and g4 one plan, ♜h3-g3 another), but here 9 ♞c3? ♛xe4 doesn't give White enough for the pawn, so he has to go 9 ♝d2.

Here 9...♝xd2+ 10 ♞xd2 ♞e7! prepares the classical counter ...d5. This has often worked out well in practice, with 11 0-0-0?! 0-0 12 ♛e3 d5 13 f3 ♜e8 already favouring Black in J.Zezulkin-V.Malaniuk, Koszalin 1997. Thus White usually goes 11 g3, but after 11...0-0 12 ♝g2 ♛b6! (12...d5 is tempting and has been more popular, but after 13 0-0! dxe4 14 ♞xe4 c6 15 ♜fe1 ♝g4 16 ♛d2 followed by ♞c5 White was slightly better despite the

IQP in B.Golubovic-O.Romanishin, Cannes 1998, and here 15...♘d5 16 ♘c3 ♘xc3 17 bxc3 ♗e6 18 ♖ab1 ♖ab8 19 c4 also saw Black fail to equalize in S.Brunello-O.Romanishin, Frascati 2006) 13 ♘f3 (White should give serious consideration to 13 d5!? ♕xb2 14 0-0 and after 14...d6 15 ♕d3 ♘g6 in S.Brunello-V.Golubenko, Sibenik 2007, with 16 ♖fc1 he would have had enough for the pawn) 13...d5! 14 e5 ♗d7 15 a4 ♘c6 16 0-0 ♗g4 Black had the initiative in J.Zawadzka-M.Szydlowska, Bartkowa 2002. If White wants to try and resurrect this approach, as well as Brunello's gambit idea, he should examine the 11 ♕c4!? c6 of A.Motylev-P.Simacek, Yerevan 1997, and then 12 ♕b4 a5 13 ♕a3, fighting to prevent Black from castling.

Returning to the more ambitious 8 ♗xd4:

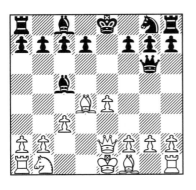

8...♗xd4

White's knight will reach c3 after this, but Black should still likely prefer it to 8...♗b6 when 9 ♗xb6 axb6 10 ♘a3! ♘f6 was seen in E.Berg-F.Vallejo

Pons, Aviles 2000, and now 11 e5 gives White an early initiative.

9 cxd4 ♘e7

Black usually prepares ...d5 thus. He preferred 9...♘f6 10 ♘c3 0-0 in L.Paulsen-E.Schallopp, Braunschweig 1880, but after 11 f3 clearly 11...d5?! is inadvisable on account of 12 e5 and 11...c6 12 0-0-0 b5 13 ♕d2 leaves White with the superior attacking chances.

10 ♘c3 0-0 11 0-0-0

The most aggressive and popular continuation. Here too White has tested 11 g3, but after 11...d5 12 e5 ♗g4 (12...f6 13 ♗g2 c6 should also be okay for Black) 13 f3 ♗f5 14 ♕b5 (M.Vasic-N.Kosintseva, Oropesa del Mar 1998) 14...♕b6 Black has enough counterplay.

11...c6

The final preparation for ...d5, but the break might even be played without delay: 11...d5!? 12 exd5 ♖e8 13 ♕e5 (or 13 ♕e3 ♗f5 14 ♕g3 ♕h6+ 15 ♕e3 and now Black avoided the repetition with 15...♕d6!? in S.Mozaliov-I.Ibragimov, Moscow 1996) 13...♗f5 14 ♗c4 ♘c6! 15 ♕g3 (clearly White must avoid 15 ♕xc7? ♕h6+ 16 ♖d2 ♖ac8) 15...♕h6+ likely gave Black enough play for his pawn in E.Schmittdiel-O.Romanishin, Bad Endbach 1995.

12 ♕d2

Ivanchuk once preferred 12 ♕e3, but after 12...d5 13 f3 (13 e5?! f6! 14 f4 fxe5 15 dxe5 ♘f5 16 ♕d2 d4 leaves White vulnerable on e3, as pointed out by Wells) 13...dxe4 14 fxe4 ♗g4! 15 ♖d2

♜ad8 16 h3 ♝c8 Black had enough counterplay down the central files and with his b-pawn in V.Ivanchuk-V.Smyslov, Tilburg 1994.

12...d5

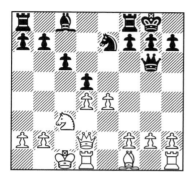

Now 13 e5 once again gives Black easy and fairly effective counterplay after 13...f6! 14 f4 fxe5 15 fxe5 ♝g4, but 13 f3 dxe4 14 fxe4 ♜d8 15 ♝e2 ♝e6 16 ♝f3 b5 also left Black with a small initiative in L.Goldgewicht-G.Flear, French League 1999.

C214) 7 ♛f3!?

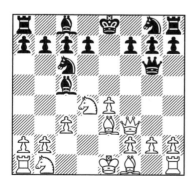

An active way of defending the e-pawn and an approach which is some-what more convincing than with the preliminary 7 ♞d2 ♞f6 thrown in.

7...♞e5

Black doesn't want to let the queen settle and for White to develop his remaining bishop without difficulty. This isn't forced, but of the alternatives only really 'f' deserves attention:

a) It's surprising how often 7...♞ge7? hasn't been punished by 8 ♞b5, which was surely one of White's main ideas behind 7 ♛f3. Now 8...♝d6 9 ♞d2 a6 10 ♞xd6+ ♛xd6 11 ♝f4 is clearly pretty good for White, but so too was 8...♝xe3 9 ♛xe3 (9 ♞xc7+!? may also be promising) 9...♚d8 10 ♞d2 f5?! (10...a6 improves and restricts White to just an edge after 11 ♞d4 ♞xd4 12 ♛xd4) 11 0-0-0 d6 12 ♞c4 ♝d7 13 ♞cxd6! cxd6 14 ♜xd6 in V.Baklan-D.Van Leent, Hoogeveen 2004.

b) After 7...♝b6?! White should go 8 ♞b5! regardless and 8...♚d8 (8...♞d8? 9 ♞d2 a6 10 ♝xb6 ♛xb6 11 ♞c4! ♛c6 12 ♞d4 ♛f6 13 ♛e3 leaves White some-what in front, but even worse for Black here was 9...♞e6? 10 ♝xb6 axb6 11 ♝c4 ♚e7 12 ♝xe6 fxe6 13 ♞xc7 ♜a5 14 b4 when White already enjoyed a near-decisive advantage in E.Sutovsky-J.Hector, Malmo 2003) 9 ♞d2 must leave him at least slightly for choice thanks to his better king position.

c) 7...♞xd4 8 cxd4 ♝b4+ (moving the queen again with 8...♛b6? fails to 9 dxc5! ♛xb2 10 ♝c4 ♞f6 11 ♛d1! ♛xa1 12 ♝d4, which traps the queen, as pointed out by Davies) 9 ♝d2 (9 ♞c3 isn't so effective on account of 9...d5! 10 exd5 ♗g4 11 ♕g3 and now in J.Tomczak-M.Krasenkow, Warsaw 2006, with 11...0-0-0 Black would have retained decent play for the pawn) 9...♗xd2+ 10 ♘xd2 ♘e7 avoids any problems with an early ♘b5 raid.

The downside to Black's play is that White has been given an ideal centre and after 11 ♗d3! it isn't so easy for him to get in an effective ...d5. The game D.Moreno Gracia-I.Salgado Lopez, Formigal 2002, continued 11...♕b6 12 ♘b3 (White can also consider the 12 0-0!? ♕xd4 13 ♕e2 ♘c6 of N.Blum-V.Paul, French League 2001, when 14 ♘f3 ♕b6 15 e5 gives him a handy lead in development for the pawn) 12...0-0 13 0-0 a5 14 e5 a4 15 ♕e4 g6 16 ♘c5 with slightly the better chances for White.

d) Naturally White should meet 7...♘f6 with 8 ♘b5 and with 8...♗xe3 9 ♕xe3 ♔d8 10 f3 ♖e8 11 ♘d2 a6 12 ♘d4 d6 13 0-0-0 ♔e7 14 g4 ♔f8 15 h4 he continued to attack in N.Fercec-C.Luciani, Nova Gorica 2001.

e) 7...d6 8 ♘b5 ♗g4 9 ♕f4 ♗xe3 10 ♕xe3 is also slightly in White's favour after 10...♖c8 11 ♗d3, but Black should prefer that to 10...0-0-0? 11 f3 ♗d7 12 ♘xa7+ or 10...♔d7 11 ♘d2 ♘ge7 12 ♗c4 12...♗e6?! (12...a6 13 ♘d4 ♖ae8 14 0-0 would have restricted White to an edge) 13 0-0 ♗xc4 14 ♘xc4 which left White clearly for choice in R.Ponomariov-L.Winants, Neum 2000.

f) As mentioned above 7...♗xd4!? is Black's best alternative to our main line and now White faces the usual dilemma over how to recapture:

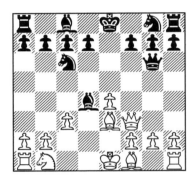

f1) 8 ♗xd4 ♘ge7 9 ♘d2 0-0 (Black also enjoyed the initiative after 9...d5 10 ♗b5 0-0 11 ♗e3 dxe4 12 ♕xe4 ♗f5 13 ♕f3 ♘e5 14 ♕g3 ♘g4 in E.Schmittdiel-V.Kupreichik, Bad Wörishofen 1995) 10 ♗c4 d5! 11 exd5 ♘xd4 12 cxd4 ♗g4 13 ♕f4 b5 14 ♗b3 a5 15 a3 a4 saw some very energetic play from Black give him the upper hand in M.Schaefer-J.Hector, German League 2006.

f2) Thus White should prefer 8 cxd4!, not worrying about his vulnerability on c2.

Black has usually taken up the challenge with 8...♘b4 (8...d5?! 9 ♘c3 dxe4 10 ♛f4! ♘f6 11 d5 leaves White doing pretty well, as 11...♘b4 can be met by the forceful 12 ♛e5+ ♚d8 13 d6!), leading to a final divide:

f21) 9 ♛e2!? ♛xe4 10 ♘c3 ♛f5 (or 10...♛e6 11 a3 ♘d5 12 ♘xd5 ♛xd5 13 ♛g4 ♚f8 14 ♖c1 ♘f6 15 ♛f4 when White's bishop-pair, safer king and much more active pieces gave him good compensation in S.Rublevsky-O.Romanishin, Warsaw 2005) 11 0-0-0 ♘e7 12 d5 b6 13 g4 ♛g6 14 a3 looks like pretty decent compensation.

f22) White doesn't have to sacrifice, though, and 9 ♘a3 ♘e7 (or 9...d5 10 ♘b5! ♘a6 11 exd5 ♘f6 12 ♗c4 0-0, as in H.Banikas-O.Romanishin, Chalkida 2009, and then 13 0-0 when Black hasn't enough for the pawn) 10 ♗d2 (stronger than 10 ♗e2?! d5 11 exd5 ♘bxd5 12 0-0 ♗f5 13 ♘c4 ♗e4 14 ♛h3 ♗f5 15 ♛g3 ♛xg3 16 hxg3 ♘xe3 17 fxe3 0-0 which enabled Black to equalize in Y.Dembo-B.Yildiz, Beijing (rapid) 2008) 10...a5 11 ♘b5 0-0 12 ♗xb4 axb4

13 ♘xc7 ♖a5 14 ♗c4! ♛c6 15 ♘d5 kept White's nose in front in J.Skoberne-O.Romanishin, Budapest 2008.

We now return to 7...♘e5:

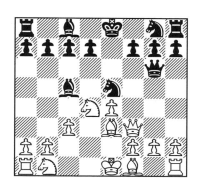

8 ♛e2!

An effective retreat, as White will follow up with a powerful advance of the f-pawn. Instead 8 ♛f5?! ♛xf5 9 ♘xf5 ♗xe3 10 ♘xe3 d6 seems fine for Black, but 8 ♛g3!? d6 (8...♘g4? runs into 9 ♘b5! ♘xe3 10 ♛e5+ which looks pretty good for White) 9 ♘b5 was seen in M.Visschedij-J.Jackova, German League 2000, and now 9...♗xe3 10 ♛xe3 ♚d8 11 ♘d2 would have left White slightly for choice.

8...♘e7

Fairly necessary, but in practice Black has more often than not lost his way at this point:

a) 8...♘h6?! 9 h3! (9 f4 ♘eg4 10 f5 ♛g6 11 ♗g1 0-0 12 ♘d2 ♘e5 wasn't so bad for Black in R.Ponomariov-I.Sokolov, Istanbul Olympiad 2000) 9...0-0 10 ♘d2 d5!? 11 exd5 ♘f5 12 0-0-0 shouldn't give Black enough for the pawn.

b) 8...♘f6?! forgets about the weakness of c7 and after 9 ♘b5 ♗xe3 10 ♕xe3! 0-0!? 11 ♘xc7 ♘fg4 12 ♕d4 Black's compensation again seems insufficient.

c) 8...♕xe4? 9 ♘b5! ♗d6 (Davies points out that White wins material after both 9...♕c6 10 ♗xc5 ♕xc5 11 b4 and 9...♗xe3 10 ♘xc7+ ♔d8 11 ♘xa8) 10 ♘d2 ♕f5 11 f4 ♘g4 12 ♘c4 is pretty horrendous for Black.

d) 8...♘g4?! 9 ♗f4 d6 was seen in A.Caruso-S.Skembris, Padova 2000, and here 10 f3 ♕f6 11 ♕d2 ♘e5 12 ♗g5 leaves White somewhat in front.

9 f4 ♘g4 10 f5!

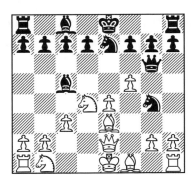

The f-pawn charges on and now 10...♕b6 11 ♗g1 leaves White with the initiative, but Black should probably prefer that to 10...♕h5 11 ♘d2 g6 12 0-0-0 ♘xe3 13 ♕xe3 ♕h4 14 ♘2f3 ♕f6 as was seen in E.Wiersma-D.Van Leent, Dieren 2003, when the direct 15 e5 would have left Black in serious trouble.

C22) 6...♘ge7

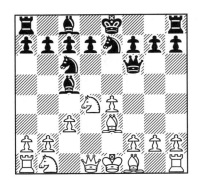

We are now rapidly descending on the main line of the 4...♗c5 5 ♗e3 variation and, indeed, 7 ♗c4 will be the subject of our next chapter. Here we will focus on:

C221: 7 ♗e2
C222: 7 ♘c2
C223: 7 ♕d2
C224: 7 g3

White has actually tried a pretty wide range of moves here, including too:

a) 7 f4?! is too ambitious on account of 7...♕g6! and after 8 ♕d3 ♗xd4! 9 ♗xd4 d5 10 exd5 ♗f5 Black is better, as pointed out by Wells.

b) 7 b4?! ♗b6 8 ♗c4 (trying to prevent ...d5; meanwhile it's too late for 8 ♘b5?! when Black is somewhat for choice after 8...♗xe3 9 fxe3 ♕h4+) 8...a5 reveals the drawback to White's ambitious approach and after 9 b5 ♘e5 10 ♗e2 d5 Black has the initiative.

c) 7 ♘f5?! d6! 8 ♗d4 (8 ♗xc5 is

rather well met by 8...♗xf5 and 8 ♘xe7 by 8...♗xe3) 8...♘xd4 9 ♘xd4 saw White losing time and the bishop-pair in A.Rubio Fornes-A.Ehsan, Cullera 2005, and after 9...0-0 followed by 10...♘c6 Black is doing very well.

d) 7 ♕a4 ♘e5 8 ♗e2 0-0 9 ♘d2 d5 10 ♘c2 ♗d7 11 ♕b3 left Black's pieces the more active in E.Bebchuk-V.Fedorov, Belgrade 1988, and after the simple 11...♗xe3 12 ♘xe3 dxe4 13 ♘xe4 ♕c6 he would have enjoyed an edge.

e) 7 ♕f3 has been quite rare here. After 7...♘xd4 8 ♕xf6 ♘c2+ 9 ♔d2 ♗xe3+ 10 fxe3 gxf6 11 ♔xc2 ♘g6 both sides' structures are a mess and the chances are likely balanced.

f) 7 ♗b5 0-0 8 0-0 ♗b6 sees Black safeguarding his bishop and so preparing ...d5.

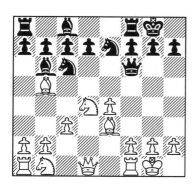

White's bishop just looks a little misplaced on b5 and after 9 ♕a4 (otherwise, 9 ♘a3 d5 10 ♘xc6 bxc6 11 ♗d3, as in D.Khamrakulov-S.Tanrikulu, Denizli 2003, and then 11...♗xe3 12 fxe3 ♕e5 leaves Black slightly for

choice, as did 9 ♖e1 d6 10 ♗a4 ♘e5 11 f3 ♘c4 in P.Kuijpers-R.Von Saldern, Les Dicqs 2002) 9...♕g6 10 ♘f5 ♘xf5 11 exf5 ♕xf5 12 ♗xb6 cxb6 13 ♘a3 ♕c5 14 ♖fe1 d5 15 ♗d3 d4! Black had a pull in R.Zelcic-D.Pavasovic, Rabac 2004.

C221) 7 ♗e2?!

A rather meek move and one which does nothing to prevent Black carrying out his plan of advancing in the centre and equalizing.

7...0-0 8 0-0 d5!

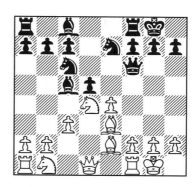

Already it's not hard to see that Black hasn't any problems.

9 ♘xc6

Wisely playing for exchanges. Instead 9 exd5? ♘xd5 10 ♗f3 (10 ♘c2 ♘xe3 11 ♘xe3 ♕g5 isn't exactly much of an improvement) 10...♘xe3 11 fxe3 ♕h6 already leaves White somewhat worse, while 9 ♗f3?! ♘e5 10 ♘d2 ♘xf3+ 11 ♕xf3 ♕xf3 12 gxf3 ♗b6 13 a4 c6 gave Black a pleasant pull with his bishop-pair in W.Zagema-R.De Graaff, Dutch League 2000.

9...♕xc6 10 ♗xc5

Again White should make a piece exchange and, indeed, about the only good thing one can say about 7 ♗e2 is that it can be hard for Black to generate any winning chances here.

10...♕xc5 11 ♘d2

The alternative is 11 exd5 ♘xd5 which leaves Black slightly the more active.

Indeed, White has often drifted into trouble here, as he did with 12 b4?! ♕c6 13 ♗f3 ♗e6 14 ♕d2 ♖fd8 15 ♖d1 ♖d6, which left Black beginning to take control of the position in E.Vegetti-R.Ekstroem, Mendrisio 1988. Instead the best defence is probably 12 ♘d2 ♘f4 13 ♗f3, as in D.Zapata-E.Ramos, Lima 2004, and do note how we are already referring to a 'defence' for White.

11...♗e6 12 ♕c2!

Good defence, getting off the d-file.

Alternatively, 12 ♗f3 ♖ad8 13 ♘b3 ♕b6 14 ♕c2 c5 15 exd5 ♗xd5 was about equal in A.Brovkin-M.Novikov, Donskoj 2003. So too was 12 ♘b3 ♕b6 13 exd5 ♗xd5 14 ♕d4 ♕c6 in

R.Cappallo-J.Curdo, Marlborough 1997, but in both cases Black enjoyed slightly the more pleasant position to play.

12...♖ad8

Black clearly enjoys comfortable equality, but White too was fine after 13 ♘b3 ♕b6 14 ♗d3 h6 in A.Baranyai-L.Trembacz, Hungarian League 1995.

C222) 7 ♘c2

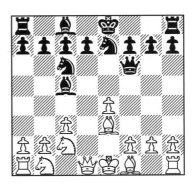

This may also appear a little meek at first sight, but White wants to remove one of Black's active pieces while bringing his knight to e3, clamping down on the d5-square.

7...♗xe3

Seemingly falling in with White's aims, but this is by far the easiest way for Black to equalize.

8 ♘xe3 ♛e5!

The point of Black's play. Once again we find White without a particularly attractive method of defending his e-pawn.

9 ♘d2

Alternatively:

a) 9 ♛d3 f5! 10 exf5 d5 11 ♗e2 ♗xf5 12 ♘xf5 ♘xf5 13 ♘d2 was seen in S.Tartakower-P.Johner, Teplitz Schoenau 1922, and now with another active move, 13...0-0-0, Black would have enjoyed full equality.

b) 9 ♛f3 is also quite well met by 9...f5! and after 10 exf5 (or 10 ♘xf5 ♖f8 11 ♛e2 ♘xf5 12 exf5 ♖xf5 13 ♘d2 d6 with easy play for Black in L.Ljubarskaya-K.Zvorykina, Cheliabinsk 2004) 10...d5 11 ♗e2 ♗xf5 12 ♘xf5 ♘xf5 13 0-0 0-0 Black clearly didn't have any problems in A.Strikovic-J.Hector, La Corunna 1995.

9...d5

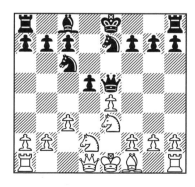

Once more this thematic counter-

strike fully solves Black's problems.

10 ♗d3

At least this activates the bishop. Instead after 10 exd5 ♘xd5 11 ♘dc4 ♘xe3 12 ♘xe3 ♗e6 13 ♛a4 (and not 13 ♗e2 0-0 14 0-0 ♖ad8 15 ♛c2 f5! which saw White drifting into a little trouble in E.Dolukhanova-A.Burtasova, Kharkov 2007) 13...0-0 14 ♗c4 ♖ad8 15 0-0 ♛e4 the pin was a touch awkward, although White was still able to claim equality in E.Sveshnikov-V.Korchnoi, USSR Championship, Moscow 1973.

10...dxe4 11 ♗xe4 ♗e6 12 ♛c2

The safest square. White preferred 12 ♛a4 in the elite encounter V.Ivanchuk-V.Anand, Monte Carlo (blindfold) 2005, but after 12...0-0-0 13 ♘f3 ♛h5 14 0-0 f5 15 ♗xc6 ♘xc6 only Black had chances to be better, in view of his superior minor piece.

12...0-0-0

Black continues to develop actively and at full speed. Now White must avoid 13 0-0? ♖xd2 14 ♛xd2 ♛xe4 and so he wisely went 13 ♘f3 in A.Morozevich-K.Georgiev, Fuegen 2006.

Then 13...♕b5 14 b4! ♖he8 15 a4 wasn't so clear in the game, so perhaps Black should again prefer 13...♕h5!? followed by pursuing the initiative with ...f5.

C223) 7 ♕d2

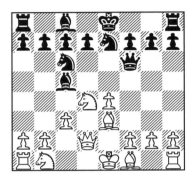

It may seem a little strange to remove the d2-square from the knight, but White covers the bishop and so renews the idea of ♘b5.

7...0-0!

Black continues to develop, keeps the ...d5 break in mind and provokes White's knight to visit b5. In practice he has tried a number of other approaches, but there is little doubt that the text is critical and best, as we can see from:

a) 7...♘e5?! hopes to snare the bishop-pair with ...♘g4, but underestimates White's main idea and after 8 ♘b5 ♗xe3 9 ♕xe3 ♕c6 10 ♘xa7 Black clearly hasn't enough for the pawn.

b) 7...♗xd4 8 cxd4 d5 strikes back in the centre, but at the cost of the bishop-pair and after 9 ♘c3 0-0

(9...dxe4? 10 d5! ♘e5 would have been even worse for Black in I.Kashdan-S.Reshevsky, New York 1936, had White found 11 ♗g5! ♕b6 12 ♗xe7 ♔xe7 13 ♕g5+ ♕f6 14 d6+!) 10 exd5 ♘b4 11 ♗c4 ♕f5 12 0-0 ♘exd5 (or 12...♘bxd5, as in L.Paulsen-B.Englisch, Wiesbaden 1880, and then 13 ♖fe1 retains a pull) 13 a3 ♘b6 14 ♗e2 ♘4d5 15 ♗d3 ♕h5 16 ♘e2 White has an edge.

c) 7...♗b6 hopes to dissuade ♘b5, but doesn't and after 8 ♘b5! ♗a5 (8...♗xe3?! 9 ♕xe3 ♕e5 10 ♘d2 ♔d8 11 ♘f3 is even worse for Black) 9 ♘1a3 a6 10 ♘d4 ♗b6 in M.Goodger-D.Ledger, Hastings 2008/09, the simple 11 ♗e2 0-0 12 0-0 would have sufficed for an edge.

d) 7...a6!? when followed up with 8 f4 ♗xd4 9 cxd4 d5 is the most creative and challenging of Black's alternatives. The critical response is 10 ♘c3!, but even here matters aren't so clear.

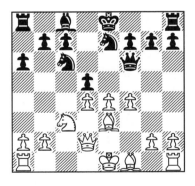

Indeed, after 10...0-0! (but not 10...dxe4? 11 d5 when White dominated the centre with some advantage in D.Szopka-M.Twardon, Lublin 1988)

11 ♗d3 dxe4 12 ♘xe4 ♛g6 13 d5 in T.Mifsud-C.Fucek, Bratislava 1993, Black would have retained decent counterplay had he gone 13...♗f5.

8 ♘b5!

Taking up the challenge. White has tested a number of alternatives, but without making much impression: for example, 8 f4 d6 9 ♘xc6 ♘xc6 10 ♗xc5 dxc5 11 ♛e3 ♖e8 gave Black enough counterplay against e4 in X.Mellgren-J.Moller, Stockholm 1897, while somewhat more recently 8 ♘c2 ♗xe3 9 ♘xe3 d6 10 ♘a3 a6 11 ♗d3 ♘e5 12 ♗c2 b5 gave Black easy equality in M.Godena-L.Fressinet, French League 2003.

8...♗xe3 9 ♛xe3

White is ready to meet 9...♛e5?! with 10 ♘d2! followed by 11 f4 or 11 ♘f3, but not the immediate 10 f4?! on account of 10...♘d5!. Indeed, it might seem that Black is in some trouble, but both members of White's royal family are lined up on the e-file and thus it's not so hard to see that Black would like to strike out in the centre:

9...d5! 10 ♘d2!

A prudent response. Of course, the critical test is 10 ♘xc7?! ♖b8, but practice has shown that this gives Black dangerous compensation:

a) 11 ♘xd5?! ♘xd5 12 exd5 ♘b4! 13 ♛d2 (13 cxb4? ♛xb2 14 ♛c3 ♖e8+ 15 ♔d1 ♛xf2 gives Black a tremendous attack, as pointed out by Miles) 13...♖e8+ 14 ♗e2 ♗g4 15 f3 ♘xd5! gave Black a strong attack for the piece in M.Lupu-A.Miles, Cappelle la Grande 1994, and was even stronger than forcing a draw with 15...♗xf3 16 gxf3 ♛xf3 17 ♖g1 ♘d3+ 18 ♔d1 ♘f2+.

b) 11 ♘d2 dxe4 12 0-0-0 ♛e5 13 ♘b5 ♗f5 14 f4 ♘d5 also gave Black the initiative in N.Ninov-V.Georgiev, Sunny Beach 2009.

c) 11 exd5 might be White's best, but he must still take care after 11...♘f5:

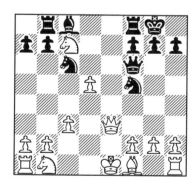

Indeed, one of your authors failed to in Y.Dembo-K.Lahno, Novi Sad 2009, where 12 ♛f4? ♘e5 left White in trouble, with the point that 13 ♛e4 is well met by 13...♘g6!, creating problems down the e-file as well as for the errant knight on c7. Correct is 12 ♕e2, although after 12...♘a5 Black still enjoys pretty decent play for the pawn.

10...dxe4

Black's simplest approach, but it may well be that the 10...♗d7!? of Y.Dembo-N.Kosintseva, Ohrid 2009 is preferable, with the idea of 11 0-0-0 ♖ac8 which is fine for Black.

11 ♘xe4 ♕e5 12 ♘c5!

Wisely forcing the queens off, rather than allow Black an active knight and good compensation with 12 f4 ♘d5 13 fxe5 ♘xe3 (A.Kim-P.Malysheva, Kazan 2000) 14 ♘xc7 ♖b8.

At this point 12...♕xe3+ 13 fxe3 ♘d5?! (13...♗g4 improves, but 14 h3 ♗h5 15 ♘xc7 ♖ad8 16 ♗e2 is still slightly better for White) 14 e4 ♘e3 15 ♘xc7 now failed to give Black enough for the pawn in D.Smerdon-S.Solomon, Gold Coast 2009. Thus theory has indicated that he should prefer to defend c7 with 12...♘d5, but after 13 ♕xe5 ♘xe5 14 0-0-0 (14 c4?! ♘b4 15 ♘xc7 was quite a risky pawn snatch after 15...♖b8 16 ♔d2 b6 in A.Mihailidis-

K.Markidis, Kallithea 2008) 14...c6 with 15 ♘d6! (15 ♘d4 ♘d7 16 ♘cb3 a5 was fine for Black in S.Rublevsky-A.Grischuk, Moscow (blitz) 2007) 15...b6 16 ♘xc8 ♖axc8 17 ♘d3 White can still aspire to a small edge on account of his superior minor piece.

C224) 7 g3!?

White aims to restrain the ...d5 break by placing his bishop on g2, where it will be less exposed than on c4 and more usefully placed than on e2. Over the past five years or so this continuation has become pretty popular, with a number of grandmasters adding it to their repertoires as well as or even instead of 7 ♗c4.

Once White completes the fianchetto, Black may struggle for counterplay, so he usually begins some right away:

C2241: 7...h5
C2242: 7...d5

Solid approaches are often seen too, but rather risk leaving Black a little passive and worse:

a) 7...♘g6?! 8 ♗g2 ♗b6 9 0-0 d6 10 f4 ♗d7 11 ♘a3 illustrates White's ideal method of development and after the 11...h5 of D.Swieszek-B.Blach, Sielpa 2004, 12 ♘c4 would have left him clearly for choice.

b) 7...b6 8 ♗g2 ♗b7 (or 8...♗a6 9 ♕a4! ♗d3 10 ♘a3, as in A.Kolev-J.Friedel, Las Vegas 2007, when Black's bishop is more misplaced than active on d3 and 10...0-0 11 ♖d1 ♗xa3 12 ♕xa3 ♗c4 13 b3 ♗e6 14 0-0 leaves White doing pretty well with the bishop-pair) 9 0-0 0-0-0 10 b4! ♗xd4 11 cxd4 ♘xb4 12 ♕d2 ♘bc6 13 ♘c3 h6 14 ♖fc1 ♔b8 15 ♘b5 gave White a strong attack for the pawn in N.Jakubovic-M.Vucic, Bihac 1999.

c) 7...d6 8 ♗g2 h5 (finally, Black decides to undertake something active; otherwise, 8...♘e5 9 0-0 0-0 10 ♘c2 ♗b6 11 ♗xb6 axb6, as in the game K.Krondraf-Z.Vojacek, Havlickuv Brod 2006, and then 12 f4 gives White an edge, as does 8...♘xd4 9 cxd4 ♗b6 10 ♘c3 0-0 11 0-0 ♕g6 12 ♘a4 ♗a5 13 f4) 9 h3! leaves Black less actively placed than in Line C2241, below, and after 9...♗d7 10 0-0 h4 11 g4 White keeps control of the position, with a definite edge.

d) After 7...0-0 8 ♗g2 Black has tried a number of ideas, but it's not easy for him to obtain counterplay with piece-play alone:

d1) 8...♘e5 9 0-0 ♘c4 (White enjoyed a comfortable edge too following 9...a6 10 ♘d2 d6 11 h3 ♕g6 12 ♕e2 ♗d7 13 f4 in V.Baklan-M.Larmuseau, Ghent 2007) 10 ♗c1! d6 (better than 10...♘c6 11 ♕e2 ♘4e5 12 ♗e3 d6 13 ♘xc6 ♘xc6 14 ♗xc5 dxc5 15 f4 which left White much better in D.Pavasovic-I.Zaja, Celje 2003) 11 b3 ♘e5 drove back the black knight in V.Schneider-T.Shadrina, Szeged 2006, and now 12 ♘a3 would have left White with the initiative.

d2) 8...♗b6 9 0-0 ♘e5 10 ♘d2 d6 11 h3 ♗e6 12 ♕e2 ♘5c6 was seen in E.Solozhenkin-P.Martynov, Finnish League 2008, and now 13 ♘xe6 ♕xe6 14 ♘b3 would have secured the bishop-pair and an edge.

d3) 8...♘xd4?! 9 cxd4 d5!? works elsewhere in this chapter, but not here and 10 exd5 ♘b4 11 ♕b3 ♕d6 12 ♗f4 ♕b6 13 0-0 just left White clearly better in P.Piscopo-D.Isonzo, Saint Vincent 2002.

d4) 8...♘xd4 9 cxd4 ♗b4+ 10 ♘c3 d5 is a better version of the central counterstrike, but with 11 0-0 dxe4 12 ♘xe4 ♕g6 13 ♕b3 a5 14 ♘c5 White retained an edge in M.Hoffmann-J.Fleck, German League 1991.

d5) 8...d6 9 0-0 ♗d7 (or 9...♕g6 10 ♘d2 a6, as in K.Ambarcumova-T.Mamedjarova, Peniscola 2002, and then 11 ♘2b3 ♗a7 12 f4 gives White a pleasant edge) 10 f4 again sees White expanding with a nice position, while Black finds himself a little low on counterplay.

C2241) 7...h5!?

With theory expanding at a rate of knots after 7...d5, it's not such a surprise that this active alternative has gone from being considered pretty ambitious to fairly respectable as it has gained adherents.

8 h3

White elects to keep the kingside closed by meeting ...h4 with g4. This is a pretty sensible approach, but practice has also seen:

a) 8 ♗g2?! h4 9 0-0 (or 9 ♖f1 hxg3 10 ♘b5 ♗xe3! 11 ♘xc7+ ♔d8 12 fxe3 ♕g5 13 ♘xa8 ♕xe3+ 14 ♕e2 ♕c1+ and Black enjoyed a strong initiative for the rook in J.Dworakowska-S.Haslinger, Port Erin 2006) 9...hxg3 10 hxg3 (after 10 fxg3 ♕g6 11 ♘d2 ♘e5 the initiative belongs to Black with ...♘g4 on its way) 10...♘e5 11 f4 (11 ♘c2?! d6 12 ♗xc5?! ♕h6 13 f3 ♕h2+ followed by 14...♖h3 was something of a disaster for White in M.Hrabinska-V.Bhat, Cappelle la Grande 2009) 11...♘c4 12 ♕e2 ♘xe3 13 ♕xe3 was seen in D.Villarraga-S.Kolosovas, Barquisimeto 2001, and now 13...d5 14 exd5 ♗h3 followed by ...0-0-0 would have left Black attacking and undoubtedly for choice.

b) 8 f4 d6 (Black should also give consideration to 8...♗xd4!? 9 cxd4 d5 10 ♘c3 ♗g4) 9 ♗g2 (or 9 ♗e2 ♗h3 10 ♕d3 0-0-0 11 ♘d2, as in P.Pazos Gambarrotti-Tsang Hon Ki, Dresden Olympiad 2008, where 11...♘e5! would have seized the initiative) 9...h4 10 ♕d3 hxg3 11 hxg3 ♖xh1+ 12 ♗xh1 g5! 13 ♘xc6 ♕h8 14 ♗g2 ♘xc6 15 ♗xc5 dxc5 again left White on the defensive and Black with the initiative in C.Krogh-J.Furhoff, Copenhagen 1993.

c) 8 h4 halts Black on the h-file, but does rather weaken the g4-square. Indeed, 8...d5 (or the logical 8...♘e5 and following 9 ♗e2 d5 10 ♘d2 ♘g4 11 ♗xg4 ♗xg4 12 ♕a4+ ♗d7 13 ♕b3 ♕a6 14 exd5 ♗a4 Black had a definite edge in A.Suarez Real-A.Naiditsch, Leon 2008) 9 ♗g2 ♗g4! made good use of the drawback to White's 8th in J.Anglada Lobarte-S.Roa Alonso,

Zaragoza 1993, and after 10 ♕a4 ♗d7 Black enjoys the initiative with ...♘e5-g4 as well as ....0-0-0 high on the agenda.

8...d5!

Only now does Black strike out in the centre, hoping that the inclusion of h3 and ...h5 will be in his favour. Indeed, White may not find it so easy to expand with f4.

Instead 8...d6 9 ♗g2 was seen in note 'c' to Black's 7th move at the start of Line C224, above, but pushing on with 8...h4 9 g4 ♘g6 has been quite a popular alternative.

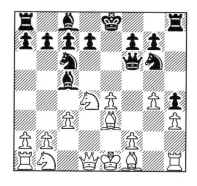

White is clearly a little vulnerable on f4 here, but is not without chances to take control of the central situation:

a) 10 ♕a4 0-0 (10...♘ge5!?, eyeing another weak square, f3, may be better) 11 ♘d2 a6 12 0-0-0 (preferable to 12 g5 ♕e5 13 0-0-0 b5! 14 ♘xb5 ♗xe3 15 fxe3 ♖b8 16 ♘d4 ♕xg5 which favoured Black slightly in A.Bitalzadeh-C.D'Amore, Palau 2009) 12...♗a7 13 g5 ♕e5 was seen in T.Burg-M.Bensdorp, Groningen 2008, and now the prudent

14 ♕c4 might have left White slightly for choice.

b) 10 g5!? ♕e5 11 ♘d2 is the active defence and after the 11...♗xd4 (otherwise, 11...♘xd4!? 12 cxd4 ♗xd4 13 ♘c4 ♕xe4 14 f3 ♕xe3+ 15 ♘xe3 ♗xe3 16 ♗c4 likely doesn't give Black quite enough for the queen and 11...♗b6 12 ♕a4! 0-0 13 0-0-0 d5 14 ♘4f3 left White slightly for choice in K.Klokas-A.Stefanova, Gibraltar 2007) 12 cxd4 ♘xd4 of N.Savushkina-I.Kazarova, Kolontaevo 1997, Postny has pointed out that 13 f4! ♘xf4 14 ♘c4! ♕xe4 15 ♕xd4 ♕xh1 16 ♗xf4 d6 17 0-0-0 solves White's development issues and gives him the initiative.

c) 10 ♗g2 ♘f4 11 0-0 is a solid choice, but after 11...♘e5 12 ♘d2 d6 13 ♘c4 ♘xc4 14 ♕a4+ c6 15 ♕xc4 0-0 Black was fine thanks to his control of f4 in R.Kalod-A.Mikhalchishin, Austrian League 2007.

d) Neither is 10 ♘f5 ♗xe3 11 ♘xe3 the solution for White: 11...0-0 (or 11...♘ce5 12 ♘d2 c6 13 ♕c2 0-0 14 ♖g1 d5 and Black had the initiative in M.Meinhardt-V.Georgiev, German League 2008) 12 ♘d2 (W.Madeira-Y.Marrero Lopez, Sao Paulo 2004) 12...♘f4 13 ♕c2 d6 followed by ...♘e5 leaves Black slightly for preference, in view of the holes in White's camp.

e) 10 ♕d2 has been White's most usual, but after 10...♘ce5!? (ambitiously eyeing the f3-square, but a good case can be made for 10...0-0! when 11 f4?! ♖e8 12 ♗g2 d5 left Black already somewhat ahead in S.Rublevsky-V.Kramnik, Moscow (blitz) 2007, and 11 g5 ♕e7 12 ♗g2 d5 13 ♘xc6 bxc6 14 ♗xc5 ♕xc5 15 ♘a3 dxe4 was hardly ideal either for White in L.Rojas-M.Gongora Reyes, Sabadell 2008) 11 ♗e2 ♗xd4 12 ♕xd4 (12 cxd4 ♘f3+ 13 ♗xf3 ♕xf3 14 ♖h2 ♕xe4 15 f4 would have left White a little worse in T.Radjabov-A.Beliavsky, Warsaw 2005, had Black blocked the kingside with Postny's 15...f5! 16 ♘c3 ♕f3) 12...♘f4 13 ♘a3 0-0 14 ♘b5 ♘e6 15 g5! ♘f3+ 16 ♔d1 was a decent-enough pawn sacrifice and rather unclear in J.Smeets-E.L'Ami, London 2007.

Before we return to 8...d5, we should note that 8...b6!? has appealed to Shirov.

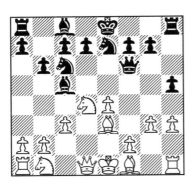

Black wants to house his king on the queenside while keeping open the option of advancing with ...d5 in one move. This creative approach undoubtedly deserves further attention and in S.Movsesian-A.Shirov, Sarajevo 2004, 9 ♗g2 ♗b7 10 0-0 0-0-0 11 b4! (White cannot tarry; 11 a3?! d5 12 ♘xc6 ♕xc6 13 ♗xc5 ♕xc5 left Black calling the

shots in F.Steil Antoni-A.Karlovich, Dresden 2007) 11...♘xd4 12 bxc5 (White might consider Postny's idea 12 cxd4!? ♗xb4 13 ♕a4 ♗a5 14 ♘d2 with some play for the pawn, but his alternate suggestion, 12 ♗xd4 ♗xd4 13 cxd4, looks promising for Black after 13...h4!) 12...♘dc6 13 ♘a3 d5! 14 cxd6 (and not 14 exd5? ♘xd5 15 ♗xd5 ♖xd5! 16 ♕xd5 ♘e5 with a massacre on the long diagonal) 14...♖xd6 15 ♕a4 (White tried to improve with 15 ♕e2!? in S.Rublevsky-K.Sasikiran, Khanty-Mansiysk 2005, but matters are hardly clear here after 15...♗d7) 15...♖d3 16 ♘b5 a6 gave Black enough counterplay in an unclear struggle.

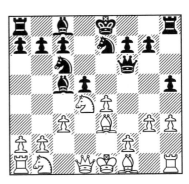

9 ♗g2 dxe4

The position clearly needs to be compared with the analogous ones in Line C2242, below, and here Black has:

a) 9...♘xd4 10 cxd4 ♗b4+ 11 ♘c3 c6 was seen in O.Von Bahr-J.Furhoff, Swedish Team Championship 2005, and here 12 e5! ♕g6 13 0-0 gives White the initiative with Black's early h-pawn advance not especially helping him.

b) 9...♗xd4!? 10 cxd4 dxe4 11 ♘c3 (11 d5? fails to 11...♕xb2) 11...♗f5 12 0-0 (or 12 ♕a4, as in E.Epstein-J.Friedel, Connecticut 2004, and then 12...0-0-0 13 0-0-0 ♘d5! 14 ♘xe4 ♗xe4 15 ♗xe4 ♕e6 regains one bishop with an edge) 12...0-0-0 13 f3 exf3 14 ♕xf3 and now in F.Bentivegna-V.Malaniuk, Cutro 2009, 14...♕d6 would have left Black slightly for choice.

10 ♘d2 ♗xd4 11 cxd4 ♗f5 12 ♘xe4 ♗xe4 13 ♗xe4 0-0-0

After quite a logical sequence an unbalanced position has been reached. White has two unopposed bishops, but d4 is vulnerable and Black's knights are hardly at all shabby here. Indeed, practice has shown that he enjoys good counterplay:

a) 14 ♕b3 ♘f5 15 0-0-0 ♖he8 gave Black the initiative in M.Mahjoob-P.Harikrishna, Beijing (rapid) 2008.

b) 14 0-0!? ♘d5 (Black can also test White's compensation with 14...♘xd4!?) 15 ♗g2 ♘ce7 16 ♖c1 c6 was solid for Black and about equal in Ni Hua-V.Zvjaginsev, Taiyuan 2007.

C2242) 7...d5

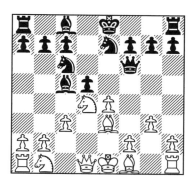

Black's most logical approach, exploiting the absence of the bishop from c4.

8 ♗g2

Now, with apologies to the reader, we come to a final divide:

> **C22421: 8...♗xd4**
> **C22422: 8...dxe4**
> **C22423: 8...♘xd4**

The only other move that makes any real sense is 8...♘e5?! when matters aren't so clear after 9 exd5 ♗g4!. However, with 9 0-0 0-0 10 ♘d2 c6 (or 10...♗b6 11 exd5 ♖d8, as in M.Ashley-Y.Lapshun, New York 1997, and then 12 c4 with a clear extra pawn) 11 h3 ♘d7 12 f4 ♕g6 13 g4! White was expanding with some advantage in M.Kislov-O.Korneev, Polanica Zdroj 1993.

C22421) 8...♗xd4 9 cxd4 dxe4

Black gives up the bishop-pair to saddle White with an IQP and now play is closely related to Line C22422 and may even transpose.

10 ♘c3 0-0

An ambitious alternative is 10...♗f5 11 d5 0-0-0!? (11...♖d8 12 ♕b3 ♘e5 13 ♘xe4 just gave White a pull in Y.Marrero Lopez-J.Cueto, Havana 2004), but after 12 ♕b3 Black must take care of his king and 12...♘e5 (or 12...♘d4 13 ♕a4 ♘f3+ 14 ♗xf3 exf3 15 ♕xa7 ♕a6 16 ♕xa6 bxa6 17 0-0-0 which saw White regain her pawn with a pull in J.Dworakowska-A.Onischuk, Skopje 2002) 13 ♘xe4 ♕a6 14 0-0-0 ♖he8 15 ♖he1 leaves White with the initiative, as analysed by Lybin.

11 ♘xe4 ♕g6 12 0-0

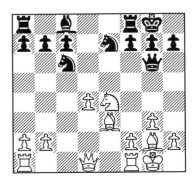

White's light-squared bishop is quite strong here and he'd like to increase the pressure with ♘c5. Indeed, it's not so easy for Black to equalize as we can see from:

a) 12...♘d5?! 13 ♕b3 (13 ♘c5 ♘ce7 14 ♖e1 c6 15 ♖c1 also sufficed for a pull in A.Areshchenko-M.Kobalia, Port Erin 2005) 13...♘ce7 14 ♘c5 c6 was seen in J.Bosch-Y.Marrero Lopez, Ma-

tanzas 1998, and now 15 ♖ac1 would have kept the pressure up with an edge.

b) 12...♗g4 13 ♕b3 took aim at b7 and gave White the initiative in M.Santo Roman-J.Gomez Esteban, Linares 1995.

c) 12...♗e6 might be a better square for the bishop, but as we'll see by transposition in note 'a' to Black's 10th move in our next section, White can still aspire to an edge.

d) After 12...♗f5 White should consent with 13 ♘c3 to a transposition to the notes to Black's 11th move in Line C22422, since 13 ♘c5?! b6 14 ♘b3 ♖ad8 15 ♖c1 ♗e4 16 ♗xe4 ♕xe4 17 ♕c2 ♕d5 was fine for Black in E.Sevillano-J.Egger, Manila Olympiad 1992.

C22422) 8...dxe4

Black's main move and one which keeps open the option of when to exchange on d4 and with which piece.

9 ♘d2

The main response, although there are alternatives:

a) White should not hurry to regain the pawn with 9 ♗xe4?! because of 9...♗xd4 10 cxd4 ♗f5 and after 11 ♘c3 (or 11 ♗g2 0-0-0 12 ♕b3 ♗e6 13 ♕b5 ♗d5 with some advantage for Black in A.Shalagina-V.Yakkimaienen, Petrozavodsk 2007) 11...0-0-0 12 ♗xf5+ in R.Roszkowski-M.Kwiatkowski, Augustow 2004, 12...♕xf5 would have left Black somewhat for choice.

b) 9 ♘b5 ♗xe3 (Black should take up the challenge; 9...♗d6? 10 ♘d2! is just in White's favour: for example, 10...♗e5 11 ♘xe4 ♕g6 12 0-0 a6 13 ♘d4 0-0 14 ♘xc6 ♘xc6, as in A.Dubinsky-A.Ivanov, Moscow 1973, and then 15 f4 gives White a pleasant edge and 10...♕e5?! 11 ♘xd6+ ♕xd6 12 ♘xe4 ♕xd1+ 13 ♖xd1 was, if anything, even worse for Black in T.Ananjeva-T.Makeeva, Russia 2004) 10 ♘xc7+ ♔f8 gives White a choice of ways to avert mate:

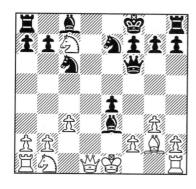

b1) 11 0-0 ♖b8 (Black might also consider the exchange sacrifice 11...♗c5!? 12 ♘xa8, as in W.Cugini-P.Svacina, Imperia 2003, as then 12...e3

gives him the initiative) 12 fxe3 ♕e5 13 ♕b3 f5 14 ♘b5 reaches quite an unbalanced position where one decent method for Black is 14...h5!? ♘d2 ♗e6 16 ♕a4 (A.Vatanski-J.Salimaki, Vantaa 1996) 16...♔g8 17 ♘c4 ♕c5 with rough equality.

b2) 11 fxe3 ♖b8 12 ♘a3 (the alternative is 12 ♘d5 when 12...♕g5 13 ♘f4 ♕c5 14 0-0! ♕xe3+ 15 ♖f2 g6 16 ♘d2 saw White regain his pawn with an ongoing pull in E.Cosma-A.Botsari, Chania 1989, but 12...♕e5! 13 ♘xe7 ♔xe7 14 ♘d2 ♖d8 improved and equalized in F.Izeta Txabarri-J.Lakunza Oyarbide, San Sebastian 1991) 12...♕e5 (here 12...h5 just seems too ambitious and 13 ♘c4 ♗g4 14 ♕d6 left White slightly for choice in M.Narciso Dublan-S.Azarov, Leon 2001) 13 ♘cb5 was seen in A.Bitalzadeh-C.Hanley, Groningen 2006, where 13...g6 followed by ...♗g7 would have been about equal.

c) 9 0-0 and then:

c1) 9...♘xd4?! 10 cxd4 ♗b6 (or 10...♗d6 11 ♘c3 ♗f5 12 ♘xe4 ♗xe4 13 ♗xe4 when White dominated with his bishops in D.Pavasovic-A.Bernei, Hungarian League 2003) 11 ♘c3 ♗f5 (Kuzmin points out that 11...0-0 12 ♘xe4 ♕g6 13 ♘c5 ♘f5 14 ♖e1 is slightly in White's favour) 12 ♘xe4 ♗xe4 13 ♗xe4 c6 14 a4!? ♖d8 and now in M.Villanueva-R.Hungaski, Avellaneda 2007, 15 ♕d3 ♗xd4 16 ♖ad1 ♗b6 17 ♕b3 ♗xe3 18 ♖xd8+ ♔xd8 19 ♕xe3 would have left White with promising play for the pawn.

c2) 9...0-0 10 ♘d2 ♗b6 (10...♗xd4 11 cxd4 ♕g6 will be seen in note 'a' to Black's 10th move in our main line) 11 ♘xe4 (after 11 ♖e1 Black has usually gone 11...♘xd4 12 ♘xe4 ♕g6 13 ♗xd4, which we'll see by transposition in note 'd3' to Black's 9th move in our main line, but here 11...♖d8!? 12 ♘xe4 ♕g6 13 ♕e2 ♗g4 was an easy equalizer in S.Rublevsky-J.Hammer, Kemer 2007) 11...♕g6 12 ♖e1 ♗g4! has seen White try a number of ideas without really managing to trouble Black:

c21) 13 ♕a4 ♘e5 14 ♕b5 (or 14 h3 ♗d7) 14...♕h5 was fine for Black in Y.Berthelot-J.Lautier, French League 2007.

c22) 13 f3 ♗d7 should be met by 14 ♕d2, maintaining the balance, whereas 14 ♘xc6?! ♗xe3+ 15 ♖xe3 ♗xc6 allowed Black to generate some pressure down the central files in D.Pavasovic-J.Lautier, Turin Olympiad 2006.

c23) 13 ♕b3!? ♖fe8 (now 13...♘e5 can be met by 14 h3 with a pull) 14 ♘xc6 ♘xc6 15 ♘c5 ♖ab8 is unclear according to Alexey Kuzmin.

c3) 9...♗xd4 10 cxd4 ♗f5! is another decent method for Black and after 11 ♘c3 he might even become ambitious with 11...0-0-0!? (11...♖d8 12 ♘xe4 ♗xe4 13 ♗xe4 0-0 is a solid, respectable alternative). Following 12 ♘xe4?! ♗xe4 13 ♗xe4 ♘xd4! 14 ♕a4 ♘ec6 15 ♖ad1 (or 15 ♖ac1 a6 16 ♖c4, as proposed by Kuzmin, and then 15...♖he8 when White shouldn't have enough compensation) 15...a6 16 ♔h1 ♖he8 17 ♗g2 was seen in E.Solozhenkin-J.Norri, Jyvaskyla 2008, where 17...h5! would have confirmed Black's advantage. White does better with 12 f3, although after 12...exf3 13 ♕xf3 ♗e6! 14 ♕d1 ♖xd4 15 ♗xd4 ♕xd4+ 16 ♕xd4 ♘xd4 Black had two good pawns and full compensation for the exchange in E.Sutovsky-E.Postny, Israeli Championship 2000.

After that important digression, we return to 9 ♘d2:

9...♗xd4!

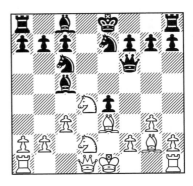

Black's simplest solution, giving White an isolated queen's pawn, but again there are alternatives:

a) 9...♕g6? 10 ♗xe4 f5 11 ♗f3 gave White a powerful early initiative in M.Sebag-B.Kadziolka, Peniscola 2002.

b) 9...♗f5? 10 ♘xf5 ♕xf5 11 ♗xe4 gives White a pleasant bishop-pair advantage, as shown by the further 11...♕e5 12 ♗f4 ♕e6 13 0-0 0-0-0 14 ♕c2 f5 15 ♗g2 of A.Seyb-L.Baumgardt, Dittrichshuette 2004.

c) 9...♘xd4 10 ♘xe4 ♕g6 11 cxd4 ♗b4+ 12 ♘c3 0-0 (12...♗g4?! 13 ♕a4+ ♘c6 14 0-0 only made matters worse for Black in N.Napoli-A.Longo, Porto San Giorgio 2004) 13 0-0 c6 14 ♕b3 generated a bit of pressure down the b-file and gave White a pull in O.Castro Rojas-D.Campora, Bogota 1979.

d) Retaining the bishop-pair with 9...♗b6!? 10 ♘xe4 ♕g6 is the best of these alternatives and after 11 0-0 (or 11 ♘xc6 ♘xc6 12 ♗xb6 axb6 13 0-0 0-0 14 ♕d2 ♗f5 15 ♕f4 ♖fe8 16 ♖fe1 ♖e7 which was fine for Black in Y.Afek-F.Levin, La Fere 2004) 11...0-0 it's not so easy for White to generate anything in this symmetrical structure.

♗g4 15 ♕b3 ♘e5! saw Black beginning to take over the initiative in C.Jahn-B.Von Herman, German League 2007.

d2) The 12 ♕b3 of F.Steil Antoni-A.Van Weersel, Dresden 2007, should be met by the solid 12...♘xd4 13 ♗xd4 ♗e6 with full equality.

d3) 12 ♖e1 ♘xd4 13 ♗xd4 ♘c6 14 ♗xb6 axb6 15 ♕d2 f6!? (15...♕f5 16 h3! had given White a pull in V.Ivanchuk-P.Leko, Morelia 2007) 16 ♕f4 ♕f7! 17 ♖ad1 ♘e5 18 a3 ♗g4 sees Black obtaining decent-enough counterplay, as pointed out by Kuzmin.

d4) 12 ♘c5 ♘xd4 13 ♗xd4 (or 13 cxd4 c6 14 ♖e1 ♖d8! preparing ...♘d5 which is very solid for Black) 13...♘c6 14 ♖e1 ♘xd4 15 ♕xd4 c6 gave Black solid equality in J.Smeets-V.Kramnik, Dutch League 2007.

10 cxd4

The correct recapture, as 10 ♘xe4?! allows the intermezzo 10...♗xc3+! and 10 ♗xd4 ♘xd4 11 ♘xe4 ♕b6 12 ♕xd4 ♕xd4 13 cxd4 ♗e6 is clearly fine for Black.

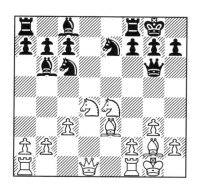

d1) 12 ♘xc6 ♘xc6 13 ♘c5 ♖e8 14 b4

10...♗f5

Black's main move, preparing a further piece exchange, but he has a number of alternatives:

a) 10...0-0 11 ♘xe4 (Black is fine after 11 0-0 ♕g6 12 ♗xe4 ♗f5) 11...♕g6 12 0-0 ♗e6 13 ♘c3! (trying to force through d5; the alternative is 13 ♘c5, but after 13...♗d5! 14 ♗xd5 ♘xd5 15 ♕b3 ♘ce7 the b-pawn remains pretty much taboo and 16 ♖ac1 b6 17 ♘d3 ♖fe8 18 ♗f4 ♖ac8 was okay for Black in R.Swinkels-P.Doggers, Amsterdam 2006) 13...♖ad8 14 ♖e1 (unfortunately for White, 14 d5 ♘xd5 15 ♘xd5 ♗xd5 16 ♗xd5 ♕f5! regains the piece, after which 17 ♗xf7+ ♕xf7 led to a pretty level endgame in P.Kalaitzoglou-K.Tsiamis, Ermioni 2006) 14...♖fe8 (Wang was also a little better after both 14...♘f5 15 d5 ♘xe3 16 fxe3, M.Wang-G.Arias Duval, correspondence 1998, and 14...♘d5 15 ♘xd5 ♗xd5 16 ♗xd5 ♖xd5 17 ♕b3 in M.Wang-K.Elison, corrrespondence 1997) 15 ♖c1 ♘xd4 was seen in M.Wang-C.Van Wieringen, correspondence 1999, and now 16 ♗xd4 c5 17 ♘b5! would have seen White retain a pull.

b) 10...♘d5 11 ♘xe4 ♕e7 12 ♕b3! ♘xe3 (12...♘b6? runs into 13 d5, while 12...♕b4+ 13 ♘c3 ♕xb3 14 axb3 ♘xe3 15 fxe3 sees White obtaining a pull despite the exchanges) 13 fxe3 ♘d8 14 0-0 c6 15 ♕d3 gave White a small but clear edge in M.Heidrich-R.Slobodjan, German League 1997.

c) 10...♘f5 11 ♘xe4 ♕e7 12 0-0 again sees White not fearing an exchange on e3 and with 12...0-0 13 d5! ♘xe3 14 fxe3 ♘e5 15 d6 he obtained an edge in S.Granara Barreto-H.Van Riemsdijk, Mendoza 2008.

d) Slightly surprisingly 10...♗e6!? hasn't been too common, but after 11 ♘xe4 ♕f5 12 0-0 ♗d5 Black seemed to be okay in Y.Afek-Y.Duhayon, Leuven 2004.

e) The critical 10...♕d6!? could also do with further attention. After 11 ♘xe4 ♕b4+ 12 ♗d2 ♕xd4 13 0-0 0-0 14 ♕c1 White's bishop-pair compensated for the pawn, but surely not more than that in A.Cioara-G.Olarasu, Felix Spa 2007.

11 ♘xe4

11...♗xe4!

Black gives up a second bishop, but will obtain counter-pressure down the d-file and crucially is able to maintain a hold over the key d5-square.

The alternative is 11...♕g6?!, but after 12 ♘c3 0-0 13 0-0 White's d-pawn is ready to advance and Black has struggled a number of times in practice, as he did with 13...♘b4 (otherwise,

13...♖ad8?! 14 d5 ♖d7 15 ♛a4 ♘e5 16 ♛xa7 saw White net a pawn in L.Goldgewicht-J.Tersarkissoff, French League 1995, while 13...♗g4!? 14 ♛b3 ♘f5 15 ♘d5 maintained a pull in B.Kharashkina-B.Aliabiev, Serpukhov 2003) 14 ♛b3! (stronger than 14 d5 ♘c2 15 ♖c1 ♘xe3 16 fxe3 which was only a little better for White, M.Bluvshtein-T.Krnan, Toronto 2006) 14...a5 15 a3, which left White calling the tune and with a pretty pleasant advantage in V.Baklan-Z.Gyimesi, Austrian League 2006.

12 ♗xe4 0-0-0

Black's main move, although he can also consider both 12...0-0 13 0-0 (T.Ananyeva-M.Molchanov, St Petersburg 2007) 13...♖ad8 14 ♛c2 h6, which doesn't seem too bad, and 12...♛e6 13 ♗g2 ♘d5 14 ♛b3 0-0-0 15 0-0 ♖he8, which was pretty solid in N.Sedlak-E.Ovod, Budapest 2002. In the latter line 13...♛c4 has been more common, but after the simple 14 a3! 0-0 15 ♖c1 White was slightly for choice in V.Svoboda-J.Krejci, Sec u Chrudimi 2008.

13 ♛b3

Continuing to fight for the key square, since 13 d5? ♘xd5!, with the idea of 14 ♗xd5 ♛f5, left White with clearly insufficient compensation in G.Ligterink-V.Korchnoi, Leeuwarden 1977.

13...♛e6! 14 ♛xe6+ fxe6

Thus Black has had to accept a small structural weakness in his own camp too, but in return can be pretty happy with his control over d5 and might hope one day to reach a good knight against bad bishop ending.

15 0-0-0 h6

There's also nothing wrong with the immediate 15...♖d7 or with 15...♘d5 16 h4 h6 17 g4 when in E.Sveshnikov-A.Bonte, Predeal 2006, 17...♖hf8 would have been fine for Black.

16 ♔b1 ♖d7

Black prepares to double rooks and had clearly solved all his opening problems in E.Szurovszky-Z.Gyimesi, Hungarian League 2004.

C22423) 8...♘xd4

A solid alternative to the capture on e4.

9 cxd4

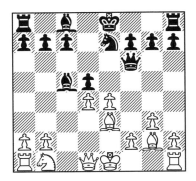

White should recapture this way, since after 9 ♗xd4?! ♗xd4 10 cxd4 dxe4 11 ♘c3 0-0 he doesn't have the bishop-pair to help offset the IQP.

9...♗b4+

Black plans to exchange on c3 and e4 before blockading on d5. An ambitious alternative is 9...♗b6, but after 10 exd5 ♘f5 11 0-0 0-0 12 ♘d2! (12 ♘c3 ♗xd4 13 ♘e4 ♕b6 14 ♗xd4 ♘xd4 15 ♖c1 ♗f5 was okay for Black in J.Nunn-S.Smagin, German League 1991) 12...♗xd4 13 ♗xd4 ♘xd4 (or 13...♕xd4 14 ♕c2, beginning to target c7) 14 ♖c1 White is slightly for choice, as pointed out by Gutman.

10 ♘c3

Invariably played, but there are alternatives:

a) 10 ♔f1?! 0-0 11 a3 ♗a5 unsurprisingly gives Black the initiative thanks to his better king position.

b) However, 10 ♘d2!? deserves attention and after 10...♗xd2+ (or

10...0-0, as in M.Steinhauser-A.Prizker, Nickenich 2007, and then 11 0-0 ♗xd2 12 ♕xd2 dxe4 13 ♗xe4 with a pull) 11 ♕xd2 dxe4 12 ♗xe4 0-0 13 0-0 White's activity and bishop-pair slightly outweighed the presence of an IQP in D.Bojovic-M.Pavlovic, Belgrade 2007.

10...♗xc3+!

A precise follow-up. Alternatively:

a) 10...dxe4? is not the right move order because of 11 ♕a4+! ♘c6 12 0-0! ♗xc3 (12...♗d7? 13 ♘xe4 ♕e7 14 a3 cost Black material due to his line-up down the e-file in J.Gutierrez Masdeu-C.Fontgivell Dalmau, Tarragona 1994) 13 bxc3 0-0 14 ♗xe4 when Black hasn't a blockade of d5 and White has done pretty well in practice.

b) 10...c6 is also slightly imprecise: 11 0-0 ♗xc3 (after 11...dxe4?! 12 ♘xe4 ♕g6 13 ♕b3! the bishop rather floats in mid-air on b4 and 13...♘d5 14 ♘c3! ♗xc3 15 bxc3 0-0 16 c4 left White much better in G.Sax-P.Blatny, Lazne Bohdanec 1995) 12 e5!? (avoiding a transposition to our main line with 12 bxc3 dxe4 13 ♗xe4 0-0) 12...♕g6 13 bxc3 ♗f5 14 ♕b3 gave White an edge despite Black's hold on the light squares in A.Seyb-A.Hammerschmidt, Oberhaching 2006.

c) 10...♕a6!? stops White going short and after 11 exd5 (11 ♕e2 ♕xe2+ 12 ♔xe2 dxe4 13 ♗xe4 c6 was okay for Black in J.Buenafe Moya-R.Oltra Caurin, Mislata 1993) 11...0-0 12 ♕b3 ♗a5 13 0-0-0 in Y.Afek-J.Hartung, Belgian League 2006, 13...♗xc3 14 bxc3 c6 15 d6 ♘d5 would have given Black some compensation with his own light-squared bishop then quite strong.

11 bxc3 dxe4 12 ♗xe4

12...c6

Beginning to construct the blockade, although Black can also employ the move order 12...0-0 13 0-0 c6.

13 0-0 0-0

Black keeps his light-squared bishop's options open, but he has also developed it with:

a) 13...♗f5 14 ♗g2 0-0 15 ♛b3!? (one can also make a pretty good case for the immediate 15 c4 and after 15...♗e6? 16 d5 White was doing pretty well in Z.Azmaiparashvili-R.Kasimdzhanov, Moscow 2001; here Black does better with 15...♖ad8!, as played by Leko, although after 16 ♛b3!? ♗e6 17 ♛xb7 ♗xc4, as in M.Godena-O.Korneev, Istanbul 2003, White might still claim an edge with Kuzmin's 18 ♖fc1) 15...b5 (trying to blockade; 15...b6 16 c4 is just quite pleasant for White) 16 ♖fe1 ♗e6 17 ♛a3 menaced ideas of ♛a6 and a4, and left White slightly for choice in

R.Hoen-J.Rubinetti, Lucerne 1982.

b) 13...♗e6 14 ♖e1 h6?! 15 ♖b1 left Black without a particularly good way of defending b7 in M.Zuriel-L.Piarnpuu, Istanbul 2000.

c) Likewise, 13...♘d5 is a little misguided, here because of 14 ♗d2 followed by c4.

14 ♖b1

White hopes to tie Black down to b7, but this is by no means the only way he might pursue the advantage:

a) 14 a4?! ♗f5 15 ♗g2 (naturally White wants to retain the light-squared bishops; otherwise, he can easily suffer with bad bishop against good knight) 15...♖ad8 16 ♛b3 ♖d7 defended b7 from the side and was fine for Black in V.Salov-A.Karpov, Reggio Emilia 1992.

b) 14 c4?! ♖d8 15 ♛h5 h6 16 ♖ad1 ♗f5 was also enough for equality in J.Zorko-G.Podkriznik, Murska Sobota 2007.

c) 14 ♖e1!? ♗f5 15 ♗g2 keeps White's options open and asks Black what set-up he has in mind:

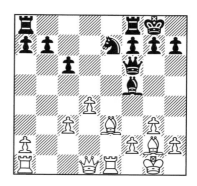

c1) 15...♖fd8 looked solid enough in S.Movsesian-Z.Gyimesi, Sibenik 2006, but now White might have sounded the charge 16 h4! when 16...h6 (the h-pawn space-gainer is hardly out of place after 16...♕d6 17 ♕b3, with a pull) 17 g4 ♗d7 18 g5! (Kuzmin) suddenly gives White a strong initiative on the kingside.

c2) 15...♗e6 16 ♕b1! (16 a4 ♗d5 17 ♕g4 ♗xg2 18 ♔xg2 ♕d6 forced a favourable trade and was fine for Black in Zhang Pengxiang-D.Jakovenko, Ergun 2006) 16...b5 (after 16...b6 White might begin to probe with 17 ♕c1!? h6 18 ♗f4) 17 a4 gave White some queenside pressure and an ongoing edge in V.Bakla-A.Vul, Cappelle la Grande 2006.

14...b6

This might be a little too compliant. Instead 14...♘d5 15 ♗d2 ♖e8 gives Black ideas of an exchange sacrifice in the event of 16 ♖e1 and the 14...b5!? of M.Neubauer-S.Baumegger, Gmunden 2005, definitely deserves attention, as 15 ♖xb5 cxb5 16 ♗xa8 ♗h3 17 ♗g2 ♗xg2 18 ♔xg2 ♘d5 would leave Black with full positional compensation for the pawn.

15 ♖c1

White sidesteps the threat of 15...♗f5 (which can now be met by 16 ♗g2), supports a central advance and might even probe on both flanks with 15...b5 16 ♕h5, which left him slightly for choice in I.Smirin-V.Malakhov, Khanty-Mansiysk 2009.

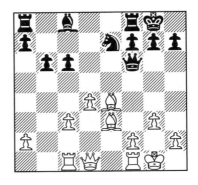

Conclusion

If White wants to go 5 ♗e3 but not engage in the main line 5...♕f6 6 c3 ♘ge7 7 ♗c4, he has a number of options. The sharp approach 6 ♘b5!? remains relatively unexplored and is perhaps a more fertile ground than White's 7th-move options after 6 c3 ♘ge7, against which Black has worked out some good defences. That said, an endgame lover may find a little mileage in 7 ♕d2, and 7 g3 has been pretty popular in recent years, although then both 7...d5 and 7...h5!? should promise Black decent-enough counterplay.

As for Black, his 5th-move alternatives aren't particularly attractive, but 6 c3 ♕g6 has caught out a number of Scotch players over the years. Moreover, it's surprising that so much attention there has been focussed on 7 ♘d2 and 7 ♕e2, neither of which is especially impressive, but with 7 ♘b5, 7 ♕f3 and even 7 ♗e2 White has good chances of emerging with the initiative.

Chapter Nine
The 4...♝c5 Variation:
5 ♗e3 ♛f6 6 c3 ♞ge7 7 ♗c4

1 e4 e5 2 ♞f3 ♞c6 3 d4 exd4 4 ♞xd4
♝c5 5 ♗e3 ♛f6 6 c3 ♞ge7 7 ♗c4

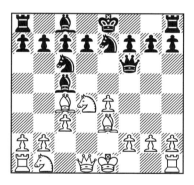

White's main move in this, the traditional main line of 4...♝c5. He develops his bishop as actively as possible, while making it harder for Black to equalize with an early ...d5. At this point Black's most common response involves driving White's bishop from c4, but that's by no means his only option as we shall see when we consider the following:

The remaining alternatives are generally pretty unimpressive, either failing tactically or leaving Black a little planless and White in control of the central situation:

a) 7...♛g6? 8 ♞xc6! ♛xc6 (White wins material after both 8...♝xe3? 9 ♞xe7 and 8...♛xg2? 9 ♖f1) 9 ♛h5! ♝xe3 (the only other move is 9...d5 which just leaves White a pawn to the good after 10 exd5) 10 ♛xf7+ ♚d8 11 fxe3 ♛xe4 was seen in Hoang Xuan Thanh-Nguyen Thi Dieu Hanh, Vietnam 2002, and now 12 ♛xg7 would have left White doing very well. The e-file opens to his advantage after 12...♛xe3+ 13 ♚d1, but 12...♖e8 13 ♗f7 can hardly be described as a panacea for Black.

b) 7...♘xd4?! 8 cxd4 ♗b4+ 9 ♘c3 leaves White with a perfect centre and ideal development.

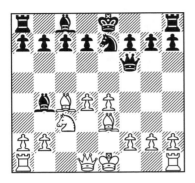

Unsurprisingly Black has rather struggled from here, as he did with 9...♗xc3+ 10 bxc3 0-0 11 0-0! ♕g6 ♕c6 12 ♗d3 d5 13 ♕c2 ♕g6 14 exd5 ♗f5 15 ♗xf5 ♘xf5 16 ♖fe1 in E.Schmittdiel-O.Romanishin, Groningen 1991, while 9...c6 10 0-0 ♗xc3, as in R.Smith-O.Mina, Moscow Olympiad 1994, should be met by 11 e5 ♕g6 12 ♗d3, again with a clear advantage.

c) 7...d5?! 8 ♗xd5 ♘xd5 9 exd5 ♘e5 was quite an active try in A.Fernandes-R.Damaso, Portugal 1992, but after 10 0-0 Black hasn't enough for the pawn.

d) 7...♘g6 8 0-0 ♘ce5 9 ♗b3 d6 10 ♘b5 ♕e7 11 ♗xc5 dxc5 was J.Hansen-I.Grueneberg, Dortmund 2006, where 12 f4 would have confirmed that White enjoys a small but clear advantage.

e) 7...a6 8 0-0 ♘g6!? (otherwise, 8...b5? failed to 9 ♘xc6 ♕xc6 10 ♗xf7+! ♔xf7 11 ♕h5+ in L.Lysiniuk-B.Bebchuk,

St Petersburg 2007, and 8...♗b6 9 ♘xc6 ♕xc6 10 ♕b3 was hardly ideal either for the second player in C.Jaureguiberry-S.Chauvin, French League 2007) 9 ♘xc6 ♕xc6 10 ♗d5 ♕d6 11 e5 ♕e7 12 ♗xc5 ♕xc5 13 ♕d4! again sees White emerging from the opening with a pleasant pull.

f) 7...♗b6 safeguards the bishop, but is a little slow.

Indeed, after 8 0-0 ♘e5 (otherwise, White would increase the pressure with 9 ♘b5, but Black should prefer the solid 8...0-0, transposing to Line C3, below) 9 ♗e2 d5 (9...♕g6? was preferred in J.Konnyu-R.Kaufman, Budapest 2006, but it's by no means clear what Black intended after 10 ♘b5) 10 f4 White was expanding from an ideal base in M.Visschedijk-F.Glerum, Leiden 1997, where 10...♘5c6 11 e5 would have confirmed his ascendency.

A) 7...d6 8 0-0

Now 9 ♘b5 is most certainly a threat and not only must Black counter that, but he must also try to find a way to obtain some counterplay, which isn't so easy with f4 set to augment White's central control.

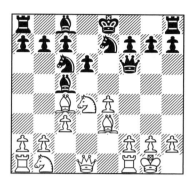

8...♘e5

Forcing the bishop to move, but White will, of course, regain some time once he gets in f4. The alternatives are:

a) 8...♗b6? 9 ♘b5 ♗a5 10 b4 a6 11 ♘xd6+ ♛xd6 12 ♛xd6 cxd6 13 bxa5 ♘xa5 14 ♗e2 left White doing pretty well with his bishops in B.Mews-J.Chudnovsky, Newark 1995.

b) 8...♘g6? enables Black to meet 9 ♘b5 with 9...♛e7, but White has another threat and 9 ♘xc6 bxc6 10 ♗xc5 dxc5 11 f4 leaves Black with a pretty disgusting structure.

c) 8...a6?! avoids ♘b5 issues too, but 9 ♘xc6 ♘xc6 10 ♗xc5 dxc5 11 f4 ♗e6 12 ♘a3 again gave White a pleasant structural advantage in V.Vuelban-R.Failli, Rome 2006.

d) Likewise 8...0-0 9 ♘xc6 ♘xc6 10 ♗xc5 dxc5 11 f4 ♗e6 12 e5 ♛e7 13 ♛e2 ♖fd8 14 ♘a3 a6 15 ♖ad1 left White with a pleasant edge in K.Lalic-A.Matardzic, Zupanja 2008.

e) 8...♛g6 9 ♘xc6! (even better than taking play into the main line, Line D223 below) 9...♘xc6 10 ♗xc5 dxc5 11 f4 0-0 was tried in V.Forcen Esteban-J.Villanueva Toral, Zaragoza 2005, where 12 ♛e2 would again have left White slightly for choice.

9 ♗e2

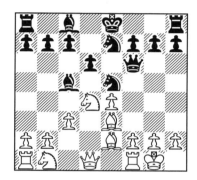

As we'll see, this is almost always the correct retreat for the bishop, taking control of g4 and so enabling him to advance with f4.

9...0-0

Again practice has seen some alternatives, but White's last renewed 10 ♘b5 as a threat and 9...c6? 10 f4 ♘5g6 11 b4 ♗b6 12 ♘d2 0-0 would have been pretty grim for Black in S.Petrosian-R.Vinsot, Cannes 2007, after just 13 g3, while 9...a6 10 f4 ♘5c6, as in A.Szieberth-A.Karacsony, Eger 1993, leaves Black a little low on counterplay and White better after 11 ♘a3.

10 f4 ♘5g6

White enjoyed control and a pleasant plus after 10...♘d7 11 ♘d2 ♘c6 12 ♘2b3 ♗b6 13 ♛d2 in S.Silov-F.Stluka,

Pardubice 1994, just as he does after 10...♘5c6 11 ♘a3, but these may be better options for Black.

11 ♕d2 h6 12 b4! ♗b6 13 ♘a3 ♘c6 14 ♘c4

White's queenside expansion is instructive and having chased down the bishop-pair, he found himself a little better, R.Smith-P.Beach, Auckland 1997.

B) 7...b6!?

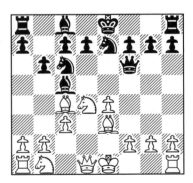

Black's most-creative option in this chapter. By fianchettoing his queen's bishop, he not only gives himself the option of going long, but also gives support to the ...d5 break. However, his play is also quite provocative, allowing White to expand with f4, while leaving the dark-squared bishop a little vulnerable to ideas of b4.

8 0-0

White hurries his king safety, which is prudent, but there are alternatives:

a) It's a little too early for 8 b4?! and after 8...♘xd4! (but not 8...♗xd4 9 cxd4 ♘xb4 10 0-0 followed by ♘c3 when White definitely has decent compensation) 9 ♗xd4 ♗xd4 10 ♕xd4 in L.Zimmerer-S.Titgemeyer, Willingen 2006, Black might have seized the initiative with 10...♕xd4 11 cxd4 d5.

b) 8 ♘b5?! doesn't work either yet and 8...♗xe3 9 fxe3 ♕h4+ 10 ♔f1 ♔d8 leaves Black doing pretty well.

c) 8 ♘c2 ♗xe3 (8...♘e5!? was preferred in M.Drobne-Z.Tomazini, Celje 2008, where 9 ♗e2 ♗b7 would have given Black an early initiative) 9 ♘xe3 ♗b7 10 ♘d2 ♘e5 11 ♘g4 ♘xg4 12 ♕xg4 ♘g6 13 ♕g3 ♘e5 was equal in M.Chlost-M.Szydlowska, Wisla 2000.

d) 8 ♕d2 renews the idea of ♘b5, but gives Black a fairly pleasant choice:

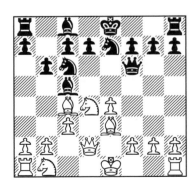

d1) 8...♗b7 9 b4!? is White's main idea, but even this doesn't seem too bad for Black after 9...♗d6! (White has, though, done pretty well after 9...♗xd4 10 cxd4: for example, 10...♕g6 11 f3 h5 12 a3 h4 13 ♘c3 h3 14 g4 left him clearly better in H.Nakamura-R.De Guzman, Reno 2003, and here even the superior 11...0-0-0 12 b5 ♘a5 13 ♗d3 d5 of R.Lau-P.Juergens, Dortmund 1992, leaves White better after 14 e5) 10 f3 (10 f4?! ♘xd4 11 ♗xd4 ♕h4+ 12 g3 was an aggressive try in K.Olsson-B.Adler, Stockholm 1993, but White's light squares just look a little too weak after 12...♕h3) 10...a5 11 b5 which was seen in J.Tomczak-B.Socko, Opole 2007, where 11...♘e5 12 ♗e2 ♕g6 would have given Black the initiative with ...f5 on the agenda.

d2) Theory has generally approved of 8...♕g6, but after 9 0-0! (and not 9 f3?! ♘e5 10 ♗f1 when 10...0-0 is just one approach which leaves Black with the initiative) 9...♘e5 (White enjoys decent play for a pawn after 9...♕xe4 10 ♗d3 ♕h4 11 ♘b5 ♗xe3 12 ♕xe3, but Black might consider 9...0-0!?, with a transposition to variation 'd3') 10 ♗e2 ♕xe4 11 b4 ♗d6 12 f3 ♕g6 13 ♘b5 0-0 14 ♘xd6 cxd6 15 ♘a3 ♗b7 16 ♗f4 one of your authors had enough compensation for the pawn in Y.Dembo-S.Haslinger, Liverpool 2008.

d3) 8...0-0!? 9 0-0 (after 9 b4?! ♗xd4 10 cxd4 ♕g6 Black is ready to meet 11 f3?! with 11...d5! 12 exd5 ♘xb4, but 11 ♘c3 d5! 12 ♘xd5 ♕xg2 13 0-0-0 ♕xe4

still favoured Black slightly in P.Wells-S.Azarov, Ohrid 2001) 9...♕g6 takes aim at e4.

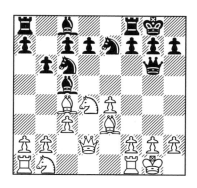

As it's not clear that the inclusion of 10 ♗f4 ♗b7 especially helps him, White has usually gone 10 f3, but after 10...d5!? (this can also be prepared with 10...♖d8 whereupon 11 ♗d3 ♘e5 12 ♗e2 d5 13 f4 was seen in V.Baklan-V.Golod, German League 2006, and now 13...♘c4!? 14 ♗xc4 dxc4 15 f5 ♕d6 would have given Black decent counterplay) 11 ♗xd5 ♘xd5 12 exd5 ♘e5 Black's pieces are pretty active and he should have enough for the pawn.

Returning to 8 0-0:

8...♗b7

Invariably played and clearly best. Naturally Black must avoid 8...d6? on account of 9 ♘xc6 ♘xc6 10 ♕d5 ♗b7 11 ♗b5 ♔d7 12 ♗xc5 bxc5 13 ♘d2 when the pin is a killer and 8...♘e5? 9 ♗e2 ♕g6 10 ♘d2 d5 11 ♗h5 ♕d6 would have been shown up as far too ambitious in G.David-A.Heymann, Pinneberg 1996, had White gone 12 ♗f4. However, 8...0-0!? is very playable, taking play into Line C2 below.

After 8...♗b7 White has three main methods with which to try and refute Black's ambitious play:

> **B1: 9 b4**
> **B2: 9 f4**
> **B3: 9 ♘b5**

a) Slow approaches are generally not especially impressive and, for instance, 9 ♕d2?! gives Black the initiative after Panczyk and Ilczuk's 9...♘e5, unfurling the fianchettoed bishop with some effect.

b) Likewise, 9 ♘c2?! ♘e5 10 ♗xc5 bxc5 11 ♗d5 ♘xd5 12 exd5 would have left Black doing very well on the light squares in Thorhallsson-A.Grischuk, Internet (blitz) 2000, had he gone 12...♗a6 13 ♖e1 0-0.

c) 9 f3 0-0! (this seems safer than 9...0-0-0 when 10 b4! ♗xd4 11 cxd4 d5, as in D.Kononenko-M.Serik, Donetsk 2008, and then 12 ♗e2 ♘xb4 13 ♘c3 gives White decent compensation, as pointed out by Panczyk and Ilczuk) 10 a3 (10 ♕d2 is also well met by 10...d5) 10...d5! sees Black enjoying an early initiative, with White's pieces a little vulnerable down the central files.

d) 9 ♘xc6 is fairly well met by 9...♕xc6 10 ♗xc5 ♕xc5.

It's hard to believe that Black is especially troubled by the early simplification and after 11 ♘d2 (or 11 ♕e2 0-0 12 ♘d2 when both 12...d5 and 12...♘g6!? are fine for Black) 11...0-0 12 ♖e1 ♘g6!? he enjoys any initiative that's going, whereas 12...d6 13 ♕e2 ♘g6 14 ♕e3 ♕xe3 15 ♖xe3 ♖fe8 was sufficient only for solid equality in H.Kummerow-F.Levin, Recklinghausen 2000.

e) 9 ♘b3 looks quite attractive at first, since 9...♗xe3?! 10 fxe3 ♕g5 11 ♗xf7+ ♔d8 12 ♖f4 failed to give Black enough for his pawn in W.Watson-P.Wells, Walsall 1992. However, he should not mind giving up bishop for knight with the active 9...♘e5! 10 ♘xc5 (Black enjoyed easy and full equality after 10 ♗xc5 ♘xc4 11 ♗d4 ♕g6 12 f3 a5 13 ♘1d2 ♘xd2 14 ♘xd2 0-0 in Y.Dembo-Z.Korpics, Hungarian League 2001) 10...bxc5.

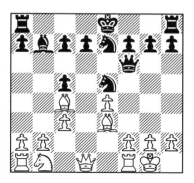

Here White should avoid 11 ♗d5?!, which gives Black the initiative on the light squares after 11...♘xd5 12 exd5 ♗a6!, preferring either 11 ♗e2!? ♗xe4 12 f3 when 12...♗b7 (12...♗xb1?! 13 ♖xb1 d6 14 f4 followed by ♗f3 gives White promising play for the pawn) 13 ♗xc5 0-0 14 ♘d2 d6 was fine for Black in R.Ponomariov-A.Grischuk, Lausanne 2000, or 11 ♘d2 ♘xc4 12 ♘xc4 ♗a6 13 b3, as in E.Sveshnikov-P.Ponkratov, Satka 2008, when Black might have equalized with 13...♗xc4 14 bxc4 ♕c6.

f) 9 ♖e1 0-0 (fans of 7...b6 are often attracted to quite aggressive play, but here 9...0-0-0?! is likely too risky on account of 10 b4! ♗xd4 11 cxd4 ♘xb4 12 ♘c3 with good play for the pawn, as indicated by Panczyk and Ilczuk) 10 ♗f1 (Black was fine after 10 ♘xc6 ♗xc6 11 ♘d2 ♘g6 12 ♕f3 ♕d6 in H.Ponce-W.Arencibia Rodriguez, Fuerteventura 1992) 10...d5 (10...♖fe8!? is also reasonable and 11 ♘c2 ♘e5 12 ♘d2 d5 13

♗xc5 bxc5 equalized in Y.Dembo-M.Godena, Solin 2007) 11 ♘xc6 ♕xc6 12 ♗xc5 ♕xc5 13 e5!? (more challenging than 13 ♘d2 dxe4 14 ♘xe4 ♕c6 15 ♕f3 ♘g6 which was pretty level in G.Szabo-A.Pashikian, Novi Sad 2009) 13...♘g6 14 ♘d2 ♕e7 15 ♕h5 was once advocated for White by Oll, but after 15...♖ad8 16 ♘f3 c5 Black shouldn't have any problems.

B1) 9 b4?!

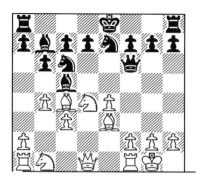

A bold gambit, but not an especially convincing one should Black know how to respond.

9...♘xd4!

Wisely declining the gambit. Clearly 9...♗d6? runs into 10 ♘b5, but a few brave souls have gone in for 9...♗xd4 10 cxd4 ♘xb4 even though White must have at least good compensation with his strong centre. Here 11 ♘c3 0-0 12 a3 ♘bc6 13 ♖c1 left Black under a bit of pressure in T.Shadrina-M.Shukurova, Kusadasi 2006, and 11 ♕d2!? ♘bc6 12 ♘c3 may be even stronger.

10 bxc5

White would prefer to gambit with 10 cxd4?! ♗xb4, but he doesn't have the bishop-pair here and has generally struggled to demonstrate enough compensation in practice:

a) 11 a3 ♗a5 12 d5 0-0! 13 ♖a2?! (13 ♘d2 improves, but still looks better for Black after 13...c6) 13...c6 14 ♗d4 ♕g6 15 f4 cxd5 16 f5 ♕g5 saw White coming up somewhat short in E.Schmittdiel-R.Tischbierek, German League 1992.

b) 11 ♕b3 ♗a5 12 f3 d5 (or 12...0-0 13 ♘c3, as in J.Zezulkin-M.Kolasinski, Rowy 2000, when 13...c6 favours Black, as pointed out by Panczyk and Ilczuk) 13 ♗d3 0-0 14 e5 was seen in K.Toma-P.Staniszewski, Polanica Zdroj 2001, where 14...♕e6 would have left Black with a strong blockade and somewhat for choice.

10...♘e6 11 cxb6 axb6

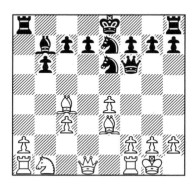

12 ♗d5

This isn't especially impressive, but Black's position is slightly the easier to play after both 12 f3 ♖d8 13 ♕d2 0-0 and 12 ♘d2 0-0.

12...♗c6

Black may do better with 12...♘xd5!? 13 exd5 ♘f4 14 ♗xf4 ♕xf4 15 ♖e1+, as in D.Margraf-M.Meyer, Bockenem 2003, and then 15...♔d8, which should give him an edge.

13 f4 ♖a5 14 ♗xc6 ♘xc6

Black clearly hasn't any problems here, but rather than allow a blockade with 15 e5?! ♕f5, as he did in V.Baklan-C.Marcelin, French League 2001, White should prefer 15 ♕c2 0-0, which led to an unbalanced, roughly level game in C.Rzayev-S.Das, Vung Tau 2008.

B2) 9 f4 0-0!

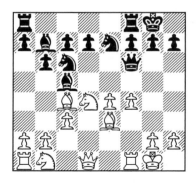

Black renounces ideas of going long, but now it's not so easy for White to develop his remaining knight without making a concession. Indeed, Black seems to be able to obtain sufficient counterplay after the text, not that that has stopped him from experimenting with the alternatives on occasion:

a) If 9...d5?! worked everyone would play it, but after 10 exd5 ♗xd4 11 cxd4 White must be slightly better at least.

b) 9...♕g6 10 ♘d2 (10 f5!? ♕f6 11 b4 ♗d6, as in A.Chernobai-P.Ponkratov, Satka 2005, and then 12 ♘d2 should also be slightly in White's favour) 10...♘xd4 (after 10...f5?! Panczyk and Ilczuk's idea of 11 ♖f3!? is pretty tempting) 11 cxd4 ♘f5! was seen in D.Khamrakulov-M.Ragger, Belfort 2005, where 12 ♕e2 ♘xd4 13 ♕f2 would have kept White in front.

c) 9...d6 might well be met by the logical 10 e5!?, securing an early initiative for White.

d) 9...0-0-0

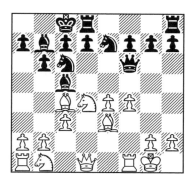

10 ♕d2! (White might like to go 10 b4, but after 10...♗xd4! – White has decent chances to secure the initiative after 10...♘xd4 11 bxc5! ♘e6 12 ♕a4 – 11 cxd4 ♘xb4 12 d5 Black found the awkward 12...♘bxd5! in I.Gushpit-V.Bezman, Yalta 1996, whereupon 13 ♗d4 ♕c6 14 ♗xd5 ♘xd5 15 exd5 ♕xd5 16 ♕d2 c5 17 ♗e5 ♕xd2 18 ♘xd2 d6 19 ♗b2 f6 would have left Black with three good pawns for the piece and the better prospects in the resulting endgame, as pointed out by Postny; if

White wants to resurrect this line he should investigate 12 a3!? d5 13 ♗e2 ♘bc6 14 e5 when his strong centre compensates for the pawn, as suggested by Panczyk and Ilczuk) and then:

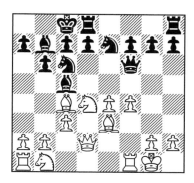

d1) 10...g6?! 11 b4 ♗xd4 12 cxd4 d5 13 e5 ♕e6 14 ♗e2 illustrated White's main idea and left him better in F.Amonatov-J.Prizant, Vladimir 2004.

d2) 10...d5 11 e5 ♕h4 12 ♗d3 f6 (trying to obtain some counterplay; instead 12...g6?! 13 ♗f2 ♕h6 14 b4 ♗xd4 15 cxd4 gave White a strong attack in J.Tomczak-A.Tomazini, Szeged 2008) 13 b4 fxe5 and now in K.Van der Weide-Y.Duhayon, Triesen 2007, the best way for White to maintain control was the intermezzo 14 g3!.

d3) 10...♕h4 hopes to break with ...d5, but after 11 ♗d3! White stays front, J.Tomczak-M.Olszewski, Chotowa 2009.

d4) 10...♕g6 was tried in A.Grischuk-V.Milov, Spanish Team Championship 2007, where White might have continued aggressively: 11 f5!? ♕f6 12 b4 d5 (12...♗d6? is, as so often, rebuffed by 13 ♘b5) 13 bxc5 dxc4 14 ♘a3 which isn't too clear, but should be slightly in White's favour.

Returning to the safer 9...0-0:

10 ♘c2

Not perhaps the move White wanted to make, but 10 b4?! ♘xd4 11 bxc5 ♘e6 favoured Black in B.Reefat-A.Miles, Calcutta 1994, and if he prepares ♘d2 with 10 ♕d3?! then Black can strike back with 10...♗xd4! 11 ♗xd4 ♘xd4 12 cxd4 d5.

10 e5 ♕h4 seems okay for Black, but 10 ♕d2!? Is possible. Then 10...♖ae8 and 10...♕g6 look like critical responses, rather than 10...♗xd4?! 11 cxd4 d5 12 e5 ♕e6 of A.Cioara-L.Sobolevsky, Jena 2005, when 13 ♗e2 would have left White slightly for choice.

10...♖ad8

Black can also break straight away and 10...d5!? was seen in R.Kuczynski-R.Hübner, German League 1993, where the position would have been quite unbalanced and unclear after 11 ♗xd5 ♘xd5 12 ♗xc5 bxc5 13 exd5 ♖ad8.

11 ♘d2

We've followed the game R.Brunello-M.Brunello, Bratto 2008, in which there was no good reason for Black not to equalize with 11...d5.

B3) 9 ♘b5

White wastes no time going after c7. This is quite critical and likely his strongest try, although even here Black has his resources.

9...0-0-0!

Now this is the right side for the king and by far the best way of dealing with the threat to c7, as we can see by comparing:

a) Perhaps surprised by his opponent's choice of first move, 9...♘e5? saw Black blunder a pawn to 10 ♘xc7+ ♔d8 11 ♘d5 in K.Arkell-J.Guasch Murtra, Olot 1993.

b) 9...♕e5? 10 ♕f3 ♗xe3 11 ♕xf7+ ♔d8 12 fxe3 ♖e8 13 ♘d2 was pretty bad too for Black in B.Trabert-B.Kovacevic, Budapest 1994.

c) 9...♖c8 10 b4!? (10 ♗xc5 bxc5 11 ♘d2 0-0 12 f4 is the sensible alternative, but with 12...a6 13 ♘a3 ♘a5 14 ♗d3 d5

Black developed counterplay in P.Krupkova-S.Joy Lomibao, Elista Olympiad 1998; now the critical line appears to be 15 exd5 ♘xd5 16 ♕a4, as proposed by Panczyk and Ilczuk, and then the active 16...♖cd8!, maintaining a rough balance) 10...♗xb4 (Black may do better with the 10...♘e5!? of R.Alias Franco-L.Bermejo Arruego, San Sebastian 1995; then 11 ♘xa7!? ♖a8 12 ♘b5 ♘xc4 13 ♘xc7+ ♔d8 14 bxc5 ♗xc7 15 cxb6+ ♘xb6 16 ♘d2 gives White two pawns and an attack for the piece, but is hardly clear) 11 cxb4 ♕xa1 12 ♘xa7 ♕e5! (wisely rescuing the queen from danger; instead 12...♖d8? 13 ♘xc6 dxc6 14 ♗xf7+ ♔xf7 15 ♕b3+ ♔e8 16 ♘c3 left Black in some trouble in I.Balinov-E.Reichmann, Finkenstein 1992, just as is he is too after 12...♕f6?! 13 ♘xc8 ♗xc8 14 b5) 13 ♘xc8 ♘xc8 14 ♗d2 gives White a pull with his bishop-pair.

10 ♗xc5 bxc5

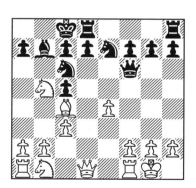

11 ♘d2

Continuing to develop, but there are alternatives:

a) With 11 ♗d5?! White hopes to

follow up with 12 c4, thereby allowing his knight to retreat to c3 if needs be. However, 11...♘xd5! 12 exd5 ♘e5 was a strong riposte in G.Kjartansson-A.Gunnarsson, Reykjavik 2001, and after 13 ♘xa7+ ♔b8 14 ♘b5 c6 15 ♘5a3 cxd5 16 ♘d2 ♖de8 17 ♘b5 ♕g6 Black regains his pawn while taking over the initiative.

b) 11 ♕a4

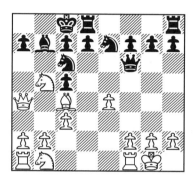

11...a6! (fairly effective, but by no means forced: 11...♔b8 12 ♘d2 d5 13 ♗e2 ♘c8 14 exd5 ♘b6 saw Black equalize in P.Sedy-K.Olsarova, Ostrava 2006; he might consider Panczyk and Ilczuk's idea of 11...♕g6 12 ♘d2 d5!?; and 11...d5 can even be played without delay, after which 12 ♗e2 dxe4! 13 ♘xa7+ ♘xa7 14 ♕xa7 ♕b6 15 ♕xb6 cxb6 16 a4 ♘c6 17 ♘a3 ♘e5 was again fine for Black in B.Yildiz-Y.Yagiz, Antalya 2008) 12 ♘5a3 ♘e5 13 ♗e2 (neither is 13 ♘d2?! a panacea for White: 13...d5! 14 exd5 ♘xd5 gave Black a strong initiative with the knight a little loose on d2 in D.Alexakis-S.Kapnisis, Athens 2006) 13...♘7g6 14 g3 saw White trying to

keep Black out of f4 in A.Cieri-
J.Morasso, Chivilcoy 1997, but with
14...♘f4! 15 gxf4 ♕xf4 Black might
have obtained a strong attack for the
piece.

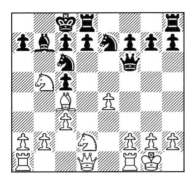

11...a6

Black usually kicks the knight without delay, although he doesn't have to:

a) 11...g5?! prepares the way for
...♘e5 and hopes to launch an attack,
but after 12 ♖e1 ♔b8 13 ♗d5! the initiative is with White.

b) 11...♔b8?! 12 f4 (thematic, but 12
♗d5!? a6 13 ♘a3 ♘xd5 14 exd5 ♘e7 15
c4 also gave White the initiative in
J.Granda Zuniga-E.Righi, Bled Olympiad
2002) 12...d5 (quite possibly Black
should look into Postny's suggestion of
12...a6!? 13 ♘a3 d5 14 exd5 ♘xd5) 13
exd5 ♘xd5 14 ♘e4 ♘xc3 (14...♕f5? 15
♘bd6! cxd6 16 ♗xd5 only made matters worse for Black in S.Ganguly-
D.Sharma, Calcutta 2001) 15 ♘bxc3
♖xd1 16 ♘xf6 ♖xa1 (16...♖d4 17 ♗xf7
gxf6 would restrict White to just an
edge on account of his superior structure, as pointed out by Postny) 17 ♖xa1

gxf6 18 ♗xf7 ♖d8 was optimistically
assessed as unclear by Postny, but after
the simple 19 ♖e1 White must be a lot
better, since all of Black's pawns are
isolated.

c) 11...♘e5!? gives up a7 to fight for
counterplay.

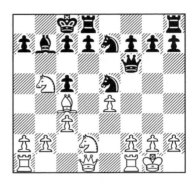

Now:

c1) 12 ♘xa7+? ♔b8 13 ♘b5 d5 reveals Black's main idea and left him
doing pretty well down the d-file in
P.De Kaey-Y.Duhayon, Leuven 2003.

c2) 12 f4 ♘xc4 13 ♘xc4 d5 14 exd5
(otherwise, 14 ♕g4+ ♔b8, as in
S.Kristjansson-Bj.Thorfinnsson, Haf-
narborg 2003, is also quite unclear after 15 exd5 ♖xd5, while 14 ♘e5 a6 15
♕g4+ ♔b8 16 ♘a3 dxe4!? gave Black
full compensation for the exchange in
S.Kristjansson-A.Shirov, Reykjavik 2003)
14...♘xd5 wasn't clear, but did leave
Black with a small initiative in J.Cubas-
L.Perdomo, Sao Paulo 2007.

c3) Thus White should consider
safeguarding his bishop while preparing to advance the f-pawn with 12
♗e2!? (Panczyk and Ilczuk).

d) The closely-related 11...d5 12 exd5 ♘e5!? is another idea Black might consider, as again pointed out by the indefatigable Polish analysts.

12 ♘a3 ♘e5

Once again the other method of striking back is 12...d5?, but that's premature here: 13 exd5 ♘e5 (or 13...♘xd5 14 ♘e4 ♕e5 15 ♕f3 ♘b6 16 ♖fe1 when White's pieces dominate the centre for once) 14 ♘e4 ♕g6 15 ♘xc5 ♘xc4 16 ♘xb7 ♖xd5 17 ♕e2 ♘xa3 18 bxa3 left White somewhat for choice in J.Boada Llombart-E.Leeuwen, correspondence 1992.

13 f4

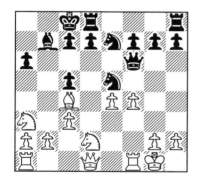

The critical try. White has also gone 13 ♕e2?!, but after 13...d5 14 exd5 ♘xd5 15 ♗xd5 ♖xd5 the initiative belonged to Black in F.De Gleria-D.Ciornei, Duisburg 2006.

Once again the idea of retaining the bishop with 13 ♗e2!? deserves serious attention, although here 13...d5 (13...g5?! 14 ♘b3! ♕b6 kept White's knight out of a5 and c5 in J.Rabier-J.Demarre, Issy les Moulineaux 1996,

but the simple 15 ♘c4 ♘xc4 16 ♗xc4 would have given White a pleasant pull) 14 f4 ♘5g6 15 e5 (this position is quite critical; indeed, White might do better with Panczyk and Ilczuk's 15 ♕c2!? or the 15 ♕a4 ♔b8 of E.Matsuura-D.Lima, Teresina 2000, and then 16 f5 ♘e5 17 ♘b3!, fighting for the initiative) 15...♕b6 seemed okay for Black, with his f-pawn ready to advance and ...♘h4-f5 another idea in S.Ivanets-M.Evchin, Kiev 2005.

13...♘5g6!

Much more often in practice Black has preferred 13...♘xc4?! 14 ♘axc4 d5, but after 15 ♕g4+! (15 e5!? ♕g6 16 ♘a5 ♗a8 17 ♖f2 d4, as in D.Pilz-M.Nemeth, Szentgotthard 2001, and then 18 cxd4 ♖xd4 19 ♕e2 is also quite promising) 15...♔b8 16 e5 ♕f5 17 ♕xf5 ♘xf5 18 ♘a5 White was doing pretty well on account of his probing knights and better structure in A.Cioara-R.Bernhardt, German League 2003.

14 ♕g4

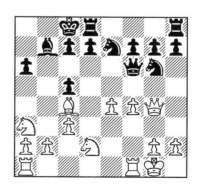

This unbalanced position was reached in A.Grosar-M.Magomedov,

Ljubljana 1992, and now Black should have kicked the queen while beginning counterplay with 14...h5!.

C) 7...0-0

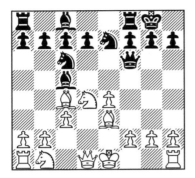

Black elects to house his king without delay, keeping open the option of whether to gain counterplay with ...♕g6, ...b6, ...♘e5, ...d5 or, most likely, a combination of those ideas.

8 0-0

Once again there's nothing better: 8 ♘xc6 ♕xc6 9 ♗xc5 ♕xc5 is clearly fine for Black and the optimistic 8 f4? d5 9 exd5 of R.Garcia Bueno-J.Garcia Fernandez, Terrassa 1996, should have been punished by 9...♖e8!.

After 8 0-0 Black has:

> **C1: 8...♕g6**
> **C2: 8...b6**
> **C3: 8...♗b6**

In practice, however, a whole number of lesser options have been seen, possibly because the second player has failed to do his homework in the main line of the 4...♗c5 Scotch:

a) 7...d6 8 0-0 0-0 allows White a pleasant edge, as we saw in note 'd' to Black's 8th move in Line A.

b) 8...♘e5 9 ♗e2 leads to a couple of more important transpositions: after 9...♕g6 to Line D222 and after 9...d5 to Line D21, below.

c) 8...♖d8? fails to grasp what move White's last prepared and after 9 ♘b5 Black has nothing better than 9...d5 (9...♗b6? 10 ♗xb6 cxb6 11 ♘d6 would just be positional suicide) 10 exd5 ♗xe3 11 fxe3 with an extra pawn for White.

d) 8...d5? 9 ♘xc6 ♗xe3 10 ♘xe7+ ♕xe7 (P.Toropov-A.Vlasov, Kazan 2009) 11 exd5 also leaves White a clear pawn to the good.

e) After 8...♗xd4? 9 cxd4 if Black goes 9...d6 White will just dominate with his strong centre after 10 ♘c3 and 11 f4. Thus Black has usually tried 9...d5!? 10 exd5 ♘a5, but this is hardly an ideal solution either:

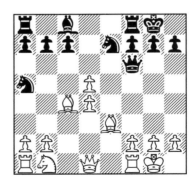

The main problem is that 11 ♗d3

♘xd5?? loses to 12 ♕h5. Thus Black tried 11...♕d6 in M.Korhonen-T.Ronnqvist, Finnish League 2006, but he remained significantly worse after 12 ♘c3 a6 13 ♕f3.

f) 8...♕e5?! 9 ♘d2 d6 10 f4 ♕f6 11 ♘2b3 ♗b6 12 ♕d2 saw Black losing time, while White was ready to continue with ideas such as a4 and/or ♖ae1 in R.Hasangatin-R.Ondo, Presov 2002.

g) 8...a6 prevents ♘b5 ideas, gives the bishop an extra retreat square and prepares to meet 9 f4?! with 9...d5!. Thus White should prefer the prophylactic 9 ♔h1! with which he obtained an edge after 9...♗a7 10 f4 d6 11 ♘a3 ♘xd4 12 ♗xd4 ♗xd4 13 cxd4 d5 14 e5 ♕g6 15 ♗d3 ♗f5 16 ♗xf5 ♘xf5 17 ♘c2 h5 18 ♕d3 in W.Watson-A.Zude, German League 1992. That's probably Black's best try, though, as both 9...♘e5 10 ♗e2 d6 11 f4 (I.Picazo Lopez-D.Gil Quilez, Cullera 2004) 11...♘5g6 12 ♘d2 and 9...b5 10 ♗e2 ♗b7 11 f4 d6 12 ♗f3 ♘g6, as in J.Hjartarson-A.Goldin, Philadelphia 1991, and then 13 ♘xc6 ♗xc6 14 ♗xc5 dxc5 15 e5 ♗xf3 16 ♕xf3 (Hjartarson) are pretty pleasant for White.

C1) 8...♕g6

Black removes his queen from the f-file to dissuade 9 ♘b5, while attacking the e-pawn. This makes a fair degree of sense, but is a little too simplistic an approach here.

9 ♘d2

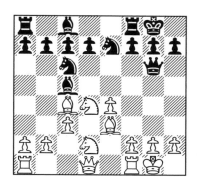

9...♗b6

Safeguarding the bishop. Black has tried a number of alternatives, but without finding a satisfactory way to obtain enough counterplay:

a) 9...♖d8? 10 ♘xc6 ♕xc6 11 ♗xf7+! exploited the loose bishop on c5 to win a pawn in A.Seidl-J.Jancarik, Sec 2007.

b) 9...d5 10 exd5 ♘xd4 11 ♗xd4 ♗xd4 (11...♗h3?! 12 ♕f3 ♗g4 13 ♕f4 ♗d6 14 ♗e5 leaves White a clear pawn in front) 12 cxd4 shreds White's pawns, but the extra one on d5 exerts a certain cramping effect and after 12...b5!? (12...♗g4 13 ♕b3 leaves White in control) 13 ♗xb5 ♖b8 in D.Stojanovski-S.Hamalainen, Rethymnon 2003, 14 ♗c4 would surely have left White at least slightly for choice.

c) 9...b6?! 10 ♘b5 leaves Black unable to defend his c-pawn.

d) 9...♘e5?! looks quite active and thematic, but runs into the powerful 10 ♘f5! ♘xf5 11 exf5 ♕c6 12 ♗xc5 ♕xc5 13 ♗b3 d5 14 ♖e1! ♘d7 (after 14...♘d3 Smyslov was intending 15 ♖e3 ♘xb2 16 ♕h5 ♘c4 17 ♖h3 h6 18 ♖g3 with good attacking prospects for the pawn) 15 ♕f3 ♘f6 16 g4!, which gave White a strong initiative in V.Smyslov-N.Ioseliani, Prague 1995.

e) 9...♘xd4 10 cxd4 ♗b6 hopes for 11 f4?! d5, but after 11 ♖e1! White has a pleasant edge.

f) 9...♗xd4 10 cxd4 d5 11 exd5 ♘b4 is another reasonable-looking idea, but after 12 ♘f3 ♘bxd5 (A.Murariu-B.Abramovic, Sozina 2004) 13 ♕b3 ♕d6 14 ♗g5 White's bishop-pair and active pieces more than offset the IQP.

10 ♔h1!

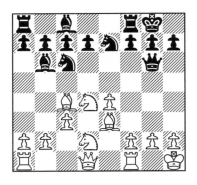

Again this is a useful prophylactic move and one which here also prevents any notion Black might have entertained of following up ...d5 or ...d6 with ...♗h3.

10...d5

This turns out to be too ambitious, but after the 10...♘e5 11 ♗e2 d5 12 ♗h5 ♕d6 13 f4 ♘5c6 of W.Murawski-M.Kawala, Wroclaw 2008, with 14 ♘b5 White would have kept his nose slightly but definitely in front.

Black has also tried 10...♘xd4 11

♗xd4 ♗xd4 12 cxd4 ♕b6, but 13 ♘b3 defends both en prise pawns and after 13...a5 14 d5 a4 15 ♘d4 c5 16 ♘b5 ♖a5 17 ♕e2 White enjoyed an edge in the battle of the Scotch experts, T.Nedev-V.Baklan, Ohrid 2001.

11 exd5 ♘e5?!

Making matters worse. With 11...♘xd4 12 ♗xd4 ♗xd4 13 cxd4 White would have been restricted to just small advantage. After the text, in R.Zelcic-S.Fedorchuk, Cannes 2006, 12 ♘4f3! would have been strong, not that 12 ♗b3 ♘g4 13 h3 ♘xe3 14 fxe3 exactly turned out badly in the game.

C2) 8...b6!?

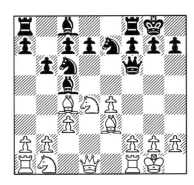

We've already seen that it's not so easy for White to obtain anything after 7...b6 8 0-0 ♗b7 and, partly building on that no doubt, the delayed queenside fianchetto has begun to receive attention at grandmaster level of late.

9 ♘xc6

White hopes that he will emerge from the exchanges with slightly the better structure and a pull, but by no means everyone has been so keen to simplify:

a) 9 ♔h1?! is a little mysterious since after 9...♗b7 Black is ready to meet 10 f4 with 10...d5!. Thus 10 ♘xc6 ♕xc6 11 ♗xc5 ♕xc5 12 ♘d2 was tried in A.Areshchenko-G.Sargissian, Ohrid 2009, but after 12...♖ad8 13 ♗e2 d5 Black was slightly for choice.

b) 9 b4 ♗xd4 10 cxd4!? (again we see White keen to gambit...) 10...d5! (...and Black equally keen to decline) 11 exd5 ♘xb4 12 ♘c3 c6 13 ♕b3 ♘bxd5 14 ♗xd5 ♘xd5 15 ♘xd5 cxd5 16 ♕xd5 ♗e6 saw Black equalize completely in Z.Vukovic-J.Nikolac, Pula 1999.

c) 9 ♘c2 has been fairly popular, but doesn't seem especially challenging:

c1) 9...♕g6 10 ♘d2 ♗b7 (or 10...♘e5!? 11 ♗e2 d5 12 ♗xc5 bxc5 13 f4 ♘5c6 14 ♗h5 ♕h6 15 ♗f3 ♗a6 which was unclear in J.Smeets-R.Ponomariov, Nice (rapid) 2010, especially once White sacrificed the exchange with 16 exd5!?) 11 ♗xc5 bxc5 12 ♘e3 ♘e5 sees Black's active pieces compensating for his slightly inferior structure.

Now 13 ♗b3 ♗a6 14 c4 ♘5c6 was fine for Black in A.Zapata-A.Miles, Linares 1994. However, 13 ♖e1 d6 14 ♗f1!? ♗xe4 15 ♘xe4 ♕xe4 16 ♘c4 gave White good play for the pawn in E.Wiersma-M.Dutreeuw, Belgian League 2007.

c2) 9...♘e5 10 ♗e2 ♘5g6 again sees Black not fearing an exchange on c5, which gives him a half-open b-file and useful control of d4, while taking steps against f4, and after 11 ♘d2 ♗xe3 12 ♘xe3 ♗b7 13 ♖e1 d5 14 ♕c2 ♘f4 he was fine in E.Najer-A.Pashikian, Ohrid 2009.

c3) 9...♗b7 10 ♘d2 (10 ♗xc5 bxc5 11 ♘d2 ♘e5 12 ♗e2 was preferred in J.Tomczak-A.Panocki, Wroclaw 2009, but now 12...d5! 13 f4 ♘5g6 would have given Black the initiative) 10...♖ad8 11 ♗xc5 (White can also try to reach a fractionally better structure with 11 ♗d5, but after 11...♘xd5 12 exd5 ♘e7 13 ♗xc5 bxc5 14 c4 d6 Black was okay in Y.Dembo-A.Karpatchev, Corfu 2007) 11...bxc5 12 ♘e3 ♘e5 again leaves Black's pieces quite well coordinated and after 13 ♕b3 ♘xc4 in D.Pavasovic-L.Fressinet, Heraklion 2007, he was ready to take over the initiative, such as with 14 ♘exc4 ♗a8 followed by 15...d5.

d) 9 f4?! is the move White would like to play. Indeed, 9...♗b7 10 e5 ♕h6 11 ♕d2 ♗xd4 12 cxd4 ♘f5 13 ♘c3 gave him an edge in J.Bryant-M.Brown, Los Angeles 2009, and he might meet the 9...♗xd4 10 cxd4 d5 of E.Ozatakan-

E.Kayar, Kocaeli 2002, with 11 exd5 b5 12 dxc6! bxc4 13 d5, thereby seizing the initiative. However, not for the first time in this chapter, Black should prefer 9...d5!.

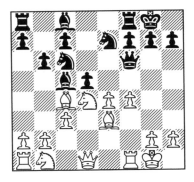

Now the fiendish 10 e5? ♕h6! costs White a pawn after 11 ♗e2 ♘xe5, but in any case Black appears to have the easier game: 10 ♗xd5 ♘xd5 11 exd5 ♘e7 12 ♘c2 ♖d8 13 ♕f3 ♘xd5 14 ♗xc5 bxc5 slightly favoured him thanks to his strong light-squared bishop in E.Wiersma-F.Levin, Triesen 2006, and 10 exd5 ♘a5! (10...♘xd4 wouldn't have been so effective in J.Sanchez-M.Godena, Bratto 2004, had White found 11 ♗xd4 ♗b7 12 ♗xc5 bxc5 13 ♘a3, with an edge) 11 ♗d3 ♖d8 12 ♘d2 ♘xd5 13 ♗f2 ♕xf4 14 ♕c2 ♕h6 failed to give White quite enough for his pawn in R.Zelcic-M.Godena, Lugano 2007.

e) 9 ♕d2!? has in mind the idea of meeting 9...♗b7 with 10 b4, which could really do with a test. Black preferred 9...♕g6 in B.Predojevic-A.Brkic, Rijeka 2010, and after 10 f3 a5

(10...♘e5!? 11 ♗e2 ♗b7 12 ♘a3 prepares to meet 12...d5? with 13 b4 when 13...♗d6? 14 f4 would embarrass Black's pieces, but after 12...♗xa3 13 bxa3 f5! Black develops counterplay) 11 ♘a3! ♘xd4 12 cxd4 ♗xa3 13 bxa3 d5 14 ♗xd5 ♘xd5 15 exd5 ♗b7 16 ♗f4 was a little worse, although he made good use of the presence of opposite-coloured bishops to hold the draw.

We now return to 9 ♘xc6:

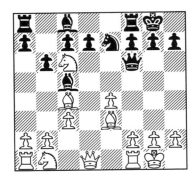

9...♕xc6

Invariably played, but it's not clear that Black needs to worry about having doubled c-pawns and 9...♘xc6!? 10 ♗xc5 bxc5 11 ♘d2 ♖b8 12 ♖b1 ♘e5 13 ♗e2 ♗a6 was very solid and seemed fine for him in a rare test, J.Baillot-A.Karpatchev, Metz 2008.

10 ♗xc5

The only other real move is 10 ♗d5, but after 10...♘xd5 11 exd5 (11 ♕xd5? ♗xe3 12 fxe3 ♗b7 would just be very good for Black on account of his pressure down the long diagonal) 11...♕b5 (or 11...♕g6 12 ♗xc5 bxc5 13 c4 d6 14 ♘c3 ♗h3 15 ♕f3 ♗d7 with which Black equalized in O.Saez Gabikagogeaskoa-D.Bosch Porta, Barcelona 1996) 12 ♗xc5 ♕xc5 13 ♕d3 ♗b7 in V.Korchnoi-J.Platzek, Berlin (simul) 2001, Black was ready to keep his bishop active, with a small initiative after 14 c4 c6.

10...♕xc5

11 ♕d4

White has also tried keeping the queens on, but with all of 11 ♕d3 d6 12 ♘d2 ♗b7, 11 ♗b3 d6 12 ♘d2 ♖e8 13 ♕f3 ♗e6, as in T.Troestrum-L.Ebner, Ueberlingen 2000, intending 14 ♗xe6 fxe6, and the 11 ♘a3 ♘g6 12 ♕d5 ♖b8 13 ♕xc5 bxc5 14 b3 d6 15 ♖fe1 ♗d7 of H.Odeev-C.Arduman, Elista Olympiad 1998, he fails to obtain any advantage.

11...d6!

Keeping the bishop flexible. Instead 11...♗b7 12 ♕xc5 bxc5 13 ♘d2 a5 was seen in S.Movsesian-I.Sokolov, Sarajevo 2004, and now with 14 f4 a4 15 ♖fe1 White might have obtained a pull.

12 ♕xc5 bxc5 13 ♘d2 ♖b8

By no means the only approach and 13...a5!? 14 b3 ♗a6 15 ♖ab1 ♖fb8 16 ♖fe1 ♔f8 17 f3 f6 was very solid for

Black and soon agreed drawn in T.Nabaty-D.Howell, Rijeka 2010.

14 ♖ab1

Perhaps White might consider 14 b3!?, enabling him to centralize his queen's rook and push f4.

14...♖d8 15 ♖fe1

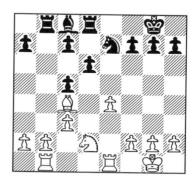

We've followed the game V.Gorkavij-A.Aleksandrov, St Petersburg 2009, in which the easiest way for Black to equalize was the simple 15...♗e6 16 ♗xe6 fxe6.

C3) 8...♗b6

A very solid choice. Black safeguards his bishop, exploits the fact that with

White's bishop on c4 he can meet 9 ♘b5?! with 9...a6 and keeps his options for counterplay open.

9 ♘a3

White develops his last piece, but unsurprisingly this is by no means forced, with practice having seen a large array of alternatives:

a) 9 a4 d6 10 ♕d2 ♕g6 11 f3 ♘e5 12 ♗b3 saw the early a-pawn advance fail to especially trouble Black in S.Khukhashvili-P.Reyes Jara, Heraklion 2002, where 12...♘7c6 would have left Black comfortably placed.

b) 9 ♘xc6 ♕xc6 10 ♗xb6 axb6 11 ♕e2 d5 12 exd5 ♘xd5 gave Black good counter-activity and easy equality in M.Brunello-V.Sokolova, Budva 2003.

c) 9 ♕d2 d6 10 ♔h1 ♗e6 11 ♘xe6 fxe6 was very solid for Black, with his knight-pair in no way inferior to White's bishops in F.Haeusler-M.Voelz, Sebnitz 2004.

d) 9 f4

9...♘xd4 10 cxd4 (Black should also meet 10 ♗xd4 with 10...d5 11 exd5 ♖d8, regaining the pawn with a good

game) 10...d5 11 e5 ♕g6 12 ♗b3 was seen in L.Jaime Montalvan-J.Garcia Munoz, Malaga 2003, where 12...♕e4 would have left Black with a strong blockade and decent-enough counterplay.

e) 9 ♔h1?! achieves less than nothing here, since Black will go 9...♖d8! threatening 10...d5.

Following 10 ♕h5 h6! 11 ♘d2 d5 12 exd5 ♘xd4 13 cxd4 ♗f5 the World's leading Scotch exponent even found himself a touch worse in G.Kasparov-G.Kamsky, Tilburg 1991. White can do better with the 10 ♕d2 h6 11 f4 of G.Timmerman-P.Herb, Belfort 1991, not that Black has any problems here after 11...♘xd4 12 ♗xd4 ♗xd4 13 cxd4 d5 14 e5 ♕g6.

f) 9 ♘c2 sees White hoping to obtain a grip on the d5-square, but 9...♘e5, while by no means invariably played, is a good antidote: 10 ♗e2 (or 10 ♗b3 ♗xe3 11 ♘xe3 ♕b6 12 ♕e2 d6 13 ♔h1 ♗e6 14 f4, as in R.Zelcic-J.Klovans, Schwarzach 2005, where 14...♘d7 would have left Black solidly placed) 10...♘5g6! (the point of Black's play; rather than a white pawn, it will be a black knight making good use of the f4-square) 11 ♗xb6 (after 11 ♗d4 ♕g5 12 g3 ♘f4 13 ♗f3 d6 it was Black who enjoyed a light initiative in K.Toma-J.Sosna, Brno 2006) 11...♕xb6 12 ♘ba3 ♘f4 13 ♗f3 ♘eg6 gave Black easy counterplay in R.Tischbierek-S.Smagin, Dortmund 1992, and here he might do even better with 11...axb6!? 12 ♘e3 ♘f4.

g) 9 ♗b3 prepares to meet 9...d6 with 10 ♘b5, but 9...♘a5 scotches such ideas and 10 ♗c2 (Black was clearly fine after 10 ♘c2 ♕g6 11 ♖e1 d6 12 ♘d2 ♘xb3 13 axb3 ♗h3 in F.Nijboer-J.Van der Wiel, Eindhoven 1991, but White should likely prefer this) 10...♘c4 11 ♗c1 ♘c6! 12 ♘e2 d6 13 ♘g3 ♘6e5 14 h3 ♗d7 15 a4 a6 left Black much the more active and doing quite well in A.Morozevich-V.Ivanchuk, Moscow (blitz) 2008.

We now return to 9 ♘a3:

9...♕g6

Black hurries to create some pres-

sure against e4 and even g2. This is likely best, as we can see by comparing:

a) 9...♘xd4?! 10 ♗xd4! (but 10 cxd4?! d5! was somewhat less effective in M.Chandler-N.Short, London 1991) 10...♗xd4 11 cxd4 d5 12 exd5 (12 ♗xd5!? also comes into consideration) 12...♘f5 13 ♘c2 failed to give Black quite enough for the pawn in L.Oll-Peng Xiaomin, Beijing 1997.

b) 9...a6 10 ♘ac2 ♘e5 11 ♗e2 d6 12 f4 ♘5g6 saw White achieve his ideal expansion in C.Mohineesh-S.Moosavi, Teheran 2006, where 13 ♕d2 would have left him with a pretty pleasant edge.

c) 9...♖d8?! ran into the powerful 10 ♘db5! ♘e5 (Black must avoid 10...a6? 11 ♘d6! and in Z.Vukovic-D.Mozetic, Niksic 1996, 10...d5 11 exd5 ♘e5 12 ♗xb6 favoured White, with the idea of 12...axb6 13 ♗b3, maintaining control) 11 ♗b3! (11 ♕h5!? looks dangerous and has been supported by Wells, but with 11...d5! 12 ♗g5 ♕g6 13 ♕xg6 ♘5xg6 14 exd5 a6 Black was able to equalize in J.Tomczak-M.Grabarczyk, Opole 2007) 11...a6?! in R.Hasangatin-J.Filipek, Frydek-Mistek 1997, where 12 ♘d6 would have left White doing pretty well indeed.

d) 9...d6 10 ♕d2! (10 ♘db5 doesn't seem so clear in view of 10...a6! 11 ♘xd6 ♗xe3 12 ♘xc8 ♘xc8 13 fxe3, as in J.Rosito-R.Servat, Buenos Aires 1991, where 13...♕e7 would have been okay for Black) 10...♕g6 (or 10...♘e5 11 ♗g5 ♕g6 and now in A.Eaker-F.Vlugt, Curacao 2002, White might have seized the initiative with 12 ♗xe7 ♗xd4 13 ♔h1) 11 ♖ae1 ♘xd4 12 ♗xd4 ♘c6 13 ♗xb6 axb6 14 f4 left White with a small but clear edge in Z.Lapeginas-A.Vasilkis, correspondence 2004.

e) 9...♘e5!? is the most active and best of Black's alternatives and after 10 ♗b3 (10 ♗e2 d5 11 f4 ♘5c6 12 e5 ♕h6 13 ♘ac2 ♘xd4 14 cxd4 ♘f5 gave Black a blockade and full equality in M.Pila Diez-M.Perez, Spain 1996) 10...d6 (or 10...♕g6 11 f3 d6 12 ♘dc2 when in B.Trabert-V.Yemelin, Hamburg 2000, Black would have been okay after 12...♗d7) 11 ♘c4 was seen in A.Hemmer-L.Beck, Leiden 1999, where it was time for Black to continue his counterplay with 11...♕g6, thereby maintaining a rough balance.

Returning to the immediate 9...♕g6:

10 ♖e1

Indirect defence of the e-pawn, but again there are alternatives:

a) 10 ♕d2!? ♘e5 (10...♘xd4 11 ♗xd4 ♗xd4 12 cxd4 d5 13 exd5 ♗h3 14 f4 was slightly better for White despite his sub-optimal structure in R.Mainka-P.Van der Sterren, Prague 1992) 11 f3 d6 is very solid for Black, although it's surprising that White hasn't tried this more often.

b) 10 ♘ac2 ♘e5 11 ♗e2 d5! 12 f4 ♘g4 saw Black seizing the initiative in M.Aigner-A.Stein, San Francisco 2005.

c) 10 ♘xc6 bxc6! (but not 10...♘xc6? 11 ♗xb6 axb6 12 ♘b5 which left White somewhat for choice in N.Borge-B.Hedlund, Gausdal 1992, while 10...♕xc6 11 ♗d4 gives him a small pull) 11 ♖e1 d6 (White is slightly for choice after the 11...♔h8 12 ♗d3 d6 of J.Van der Wiel-D.De Vreugt, Wijk aan Zee 1999, and then 13 ♘c4 f5 14 e5 or 13...♗h3 14 ♕f3 ♗g4 15 ♕g3, but Black might consider 11...d5!? 12 exd5 ♗g4! 13 ♕d2 ♗f3 14 ♗g5 ♘xd5 15 ♗d3! f5 16 gxf3 h6 17 c4 ♘f6, as analysed by Mikhalevski, with something of a mess, although 18 h4 should keep White's nose in front) 12 ♗d3 ♗g4 was solid and okay for Black in N.Fercec-L.Zsinka, Oberwart 2001.

d) Black has tried a number of moves after 10 f3, but not for the first time 10...♖d8! looks rather to the point and after 11 ♘dc2 ♘e5 12 ♗b3 d5 13 exd5 (as played in G.Hernandez-G.Milos, Guarapuava 1992; later White preferred 13 ♗xb6 ♕xb6+ 14 ♔h1 ♗e6, not that this especially trouble Black in G.Timoscenko-B.Trabert, Bolzano 2000) 13...♗h3! followed by 14...♘xd5 Black has the initiative, as pointed out by Mikhalevski.

10...♘e5 11 f4

White has also tried the more sedate 11 ♗f1, but after 11...d5 (Wells' idea of 11...d6 12 ♘ac2 ♘g4!? is a decent alternative) 12 ♗f4 in K.Arakhamia Grant-J.Jackova, Elista 1998, Black might have equalized with 12...♘5c6 13 ♘xc6 bxc6.

11...d5!

The correct method. 11...♘g4? may also look tempting, but after 12 f5 ♘xe3 13 fxg6 ♘xd1 14 gxf7+ ♔h8 15 ♖axd1 d6 16 ♖f1 White is doing rather well, as analysed by Bruzon.

12 fxe5 dxc4 13 ♘xc4 ♗e6 14 ♘xb6 axb6

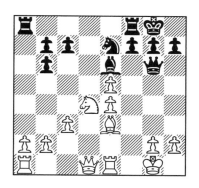

Following a few semi-forced moves, the game Zhang Pengxiang-L.Bruzon Bautista, Skanderborg 2005, reached this position in which it was clear that Black was pretty solidly placed and had enough positional compensation for the pawn.

D) 7...♘e5

At last we come to Black's main and most active approach. Clearly White must retain his bishop if he wants to fight for the initiative and the choice is between:

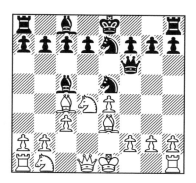

D1: 8 ♗b3
D2: 8 ♗e2

D1) 8 ♗b3

The move White would like to play, keeping the ...d5 break under control, but the bishop will be missed on the kingside.

8...♕g6

Immediately exploiting the downside to White's last. This is pretty logical, although there are alternatives.

a) One good response to the overly-routine 8...0-0?! is 9 f4!? ♘5g6 10 0-0 d6 and now in A.Malienko-V.Gerber, Kyiv 2007, 11 ♕d2 h6 12 ♘b5 would have left White with a small but clear edge.

b) 8...d6!? doesn't look especially impressive, but forces White to take care. Indeed, in S.Rabaev-W.Lukas, Berlin Pankow 2005, 9 ♘c2? should have been punished by 9...♗g4! 10 ♕d2

♗f3!. Likewise, it's not a good idea to keep Black out of g4 with 9 h3? on account of 9...♕g6.

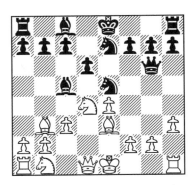

Suddenly White is losing a pawn and after 10 ♔f1 ♕xe4 11 ♘d2 ♕d3+ 12 ♔g1 (A.Ac-J.Hartl, Slovakian League 2002) 12...0-0 Black is just doing rather well. Thus White should likely prefer the prudent 9 f3, although after 9...♗d7 (9...♕h4+!? 10 ♗f2 ♕g5 may also be okay, since 11 0-0 0-0 doesn't exactly leave White with a great plan) 10 0-0 in J.Dufour-P.Rouveret, Issy les Moulineaux 1997, with 10...0-0 Black would have been fine, with ...♘eg6-f4 one plan.

c) 8...♕a6!? prevents White castling and after 9 ♗c2 0-0 10 b4 ♗xd4 11 cxd4 ♘c4 12 0-0 d5 Black enjoyed decent counterplay in F.Amonatov-E.Safarli, Moscow 2010.

9 0-0 d5!

The correct method of obtaining counterplay, especially as 9...♕xe4?! is rather risky on account of 10 ♖e1!.

Black's pieces are rather lined up on the e-file here and without his bishop on e2 White is well placed to take advantage.

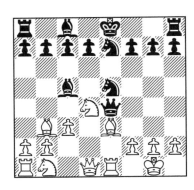

Now 10...0-0?? 11 ♗g5 costs Black a piece and 10...♕h4? 11 ♘f5 ♘xf5 12 ♗xc5 d6 13 ♗a4+ c6 14 ♗xd6 was hardly much of an improvement in A.Pruneda-F.Sanchez Guirado, Asturias 1992. Neither is 10...♕g4? 11 ♘b5, although with 10...d6 Black can keep White's initiative and advantage within bounds after 11 ♗c2 followed by 12 ♘b5.

Here we should also note that 9...♘g4 fails to trouble White and after 10 ♗f4 d6 11 ♘b5 ♗b6 in D.Quernheim-A.Karmann, Bergneustadt 2001, he might have seized the initiative with 12 ♗xd6!? cxd6 13 ♘xd6+ ♔f8 14 ♘xf7.

10 ♗f4

Now it's White's turn to be careful: both 10 exd5?? and 10 ♘b5?? perish on the spot to 10...♗h3. Meanwhile 10 ♘f3?! ♘xf3+ 11 ♕xf3 ♗g4 12 ♕f4 ♗xe3 13 fxe3 0-0-0 left Black with the initiative in A.Petrushin-P.Kotenko, Russia 2002, but White might consider

10 f3!? ♛xe4 (10...♗h3?! 11 ♛e2 0-0-0 12 ♔h1 repulsed Black's attacking ambitions in T.Wallis-L.Juen,L Austrian League 1994) 11 ♘d2 exf3 12 ♘2xf3 ♘xf3+ 13 ♛xf3 0-0 14 ♖f2 followed by 15 ♖af1 with decent play for the pawn.

10...♗g4

Black's main move, continuing to develop with tempo. Again the e-pawn was en prise, but after 10...♛xe4 both 11 ♛d2 ♘c4 12 ♗xc4 dxc4 13 ♖e1 ♛g6 14 ♘a3 (Marin) and 11 ♗g3 f6 12 ♘d2 ♛g6 13 ♖e1 (Kosten) give White the initiative and at least enough compensation.

11 ♛c2

Again White must be careful: 11 f3? ♘xf3+! 12 ♖xf3 dxe4 would not be the way to go.

11...f6 12 ♗a4+

After 12 ♘d2 Black might well have gone 12...0-0-0, so White dissuades queenside castling with this check.

12...c6 13 ♘d2 0-0

Black hardly minds going short, whereas 13...0-0-0 14 b4! (Golubev) would allow White to carry out the

main idea behind his 12th.

14 f3 ♗d7 15 ♔h1

White tried to improve with 15 ♖ae1 in F.Amonatov-N.Kosintseva, Moscow 2010, but 15...♖fe8 kept e5 covered and after 16 ♔h1 ♖ad8 17 ♛b1 ♛f7 18 ♗c2 ♘5g6 19 ♗c7 ♖c8 20 ♗g3 ♗b6 both sides continued to jockey for position with the chances finely balanced.

15...♗b6 16 ♖ae1 ♖ae8

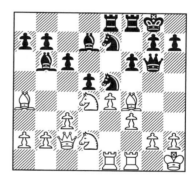

Black is pretty solidly placed here and didn't really face any problems in A.Morozevich-P.Leko, Mexico City 2007.

D2) 8 ♗e2!

White's main move, taking control of the g4-square and so preparing an advance of the f-pawn. The move does entail a pawn sacrifice, though, and Black must now decide whether to fork e4 and g2 or to prefer an ambitious idea of his own.

> **D21: 8...d5**
>
> **D22: 8...♕g6**

By and large Black's lesser options are pretty unimpressive:

a) 8...h5?! prepared to meet 9 f4 with 9...♘g4 in G.Hernandez-C.Garcia Fernandez, Cullera 2003, but White must be at least slightly for choice after Postny's prudent 9 ♘d2, allowing him to consider ideas of b4, as well as of f4.

b) 8...g5? 9 0-0 ♘5g6 clamps down on the f4-square, but after 10 ♘b5 Black found himself losing a pawn in F.Amonatov-H.Abbasifar, Elista Olympiad 1998.

c) 8...♘5g6 9 0-0 ♘f4 was seen in G.Zentai-B.Lengyel, Budapest 1999, and now 10 ♗g4 followed by 11 ♕d2 or 11 g3 would keep control and an edge.

d) Likewise 8...♘7g6 9 ♕d2 h6 10 0-0 (R.Ibanez-S.Riera, Spain 1993) 10...d6 11 b4 (or 11 f4) 11...♗b6 12 a4 gives White a pleasant pull.

e) 8...d6 9 0-0 takes play back into Line A, above.

f) 8...0-0 9 0-0 is also likely to transpose elsewhere:

f1) 9...d6 is Line A again.

f2) 9...♕g6 will be seen in Line D222, below.

f3) 9...d5 takes play into our next section (Line D21).

f4) 9...♗b6?! 10 f4 ♘5c6 11 ♕d2 d6 12 ♘b5 left White in control and beginning to press in R.Pokorna-L.Sepulveda, St Lorenzo 1995.

D21) 8...d5

Black carries out his ideal break, but unfortunately for him White can just ignore it.

9 0-0!

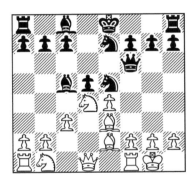

9...0-0

Black brings his king to safety, albeit at the cost of allowing White to expand in the centre. There are alternatives though:

a) 9...♕g6 transposes to Line D221, below.

b) The anti-f4 measure 9...h5? is again far too ambitious and after 10 ♘b5 ♗xe3 (or 10...♕b6 11 ♗xc5 ♕xc5 12 ♕d4 and 1-0 in A.Khasin-A.Lilienthal, Moscow 1955) 11 ♘xc7+ White's advantage was already pretty much decisive in P.Kotsur-M.Logunov, Krasnoyarsk 1998.

c) 9...♗d7?! saw Black hoping to go long in A.Garaud-F.Forgues, Mont de Marsan 2005, but after 10 f4 (the vigorous 10 exd5 ♘xd5 11 ♘b5!? is also quite tempting) 10...♘5c6 11 e5 White must be at least slightly for choice.

d) 9...dxe4?! is in a sense quite critical, but after 10 ♘b5! ♗d6! (naturally not 10...♗xe3?? 11 ♘xc7+ ♔f8 12 ♛d8 mate, while Black loses material after both 10...♗b6 11 ♗xb6 ♛xb6 12 ♛d4 and 10...♛b6 11 ♗xc5 ♛xc5 12 ♛d4) 11 ♗c5! 0-0 (or 11...a6 12 ♗xd6 axb5 13 ♗xc7 with some advantage) 12 ♘xd6 cxd6 13 ♛xd6 ♛xd6 14 ♗xd6 ♘5g6, as in H.Kummerow-R.Ziatdinov, Biel 1992, and then 15 ♘d2 White enjoys a pleasant, long-term edge with his bishop-pair.

10 f4! ♘5c6

The best square for the knight, as 10...♘c4? 11 ♗xc4 dxc4 12 ♘d2 just leaves Black in some trouble.

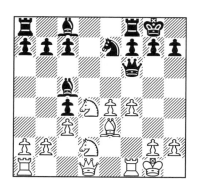

After 12...♛a6 13 ♛e2 and 12...♖d8 13 ♛h5 he is somewhat worse, while

12...b5 13 a4!? (13 ♛h5 is also pretty effective) 13...♗d7 14 axb5 ♗xb5 15 e5 left White with a strong initiative in R.Zelcic-D.Sulc, Bosnjaci 2010.

Before returning to 10...♘5c6, we should note that 10...♛h6!? 11 ♛d2 wouldn't have been too bad for Black in J.Kochetkova-I.Semenova, Miass 2007, had she gone in for the critical line 11...♘g4! 12 ♗xg4 ♗xg4 13 f5! ♛h5 14 h3 ♗xh3 15 gxh3 ♛xh3 16 ♖f3 ♛g4+ 17 ♛g2 ♛xg2+ 18 ♔xg2 dxe4 19 ♖f4, thereby restricting White to just a pull in the resulting endgame.

11 e5 ♛h6

Black should avoid 11...♛g6? because 12 f5 ♗xd4 13 fxg6 ♗xe3+ 14 ♔h1 hxg6 15 ♗g4 didn't give him enough for the queen in J.Zezulkin-J.Lechtynsky, Czech League 2006, but 11...♛h4 is possible and after 12 ♛d2 ♗g4 13 ♗d3 (S.Rublevsky-V.Popov, Warsaw 2005) 13...f6!? 14 ♘xc6 ♗xe3+ 15 ♛xe3 ♘xc6 16 h3 ♗c8 17 ♘d2 fxe5 18 fxe5 ♗e6 19 ♘f3 White is only slightly for choice.

12 ♛d2 ♗xd4 13 cxd4 ♛g6 14 ♘c3 ♗f5

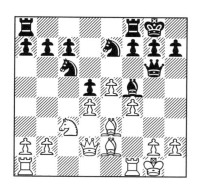

Black has given up the bishop-pair to achieve a central blockade, but White has options on both flanks and in J.Sanchez-N.Dobrev, French League 2007, 15 ♖ac1 would have left him with a small but clear edge.

D22) 8...♕g6

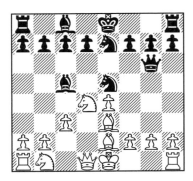

The critical test of the retreat to e2.

9 0-0!

White must sacrifice: 9 ♗f3?! d5! 10 ♘d2 (10 exd5?! ♘xf3+ 11 ♕xf3 ♗g4 12 ♕f4 ♗d6 would just be very good for Black with his active pieces and bishop-pair) 10...♘d3+ 11 ♔f1 0-0 misplaces White's king and leaves Black with an early initiative.

After the text move, Black has three main approaches:

D221: 9...d5
D222: 9...0-0
D223: 9...d6

Of course, White's whole approach would fail if 9...♕xe4? was a good move,

but it isn't: 10 ♘b5 (10 ♘d2!? ♕g6 11 ♘b5 is also pretty good and so too here is Emms' idea of 11 ♗h5!? ♕d3 12 ♘4f3! with a strong initiative) 10...♗xe3 (10...♕c6? 11 ♗xc5 ♕xc5 12 ♕d4 won material in E.Grosse Kloenne-U.Wiechen, German League 1999) 11 ♘xc7+ ♔d8 12 ♘xa8 sees White picking up the exchange while displacing Black's king.

Admittedly the knight is stuck in the corner, but with Black's pieces not especially well coordinated, White should emerge with some advantage after 12...♗f4 13 g3, but that looks a better try for Black than 12...♗g5? 13 ♘d2 ♗xd2 14 ♕xd2 which was pretty good for White in E.Betz-H.Doehner, Bad Wiessee 2003, since 14...b6 15 f4! ♗b7 16 ♖f2 ♘c4 17 ♕d1 ♗xa8 18 ♗f3 would have seen him emerging ahead in the material stakes.

Likewise, 9...h5? 10 ♘b5! (again the punishment of an early ...h5) 10...♗xe3 11 ♘xc7+ ♔d8 12 ♘xa8 ♗f4 13 ♕a4 left White somewhat better despite the cornered knight in M.Bouhlel-L.Linnemer, French League 2005.

D221) 9...d5?!

Rather than play to win the e4-pawn under improved circumstances or move his king into safety, Black strives for the initiative, but just as when played a move earlier, such a policy turns out to be too ambitious.

10 ♗h5!

White forces Black to take the pawn after all. This isn't forced, but of the alternatives only 'd' and 'e' deserve further attention:

a) 10 ♘b5?? ♗h3 11 ♗f3 dxe4! 12 ♘xc7+ ♔f8 cost White the game in F.Fernandez-F.De la Paz Perdomo, Collado Villalba 2001.

b) 10 exd5?! ♗h3 11 ♗f3 0-0-0 gives Black an early initiative, although after 12 c4 ♘xc4 13 ♘c3 ♘xe3 14 fxe3 ♔b8 the position wasn't too clear in Nguyen Hoang Tuan-Hoang Nam Thang, Vung Tau 2000.

c) 10 f3?! dxe4 11 fxe4 ♗h3 12 ♗f3 0-0-0 was, however, definitely slightly better for Black in F.Shiraliyeva-S.Allahverdieva, Baku 2001.

d) 10 ♔h1 avoids problems on the g2-square, but is a little slow and after 10...0-0! (wisely resisting temptation; indeed White is slightly for choice after both 10...dxe4 11 ♘b5 ♗d6 12 ♗c5 and 10...♕xe4 11 ♘d2 ♕g6 12 ♘b5) 11 ♘f5 ♗xf5 12 exf5 (12 ♗xc5? ♗xe4 13 f3 ♗c2 cost White a pawn in J.Wengler-M.Hock, German League 2003) 12...♕b6 13 f6 gxf6 didn't give White quite enough for his pawn in M.Ashley-E.Moskow, New York 1993.

e) 10 ♗f4!? ♕f6 (alternatively, 10...♕xe4 11 ♗g3 ♗xd4?! was seen in N.Kopaev-L.Abramavicius, Ivanovo 1951, where White would have been doing very well had he gone 12 cxd4 ♘5c6 13 ♘c3; likewise, 10...♗d6 11 exd5 ♘xd5, as in A.Nicolini-S.Marek, Slovakian League 1997, and then 12 ♗h5! ♕f6 13 ♗xe5 ♗xe5 14 ♖e1 is somewhat in White's favour) 11 ♗g3 ♗e6 12 ♕a4+ c6 13 ♘d2 looks a little better for White.

f) 10 f4!? ♕xe4 (10...♗h3?! 11 ♖f2 ♕xe4 12 ♗c1! didn't give Black enough compensation in Z.Runic-B.Topic, Jahorina 2001) 11 ♕d2 (without there being a loose bishop on h3, 11 ♗c1? ♗xd4+ 12 cxd4 ♘5c6 is clearly good for Black) 11...♘g4 was seen in S.Cardenas Serrano-J.Cruz Gomez, Cordoba 1995, and 12 ♗xg4 ♗xg4 13 f5! would have given White decent play for his pawn.

10...♕xe4

Taking up the challenge. This might not be what Black wants to do, but neither are the alternatives exactly ideal for him:

a) 10...♕f6? 11 ♘b5 ♕b6 (10...♕d6? 11 ♘b5 ♕b6 is another move order) 12 ♗xc5 ♕xc5 13 ♘1a3 left Black without a particularly good defence to the threat of 14 ♕d4 in T.Shadrina-O.Kim, Moscow 1996.

b) 10...♕b6? 11 b4! was even worse for Black in S.Chekhov-A.Galdin, Voronezh 2007.

c) However, 10...♗g4!? might be Black's best try, even though 11 ♗xg6 ♗xd1 12 ♗xf7+ ♔xf7 13 ♖xd1 ♘c4 (disruption is the only policy; instead 13...dxe4? 14 ♘d2 would just be rather good for White, as pointed out by Wells) 14 b4! leaves White a pawn up.

Now 14...♗b6 15 ♘d2 ♘xe3 (15...♘xd2!? 16 ♖xd2 dxe4 17 ♘b5 might be a better defensive try, J.Eslon-A.Martinez Cebolla, Zaragoza 1992) 16 fxe3 ♖he8 17 c4! dxc4 18 ♘xc4 ♖ad8 19 ♘xb6 axb6 20 ♘b5! left White somewhat ahead in S.Rublevsky-H.Gretarsson, Yerevan Olympiad 1996, and so Black might try 14...♗xd4, although 15 ♖xd4 ♖hd8 16 ♘d2 was surely at least slightly better for White in F.Hamperl-

M.Van der Sanden, Guernsey 2008.

11 ♘d2

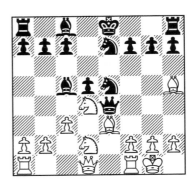

White begins to gain time against Black's queen.

11...♕d3

This looks like a better try than 11...♕h4?! when 12 ♗xf7+! ♘xf7 13 ♘4f3 ♕f6 14 ♗xc5 0-0 15 ♖e1 ♘d6 (or 15...♖e8, as in P.H.Nielsen-J.Hector, Stavanger 1991, and then 16 ♕b3) 16 ♕b3 left Black under heavy pressure in G.Hernandez-O.Castro Rojas, Bucaramanga 1992.

12 ♘4f3!

A powerful retreat which takes full advantage of the unprotected bishop on c5.

12...♗d6

Again the alternatives only make matters worse: 12...♗xe3?! 13 ♘xe5 ♕xd2 would have left White somewhat for choice in R.Tischbierek-A.Maier, Munich 1992, had he gone 14 ♕a4+, and 12...♘xf3+ 13 ♕xf3 ♗xe3 14 ♕xf7+ ♔d8, as in J.Lampe-O.Link, Hamburg 1997, and then 15 ♖ae1 is also clearly in White's favour.

13 ♘xe5 ♗xe5 14 ♗c5! ♕f5

The pressure down the a3-f8 diagonal is rather awkward for Black and he has also struggled rather after:

a) 14...g6 15 ♗e2 ♕f5 16 ♖e1! ♕d7 17 ♗xe7 ♕xe7 18 ♗b5+ left Black in trouble down the central files in A.Murariu-A.Bochkarev, Bucharest 2001.

b) 14...♗f6 15 ♖e1 g6 16 ♗e2! ♕f5 17 ♕a4+! c6 (17...♕d7? 18 ♕f4! cost Black a piece in J.Hoogendoorn-H.Jonkman, Hengelo 1994) 18 h3 threatens 19 ♗g4 to which Black lacks a particularly satisfactory defence.

c) 14...♗d6 15 ♗xd6 cxd6 dealt with one strong form of pressure, but only by allowing another with 16 ♖e1 in S.Chekhov-V.Sokolovsky, Voronezh 2007.

15 ♖e1

Black is clearly in some trouble down the e-file and in E.Sveshnikov-V.Varavin, Anapa 1991, he collapsed with 15...g6? 16 ♗xe7! ♔xe7 17 ♘f3. Relatively better defences are the 15...♗e6 16 ♘f3 of S.Ivanets-V.Roman-

ov, Kiev 2004, and 15...♗f6 16 ♘b3, not that there can be any doubt that White enjoys a clear advantage in both cases.

D222) 9...0-0

Black continues his development. This can't be too bad, but isn't especially challenging and allows White time to defend his e-pawn and emerge with an edge.

10 ♘d2

10...d5

Black tries to strike back in the centre after all. He has also been known to try:

a) The 10...♕b6? of L.Braggaar-E.Gorter, Venlo 2007, should have been punished by 11 b4.

b) 10...d6 11 ♗h5! ♕f6 (11...♗g4? 12 ♗xg6 ♗xd1 13 ♗xh7+ ♔xh7 14 ♖axd1 cost Black a pawn in P.Wojciechowski-Kim Youngsoo, Turin 2006) 12 f4 ♘5c6 (otherwise, 12...♕h6? 13 ♕e2 just left Black's queen misplaced on h6 in D.Mieles Palau-W.Palencia, Guayaquil 2003, while after 12...♘5g6 13 b4 ♗b6 in S.Sommer-R.Pascua, Yerevan 1996, White could have obtained a pleasant edge with 14 ♘c4) 13 ♘c4! ♗xd4 14 cxd4 d5 (White's main idea is revealed after 14...♕e6 15 ♖c1 ♕xe4 16 ♗f3 ♕g6 17 d5 ♘b4 18 ♕d2 with strong pressure and good play for the pawn) 15 e5 left White slightly for choice with his bishops in T.Nabaty-K.Lerner, Israeli League 2008.

11 ♗h5!

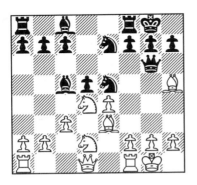

Again this active raid is the best way to prevent 11...♗h3 and poses problems.

11...♕d6

Keeping the queen centralized, but practice has also seen:

a) 11...♕b6? 12 b4 ♗xd4 13 ♗xd4 ♕d6 (or 13...♕e6 14 f4 ♘5c6 15 f5 with a strong initiative in O.Dancevski-C.Solinas, Jesolo 1999) 14 ♗c5! ♕d8 15 exd5 ♖e8 16 ♖e1 gave White a clear advantage in H.Stevic-D.Bubalovic, Belisce 1999.

b) 11...♕a6? 12 ♘f5 ♘xf5 13 ♗xc5 ♘d6 14 exd5 also left White somewhat for choice in P.Sedy-V.Koubek, Czech League 2006.

c) 11...♕f6 12 f4 ♘5c6 (stronger than 12...♘d3? 13 ♕b1!, E.Matsuura-

S.Pereira, Curitiba 1999, and the 12...♘c4? 13 ♘xc4 dxc4 14 ♕e2 of D.Pavasovic-M.Bosiocic, Trieste 2006, with a clear advantage for White in both cases, while 12...♘5g6 13 e5 ♕h4 14 g3 ♕h3 15 ♗f3 ♗b6 16 ♗g2 gave him an edge in D.Pavasovic-D.Jakovenko, Dresden 2007) 13 e5 ♕h6 14 ♘2b3! ♗xd4 15 cxd4 (one can also make a good case for 15 ♘xd4!? ♘xd4 16 ♗xd4) 15...♘f5 16 ♗d2 looks a little suspicious for White at first sight, with his queen tied down and d-pawn en prise.

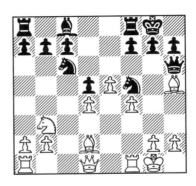

However, after Wells' 16...♘cxd4 17 ♘xd4 ♘xd4 18 f5 ♕b6 (or 18...♕a6 19 f6, beginning an attack) 19 ♗e3 c5 20 ♗xd4 cxd4 21 ♕d2 White is for choice and perhaps even clearly for choice following 21...d3+ 22 ♔h1 ♕d4 23 ♖ae1 in view of his much safer king. Thus in S.Rublevsky-Peng Xiaomin, Yerevan Olympiad 1996, Black tried 16...♕e6, but after 17 ♖f2! g6 (and not 17...♘cxd4? 18 g4) 18 ♗g4 White had managed to save his pawn while taking over the initiative.

12 f4 ♘5c6 13 e5 ♕h6

Black has also retreated down the d-file, but White retained an edge after 13...♕d8 14 ♘2b3 ♗b6 15 ♗f3 ♘xd4 16 cxd4 in I.Sofronie-C.Cozianu, Singeorz 1993, and with 13...♕d7 14 ♘2b3 ♗xd4 15 ♘xd4 in P.Charbonneau-E.Cormos, Quebec 2000.

14 ♘2b3 ♗b6

White also enjoys a small but clear pull after 14...♗xd4 15 ♘xd4 ♘xd4 (15...♘xe5?! makes use of the pin down the c1-h6 diagonal, but after 16 ♘b5 White will at least regain his pawn while maintaining the upper hand) 16 ♗xd4.

15 ♕e2! ♘f5 16 ♘xf5 ♗xf5 17 ♘d4

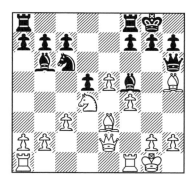

We've followed the game S.Movsesian-E.Bacrot, Kemer 2007, in which Black, under pressure, blundered a pawn with 17...♗d3? 18 ♗xf7+. However, 17...♘xd4 18 cxd4 would have left White clearly better thanks to his strong centre and kingside possibilities, while 17...♗xd4 18 cxd4 ♘b4 gives White a pleasant choice between 19 ♖ad1 ♗d3 20 ♖xd3 ♘xd3 21 f5 ♕a6 22 f6 (Movsesian) with a dangerous attack

and 19 ♗f3!? ♗d3 20 ♕d2 ♗xf1 21 ♕xb4 ♗a6 22 ♗xd5 with the bishop-pair, a dominating centre and more than enough for the exchange.

D223) 9...d6

Having seen that ideas with an early ...d5 don't really work for Black, it's not a surprise that the sensible text move has evolved into his main choice.

In this important tabiya White must decide how energetic he's feeling:

> **D2231: 10 f3**
> **D2232: 10 ♔h1**
> **D2233: 10 f4**

Those are White's three main moves, although perhaps unsurprisingly practice has also seen a fair bit of the alternatives:

a) 10 ♘b5?! tries to seize the initiative, but after 10...♗h3! 11 ♗f3 Black's king will reach safety and, indeed, he has a pleasant choice here: 11...0-0-0 12 ♘d4 (as played in D.Eschbach-G.Tammert, German League 1997; otherwise, 12 ♕e2? ♘xf3+ 13 ♕xf3 ♗g4 14 ♕f4 ♗e2 costs White material) 12...f5 gives Black a strong kingside initiative and 11...0-0!? 12 ♘xc7 (12 ♗xc5 dxc5 13 ♘xc7 ♖ad8 14 ♘d5 ♘xd5 15 exd5 ♘xf3+ 16 ♕xf3 ♗g4 was quite good for Black in J.Baeza Escudero-D.Franco Rincon, Collado Villalba 2009) 12...♗xe3 13 fxe3 ♖ac8 looks like pretty good value for a pawn.

b) 10 ♘d2?! works well when Black has castled, but here his light-squared bishop can move and 10...♗h3 11 ♗f3 0-0 leaves White on the back foot:

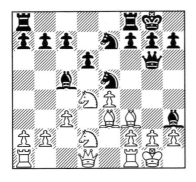

b1) 12 ♘c2 f5 13 ♔h1 ♘xf3 14 ♕xf3 ♗g4 gave Black an edge with his bishop-pair in H.Contreras Rodriguez-M.Lacrosse, Benidorm 2002.

b2) 12 b4 ♗b6 13 ♘c2 f5 14 ♗xb6 axb6 also leaves Black for choice, B.Nuber-M.Dapprich, Kelheim 2007.

b3) 12 ♔h1 is likely White's best move, but is quite well met by 12...♘xf3 13 ♕xf3 ♗g4 (or 13...♗d7!? when 14 ♕g3 ♕xg3 15 hxg3 f5 16 ♖fe1 fxe4 17 ♘xe4 was seen in A.Hadzipasic-M.Bosiocic, Rabac 2003, where 17...♗b6

would have retained an edge; here White has also tried some other 14th moves, but after, for example, 14 b4 ♗b6 15 a4 a5! 16 b5 Black could have seized the initiative in K.Ogonowska-M.Chrzaszcz, Sielpa 2004, with 16...d5) 14 ♕g3 ♗d7 15 ♕h4 ♖ae8 16 ♖ae1, as in G.Kovacs-Z.Gyimesi, Budapest 1993, where 16...f5 would again have left Black with the initiative.

c) 10 ♖e1 ♗h3! (10...♕xe4 is still quite a risky grab and 11 ♘d2 ♕g6 12 ♗h5 gives White the initiative) 11 ♗f1 ♗g4 12 ♗e2 ♗h3 13 ♗f1 ♗g4 clearly gave Black no problems whatsoever in A.Rios-F.De la Paz Perdomo, Barbera del Valles 2004.

d) 10 ♗f3 ♘xf3+ 11 ♕xf3 ♗g4 12 ♕f4 0-0 13 ♘d2 ♖fe8 was pretty comfortable for Black in D.Fernandes-M.Coimbra, Lisbon 1998.

e) 10 ♗h5 works after 9...d5, but here Black's e5-knight and dark-squared bishop are much better defended, so he should go in for 10...♕xe4.

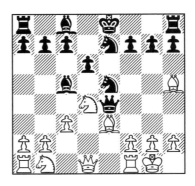

White's best try is 11 ♘d2 (otherwise, 11 ♗g5? ♗g4! 12 ♕a4+ ♗d7 13

♕d1 ♗c6 left Black doing rather well in J.Paszler-P.Acs, Hungarian League 1994, and 11 ♖e1 ♕h4 12 g3 ♕h3 13 ♗g5 ♗e6 14 ♗xe7 ♔xe7 15 f4 g6 saw White coming up slightly short in R.Vevera-V.Koubek, Klatovy 2002) 11...♕h4!? (Black might well prefer to repeat moves with 11...♕d3 12 ♗e2 ♕g6 13 ♗h5 ♕d3 and it's not at all easy for White to improve over this sequence: for example, 13 ♘b5? ♗h3 14 ♗f3 ♗xe3 15 fxe3 0-0-0! is somewhat better for Black and, a move earlier, 12 ♖e1 0-0 13 ♗e2 ♕g6 14 ♗h5 ♗g4!? gives Black the initiative) 12 ♘b5 when he obtains enough play for the pawn:

e1) 12...♗xe3!? 13 ♘xc7+ (13 fxe3?! ♔d8! 14 ♖f4 ♕g5 didn't give White quite enough compensation in G.Chandanani-G.Joshi, Calcutta 2000) 13...♔d8 14 ♘xa8 ♗g4 is pretty unclear, although one would be surprised if Black was worse after, say, 15 ♗xg4 ♘xg4 16 ♘f3 ♗xf2+ 17 ♔h1 ♕h6.

e2) 12...0-0 13 ♗xc5 dxc5 returns the pawn, but gives Black chances to seize the initiative.

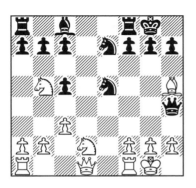

That said, with 14 ♘xc7 (otherwise, 14 ♖e1?! ♗g4 didn't help in B.Werner-I.Ibragimov, Reykjavik 1994, and 14 ♕e2 ♘7c6 15 ♘xc7 ♖b8 16 f4 ♘g4 17 ♗xg4 ♗xg4 18 ♘f3 ♕d8 also turned out slightly in Black's favour in G.De Vita-F.Ferretti, Verona 1997) 14...♖b8 15 ♖e1 ♗g4 16 f3 ♕xh5 17 fxg4 ♕g5 White was able to maintain equality, S.Huguet-M.Sanchez, Mislata 2008.

D2231) 10 f3

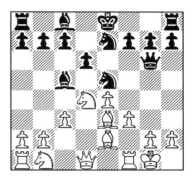

White defends his e-pawn and is happy to play to slowly improve his position.

10...0-0

Invariably played, although Black might consider 10...d5!? when 11 ♘d2 (11 ♔h1 dxe4 12 fxe4 was preferred in G.Buchicchio-S.Brunello, Porto San Giorgio 2004, but now Black might have seized a small initiative with 12...♗h3! 13 ♗f3 ♘xf3 14 ♕xf3 ♗g4) 11...0-0 doesn't seem to leave White with anything better than 12 ♔h1, taking play into note 'c' to Black's 11th move, below.

11 ♘d2

White develops his last minor piece, but this is by no means his only option:

a) 11 ♔h1 is quite a common alternative:

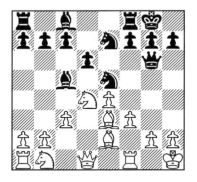

a1) Play often transposes to our main line after 11...♗b6 12 ♘d2. Here White has also tried 12 a4, but after 12...♘5c6 (12...c6!? 13 ♘d2 d5 is a decent alternative and after 14 a5 ♗c7 15 ♗g1 dxe4 16 fxe4 ♗g4 Black had clearly solved all his problems in T.Nedev-J.Lautier, Ohrid 2001) 13 ♘a3 (White might explore 13 ♘d2 f5 14 b4!? when 14...d5!? looks like the critical response, whereas fxe4 15 ♕b3+ ♔h8 16 fxe4 ♗g4 17 ♗xg4 ♕xg4 18 a5 turned out slightly in White's favour in R.Zelcic-Z.Gyimesi, Banja Vrucica 2009) 13...f5 14 ♘ab5 fxe4 15 fxe4 ♖xf1+ 16 ♕xf1 ♗d7 17 ♗c4+ ♔h8 Black was fine in Wang Hao-A.Beliavsky, Amsterdam 2006.

a2) 11...f5!? 12 exf5 (Black is okay after 12 f4 ♘g4 13 ♗xg4 ♕xg4 14 ♕xg4 fxg4, as in J.Zezulkin-S.Fedorchuk, Ustron 2004, since White's centre can't really advance, while 12 ♘d2 will be seen by transposition in note 'b' to Black's 11th move in our main line) 12...♗xf5!? (likely even stronger than 12...♘xf5 13 ♘xf5 ♕xf5 14 ♗xc5 dxc5 15 ♕d5+ ♘f7 which equalized in H.Tikir-E.Thorfinnsdottir, Kemer 2007) 13 ♘xf5 (13 ♘d2 ♗xd4! 14 ♗xd4 ♗c2 is a little awkward for White) 13...♘xf5 14 ♗xc5 dxc5 favoured Black with his active knights, if anyone, in A.Areshchenko-V.Rogovski, Simferopol 2003.

a3) After 11...d5 White can take play into note 'c' to Black's 11th move in our main line with 12 ♘d2, but here he also has 12 f4!?:

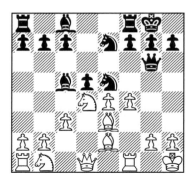

a31) 12...♕xe4 is risky: 13 b4! ♗b6 (13...♕xe3?! 14 bxc5 b6?! 15 cxb6 was pretty good for White in F.Amonatov-A.Aleksandrov, Zvenigorod 2008, and here 14...f6 15 fxe5 fxe5 16 ♖xf8+ ♔xf8 must also favour him, as pointed out by Mikhalevski) 14 ♗g1! ♕h3 15 ♖f2 ♗xd4 16 cxd4 ♘g4 17 ♖f3 saw the complications favour White slightly in E.Najer-A.Naiditsch, Kallithea 2008.

a32) 12...♘g4! 13 ♗g1 ♗xd4 14 f5! ♕g5 was seen in S.Movsesian-P.Eljanov, Sarajevo 2009, and now 15 ♕xd4 dxe4 16 ♕xe4 ♘f6!? 17 ♕xe7 ♖e8 18 ♕xc7 ♖xe2 19 ♖f2! ♖e8 20 ♘d2 ♗xf5 21 ♕xb7 ♖ad8 22 ♘f3 ♕h5 (Mikhalevski) leaves Black quite active and with play for the pawn.

b) 11 ♘c2 ♗h3! 12 ♖f2 ♖ad8 13 b4 ♗xe3 14 ♘xe3 ♗e6 followed by ...f5 was comfortable for Black in M.Quast-S.Galdunts, German League 1998, and in general after 10 f3 White should be trying to maintain the tension, not allowing too many early exchanges.

c) 11 c4 ♗e6 12 b3 ♕f6! 13 ♕d2 ♘5c6 14 ♘c2 ♘b4 15 ♘ba3 was seen in I.Hakki-P.Harikrishna, Abu Dhabi 2004, and now 15...♘ec6 would have kept Black's early initiative going.

Returning to 11 ♘d2:

11...♗b6!

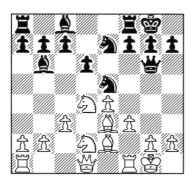

Black's safest approach, retreating his bishop to a secure square while keeping all his options open, but again there are alternatives:

a) 11...c6!? 12 ♔h1 (White can change gear, but 12 f4 ♘g4 13 f5 ♘xe3 14 fxg6 ♘xd1 15 gxh7+ ♔xh7 failed to trouble Black in L.Bravo-C.Fonseca, Cali 2008) 12...f5 13 f4 was seen in M.Narciso Dublan-E.Janev, Barbera del Valles 2005, and now 13...♘g4 14 ♗xg4 ♕xg4 would likely have been fine for Black.

b) The immediate 11...f5!? also deserves further attention and after 12 exf5 (otherwise, 12 ♘xf5? ♗xf5 13 ♗xc5 fails to 13...♗h3, while 12 ♔h1 can be met by 12...f4!? or 12...fxe4 13 ♕b3+ ♕f7 14 ♘xe4 ♗b6 15 f4 and now in S.Movsesian-K.Georgiev, Bled Olympiad 2002, Black could have equalized with 15...♕xb3 16 axb3 ♘5g6 followed by ...d5) 12...♘xf5 (12...♗xf5?! doesn't work so well here on account of 13 ♘xf5 ♘xf5 14 ♗xc5 dxc5 15 ♕b3+!) Black is contesting the key central squares.

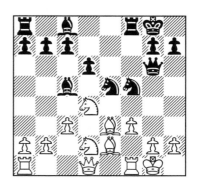

Indeed, it's surprising that this simple approach hasn't been seen more and 13 ♘xf5 ♗xf5 14 ♗xc5 dxc5 15 ♕b3+ ♕f7 saw Black's slightly more active pieces offset the doubled pawns in S.Bogatyrev-K.Bryzgalin, Kolontaevo 1998.

c) 11...d5 is a much more common alternative and after 12 ♘d2 Black must decide whether to take action in the centre or to continue waiting:

c1) 12...dxe4 13 fxe4 (several tests have shown 13 ♘xe4 ♘d5! to be fine for Black) 13...♗g4! (by no means Black's only approach, but it makes a lot of sense to simplify) 14 ♗f4 (White must avoid 14 ♘f5?? ♘xf5 15 exf5 on account of 15...♕h5 and 14 ♗f3?! ♖ad8 15 ♕e2 ♘7c6 saw Black exerting a bit of pressure in K.Van der Weide-T.Nyback, Dresden 2007; a better alternative is 14 h3, after which 14...♗xe2 15 ♕xe2 ♖ae8 16 b4 ♗b6 17 a4 c5 was balanced in P.Charbonneau-M.Adams, British League 2005) and then:

c11) 14...♗xe2 15 ♕xe2 ♗d6 is very solid for Black and after 16 ♖ad1 ♖ae8 17 ♗xe5 (Rublevsky had earlier failed to achieve anything with 17 ♕b5 ♘g4 18 e5 c6 19 ♕xb7 ♗xe5 in S.Rublevsky-E.Najer, Warsaw 2005, and with 17 ♗g3 a6 18 ♘2b3 b5 in S.Rublevsky-M.Kobalia, Kazan 2005) 17...♗xe5 18 ♕b5 ♗xd4 19 cxd4 ♕b6 20 ♕d3 ♕xb2

21 ♖b1 ♕xa2 22 ♖xb7 f5! 23 e5 ♘d5 24 ♘b3 ♖f7 he was fine in S.Rublevsky-K.Georgiev, Saint Vincent 2005.

c12) However, 14...♗d6 is probably less effective on account of 15 ♗xg4! (by no means invariably played, but best) 15...♘xg4 16 ♘f5 ♖fe8 17 ♘xd6 cxd6, as in Wang Yu-Zhao Xue, Beijing 2005, and then 18 ♕b3 with a small pull.

c2) 12...♗b6 13 a4! (alternatively, 13 ♗f4 ♕f6 14 ♗g3 c5 15 ♘c2 ♖d8 16 ♕e1 ♘5g6 was fine for Black in J.Hector-G.Sargissian, Bled Olympiad 2002, but the other queenside probe, 13 b4!?, deserves attention; then Black may do best with 13...a5 14 b5 ♗d7, since 13...dxe4 14 fxe4 ♗g4 15 ♗f4 ♗xe2 16 ♕xe2 ♘7c6 17 ♘xc6 ♘xc6 18 a4 a5 19 b5 ♘d8 20 ♘c4 gave White a little something in F.Amonatov-L.Lenic, Moscow 2010) 13...a5 14 ♗f4 ♕f6 15 ♗g3 ♘5g6 16 exd5! (stronger than 16 ♘2b3 ♘f4 17 ♕d2 ♘xe2 18 ♕xe2 ♗d7 which was about equal in T.Nedev-N.Mitkov, Stip 2002) 16...♘xd5 (16...♗xd4? ran into 17 ♘e4 ♕b6 18 ♗xc7 ♕xc7 19 d6 with some advantage in T.Nedev-D.Arngrimsson, Novi Sad 2009) 17 ♘e4 leaves White with a small initiative, M.Heika-C.Eichler, German League 2007.

Finally we can return to 11...♗b6:

12 ♔h1

Again we see White making this useful move. He has also tried 12 ♘c4 ♘xc4 13 ♗xc4 which removes Black's well-placed knight from e5 and pins the f-pawn.

However, that pawn is easily un-pinned with 13...♔h8 and after 14 ♕d2 f5 15 ♗d3 (Black was okay too after 15 ♖ae1 fxe4 16 fxe4 ♗d7 in D.Pavasovic-I.Ibragimov, Bled 1996) 15...♕f7 16 a4 f4 17 ♗f2 a5 Black was fine in J.Van Rosmalen-Y.Gorter, Leiden 2007.

12...f5!

Once again Black frees his position with this tempting break.

13 f4!?

White hopes to pose at least a few problems with this. Instead 13 exf5 ♘xf5 14 ♘xf5 ♗xf5 15 ♘c4 ♘xc4 16 ♗c4 saw the exchanges give Black full equality in S.Maze-E.Tomashevsky, Budva 2009.

13...♘5c6

Black's main move, but he can also consider 13...♘g4!? 14 ♗xg4 (14 exf5 ♘xf5 15 ♘xf5 ♗xf5 favoured Black if anyone in M.Zuberec-V.Marman, Slovakia League 2001) 14...♕xg4 (but not 14...fxg4? 15 f5) 15 ♕xg4 fxg4 which was very solid for him in D.Roberts-R.James, Exmouth 2007.

14 ♘xc6

Otherwise, 14 exf5 ♘xf5 15 ♘xf5 ♗xf5 16 ♗xb6 axb6, as in J.Ruano Marco-S.Roa Alonso, Madrid 2005, just leads to drawish exchanges once again, while after 14 ♗d3 ♗xd4 15 ♗xd4 in R.Zelcic-L.Schandorff, Heraklion 2007, Black could have equalized with 15...fxe4 16 ♗xe4 ♕f7.

14...♘xc6 15 ♗xb6 axb6

White's set-up isn't particularly challenging here and both 16 ♗f3 ♗d7 17 ♕c2 fxe4 18 ♗xe4 ♗f5 in A.Bodnaruk-N.Kosintseva, Moscow 2008, and the 16 ♗d3 fxe4 17 ♗xe4 ♗f5 of D.Pavasovic-J.Borisek, Murska Sobota 2008, failed to pose Black any real questions.

D2232) 10 ♔h1

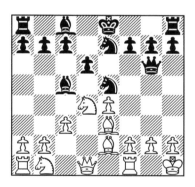

White sidesteps the threat of 10...♗h3 and prepares to push Black back with f4, but this does, of course, entail a pawn sacrifice.

10...♕xe4!

Acceptance must be critical, although by no means everyone has been so keen to accept:

a) 10...c6?! 11 ♘d2 (11 f4!? may be even stronger and 11...♕xe4 12 ♗g1 ♗h3 13 ♖f2 is certainly somewhat in White's favour) 11...0-0 12 ♗h5 ♕f6 was seen in M.Ostojic-Z.Maslov, Pula 2002, and now 13 f4 sees White expanding with an ideal set-up.

b) 10...a6?! is also quite well met by 11 f4! and after 11...♕xe4 12 ♘d2 ♕xe3 13 ♘c2 ♘g4 14 ♘xe3 ♘xe3 15 ♕e1 ♘c2 16 ♕g3 ♘xa1 17 ♕xg7 ♖g8 18 ♕h6 Black is worse, despite having three pieces for the queen, since ♘e4 is on its way.

c) After 10...♗g4?! 11 f3 ♗d7, as in R.Pokorna-F.Steil Antoni, Dresden 2008, White can go 12 a4 a6 13 f4, with an edge.

d) 10...♘g4 makes a fair degree of sense, trying to hunt down the bishop-pair:

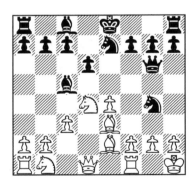

d1) 11 ♗xg4 ♗xg4 12 f3 ♗d7 13 ♘d2 (Black was okay too after 13 c4 0-0 14 ♘c3 ♖ae8 15 ♕d2 a6 in D.Pavasovic-K.Georgiev, Sibenik 2006) 13...0-0 14 ♕b3 ♗b6 is very solid for Black who can meet both 15 ♘c4 and 15 f4 (R.Zelcic-

L.Fressinet, Cannes 2006) with 15...♘c6.

d2) However, White can preserve his dark-squared bishop and after 11 ♗c1! ♘f6? 12 ♘b5 Black finds himself in trouble once again on c7. Better is 11...♗d7, although after 12 b4 (but not the 12 f4?! h5! of S.Rublevsky-B.Macieja, Polanica Zdroj 1998, when 13 b4 ♗b6 would have left Black with the initiative) 12...♗b6 13 f3 ♘f6 14 ♘d2 White must be slightly for choice.

e) A popular choice is 10...0-0 and:

e1) 11 f3 transposes to note 'a' to White's 11th move in Line D2231.

e2) 11 ♘b5?! c6 12 ♗xc5 dxc5 13 ♘d6 ♖d8 gave Black the initiative down the d-file in O.Centeno-N.Mitkov, Alajuela 2006.

e3) 11 ♘d2 has been quite topical of late and after 11...♘g4 (but not 11...d5? 12 ♘f5! ♘xf5 13 ♗xc5 and White won material in A.Naiditsch-D.Jakovenko, Odessa (rapid) 2009, while 11...f5?! 12 ♗h5 ♕f6 13 exf5 should be slightly better for White) 12 ♗f4 ♘c6 (this may not be best; instead 12...f5!? 13 f3 ♘e5 14 ♘2b3 ♗b6 seemed okay for Black in B.Smieszniak-J.Tobolski, Leba 2008, and 12...♘f6 13 ♗d3 ♕g4! 14 ♕xg4 ♘xg4 was too in P.Svidler-V.Arkhipov, Elista 1994) 13 f3 ♘ge5 (perhaps Black does better with 13...♘f6, although 14 ♘2b3 ♗b6 15 a4! secured a pull in T.Thiel-I.Semenova, Balatonbereny 1994) 14 ♗e3! (14 ♘xc6 ♘xc6 seems fine for Black) 14...♗b6 15 f4 White began to expand in D.Howell-T.Nyback, Wijk aan Zee 2010.

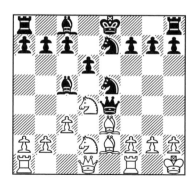

White's strong centre leaves him somewhat for choice here and after 15...♘xd4 16 cxd4 ♘c6 Howell broke through with 17 f5! ♕f6 18 e5! dxe5 19 ♘e4, thereby obtaining a very strong attack.

e4) 11 f4! ♘g4 (again after 11...♕xe4?! 12 ♘d2 ♕xe3 13 ♘c2! Black is forced to give up his queen and following 13...♘g4 14 ♘xe3 ♘xe3 15 ♕a4! ♘xf1 16 ♖xf1 practice has shown White's chances to be slightly superior and here, for example, 16...d5 17 ♗d3 ♗f5 18 ♕c2 forced a favourable trade in S.Ganguly-G.Joshi, Calcutta 2000) 12 ♗g1 ♘f6 (the prudent choice, but strangely Black has preferred 12...f5?? in practice and after 13 exf5 ♘xf5 14 ♗xg4 ♘g3+ 15 hxg3 ♗xg4 16 ♕b3+ ♔h8 17 ♘d2 ♖ae8 18 ♖fe1 White was just a piece up in C.Vitoux-N.Saez, Calvi 2005) 13 ♘d2 sees White keeping control of his centre and so leaves him slightly for choice.

We now return to the critical pawn grab:

11 ♘d2

11...♕g6

Black has also gone 11...♕h4, but after 12 ♘2f3! (better than 12 ♘b5 0-0 13 ♘xc7 ♖b8 14 ♗xc5 dxc5 which was fine for Black in E.Can-E.Musakaev, Herceg Novi 2006) 12...♘xf3 13 ♘xf3 ♕g4 (and not 13...♕h5?? 14 ♘g5, while 13...♕f6 14 ♗g5 ♕f5 15 ♗d3 ♕d7 16 ♖e1 f6 17 ♗e3 left Black tied up and White with promising compensation in R.Zelcic-K.Georgiev, Kusadasi 2006) 14 ♘g5 ♕f5 15 ♗d3 White had the initiative and decent compensation in N.Fercec-D.Bubalovic, Bizovac 2000.

12 ♘b5

Going after c7. The alternative is 12 ♗h5, but 12...♗g4!? (12...♕d3 13 ♗e2 ♕g6 has led to an early draw in a number of games) 13 ♗xg6 (13 ♕a4+ ♗d7 14 ♕d1 ♗g4 is another repetition) 13...♗xd1 14 ♗xf7+ ♔xf7 15 ♖axd1 ♗xd4 16 ♗xd4 ♘5c6 gives Black solid equality, G.Batista-G.Frederico, Passos 2007.

12...0-0!

Black should return the pawn. Indeed, 12...♗xe3? 13 ♘xc7+ ♔d8 14

♘xa8 seems to be too risky for him with 14...♗f4 15 ♘f3 ♗d7 16 g3! ♗h6 17 ♘xe5 dxe5 18 ♗b5 somewhat in White's favour despite the cornered knight.

13 ♘xc7 ♖b8

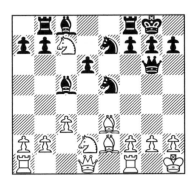

14 ♗f4

White has also investigated a couple of alternatives in his so far generally unsuccessful quest for an advantage:

a) 14 ♗h5!? ♕f5! (but not here 14...♕d3?! because of 15 ♖e1! when 15...♘7c6 16 ♘e4! ♕xe4 17 ♗xc5 favoured White in Ni Hua-A.Kunte, Cebu City 2007) 15 f4 has been quite topical of late:

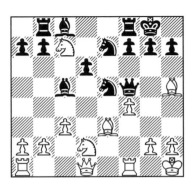

a1) 15...♘g4 16 ♗xg4 ♕xg4 17 ♕xg4 ♗xg4 18 ♖ae1 left White with a small initiative and the better pawn structure in D.Pavasovic-T.Sakelsek, Ljubljana 2007.

a2) 15...♘5c6 16 ♘c4 b5!? (more uncompromising and likely stronger than 16...♗e6 17 ♘xe6 ♕xe6 18 ♕e2 g6 19 ♗xc5 ♕xe2 20 ♗xe2 dxc5 21 ♖ad1 which gave White an edge in V.Laznicka-K.Georgiev, Heraklion 2007) 17 ♗xc5 bxc4 18 ♗xd6 ♖d8 gave Black full compensation for the pawn, with White's pieces far from well coordinated in S.Rublevsky-I.Khenkin, Dagomys 2008.

a3) 15...♗xe3 16 fxe5 ♕xe5 17 ♘c4 ♕c5 18 ♘xe3 ♕xc7 (better than 18...♕xe3?! 19 ♖e1 ♕g5 20 ♕xd6 ♕xh5 21 ♖xe7 when White was pretty active in S.Movsesian-A.Grischuk, Kemer 2007) 19 ♗xf7+!? ♖xf7 20 ♖xf7 ♔xf7 21 ♕h5+ g6 22 ♕xh7+ ♔e8 23 ♖e1 gave White enough for the piece, but probably no more than that in B.Jobava-S.Movsesian, Pamplona 2007.

a4) 15...♘d3 16 ♕e2 ♘xb2!? (more critical than 16...♗xe3 17 ♕xe3 ♕xh5 18 ♕xd3 ♕c5 19 ♘b5 ♗f5 20 ♕e2 ♘d5 21 ♖ae1 which was perhaps a touch better for White in S.Haslinger-L.Johannessen, German League 2010) 17 ♗xc5 dxc5 was pretty unclear in D.Pavasovic-L.Mazi, Trieste 2007.

b) 14 ♘c4 is fairly well met by 14...♗h3! and after 15 ♖g1 ♘xc4 16 ♗xc5 (the best way to simplify, as 16 ♗xc4 ♗xe3 17 fxe3 ♗f5 left Black with a small initiative in S.Ganguly-A.Khalifman, Moscow 2001) 16...dxc5 17 ♗xc4 ♕b6 18 ♘d5 ♘xd5 19 ♗xd5 ♗e6 the position is equal, as noted by Mikhalevski.

14...♗d7!

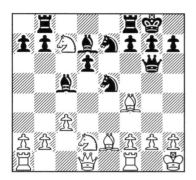

This seems quite promising, although 14...♗f5 15 ♘b3 ♗b6 16 ♘b5 ♖bd8 also left Black with a small initiative in J.Lautier-P.Van der Sterren, Amsterdam 1994.

15 ♗g3

Safer is 15 ♘b3 ♗c6 16 ♗g3 ♗b6 (perhaps Black does even better with the 16...♘f5!? 17 ♘d5 ♖fe8 of R.Hasangatin-N.Maiorov, Pardubice 2001) 17 ♘b5 ♘f5, although Black must be slightly for choice here, in view of his somewhat more active pieces, L.Wely-J.Piket, 2nd matchgame, Monte Carlo 1997.

15...♗c6 16 ♘b5?

It still wasn't too late for 16 ♘b3, taking play into our last note.

16...♘f5 17 ♘b3

Hardly ideal, but 17 c4 ♘xg3+ 18 fxg3 ♘d3 would have been pretty good too for Black.

17...♗xf2!

This fine tactical blow exploited White's careless defence to leave him in serious trouble in D.Mussanti-F.Pierrot, Mar del Plata 2009.

D2233) 10 f4!?

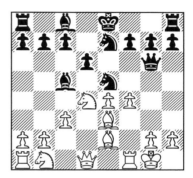

White's most aggressive continuation, driving the knight from e5 at the cost of a pawn.

10...♕xe4

This must be critical and has been Black's most popular choice by some margin, but the alternatives are quite sharp and deserve further attention:

a) 10...♘g4 11 ♗c1! (otherwise, 11 f5?! ♘xe3 12 fxg6 ♘xd1 13 gxf7+ ♔f8 14 ♖xd1 ♔xf7 15 ♘d2 ♘c6 gave Black an edge in J.Tomczak-L.Lenic, Warsaw 2008, and 11 ♗xg4 ♕xg4 12 ♕d3 ♗d7, as in G.Vescovi-C.Oblitas Guerrero, Sao Paulo 2000, should be okay for Black after 13 ♘d2 0-0) 11...h5 (this may not be best and 11...f5!? 12 h3 h5! could do with some testing) 12 ♘a3! threatening 13 ♘ab5 should be slightly better for White and seems clearer than the

12 h3 ♘e5!? 13 f5 of P.Vas-O.Krivonosov, Gothenburg 2008, when 13...♘xf5! 14 exf5 ♗xf5 would have given Black decent play for the piece.

b) 10...♗h3!? 11 ♖f2! (White has also tried 11 ♗f3 ♘xf3+ 12 ♕xf3 ♗g4, but 13 f5 ♗xf3 14 fxg6 ♗xe4 15 gxf7+ ♔d7 was fine for Black in C.Kedziora-S.Galdunts, Sueder 1996, and 13 ♕f2 ♕xe4 14 ♘d2 ♕d3 didn't give White quite enough compensation in M.Brunello-D.Quinn, Glasgow 2008) 11...♕xe4 (but not 11...♘g4?? 12 f5 ♘xf2 which blundered the queen to 13 ♕a4+ in H.Silber-G.Voropaev, German League 2006) 12 ♕d2 ♘d5 13 fxe5 was seen in R.Crespo-A.Ramirez, Argentina 1996, and now Stohl has suggested that 13...♕xe3 is equal. The critical continuation runs 14 gxh3 dxe5 (14...♕xd2 15 ♘xd2 dxe5 16 ♘2b3 ♗b6 17 c4! must favour White) 15 ♕xe3 ♘xe3 16 ♘b3 ♗b6 17 ♔h1 when Black has the better structure, two good pawns and an active knight for the piece, but a piece is a piece and White certainly has chances to be better here.

11 ♗f2

Clearly the right retreat, as 11 ♗c1? ♗xd4+ 12 cxd4 ♘5c6 sees Black taking aim at d4 and must be pretty good for him.

11...♗xd4!

Black must simplify to buy his queen a retreat square. Otherwise:

a) 11...♘5c6? 12 ♗d3 ♕d5 gives White a couple of dangerous options as follows:

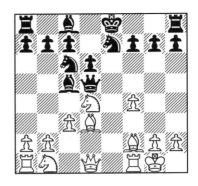

a1) 13 ♘b5? ♔d8 14 b4 ♗xf2+ 15 ♖xf2 ♗f5 with some advantage for Black was not the refutation in T.Deflesselle-M.Mancini, Paris 1999.

a2) The critical line is 13 c4 ♕xd4 14 ♗xd4 ♗xd4+ 15 ♖f2! (and not 15 ♔h1? ♗xb2 16 ♘d2 ♗xa1 17 ♕xa1 0-0 when Black had enough for the queen in M.Rev-M.Milicevic, Logrono 1998) 15...0-0 16 ♘c3 was at least slightly in White's favour, with queen against rook, knight and pawn in Y.Dembo-M.Mancini, Cappelle la Grande 2008.

a3) White may do even better with Stohl's idea of 13 ♖e1!? ♗d7 (13...0-0? fails to 14 ♘xc6 ♘xc6? 15 ♗xh7+ and 13...♗xd4 14 cxd4 followed by 15 ♘c3 gives White a pretty strong initiative) 14 ♗e4 ♕c4 15 ♘d2 ♕a6 16 ♗xc6 bxc6 17 ♘e4 which the Slovak Grandmaster and theoretician has unsurprisingly assessed as a clear advantage for White.

b) 11...♕xf4? 12 ♘b5 ♘g4 (as tried in G.Halvax-H.Knoll, Jenbach 2009; otherwise Black just loses a piece for nothing) 13 ♘xc7+ ♔d8 14 ♗xg4 ♗xg4 15

♕e1 costs Black material.

c) 11...♘5g6? 12 ♘d2 ♕xf4 13 ♘b5 was similarly rather effective in J.Tomczak-J.Kociscak, Kemer 2007.

d) 11...♘d7? 12 ♗d3 ♕d5 13 c4 (again 13 ♖e1!? is very much an option too) 13...♕xd4 14 ♗xd4 ♗xd4+ 15 ♖f2! ♘f6 16 h3 ♗xf2+ 17 ♔xf2 ♗e6 18 ♘c3 didn't give Black enough for the queen in F.Rinkewitz-E.Pilz, correspondence 2004.

12 cxd4

White should preserve his bishop, inactive though it may currently appear on f2. Instead 12 ♗xd4? ♘5c6! 13 ♘d2 ♕g6 fails to supply enough compensation.

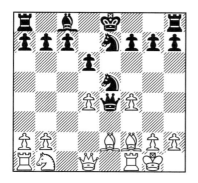

12...♘5g6!

Again Black must be quite accurate:

a) 12...♘5c6? 13 ♘c3! ♕xf4 (or 13...♕g6 14 d5! ♘b8 15 ♗h4 h5 16 ♖e1 with a crushing initiative in M.Müller-S.Kalinitschew, German League 2002) 14 d5 followed by ♘b5 is somewhat in White's favour, F.Helmond-V.Nowik, Goch 1993.

b) 12...♘d7?! 13 ♘c3 (one can also

make a good case for the simpler 13 ♕d2!?) 13...♕xf4 14 ♘b5 ♘d5 15 ♗f3 ♘7f6 16 ♖e1+ ♗e6 17 ♗g3 gave White at least enough compensation in D.Merlini-T.Andresen, correspondence 1997.

13 g3!

This calm approach has evolved into White's most promising. There has also been a fair amount of testing with 13 ♘c3, but after 13...♕xf4 14 ♘b5 0-0! 15 ♘xc7 ♖b8 Black is quite solid and should be fine:

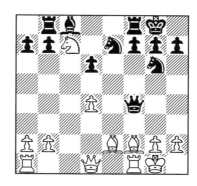

a) 16 ♘b5 ♘f5 (or 16...♗d7 17 ♘xa7 ♕g5 18 a4 ♘f5 19 ♔h1 ♖fe8 transposing to variation 'b') 17 ♘xa7 ♗d7 18 g3 ♕g5 19 ♕c1 ♕f6 20 ♕d2 ♖fe8 was about equal in J.Hinken-W.Schueler, correspondence 2007.

b) 16 ♔h1 ♕g5 17 ♘b5 ♘f5 18 ♘xa7 ♗d7 19 a4 ♖fe8 20 ♗b5 ♘gh4 was also fine for Black in R.Zelcic-D.Bubalovic, Zagreb 1993.

c) 16 d5?! b6! 17 ♘b5 ♕g5 18 ♘xa7 ♗b7! has turned out well for Black in a number of games with, for example, 19 ♘c6 ♘xc6 20 dxc6 ♗xc6 21 ♗g3 ♖be8 failing to give White enough for his pawn in R.Maur-S.Zielinski, correspondence 2005.

13...0-0

A very natural choice, but again there are alternatives and quite important ones at that:

a) 13...♗h3 14 ♗f3 ♕f5 15 ♖e1 sees White activating his bishop, while developing some pressure down the e-file:

a1) 15...0-0 16 ♗xb7 (J.Smeets-H.Koneru, Wijk aan Zee 2008) 16...♖ab8 17 ♗e4 regains the pawn with a pull.

a2) 15...c6 16 d5 ♕d7 (16...c5 was preferred in H.Namyslo-M.Plomp, correspondence 2000, and now White should consider 17 b4!? cxb4 18 ♕a4+ ♕d7 19 ♕xb4 0-0 20 ♘a3, retaining the initiative) 17 ♘c3 0-0 18 dxc6 bxc6 19 ♘e4 gave White good play for the pawn in H.Namyslo-D.Gutsche, correspondence 2001.

a3) 15...d5 16 ♘c3! (stronger than 16 ♕b3 0-0 17 ♘c3 ♗g4! 18 ♗xd5 ♘xd5 19 ♕xd5 ♕xd5 20 ♘xd5 c6 which returned the pawn for full equality in B.Macieja-L.Johannessen, Novi Sad 2009) 16...c6 17 b4! gave White full compensation for the pawn, but was agreed drawn here in S.Brunello-I.Naumkin, Montecatini Terme 2006. I (YD) preferred to continue in Y.Dembo-P.Papp, Rijeka 2010, where matters were quite unclear after 17...h5 18 ♕e2 ♗g4 19 ♘d1 ♗xf3 20 ♕xf3 0-0-0 21 b5 until Black allowed me to begin to take control with 21...h4? 22 g4 ♕f6 23 f5!.

b) 13...♘xf4!? 14 gxf4 ♗h3 is suggested by the computer and could do with a test, although after 15 ♗f3 ♕g6+ 16 ♔h1 ♗xf1 17 ♕xf1 0-0 18 ♘c3 White should be slightly for choice with his bishops and active pieces in general.

c) 13...c6 14 ♘c3 ♕f5 15 ♗d3 ♕a5 16 a3! followed by b4 gave White good compensation right across the board in R.Biros-R.Lukac, Slovakian League 2006.

d) 13...♕f5!? has been explored a little of late and after 14 ♘c3 d5 15 ♗f3 (15 h4 h5 16 ♖e1 c6 17 ♗d3 ♕f6 18 ♗e2 ♔f8!? 19 ♗xh5 ♘f5 gave Black good counterplay in R.Mamedov-A.Naiditsch, Moscow 2010) 15...c6 16 ♖e1 h5 17 h4 ♕h3 18 ♗g2 ♕g4 19 ♕d2 ♗e6 chances were about equal in A.Areshchenko-L.Lenic, Rijeka 2010.

14 ♘c3 ♕f5 15 d5!

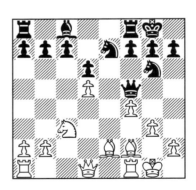

Beginning to cramp Black.

15...a6

Black's pieces are a little jumbled up and he has also tried to coordinate them with:

a) 15...♕d7 16 h4! h6 17 h5 ♘h8 18

♖e1 entombed Black's knight and gave White promising compensation in S.Brunello-I.Naumkin, Verona 2006.

b) 15...♗d7 16 ♖e1 ♖fe8 17 ♖c1 a6 18 ♗f3 ♖ac8 19 a4 (White can also play on the other flank and 19 h4!? h6 20 h5 ♘xf4!? 21 gxf4 ♕xf4 22 ♖e4 ♕g5+ 23 ♔h1 ♘f5 24 ♕g1 leaves him slightly for choice, as analysed by Stohl) 19...♔f8 20 a5 saw White calmly increasing the pressure with the upper hand, since it wasn't so easy for Black to free himself in S.Ganguly-P.Acs, Paks 2009.

c) 15...♖d8 16 ♗f3 ♗d7 (Black preferred 16...c5?! in Y.Dembo-A.Stefanova, Solin 2007, but now 17 h4! ♗d7 18 ♖e1 would have been pretty good for White) 17 ♖e1 (Stohl) keeps Black tied up and so White maintains at least full compensation, while enjoying the easier-to-play position.

16 ♖e1 ♔h8

A little slow and Black may do better with either 16...b6 or Mikhalevski's 16...♖e8 17 ♖c1 b5!?, thereby obtaining some counterplay.

17 ♖c1 ♗d7 18 ♗f3 ♖ac8 19 ♕b3

We've followed no less a game than M.Carlsen-P.Leko, Nanjing 2009, in which White kept increasing the pressure and went on to achieve a crushing positional victory.

Conclusion

7 ♗c4 remains a critical test of Black's fairly ambitious approach with 5...♕f6 6 c3 ♘ge7. In this millennium 7...b6!? has been quite popular when 8 0-0 ♗b7 9 ♘b5 looks like the critical line and may be why Black has begun to prefer the closely-related 7...0-0 8 0-0 b6!? of late. That's currently in pretty good health and neither is it at all easy for White to crack the solid 8...♗b6.

Black's main response remains 7...♘e5 when after 8 ♗e2 ideas with an early ...d5 fail to convince. Instead Black should go in for the key tabiya which arises after 8...♕g6 9 0-0 d6 where 10 f3 gives rise to a manoeuvring struggle in which Black should be able to maintain a rough balance, whether he opts for an early ...d5 or ...f5. Thus of late White has often preferred more vigorous measures, but 10 ♔h1 likely doesn't lead anywhere unless White comes up with some new ideas in the critical note 'a' to his 14th move in Line D2232. However, it looks like 10 f4!? will continue to attract adherents, following in Carlsen's footsteps. The main line there gives White an easy-to-handle set-up and good compensation, but Black may do better with the alternatives on his 13th move.

Chapter Ten
The 4...♗c5 Variation: Early Alternatives

1 e4 e5 2 ♘f3 ♘c6 3 d4 exd4 4 ♘xd4 ♗c5

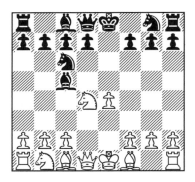

Having examined White's two main continuations, we now turn our attention to the remaining less-popular and generally less-critical ways to deal with the early attack on his knight.

> **A: 5 ♘f5**
> **B: 5 ♘b3**

Line A has aggressive intent, but backfires in the face of forceful play from Black. However, Line B has recently received some attention thanks to an aggressive new plan championed by Magnus Carlsen.

Otherwise, 5 ♘f3 ♘f6 6 ♗d3 (and not 6 e5? ♘g4 with a double-attack) 6...0-0 7 0-0 already allows Black at least full equality with 7...d5, as does 5 c3?! ♘f6 6 ♘xc6 bxc6 7 ♗d3 (O.Ottesen-R.Berg, Reykjavik 2009) 7...d5.

A) 5 ♘f5?! d5!

This powerful pawn sacrifice has pretty much consigned White's aggressive approach to the bin.

6 ♘xg7+

Neither does declining the pawn help White, as Black also obtains the initiative after both 6 exd5 ♗xf5 7 ♕e2+ ♘ge7 8 dxc6 bxc6 and 6 ♘c3 ♗xf5 7 exf5 ♕e7+ 8 ♗e2 0-0-0.

6...♚f8

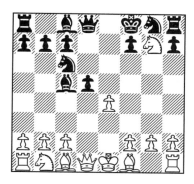

7 ♘h5

The best try, especially as 7 exd5?? ♚xg7 8 dxc6 ♝xf2+! forced an embarrassing early resignation in R.Bana-G.Olarasu, Varna 1994, and 7 ♘f5? ♝xf5 8 exf5 ♛h4 is also best avoided: for example, 9 ♛f3 (or 9 ♛d2 ♜e8+ 10 ♚d1 ♝xf2 11 ♝e2 and now in P.Dukaczewski-M.Sakic, Ustron 1994, 11...♝e3 would have left Black firmly in the driving seat) 9...♜e8+ 10 ♚d1 ♘f6 11 g3 was O.Castro Rojas-G.Garcia, Bogota 1986, in which it's hard to believe that White would have survived after 11...♛d4+.

7...♛h4! 8 ♘g3 ♘f6!

While White has spent six tempi moving his knight around, Black has developed his queen and minor pieces to very active squares, thereby already giving him a highly-dangerous initiative.

9 ♝e2

Wisely directed against the threat of 9...♘g4 and once again White has hardly prospered with the alternatives:

a) 9 exd5? ♝g4 10 f3 ♜e8+ 11 ♝e2 ♘d4 12 ♘c3 ♝xf3! saw White being crushed in the old game J.Minchin-W.Wayte, London 1900.

b) The desperate counter-gambit 9 b4? was tried in J.Bauma-P.Zvara, Czech League 2007, but after just 9...♘xb4 Black's initiative has scarcely been diminished.

9...dxe4!

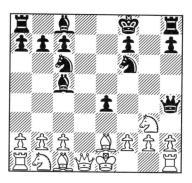

The simplest reaction, regaining the pawn and preparing to occupy the d-file. Unsurprisingly Black has scored well from here in practice, with White facing problems housing his king and developing his queenside:

a) 10 ♝e3 ♝xe3 11 fxe3 was an attempt to reduce the attacking force in A.Grekh-A.Tukhaev, Simferopol 2000, but with 11...♝g4 Black retains a strong initiative.

b) 10 0-0 is best met by 10...♜g8, menacing an exchange sacrifice, as well as ideas of ...♘g4.

c) 10 b4?! ♝xb4+ 11 c3 ♝c5 12 ♝a3 ♝xa3 13 ♘xa3 ♛f4 14 ♘c4 ♝e6 saw Black go a pawn ahead for no real compensation in W.Puntier-C.D'Amore, Calvia Olympiad 2004.

d) 10 ♘c3 ♗e6 11 ♗e3 (otherwise, 11 ♕d2? e3! 12 fxe3 ♖d8 13 ♗d3 ♖g8 was a disaster for White in A.Damia-J.Tuma, Brno 2006, while the 11 ♗d2 of H.Strehlow-R.Rabiega, Berlin 2007, should just be met by 11...♖g8, retaining the initiative) 11...♗xe3 12 fxe3 ♖d8 13 ♕c1 h5 14 b3 ♕g5 saw Black maintain the initiative and the upper hand in Y.Yakovich-A.Goldin, Moscow 1994.

B) 5 ♘b3

A much more sensible approach, removing the knight from attack with gain of tempo.
5...♗b6

Here White must decide whether or not to harass Black's bishop on b6:

B1: 6 a4
B2: 6 ♘c3
B3: 6 ♕e2

White's remaining options are generally a little planless and unimpressive:

a) 6 ♗d3 ♕h4 7 0-0 ♘f6 8 h3 d6 gives Black good, active development and full equality. Moreover, it's White who must be careful here, as was shown by 9 ♘1d2? ♗xh3! 10 ♕f3 (10 gxh3? ♕g3+ 11 ♔h1 ♕xh3+ 12 ♔g1 ♘g4 13 ♘f3 ♕g3+ 14 ♔h1 ♗xf2 is crushing) 10...♗e6 and Black won in G.Seils-M.Heintze, Stralsund 1988.

b) 6 ♗c4?! ♕h4 7 0-0 (or 7 ♕e2 ♘e5! when Black seizes the initiative) 7...♘f6 8 h3?! ♘xe4 9 ♕e2 0-0 simply left White a pawn down in J.Gonczi-E.Szurovszky, Heves 1999.

c) 6 c4 is the most popular of these lesser options, clamping down on the d5-square.

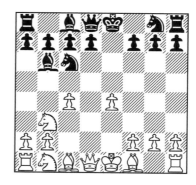

However, after 6...d6 7 ♘c3 (otherwise, 7 ♗e2 ♕h4 8 0-0 ♘f6 9 ♘c3 ♘g4!? 10 ♗xg4 ♗xg4 11 ♕c2 a5 12 ♗f4 0-0 13 ♗g3 ♕h5 gave Black good activity in D.Genocchio-M.Lazic, Cortina d'Ampezzo 2004, and the 7 ♗d3 ♕h4! 8 0-0?! ♘f6 9 ♕e2 of H.Murtez-

D.Gurtner, Geneva 2004, should have been met by 9...♘e5, menacing 10...♘fg4 with dangerous attacking prospects) Black should not be too unhappy thanks to his strong presence on the dark squares:

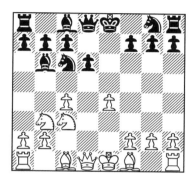

c1) 7...♘ge7 8 ♗e2 (8 ♕e2?! 0-0 9 ♗e3 was a rather ambitious idea in G.Kuzmin-O.Kulicov, Kramatorsk 2003, and might have been punished by 9...♖e8 10 0-0-0 ♗xe3+ 11 ♕xe3 a5 when Black is the first to attack) 8...0-0 was solid and fine for Black in S.Kalygin-V.Malaniuk, Alushta 2004.

c2) 7...♘f6 8 ♗e2 0-0 (but not 8...♘e5?! because of 9 c5! dxc5 10 ♕xd8+ ♔xd8 11 f4 ♘g6 12 e5 with more than enough for the pawn) 9 ♗g5 was seen in D.Szopka-T.Dziadykiewcz, Czestochowa 1994, and after 9...h6 10 ♗h4 ♖e8 the pressure against e4 gives Black the initiative.

c3) 7...♕h4 was once employed by Bronstein. It isn't quite as effective as elsewhere in this chapter, but even so after 8 g3 ♕f6 9 ♕e2 ♘ge7 Black cannot be worse.

c4) 7...♕f6! 8 f3 (otherwise, the 8 f4 ♘ge7 9 ♗e2 0-0 10 ♘a4 of F.Riemann-E.Flechsig, Breslau 1886, should be met by 10...♕g6 11 ♗f3 f5 with the initiative, while 8 c5?! dxc5 9 ♘d5 ♕e5 10 f3 ♘ge7 11 ♗f4 ♕xb2 12 ♗c1 ♕e5 failed to give White enough for his pawns in J.Szabo-B.Tomisa, Hungarian League 1999) 8...♘ge7 9 ♘a4 sees White hunting down Black's powerful bishop, but at some cost in terms of time.

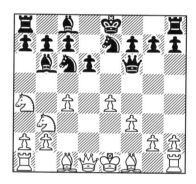

Indeed, after 9...0-0! (9...♗e6 10 ♘xb6 axb6 11 ♗e2, as in J.Martinez-M.Cardena, Merida 1997, and then 11...♘e5 also sees Black seizing the initiative) 10 ♘xb6 (or 10 ♕c2 ♕h4+ 11 g3 ♕h5 and suddenly White comes under pressure on the light squares) 10...axb6 11 ♗e2 ♕h4+ 12 g3 ♕h3 followed by ...f5 White's position remains under pressure.

B1) 6 a4

Until quite recently it was believed that this push represented White's only real attempt to make something out of his fifth move.

6...a6!

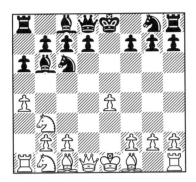

The most flexible and popular response. That said, 6...a5 is also playable and after 7 ♘c3 ♘ge7 (the ambitious 7...♕f6 8 ♕e2 ♘b4 could have backfired in J.Isaev-J.Piket, Elista 1998, had White seized the initiative with the logical 9 ♘b5) 8 ♗g5 f6 9 ♗h4 0-0 10 ♕d2 d6 11 ♗e2 ♘b4 the respective queenside holes roughly cancelled each other out in V.Samolins-J.Klovans, Riga 2009.

7 ♘c3

Invariably played, especially because pushing the a-pawn on doesn't achieve much: 7 a5 ♗a7 8 ♗d3 d6 9 0-0 ♘f6 10 ♗g5 h6 11 ♗xf6 ♕xf6 12 ♘c3 was seen in N.Bozilov-V.Stoimenov, Dimitrovgrad 2003, and now 12...♘e7 would have left Black fully equal.

7...d6

Again the most flexible and likely the best, but there are alternatives:

a) 7...♕f6 8 ♕e2 ♘ge7 9 ♘d5!? (trying to punish Black's slightly ambitious approach; earlier 9 h4 h6 10 g4 ♘d4 11 ♘xd4 ♗xd4 12 ♗d2 d6 13 f4 g6 14 ♗g2 ♗d7 had also led to a rather unclear

middlegame in S.Ansell-S.Ganguly, Edinburgh 2003) 9...♘xd5 10 exd5+ ♘e7 11 a5 ♗a7 12 h4 d6?! (natural, but 12...h6!? is probably an improvement; then 13 ♖a4?! is much less effective on account of 13...0-0 14 ♖f4 ♕d6) 13 ♖a4! saw White seize the initiative in J.Van der Wiel-M.Merbis, Leiden 2010, with the creative idea of 13...0-0? 14 ♖f4.

b) 7...♘ge7 8 ♗e2 0-0 9 0-0 d6 10 ♗g5 ♗e6 11 ♘d5 ♗xd5 12 exd5 ♘e5 13 ♔h1 h6 was very solid for Black in H.Velchev-M.Vasilev, Sunny Beach 2009.

c) 7...♘f6

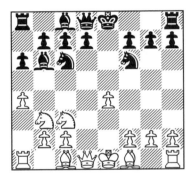

8 ♗e2 (White may do better with 8 ♗d3 d6 9 ♗g5!?, since 9...h6 10 ♗h4 g5 11 ♗g3 ♕e7 12 0-0 ♗e6 13 ♘d5 ♗xd5 14 exd5 ♘e5 15 ♖e1 gave him the initiative in C.Debray-L.Fressinet, Paris 2007, but the immediate 8 ♗g5 allowed Black to obtain decent counterplay with 8...h6 9 ♗h4 d6 10 ♗e2 ♗e6 11 0-0 g5!? – only now! – 12 ♗g3 h5 in J.Poenisch-V.Malaniuk, Dresden (rapid) 2010) 8...d6 9 0-0 h6 10 ♔h1 0-0 11 f4 ♖e8 12 ♗f3 ♗e6 13 a5 ♗a7 left both

sides with trumps and was about equal in J.Gallagher-S.Brunello, Dresden Olympiad 2008.

8 ♘d5

Continuing to harass the bishop, but White has also tested a number of alternatives:

a) 8 a5 again fails to impress: 8...♗a7 9 ♗e2 (Black was also better after 9 ♗d3 ♘f6 10 ♕e2 ♗e6 11 ♘d5 0-0 12 0-0 ♗xd5 13 exd5 ♖e8! 14 ♕f3 ♘e5 in E.Velazco-S.Ludena, Arequipa 2003, and after the 9 ♕e2 ♗e6 10 ♘d5 of V.Vigfusson-L.Blomstrom, Copenhagen 2007, one simple route to easy equality is 10...h6 11 ♗e3 ♗xe3 12 ♕xe3 ♘f6) 9...♘f6 10 g4?? (a shocking decision; correct was the simple 10 0-0 with equality) 10...♘xg4! 11 ♗xg4 ♕h4 unfurls a double-attack against the bishop and f2.

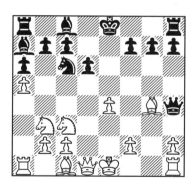

Unsurprisingly White was swiftly routed after 12 ♕d2 ♗xg4 13 ♕f4 ♘e5 14 h3 ♘f3+ in G.Trkulja-S.Atalik, Neum 2005.

b) The 8 ♕e2 ♗e6 9 ♗e3 ♗xe3 10 ♕xe3 of G.Botterill-A.Perkins, Clacton on Sea 1974, isn't a particularly inspiring approach and is a little illogical after the earlier 5 ♘b3 and 6 a4. Here 10...♘f6 11 ♗e2 0-0 12 0-0 ♖e8 should unsurprisingly be fine for Black.

c) 8 ♗c4 ♘f6 9 ♗g5 ♗e6 is also equal, but White must now avoid the trap 10 ♘d5? ♗xf2+!.

d) 8 ♕f3?! ♘e5 9 ♕f4 (9 ♕g3 ♘g4 seizes the initiative) 9...♘f6 10 ♗e2 0-0 11 0-0 was seen in S.Naranjo Espinosa-F.Gomez, Havana 2007, and now 11...♖e8 would have left Black, if anyone, slightly for preference.

8...♗a7

9 ♗e2

White settles for simple development. Such an approach is unlikely to trouble Black, but in any case the position appears fairly level:

a) 9 ♗e3 ♗xe3 (there's no real reason to allow White to exchange on a7) 10 ♘xe3 ♘f6 11 ♗d3 (but not the 11 f4? ♘xe4 12 ♕f3 ♘f6 13 0-0-0 0-0 14 g4 of W.Danneck-R.Kurz, Hockenheim 1994, because 14...♗e6 15 g5 ♘d7 would have shown up White's play as being too ambitious) 11...0-0 12 0-0 ♖e8 leaves White quite strong on the light squares, but Black with sufficient counterplay down the e-file and potentially on the dark squares.

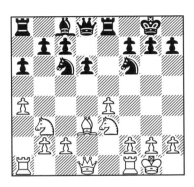

Indeed, with 13 f3 (13 ♘d2 was preferred in J.Rodriguez-Y.Kraidman, Siegen 1970, but 13...♘e5 would have attacked White's remaining bishop while preparing ...d5) 13...♗d7 14 c4 ♕b8! 15 ♖f2 ♕a7 Black had found his queen a dark-square role and enjoyed good counterplay in J.Hector-B.Sahl, Vejle 1994.

b) 9 ♕e2 ♗e6 10 ♗e3 ♗xe3 11 ♕xe3 ♘f6 12 ♗c4 (after the 12 0-0-0?! 0-0 13 f4 of T.Halasz-P.Lukacs, Budapest 1979, 13...♗xd5 14 exd5 ♘e7 gives Black strong play against the vulnerable pawns on a4 and d5) 12...0-0 13 0-0 ♖e8 14 ♕f3 ♗xd5 15 exd5 ♘e5 16 ♕f4 saw White trying to exchange his way to a draw in A.Vuckovic-A.Karpatchev, German League 2005, but here 16...♘xc4 17 ♕xc4 ♖e4 was one way for Black to retain an edge.

c) 9 ♕f3!? is an ambitious try, dis-

suading ...♘f6 and provoking complications. However, after 9...♗e6 Black seems to be able to obtain enough counterplay:

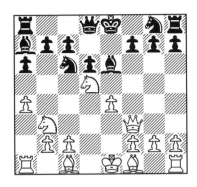

c1) 10 ♕c3 ♘f6! 11 ♘xf6+ (11 ♗e3 was preferred in A.Martorelli-F.Bellini, Arvier 2008, but 11...♗xd5 12 exd5 ♗xe3 13 ♕xe3+ ♘e7 strikes against d5 and leaves Black slightly better) 11...♕xf6 12 ♕xf6 gxf6 gives Black the initiative as ...f5 is next up.

c2) Zhang Pengxiang's 10 ♗d2 prepares ♗c3, but Black shouldn't have any problems after 10...♘ge7.

c3) 10 ♕g3 is critical, but 10...♗xd5! 11 exd5 ♘b4 12 ♕xg7?! (White should prefer 12 ♗c4 ♘e7! 13 0-0 0-0, retaining equality) 12...♕f6 13 ♕xf6 ♘xf6 14 ♗d3 (and not 14 ♔d1? ♘g4, as in R.Chalmeta Ugas-H.Mestre Bellido, Barbera del Valles 2008) 14...♘xd3+ 15 cxd3 ♘xd5 saw Black regaining his pawn with a pull in I.Salonen-I.Skrjabin, Espoo 2006.

d) 9 ♗g5?! might appeal to some ambitious or just weak players, but 9...♕xg5! 10 ♘xc7+ ♔e7 11 ♘xa8 ♘f6

12 ♕d2 ♕e5 should turn out rather well for Black, since the knight is in some trouble on a8: for example, 13 f3 d5 with some initiative or 13 ♗d3 ♘xe4 14 ♗xe4 ♕xe4+ 15 ♔d1 ♕xg2 16 ♖e1+ ♗e6 17 ♘c7 ♗xf2 and Black has far too much for the exchange.

We now return to 9 ♗e2:

9...♘f6! 10 0-0

White must always beware tactics on f2 in this line and here 10 ♗g5? ♗xf2+ 11 ♔f1 (11 ♔xf2? ♘xe4+ 12 ♔e1 ♘xg5 regains the piece with a two-pawn surplus) 11...♗a7! 12 ♗xf6 gxf6 13 ♕d2 ♗e6 14 ♕h6 ♔d7! 15 ♘xf6+ ♔c8 leaves Black on top. So too does 10 ♘xf6+ ♕xf6 11 0-0 0-0 12 ♔h1 ♖e8 13 f3 ♗e6 14 c4 (H.Velchev-M.Stoinev, Plovdiv 2003) 14...♕g6! followed by ...f5 with the initiative.

10...♘xd5 11 exd5 ♘e5

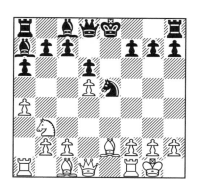

Thus Black has managed to leave White with a pawn not a piece on d5, while bringing his own knight to a promising square.

12 ♘d4

White hurries to recentralize his

knight, but in any case Black is already slightly the more comfortable.

12 ♗f4 was preferred in R.Wade-E.Mulcahy, Munich 1954, but after 12...0-0 13 ♕d2 ♗f5 14 ♖a3 ♕d7 15 c4 ♖fe8 Black had the initiative and should have met 16 ♘d4? with 16...♘xc4! 17 ♗xc4 ♗xd4 18 ♕xd4 ♖e4.

Much more recently 12 ♔h1 was tried in D.Eggleston-P.Doggers, Budapest 2007, but after the continuation 12...0-0 13 f4 ♘d7 followed by ...♘f6 and ...♗f5 Black can have no complaints whatsoever.

12...0-0 13 f4?!

Too ambitious. White had to settle for 13 ♗e3, pretty pleasant though 13...♕h4 would have been for Black.

13...♘g4!

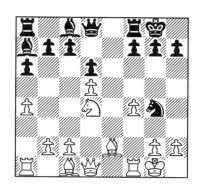

This strong blow left White in trouble in H.Pfleger-P.Keres, Tallinn 1973, and after 14 ♗xg4?! ♗xg4 15 ♕xg4 ♗xd4+ 16 ♔h1 f5! the legendary Estonian was well on his way to the full point, but even the more prudent 14 h3 ♘f6 15 ♗f3 ♖e8 16 ♔h2 ♗d7 would have given Black an edge.

B2) 6 ♘c3

White keeps his options open for a move: 7 a4 or 7 ♕e2 may yet follow.

6...d6

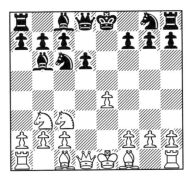

This looks like Black's best move order, although his choice does partly depend on how he likes to meet 6 ♕e2 (Line B3). Otherwise:

a) The misguided 6...a6?! 7 ♘d5 ♗a7 was brutally punished by 8 ♕g4! g6?! 9 ♕g3 d6 10 ♗g5 f6 11 ♕c3! ♔f7 12 0-0-0 in H.Odeev-H.Mikati, Guangzhou 2010.

b) 6...♘f6 7 ♗g5 (for 7 ♕e2 see Line B3) 7...h6 8 ♗h4 doesn't seem to be too scary a pin and after 8...d6 9 ♗d3 g5 10 ♗g3 ♕e7 11 h4 ♖g8 12 hxg5 hxg5 13 ♕d2 ♗e6 14 0-0-0 0-0-0 Black enjoyed full equality in K.Lahno-B.Bok, German League 2010.

c) 6...♕f6!? echoes Black's play after 5 ♘xc6 and is a slightly awkward attack on f2. White usually responds 7 ♕e2 and so we'll consider this position in Line B3.

7 ♘d5

White chases down the bishop, which this time has no escape. Others

here are:

a) 7 a4 a6 is another route into Line B1.

b) 7 ♕e2 transposes to Line B3.

c) 7 ♗d3 ♕h4! (we will see plenty more of this aggressive, logical and strong deployment below) 8 g3 ♕f6 9 f4 ♘ge7 10 ♕e2 0-0 11 ♗e3 ♗xe3 12 ♕xe3 a5 13 a4 ♗e6 14 ♘d2 was seen in L.Kernazhitsky-V.Romanov, Kiev 2004, and now 14...♘b4 would have been fine for Black.

d) 7 g3 ♘f6 8 ♗g2 (A.Teuschler-W.Halser, Austria 1991) 8...0-0 9 0-0 ♗g4 is clearly very comfortable for Black.

e) 7 ♗f4 (F.Anton-K.Tsoumanis, Mecklenburg 2006) 7...♘f6 8 ♕d2 0-0 9 f3 a5! also sees Black beginning to assume the initiative.

f) And so does 7 ♗c4 ♘e5! 8 ♗e2 (and not 8 ♕e2?, as White played in M.Lugosi-T.Simon, Hungarian League 2007, because of 8...♕h4! with the nasty idea of 9...♗g4, not to mention the attacked bishop) 8...♘f6 9 0-0 h6 10 h3 0-0 11 ♔h1 (N.Greb-M.Muskardin, Bjelolasica 2008) 11...♖e8 12 f4 ♘c6 13 ♗f3 a5!. Indeed, an early a-pawn advance can be used by both sides in this variation to weaken the opponent's queenside, with the b4-square a particularly good outpost for a black knight.

7...♕h4!

Just when White thought he was picking up the bishop-pair, Black counters in time against e4 and f2.

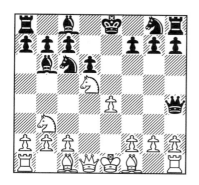

8 ♕f3

The alternative is 8 ♕e2?!, but after 8...♝g4 9 ♕d2 (and not the 9 g3? of T.Vasile-M.Burakovsky, Eger 2005, because of 9...♝xe2 10 gxh4 ♝f3) 9...♝e6 10 ♝d3?! (10 ♘f4 0-0-0 would restrict Black to just a pull) 10...♞xd5! 11 exd5 ♘e5 12 0-0 ♘f6 13 ♝b5+ ♚f8! 14 ♝e2 ♜e8 Black enjoyed a dangerous initiative in V.Kupreichik-Y.Razuvaev, USSR 1977.

8...♘f6!

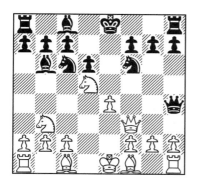

9 ♘xf6+

White changes tack. He can remain true to his initial idea, but after 9 ♘xb6 axb6 10 ♝d3 0-0 11 0-0 Black clearly

doesn't have any problems. Indeed, he might even try to seize the initiative by attacking e4 with the unstereotyped 11...♜a4!?.

9...♕xf6 10 ♕xf6 gxf6

Taking stock we can see that White has fractured Black's kingside, but at a slight cost in terms of time. Moreover, ...f5 is imminent and after 11 c3 (11 ♝b5 f5 12 exf5 ♝xf5 13 c3 0-0-0 left Black with the safer king and beginning to attack in I.Radulov-S.Gligoric, Vrbas 1977) 11...♝e6 (11...f5!?) 12 ♝f4 0-0-0 13 ♝g3 f5 14 exf5 ♝xf5 15 0-0-0 ♜de8 Black clearly had no problems whatsoever in P.Simacek-D.Schwarz, Slovakian League 2005.

B3) 6 ♕e2!?

This aggressive sideline (White plans 7 ♝e3, 8 ♘c3 and 9 0-0-0) was used with some success by Magnus Carlsen in the 2009 World Blitz Championship. It had actually been introduced into top-flight praxis by Ivanchuk back in 2004, after which 6 ♕e2 began to gain a few adherents, but only over the past year has it become quite topical.

Before we discuss 6 ♕e2, we should examine a question of move order: should White start with 6 ♕e2 or prefer 6 ♘c3 followed by 7 ♕e2? It is still a little too early to be able to supply a definitive answer, but Carlsen himself did begin with 6 ♘c3 in a recent game. After 6 ♘c3 Black has:

a) 6...d6 7 ♕e2 ♘f6 transposes to our main line after 8 ♗e3 or to the notes to Black's 7th move, below, in the case of 7...♘ge7 8 ♗e3.

b) 6...♕f6 rather forces 7 ♕e2 and after 7...♘ge7 8 ♗e3 the aggressively-placed black queen may well turn out to be exposed on f6. Following 8...♘d4 (hurrying to simplify; 8...0-0 9 0-0-0 d6 10 h4 ♗xe3+ 11 ♕xe3 ♗e6 12 ♗e2 a5 was an attempt to counterattack in D.Lima-J.Cori, Cali 2010, but after 13 ♘d4! ♘xd4 14 ♖xd4 ♖fe8 15 ♖d2 a4 16 a3 ♖a5 17 f4 ♗d7 18 g4 it had become clear that White's attack was somewhat the more potent, partly due to that by now misplaced queen on f6) 9

♘xd4 ♗xd4 10 ♗xd4 (10 ♕d2!? would be a more aggressive approach) 10...♕xd4 11 ♖d1 ♕b6 12 ♕b5 0-0 13 ♗e2 Black was quite solid, but White undoubtedly had a small pull in E.Ghaem Maghami-P.Harikrishna, Guangzhou 2010.

c) 6...♘f6 7 ♕e2 0-0 8 ♗g5 h6 9 ♗h4 (the far too ambitious 9 h4?! d6! 10 f3?! failed to 10...hxg5 11 hxg5 ♘g4! 12 fxg4 ♕xg5 in S.Rublevsky-V.Anand, Bastia (rapid) 2004) 9...a5 10 a4 ♘d4 (tempting but Carlsen doesn't fear the doubled b-pawns; perhaps 10...d6!? is more critical when one rather unclear line runs 11 ♘d5!? g5 12 ♘xb6 cxb6 13 ♗g3 ♘xe4 14 0-0-0 ♗f5 15 ♘d4 ♘xd4 16 ♖xd4 when White's kingside is still asleep, but Black's wrecked structure should grant him decent compensation) 11 ♕d3! ♘xb3 12 cxb3 ♖e8 13 0-0-0 reaches an original and fairly unclear position.

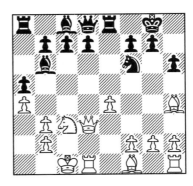

White's queenside may not make a pretty picture, but his king is safe and e-pawn mobile; factors which combined to leave him somewhat for choice after 13...d6 14 ♕c2 ♗d7?! (slow; Black had to avoid 14...♗e6?! 15 e5, but 14...c6!? 15 ♗c4 ♕e7 would have kept matters fairly unclear: for example, 16 ♖he1 ♗e6 17 ♘d5!? cxd5 18 exd5 g5! 19 dxe6 d5 and Black seems to be holding his own in the resulting tactical flurry) 15 ♗c4 ♗e6 16 ♖he1 ♕e7 17 e5! dxe5 18 ♖xe5 ♕f8 19 ♗xf6 gxf6 20 ♖e2 in M.Carlsen-E.Bacrot, Nanjing 2010.

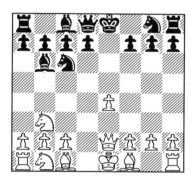

6...d6

Black's invariable choice, but this is by no means forced:

a) As elsewhere in the 5 ♘b3 variation, 6...a5!? deserves attention. Certainly 7 a4 (Black doesn't have any problems after 7 ♗e3 a4 8 ♘3d2 ♗xe3 9 ♕xe3 ♘f6) 7...♘ge7 8 ♘c3 ♘b4 9 ♗g5 (freeing the c-pawn with 9 ♘b5!? may be critical) 9...f6 10 ♗h4 0-0 11 0-0-0 d5 gave Black decent-enough counterplay in S.Novikov-A.Aleksandrov, Sochi 2005.

b) 6...♘d4 7 ♘xd4 ♗xd4 is a little too simplistic: 8 c3!? (the more straightforward 8 ♘c3 d6 9 ♕d3 should also suffice for an edge) 8...♗b6 9 ♘a3! a6?! (Black doesn't have time to pre-

serve her bishop so) 10 ♘c4 ♗a7 11 e5! b5 saw one of your authors gain a strong, early initiative in Y.Dembo-A.Stefanova, Rijeka 2010, and now 12 ♕e4!? ♖b8 13 ♗e3! ♗xe3 (or 13...♗b7 14 ♕g4, taking aim at that ever-sensitive g7-pawn) 14 ♘xe3 ♘e7 15 ♗d3 would have left White in charge of the position.

7 ♗e3 ♘f6

The main line, but it may be that Black does better with 7...♘ge7!? 8 ♘c3 0-0 9 0-0-0, thereby obtaining quite a solid set-up and one in which the f-pawn may be employed to begin counterplay.

Yet another recent high-level encounter, T.Radjabov-E.Tomashevsky, Plovdiv 2010, continued 9...♗e6 (9...f5!? looks more consistent and after 10 ♕d2 ♗e6 11 ♔b1 ♔h8 12 ♗b5 fxe4 13 ♘xe4 ♘f5 14 ♗g5 White was at most a touch better in T.Thorhallsson-G.Sargissian, Copenhagen 2007) 10 f4 ♔h8 11 ♔b1 ♕e8 12 ♗xb6 (12 h4!? is also tempting, provoking 12...f5, as then White has 13 ♘b5! ♕d7 14 ♗xb6 axb6 15 e5 with a central breakthrough) 12...axb6 13 g4 f6 14 h4 ♕f7 15 f5 ♗xb3 16 cxb3 ♘e5 17 g5 and White must be slightly better here, although in the game Black's solid defences held.

8 ♘c3 0-0

Black has also gone long with 8...♕e7 9 0-0-0 ♗e6 (or 8...♗e6 9 0-0-0 ♕e7 with a transposition) 10 f3 0-0-0 (10...h6 11 ♔b1 ♗xe3 12 ♕xe3 a6 13 ♘d4 ♘xd4 14 ♕xd4 0-0 15 ♗c4 ♖fe8 was fine for Black in N.Fercec-V.Erdos, Rijeka 2010, but here White might have begun to advance his kingside pawns with 13 h4!?, which should retain a small pull) 11 ♗xb6 axb6 12 ♘d4 ♔b8 13 ♕e3 ♖he8, thereby reaching another quite solid set-up, but again one where White's space advantage persists and gives him a small edge.

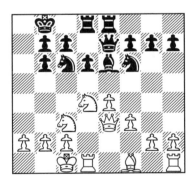

Indeed, with 14 ♘xe6 (it's logical to trade the bishop, but 14 ♗b5 ♗d7 15 ♘de2 ♕e5 16 ♕f4 ♕xf4+ 17 ♘xf4 was also enough for a small edge in M.Carlsen-V.Tkachiev, Moscow (blitz) 2009) 14...♕xe6 15 ♕d2 ♕e5 16 ♗c4 ♖e7 17 ♘d5! ♘xd5 18 exd5 ♘a7 19

♖he1 White had obtained the superior minor piece and begun to take control in E.Berg-M.Carlhammar, Gothenburg 2010.

9 0-0-0

We've now reached a position which is fast becoming a critical tabiya for this sub-variation.

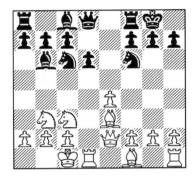

9...♖e8

Thematic, but Black might again turn to his a-pawn in the bid for counterplay with 9...♗xe3+ 10 ♕xe3 a5. This also appears quite logical, but with the precise 11 ♘d4 ♕e7 12 ♗b5! ♘xd4 13 ♕xd4 ♕e5 14 f3 ♗e6 15 ♕xe5 dxe5 16 ♘a4! White obtained an edge which he went on to convert in M.Carlsen-R.Ponomariov, Moscow (blitz) 2009.

That may help to explain why active players have recently begun investigating 9...♗e6 10 f3 ♘d7!?, relying on piece-play. Moreover, White must not underestimate the strength of the knight coming to e5, as he appeared to with 11 g4?! (11 ♘d4 ♘xd4 12 ♗xd4 is a more prudent approach and after 12...♕g5+ 13 ♕d2 ♕xd2+ 14 ♖xd2 a6

15 f4 f6 16 ♗e2 ♖fe8 17 ♘f3 White even had an edge in E.Berg-M.Ivanov, Gothenburg 2010, but here Black might do better to secure some counterplay with 15...f5!?) 11...♘de5 12 ♖g1 in H.Nakamura-N.Kosintseva, Cap d'Agde (rapid) 2010, whereupon 12...♕f6! 13 ♖g3 ♘c4 would have left White on the back foot.

10 f3 ♗e6

This may be a little too routine and once again there are alternatives:

a) 10...♘e5!? 11 ♕d2 ♗e6 12 ♗e2 ♗c4 13 g4 ♗xe3 14 ♕xe3 c6 15 g5 was seen in the stem game V.Ivanchuk-V.Topalov, Monte Carlo (blindfold) 2004, and now Black would have been okay in the complications after 15...♘d5!, as pointed out by Mikhalevski. Thus the critical line is likely 15 ♘d4!? d5 16 g5 ♘fd7 17 b3, which may be slightly in White's favour.

b) 10...♗xe3+ 11 ♕xe3 a5 12 ♔b1?! a4! 13 ♘c1 a3 gave Black good counterplay in G.Arzumanian-Y.Balashov, Tula 2004, but White should have recentralized with 12 ♘d4, as again Mikhalevski has pointed out in his excellent column for ChessPublishing.com.

11 ♗xb6!?

White doesn't fear the resulting half-open a-file, but one can certainly also make a decent case for the immediate 11 ♕d2.

11...axb6 12 ♕d2

White has managed to prevent Black from breaking with ...d5, but Black's position remains pretty solid

and he can look to the a-file for counterplay. Perhaps White is a touch better, but it would be surprising if there weren't further developments here over the coming months. For now let's examine Carlsen's two experiences from this position in the 2009 World Blitz Championship:

a) 12...♗xb3 13 cxb3 ♕e7 (Mikhalevski's 13...♘d7!? intending ...♘c5 would at least give Black some counterplay against White's slightly vulnerable king position) 14 ♗b5 ♕e5 15 ♔b1 ♖ed8 16 a3! saw White keeping the queenside situation under control while preparing ♘d5 with a pull in M.Carlsen-A.Naiditsch, Moscow (blitz) 2009, but after 16...♘e7?! the breakthrough 17 f4 ♕e6 18 e5! gave him even more than that.

b) A few rounds later 12...♘d7 13 ♗b5 ♘c5 was preferred in M.Carlsen-D.Jakovenko, Moscow (blitz) 2009, but 14 ♘d4! ♗d7 15 ♔b1 ♘xd4 16 ♕xd4 ♗xb5 17 ♘xb5 ♕d7 18 c4 saw White retain a pull thanks to his bind and extra space.

Conclusion

When I (YD) started work on this book in 2008, 5 ♘b3 looked more respectable than 5 ♘f5, but that was about it. Indeed, practice has shown that the plan of 5...♗b6 6 a4 isn't too challenging, especially when compared with White's approaches in our last four chapters. However, thanks to the patronage of Ivanchuk and Carlsen, 6 ♕e2 and the closely-related 6 ♘c3 d6 7 ♕e2 has evolved into quite a dangerous weapon. Despite the fact that the players generally castle on opposite sides, White must be happy with quite a small edge in a manoeuvring middlegame, but we are talking about decent prospects of an edge for White... at least at the time of this book going to press! Undoubtedly the ball is currently in Black's court here, but he may be able to hit back, especially by pursuing a more active approach than Carlsen's opponents have generally done.

Chapter Eleven

The Check on b4

1 e4 e5 2 ♘f3 ♘c6 3 d4 exd4 4 ♘xd4
♗b4+

With this old favourite of Tony
Miles, Black usually intends to place his
bishop on c5 after all, having first induced White to take away his queen's
knight's natural development by moving his c-pawn; the point being that 5
♘c3 ♘f6 transposes to the Scotch Four
Knights.

5 c3

Now we will consider:

A: 5...♗c5
B: 5...♗e7

Line A is Black's usual choice, but in
both cases White has decent chances of
emerging with an edge so long as he
knows his stuff and hasn't been caught
too much by surprise by the check.

It should also be pointed out that
5...♘xd4? 6 ♕xd4 forces 6...♗f8, which
hardly impresses. Neither does 5...♗a5
particularly impress after 6 ♘xc6
(White can also play the natural 6 ♗c4
and after 6...♘f6 he has 7 ♘xc6 bxc6 8
e5 ♘e4 9 ♕g4 with a big plus) 6...bxc6
(and not 6...dxc6? 7 ♕xd8+ ♔xd8 8 ♘a3
when ♘c4, ♗g5+ and 0-0-0 are coming) 7 ♗c4 (again the most natural, but
one should also pay attention to Barsky's idea of 7 a4!? ♗b6 8 a5 ♗c5 9 b4
♗e7 10 ♗c4 with an edge for White)
7...♕h4 (White has some tactical

threats on f7 in view of the loose position of the bishop on a5, so care is required from Black) 8 0-0 ♞f6 9 ♞d2 0-0 and now the simple 10 e5 gives White an edge.

A) 5...♝c5

Just as after 4...♝c5, the standard methods for White are:

> **A1: 6 ♞xc6**
> **A2: 6 ♝e3**

However, with Black not actually threatening to capture on d4 here, White has also been known to consider:

a) 6 ♝b5?! is a very strange move, with the single merit that it temporarily discourages an advance of the black d-pawn. Following 6...♞ge7 (6...♞f6 also looks good) 7 0-0 0-0 8 ♝g5 ♝b6 9 ♜e1 Black played the obvious 9...♞xd4 10 cxd4 d5 and after 11 ♞c3 f6 12 ♝e3 ♚h8 13 ♛d2 c6 14 ♝d3 dxe4 15 ♝xe4 ♝f5 he was better in M.Ashley-E.Bacrot, Bermuda 1999.

b) 6 ♞f5?! is, just like after 4...♝c5, hardly any good. The best reaction for Black here is 6...d6! and after 7 ♞xg7+ ♚f8 8 ♞f5 ♝xf5 9 exf5 ♛h4 10 ♛f3 ♜e8+ 11 ♚d1 ♞e5 he has very good compensation.

c) 6 ♝c4 is more logical. Play may continue 6...♞f6 (6...d6 is also possible: for example, 7 0-0 ♞ge7 8 ♝e3 0-0 9 ♞d2 ♝xd4 10 cxd4 d5 was seen in S.Zikeli-A.Guadamuro Torrente, Herceg Novi 2006, and after 11 exd5 ♞xd5 Black is fine) 7 ♞xc6 (7 0-0 0-0 8 ♝g5?! fails to 8...h6 9 ♝h4?! g5 10 ♝g3 ♞xe4) 7...bxc6 and now:

c1) Black is not troubled by 8 e5 ♛e7 9 0-0 (or 9 ♛e2 ♞d5 10 0-0 0-0 11 ♜e1 ♜e8 12 ♞d2 d6 with good play, especially since 13 exd6? runs into 13...♝xf2+! 14 ♚f1 ♛xe2+ 15 ♜xe2 ♜xe2 16 ♝xe2 ♝b6 with the advantage) 9...♛xe5 10 ♜e1 ♞e4 11 ♝e3 ♝xe3 12 ♜xe3 0-0 13 ♛e1 d5 14 ♝d3 ♛g5 15 ♝xe4 dxe4 16 ♜xe4 ♝h3 17 g3 ♜ab8 18 b3 ♜bd8 when he had the advantage in G.Arzumanian-O.Kulicov, Kramatorsk 2003.

c2) 8 0-0 0-0 9 e5 ♘e4 10 ♕f3 ♕h4 and Black's active pieces give him good play: for instance, 11 g3 (11 ♗f4 ♘g5 12 ♕g3 ♕xg3 13 hxg3 ♘e6 is equal) 11...♘g5! (11...♘xg3?! loses material after 12 ♕xg3 ♕xc4 13 ♗h6 g6 14 ♘d2)

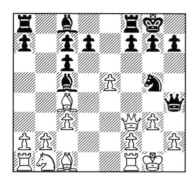

12 ♗xg5 (Postny shows that all the alternatives fail: 12 ♗xf7+? ♔h8!, 12 ♕xf7+ ♘xf7 13 gxh4 d5 and 12 ♕e2 ♘f3+! 13 ♕xf3 ♕xc4) 12...♕xc4 13 ♘d2 ♕e6 14 ♖fe1 ♖e8 and Black is certainly not worse.

d) 6 g3 ♘f6 7 ♗g2 0-0 8 0-0 ♖e8 with equality.

e) 6 ♗e2 ♘f6 7 ♘xc6 bxc6 8 e5 ♘d5 and again Black has no problems.

f) Finally, after 6 ♘b3 ♗b6 the only sensible move is 7 c4. This transposes to the variation 4...♗c5 5 ♘b3 ♗b6 6 c4 in which Black is fine, as we saw at the start of Line B of Chapter Ten.

A1) 6 ♘xc6

Just as in most Scotch systems, this move is critical. Moreover, here, unlike after 4...♗c5 5 ♘xc6, Black can't respond 6...♕f6?? on account of 7 ♘d4.

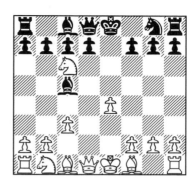

6...bxc6 7 ♗d3

The most obvious square for the bishop, as ♗c4 is liable to be met by ...d5 at some point:

a) Black has no problems after 7 ♘d2 ♘f6! (7...♘e7 8 ♘b3 ♗b6 9 c4!? makes things trickier for the second player, as his bishop is about to be shut off from the game for a while) 8 e5 ♕e7 9 ♕e2 ♘d5 10 ♕e4 d6.

b) However, in fact 7 ♗c4!? deserves attention. After 7...d6 (7...♕f6 8 0-0 ♘e7 9 ♕h5 d6 10 ♗e3 supplies some edge, while after the critical 7...d5 8 exd5 ♗xf2+ 9 ♔xf2 ♕h4+ 10 g3 ♕xc4 11 ♖e1+ ♘e7 12 ♘a3 ♕c5+ 13 ♗e3 ♕xd5 14 ♕xd5 ♘xd5 15 ♗d4+ White is again slightly better) 8 0-0 ♘e7 (most likely 8...♘f6 is preferable, not allowing the white queen to h5) 9 ♘d2 0-0 10 ♕h5 White has a slight initiative.

7...♘e7

The most logical move in this important tabiya. Black develops the knight safely out of harm's way (away from e4-e5), and may later transfer it to g6 and e5.

One of the first top-level tests of this line saw the typical 7...♕h4?! here. However, in this particular position, White can demonstrate its drawbacks with some accurate play: 8 ♕e2! ♘f6 (8...d6 9 ♘d2 ♘e7 10 b4 ♗b6 11 a4 was also better for White in A.Zontakh-M.Lazic, Jahorina 2000) 9 h3! and suddenly White, having prevented ...♘g4, threatens g3 and will push the black pieces back.

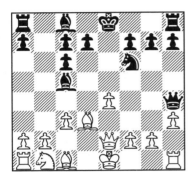

Indeed, after 9...0-0 (9...d6? is met by 10 e5 and if 10...♗g4? 11 ♕f1 White wins, while 9...d5? loses to 10 exd5+ ♔d8 11 g3 ♕a4 12 b3, as pointed out by Kasparov) 10 g3 ♕h5 11 g4! (not, of course, the tame 11 ♕xh5 ♘xh5) 11...♕e5 (Black loses after the alternative 11...♕h4? 12 ♘d2 d5 13 ♘f3 ♕xf2+ 14 ♕xf2 ♗xf2+ 15 ♔xf2 dxe4 16 g5 – Kasparov) 12 g5 ♘e8 (and here no good is 12...♘xe4? 13 ♗xe4 ♖e8 14 ♗f3 ♕xe2+ 15 ♗xe2 ♗a6 16 c4 ♗xc4 17 ♘c3, with an extra piece for White and no real compensation for Black in G.Kasparov-P.Leko, Tilburg 1997) 13 f4 White's massive pawn advance had put

Black in a very difficult position in E.Frisk-V.Breen, Stockholm 2003.

Instead 7...♘f6?! is unsurprisingly incorrect in view of 8 e5 ♘d5 9 ♕g4, but 7...d6!? deserves serious attention. Black prepares to develop the knight to its optimal square, f6, from where it has more influence in the centre and prevents the white queen from attacking the black kingside.

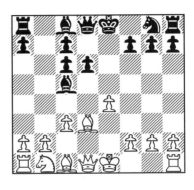

Now:

a) 8 0-0 ♘f6 9 ♘d2 (White achieves nothing with 9 ♗g5 h6 10 ♗h4?! because of 10...g5! 11 ♗g3 h5 12 e5 h4! 13 ♗xh4 ♖xh4 14 exf6 ♕xf6 with a strong attack for Black) 9...0-0 10 h3 ♖e8 11 ♖e1 ♘d7 12 ♘f3 ♘e5 13 ♘xe5 dxe5 was equal in L.Shytaj-S.Atalik, Turin Olympiad 2006.

b) 8 ♘d2! seems White's most promising course: 8...♘f6 (once again the aggressive 8...♕h4 fails to 9 0-0 ♘e7 10 b4 ♗b6 11 a4 a5 12 ♘c4 when White has a clear plus) 9 ♘b3 ♗b6 (9...♘d7 10 ♘xc5 ♘xc5 11 ♗c2 0-0 12 0-0 is a simple edge for White), and now White can finally play 10 ♗g5 h6

11 ♗h4 0-0 12 0-0 ♖e8 13 ♖e1 with a slight but steady edge; he plans h3, ♕f3 and ♖ad1.

Returning to 7...♘e7:

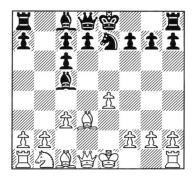

8 0-0

Logical development is the obvious course, although in the Scotch there are, of course, many exceptions to such an approach!

The attempt to exploit the absence of the knight from f6 and hinder castling by playing 8 ♕h5 does not bring too much after 8...d6 (8...d5?! 9 0-0 0-0 10 ♘d2 is inferior) 9 0-0 0-0 10 ♘d2 ♘g6 11 ♘f3 when Black is generally okay after something like 11...♕d7 12 h3 f6, although White may be able to lay claim to a tiny edge.

Likewise, 8 ♘d2 is fairly inoffensive after 8...0-0 (but not 8...d5?! 9 0-0 0-0 10 ♘b3 ♗b6 when White has the strong 11 c4!, forcing 11...dxe4 12 ♗xe4 ♕xd1 13 ♖xd1 ♗e6 14 ♗d3 ♖ad8 15 ♗f4 ♘g6 16 ♗g3 with the threat of c5 and an edge, E.Bacrot-R.Fontaine, Aix les Bains 2003) 9 ♘b3 ♗b6 10 c4 c5 11 0-0 d6. The bishop on b6 is shut off

from the game for now, but Black has good control over the dark squares: 12 ♖e1 (or 12 ♕h5 ♘c6 13 ♗g5 ♕e8 14 e5 f5 15 ♕xe8 ♖xe8 16 exd6 cxd6, which was equal in Y.Dembo-D.Baramidze, Liverpool 2008) 12...♘g6 13 ♗f1 ♗b7 14 ♗d2 (E.Vorobiov-V.Yandemirov, St Petersburg 2002) 14...♖e8 15 f3 a5 and Black has the initiative. Generally this idea of ♘d2-b3 and c4-c5 is ineffective, unless it causes Black immediate difficulties.

The most interesting alternative is the deeply prophylactic advance 8 h4!?, intending to harass Black's knight on g6 while supporting ♗g5 in the case of ...f5.

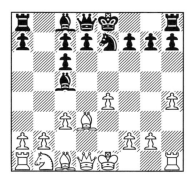

Now:

a) 8...0-0 9 h5 threatens h6, after which the mechanical 9...h6? (better is 9...f5, answering a flank attack with a counterattack in the centre, and after 10 e5 ♘d5 Black has counterplay, but less effective is 9...d5 in view of 10 h6! g6 11 ♘d2 ♖e8 12 0-0 ♕d6 13 ♖e1 ♕g3 14 ♕f3 with some advantage for White) runs into 10 ♗xh6!.

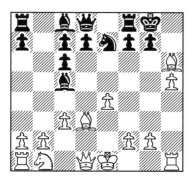

The reader will be spared a fair amount of analysis here, but should note that Black's best is 10...f5! (10...gxh6 11 ♕g4+ ♔h8 12 ♕f4 regains the piece and is the point of White's play, although 12...f5 13 ♕e5+ ♔g8 14 ♕xc5 fxe4 15 ♗xe4 d6 is still not entirely clear) 11 ♗xg7 ♔xg7 12 exf5 ♔h8 when Nataf considered White's position as won after 13 g4. Matters do not seem quite so clear after 13...♘d5 14 ♕f3 ♖e8+, although even so Black's position does not inspire much confidence.

b) Black's best reaction is 8...♘g6!, not fearing 9 b4 ♗b6 10 h5.

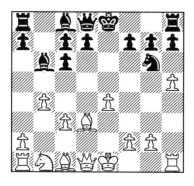

The reason for this is the strong intermediate move 10...♕f6! and after 11 0-0 (11 ♕f3? ♘e5 12 ♕xf6 ♘xd3+ 13 ♔d2 gxf6 14 ♔xd3 ♗xf2 is just bad for White, as is 11 ♕e2 ♘e5 12 ♗c2 d6! 13 f4 ♘g4) 11...♘e5 12 ♗e2 d6 Black has the initiative – sometimes the most logical moves are, indeed, the best!

c) One also has to wonder about the merits of 8...d5!?: 9 ♘d2 0-0 10 h5 was seen in M.Agopov-P.Royset, Gausdal 2002, when 10...h6 11 0-0 ♗b6 looks fine for Black.

We now return to the main line, 8 0-0.

8...0-0

For Black it is also logical to castle before anything else. Alternatively:

a) 8...♘g6 9 ♘d2 0-0 10 ♘b3 ♗b6 11 ♘d4 ♖b8 12 ♗e3 and White is better according to Barsky.

b) After 8...d6 9 ♗g5 h6! 10 ♗h4 (neither does 10 ♗d2 especially trouble Black) 10...g5 11 ♗g3 h5 12 h3 ♘g6 13 b4 ♗b6 14 e5 h4 15 ♗h2 ♘xe5 16 ♗xe5 dxe5 17 ♖e1 White had some compensation in J.Skoberne-D.Baramidze, Rogaska Slatina 2009, but Black had his trumps as well. Thus here 9 b4!? ♗b6 10 a4 a5 11 ♘d2 is perhaps more promising: 11...axb4 12 cxb4 0-0 13 ♗b2 ♘g6 was seen in A.Motylev-A.Hauchard, Linares 2000, and now 14 ♘c4 ♗a7 15 ♕d2 would have secured the advantage. Of course, White can also consider the straightforward 9 ♘d2 when 9...0-0 would take play back into our main line.

c) Yet again 8...d5 is not the most effective move: 9 c4 dxe4 10 ♗xe4 ♕xd1 11 ♖xd1 ♗g4 12 ♖e1 0-0-0 13 ♘c3 ♗e6 14 b3 ♗b4 15 ♗b2 ♖d2 16 ♘a4 ♖xb2 17 ♘xb2 ♗xe1 18 ♖xe1 saw White retain an edge in D.Pavasovic-O.Jovanic, Nova Gorica 2006.

9 ♘d2

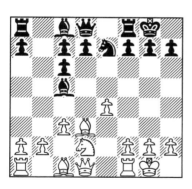

The obvious developing move and one which promises White good chances for an advantage. Other tries:

a) One logical move is 9 ♗g5, trying to extract a kingside concession, but Black appears comfortable enough after 9...h6 (even 9...f6 should be okay, provided Black follows up with 10 ♗h4

♘g6! 11 ♗g3 ♘e5 12 ♗e2 d5, but not 10...d6?! when 11 ♘d2 ♘g6 12 ♗g3 f5 13 exf5 ♗xf5 14 ♗xf5 ♖xf5 15 a4 gave White an edge in A.Morozevich-I.Sokolov, Sarajevo 2008) 10 ♗h4 d6 11 ♘d2 ♕e8 12 a4 ♘g6 13 ♗g3 a5 with approximate equality.

b) 9 ♔h1 frees the f-pawn, but can be met well enough by a timely ...f5: 9...d6 10 f4 f5 11 ♘d2 and now the simplest is 11...fxe4 (Black can also play 11...♗b6 12 ♕c2 h6 13 ♘f3 fxe4 14 ♗xe4 ♗f5 15 ♗d2 ♕e8 intending ...♕h5 with equal chances, M.Godena-I.Morovic Fernandez, Havana 1999) 12 ♘xe4 ♗b6 13 ♘g3 ♘f5 14 ♕f3 ♘xg3+ 15 ♕xg3 ♗f5 with equality, A.Hauchard-A.Miles, Cappelle la Grande 1998.

c) As we have seen elsewhere, one good plan is that of queenside expansion, trying to take advantage of Black's structural weaknesses there. Moreover, after the 9 b4!? ♗b6 10 a4 a5 11 ♘d2 d5 of A.Drei-A.Miles, Reykjavik 2000, White could have obtained the advantage with the consistent 12 ♘b3! ♖e8 (or 12...dxe4 13 ♗xe4 ♗f5 14 ♗xf5 ♘xf5 15 ♕xd8 ♖fxd8 16 ♗f4) 13 bxa5 ♗xa5 14 ♘xa5 ♖xa5 15 c4 thanks to his two bishops and passed a-pawn.

9...d6

Alternatively, White had the better position after 9...♘g6 10 ♘b3 ♗b6 11 ♘d4 ♕f6 12 ♗e3 (but not 12 ♕c2 d5! 13 ♘f3 ♗g4 14 ♗g5 ♕d6 with the initiative for Black in D.Pavasovic-M.Godena, Portoroz 1998) 12...♘f4 13

♗c2 ♗a6 14 ♖e1 ♖fe8 15 ♕d2 in Z.Zhao-M.Chapman, Melbourne 2000.

10 b4!

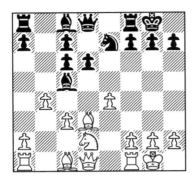

Again the queenside advance is logical and likely the correct way forward for White. Note that White starts with b4, as 10 a4 can be met by 10...a5.

Instead White didn't get much out of 10 ♘b3 ♗b6 11 c4 ♗e6 12 ♕e2 ♘g6 13 ♗e3 ♗xe3 14 ♕xe3 ♘e5 15 ♖ac1 ♕h4 with equality in Y.Dembo-E.Paehtz, Beijing (rapid) 2008.

10...♗b6 11 a4

Proceeding with the plan without delay.

11...a5

Black must not allow White to push a4-a5, but now his entire queenside structure is weakened.

12 ♘c4 ♗e6

12...axb4 13 ♘xb6 cxb6 14 cxb4 is simply better for White, in view of his better structure and bishop-pair.

13 ♕e2

Here White should prefer Barsky's simple suggestion of 13 ♘xb6! cxb6 14 b5 with a slight but permanent advan-

tage. Likewise, 14 ♗e3 should retain an edge, as did 14 ♕c2!? ♕c7 15 ♖d1 ♖ad8 16 ♖b1 h6 17 ♗f4!? ♘g6 18 ♗e3 in the recent V.Kotronias-A.Mastrovasilis, Vrahati 2010. However, the text gives Black an opportunity to equalize...

13...♔h8?

...which he misses. The correct 13...♗xc4! 14 ♗xc4 d5 15 exd5 ♘xd5 would have equalized the chances in view of the weakness of White's queenside structure – quite a reversal!

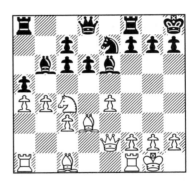

In F.Amonatov-A.Zubarev, Ohrid 2009, White continued 14 ♗g5, but again the obvious 14 ♘xb6! cxb6 15 b5 would have been stronger, since 15...c5 16 c4 results in a weak pawn on d6 and thus a large advantage for White.

A2) 6 ♗e3

A natural developing move, creating the threat of 7 ♘xc6 and in general neutralizing the activity of the bishop on c5. Moreover, the additional support given to the knight on d4 allows White's other pieces greater freedom, especially the queen.

6...♗b6

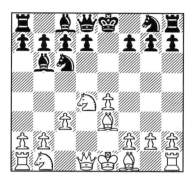

The only logical move, defending against 7 ♘xc6. Black can now consider playing ...♘f6, as he can meet ♘xc6 bxc6; e5 with ...♘d5, hitting the bishop on e3. Now White again faces a large choice:

A21: 7 ♘xc6
A22: 7 ♘f5
A23: 7 ♕g4

The aggressive Line A23 is unsurprisingly the most dangerous continuation, but on occasion White has preferred one of:

a) 7 ♗e2 fails to trouble Black: 7...♘f6! 8 ♘d2 0-0 9 0-0 d5 sees Black comfortably equalize. After the further 10 ♘xc6 bxc6 11 ♗xb6 axb6 12 e5 ♘d7 13 f4 ♕e7 he intends ...f6 and has the initiative.

b) 7 ♗d3 ♘ge7 8 0-0 0-0 is fine too for Black: for example, 9 ♕h5 ♘xd4 10 cxd4 (or 10 ♗xd4 ♘g6! 11 ♗xb6 axb6 12 f4 d6 13 ♘d2 ♖e8 with equality)

10...d5 11 exd5 g6 12 ♕f3 ♘xd5 and Black has the initiative.

c) 7 ♘d2 is also hardly threatening. Black prepares ...d5 with 7...♘ge7 8 ♗d3 (Black is fine too after 8 ♘c4 ♗xd4! 9 ♗xd4 0-0) 8...♘e5 9 ♗e2 (9 ♘c4 was tried in Z.Zahariev-A.Miles, Chania 1997, and now 9...♘xd3+ 10 ♕xd3 d5 11 ♘xb6 axb6 is fine for Black) 9...d5 10 f4 ♘5c6 11 ♘xc6 bxc6 12 ♗xb6 (D.Lintchevski-N.Nestorovic, Vojvodina 2005) 12...axb6 13 0-0 0-0 and by now he stands well.

d) 7 g3 ♘f6 8 ♗g2 0-0 9 0-0 is a solid set-up, but does nothing to prevent ...d5:

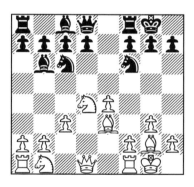

9...♖e8 10 ♘d2 (or 10 ♖e1 d5 11 ♘xc6 bxc6 12 ♗xb6 axb6 13 exd5, G.Borgo-C.Garcia Palermo, Cremona 2006, and now 13...♖xe1+ 14 ♕xe1 ♘xd5 is equal) 10...d5 11 ♘xc6 (11 exd5 ♘xd4 12 ♗xd4 ♗xd4 13 cxd4 ♘xd5 14 ♘e4 c6 15 ♖e1 ♗f5 16 ♕b3 ♗xe4 17 ♖xe4 ♖xe4 18 ♗xe4 ♘f6 turned out well for Black in L.Shytaj-J.Rowson, Verona 2006) 11...bxc6 and Black is fine: for example, 12 ♖e1 ♗e6 13 ♕a4

(J.Zhang-G.Lane, Kuala Lumpur 2007)
13...♘g4! 14 ♗xb6 axb6 15 ♕xc6 dxe4
16 ♘xe4 ♘e5 17 ♕b7 ♖a5 with excellent compensation.

e) 7 f4?! was tried in A.Naiditsch-
M.Roiz, Eppingen 2009, but is not good
in view of 7...♘f6! when Black obtains
excellent play after all of 8 e5 ♘d5, 8
♘d2 0-0 intending ...♖e8 and ...d5, 8
♕f3 d5 9 e5 ♘g4 10 ♗g1 0-0 11 h3
♘gxe5! 12 fxe5 ♘xe5 13 ♕g3 ♖e8, 8
♗d3 d5 9 e5 ♘g4 10 ♘xc6 ♕h4+ 11 g3
♘xe3 and, finally, 8 ♕d3 d5 9 e5 ♘g4.

f) 7 ♕a4?! renews the threat of 8
♘xc6, as then 9 ♗xb6 will follow and
Black cannot recapture with the a-
pawn. Unsurprisingly, though, this
strange move achieves nothing after
the simple 7...♖b8!.

bad for White, as pointed out by Sokolov) 11...♖xb6 12 0-0 ♗a6 13 ♖e1 ♘e5
14 ♕d4 ♕f6 gives Black good, active
play.

g) 7 ♗c4 is the most logical of these
minor options and has the benefit of
controlling the d5-square. Play may
continue 7...♘ge7 (alternatively, 7...♘f6
is, of course, met by 8 ♘xc6 bxc6 9
♗xb6 axb6 10 e5, but Black can handle
it: 10...♘d5 11 0-0 0-0 12 ♘d2 ♘f4 13
♕g4 ♘g6 14 ♕g3 d6 and Black was fine
in F.Samaritani-M.Godena, Jesolo 1999;
possible too is 7...♘e5 which kicks the
bishop from c4 and after 8 ♗e2 ♘f6 9
f4 ♘c6 10 ♗f3 Miles once played the
solid 10...d6, but must have been
tempted by 10...d5!?) 8 0-0 0-0 when
Black is ready for ...d5.

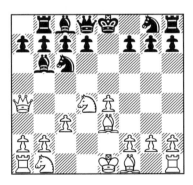

Black was fine after 8 ♘d2 ♘ge7 9
♗e2 0-0 10 0-0 d6 11 ♘xc6 bxc6 12
♗xb6 axb6 13 f4 f5 14 ♗d3 fxe4 15
♘xe4 ♗f5 in G.Garcia-A.Miles, Ubeda
1997. Thus 8 g3 ♘f6 9 ♗g2 was tried in
J.Smeets-I.Sokolov, Enschede 2006, but
here 9...♘g4! 10 ♘xc6 bxc6 11 ♗xb6
(11 ♗d4? c5 12 ♗xg7 ♖g8 13 h3 ♘xf2 is

Thus White usually opts for the aggressive for 9 ♕h5, but 9...d6 (another
solution is 9...♘xd4!? 10 cxd4 d5 11
exd5 ♘f5 12 ♘c3 ♘xd4 13 ♘a4 ♘c2
when Black stands well) 10 ♘d2 (10
f4?! runs into 10...♘xd4 11 ♗xd4
♗xd4+ 12 cxd4 d5! 13 exd5 ♘f5 14
♘d2 ♕d6 with excellent compensa-

tion) 10...♘xd4 11 ♗xd4 (if 11 cxd4 Black equalizes with the simple 11...c6! 12 ♗d3 d5) 11...♗e6! 12 ♗b3 ♗xb3 13 ♘xb3 ♘c6 14 a4 ♕e7 15 ♖fe1 ♕e6 was equal in I.Yagupov-V.Yandemirov, Tula 2003.

A21) 7 ♘xc6 bxc6

The exchange on c6 doesn't achieve much, as White must now attend to the tension between the bishops.

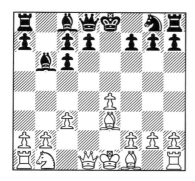

8 ♗d4!?

An ambitious attempt to cut across Black's plan of ...♘e7, ...0-0 and ...d5.

Otherwise, 8 ♗xb6 axb6 9 ♗c4 ♘e7 10 0-0 0-0 11 ♘d2 d5 12 exd5 cxd5 13 ♗b3 ♕d6 14 ♘f3 ♗b7 15 ♖e1 ♘g6 16 ♕d2 ♖fd8 17 ♖ad1 c5 was slowly but steadily becoming quite pleasant for Black in A.Rodriguez Perez-D.Pardo Simon, Linares 2007, while both 8 ♕d2?! ♘f6 9 ♗d3 0-0 10 0-0 ♖e8 11 c4 ♗xe3 12 ♕xe3 d5 13 ♘d2 ♕d6 and 8 ♕f3 ♕f6 9 ♗c4 ♕xf3 10 gxf3 ♘e7 11 ♘d2 d5 12 ♗e2 0-0 13 0-0-0 (M.Jelica-R.Pokorna, Krk 2004) 13...f5 are at least okay for Black.

8...♘f6!

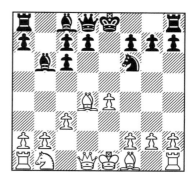

A simple and strong response.

8...♕h4!? 9 ♗d3 ♘e7 10 0-0 0-0 is also fine for Black: 11 a4 ♖b8 12 ♗e5 (trying to evict the black queen from the kingside; 12 ♕c2 d6 13 ♘d2 ♘g6 14 ♘f3 ♕h6 is equal according to Postny) 12...a5 13 ♘d2 d5 14 c4 ♘g6 15 ♗g3 ♕d8 16 exd5 f5! and Black had the advantage in M.Llaneza Vega-I.Sokolov, Budapest 2009, as White's bishop was trapped.

9 e5

Alternatively:

a) 9 ♕f3 ♗xd4 10 cxd4 ♕e7 11 ♘c3 0-0 12 0-0-0 d6 13 h3 a5 14 ♗d3 ♗a6 15 ♖he1 ♗xd3 16 ♕xd3 ♖fb8 saw Black obtaining good play in N.Miasnikov-I.Grinberg, Moscow 1999.

b) 9 ♗d3 0-0 10 0-0 d5!? (10...d6 is also playable, of course) 11 exd5 and now in D.Dochev-A.Vouldis, Kavala 2001, Black could have played 11...♘xd5!, intending ...♘f4 when his pieces are very active on the kingside.

c) The 9 ♘d2 0-0 10 ♗d3 of G.Szabo-J.Gustafsson, Plovdiv 2008, should be met by 10...d5! 11 0-0 ♗xd4 12 cxd4 dxe4 13 ♘xe4 ♕xd4 14 ♘xf6+ ♕xf6 15 ♕a4 with equality.

9...♘d5 10 ♗c4 0-0!

This pawn sacrifice is the real point of Black's play.

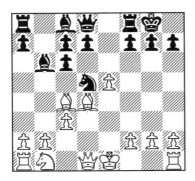

11 0-0

Accepting the pawn with 11 ♗xd5?! cxd5 12 ♗xb6 axb6 13 ♕xd5 doesn't turn out well after 13...♖a5 14 ♕d4 ♖e8 15 f4 ♕h4+ 16 g3 ♕h3 when White is in big trouble on the light squares. Relatively better here is 13 0-0, although after 13...♖e8 14 ♖e1 ♕g5 15 ♕d4 d6 16 ♕xd5 ♖b8 17 ♕d2 ♖xe5 18 ♖xe5 ♕xe5 Black had a slight edge in Zhang Zhong-G.Sargissian, Merida 2008.

11...d6 12 a4?!

Safer is 12 exd6 ♕xd6 13 ♖e1 with rough equality.

12...♗e6

Black is certainly fine and was more than that once White continued his misguided approach with 13 a5?! ♗xd4 14 ♕xd4 ♕g5! in E.Sutovsky-A.Onischuk, Polanica Zdroj 1999.

A22) 7 ♘f5

White wants to exchange the bishops and bring his knight to e3, after which he will play c4 and ♘c3, preventing ...d5 altogether.

Black is in serious danger of falling into a bind and being deprived of all counterplay, as has happened several times in practice. Therefore, he must react in a very precise way.

7...g6!

Instead 7...♗xe3 8 ♘xe3 has been the most popular course by far, but Black has been unable to prove equality with it. As ...d5 is impossible to achieve, the only central break available is ...f5, but that may weaken Black's position:

a) 8...♘f6 blocks the f-pawn and so White retains his bind after 9 f3 0-0 (or 9...d6 10 c4 ♕e7 11 ♘c3 ♕e5, as in S.Ansell-D.De Vreugt, Hilversum 2008, and then 12 ♘ed5 ♘xd5 13 cxd5 ♘e7 14 ♕d2 intending f4, with an edge) 10 c4! d6 (note that 10...♘xe4? fails to 11 fxe4 ♕h4+ 12 ♔d2 ♕xe4 13 ♘d5!, while after 10...♘e5 11 ♘c3 Black's attempt to prepare ...d5 by means of

11...c6? runs into 12 ♕d4! ♖e8 13 0-0-0 with a big plus, as pointed out by Golod) 11 ♘c3

11...♘d7 (another try was 11...♘h5 12 ♕d2 ♘f4 13 0-0-0 a6 14 ♘ed5 ♘e6 15 ♕e3 ♗d7 16 f4, which saw Black waste a lot of time with his knight and end up clearly worse in R.Kasimdzhanov-L.McShane, German League 2006) 12 ♕d2 ♘c5 13 ♗e2 f5 (Black achieves the desired break, but...) 14 exf5 ♗xf5 15 ♘xf5 ♖xf5 16 0-0 ♕h4 17 f4 ♖af8 18 ♗f3 ♔h8 19 g3 ♕d8 20 ♖ae1 and by now White had an obvious advantage in M.Palac-V.Vaisman, Cap d'Agde (rapid) 1998.

b) 8...d6 9 c4 ♘ge7 10 ♗d3 0-0 11 0-0 ♘b4 12 ♘c3 ♘xd3 13 ♕xd3 f5 was tried in N.Fercec-R.Kasimdzhanov, Fuegen 2006. Black has managed to exchange White's remaining bishop, but would still have been clearly worse after 14 c5! ♗e6 (or 14...dxc5 15 ♕c4+ ♔h8 16 ♖ad1) 15 exf5 ♘xf5 16 ♘xf5 ♖xf5 17 ♖fe1 ♕d7 18 cxd6 cxd6 19 ♖ad1.

c) 8...♘ge7 9 c4 0-0 10 ♘c3 d6 is

Black's best set-up, angling for ...f5.

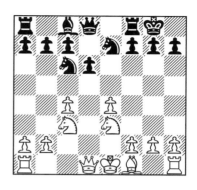

That said, with 11 ♗d3! (11 ♗e2 f5 12 exf5 ♘xf5 13 ♘xf5 ♗xf5 was okay for Black in J.Sanchez-E.Bacrot, Ajiaccio (rapid) 2008) 11...♘d4 (Black also failed to solve his problems after 11...♗e6 12 0-0 ♕d7 13 f4 f5 14 ♕d2 ♖ae8 15 ♖ae1 ♔h8 in M.Sorokin-V.Yandemirov, Cheliabinsk 2005, as White could now have played 16 ♘cd5 with a clear plus) 12 0-0 White retains an edge, since the dynamic 12...c5 (if 12...♖e8 then 13 f4 intends ♕h5 with the initiative) 13 ♕h5 g6 14 ♕h6 ♔h8 15 ♖ae1 a6 16 ♘cd5 ♘g8 17 ♕f4 ♗e6 failed to bring Black any joy after the strong 18 e5! in B.Savchenko-M.Sorokin, Sochi 2004.

8 ♗xb6

White must clear e3 for his knight.

8...axb6

Naturally not 8...gxf5? 9 ♗d4 ♘xd4 10 ♕xd4 ♕f6, as in K.Klokas-D.Delithanasis, Athens 2007, in view of 11 e5.

9 ♘e3 ♘f6 10 f3

More accurate than 10 ♘d2?! which allowed 10...d5 11 exd5 ♘xd5 12 ♘dc4

♗e6! 13 ♘xd5 in S.Movsesian-I.Sokolov, Sarajevo 2007, and now simply 13...♗xd5 would have left Black on top.

10...0-0

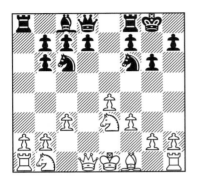

Compared with variation 'a' to Black's 7th move, the difference is that Black has gained time, an open file for his queen's rook and good chances for counterplay. For example:

a) 11 ♕d2 d6 12 c4 ♘d7! (this manoeuvre of the knight to c5 is very annoying for White, precisely because the open a-file creates the threat of ...♘b3; worse is 12...♘h5 13 ♘c3 ♗e6 14 0-0-0 ♘e5 15 ♔b1 with the initiative for White in D.Brandenburg-E.L'Ami, Dieren 2007) 13 ♘c3 ♘c5 14 ♖d1 (White must avoid the obvious 14 ♗e2?? ♘b3 15 axb3 ♖xa1+, as well as the pretty 14 0-0-0?? ♖xa2! 15 ♘xa2 ♘b3+) 14...f5 and Black is at least slightly better.

b) A safer approach is 11 ♗e2 d6 12 0-0, although the further 12...♖e8 13 c4 ♘h5 14 ♘d5 ♘e7 15 ♘xe7+ ♕xe7 16 ♘c3 ♕e5 still gave Black some initiative in M.Velcheva-M.Makropoulou, Heraklion 2007.

A23) 7 ♕g4

Finally we come to White's most critical option, hitting the vulnerable point on g7.

7...♕f6

This has traditionally been the main move, but it's not clear that it is best:

a) 7...♘f6!? has been suggested by Postny and it appears quite playable. His analysis runs 8 ♕xg7 ♖g8 9 ♕h6 d5!? (or 9...♖g6 10 ♕f4 ♘xd4 11 cxd4 – 11 ♗xd4 is met by 11...♘xe4! and if 12 ♕xe4+? ♖e6 13 ♗e5 d5 14 ♕e2 f6 White is much worse – 11...d5 12 ♘c3 dxe4 13 ♘xe4 ♕e7 14 ♘c3 c6 15 g3 ♗e6 16 ♗g2 ♗c7 17 ♕h4 ♖g4 18 ♕h6 ♖g6 with a repetition) 10 ♗b5 (10 ♘xc6 bxc6 11 ♘d2 ♕e7 12 h3 ♖g6 13 ♕f4 dxe4 gives Black good counterplay) 10...♗d7 11 ♗xc6 bxc6 12 e5 ♖g6 13 ♕h4 ♘g4 14 ♕xd8+ ♖xd8 15 ♗f4 c5 16 ♘f3 c4 17 ♗g3 ♔f8 18 h3 ♘e3 19 fxe3 ♖xg3 20 ♔f2 ♖g6 with compensation. All these lines are, of course, not forced and require further analysis, but the main point is that 7...♘f6 has potential!

b) 7...g6 is the simple response, but it seems inadequate for equality: 8 ♘d2! d6 (8...♕e7 was preferred in T.Radjabov-L.Aronian, Sochi 2008, but after Postny's 9 0-0-0! d6 10 ♕f3! ♘e5 11 ♕g3 ♘f6 12 ♗g5 White is better, while Black cannot afford 8...d5?! because of 9 ♕g3 ♘xd4 10 ♕e5+ ♔f8 11 cxd4 with a clear plus) 9 ♕g3 ♘f6 10 ♗e2 ♕e7 11 0-0 ♗d7 and now in J.Rosito-C.Garcia Palermo, Pinamar 2002, White could have retained a slight plus with 12 ♕h4.

8 ♕g3

Wisely moving out of the way of ...d5. Only once, though, has White tested 8 ♘b5!? which is surprising, because after 8...♗xe3 9 fxe3 ♔d8 10 ♘d2 d6 11 ♕g3 play has transposed to our next note, which is a line Black usually tries to avoid.

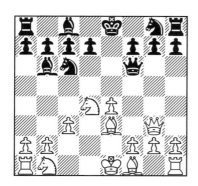

8...♕g6

Black seeks a queen exchange and clears f6 for his knight. He can also try 8...d6, but now White puts into effect his main idea of 9 ♘b5 ♗xe3 10 fxe3!?, creating some problems (10 ♕xe3

might appear more natural, but after 10...♕e7 11 c4 a6 12 ♘5c3 ♘b4 13 ♕d2 f5 14 a3 ♘c6 15 ♗e2 ♘f6 16 ♘d5 ♘xd5 17 exd5 ♘e5 Black had equalized in R.Zelcic-A.Stefanova, Cutro 2003, while 10 ♘xc7+ ♔d8 11 ♘d5 − 11 ♘xa8? ♗c1 12 ♘d2 ♗xb2 13 ♖d1 ♗xc3 will eventually leave White with a material deficit after the knight on a8 is rounded up − 11...♕xf2+ 12 ♕xf2 ♗xf2+ 13 ♔xf2 ♘ge7 is equal according to Postny). Black must now play 10...♔d8 and after the further 11 ♘d2 ♕e5 12 ♕h4+ ♘f6 of E.Najer-D.Baramidze, German League 2009, White can try Postny's suggestion of 13 ♘d4!? ♕h5 14 ♘xc6+ bxc6 15 ♕xh5 ♘xh5 16 e5! dxe5 17 ♘c4 with good compensation. Thus here the tireless Israeli analyst has suggested too 12...♕f6!? 13 ♕f4 ♗d7, which could also really do with a test or two.

Before we continue, note that Black cannot take the pawn on d4: 8...♘xd4? 9 cxd4 ♗xd4?! (9...d5 10 ♘c3 is also very unpleasant, as was 9...♘e7 10 ♘c3 ♕g6 11 ♕h4 ♗a5 12 ♗d3 ♘d5 13 0-0 ♘xe3 14 fxe3 in L.Trent-M.Erwich, Millfield 2002) 10 ♗xd4 ♕xd4 11 ♘c3 ♘e7 (11...♘f6 12 ♖d1 ♕b6 13 e5 ♘h5 14 ♕g4 ♕g6 15 ♕h4 threatens ♗e2 and pretty much wins, while 11...d6 12 ♖d1 ♕e5 13 f4 is also very bad for Black) 12 ♕xc7 0-0 13 ♖d1 ♕b4 14 ♖d2 and Black was completely lost, being unable to develop his queenside in G.Kasparov-W.Unzicker, Zurich (rapid) 2001.

Thus the queen move is a very prudent course and the resulting positions have generally proved fine for Black, which helps explain why there was a burst in the popularity of 7 ♘f5 before White turned his attention to 6 ♘xc6.

9 ♗c4

Neither have the alternatives brought any dividends to White:

a) 9 ♘f5 is best met by the pawn sacrifice 9...d6!, though 9...♘f6 10 ♘xg7+ ♔f8 11 ♘f5 ♘xe4 12 ♕f4 d5 also looks playable.

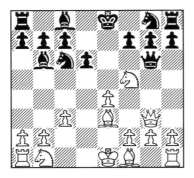

Following 10 ♗xb6 (10 ♘xg7+ ♔f8 11 ♘f5 ♗xf5 12 exf5 ♕xg3 13 hxg3 ♗xe3 14 fxe3 ♘f6 gives Black excellent compensation for the pawn) 10...axb6 11 ♘e3 (again White gains nothing from 11 ♘xg7+ ♔f8 12 ♘f5 ♗xf5 13 exf5 ♕xf5 14 ♗d3 ♕e6+ 15 ♕e3 with equality according to Afek) 11...♘f6 Black was okay in H.Nakamura-A.Goldin, Buenos Aires 2003.

b) 9 ♘xc6 bxc6 10 ♗xb6 axb6 11 ♕xc7 is quite critical, but after 11...♕xe4+ 12 ♔d1 ♘e7 13 ♘d2 ♕g6 14 ♕xb6 0-0 Black had excellent compensation in A.Danin-V.Yemelin, Sochi

2007, in view of White's misplaced king.

c) 9 ♘b5 is always a move to look out for, but here it is harmless: 9...♕xg3 10 hxg3 ♔d8 11 ♗xb6 axb6 12 f3 d6 13 g4 ♗e6 was equal in I.Nataf-L.Fressinet, Aix-les-Bains 2007.

d) 9 ♕f4 again avoids the exchange of queens, but Black can simply play 9...♘xd4 10 cxd4 ♘f6 11 ♘c3 0-0 12 0-0-0 ♘g4 with good play.

e) 9 ♗d3 ♘f6 10 ♘f5 d5! was promising for Black in N.Laursen-M.Godena, Copenhagen 2007. A possible continuation is 11 exd5 ♗xf5 12 ♗xf5 ♕xf5 13 dxc6 bxc6 14 0-0 ♘e4 15 ♕xg7 0-0-0 with great compensation.

f) 9 ♘d2 ♘ge7 (9...♕xg3 10 hxg3 ♘xd4 11 ♗xd4 f6 also looks okay) 10 ♗c4 (10 ♘xc6 ♘xc6 11 ♗xb6 ♕xg3 12 hxg3 axb6 is equal) 10...♘xd4 11 cxd4 d6 12 0-0 c6 13 ♕f4 0-0 14 ♕h4 ♗d8 was about equal in J.Smeets-J.Bosch, Hilversum 2006.

9...♕xg3

Black relieves the pressure with this exchange and can develop easily.

10 hxg3 ♘f6 11 f3 0-0 12 g4

It seems that White has some initiative. He can gain space on the kingside and Black is unable to break in the centre – or is he?

12...d5!

A very creative and strong idea! Black sacrifices a pawn to exploit the fact that White is behind in development and that his centralized king is exposed.

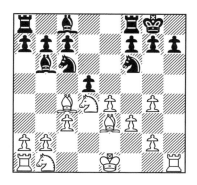

13 exd5 ♘e5 14 ♗b3 ♖e8 15 ♔d2 c5!

Another strong move, forcing open more lines. E.Najer-G.Sargissian, German League 2008, continued 16 dxc6 (16 ♘e2 ♘exg4 17 fxg4 ♘e4+ 18 ♔c2 ♘f6 forces White to repeat, and here Black might even prefer the alternative sacrifice, 16...♗xg4!? 17 fxg4 ♘exg4 18 ♗f4 g5 19 ♗g3 ♖e3 with good compensation) 16...bxc6 17 g5 and now perhaps best is 17...♘d5!? 18 ♗xd5 cxd5 threatening 19...♘c4+ and if 19 b3 (19 ♘a3 ♗c5) 19...♗c5 White has problems developing his queenside pieces.

B) 5...♗e7

A rather passive move compared to 5...♗c5 and one which allows White greater freedom of action.

6 ♗c4

This is, as usual, the most active post for the bishop. However, it is by no means the only good move. Indeed, most logical, developing set-ups suffice for an edge:

a) 6 ♗d3 ♘f6 (alternatively, 6...♗f6 7 ♘xc6 bxc6 8 0-0 d6 9 f4 ♘e7 10 ♘d2 is better for White, who will follow up with ♘f3, perhaps after first ♕h5, while the 6...d5 of M.Sorokin-V.Yandemirov, Linares 2000, is well met by 7 ♘xc6 bxc6 8 e5! with the advantage) 7 0-0 d6 (7...0-0 allowed 8 ♘f5 d5 9 ♘xe7+ ♘xe7 10 exd5 ♕xd5 in R.Reinaldo Castineira-F.Sanz Alonso, Barreiro 2001, and after 11 c4 ♕d6 12 ♗e2 White is slightly better thanks to his two bishops), and now 8 ♘xc6 bxc6 9 c4 is one good approach, 8 f4! a more dangerous one.

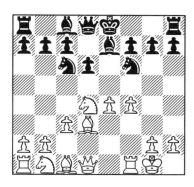

Following 8...0-0 (it's no good to play 8...d5?! 9 e5 ♘e4 10 ♘xc6 bxc6 11 ♗xe4 dxe4 12 ♕xd8+ ♔xd8, as in

D.Bryson-A.Rizouk, Cappelle la Grande 1994, because after 13 ♖d1+ ♔e8 14 ♖e1 White is much better) 9 ♕c2 ♗d7 10 ♘d2 ♖e8 11 ♘2f3 White is comfortably better: for example, 11...h6 (or 11...g6 12 e5 dxe5 13 fxe5 ♘xd4 14 ♘xd4 ♘g4 15 e6 ♗xe6 16 ♘xe6 fxe6 17 ♗xg6 with a strong attack in D.Shevelev-I.Ibragimov, New York 2002) 12 ♗d2 ♘xd4 13 cxd4 d5 14 e5 ♘e4 15 ♗xe4 dxe4 16 ♕xe4 ♗c6 17 ♕e3 and Black did not have sufficient compensation in P.Zarnicki-R.Garcia, Buenos Aires 1990.

b) 6 ♘f5!? is another tempting move. White brings the knight to e3, clamping down on the d5-square, and follows up with ♘d5 and perhaps c4. This plan takes some time to carry out, but Black is rather passive anyway and placing him in a bind is worth the time invested.

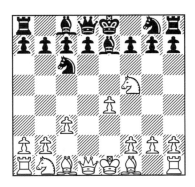

The game V.Varavin-V.Yandemirov, Nizhny Novgorod 1999, continued 6...♗f6 7 ♘e3 (White can also play 7 ♗c4 ♘ge7 8 ♘e3 d6 9 0-0 ♗e6 and now 10 ♘d5!? with an edge) 7...d6 (al-

ternatively, 7...♘ge7 8 ♘g4 finally grabs the bishop and after 8...♘g6 9 ♘xf6+ ♕xf6 10 ♗e3 0-0 11 ♘d2 d6 12 ♕c2 ♘ge5 13 h3 ♕g6 14 g4 White threatened 0-0-0 followed by f4 and was better in O.Kulicov-E.Ovod, St Petersburg 2000, while after 7...g6 8 ♘d5 ♗g7 9 ♘a3 a6 10 ♘c4 d6 11 ♗g5! White had a clear edge in D.Rombaldoni-M.Godena, Sarre 2009) 8 ♘d5 ♗e7 9 c4 ♘f6 and now after 10 ♘bc3 0-0 11 ♗e2 ♗e6 12 0-0 White has a very good position, with the idea of ♗e3 and f4.

c) 6 ♘xc6 bxc6 is, of course, quite possible too. Indeed, play may well transpose to our main line after 7 ♗c4 ♘f6.

Returning to 6 ♗c4:

6...♘f6

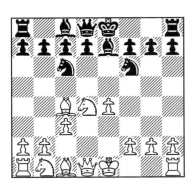

The logical way to develop. Other tries:

a) 6...♗f6? leaves Black in trouble after 7 ♘xc6! dxc6 (even worse is 7...bxc6 8 ♕b3 ♕e7 9 0-0 ♕xe4 10 ♗xf7+ ♔f8 11 ♘d2 ♕e7 12 ♗c4 with a huge edge for White in E.Anka-Y.Balashov, Wisla

1992) 8 ♕xd8+ ♗xd8 (V.Baklan-U.Garbisu, Sabadell 2007) 9 ♗f4! (tying Black down to his pawn on c7) 9...♘f6 10 ♘d2 0-0 11 0-0 with a serious advantage for White.

b) 6...♘e5?! just exposes the knight to attack: 7 ♗b3 ♘f6 8 f4 ♘g6 was R.Zelcic-I.Efimov, Bratto 1997, and now 9 e5 ♘e4 10 0-0 0-0 11 ♘d2 would have been strong.

c) 6...d6 is best met by 7 ♘xc6 bxc6 8 ♕b3!, striking against f7.

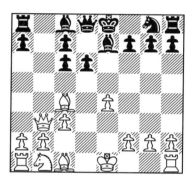

Black must sacrifice the pawn with 8...♘f6 (8...d5? 9 exd5 ♘f6 10 dxc6 0-0 11 0-0 ♗d6 12 ♘d2 was a disaster in A.Rios-F.De la Paz, Barbera des Valles 2003, as is 8...♗e6 9 ♗xe6 fxe6 10 ♕xe6 ♕d7 11 ♕xd7+ ♔xd7 12 0-0) 9 ♗xf7+ (much worse is 9 e5? ♘d5 10 ♗xd5 cxd5 11 ♕xd5 ♗e6 with compensation for Black) 9...♔f8, but now the simplest is 10 ♗e6! ♘xe4 11 ♗xc8 ♕xc8 (the intermediate 11...♘c5 is good for White after 12 ♕c2 ♕xc8 13 0-0 ♕e6 14 ♗e3 d5 15 ♗xc5 ♗xc5 16 ♘d2 due to the misplaced black king) 12 0-0 d5 13 ♘d2 and the exposed nature of Black's king

will keep troubling the second player, A.Grosar-D.Sermek, Portoroz 1993.

However, after 6...♘f6 White must be a little careful. Black intends ...♘xd4; cxd4 d5, either immediately or after castling, which White must really prevent. The most natural way to do so is by exchanging on c6:

7 ♘xc6

Alternatively, White can play the simple 7 0-0 0-0 (7...♘xe4?! fails to 8 ♘f5 ♗f6 9 ♕d5 0-0 10 ♕xe4 d5 11 ♗xd5 ♗xf5 12 ♕xf5 ♘e7 13 ♗xf7+ ♖xf7 14 ♕b5 with an extra pawn for White) 8 ♘f5, but Black should be able to handle this position quite easily:

a) 8...♘xe4? again fails, this time to 9 ♕g4 ♘g5 (or 9...g6 10 ♘h6+ ♔g7 11 ♕xe4) 10 ♘xe7+ ♕xe7 11 ♕xg5.

b) 8...♗c5 9 ♗g5 d6 (also interesting is 9...h6!? 10 ♗h4 ♘e5 11 ♗b3 d5 with some initiative) 10 ♗b3 h6 11 ♗h4 ♘e5 12 ♘d2 ♘g6 13 ♗g3 ♖e8 14 ♕f3 a5 15 a4 ♗e6 and Black was fine in R.Zelcic-V.Malaniuk, Bolzano 1992.

c) 8...d5!? also deserves attention. After 9 ♘xe7+ ♘xe7 10 exd5 ♘exd5

White has the two bishops, but his edge is very small, if indeed it exists.

7...bxc6

The usual response, aiming for complex play. The other recapture condemns Black to a difficult defence, in view of his structural disadvantage and lack of counterplay: 7...dxc6?! 8 ♕xd8+ ♚xd8 9 f3 ♘d7 (Black tries to solve the problem of defending the c7-pawn; alternatively, 9...0-0 10 ♗f4 is unpleasant, while 9...♗e7 10 ♗e3! ♘d7 11 ♘d2 ♗c5 12 ♚e2 b5 13 ♗d3 ♗xe3 14 ♚xe3 ♘c5 15 ♘b3 ♘a4 16 ♖ab1 a6 17 ♘a5 was steadily better for White in B.Pawlowski-K.Bulski, Wisla 2000) 10 ♗f4 ♘c5 11 ♘d2 b5 (or 11...♗d7 12 0-0-0 ♘e6 13 ♗e3 ♗e7 14 f4 ♘c5 and now the strong 15 ♘b3! with advantage, after which 15...♘xe4? failed to 16 ♗xf7+ ♚xf7 17 ♖xd7 ♖ac8 18 ♖e1 in J.Gonzalez-N.Delgado, Santa Clara 2003) 12 ♗e2 a5 and now in L.Milov-T.Preziuso, Lenk 1995, 13 ♘b3 ♘xb3 14 axb3 would have sufficed for a permanent edge.

8 e5

Naturally White takes up the opportunity to harass Black's development, especially since Black was ready for ...d5.

8...♘d5!

The best reply, sacrificing a pawn for compensation. The alternative, 8...♘e4, is also not so easy to refute. White likely does best to play simply with 9 ♘d2 (9 ♕f3 is not so effective after 9...d5 10 exd6 ♘xd6 11 0-0 0-0 12 ♗d3 ♗b7 13 ♗e3 when White is only slightly better and Black has some counterplay) 9...♘xd2 (9...d5 10 ♘xe4 dxc4 11 ♕xd8+ ♗xd8 12 ♗f4 ♗e6 13 0-0-0 ♗d5 14 ♖he1 0-0 15 f3 gave White an edge in M.Heidrich-E.Zude, German League 2000) 10 ♗xd2 and after 10...0-0 (or 10...d5 11 ♗d3 0-0 12 0-0 ♗e6, as in P.Charbonneau-E.Dumesnil, Montreal 1998, and now 13 f4 ♗c5+ 14 ♚h1 is slightly better for White) 11 0-0 d6 12 ♗f4 (12 exd6 cxd6 should be okay for Black) 12...♗f5 13 ♖e1 d5 14 ♗d3 ♕d7 15 ♕c2 ♗xd3 16 ♕xd3 White was slightly better in R.Asylguzhin-B.Markun, Bled 2001; he will retreat the bishop to e3 and push ahead with f4-f5.

After 8...♘d5, White must play energetically because Black is ready to castle and hit back in the centre. Another idea for Black is to play ...♘b6 with tempo and then ...d5. Naturally, White should thus focus on the weak spot in Black's position: g7.

9 ♕g4!

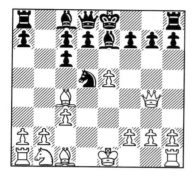

Instead 9 0-0 ♘b6 10 ♗d3 0-0 11 ♘d2 d6 12 exd6 cxd6 13 ♕c2 g6 14 ♘f3 ♘d7 15 ♗f4 ♘c5 (M.Calzetta-R.Turauskiene, Bled 2002) is a good example of how Black obtains easy play in the case of a slightly planless approach from White, and accepting the pawn with 9 ♗xd5 cxd5 10 ♕xd5 allows Black too much counterplay after 10...♗a6, as White cannot castle.

9...g6

The most logical, but after White's next move Black will be unable to castle for a long time. On the other hand, he is able to create counterplay and this is likely his best choice:

a) 9...♗f8?! is plain bad: 10 0-0 ♕e7

11 ♘d2 gives White an obvious edge, since 11...♕xe5? 12 ♘f3 followed by 13 ♖e1 is very difficult to meet.

b) 9...♔f8 is the real alternative, but why give up castling rights for good? White should now move the queen as ...d6 is threatened: 10 ♕h5! (this seems the most promising, especially as 10 ♕f3 d6 11 exd6 ♗xd6 gives Black plenty of play) 10...d6 11 0-0 (after 11 f4 g6 12 ♕e2 ♔g7 13 0-0 ♖e8 14 ♕f3 dxe5 15 fxe5 Black had good counterplay in J.Kis-L.Kotan, Eger 2004) 11...dxe5 12 ♕xe5 ♗e6 13 ♘d2 ♗d6 14 ♕d4 c5 15 ♕e4 c6 16 ♘f3 and White had avoided all the pitfalls, thereby securing an edge in J.Sondermann-L.Kotan, Znojmo 2006.

10 ♗h6 ♘b6

Worse is 10...d6 11 ♕e2 dxe5 12 ♗g7 ♖g8 13 ♗xe5 ♔f8 14 ♘d2 f6 15 ♗g3 ♔g7 16 0-0 and White was much better in V.Golod-V.Yandemirov, Alushta 1993.

11 ♗d3 d5

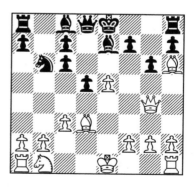

Black claims his share of the centre and hopes to activate his pieces. White must spend some time moving his own pieces around, but his structural advantage will persist.

12 ♕f4

Also possible is 12 ♕g3 ♘a4 (or 12...♘d7 13 0-0 ♘c5 14 ♗c2 ♘e6 15 ♘d2 ♖b8 16 b4 with a clear plus for White in D.Lintchevski-M.Matlakov, St Petersburg 2006) 13 b3 ♘c5 14 ♗c2 ♗a6 15 ♘d2 ♘e6 16 0-0-0 and White retained a slight edge in J.Sanchez-V.Yandemirov, Ubeda 2001.

12...♘d7

Black regroups the knight to the influential e6-square. Inferior is 12...♗e6 13 0-0 ♕d7 14 ♗a6 c5 15 a4 and Black was in trouble in F.Barglowski-V.Bogdanov, Bydgoszcz 2001.

13 ♘d2 ♘c5 14 ♗c2 ♘e6 15 ♕a4 ♗d7

Black has managed to mobilize his forces, but White retains some edge, as he has the better structure and Black is still unable to castle. Now in S.Bouaziz-V.Malaniuk, Calimanesti 1992, White prevented ...♗g5 with 16 ♘f3 and then went long, but I don't understand this decision. Instead, simple and good was 16 0-0!? ♗g5 (or 16...c5 17 ♕a6) 17 ♗xg5 ♕xg5 18 f4 ♕g4 19 ♖ae1 with a steady edge.

Conclusion

After 4...♗b4+ 5 c3 ♗c5 the main move for a long time was 6 ♗e3, but the trend is now shifting away from it. Indeed, after 6...♗b6 the older 7 ♕g4 no longer holds any terrors for Black after 7...♕f6 and Postny's 7...♘f6!? looks like a viable alternative. However, neither does the critical alternative, 7 ♘f5, lead to any advantage after the accurate response 7...g6!. That explains why 6 ♘xc6 is becoming more and more popular. It allows Black to obtain counterplay with his central pawns and active pieces, but Black's weakened queenside gives White a clear-cut plan for the middlegame and he should emerge with an advantage, even if only a very slight one.

Whereas 5...♗c5 allows Black to obtain some counterplay, 5...♗e7 is generally a solid and unambitious line. White retains the better chances with all of 6 ♗d3, 6 ♘f5 and 6 ♗c4. The last of those is the most forcing and can easily lead to a passive and slightly prospectless position for Black.

Chapter Twelve
Odds and Ends

1 e4 e5 2 ♘f3 ♘c6 3 d4

The majority of this chapter will be devoted to Black's fairly rare defences after 3...exd4 4 ♘xd4, but first a brief mention should be made of his various third moves.

3...exd4

This is clearly best. Alternatives which are occasionally seen at club level are:

a) 3...♘f6 4 dxe5 ♘xe4 5 ♗c4 is good for White, especially after 5...d6

(safer is 5...♗c5 6 0-0 with just an edge for White) 6 ♗xf7+! ♔xf7 7 ♕d5+ ♗e6 8 ♕xe4 with a clear advantage.

b) 3...f6? 4 ♗c4 ♘ge7 5 dxe5 fxe5 6 0-0 is obviously bad for Black, whose king is exposed.

c) 3...f5? is also a bad idea: 4 exf5 e4 5 ♘e5 ♘f6 and now the most incisive is 6 g4! and if 6...h5 then 7 ♘g6 ♖h7 8 g5 ♘g8 (or 8...♘g4 9 ♘xf8 ♔xf8 10 h3 and wins) 9 d5 ♘ce7 10 d6 cxd6 11 ♕xd6 when White's superiority is almost decisive.

d) 3...♗d6?! is simply met by 4 dxe5 ♘xe5 5 ♘xe5 ♗xe5 6 f4 ♗f6 (or 6...♗d6 7 ♗c4 f6 8 0-0 ♘e7 9 ♗e3 with an obvious plus) 7 e5 with an indisputable edge.

e) One way to meet the weird 3...♕e7?! is 4 d5 ♘b8 5 ♘c3 d6 6 ♗d3 with an edge, as suggested by Barsky.

f) 3...♕f6 is more logical, but still inadequate after 4 d5 ♘d4 (or 4...♘ce7 5

♘c3) 5 ♘xd4 exd4 6 ♗d3 ♗b4+ 7 ♘d2 with a clear edge.

g) 3...d5?! fails to the forcing 4 ♘xe5 ♘xe5 (4...dxe4 5 ♗b5 ♘ge7 6 ♘c3 is also very good for White) 5 dxe5 dxe4 (no better is 5...d4 6 c3 ♗c5 7 ♗c4 ♕h4 8 0-0) 6 ♕xd8+ ♔xd8 7 ♗c4 ♔e7 8 ♘c3 ♗e6 9 ♗b3 ♗xb3 10 axb3 ♔e6 and now the strong 11 ♖a4! with a clear advantage.

h) The most reasonable of these options, though still passive, is 3...d6.

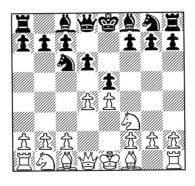

Now 4 ♗b5 transposes to the Steinitz Defence to the Ruy Lopez, but the simplest response is 4 dxe5 ♘xe5 (or 4...dxe5 5 ♕xd8+ ♔xd8 6 ♗c4 f6 7 ♗e3 ♗g4 8 ♘bd2 ♘ge7 9 0-0-0 ♘c8, as in B.Kovac-Z.Mestrovic, Radenci 1998, and now after Barsky's 10 h3 ♗d7 11 a3 ♘d6 12 ♗d5 White is slightly better) 5 ♘xe5 dxe5 6 ♕xd8+ ♔xd8 7 ♗c4 f6 (Black can accept a slight but permanent disadvantage with 7...♗e6 8 ♗xe6 fxe6 9 ♗e3 ♘f6 10 f3 ♘d7 11 ♘d2) 8 ♗e3 ♗d6 9 ♘c3 c6 10 0-0-0 ♔c7 and now the most logical plan is 11 ♖d3 ♘e7 12 ♖hd1 ♗b4 13 a3 ♗xc3 14 ♖xc3

when White was obviously better in E.Moser-M.Marin, Barcelona 2007.

Returning to the main line:

4 ♘xd4

Apart from the main moves, 4...♘f6 and 4...♗c5, and the important alternative 4...♗b4+, Black has tried almost every legal move here. Most of them are clearly inferior to the main lines, though, either because they are passive or too ambitious. Here we will focus our attention on:

> **A: 4...♘ge7**
> **B: 4...♕h4**
> **C: 4...g6**

Note that 4...d6 followed by ...g6 will be considered in Line C. Even rarer are:

a) 4...♘xd4 5 ♕xd4 is a little too simplistic from Black, but isn't entirely unknown at club level:

Now:

a1) 5...♘e7 6 ♘c3 transposes to Line A.

a2) 5...♘f6 runs into 6 e5 when there are no benefits for Black from 6...♕e7 (6...c5 7 ♕e3 ♘d5 8 ♕e4 sees the white queen find a safe home in the centre, leaving Black's position a mess) 7 ♗e3! ♘g8 (7...c5?? 8 exf6 loses a piece, as do both 7...♘h5?? 8 g4 and 7...♕b4+?? 8 ♕xb4 ♗xb4+ 9 c3) 8 ♘c3 c6 (8...♕b4 9 ♗c4 ♗e7 10 0-0-0 reminds one of positions from 19th Century games, while 8...d6 is strongly met by 9 ♘d5 and then exd6) 9 0-0-0 f6 10 f4 fxe5 11 fxe5 g6 12 ♘e4 with a decisive advantage.

a3) 5...d6 6 ♘c3 ♘f6 7 h3 (the plan of 7 f3 and then ♗e3 followed by 0-0-0 is also quite good) 7...♗e7 8 ♗e3 0-0 9 0-0-0 ♖e8 10 f4 ♘d7 11 ♘d5 and White is steadily better.

a4) 5...♕f6 sees Black continuing his policy of exchanges, but White retains the advantage with 6 e5!. Black can insist on an exchange of queens with 6...♕b6 (6...c5 7 exf6 cxd4 8 fxg7 ♗xg7 9 ♗d3 ♘f6 10 0-0 is much better for White, as was 6...♕g6 7 ♘c3! ♗e7 8 ♗d2 ♘h6 – the overly-greedy 8...♕xc2? loses to 9 ♗d3 ♕xb2 10 ♖b1 ♕a3 11 ♘b5 – 9 0-0-0 c6 10 ♗d3 in G.Dominguez Aguilar-J.Garcia Correa, Aguascalientes 2007), but after 7 ♕xb6 axb6 8 ♘c3 White threatens 9 ♘b5 and Black is unable to equalize.

For example, 8...♗b4 (or 8...c6 9 ♗e3 b5 10 0-0-0! f6 11 f4 ♘e7, as in B.Predojevic-S.Drazic, Subotica 2003, and White is better after 12 exf6 gxf6 13 ♗e2, as indicated by Barsky) 9 ♗d2 f6 (9...♘e7 10 ♘b5 ♗xd2+ 11 ♔xd2

♔d8 12 ♗c4 is good for White, as was 9...♗xc3 10 ♗xc3 ♘e7 11 ♗d3 0-0 12 0-0 ♘c6 13 f4 d6 14 exd6 cxd6 15 f5 in A.Szieberth-S.Stupar, Budapest 1994) 10 ♘d5 ♗xd2+ 11 ♔xd2 ♔d8 12 exf6 ♘xf6 13 ♘xf6 gxf6 14 ♗d3 and White had retained an edge in A.Areshchenko-S.Ovsejewitsch, Ordzhonikidze 2001.

b) 4...d5?! is in a sense a critical move; if it was playable, then the entire Scotch Game would be consigned to the archives! Thankfully, it is not too promising. The best reaction is 5 ♗b5! dxe4 (both 5...♘ge7 6 ♕e2 and 5...♗d7 6 exd5 are plain bad for Black) 6 ♘c3.

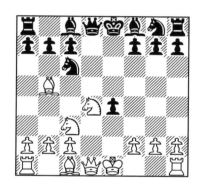

Now Black's most ambitious try is 6...♗d7 (instead 6...♗b4 7 0-0 ♗xc3 8 bxc3 ♗d7 9 ♖b1! gives White some initiative), but after 7 0-0 f5 (7...♘f6 8 ♗xc6 ♗xc6 9 ♘xc6 bxc6 10 ♕e2 sees White regain the pawn with an edge) 8 ♗xc6 bxc6 9 f3 c5 (9...exf3? 10 ♕xf3 has all the makings of a disaster for Black) 10 ♘b3 c4 (Barsky analyses both 10...exf3 11 ♕xf3 ♘f6 12 ♗g5 and 10...♗d6 11 fxe4 ♕h4 12 g3! ♗xg3 13

♕e2! ♗d6 14 e5 ♗e7 15 ♘d5 as much better for White) 11 ♘d2 Black's position is not to be envied.

c) 4...♕e7?! doesn't make much sense, as it puts the queen on an exposed square and blocks Black's natural development: 5 ♘c3 ♘f6 6 ♗f4! d6 (6...♘xe4? 7 ♘d5 wins on the spot) 7 ♗b5 ♗d7 8 0-0 and already White is much better.

d) 4...♗e7 is a normal and solid move, but also a little passive. White should meet it with standard development, which will enable him to claim a plus: 5 ♘c3 ♗f6 (5...♘f6 runs into 6 ♘xc6! dxc6 7 ♕xd8+ ♗xd8 8 ♗f4 0-0 9 0-0-0 ♗e6 10 f3 ♘h5 11 ♗e3 ♗f6, as played in M.Petras-J.Pastorek, Liptovsky Mikulas 2007, and now after the powerful 12 ♘a4!, heading for c5 and also threatening 13 g4, White has a large advantage) 6 ♗e3 ♘ge7 (6...♘xd4 7 ♗xd4 ♕e7 8 ♗e2 intending f4 seems difficult for Black) 7 ♕d2 0-0 8 0-0-0 d6 9 ♗e2 a6 10 f4 ♘xd4 11 ♗xd4 ♗xd4 12 ♕xd4.

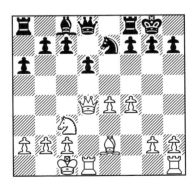

This is very pleasant for White: for example, 12...♖e8 (worse was 12...♕e8? 13 g4 b5 in M.Wiedenkeller-K.Engstrom, Karlskrona 1983, because after 14 h4 White has a very strong attack) 13 h4 and White is attacking while Black can only watch.

e) 4...♕f6 often transposes to the 4...♗c5 variation. Several players use 4...♕f6 in this manner, but it's not entirely clear why: all Black avoids this way is the 4...♗c5 5 ♘b3 line, which is arguably White's least dangerous option. Moreover, here White can try the independent and seemingly promising 5 ♘b5!? (both 5 ♗e3 ♗c5 and 5 ♘xc6 ♗c5 transpose to the main lines of the 4...♗c5 variation) 5...♗c5 6 ♕d2 ♗b6 7 ♘1c3.

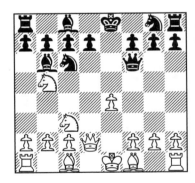

Following 7...♘ge7 (the other option is 7...♕e5 and now 8 f4 ♕e6 9 f5 ♕e7 10 ♕e2 gives White a nice advantage, with ♗f4 and ♘d5 on their way) 8 ♕f4 ♕xf4 9 ♗xf4 d6 10 ♗e3 ♗a5 White would have had an advantage in S.Mannion-P.Motwani, Edinburgh 1999, had he gone in for 11 a3 a6 12 b4.

A) 4...♘ge7

This approach has even been tried by some strong players. The idea behind it is very simple: Black wants to exchange knights on d4 and bring his other knight to c6 with tempo. The exchange of a pair of pieces will serve to relieve Black's cramp, but also deprives him of chances for counterplay. Most importantly, Black's set-up surrenders complete control of the d5-square.

5 ♘c3

White should not refrain from this move, as Black also had the idea of 5...d5.

5...♘xd4

One should take note of the blunder 5...g6?? 6 ♗g5 followed by ♘d5 when White wins. Moreover, he does so in style after 6...♗g7 7 ♘d5! ♗xd4 8 ♕xd4! as 8...♘xd4 9 ♘f6+ ♔f8 10 ♗h6 is mate!

6 ♕xd4

6...♘c6

Instead 6...♘g6 7 ♗e3 followed by 0-0-0 is excellent for White, while after 6...d6 7 ♗f4 ♘c6 8 ♕e3 ♗e6 9 0-0-0

♗e7 (D.Alvarez Hernandez-R.Vindas Moran, Moravia 2008) 10 h4 White enjoys a strong initiative, with the point that 10...♗xh4? fails to 11 e5 ♗e7 12 exd6 cxd6 13 ♘d5 with a clear plus.

7 ♕d3 ♗c5

All of 7...♗b4 8 a3 ♗xc3+ 9 ♕xc3, 7...d6 8 ♗e3 ♗e6 9 0-0-0 and 7...♘b4 8 ♕e2 ♗c5 9 a3 ♘c6 10 ♗e3 ♗xe3 11 ♕xe3 0-0 12 0-0-0 are good for White, the last-named appearing in G.Vescovi-V.Ramon, Sao Paulo 1999.

8 ♕g3 0-0 9 ♗g5!

Provoking a weakening pawn move.

9...f6 10 ♗h6 ♕e7 11 0-0-0 d6 12 ♗c4+ ♔h8 13 ♘d5 ♕d7 14 ♗e3

Another highly logical decision, exchanging Black's only active piece.

14...♗xe3+ 15 ♕xe3

White is obviously better. Moreover, Black is completely unable to create any play, although he did later manage to turn things round in E.Van den Doel-I.Sokolov, Dutch League 1995.

B) 4...♕h4

Black's most ambitious and at the

same time riskiest option. By immediately attacking the pawn on e4, he practically forces White to sacrifice it, raising the stakes. However, Black makes several concessions to secure this small material gain and it is the general feeling of all experts on the Scotch that this whole approach is extremely risky for him.

As we will see, White should rely on simple and quick development while Black is winning the central pawn with his queen. Still, you can rest assured that a black player entering the main lines has done a lot of homework, likely involving deep computer analysis of the resulting positions, so accuracy and creativity are required from White. Overall, though, the excessively high risk involved in this line, especially when compared with the minute reward, has made most players shy away from 4...♛h4 in practice.

5 ♘c3!

Although not the only good option, this simple move is probably the most promising. The only other options are:

a) The meek 5 ♕d3?! looks bad – and it is. White quickly ends up worse after 5...♘f6! 6 ♘xc6 (or 6 ♘d2 ♘g4! 7 g3 ♕f6 8 ♘4f3 ♘ce5 9 ♕c3 ♗b4! 10 ♕xb4 ♘xf3+ 11 ♘xf3 ♕xf3 and Black wins) 6...dxc6 7 ♘c3 ♗b4 8 ♗d2 0-0.

b) Indeed, the only real alternative to 5 ♘c3, and a quite decent one at that, is 5 ♘b5.

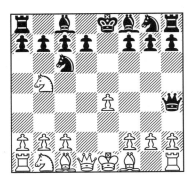

Black can, of course, capture the e4-pawn with check, but White's idea is to start creating threats as quickly as possible. Moreover, if Black can be forced to play ...♚d8, then White's compensation will be fairly enduring.

Now:

b1) The immediate 5...♕xe4+ is unsatisfactory in view of 6 ♗e2! ♚d8 (6...♗b4+ 7 ♘1c3 transposes to Line B3, below, but White can definitely also consider Wells' suggestion of 7 ♗d2!?; note too that both 6...♕e5? 7 f4 and 6...♕xg2? 7 ♗f3 lose immediately) 7 0-0 a6 8 ♘d2 ♕e8 9 ♘c3 f5 10 ♖e1 ♗e7 11 ♘c4 ♘f6 12 ♗f3 and considering that Black is not entitled to request a replay on the grounds of an incorrect placement of the king and queen, his task for the rest of the game is hardly enviable. Most certainly White had a powerful initiative here in R.Lau-H.Elstner, Bad Wörishofen 1992.

b2) 5...♗b4+ is a standard idea, trying to disturb White's development, and now White has to remain bold, as well as precise:

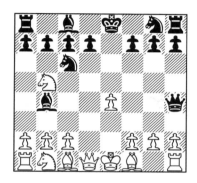

b21) 6 ♘1c3?! leads to the line 5 ♘c3 ♗b4 6 ♘db5, which is suboptimal, as we'll see in the notes to White's 6th move in our main line, below.

b22) 6 c3?! ♗a5 solves the issue of c7 and suddenly Black has the upper hand.

b23) 6 ♘d2?! fails to 6...♕xe4+ 7 ♗e2 ♕xg2! 8 ♗f3 ♕h3 and now after 9 ♘xc7+ (9 ♗g4 ♕h4 10 ♘xc7+ ♔d8 11 ♘xa8 ♘f6 12 ♗e2 ♖e8 13 c3 ♘e5 is similar and here Black's attack is very strong, as analysed by Gutman) 9...♔d8 10 ♘xa8 ♘f6 11 c3 ♖e8+ 12 ♗e2 ♘e5 Black was already winning in W.Stassen-C.Taberner, correspondence 1997.

b24) Thus 6 ♗d2! is correct and after 6...♕xe4+ (6...♗c5 7 ♕e2 sees White solve all his problems and force Black to deal with the threat to c7; moreover, here Black cannot afford play aggressively with 7...d6?! 8 ♘xc7+ ♔d8 in view of Wells' forcing line 9 ♘xa8! ♗g4 10 g3 ♕h5 11 ♕d3 ♘d4 12 h3! ♘f3+ 13 ♔d1 ♘e5+ 14 hxg4 ♕xh1 15 ♕e2 ♘xg4 16 ♗e1 with a winning position for White) 7 ♗e2 White has typically annoying pressure against c7.

Black can defend with 7...♔d8 (or, 7...♕xg2 8 ♗f3 ♗xd2+ 9 ♘xd2 ♕h3 10 ♗xc6 bxc6 11 ♘xc7+ ♔d8 12 ♘xa8 ♘f6 13 ♕f3 is clearly better for White, as given by Wells), but after 8 0-0 ♗xd2 9 ♘xd2 ♕e5 10 ♖e1 ♘f6 11 ♗c4 ♕f5 12 ♘f3 ♕c5 White should play the accurate 13 ♕e2! (instead of 13 ♕d3 d6 which was unclear in E.Sveshnikov-D.Sermek, Bled 1994) 13...♖e8 14 ♕d3 (Wells), which creates serious problems for Black. In general it's hard to trust these positions for Black with the king on d8 and, moreover, this one just appears objectively bad.

b3) This helps to explain why Black usually plays 5...♗c5. Now 6 ♕e2 (of course, 6 ♘xc7+?? ♔d8 just loses a piece) 6...♕d8 7 ♗e3 ♗xe3 8 ♕xe3 a6 9 ♘d4 seems okay for Black because of the active 9...♕f6!, with the point that 10 ♘xc6? fails to 10...♕xb2! 11 ♕d4 ♕c1+ 12 ♔e2 ♕xc2+ 13 ♘d2 ♕xc6 14 ♕xg7 ♕f6 15 ♕xf6 ♘xf6 and Black had a clear advantage in K.Mueller-M.Godena, Buekfuerdo 1995. Thus White should prefer 6 ♕f3!, covering e4 and f2, while not fearing ...♘d4 in response.

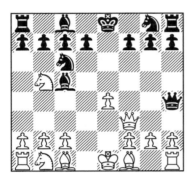

Indeed, after 6...♘d4 (otherwise, 6...♕d8? 7 ♕g3 wins material, 6...♘f6?! 7 ♘xc7+ ♔d8 8 ♕f4! is also very bad for Black, and even the relatively sane 6...♗b6 7 ♗e3 leads to a slight edge for White, since 7...♗a5+ can be met with the accurate 8 ♘d2!) 7 ♘xc7+ ♔d8 8 ♕f4 ♘xc2+ 9 ♔d1 ♕xf4 10 ♗xf4 ♘xa1 11 ♘xa8 we've reached a position that is good for White: for example, 11...♘f6 12 ♗d3 ♘g4 (or 12...b6 13 ♘c3 ♗b7 14 ♘c7 ♘h5 15 ♘7d5! which is winning for White, as analysed by Wells) 13 ♔e2

♘xf2 14 ♖c1 ♘xd3 15 ♔xd3 d6 16 ♘c7 g5 17 ♗e5! dxe5 18 ♖xc5 and Black was totally lost in O.Korneev-D.Komljenovic, Zaragoza 1996.

Overall it seems that 5 ♘b5 is adequate for a slight edge, but no more than that. We now return to the more promising and testing 5 ♘b5:

5...♗b4

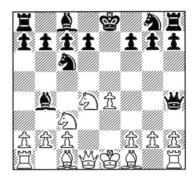

Black must continue with forcing moves, as otherwise his last move will simply prove a waste of time. For example, 5...♘f6? 6 ♘f5 is a disaster and hardly any better is 5...♗c5? 6 ♗e3 threatening 7 ♘f5, as we saw at the beginning of Chapter Eight.

6 ♗e2!

Correctly developing, rather than waste any time protecting the e4-pawn.

Note that 6 ♘db5?! comes one move too late, as Black can now reply 6...♗a5 and after 7 ♗d3 a6 8 ♘a3 b5 9 ♗d2 he would have been better in R.Schmaltz-A.Karpatchev, Cappelle la Grande 1993, had he played the simple 9...♗b6 (but not 9...b4? in view of 10

♘d5 with a strong initiative, as Black cannot capture on a3).

After 6 ♗e2 we must consider:

> **B1: 6...♘ge7**
> **B2: 6...♘f6**
> **B3: 6...♕xe4**

Of these Line B3 is unsurprisingly the most consistent and challenging option.

Instead 6...d6 7 0-0 ♘f6 transposes to Line B2 and 6...♗xc3+ 7 bxc3 ♕xe4 (but not 7...♘f6?! in view of 8 ♘f5! ♕xe4 9 ♘xg7+ ♔d8 10 0-0 ♖g8 11 ♗d3 ♕d5 12 ♗h6 d6 13 ♖e1 and White is much better according to Barsky) leaves White with nothing better than 8 ♘b5 ♔d8 9 0-0, transposing to the main line (B3).

B1) 6...♘ge7 7 0-0

White sticks with simple, straight-forward and good moves.

7...0-0

Continuing to eschew the pawn,

but Black can also consider:

a) 7...♗xc3 8 bxc3 a6 (or 8...♕xe4 9 ♘b5 ♔d8 transposing to note 'c' to Black's 9th move in Line B3, while 8...♘xd4 9 cxd4! ♕xe4 10 ♗g5 is strong) 9 ♗f3 0-0 10 g3 ♕f6 11 ♗g2 ♘g6 12 f4 d6 13 ♗b2 and White was better in Y.Dembo-A.Dimovski, Novi Sad (rapid) 2002.

b) 7...a6?! 8 ♘f3 ♕f6 9 ♗g5 ♕d6 10 ♘d5 was much better for White in A.Turzo-Z.Jonas, Zalakaros 1996.

c) 7...♗a5 8 ♘f3 ♕f6 9 ♘d5 ♘xd5 10 exd5 is also much better for White.

d) 7...d6 8 ♘f3 ♕f6 9 ♘d5 ♘xd5 10 exd5 ♘e5 11 c3 ♗c5 12 ♘xe5 dxe5 13 ♗b5+ ♔f8 14 ♕e2 (Barsky) is again very good for White.

8 ♘db5 ♗a5

Simply bad for Black is 8...♗xc3 9 bxc3 ♕xe4 10 ♘xc7 ♖b8 11 ♗a3, since he is unable to untangle.

9 ♘d5 ♘xd5

Again 9...♕xe4 10 ♘dxc7 ♖b8 (even worse is 10...♗xc7?! 11 ♘xc7 ♖b8 12 ♗d3) 11 ♗d2 is good for White.

10 exd5 ♘e5 11 f4

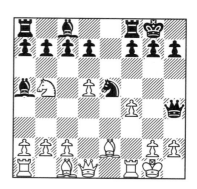

It is obvious that White has a clear advantage, due to his better development and extra space: for example, 11...♗b6+ (or 11...♘g6 12 d6 c6 13 ♘c7 ♗b6+ 14 ♔h1 ♖b8 15 ♕d3 ♕f6 16 g3 ♗c5 17 ♖d1 with a big advantage) 12 ♔h1 ♘g6 13 f5 ♘e5 14 d6 c6 15 ♖f4 ♕d8 16 ♘c3 ♖e8 17 ♘e4 and Black was completely tied up in R.Reinaldo Castineira-V.Golod, Linares 2001.

B2) 6...♘f6 7 0-0!

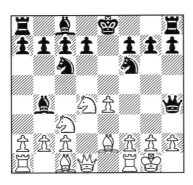

Yet more simple but consistent play from White!

7...♗xc3

Certainly not 7...0-0?? 8 ♘f5 nor 7...♘xe4? 8 ♘d5! ♗d6 (both 8...♕d8? 9 ♗f3 and 8...♗a5? 9 ♘f5 win on the spot) 9 g3 ♕d8 10 ♘b5 0-0 11 ♘xd6 cxd6 (or 11...♘xd6 12 ♘xc7 ♕xc7 13 ♗f4) 12 ♖e1 with a big plus. And not much better is 7...d6: 8 ♘f3 ♕h5 9 ♘d5 ♘xd5 10 exd5 ♘e5 (10...♘e7 loses to 11 ♘g5) 11 c3 ♗c5 12 ♗f4 and White is much better.

8 ♘f5 ♕xe4 9 ♗d3!

This duo of powerful intermediate

moves leaves Black in some trouble.

9...♕g4

Alternatively:

a) 9...♕a4 10 ♘xg7+ ♔f8 11 ♗h6 ♗e5 (White wins after both 11...♗xb2 12 ♖e1 and 11...♘g8 12 ♘e6+ ♔e7 13 ♗f8+ ♔xe6 14 bxc3) 12 f4 ♗d4+ 13 ♔h1 and White is much better (Barsky).

b) 9...♕e5 10 bxc3 causes Black serious problems: for example, 10...♔f8 (hardly any better is 10...0-0 11 ♖e1 ♕a5 12 ♖b1 and now 12...♖e8?! 13 ♖b5 ♕xa2 14 ♘xg7 ♔xg7 15 ♗h6+ was a disaster for Black in G.Pecis-M.Di Marino, correspondence 2002) 11 ♖b1 d6 12 ♖b5 ♕e6 (12...♕xc3? loses to 13 ♗b2) 13 ♖e1 ♕xa2 when White wins with the standard strike 14 ♘xg7! ♔xg7 15 ♗h6+.

10 f3 ♕a4

After 10...♕b4 11 bxc3 ♕xc3 12 ♘xg7+ ♔d8 13 ♖b1 White has a powerful attack, while 10...♗d4+? 11 ♔h1 ♕h5 just loses to 12 ♘xg7+.

11 bxc3

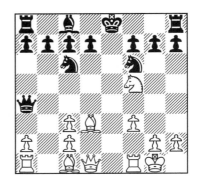

11...♔f8

Unfortunately for Black the desirable

11...0-0 runs into 12 ♘xg7! ♔xg7 13 ♗h6+! ♔g8 (there is no salvation in 13...♔xh6 14 ♕d2+ ♔h5 15 g4+ ♘xg4 16 fxg4+ ♕xg4+ 17 ♔h1 and White was winning in S.Karjakin-Malinin, Sudak 2002, or 13...♔h8 14 ♗xf8 d6 15 ♕d2 ♕h4 16 ♗h6 ♘g8 17 ♗g5 ♕a4 18 c4 ♕a5 19 ♕f4 ♘e5 20 ♗f6+ ♘xf6 21 ♕xf6+ ♔g8 22 ♕g5+ and Black resigned in Z.Vukovic-D.Mozetic, Banja Vrucica 1991) 14 ♕d2 ♕a5 (14...♕h4 15 ♗g5 wins) 15 ♗xf8 ♕xf8 16 ♕h6+ ♔e7 17 ♖ae1+ ♘e5 18 f4 (Motwani) and wins.

However, even after the text White can strike:

12 ♘xg7!

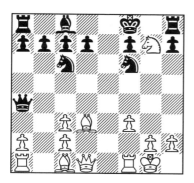

12...♔xg7 13 ♗h6+! ♔xh6 14 ♕d2+ ♔g7 15 ♕g5+ ♔f8 16 ♕h6+ ♔g8 17 ♕xf6

Black, despite being a piece up, is totally lost, as none of his pieces can help his lone king: for example, 17...d5 (or 17...d6 18 ♖ae1 ♗d7 19 ♕g5+ ♔f8 20 ♕h6+ ♔g8 21 f4, winning) 18 ♖ae1 ♗d7 19 f4 h5 (nothing is changed by 19...♕a5 20 ♖f3 ♕b6+ 21 ♔h1 ♘e5 22 ♕xe5) 20 ♖f3 (Barsky) and White wins.

B3) 6...♕xe4

The main line and likely Black's best try.

7 ♘db5

As explained earlier, White's most important idea in this line is to attack c7, trying to displace the black king.

7...♗xc3+

Black faced an unpleasant choice:

a) He cannot play 7...♗a5? because of 8 ♘xc7+! ♔d8 9 ♘xa8 ♕xg2 10 ♗f3 and White wins.

b) 7...♕xg2? 8 ♗f3 dropped the rook and was similarly winning for White in J.Timman-S.Davidov, Baku 2008.

c) 7...♘f6 is the most desirable move, but it fails to 8 ♘xc7+! (8 0-0 ♗xc3 9 bxc3 ♔d8 10 ♗e3 also supplies White with very good chances, but the text is even stronger) 8...♔d8 9 ♘xa8 ♕xg2 (9...♘d4 10 0-0 ♗xc3 11 ♗d3 leaves Black dead lost) 10 ♗f3 ♖e8+ 11 ♗e3 ♕h3 and now White has the simple 12 a3 when he is much better.

d) Finally, 7...♔d8?! is the move Black is trying to avoid. White gains a large advantage with 8 0-0 ♗xc3

(8...♛g6 9 ♘d5 wins) 9 ♘xc3! ♛d4 (no better are 9...♛g6 10 ♗h5 and 9...♛e5 10 ♖e1) 10 ♗d3: for example, 10...d6 (10...♘ge7 11 ♖e1 and 10...♘f6 11 ♖e1 d6 12 ♗e3 ♛h4 13 ♘e4 ♘xe4 14 ♗xe4 are equally unpleasant) 11 ♗e3 ♛g4 12 f3.

8 bxc3 ♚d8

Not, of course, 8...♛e5?? 9 f4 when Black loses touch with c7.

9 0-0

For the pawn White has a big lead in development, which will quickly increase because of the exposed black queen, as well as the clear target in the shape of the misplaced black king. Moreover, practice has shown that Black is generally unable to solve his problems in this position, especially in the circumstances of a tournament game.

9...a6

Alternatively:

a) Now is a better time for 9...♘f6, but as we've seen, 10 ♗e3 gives White very dangerous compensation in any case.

b) After 9...d6 10 ♖e1 ♘f6 (for 10...♘ge7 see variation 'c2', while Black cannot afford 10...♗e6?? in view of 11 ♘xd6! cxd6 12 ♛xd6+ ♚e8 13 ♗a3) 11 c4 White has a strong attack.

c) The main alternative is 9...♘ge7, but after 10 ♖e1 Black again faces difficult problems:

c1) After 10...♛h4 11 ♖b1 Black cannot play 11...d6? because of 12 ♘xd6! cxd6 13 ♛xd6+.

c2) 10...d6 again runs into 11 ♘xd6! cxd6 12 ♛xd6+ ♗d7 (or 12...♚e8 13 ♗g5) 13 ♗f4 with a winning position for White, J.Broekmuelen-M.Tan, Schagen 2003.

c3) If 10...♛d5 11 ♗d3 f6 12 c4 with a big plus.

c4) 10...a6 11 ♘d4 ♘xd4 (also unpleasant is 11...♛g6 12 ♗h5 ♛f6 in view of 13 ♗xf7!, which was rather effective in S.Smagin-D.Sermek, Vienna 1991) 12 cxd4 ♖e8 (nothing is changed by 12...d6 13 c4 or 12...♛h4 13 c4) 13 ♗xa6 with a clear advantage to White.

10 ♗f3!

As we have seen, intermediate

moves are a core component of White's play in this line. Indeed, he should never think of retreating – the motto is 'hit back'!

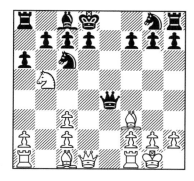

10...♕c4?

This move meets a sad but spectacular end. Black's situation is certainly difficult, but he can restrict White to just an edge with careful play. That is definitely not a good outcome for Black's choice of opening, but is the lesser evil:

a) 10...♕g6 11 ♘d4 ♘ge7 (or something like 11...♘xd4 12 ♕xd4 ♘e7 13 ♗f4 d6 14 ♖ab1 with an edge for White) 12 ♖e1 d6 (after 12...♘xd4 13 cxd4 d6 14 c4 White's initiative clearly outweighs the missing pawn, and Black must watch out for pitfalls such as 12...♖e8? 13 ♗h5) 13 ♖b1 ♖e8 14 ♗f4 ♘xd4 15 cxd4 and White retains pressure that is difficult to shake off.

b) 10...♕f5 11 ♘d4 ♘xd4 12 cxd4 ♘f6 13 c4 d6 14 ♕b3 ♖e8 15 ♗a3 and White has the usual pressure.

c) However, inferior is 10...♕e5?! 11 ♗xc6 axb5 (not 11...bxc6? 12 ♖e1! and

Black is lost) 12 ♖e1 when Black is in big trouble.

d) Finally, 10...♕a4? 11 ♘d4 ♘ge7 12 ♗xc6 bxc6 13 ♗g5 ♖e8 14 ♕g4 was a disaster for Black in R.Espinosa Flores-L.Day, Moscow Olympiad 1994.

11 ♘d6!!

A beautiful strike, highlighting Black's inability to mobilize his forces.

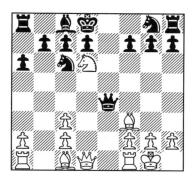

11...cxd6

11...♕e6 12 ♘xc8 ♖xc8 13 ♖e1 is plain bad.

12 ♕xd6

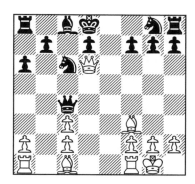

Despite his extra piece, Black has no way to oppose White's straightforward attack. The brutal encounter T.Oral-

M.Kantorik, Slovakian League 2001, concluded 12...♘f6 (12...♘ge7 13 ♗f4 gives White a very strong attack) 13 ♗e3 ♘e7 14 ♖fe1 ♘fd5 15 ♗xd5 ♘xd5 16 ♕xd5! 1-0. The queen sacrifice concludes as 16...♕xd5 17 ♗b6 is mate, as is 16...♕c6 17 ♕xc6 dxc6 18 ♗b6+ ♔d7 19 ♖ad1.

C) 4...g6

The most accurate move order if Black wants to fianchetto; the problem with 4...d6?! being 5 ♘c3 (5 ♗b5 again leads to the Steinitz Variation of the Lopez) 5...g6 6 ♘d5!.

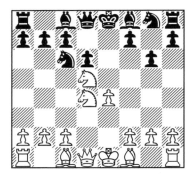

White has seized a dangerous, early initiative and, indeed, Black can easily suffer a catastrophe here:

a) 6...♗g7?? 7 ♘b5 led to a miniature in T.Christensen-B.Jacobsen, Aarhus 1991.

b) 6...a6 (I.Dahl-K.Berg, Vettre 1992) 7 ♘xc6 bxc6 8 ♕d4 f6 9 ♗c4! is somewhat better for White.

c) Likewise, 6...♘f6 7 ♗g5 ♗e7 8 ♘xe7 ♕xe7 9 f3 gives White a clear advantage.

5 ♗e3

White reinforces the knight on d4 while introducing the typical anti-fianchetto plan of ♕d2 and 0-0-0. He can also consider:

a) 5 ♘c3 ♗g7 6 ♘xc6 (6 ♗e3 transposes to our main line) 6...bxc6 7 ♗c4 ♕h4! (less stereotyped and likely stronger than 7...♘e7) 8 ♕f3 (after 8 0-0 ♘f6 White unexpectedly finds himself facing an attack) 8...♘f6 (but not 8...d5? 9 ♘xd5! cxd5 10 ♗xd5 and Black was crushed in A.Hennings-J.Rigo, Leipzig 1977) 9 ♗f4 0-0! gives Black good counterplay.

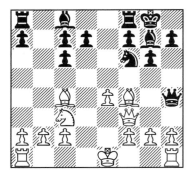

Indeed, after 10 0-0 (both 10 ♗xc7 d5! 11 ♗g3 ♕h6 12 exd5 ♗g4 13 ♕f4 ♖fe8+ 14 ♔f1 ♕xf4 15 ♗xf4 ♘xd5 16 ♗xd5 cxd5 and 10 ♗g3 ♕g5 11 ♗xc7 d5 supply decent compensation for the pawn) 10...d6 11 h3 ♘d7 12 ♕e3 ♕h5 13 ♗e2 ♕c5 Black, if anyone, had the initiative in H.Reefschlaeger-M.Steinbacher, German League 1994.

b) 5 ♘xc6!? bxc6 6 ♕d4 is a direct and quite challenging approach: 6...♕f6 (Black should avoid the 6...f6? 7 ♗c4

♗g7 8 0-0 ♕e7 9 f4 of T.Becker-G.Jacoby, Hamburg 2005, but might consider 6...♘f6!? 7 e5 ♘d5 8 ♗d3 ♗g7) 7 e5! (the critical try; Black shouldn't have any problems after 7 ♕xf6 ♘xf6 8 ♘c3 d6) 7...♕e7 8 ♘c3 ♗g7 9 ♗f4 f6 10 e6! f5! (White obtains promising compensation after both 10...d5 11 0-0-0 ♗xe6 12 ♗a6 and 10...♕xe6+ 11 ♔d2 ♔d8 12 ♖e1) 11 ♕a4! (improving over the 11 ♕c4 of J.Bejtovic-C.Hoi, Valby 2008, when 11...♖b8!? 12 0-0-0 ♖b4 gives Black the upper hand) 11...♗xc3+ 12 bxc3 ♕xe6+ 13 ♗e2 gives White good play for the pawn in the shape of his active pieces and bishop-pair.

c) 5 ♗c4 ♗g7 6 ♘xc6 bxc6 7 0-0 ♘e7 (but not 7...♘f6? 8 e5 when even 8...♘d5 9 ♗xd5 cxd5 10 ♕xd5 doesn't give Black enough compensation) 8 ♘c3 d6 9 ♖e1 (White preferred the more aggressive 9 f4!? ♗e6 10 ♗d3 ♕d7 in W.Browne-B.Larsen, San Juan 1969, and now 11 ♕e2 leaves him with the initiative) 9...0-0 10 ♗e3 ♗e6 looks quite solid for Black.

♔xg7 13 ♕d4+ sees White regain the bishop with a small but clear pull.

d) 5 c4 ♗g7 (play also rather resembles the Accelerated Dragon after 5...♘f6 6 ♘c3 d6, but for the important difference that Black has exchanged his e- not c-pawn; following 7 ♘c2 ♗g7 8 ♗e2 0-0 9 0-0 ♘d7 10 ♗d2 ♘c5 11 b4!? ♘e6 12 ♖c1 ♘ed4 13 ♘xd4 ♘xd4 14 ♗e3 ♘xe2+ 15 ♕xe2 a5 matters remained balanced in M.Carlsen-A.Diamant, Halkidiki 2003) 6 ♗e3 (the careless 6 ♘b3?! allows Black to seize the initiative with 6...a5!) 6...♘f6 7 ♘c3 0-0 (or 7...♘g4 8 ♕xg4 ♘xd4 9 ♕d1 c5 10 ♗d3 d6 11 ♕d2 0-0 12 0-0 ♖e8 13 ♘d5 ♗e6, as in I.Balinov-V.Srebrnic, Bled 1998, and now 14 ♗g5!? f6 15 ♗e3 with an edge) 8 ♗e2 ♖e8 9 f3 d6 (Emms has suggested 9...♘h5!? 10 0-0 ♘f4, but after 11 ♘xc6 ♘xe2+ 12 ♘xe2 bxc6 13 ♗d4 White is better), and now both 10 ♕d2 and 10 0-0 ♘h5 transpose to variations of the King's Indian!

Returning to 5 ♗e3:

5...♗g7 6 ♘c3

Natural and clearly best.

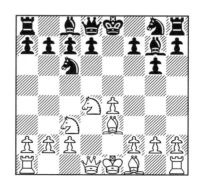

However, 11 ♗d4! ♗xc4 12 ♗xg7

Now Black must decide what to do with his king's knight: will it go to f6 as it generally does in the closely-related Larsen Variation of the Philidor (1 e4 e5 2 ♘f3 d6 3 d4 cxd4 4 ♘xd4 g6), or will he try not to obstruct the fianchettoed bishop?

> **C1: 6...♘f6**
> **C2: 6...♘ge7**

C1) 6...♘f6 7 ♘xc6!

Doubling Black's pawns at the cost of opening the b-file. However, practice has shown that Black is less likely to generate anything down that half-open file than he is with his queenside pawns after an exchange on d4: ...a6, ...b5 and ...c5. That said, by no means everyone is so convinced and practice has also seen:

a) 7 ♗c4 0-0 8 0-0 ♖e8 9 ♖e1 d6! (but not 9...♘xe4? 10 ♘xe4 ♖xe4 because of 11 ♗xf7+! when 11...♔xf7? 12 ♕f3+ ♕f6 13 ♕xe4 ♘xd4 14 ♗xd4 ♕xd4 15 ♕e8+ ♔f6 16 ♕e7+ ♔f5 17 ♖ad1 is winning for White, as analysed by Emms) 10 f3 a6 (10...♘xd4 11 ♗xd4 ♗e6 is a solid and playable alternative) 11 ♘xc6 bxc6 12 ♕d2 ♗e6 13 ♗xe6 ♖xe6 14 ♖ad1 ♘d7 15 b3 ♕b8! 16 ♘e2 ♕b7 17 ♗d4 ♗e5 saw Black equalize in V.Hort-P.Keres, Moscow 1963.

b) 7 ♗e2 isn't aggressive enough and after 7...0-0 8 ♘xc6 (White must avoid 8 f4? ♘xe4! 9 ♘xe4 ♕e7 and after 8 0-0 ♖e8! 9 f3 d5! Black equalizes)

8...bxc6 9 0-0 (the belatedly aggressive 9 e5 was preferred in Z.Fusthy-J.Boguszlavszkij, Budapest 1984, but Black could have seized the initiative with 9...♘e8! 10 f4 ♕h4+ 11 g3 ♕e7) 9...♖e8 Black has sufficient counterplay against e4 and b2.

c) 7 f3 sees White setting up just as he does in the main line of the Dragon, but Black can equalize or more with a timely ...d5:

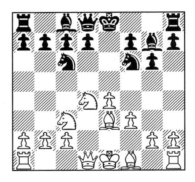

c1) 7...d5? is premature: 8 ♗b5! (8 ♘xc6 bxc6 9 exd5 ♘xd5 10 ♘xd5 ♕xd5 11 ♕xd5 cxd5 12 0-0-0 c6 is fine for Black) 8...♗d7 9 exd5 ♘b4 and now in S.Gusejnova-N.Apkhaidze, Duisburg 1992, with 10 ♗c4 White could have retained a pull.

c2) 7...0-0 8 ♗c4?! (better is 8 ♕d2, taking play into variation 'd1') 8...♖e8 9 ♕d2 (after 9 ♘xc6 bxc6 even 10 0-0 d5 gives Black the initiative, but that is better for White than 10 ♔f2? d5! 11 exd5 ♖xe3 12 ♔xe3 ♕e7+ 13 ♔f2 ♕c5+ which was a complete disaster in Y.Afek-J.Demarre, Paris 1994) 9...d5! 10 ♘xc6! (White must avoid both 10 exd5? ♘xd4 11 ♕xd4 ♘g4 and 10 ♘xd5? ♘xd5 11 ♗xd5 ♘xd4 12 ♗xd4 ♕xd5, as pointed out by Emms) 10...bxc6 11 0-0-0 ♕e7 12 ♗b3 dxe4 13 ♖he1 ♗e6 isn't wholly clear, but should be slightly in Black's favour.

d) 7 ♕d2 0-0 (Black might like to play 7...♘g4?! and did in C.Martinez-D.Lima, Sao Paulo 2004, but after 8 ♗g5 f6 9 ♗f4 White is for choice) again sees White facing the question of when to advance his f-pawn:

d1) 8 f3 d5! 9 ♘xc6! (9 0-0-0?! gives Black a decent choice between the 9...♘xd4 10 ♗xd4 dxe4 of K.Bjerring-Z.Szymczak, Trnava 1989, and Emms' 9...dxe4!? 10 ♘xc6 ♕xd2+ 11 ♖xd2 bxc6 12 fxe4 ♖e8, while 9 exd5 ♘xd5 10 ♘xc6 bxc6 11 ♘xd5 ♕xd5 12 ♕xd5 cxd5 13 0-0-0 is equal) 9...bxc6 10 0-0-0 ♗e6 (10...♖e8 transposes to variation 'd22', below) 11 ♗h6 dxe4 (White had a pull too after 11...♖b8 12 ♗xg7 ♔xg7 13 ♕e3 ♕e7 14 exd5 cxd5 15 ♘xd5 ♘xd5 16 ♖xd5 ♕f6 17 ♖e5 in I.Radulov-A.Planinec, Wijk aan Zee 1974) 12 ♗xg7 ♕xd2+ 13 ♖xd2 ♔xg7 14 fxe4 ♖ad8 15 ♗e2 ♖xd2 16 ♔xd2 saw White reach an endgame with a small edge in D.Musanti-L.Liascovich, Tres de Febrero 2003.

d2) 8 0-0-0 ♖e8! (again Black eschews the Philidorian 8...d6 and 8...d5 would be premature on account of 9 exd5 ♘xd5 10 ♘xc6 bxc6 11 ♘xd5 cxd5 12 ♕xd5 ♕f6 13 c3 with an edge) 9 f3 d5 and now:

d21) 10 exd5 ♘xd5 11 ♘xc6 bxc6 12 ♗d4 (or 12 ♘xd5 ♕xd5!? 13 ♕xd5 cxd5 14 ♗d4 ♗xd4 15 ♖xd4 ♖e1+ 16 ♖d1 ♖xd1+ 17 ♔xd1 c5 with good, ongoing activity for Black in V.Zivkovic-F.Berebora, Pula 1997) 12...♗xd4! (Black has usually preferred 12...♘xc3, but 13 ♗xc3 ♕xd2+ 14 ♗xd2 gives White an edge) 13 ♕xd4 ♕g5+! (13...♖b8 14 ♘xd5 cxd5 15 ♕xd5 ♕e7 16 h4! probably doesn't give Black quite enough) 14 ♕d2 ♕xd2+ 15 ♔xd2 ♖b8 16 b3 ♗f5 (Emms) gives Black enough activity to maintain a rough balance.

d22) 10 ♘xc6 bxc6 11 ♗g5!? (likely stronger than the more obvious 11 ♗h6 when 11...♗h8! sees Black retaining his key prelate) 11...♖b8 12 ♗c4 ♕d6 13 ♗b3 ♗e6 (13...♕b4?! 14 exd5 c5 came up short after 15 ♗xf6! ♗xf6 16 ♘e4 ♖xe4 17 fxe4 in E.Wiersma-R.Hendriks, Hoogeveen 2005) 14 ♖he1 gives White the initiative.

d23) However, the forcing 10 ♗b5 seems okay for Black after 10...♗d7! 11 exd5 ♘xd4 12 ♗xd4 (and not 12 ♗xd7? ♘xf3! 13 gxf3 ♕xd7) 12...♗xb5 13 ♘xb5 ♕xd5!.

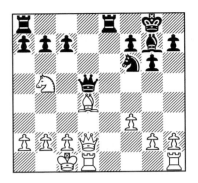

The key point being that 14 ♘xc7 ♕xa2 15 c3! (15 b3?? loses to 15...♖ec8 16 ♘xa8 ♗h6!) 15...♖ec8! forces White to tread rather carefully, although with 16 ♗xf6! (after 16 ♘xa8? ♘d5! White suffered a disaster with 17 ♕c2?? ♗h6+ 18 ♖d2 ♘b4 in Z.Jovanovic-I.Khmelniker, Pardubice 2007, and even 17 b4! ♕a1+ 18 ♔c2 ♕a4+ 19 ♔b2 ♘xc3! gives Black an initiative) 16...♖xc7 17 ♗xg7 ♔xg7 18 ♕d4+ ♔g8 he managed to reach an equal endgame in V.Malakhov-E.Geller, St Petersburg 1994.

Returning to the critical exchange on c6:

7...bxc6

Naturally Black has no interest in 7...dxc6? 8 ♕xd8+ ♔xd8 9 0-0-0+ when White is much the better developed, not to mention his structural advantage.

8 e5!

Forcing the pace, whereas after 8 ♗c4 ♕e7 9 ♕d3 0-0 10 0-0 ♘g4! it's Black who is able to seize the initiative.

8...♘g8

The sacrifice 8...♘d5? 9 ♘xd5 cxd5 10 ♕xd5 is also known from a related line of the Accelerated Dragon, but here it is clearly insufficient: 10...♖b8 11 0-0-0! 0-0 12 c3 ♗b7 13 ♕xd7 ♕xd7 14 ♖xd7 ♗xe5 (O.Nikolenko-V.Tsaturian, Podolsk 1992), and now 15 f3 leaves White fully in charge.

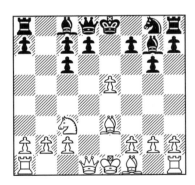

9 ♗c4!?

White continues to develop at top speed, not pausing to defend the pawn on e5. This is a very dangerous approach, but in practice he has more often preferred:

a) 9 ♗f4 ♕e7 10 ♕e2 mimics one aspect of the 4...♘f6 main line and after 10...♖b8 11 b3! (but not 11 0-0-0??

♕b4 when Black wins) 11...d6 12 0-0-0 dxe5 13 ♗e3!? (13 ♗g3 was preferred in A.Felsberger-H.Baumgartner, Austrian League 1996, but after Emms' 13...♘h6 Black has the initiative) 13...♕a3+ 14 ♔b1 ♘e7 15 h4 White has decent compensation for the pawn.

b) 9 ♗d4 ♕e7 (Black can also consider breaking the bind with 9...f6!? 10 exf6 ♘xf6 when 11 ♕e2+ ♔f7!? 12 0-0-0 d5 gives him reasonable counterplay) 10 f4 ♘h6 (10...f6!?) 11 ♗d3 0-0 12 0-0 ♕b4 13 ♘e2 d6 14 c3 ♕xb2 15 ♕a4 again gives White sufficient play for his pawn, V.Chekhov-S.Vesselovsky, Moscow 1973.

c) 9 f4 is best met by 9...d6! and then:

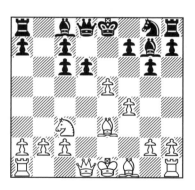

c1) 10 exd6 cxd6 11 ♕d2 ♘e7 12 0-0-0 0-0! 13 ♗d4 (13 ♕xd6? ♕xd6 14 ♖xd6 runs into 14...♗xc3! 15 bxc3 ♘f5 16 ♖d3 ♗a6 and 13 ♗e2?! ♘f5 14 ♗f2 ♕a5 15 g4 ♖b8! 16 ♗c4 d5 17 ♗b3 ♘d6 was also excellent for Black in M.Hennigan-F.Rayner, Wrexham 1994) 13...♗xd4 14 ♕xd4 ♘f5 15 ♕d2 d5 saw Black taking over the initiative in

B.Macieja-M.Bartel, Warsaw 2005.

c2) 10 ♕f3 ♘e7 11 0-0-0 0-0 12 ♗c5 ♘d5 13 ♘xd5 cxd5 14 exd6 was seen in G.Jones-F.Castaldo, Italy 2004, and now 14...♖b8 15 c3 cxd6 16 ♗d4 ♕a5 17 a3 ♗f5 (Emms) gives Black dangerous attacking prospects.

c3) 10 ♗c4 ♘h6 11 ♕f3 0-0! 12 0-0 (it's risky for White to become involved in 12 ♕xc6 ♗d7 13 ♕f3 ♗g4 14 ♕f2 ♗e6) 12...♘g4 strikes against the bishop and e5, thereby securing Black good counterplay.

9...♗xe5

In view of what follows, one might consider this too risky, but how else is Black supposed to sort out his pieces without coming under a strong attack?

10 0-0

White might also consider 10 ♕e2!?, but 10 ♕f3?! ♕f6 11 ♕e4 ♕e7 was not an effective way of demonstrating compensation in F.Eid-C.Matamoros Franco, Dresden Olympiad 2008.

10...d5

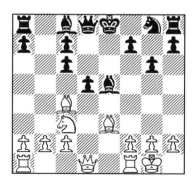

It's hard to suggest an improvement with 11 ♗d4 on its way, but now in

F.Barglowski-Z.Szymczak, Polanica Zdroj 2001, White had a powerful blow: **11 ♕xd5! cxd5 12 ♗xd5**

White has a huge attack for the piece and, indeed, Black will do very well to survive. Probably the best defence is 12...♗e6, but after 13 ♗xa8 ♕xa8 14 ♗d4! White retains a strong initiative and is likely to at least collect the important pawn on a7. Thus it may even be the case that the very direct approach with 8 e5 ♘g8 9 ♗c4 comes close to refuting the whole variation!

C2) 6...♘ge7!?

Having seen the problems Black faces against precise play after the development of the knight to f6, this alternative development may well grow in popularity. Black doesn't pressure the e4-point, but ...d5 remains on the agenda and this way the long diagonal stays open.

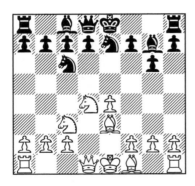

7 ♕d2

Again this must be more critical than the likes of 7 ♗c4 and 7 ♗e2.

7...0-0

Black would like to go 7...d5, but 8 ♘xc6! (8 exd5 ♘xd5 9 ♘xc6 bxc6 10 ♘xd5 ♕xd5 11 0-0-0!? may also suffice for an edge) 8...bxc6 9 0-0-0 ♗e6 10 ♗d4 (10 ♗h6 0-0 11 ♗xg7 ♔xg7 is another move order) 10...0-0 11 ♗xg7 ♔xg7 enables White to crown his systematic approach with 12 ♕d4+! (and not 12 h4?! dxe4 13 ♕f4 ♘d5 14 ♘xd5 cxd5 15 h5 ♕e7, which saw White coming up short in J.Razuvajeva-S.Efremova, St Petersburg 1999) 12...f6 (12...♔g8 was preferred in R.Backelin-M.Jonsson, Borlange 1995, when it's hard to explain why White refrained from 13 h4) 13 ♕c5 ♕d7 14 ♗c4 ♖ad8 15 ♕xa7 ♕d6 16 ♗b3 and White had picked up a pawn for insufficient compensation, although a complex fight still lay ahead in J.Nunn-A.Beliavsky, Belgrade 1991.

8 0-0-0 d5!?

With the knight on e7, it's pretty much now or never for this advance. Moreover, practice has shown via various move orders that 8...d6?! 9 h4 merely gives White a dangerous initiative.

9 ♘xc6

Again the exchange of knights is critical, whereas 9 ♘xd5?! ♘xd5 10 ♘xc6 bxc6 11 exd5 can be well met by 11...♕h4! 12 dxc6 ♕a4 when Black enjoys dangerous play for the two pawns.

9...bxc6 10 ♗d4!

Wisely removing the key bishop, rather than allow Black good compensation after 10 exd5 cxd5 11 ♘xd5 ♗e6

12 ♗c4 ♖b8.

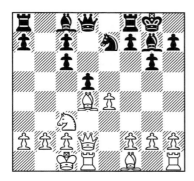

10...dxe4 11 ♗xg7 ♕xd2+ 12 ♖xd2 ♔xg7 13 ♘xe4

White's prudent approach has led to an endgame in which his centralized knight and superior structure should count for a little something. Indeed, after 13...♗f5 (perhaps Black should prefer 13...♘d5!?) 14 ♗d3 ♖fd8 15 ♖e1 ♘d5 16 ♘c5! there was no doubting his small but clear edge in A.Marechal-G.Welling, Belgian League 2004.

Conclusion

The main lines of the Scotch, as with most openings, are the main lines for a reason. Of the minor options considered in this chapter, 4...♕f6 isn't an especially impressive move order device, while after both the risky 4...♕h4 and a fianchetto approach White can obtain dangerous attacking chances with quite straightforward play.

Index of Variations